Language for Legislation and Legislation through Language

This collection teaches us how language and legislation interact to produce effective laws. It brings linguistics, lawyers, theory, and practices together to show how linguistic tools, concepts, and methodologies can be applied to improve the law's clarity, transparency, and efficiency, thus widening its social reach.

Drawing on case studies across Europe, chapters critically reflect on the dynamics of legislative drafting and the dissemination of legislation and the ways in which drafted legislation both creates laws and serves to communicate their meaning. This volume features perspectives from national and transnational examples to demonstrate the impact of varied stakeholders—legislative bodies, law interpreters, and law enforcers—on the implementation of legislation, particularly when legislative texts are translated and interpreted across different settings. Through the lens of discourse analysis, legislative texts are analyzed in lexico-grammatical and textual terms, highlighting the disparity between what is conceived and what might be expressed clearly in words and how this knowledge can inform better drafting practices. This collection charts a way forward for linguistics as a discipline to contribute to a better understanding of the nuances around effective legislative expression.

This book will appeal to scholars and stakeholders working at the intersection of language and the law, in such fields as applied linguistics, forensic linguistics, regulation, legislation, and legislative drafting.

Tímea Drinóczi is Professor of Law, Senior Researcher, Mykolas Romeris University, Lithuania and a Research Affiliate at the Law School, Federal University of Minas Gerais, Belo Horizonte, Brazil, and in the CEU Democracy Institute, Budapest, Hungary.

Giulia A. Pennisi is Professor of English Language and Translation at the Department of Political Science and International Relations (DEMS), University of Palermo, Palermo, Italy, and Associate Research Fellow at Sir William Dale Centre for Legislative Studies, London, UK.

Helen Xanthaki is a Professor at University College London, Dean of PGLaws at the University of London Worldwide, and Senior Associate Research Fellow at the Sir William Dale Centre for Legislative Studies, London, UK.

Routledge Studies in Applied Linguistics

Theory and Practice in Vocabulary Research in Digital Environments
Edited by Mark Feng Teng, Agnes Kukulska-Hulme and Junjie Gavin Wu

Concept-based Language Instruction
Usage-based Linguistics and Sociocultural Theory in Teaching Japanese
Kyoko Masuda, Amy Snyder Ohta and Rie Tsujihara

The Language of Mass Shooter Manifestos
A Corpus-Based Analysis of Pre-Crime Narratives
Emily Powell

Current Approaches to Language Ideology and Metalinguistic Discourse
Edited by Adnan Ajšić and Rachelle Vessey

Decolonizing Academic Writing through Translingualism
Walking the Talk
Edited by M. Sidury Christiansen, Zhongfeng Tian and Suresh Canagarajah

Washback Research in Language Assessment
Fundamentals and Contexts
Edited by David Allen

Language for Legislation and Legislation through Language
Edited by Tímea Drinóczi, Giulia A. Pennisi and Helen Xanthaki

For more information about this series, please visit: https://www.routledge.com/Routledge-Studies-in-Applied-Linguistics/book-series/RSAL

Language for Legislation and Legislation through Language

Edited by Tímea Drinóczi, Giulia A. Pennisi and Helen Xanthaki

Routledge
Taylor & Francis Group
NEW YORK AND LONDON

First published 2026
by Routledge
605 Third Avenue, New York, NY 10158

and by Routledge
4 Park Square, Milton Park, Abingdon, Oxon, OX14 4RN

Routledge is an imprint of the Taylor & Francis Group, an informa business

ISBN: 9781032553580 (hbk)
ISBN: 9781032553603 (pbk)
ISBN: 9781003430308 (ebk)

DOI: 10.4324/9781003430308

Typeset in Sabon
by codeMantra

To my mother, Melina, for the unconditional love that shaped my life. Forever grateful, Giulia.

Contents

Contributors

Corina Andone, Dr., is an Assistant Professor of Language and Communication at the Amsterdam Centre for Language and Communication, University of Amsterdam, Amsterdam, The Netherlands.

Gaetano Armao is Professor of Administrative Law in the Department of Political Science and International Relations (DEMS) at the University of Palermo, Palermo, Italy; a former member of the European Committee of the Regions; and coordinator of the intergroup of the European Islands.

Aysun Bolaca, Dr., is an Assistant Professor in the Private International Law Department, Faculty of Law, Ankara Yildirim Beyazit University, Turkey.

Belkis Vural Celenk, Dr., is an Associate Professor in the Private International Law Department, Faculty of Law, Ankara Yildirim Beyazit University, Turkey.

Florin Coman-Kund, Dr., is an Associate Professor of European Union Law in the Erasmus School of Law at the Erasmus University Rotterdam, Netherlands.

Tímea Drinóczi is a Professor of Law, Senior Researcher, Mykolas Romeris University, Lithuania and a Research Affiliate in the Law School, Federal University of Minas Gerais, Belo Horizonte, Brazil and in the CEU Democracy Institute, Budapest, Hungary.

Annarita Felici is an Associate Professor of Translation at the Faculty of Translation and Interpreting (FTI) of the University of Geneva, Geneva, Switzerland FTI.

Ágota Fóris is a Professor of Linguistics at Károli Gáspár University of the Reformed Church of Hungary, Terminology and Communication Research Group (TERMIK), Budapest, Hungary.

Dimitry Gegenava is a Professor of Law and Vice-Rector in the Sulkhan-Saba Orbeliani University, Tbilisi, Georgia.

Ömer Faruk Gençkaya is a Professor in the Department of Political Science and Public Administration, Istanbul Medipol University, Istanbul, Turkey.

Thiago B. V. Hermont Dr., is a researcher of Public Policies at João Pinheiro Foundation in Belo Horizonte, Minas Gerais, Brazil.

Şeref İba is an Associate Professor and Head Adviser to the President of the Grand National Assembly of Türkiye, and also Lecturer of Constitutional Law at the Ufuk University, Turkey.

Martin David Kelly, Dr., is a Lecturer in Administrative Law at the University of Glasgow, UK.

Mônica Sette Lopes is a Professor in the Law School, Federal University of Minas Gerais, Belo Horizonte, Brazil.

Xiao Lu is an Assistant Professor in the School of International Studies, Peking University, Beijing, China.

Lucas Willian Oliveira Marciano, PhD in Linguistic Studies, is a school administrator in the public education system of Belo Horizonte, Minas Gerais, Brazil.

Novitet Nezaj Dr., iur. (University of Zurich Faculty of Law), is the Director of the EU Law Department in the Kosovo Government, Republic of Kosovo.

Barnabás Novák PhD (by the Faculty of Law, University of Pécs, Hungary).

Ana Larissa Adorno Marciotto Oliveira is a Professor in the Federal University of Minas Gerais, Belo Horizonte, Brazil and in the Münster University, Münster, Germany.

John O'Shea is a Legal Translator at Jurtrans Translations Ltd, co-founder of *Lex Graeca*, and a Visiting Researcher at the University of Surrey.

Moritz Osnabrügge, Dr., is an Associate Professor in the School of Government and International Affairs, Durham University, UK.

Giulia A. Pennisi is a Professor of English Language and Translation in the Department of Political Science and International Relations (DEMS) at the University of Palermo, Palermo, Italy and Associate Research Fellow in the Sir William Dale Centre for Legislative Studies, London, UK.

Gerrit Quaremba is a PhD student in the Department of Informatics, King's College London, London, UK.

Ivan Sammut is a Professor in the Department of European & Comparative Law at the University of Malta, Malta.

Fabiana de Menezes Soares is a Professor of Law and Head of LegisLab in the Law School, Federal University of Minas Gerais, Belo Horizonte, Brazil.

Daniel Webber is a Legal Translator and Editor in Chief of *Lex Greca*.

Helen Xanthaki is a Professor at the University College London, Dean of PGLaws in the University of London Worldwide and a Senior Associate Research Fellow in the Sir William Dale Centre for Legislative Studies, London, UK.

Annalisa Zanola is Professor of English Language and Linguistics in the Department of Economics and Management and Director of the Language Centre, University of Brescia, Brescia, Italy.

Introduction to Language for Legislation and Legislation through Language

Tímea Drinóczi, Giulia A. Pennisi, and Helen Xanthaki

Message from a New Interdisciplinary Agenda

Debate on legislative expression has long been preserved for the elite, often esoteric, cast of drafting academics and practitioners, who have succeeded in discouraging other disciplines from attacking our turf, legislation. But in doing so we have failed our super goal of producing good laws. And we now need to rise to the challenge, confess that we do not have the answers to everything, and collaborate with linguistics to learn from, and borrow, know-how, experience, and resulting successes.

One of the main challenges of legislative drafters is that legislation is doing two things at the same time, viz., creating the law and communicating it and using a limited set of linguistic techniques to achieve both things. To begin with, the operation of legislation can be fully understood only in terms of its background. If an instrumental position is taken, the background can be seen to include recognition of a problem, determination of objectives, and the choice of means for their achievement. Indeed, there are inherent difficulties in the drafting of legislation. The drafter is not a mere scribe, and drafting is affected by the environment of the governmental and parliamentary process (Barnes, 2006; Karpen and Xanthaki, 2017). The implementation of legislation can be enormously affected by various filtering agents—rule enforcers, rule interpreters, and the population to whom legislation is directed. They can constrain, adapt, and modify the intentions and policies that may have motivated the passage of the legislation in the first place (Stefanou, 2011). Ultimately, if the lawmaker or someone else wishes to know how the law in question has performed and the extent to which the goals of legislation have been met, the investigation will benefit from the adoption of a broadly scientific approach (Mosmouti, 2019; Norton and De Vrieze, 2020).

Nevertheless, how language is used and how laws are communicated highly influences social acceptance, the interpretation and implementation of laws, and their translation to other languages, which is undoubtedly

DOI: 10.4324/9781003430308-1

essential in multilingual constitutional settings such as the European Union (EU) and many bi- or multilingual states and regions worldwide. How to draft and use language as a source and tool for legislative drafting is determined by various legal measures, translation, and terminological sources and the availability of well-designed terminology databases. It follows that the rules on lawmaking, including drafting, also need to follow the same general normative requirements of efficiency, clarity, and transparency to adequately guide how laws should be drafted (Witgens, 2012; Drinóczi, 2015). Acknowledging the geographical and disciplinary divides the European-focused legisprudence, i.e., the legal field dedicated to studying the theory and practice of legislation (Bar-Siman-Tov, 2020), faces, Bar-Siman-Tov and Xanthaki called for bridging them to create a global multi-disciplinary comparative field of research, comparative legisprudence (Bar-Siman-Tov and Xanthaki, 2023). By drawing on the already-existing and rich literature on the linguistic approach toward legislative drafting and the dedication of legal scholars, linguists, and terminologists committed to this field, this book lives up to this call. It is the first academic work of its kind in that it introduces and explores the first timid studies in the interdisciplinary agenda of language for legislation and legislation through language by identifying its themes, several tools, and interconnections. More specifically, the book investigates the crossroad between legislative drafting and language/linguistics with the aim of opening a new agenda: the use of teachings from the discipline of linguistics in applications useful and relevant to legislative drafting (Crystal and Davy, 1969; Bhatia, 1993; Tiersma, 1999; Garner, 2001; Gotti, 2003; Williams, 2005).

For this reason, scholars and researchers working in the field of law and language have been asked to share their knowledge and expertise, and this book represents one of the important outcomes of this collaboration in the field of legislative drafting and linguistics. Among the issues discussed, three points are particularly stressed: (i) what is clearly conceived in the first place may not be easily expressed with clarity and precision in words. The quality of legislation and its inherent drafting difficulties become crucial; (ii) drafting effective legislation is more likely to be accomplished when the efficacy of the drafted legislation is tested by a linguistic and discoursal analysis of its outcomes; (iii) the translation of normative texts raises many questions such as the need to identify the drafting aspects of language and discuss its use in legislation by reference to problems of translation in legal documents. These are the difficult questions confronting lawyers and linguists working in both national and transnational situations, who face issues such as the quality of legislative drafting and the need to identify specific aspects of drafting in the different languages and to consider how language is used in legislation to resolve problems of interpretation in legal documents. Authors also draw their data from the international context.

The focus of the investigation is centered on the analysis of discourse (very broadly construed to include lexico-grammatical analyses as well as generic and textual analyses) but with the investigation developed in specific contexts (legal, national, and international). The analysis of textual and linguistic phenomena is made considering the cross-cultural traits to highlight the transformations and/or adaptations of legal texts in different contexts.

Authors have contributed to the interdisciplinary agenda of language for legislation and legislation through language by enriching our current knowledge and advancing the field. The lessons learned may also have transformative effects on both the theory and practice of legislative drafting and how linguists and terminologists view this process. To structure this inquiry, we have identified themes, tools, and interconnections that have emerged from the chapters.

In the interdisciplinary agenda of language for legislation and legislation through language, we can identify themes that have emerged through discussing the same issue, i.e., how to make effective, clear, and transparent laws from different perspectives and methodologies. These are social practice, translation and interpretation, and legal certainty. These themes are stand-alone ones and can also be connected. Different jurisdictions identify the essential role of an adequate legal language and style of communication to express their legal and cultural diversity and strengthen cultural acceptance and democracy. They usually rely on the role of judges (EU, in Sammut, 2026), different non-judicial EU bodies (Armao, 2026), and movements supported by courts (Oliveira and Marciano, 2026 in Brazil). Others view legal language's essential role in establishing and highlighting national and legal unity, thus contributing to adequate lawmaking and social practices (Gegenava, 2026 in Georgia and Genckaya, and İba, 2026, in Turkey). Translation and law gain relevance, particularly in two areas. The first is the multilingual structures, which show how the EU multilingualism interacts with legal drafting and institutional translation in a national multilingual constitutional system (Switzerland, in Felici, 2026). The second area is the interaction between international law and national law, as poor translation practices can potentially cause problems for domestic courts when applying international agreements (Turkey, in Bolaca and Çelenk, 2026). Even though these themes are based on case studies, they do have a generalizable potential, just like the theme of legal certainty, which has also emerged through a case study focusing on legal clarity and precision as a tool to embed EU principles (Nezaj, 2026, in Montenegro).

We could detect several tools through which these (social practice, translation and interpretation, and legal certainty) themes can be approached, studied, and put into practice. These are terminology, language processing, and technology. Unlike themes, these tools are better viewed in their combination to assist the interdisciplinary agenda of language for legislation and legislation through language and its practical applicability. An adequately designed and employed terminology management could effectively assist legislative drafting. It can combine Large Language Models (LLMs) with knowledge graphs and terminology databases (Fóris, 2026) and can facilitate the use of contrastive terminology, comparative law, and terminology databases (Novák and Drinóczi, 2026). The techniques for analyzing legislative text using natural language processing is another methodological possibility (Lu et al., 2026), just like the use of multimodal design, which could serve legal language simplification (Hermont et al., 2026).

We have also established interconnections highlighting how the themes and tools come together in practice through language for effectiveness and legal certainty for language. The practical applicability features in three main areas: recommendations, guidelines, and quality criteria for drafting national (O'Shea and Webber, 2026) and EU soft law (Andone and Kund, 2026), exploring the use of the English language in drafting (Kelly, 2026; Zanola, 2026) and testing (Pennisi, 2026) and applying (Xanthaki, 2026; Annex, 2026) easification strategies.

Beyond these "Interconnections", chapters in themes and tools are also in dialogue and show some convergence in their findings, approaches, and methodologies. Five such areas can be mentioned. The first thread is the topic of translators and lawyer linguists working together in drafting, the challenges they face, and the tools that are at their disposal for efficient and socially acceptable laws through court decisions and particular methodologies of comparative law, contrastive terminology, and databases (Sammut, 2026; Fóris, 2026; Novák and Drinóczi, 2026). The second common subject is how legal discourse interacts with institutional translation practices in multilingual settings. Switzerland, a multilingual country with several ties to the EU, serves as a case study from two different directions. On the one hand, it helps explore how contact with EU languages affects Swiss translators and drafters when dealing with EU legislation and court decisions (Felici, 2026). On the other hand, it is also an example for presenting how national (Swiss) legal drafting in three languages and the use and role of databases in translation and terminological clarity could offer a best practice for EU and Member State translators, lawyer linguists, and database developers (Novák and Drinóczi, 2026). The third area is a frequently applied approach to understanding the historical development of the use of language in law and the improvement of legal language (Genckaya and İba, 2026; Gegenava, 2026; Zanola, 2026; Kelly, 2026). The societal aspects of the language of the law, and the concern for how the law can talk to all, appear in Sammut, Oliveira and Marciano, and Hermont et al.: good drafting practices and judicial interpretation, gender-sensitive language, and multimodality presented as possible methodological approaches to address these concerns. Lastly, the focus of LLM and Natural Language Processing (NLP) in two separate chapters (Luet al., 2026; Fóris, 2026) and the case study on the use of multimodality (Hermont et al., 2026) explain and further strengthen the need for the use of technology and methodological diversity.

Thus, the book proves that linguists can, and must, contribute to phronetic legislative drafting by means of supplying tried methodologies and tools toward good law, i.e., toward effective legislative expression. Linguistics investigates the way in which meaning and text functions evolve in the process of text production, finds out what the functions of the produced legislative texts are, and assesses if the texts' functions match the original intentions of the drafters. In turn, this allows drafters to become aware of how the law's functions can match the intention of drafters, thus developing techniques that can lead to the desired result. All these can be read in the 18 chapters offering case studies of analyses that cross the gap between law and linguistics. And, through the demonstration of mutually beneficial collaborations, it showcases the interconnection and interfunctionalities of interdisciplinary themes and methods for the study of legislation for and through language. The following section features the chapters' most important messages.

Message through the Chapters

Themes: Social Practice, Translation and Interpretation, and Legal Certainty

In Chapter 1"*Law, Language & Culture in the EU: A Case of Harmonisation, Reflection of Diversity or a Case for Judicial Activism?*" Ivan Sammut identifies the role of legal language within the legal and cultural diversity in EU legislation. The legal and language diversity of 27 Member States creates variances in the language versions of a multilingual EU legislation, assigning their resolution by the Court of Justice of the EU. The chapter focuses on the way in which the court resolves such variances in a creative manner, thus offering the court an opportunity to cross the border of interpretation over to judicial lawmaking. However, the analysis of court case law demonstrates that this opportunity is not taken by the court, perhaps because of the excellent work of translators and lawyer linguists in resolving as many of those variances as possible at the text level.

Ana Larissa Adorno Marciotto Oliveira and Lucas Willian Oliveira Marciano in Chapter 2 explore the various aspects of the use of gender-inclusive language in Brazil through a contextualized analysis with international comparison while applying the lenses of Brazilian Constitutional

Feminism and Critical Discourse Analysis. They set forth three main arguments, revolving simultaneously around legal questions, linguistic approaches, and social reality and movements supported by courts. The first is that the masculine default, widely used in Brazilian Portuguese, excludes the explicit representation of women and LGBT+ individuals, reinforcing a structural oversight rather than promoting intentional inclusiveness. With this, they reject the claim that the masculine form "implicitly" includes the feminine and the non-binary forms. It relates to their second claim, which is that true inclusiveness primarily requires explicitly recognizing all groups within the language itself. Lastly, they attest that gender-inclusive language in Brazil connects to discursive practices that give voice to historically underrepresented groups, which fosters pluralism and enriches democratic life, regardless of how divisive Brazilian politics and society are in the matter.

Based on a historical and contextual review, including the development and use of legal Russian in the country and the dynamics between the two languages (Georgian and Russian) in social, political, and legal life in Georgia (Georganization and Russianization), Dimitry Gegenava convincingly argues for the need for transformation and describes the challenges of "legal Georgian". In Chapter 3, he accurately documents the dynamics and central directions in developing the "legal Georgian" language adequate for the needs of democratic Georgia in the 21st century. He argues that the fact that "legal Georgian" was developed in a non-organic way and was primarily influenced by copying and literal translation from the Russian language remains one of the biggest challenges this process faces. It has been a continuous struggle as difficulties arising from the historical creation of the "legal Georgian", which the country should attempt to transcend, are persistent in judicial and legislative practices. It is because practitioners have been educated in institutions where lecturers and researchers neglected this field; i.e., the importance and implications of and innovations to the Georgian legal language have not been studied. Thus, research cannot feed policymaking.

In Chapter 4, Gaetano Armao considers the contribution that the *European Committee of the Regions* (*CoR*, the *guardian of European subsidiarity*) has given and through the entire system of local and regional authorities can and must further give to better implement of the European Commission Communications on better regulation with the aim of improving the EU's policymaking process, updating the better regulation agenda to mainstream sustainable development goals and the digital and green transition and by ensuring more foresight-based policymaking. In this area, too, the *CoR* has demonstrated the most valuable contribution it can make to the future of the EU: strengthening European democracy by bringing it closer to the citizens but also accustoming them to a new way of conceiving democracy itself. Legislating *better* is possible with the aim of giving quality to the regulatory texts and rationalizing, and systematizing the rules governing the various sectors. It is thus necessary that the different levels of government commit themselves to contributing to making life easier for citizens, families, communities, and productive sectors.

In Chapter 5, Belkis Vural Celenk and Aysun Bolaca demonstrate how translation plays a crucial role in the interpretation of law. Considering the multilingual aspect of international law, the role of translation is more critical when it comes to international legal instruments. States usually sign international agreements including their commitments to pursue common goals to improve their relations in various areas. If the official language of a contracting State is not the original language of an international agreement, the translation of this agreement to the State's own language means a lot to that State. If the text is not translated accurately or mistranslated, potential problems can occur during the application of international agreement by domestic courts of that State.

In Chapter 6, Annarita Felici attempts to outline how EU multilingualism interacts with legal drafting and institutional translation in multilingual Switzerland. Although it is not an EU Member State, Switzerland is an official trilingual country that incorporates much of the EU's legislation. Focusing exclusively on linguistic aspects and legal discourse, this study highlights the features of institutional translation and the impact of language contact. The analysis is twofold and navigates between macrotextual features, such as text structure and organization, and microlinguistics aspects, like modality and sentence structure. While the former aims to shed light on concordance with other texts in the same legal system and within the same language, the latter examines interlinguistic consistency in terms of meaning and effects across different languages. The preliminary findings show that the EU language does not have a massive impact on Swiss legal discourse and that Swiss authentic translations maintain a notable degree of autonomy.

In Chapter 7, Ömer Faruk Gençkaya and Şeref İba travel through the history of law and language in Turkey, focusing on the three constitutions in the 1920s, the 1960s, and the 1980s. Despite the continuity in the legal language throughout Turkish constitutions, the legal reform in 1924 inherited the Western language and removed some of the Persian concepts and terms used until then. But the real Turkishization of constitutional language came in the 1940s culminating with a 1961 Constitution that progressively incorporated simplification in constitutional language. The 1982 Constitution promotes linguistic integrity by using other rich and dynamic Turkish languages culling Arabic Persian and foreign terms and replacing them with their Turkish modern equivalent.

In Chapter 8, Novitet Nezaj focuses on the intersection of language for the achievement of legal clarity and precision as a tool to embed EU principles into Kosovo's governance. Legislative reform as a means of governance transformation is challenged in Kosovo by the implementation deficit and lack of key reform drivers in the country. The recommendations for regulatory governance offer a roadmap for reform in an ambitious yet feasible route for EU accession.

Tools: Terminology, Language Processing, and Technology

Ágota Fóris in Chapter 9 connects terminology management to the law and legal texts. She highlights the importance of dynamic and adaptable terminology resources and tools for legislation as they facilitate effective and comprehensible communication and ensure the clarity and comprehensibility of legal and other official documents. She suggests, first, that the comprehensibility of texts is influenced by numerous factors, including terminology, and, second, that ensuring the comprehensibility of terminology entails two main approaches. These are the intralingual translation and the creation of terminology databases, which terminology recommendations and standards can support. Fóris makes a case that standardization represents a significant advancement in implementing effective practices. It is, as she argues, because the future is the combination of LLMs with knowledge graphs and terminology databases, and it could address challenges (such as the reliability of the sources, linguistic errors, being biased and discriminatory, and fabricating incorrect information).

Barnabás Novák and Tímea Drinóczi in Chapter 10 provide a more law-oriented and less technical approach to address the multilingual challenges the drafting process faces. Their chapter drew on case studies on the Swiss and EU experiences using multilingual databases, such as the Swiss TERMDAT and the EU's IATE, and the most salient Hungarian examples of translation clashes with certain English terms used in EU lawmaking. These analyses suggest that the drafting process in multilingual jurisdictions could benefit from contrastive terminology, comparative law, and terminology databases created on these bases. They also highlight that translations and terminology databases are valuable to the legislative process but only if adequately embedded in the process, and there is a genuine collaboration between the involved parties. Through different methods and drafting mechanisms in which they are involved, both TERMDAT and IATE contribute to producing clearer, more precise, more transparent, and more accessible laws.

In Chapter 11, Xiao Lu, Moritz Osnabrügge, and Gerrit Quaremba offer a dense sample of techniques for analyzing legislative text using natural language processing. In their publication of a vast empirical sample of EU legislation across five years, they apply part of speech tagging and dependency parsing to focus on passive voice and negation. These constitute drafting anathemas and are expressly rejected in the Interinstitutional Guides for Better Law-Making. Yet 41% of sentences under study are in passive voice; 9.7% use negation. This is a bright example of how methodological tools for the study of language can identify drafting errors, calculate their extent, and inform drafting practice.

Thiago B.V. Hermont, Fabiana de Menezes Soares, and Mônica Sette Lopes, in Chapter 12, show how these approaches have implemented the simplification of the Brazilian legal language. They have argued that the combination of legal language simplification with multimodal design principles promotes transparency and ensures that official information is presented in a way that is engaging and easy to understand. Therefore, this multimodality approach ultimately contributes to a more inclusive legal system. To support their argument, the authors have analyzed the homepage of Brazil's Ministry of Environment using the Genre and Multimodality Model.

Interconnection in Praxis: Language for Effectiveness and Legal Certainty for Language

In Chapter 13, John O'Shea and Daniel Webber present the Lex Graeca project as a case study for the role of language in the achievement of effectiveness of legislation focusing specifically on clarity, precision, and unambiguity. The Lex Graeca project involves a translation of Greece's major codes into English and thus serves as a vehicle for assessing clarity, precision, ambiguity, and ultimately their effectiveness. The authors use feasible recommendations as techniques for overcoming the challenges of Greek legislation in these areas.

In Chapter 14, Martin David Kelly discusses the use of the English language in drafting, with a special focus on the challenges that its grammatical tenses, i.e., past, present, and future, and aspects, such as simple, progressive, and perfect, pose. He argues that the choice of tense in legislative drafting raises several important issues that are unduly neglected in the literature. Kelly also shows how using grammatically correct tenses and aspects poses challenges in interpretation. His case study–based analysis of tenses and aspects in legislative drafting challenges theoretical approaches of using the present tense and progressive aspect in legislative drafting, and, to do so, he discusses the arguments judges have used to highlight the complexity of the English language in drafting laws.

In Chapter 15, Annalisa Zanola analyzes the linguistic contexts in which the hendiadys "true and fair" was first used and examines the meaning of this *formula* in non-financial contexts over the centuries. The couple is first documented in literary contexts in the 16th century, subsequently becoming a hendiadys in the following centuries and finally a codified *formula* in the specialized financial field. A debate concerning the importance of interpreting the terminology employed by auditors in expressing their opinions can be found in the accounting literature. Nevertheless, this does not alter the intrinsic and enduring ambiguity of the undefined expression "true and fair view", which has been in use since its introduction in the 1948 UK Companies Act. The term has its roots in legal discourse, emerging in the 18th century, and underwent a process of translation into a legal definition concerning corporate accountability in the 20th century. The analysis of the hendiadys from a non-financial to a financial context, following the steps of the etymological and lexical research methodology, may provide support for a more complete definition of the complex concept of the "true and fair view" as set out in the Fourth Council Directive.

Corina Andone and Florin Coman-Kund's chapter concentrates on *drafting EU soft law instruments as persuasive governance tools*. The focus of their analysis is to identify, define, and operationalize drafting criteria and guidelines for EU soft law instruments. Despite their common usage and influence in a wide area of policies and a core preoccupation with the quality of EU legal acts, in general, most prominently in the context of the "better lawmaking" initiatives, the drafting of these instruments has hardly been a concern for EU drafters. This chapter first highlights the unique attributes of EU soft law instruments as persuasive governance tools. Next, concrete guidelines for the proper drafting of EU soft law instruments are outlined and explained against the background of several argumentative and legal parameters used to assess the persuasive force of these governance tools.

In Chapter 17, Giulia A. Pennisi develops *a linguistic approach to drafting legislative provisions*. The nature and extent of specification of legal scope in the expression of legislative intentions represents one of the most difficult tasks in legislative drafting. In her chapter, she takes into consideration legislative provisions from a linguistic point of view. She applies tests of language in a number of texts belonging to the current common law drafting practice to ascertain a loss of conceptual focus by legislative drafters and concludes that linguistics provides a method by which drafters can assess the effectiveness of their draft. Her analysis of simplification and "easification" strategies certainly provides interesting insights into how legislative provisions can be linguistically and textually improved depending on the communicative purposes which have originated them and the context in which they will eventually be applied.

In Chapter 18, Helen Xanthaki identifies an additional case study for the cross-fertilization between law and language. The EU Regulation on the Social Climate Fund is a recent example of a legal text produced by the

EU. It represents a body of law that is often accused of being convoluted, detached, intelligible, and inaccessible. The easification doctrine borrowed from the study of language can resolve these issues and offer another way forward for the drafting of accessible, legible, and ultimately effective EU Acts. The chapter focuses on a layered structure for EU Acts, focusing on the prioritization of regulatory messages to accommodate the needs of the three main groups of EU legislative audiences: EU citizens, Member States and their national authorities, and EU institutions and learned users. The Regulation on the Social Climate Fund is used as a case study of layered regulation, and a layered draft is put to effect by Nicole Sardiello-Zamboni, Aarohi Vikas Pillai, Denise Yasmine H. Eixas, and Kimberley Shepherd.

Final Message

The book indeed shows how joint efforts of different disciplines, methodologies, and geographic diversity can contribute to opening up a new interdisciplinary agenda of language for legislation and legislation through language. Topics have been addressed through the lens of language and law/law and language, but each has its primary orientation in legal studies, translation and terminology studies, linguistics and law, social science, and natural language processing. The book contains country-oriented case studies and some comparative exercises while speaking to both common law and civil law traditions and jurisdictions in Europe, Latin America, Caucasus, and Western Asia. It supports the statement one of us expressed in 2022:

> anything that causes drafters to challenge fixed old habits (i.e. formulaic expressions, grammar rules and social norms, repetitive use of form-meaning associations, common patterns of thought) might be seen as an opportunity for innovation and improvement (unusual collocations, unpredictable compounds).
>
> (Pennisi, 2022)

This could be the motto of this book, which, in a clear, effective, and transparent manner, brings theory and practice together, for instance, when it shows how the concept of easification can be applied to improving the clarity, transparency, and efficiency and thus widening the actual the social reach of the law. It also addresses the geographic divide by including jurisdictions like Switzerland, Hungary, Turkey, Georgia, and Brazil, which are beyond the usual suspects of any comparative exploration, such as the UK and the EU. While the book is not comparative in itself, it addresses different comparative methodologies as a useful tool for the interdisciplinary agenda of language for legislation and legislation through language and uses comparison when discussing certain case studies. It also serves as a research handbook, inspiring future research on the identified themes by using and improving the displayed tools and finding other areas of interconnections. Drafters, linguists, terminologists, lawyer linguists, and database developers can also benefit from the interdisciplinary agenda of language for legislation and legislation through language and its practical applicability.

Cited Works

Adorno Marciotto Oliveira, Ana Larissa, and Oliveira Marciano, Lucas Willian. 2026 "Gender inclusiveness: does language as a social practice meet lawmaking in Brazil?", in *Language for Legislation and Legislation through Language.*

Andone, Corina and Coman Kund, Florin. 2026 "Drafting EU soft law instruments as persuasive governance tools", in *Language for Legislation and Legislation through Language.*

Armao, Gaetano. 2026 "EU "'Better regulation': the role of European committee of the regions", in *Language for Legislation and Legislation through Language.*

Barnes, Jeffrey. 2006. "The continuing debate about 'plain language' legislation: a law reform conundrum". *Statute Law Review* 27, 85–86. https://doi.org/10.1093/slr/hml004

Bar-Siman-Tov, Ittai. 2020. "Beyond neglect and disrespect: legislatures in legal scholarship", in Cyril Benoît and Olivier Rozenberg eds. *Handbook of Parliamentary Studies.* Edward Elgar.

Bar-Siman-Tov, Ittai and Xanthaki, Helen. 2023. "Legislation, legisprudence and comparative law", in Jan M. Smits et al., eds. *Elgar Encyclopedia of Comparative Law.* Edward Elgar.

Bhatia, Vijay K. 1993. *Analyzing Genre: Language Use in Professional Settings.* Longman.

Bolaca, Aysun and Çelenk, Belkıs Vural. 2026 "Why translation matters in legal context by examining a specific case: Turkey", in *Language for Legislation and Legislation through Language.*

Crystal, David and Davy, Derek. 1969. *Investigating English Style.* Longman.

Drinóczi, Tímea. 2015. "Concept of quality in legislation—revisited: matter of perspective and a general overview". *Statute Law Review* 36(3), 211–227.

Felici, Annarita. 2026 "Institutional translation: balancing multilingual legal discourse between EU and Switzerland", in *Language for Legislation and Legislation through Language.*

Fóris, Ágota. 2026 "How can terminology management support bridging the gap between legislative language and better understanding of legislative intent for citizens?", in *Language for Legislation and Legislation through Language.*

Garner, Bryan A. 2001. *Legal Writing in Plain Language.* University of Chicago Press.

Gegenava, Dimitry. 2026 "Law, language and legal certainty: transformation and challenges of the Georgian legal language", in *Language for Legislation and Legislation through Language.*

Genckaya, Omer Faruk and İba, Şeref. 2026 "Legislative interpretation in the Ottoman and Turkish constitutions and its practice", in *Language for Legislation and Legislation through Language.*
Gotti, Maurizio. 2003. *Specialized Discourse: Linguistic Features and Changing Conventions.* Peter Lang.
Hermont, Thiago, Soares, Fabiana, and Sette Lopes, Mônica. 2026 "An empirical approach of multimodality and legal language reform in Brazil", in *Language for Legislation and Legislation through Language.*
Karpen, Ulrich and Xanthaki, Helen. eds. 2017. *Legislation and Legisprudence in Europe: A Comprehensive Guide for Scholars and Legislative Practitioners.* Hart Publishing.
Kelly, Martin David. 2026 "Tense aspects of legislative drafting", in *Language for Legislation and Legislation through Language.*
Mosmouti, Maria. 2019. *Designing Effective Legislation.* Edward Elgar.
Nezaj, Novitet. 2026 "The quest for legislative reform in Kosovo: bridging regulatory governance with legal drafting and legislative language discourses", in *Language for Legislation and Legislation through Language.*
Norton, Philip and De Vrieze, Franklin. 2020. "The significance of post-legislative scrutiny". *Journal of Legislative Studies* 26(3), 349–361. https://doi.org/10.1080/13572334.2020.1780008
Novák, Barnabás and Drinóczi, Tímea. 2026 "Making drafting clearer and more accessible in a multilingual context: the role of contrastive terminology and comparative law", in *Language for Legislation and Legislation through Language.*
O'Shea, John and Webber, Daniel. 2026 "Translation as a mirror through which to view legislation's effectiveness", in *Language for Legislation and Legislation through Language.*
Lu, Xiao, Osnabruegge, Moritz, and Quaremba, Gerrit. 2026 "Analyzing the language of legislation using natural language processing", in *Language for Legislation and Legislation through Language.*
Pennisi, Giulia Adriana. 2022. "Legislative drafting and gender: some linguistic insights into English and Italian". *The Theory and Practice of Legislation* 10(3), 305–321. https://doi.org/10.1080/20508840.2022.2139042
Pennisi, Giulia Adriana. 2026 "A linguistic approach to drafting legislative provisions", in *Language for Legislation and Legislation through Language.*
Sammut, Ivan. 2026 "Law, language & culture in the EU: a case of harmonisation, reflection of diversity or a case for judicial activism?", in *Language for Legislation and Legislation through Language.*
Stefanou, Constantine. 2011. "Legislative drafting as a form of communication", in L. Mader, Luzius and Travares-Almeida, Marta. eds. *Quality of Legislation Principles and Instruments.* Nomos Baden-Baden.
Tiersma, Peter. 1999. *Legal Language.* University of Chicago Press.
Williams, Christopher. 2005. *Tradition and Change in Legal English.* Peter Lang.
Witgens, Luc. 2012. *Legisprudence: Practical Reason for Legislation.* Routledge.
Xanthaki, Helen. 2014. *Drafting Legislation: Art and Technology of Rules for Regulation.* Hart.
Xanthaki, Helen. 2026 "Let linguists teach the drafters: easification (layering the structure) of Regulation (EU) 2023/955 establishing a social climate fund"

with Nicole Sardiello-Zamboni, Aarohi Vikas Pillai, Denise Yasmine H. Eixas and Kimberley Shepherd, in *Language for Legislation and Legislation through Language.*

Zanola, Annalisa. 2026 "Terminological controversies over a legal hendiadys: the 'true and fair' case", in *Language for Legislation and Legislation through Language.*

Part One

Themes

Social Practice, Translation and Interpretation, and Legal Certainty

1 Law, Language and Culture in the EU

A Case of Harmonisation, Reflection of Diversity or a Case for Judicial Activism?

Ivan Sammut

1.1 Law, Language and Culture in the EU

The basic unit of translation is not the word but the concept. This concept is particularly true in the European Union (EU) case, which currently has 24 language versions. Council Regulation 1/1958/EEC stipulates that once a language is recognised as official, according to Articles 2 and 4 of the Regulation, the EU institutions must communicate with citizens and enact legislation in all the recognised official languages. This includes the legislative instruments adopted for legal harmonisation. Legal harmonisation is the process by which national laws are brought closer to each other for the better functioning of the Internal Market.[1] This is mainly done through EU directives. Hence, the multilingual nature of EU law is inherently linked to the need for uniform interpretation and application of EU law. When Malta, the EU's smallest Member State, joined the EU in 2004, Maltese became the official and the national language, one of two languages, the other being English, in which law in Malta is enforced and implemented. Through Regulation 1/1958/EEC, Maltese had to become the official language of the EU. All languages in national law must become an official EU language. EU law is de facto national law, interpreted and applied in the national courts, so EU law needs to be in the same language/s as national law.

Article 1 of this Regulation established French, German, Dutch and Italian as this Community's (now Union) official and working languages, reflecting the national languages of the six founding countries, namely, France, Germany, Italy and the Benelux countries (Belgium, Luxembourg and the Netherlands). Since then, the European Economic Community has developed into the EU, the six Member States have increased to 27, and the four official and working languages have multiplied to 24, with today three main working languages, namely English, by far the most used following by French and German, a very distant second and third.

DOI: 10.4324/9781003430308-3

Article 1 of Regulation No. 1/58 has been amended accordingly and today reads as follows:

> The official languages and the working languages of the institutions of the Union shall be Bulgarian, Croatian, Czech, Danish, Dutch, English, Estonian, Finnish, French, German, Greek, Hungarian, Irish, Italian, Latvian, Lithuanian, Maltese, Polish, Portuguese, Romanian, Slovak, Slovenian, Spanish and Swedish.

However, the Regulation's substance has remained, in essence, unchanged. It comprises a concise preamble recalling the legal basis above-quoted and eight equally concise provisions.

In terms of Articles 2 and 3, written communication sent by a Member State or an individual subject to its jurisdiction to an EU institution may be drafted in any of the languages listed above, and any reply must be given in the same chosen language. Furthermore, any documents an EU institution sends to a Member State or an individual about it must be drawn up in the particular State's language. Articles 4 and 5 are of utmost importance to ensure the accessibility of European legislation to all European citizens. These provisions declare, respectively, that documents and regulations of general application must be drafted in all the official languages and that such documents and regulations must be published in all 24 languages in the Official Journal of the EU. Article 6 grants the EU institutions a degree of flexibility: they may thus "stipulate in their rules of procedures which of the languages are to be used in specific cases".

The Court of Justice is set apart from the other institutions: the languages to be used in proceedings before it are regulated by the Court's own Rules of Procedure. French is the only working language of the Court. However, these rules largely follow the general scheme of Regulation No. 1/58. Finally, this Regulation establishes that where a Member State has more than one official language, the relative Member State's general rules of law determine the language to be used.

Regulation No. 1/58 does not clearly define its scope of applicability. Article 1 speaks broadly of the languages "of the institutions of the Union" but does not explicitly State which institutions they are. They are listed in Article 13 Treaty on European Union (TEU) the European Parliament, the European Council, the Council, the Commission, the Court of Justice of the EU (CJEU), the European Central Bank and the Court of Auditors. Article 13 TEU also mentions two advisory bodies that aim to assist the Parliament, Council and Commission: the European Economic and Social Committee and the Committee of Regions. Regulation No. 1/58 thus applies to all the institutions mentioned above, barring the Court of Justice, which, as explained above, are explicitly excluded from the scope of the

Regulation under Article 7. Regulation No. 1/58 is also not applicable to several other EU bodies and agencies, such as European Union Intellectual Property Office (EUIPO). A citizen may accordingly file an application in any of the official languages of the EU but must also indicate a second language, out of the five languages of the Office, to be used in the case of subsequent proceedings.

This procedure was challenged in the case of *Christina Kik v Office* for Harmonisation in the Internal Market (Trade Marks and Designs) (OHIM), now EUIPO. The applicant, an Intellectual Property lawyer and trademark agent in the Netherlands, applied Dutch to the OHIM to register the word "KIK" as a Community Trade Mark. She also indicated Dutch as a second language. The Office dismissed her application, declaring that the formal requirement of choosing a second language had not been satisfied since Dutch was not one of the five languages of the Office. Mrs Kik appealed, claiming that the principle of equality between languages set out in Regulation 1/58 could not be derogated, not even by a subsequent regulation of the Council. Both the then-Court of First Instance heard the case, now the General Court and the Court of Justice, and both courts dismissed her argument, affirming Regulation No. 1/58 as an act of secondary law having its legal basis in Article 217 Treaty on the Functioning of the European Union (TFEU) and, as such, as one which did not establish any overriding principle.

The Court of Justice declared that the rules governing languages were not established and enshrined in the Treaty but that Article 217 TFEU allowed the Council to define, amend and establish different language rules unanimously. As such, the Court held that "it follows that the rules governing languages laid down by Regulation No. 1 cannot be deemed to amount to a principle of Community law". Furthermore, the Court highlighted the fact that although

> The Treaty contains several references to the use of language in the European Union, and these cannot be regarded as evidencing a general principle of Community law that confers a right on every citizen to have a version of anything that might affect his interests drawn up in his language in all circumstances.

Thus, although Regulation No. 1/58 establishes the EU's linguistic regime, it has limitations. It also raises several questions.

EU legal translation contributes to the harmonisation of EU law and the evolution of the European legal culture. The CJEU has regularly clarified that a uniform interpretation and application of EU law entails uniformity of all the language versions in which EU law exists. In fact, in numerous judgements, the CJEU has emphasised that the need for the uniform interpretation and application of EU law entails that EU legislation must be interpreted and applied "in the light of the versions in all .... Languages" (Case 29/69 *Stauder* [1969][2] and, more recently, Case C-375/07 *Heuschen & Schroff* [2008]).[3] In the *Regina v Bouchereau* case in 1977, the CJEU added that "the different language versions ... must be given a uniform interpretation" (Case 30/77 *Regina v Bouchereau* [1977]).[4]

Thus, the Court makes it clear that, while the EU institutions operate in various legal cultures and languages, institutional multilingualism must still result in the uniform interpretation of the law.[5] Legal harmonisation is the process of using directives, and the EU instructs the Member States to bring their national laws within the parameters set by the Directive. The national laws are written in the official language/s of the Member States, and EU law also requires directives to be available as the authentic version in the official language of the Member State. EU legal translation is not just a "standard" legal translation from one Source Language to another; it requires introducing new legal and linguistic concepts. "New" means this legal culture is created specifically for the EU legal order.

The norm "one language, one State, one people" cannot be said to apply to the EU, despite the close and almost-irreversible cooperation between the Member States. Language, in particular, becomes a key consideration for several reasons, in a discussion concerning integration between European countries with vast linguistic and cultural diversity. While language is primarily essential for communication, it is also closely linked to identity. Edwards describes language as a "powerful pillar of identity", citing language nationalist von Humboldt, who famously declared that "absolutely nothing is so important for a nation's culture as its language".[6] Joseph claims that language and identity are "ultimately inseparable",[7] and Byram confirmed, in a recent study, that language and the sense of national identity are indeed a strong link.

Therefore, for political and practical reasons, the EU boasts 24 official languages reflecting the national languages of its Member States. EU legislation is widely available in these 24 languages, ensuring that it is easily accessible to both the Member States and the citizens whom it binds. In the context of public international law, language has never been such a significant consideration. No other international entity or organisation has ever admitted or been burdened by as many working and/or official languages: the United Nations has six official languages (English, French, Arabic, Chinese, Russian and Spanish), and the Council of Europe and NATO use English and French. Language thus plays a primary role in the EU, serving both symbolic and practical purposes, as it has since the beginning of the European project.

1.2 A Single Text or a Single Meaning: Multilingual Interpretation of the EU's *acquis communautaire*

European legislation must be available in the 24 official languages of the EU and interpreted and applied uniformly throughout the Union. Amongst other functions, the Court of Justice of the EU has jurisdiction to give preliminary rulings concerning the interpretation of the Treaties and the interpretation and validity of the acts of the EU institutions, bodies, offices and agencies per Article 267 of the TFEU.

In recent years, the Court of Justice has been criticised for judicial activism,[8] a term used to denote judges who opt for a more liberal, as opposed to a restrained, interpretation of EU law. Micklitz describes such a situation as one where "judges overstep constitutional boundaries, taking over and even accepting the role of the legislator".[9] Judicial activism is often seen in decisions relating to sensitive issues which pertain to areas falling within Member States' national sovereignty, for instance, in the case of *Blaise Baheten Metock and Others v Minister for Justice, Equality and Law Reform*,[10] which concerned Directive 2004/38/EC[11] and, in particular, rules relating to the unification of migrant citizens with their families.

In this case, the Court extended the scope of Directive 2004/38/EC to spouses of migrant citizens who were third-country nationals and who did not previously reside within EU territory, holding that in the same manner as EU citizens could move and reside freely within the territory of any Member State, so could their spouses, even where such spouses were non-EU citizens. Furthermore, the Court held that the Directive mentioned above precluded domestic legislation requiring previous residence in a Member State. This judgement resulted in several Member States having to amend their respective laws and policies.[12]

Legal certainty is a general principle of EU law. Formal legal certainty implies that laws and adjudication must be predictable. Laws must satisfy the imperatives of clarity, stability, intelligibility, and predictability so that those concerned can accurately calculate the legal consequences of their actions and the outcome of legal proceedings.[13] Substantive legal certainty is related to the rational acceptability of judicial decision-making. It is not sufficient that laws are predictable. They must be accepted by the legal community in question. Legal certainty encompassing its formal and substantive elements forms an important principle in national legal systems. While principles and the national legal system do not apply automatically to EU law, one would also accept that EU law being enforced alongside pure domestic law will have similar principles. Law requires a certain degree of predictability so that those concerned can know the legal consequences of their actions in advance. The principle of legal certainty comprises a wide concept essential in EU law and the EU's legal systems. It is the ultimate necessity for the law to be clear, stable, and intelligible.

Therefore, transparency and legitimacy are seen as driving forces behind multilingualism and are closely connected to legal certainty and legitimacy. This is not so much formal validity of the legal system as substantive act ability intertwined with legitimacy. On the one hand, established law guarantees enforcement of legally accepted behaviour and the certainty of law. On the other hand, rational procedures for making and applying the law and a guarantee of legitimate expectations. Law stabilises societal behavioural expectations to create legal certainty that enables law addresses to calculate the legal consequences of their behaviour and those of others. Consequently, legal norms must assume a comprehensible, consistent and precise form and be public, made known to all addressees. They may not claim retroactivity, and they must govern the factual circumstances in general terms and connect the factual situation with legal consequences so that it is possible to apply the normal to all persons and to comparable cases in the same way.[14]

The concepts of legal certainty and the rule of law are closely connected. The notion of legal certainty is generally used in similar systems. The closest equivalent and common law appears to be the rule of law. Thus, because of its immediate connection to legal certainty, it is necessary to sketch the basic tenets of all law principles governing the power of authorities. In normative terms, the rule of law refers to the characteristics of an ideal legal system. Alternatively, it may refer to a concept that defines the content of law and the sands of a directly applicable principle of law in judicial decision-making or an interpretive principle in adjudication guiding statutory construction. However, irrespective of the legal system in which the rule of law is virtual, at least one point exists on which there is broad agreement, the principle escapes and is a precise definition. The imperatives associated with the rule of law, especially clarity, require that indeterminacy, such as vagueness and ambiguity, be avoided.

One can narrow the CJEU's approaches into literal and theological ones to address the above issues and achieve legal certainty. The literal approach' reflects the classical reconciliation method of interpretation adopted by the Court of Justice, whereby it considers diverging language versions of a particular legislative text and attempts to reconcile them and extract the intended meaning on a purely linguistic basis. The teleological approach refers to the method of interpretation adopted by the Court of Justice whereby the latter discards linguistic considerations completely and reaches its decision based on the purpose and general scheme of the rule in question instead.

1.3 The Literal Approach

Derlén and Berends refer to this method as the "classical reconciliation method"[15] and the "textual" method,[16] respectively, while, as stated above, Baaij[17] terms it "the literal approach". Berends identifies this method of interpretation as one of three which correspond to the general rule of interpretation in international law. This provides that, to interpret the terms of a multilingual treaty, one must begin from the ordinary meaning of such terms, taking into consideration the context as well as their object and purpose since it is not always straightforward to ascertain the meaning of such terms from a purely linguistic perspective. Berends likens the literal approach to examining the ordinary meaning of the terms, recalling that this is based on the presumption that the legislator's intention has been reliably expressed in the legal instrument concerned.[18] Thus, the ordinary meaning may be detected by analysing the words and language used in the text. According to Derlén's classical reconciliation method, all the language versions are compared and reconciled based on a particular principle, such as preference for a clear or majority meaning.[19] Baaij also discusses this approach in some detail, citing and echoing Derlén. He confirms that the Court, in adopting such an approach, tends to employ one of two possible arguments: the "majority argument" or the "clarity argument", and that, thus, the Court reconciles the various texts based on either the meaning expressed by the majority or the clearest text.

Various CJEU judgements deal with the literal approach, and it is not easy to be exhaustive, but one can mention some examples. One can mention *Proceedings brought by X*,[20] *Dirk Frederik Asbeek Brusse and Katarina de Man Garabito v Jahani BV*[21] and *Jager & Polacek GmbH v Office for Harmonisation in the Internal Market (Trade Marks and Designs) (OHIM)*.[22]

X involved a linguistic discrepancy between the various language versions of Article 12(a) of Directive 95/46/EC.[23] The Court declared that English and Swedish versions of this provision were ambiguous but held that neither obliged Member States to communicate information for free.[24] Furthermore, in all the other language versions of this provision, and, thus, the vast majority thereof, there was nothing to preclude communicating the said data against payment. The Court justified its conclusion as follows, echoing *Stauder*:[25]

> For the purposes of its interpretation, Article 12 (a) of Directive 95/46 cannot be examined solely in the Dutch-language version: according to settled case-law, the need for the uniform application of an EU measure and, accordingly, for a uniform interpretation of that measure makes it impossible to consider one version of the text in isolation, but requires

> that it be interpreted on the basis of both the real intention of its author and the aim which the latter seeks to achieve, in the light, in particular, of the versions in all languages.[26]

Brusse[27] concerned the interpretation of Directive 93/13/EEC.[28] In its request for a preliminary ruling, the Dutch referring Court asked whether a tenancy agreement relating to premises to be used as a residence and concluded between a landlord acting for purposes relating to his trade, business or profession and a tenant acting on a non-commercial basis, fell within the scope of this Directive. The CJEU noted a discrepancy between the various language versions of Article 1 of Directive 93/13/EEC, which set out its purpose: that of approximating national provisions relating to unfair contract terms—the Dutch version of this provision referred to contracts between a "verkoper" and a consumer. In contrast, the French version referred to contracts between a *professional*[29] and a consumer, a term reflected in the Spanish, German, Danish, Italian, Greek and Portuguese versions. The English version used the phrase "seller or supplier". The term used in the Dutch version was thus clearly more restrictive in scope.

The CJEU recalled the need for uniform application and interpretation of an EU measure, stating that, as such, the Dutch version of Article 1 could not be considered in isolation but had to be interpreted based on the author's real intention as well as the aim that the latter desired to achieve "in the light of all the language versions".[30] The Court considered the meaning expressed by the majority of the language versions of this provision and compared the definition of the relevant term in all the language versions, declaring that the Dutch term "*verkoper*" was defined in the Dutch version of the Directive in the same way as it was in the other versions. The Court thus concluded that it was not the legislator's intention to restrict the scope of this provision. It did not stop here, however: it also examined other relevant provisions within the Directive, quoted prior case law and considered the context of the legislation. In this case, the Court seems to have reached its initial conclusion based on the literal approach and confirmed it contextually.

In *Jager & Polacek v OHIM*, Jager & Polacek GmbH appealed a judgement given by the General Court, where this dismissed an action for the annulment of a decision by the Fourth Board of Appeal of the Office for Harmonisation in the Internal Market (Trade Marks and Designs) concerning opposition proceedings between Jager & Polacek and RT Mediasolutions s.r.o. The linguistic issue that arose in this case centred around the phrase "found admissible" in Rule 18 (1) of the Implementing Regulation,[31] which provides the following:

> When the opposition is found admissible pursuant to Rule 17, the Office shall send a communication to the parties informing them that

the opposition proceedings shall be deemed to commence two months after receipt of the communication.

The CJEU acknowledged that the German version of this rule varied slightly from the other language versions. It explicitly referenced the French version of the Implementing Regulation, which contained "*jugée receivable*". It maintained that an equivalent phrase was used in several other language versions of this Regulation. The Court concluded that examining the different language versions of this text "shows that the opposition must be found admissible before the inter partes proceedings can commence",[32] thus basing its reasoning on the meaning expressed in most texts. The Court did not, however, provide any justification to support its arguments in this case.

1.4 The Theological Approach

Derlén says that this approach primarily considers the "purpose" and/or "context" of the rule in question and "completely discards the linguistic aspect once a discrepancy is observed between the various language versions".[33] In cases it decides teleologically, the Court generally declares that reference must be made to the purpose and general scheme of the rules of which the provision or legislation in question forms part, which is, according to Stevens and Bredimas, as well as Berends, a "combination of teleological and systematic interpretation".[34]

An example of CJEU's use of this approach is the judgement of *Posteshop*,[35] which concerned the interpretation of Directive 2006/114/EC.[36] Here, the CJEU held that:

> The wording used in one language version of the EU law provisions cannot serve as the basis for the interpretation of those provisions. Where there is divergence between the various language versions of a European Union text, the provisions in question must thus be interpreted by reference to the general scheme and purpose of the rules of which they form a part.[37]

In this case, the French and Italian language versions of Recitals 3 and 16 to 18 of the Directive differed in that the former referred to "*pubblicita' ingannevole ed illegittimamente comparativa*". *In contrast*, the latter referred "*publicite' trompeuse et ... publicite' comparative illicite*". The Italian version thus suggested that advertising had to be misleading and unlawful, while the French version identified two separate forms of advertising. Acknowledging this discrepancy, the Court proceeded to examine Article 1, which lays out the purpose of the Directive and other relevant provisions and pointed out that the Directive contains two separate definitions for misleading advertising and unlawful comparative advertising. The CJEU also analysed the development of EU legislation in this field,[38] thus employing the historical method of interpretation to confirm its view that misleading advertising and comparative advertising are indeed two separate infringements and are not cumulative.

The reference for a preliminary ruling in *Genil 48 SL and Comercial Hostelera de Grandes Vinos SL v Bankinter SA and Banco Bilbao Vizcaya Argentaria SA*[39] concerned the interpretation of Article 19 (9) of Directive 2004/39/EC.[40] The Court noted a linguistic variance between the various language versions of this provision, whereby the English, Spanish, Danish, German, Greek, Italian, Dutch, Finnish and Swedish texts provided that "an investment service is offered as part of a financial product". In contrast, the French and Portuguese versions contained an expression similar to "offered within the framework of".

The Court acknowledged that the former wording suggested a closer, more specific link, while the latter was decidedly broader. The CJEU upheld the importance of referring to relevant rules' purpose and general scheme.[41] It then launched into an examination of the purpose of Article 19 (9), examined other provisions in the Directive, such as Section 2 of Chapter II of Title II thereof and also considered, to some extent, the wording of the provision in question, to reach its conclusion.

In *Team Relocations NV and Others v European Commission*,[42] an appeal case, several undertakings requested the CJEU to set aside a judgement of the General Courtupholding a fine imposed on them by the European Commission regarding Regulation No. 1/2003.[43] The judgement under appeal particularly concerned the interpretation of special guidelines.[44] Point 13 of the French language version of these 2006 Guidelines, like several others, refers to "sales in the relevant market". The German version, however, does not contain the word "relevant", referencing "sales in the markets concerned by the infringement".[45] The CJEU affirmed that the purpose and general scheme of the relevant rules must be considered in case of a divergence between the language versions. The General Court opted for a literal interpretation in paragraph 63 of the judgement under appeal, and the CJEU upheld this interpretation, stating that it was "fully consistent with the objective pursued by that provision, and more generally, with the objectives of EU rules on competition".[46]

The Court, however, issued an order to rectify the English language version of the above judgement. In the former version of the judgement, the Court seems to be saying that the General Court should not have reached its conclusions based on a literal interpretation since there were variances between the language versions. Such an approach would be completely against the literal method, which has been applied repeatedly by the CJEU. Under the order and subsequent correction, however, it declared that, even if the General Court's choice of literal interpretation could not be justified due to linguistic variances between the different texts, it was valid based on the purpose and general scheme of the relevant provisions.

In *Lietuvos geležinkeliai AB v Vilniaus teritorinė muitinė and Muitinės departamentas prie Lietuvos Respublikos finansų ministerijos*,[47] a reference for a preliminary ruling was made in the context of proceedings regarding VAT, additional excise duties and a fine levied on a company by a customs office. The linguistic variance in this case is featured in the definition of a "commercial motor vehicle" in Regulation 918/83.[48] The Bulgarian, Spanish, Czech, German, Estonian, English, French, Latvian, Lithuanian, Hungarian, Maltese, Polish, Portuguese, Romanian, Slovak, Slovene and Finnish language versions of this text described the vehicle in question as a "road vehicle". The Danish, Dutch and Swedish language versions did not specify such a vehicle as a "road" vehicle.[49] A similar variance exists in Article 82 (2) (a) of Directive 83/181, which determines the scope of Article 14 (1) (d) of Directive 77/388/EEC as regards exemption from VAT on the final importation of certain goods. In all the language versions of the said Article 82 (2) (a), the definition of "commercial motor vehicles" is identical to that found in Article 112 (2) (a) mentioned above.[50] Article 82 (2) (a) of the Danish, Dutch and Romanian versions, in this latter scenario, does not specify that such a vehicle is a "road vehicle", as do the other language versions thereof. The referring Court thus asked whether these two provisions also apply to locomotives.

The CJEU noted the variances between the language versions of the texts above, stating that the diverging texts could not be viewed in isolation and recalling the importance of the purpose and general scheme of the provisions in question. It cited previous case law relating to VAT matters, examined the context of the rule in question, and several related regulations and directives and general principles of EU law, particularly the principle of equal treatment, to reach its conclusion.

Considering the above, on the one hand, one may argue that regulations may not be expected to work effectively as sources of EU law because different linguistic versions may lead to a lack of uniformity. On the other hand, one may argue that directives may prove to be better tools since the transposing national legislation would ultimately be directly applicable in the national Court. However, one may counter the argument that the gaps that directives may create may lead to more judicial activism. In practice, regulations and directives are complementary legal instruments that can be used according to the particular legal base enabling that particular legislation. Language issues cannot be eliminated and will exist in both legal instruments. Thanks to the preliminary reference procedure under Article 267 TFEU, the national courts, through assistance from the CJEU, would arrive at the correct application. Judicial activism may not be needed in most circumstances but in some instances. The above theories help the CJEU develop solutions on a case-by-case basis and give it enough space to determine the best possible outcome according to the circumstances.

1.5 Conclusion—Judicial Activism or Reflection of Diversity?

Law and language in the EU are certainly not mutually exclusive: theirs may be described as a symbiotic relationship. European legislation must be expressed in terms of language, and the role of language is even more important in such a context because the law is binding on 27 Member States, each having its language and millions of citizens residing within them. European legislation creates rights and obligations on the EU Member States and their citizens, and it is therefore essential that this legislation is available in a language such citizens understand. Multilingualism in the EU, particularly regarding the availability of European legislation in various languages, guarantees democracy and ensures transparency. Although the CJEU employs various interpretative methods and mainly oscillates between the literal and teleological methods of interpretation, one may argue that it cannot be accused of judicial activism. It strives, in the majority of the cases heard and decided, to seek out the legislator's real aims and intention in the light either of the various language versions (and, thus, from a linguistic perspective) or of the purpose and the general scheme of the rules in question. There is often a strong element of subjectivity.

Translators and lawyer linguists involved in drafting the various language versions of EU legislation take a central position in realising some of the EU's most fundamental principles. Legal translation is a critical link between, on the one side, the advancement and completion of the EU's Internal Market and, on the other side, the protection and promotion of language diversity and equality in Europe. To achieve legal harmonisation within a multilingual environment, EU translators and lawyer linguists are expected to aim to achieve as much as possible "absolute concordance". Legal translation is not outside of legal harmonisation, but it is an inherent element. So, one may conclude that one need not question how translation stands in the way of harmonisation but instead think about how it can contribute. The CJEU often strikes a good balance between the different approaches possible to try and achieve unity expressed in diversity.

Notes

1 Baaij, C.J.W., *The Role of Legal Translation in Legal Harmonisation* (Wolters Kluwer: The Hague, 2012), p. 2.
2 ECR 419, para 3.

3 ECR I-8691, para 46.
4 ECR 1999, para 14.
5 Šarčević, S. (ed.), *Language and Culture in EU Law – Multidisciplinary Perspectives* (Ashgate: Surrey, 2015), p. 3.
6 Edwards, J., *Language and Identity: An Introduction* (Cambridge University Press: Cambridge, 2009), p. 205.
7 Joseph, J., *Language and Identity: National, Ethnic, Religious* (Palgrave Macmillan: Basingstoke, 2004).
8 Herzog, R. and Gerken, L., 'Stop the European Court of Justice' *EUObserver* (10 September 2008) <http://euobserver.com/opinion/26714> accessed 30 September 2024.
9 Micklitzm, H., 'Judicial Activisim of the European Court of Justice and the Development of the European Social Mode in Anti-Discrimination and Consumer Law' *EUI Working Papers LAW* 2009/19 (2009) <http://papers.ssrn.com/sol3/papers.cfm?abstract_id=1557139> accessed 30 September 2024.
10 Case C-127/08 (2008).
11 Directive 2004/38/EC of the European Parliament and the Council of 29 April 2004 on the right of citizens of the Union and their family members to move and reside freely within the territory of the Member States amending Regulation (EEC) No. 1612/68 and repealing Directives 64/221/EEC, 68/360/EEC, 72/194/EEC, 73/148/EEC, 75/34/EEC, 75/35/EEC, 90/364/EEC, 90/365/EEC and 93/96/EEC ('Directive 2004/38/EC') [2004] OJ L 158/77.
12 Brady, H., 'The Politics of European Justice' *Centre for European Reform* (1 June 2011) <http://www.cer.org.eu/publications/archive/bulletin-article/2011/politics-european-justice> accessed 30 September 2024.
13 Paunio, E., *Legal Certainty in Multilingual EU, Language, Discourse, and Reasoning at the European Court of Justice* (Ashgate: Surrey, 2013), p. 51.
14 Paunio, *Legal Certainty in Multilingual EU, Language, Discourse, and Reasoning at the European Court of Justice*, p. 52.
15 Derlén, M., *Multilingual Interpretation of European Union Law* (Kluwer Law International: The Hague, 2009), p. 43.
16 Berends, W., *The Interpretation of Multilingual EU Legislation: The Practice of the European Court of Justice and its Consequences for Legal Certainty* (Utrecht University, Utrecht The Netherlands 2011), p. 27.
17 Baaij, C., 'Fifty Years of Multilingual Interpretation in the European Union', in Tiersma, P. and Solan, L. (eds) *The Oxford Handbook of Language and Law* (Oxford University Press, Oxfrod 2012), p. 218.
18 Berends, *The Interpretation of Multilingual EU Legislation*, p. 27.
19 Derlén, *Multilingual Interpretation of European Union Law*, p. 43.
20 Case C-486/12 (2013).
21 Case C-488/11 (2013).
22 Case C-402/11 (2012).
23 Directive 95/46/EC of the European Parliament and of the Council of 24 October 1995 on the protection of individuals with regard to the processing of personal data and on the free movement of such data (1995) OJ L 281/31.
24 Case C-486/12 (2013), para 21.
25 *Stauder* (n 197).
26 *X* (n 204), para 19.
27 *Brusse* (n 205).
28 Council Directive 93/13/EEC of 5 April 1993 on unfair terms in consumer contracts (1993) OJ L95/29.

29 "Professional".
30 *Brusse* (n 205), para 26.
31 The rules implementing Regulation No. 40/94 are laid down by Commission Regulation (EC) No. 2868/95 of 13 December 1995 (OJ 1995 L 303, p. 1) as amended by Commission Regulation (EC) No. 1041/2005 of 29 June 2005 (OJ 1995 L 172, p. 4).
32 C-402/11 P—Jager & Polacek v OHIM
33 Derlén, *Multilingual Interpretation of European Union Law*, p. 47
34 Berends, *The Interpretation of Multilingual EU Legislation*, p. 35.
35 Case C-52/13 *Posteshop SpA—Divisione Franchising Kipoint v Autorità Garante della Concorrenza e del Mercato and Presidenza del Consiglio dei Ministri* (2014).
36 Directive 2006/114/EC of the European Parliament and of the Council of 12 December 2006 concerning misleading and comparative advertising (2006) OJ L 376/21.
37 *Posteshop*, para 21.
38 *Posteshop* (n 278), para 27.
39 Case C-604/11 (2013).
40 Directive 2004/39/EC of the European Parliament and of the Council of 21 April 2004 on markets in financial instruments amending Council Directives 85/611/EEC and 93/6/EEC and Directive 2000/12/EC of the European Parliament and of the Council and repealing Council Directive 93/22/EEC (2004) OJ L 145/1.
41 *Genil 48* (n 284), para 38.
42 Case C-444/11P (2013).
43 Council Regulation (EC) No. 1/2003 of 16 December 2002 on the implementation of the rules on competition laid down in Arts [81 EC] and [82 EC] (2003) OJ L 1/1.
44 Guidelines on the method of setting fines imposed pursuant to Article 23(2)(a) of Regulation No. 1/2003 (n 291) (2006) OJ C 210/02 ('2006 Guidelines').
45 *Team Relocations* (n 290), para 81.
46 *Team Relocations* (n 290), para 81.
47 Case C-250/11 (2012).
48 Council Regulation (EEC) No. 918/83 of 28 March 1983 setting up a Community system of reliefs from customs duty (1983) OJ L 105/1 as amended by Council Regulation (EEC) No. 1315/88 of 3 May 1988 (1988) OJ L 123/2.
49 *Lietuvos* (n 290), para 6.
50 *Lietuvos* (n 290), para 11.

2 Gender Inclusiveness

Does Language as a Social Practice Meet Law-Making in Brazil?

Ana Larissa Adorno Marciotto Oliveira and Lucas William Oliveira Marciano

2.1 Introduction

In this chapter, we departed from the notion that language shapes the perceptions of gender and influences the lived experiences of individuals inside and outside sexual minorities. Concerning gender-binary languages, such as Brazilian Portuguese, discussing inclusive language also combines the claim for gender equality while promoting the intersection between linguistics and law-making. As such, we hypothesize that assessing the progress of language inclusiveness is crucial to fostering the equal treatment of women and LGBT+ people, particularly in countries where the official rates of homophobia and gender violence are alarming, like Brazil, where more than one-third of women have experienced some form of physical and/or sexual violence, most of it perpetrated by their male partners.[1]

The consequences of sexism are also evident in several other aspects of social and public life, for instance, in the underrepresentation of women in elected positions, despite gender quota incentives having been in place in Brazilian legislation for at least 26 years.[2] Despite this encouragement, although women make up 51.4% of the Brazilian population, they remain outnumbered in elected positions. Party quotas are also often criticized for being misused in ways that ultimately disadvantage women. Instead of empowering qualified female candidates, they are often manipulated to meet requirements without genuine support for gender equality. Parties sometimes place women on the ballot only in unwinnable positions or choose candidates with limited resources or support, fulfilling quotas without committing to increasing female representation (Silva and Chueiri, 2023; Severi, 2022). This lack of representation significantly influences how legislators approach women's rights in Brazil, including the right to be appropriately recognized and addressed in language.

Issues related to linguistic rights also emerge and take on importance when it comes to LGBT+[3] individuals. To provide a broader perspective on this matter, it is worth mentioning that the Brazilian Ministry of Health reports

DOI: 10.4324/9781003430308-4

that 4 million people in the country identify as transgender or non-binary. These individuals face a higher risk of mental health issues when compared to the non-LGBT+ population. LGBT+ individuals are also more prone to alcohol use disorder and tobacco addiction than heterosexual individuals. They are also more likely to suffer from depression and stress and are at a greater risk of experiencing hate crimes (Walters et al., 2020; Severi, 2022). Despite some advancements, for example, the fact that, since 2018, transsexual candidates have been allowed to run for elected positions within the quotas allocated to the gender with which they identify, the rise of the far-right in 2016 has resulted in several proposed bills seeking to curtail LGBT+ rights,[4] which would reverse a 2011 Supreme Court ruling that made same-sex unions legal. It has passed one committee and now faces further debate. Proponents argue that the judiciary overstepped its authority by recognizing same-sex marriage, while opponents, including activists and progressive lawmakers, contend that the bill is discriminatory and unconstitutional. Additional proposals and policies have also emerged that could further restrict the rights of women. These include limiting educational materials on sexual orientation and reproductive rights, as well as attempts to ban abortion in cases of rape, foetal malformation, or risks to the mother's life, alongside equating abortion with homicide.[5]

All these points indicate that, despite substantial progress in protecting the rights of women and LGBT+ individuals in the past decades, Brazilian legislators still fall short of fully endorsing inclusiveness. In this matter, linguistic issues have taken centre stage since they highlight the gap in inclusiveness. This issue is especially evident in the resistance from legislators to adopt inclusive language to properly address women and LGBT+ people, along with the numerous attempts, all supported by certain societal groups, to ban its use from public life. With this in mind, in this chapter we draw on the foundations of Brazilian Constitutional Feminism and Critical Discourse Analysis to advocate that (a) adopting forms of address that recognize women and LGBT+ people in law-making and in public life connects to discursive practices that give voice to historically underrepresented groups, thereby fostering pluralism and enriching democratic life; (b) the resistance to adopting these practices, reflected in recent bill proposals, constitutes a significant setback for basic rights in the country, which has been exploited by the far-right for political gain. To do that, we first explore the tenets of Brazilian Constitutional Feminism and Critical Discourse Analysis in connection with the legal foundations and recent policy developments on women and LGBT+ people. We then characterize linguistic inclusiveness from the viewpoint of grammatical gender across languages. After that, we discuss the recent bill proposal to ban language inclusiveness in Brazil and show how they are backed up by certain sectors of society. We then lay the ground for the final remarks of the chapter.

2.2 Brazilian Constitutional Feminism and Critical Discourse Analysis in Law-Making: An Intersection

Although inclusive language has been acknowledged as a means to make legal texts more representative, this approach has not been applied to the text of the 1988 Brazilian Constitution as any adaptation in this direction would require a constitutional amendment and a corresponding legal and political discussion. As such, the Brazilian Constitutional text does not utilize gender-inclusive language; instead, it employs what was then regarded as "generic language", i.e., using masculine terms to refer to all people, such as "cidadão" (citizen/masculine) and "trabalhador" (worker/masculine) to address mixed groups.

The description of equality in the Brazilian Constitution, particularly in Article 5, also highlights the dual aspects of formal and material equality, reflecting the foundational principles of equal treatment under the law and the need for proactive measures to achieve true social and political equality. The addition of human rights declarations to the Constitution was designed to catalyse legislative actions for the fulfilment of human rights and foster the inclusive society envisioned by progressive movements. Several state objectives were also inscribed in the Constitution, including the creation of a free, just, and compassionate society; the eradication of poverty and reduction of social inequalities; and the promotion of general welfare. Despite its progressive outlook, the implementation of gender equality principles has faced challenges, particularly in embedding these ideals into infra-constitutional laws and public policies, as Silva and Chueiri (2023) call attention when advocating for what is termed Brazilian Feminist Constitutionalism.

Through the lenses of Brazilian Feminist Constitutionalism, gender inequality is seen as interconnected with other disparities affecting social life, such as racial and educational issues and social class. Brazilian Feminist Constitutionalism also extends its concern to gender violence affecting sexual minorities, like LGBT+ individuals, and advocates for a broader, more inclusive approach to addressing gender-based injustices. This comprehensive perspective seeks to guarantee that Brazil's constitutional promise of equality leads to real, impactful changes in civil life, fostering a more inclusive and less prejudiced society for all.

As can be seen, implementing gender equality principles has proven challenging, especially in integrating these ideals into infra-constitutional laws and public policies, as highlighted by Silva and Chueiri (2023). Additionally, the Constitution's language remains gender-exclusive, lacking modern, inclusive terms. One of the tenets of Brazilian Feminist Constitutionalism is that countering patriarchal norms and promoting social justice to achieve gender equality involves the joint effort of judges, litigants, and the public (Silva and Chueiri, 2023). As misogynistic and transphobic views tend to emerge from specific sectors of society, one way to unveil them is by assessing the public perception of inclusive language practices. This is how, in our view, Brazilian Feminist Constitutionalism and Critical Discourse Analysis intersect.

Critical Discourse Analysis is founded on a deep understanding of text and discourse as social practices (Fairclough, 1995; Wodak, 2001; Wodak, 2001, among others). It primarily focuses its analytical work on how power abuse, dominance, and inequality are enacted, reproduced, and resisted through language. In investigating the interconnection between discourse and social practice, Critical Discourse Analysis foregrounds the role of language use in influencing and engineering social dynamics, as well as its central impact on countering discriminatory social norms that have become "normalized" (Wodak, 2001). This theoretical framework is also interested in how ideologies and power influence language choices and contribute to determining specific social relations. From the perspective we adopt here, it is possible to claim, according to Wodak (1997), that gender is a social category and a social construct, resulting from beliefs, ideologies, and stereotyped views of men and women, which have been cemented in the minds of people through a myriad of language practices.

Along the same line, Critical Discourse Analysis examines linguistic phenomena to understand how they support and perpetuate viewpoints (Wodak and Meyer, 2001), emphasizing the connections between language, law-making, and politics. As most resistance to gender-inclusive language in Brazil stems from populist, far-right leaders and their followers, Critical Discourse Analysis, we believe, can offer an interesting viewpoint to explore how certain prejudicial views and misconceptions about sex and gender intersect with language practice and law-making, as we will show in the subsequent sections.

2.3 Legal Foundations and Recent Policy Developments on Women and LGBT+ People in Brazil

Although in Article 70 of the Brazilian Constitution discrimination in the labour market concerning job responsibilities and salaries based on sex or marital status is prohibited, gender barriers affect women's careers and professional growth. Women suffer more from the so-called invisible glass ceiling, a covert obstacle to professional advancement, rooted in various organizations and professional sectors. Due to these restrictions, many women earn lower salaries than men, even when performing the same roles. The lower earnings represent a major socioeconomic issue in the country, particularly because women head approximately 50.9% of Brazilian households, where the average income is equivalent to about 71.6% of the income received by men.[6] The low income of female household heads also confines many families to intense poverty, affecting the education and development of children and young people and limiting their future job opportunities.

Despite numerous downsides, women have fought for their rights, which have eventually been granted. An example of these advances is maternity leave, provided for in the Consolidation of Labour Laws since 1943. Although seen as an achievement, maternity leave also highlights the patriarchal understanding of society, where women are seen as solely responsible for the care of children and men are viewed as family providers. A more current understanding of childcare would need to ensure parental leave is equally shared by the caregivers of children, whether men or women (Silva and Chueiri, 2023). All of these points highlight the struggles women continue to face in Brazil, despite significant progress in protecting their rights.

As for LGBT+ people, the National Policy for Comprehensive Health of LGBT+ in 2011 marked a significant step in addressing the specific health of the LGBT+ community as a basic right. Similarly, the first National LGBT+ Health Conference Report in 2013, which emphasized the need for information on the health conditions of LGBT+ individuals to better equip the health system, and the National Policy for the Integral Health of Lesbians, Gays, Bisexuals, Transvestites, and Transsexuals, provided guidelines to prevent discrimination against LGBT+ people in public health services in Brazil.[7] Later, in 2021, the Brazilian Supreme Court issued a precautionary measure allowing medical appointments and examinations to be conducted regardless of biological sex. This measure included provisions for gender self-declaration within the Brazilian Health System and adaptations to birth certificates and civil identification documents to incorporate gender identity. The Supreme Federal Court's order also upheld the need for health services to adopt a more inclusive approach to LGBT+ individuals, countering a heteronormative perspective.

The implementation of the policies described above has also driven important changes related to inclusive language for women and LGBT+ people. For instance, a recently published decree (Decree 10.002/2024, art. 11, § 9) demands the inflection of public office names according to the gender of the officeholder, applicable to all federal normative acts. The ruling is significant because it prevents using generic masculine terms to address women holding these positions, which enhances their visibility and validates their gender. In this line, in 2016, then-President Dilma Rousseff signed a decree ensuring the use of preferred names ("nome social" in Brazilian Portuguese, Amaral, 2024) and the recognition of the identity of transsexuals in official documents. In 2018, the Ministry of Education also authorized students to use preferred names in mandatory education.

Similarly, preferred names are also allowed in the country on voter IDs and public certifications without the need for sex reassignment surgery or a court decision. Preferred names are also allowed to appear on work permits (Amaral, 2024).

Similarly, a 2018 court ruling authorized a non-binary person to have "unspecified sex" recorded on their birth certificate (Amaral, 2024), creating jurisprudence with far-reaching effects. In 2021, the Superior Electoral Court introduced the "Inclusive Language Guide for Gender-Inflection: Application and Use with a Focus on Social Communication" to comply with Resolution 376/2021 of the National Council of Justice, mandating gender inflection in the social and institutional communication of the national judiciary. These achievements are particularly notable in light of the various forms of resistance to inclusive language, as demonstrated by the bill proposals to ban such practices, which we will describe in subsequent sections. Before that, to better situate the debate, we will shed some light on grammatical gender across languages

2.4 Inclusive Language in Brazilian Portuguese and Across Languages

The impact of gender-inclusive language[8] on women is not new. It has become the focus of significant research worldwide in recent decades, with reputable works like Prewitt-Freilino et al. (2012) on language and women's empowerment; Sarrasin et al. (2012) on the relationship between sexism and the attitudes towards gender-neutral language in England, French-speaking Switzerland, and German-speaking Switzerland; Hord (2016) on sexual bias and resistance to change in English, Swedish, and French. In Germany, Stout et al. (2011) demonstrated that female job applicants tend to perceive a lack of fit when job advertisements use masculine rather than gender-inclusive expressions. In Italy, Merkel (2013) found that language descriptors of occupations with feminized terms commonly implied lower status than gender-inclusive or masculine terms. In English-speaking countries, Hellinger (2001) describes that, although singular "they" can function effectively as an epicene pronoun, higher-status occupational terms like "lawyer" or "scientist" have conventionally been associated with the generic "he", while lower-status terms like "teacher" or "nurse" were often followed by "she". In the judicial sphere, non-inclusive forms have been shown to influence court decisions, favouring men and disadvantaging women, as also observed by Hellinger (2001) and Severi (2022). In terms of LGBT+ people, although less scholarly seems to have been produced on this matter, a robust study about the effects of language inclusiveness on LGBT + people was conducted by Tavits et al. (2019), in which they show how language influences mass opinion towards gender and LGBT + equality. According to this study, evidence shows that, compared with masculine pronouns, the use of gender-neutral pronouns decreases the mental salience of males. This shift is associated with individuals expressing less bias in favour of traditional gender roles and categories, as reflected in more favourable attitudes towards women and LGBT + individuals in public life. The authors also suggest changes in the language used to address these people can help societies become more closely adhere to the ideal of gender equality.

From a linguistic perspective, grammatical gender is a system for classifying nouns into two or more categories, typically aligning with male or female distinctions for human references. Through this classification, nouns that do denote objects or collectives (e.g., door, pile) can also be categorized even without a connection to sex distinction. As grammatical gender varies across languages, in the so-called natural gender languages, like English, gender is primarily visible through pronouns ("he", "she"), as well as gendered nouns such as "mother", "uncle", or "bride", which correspond to the biological gender of the human referents (Hekanaho, 2015; Hord, 2016). In contrast, in grammatically gendered languages, like Portuguese and German, the phenomenon is visible not only in pronouns and nouns but also across other grammatical categories, e.g., adjectives and articles. Consequently, in these languages, gender is reflected in several aspects of the linguistic system, as various parts of speech, used with a semantically gendered noun, must also indicate masculine, feminine, or neuter gender.

Brazilian Portuguese, a Romance language, has two grammatical genders: masculine and feminine. In most cases, grammatical gender in Brazilian Portuguese is signified by a gender marker -o (or in some cases, -or) at the end of a noun or adjective, denoting the masculine. As for the feminine, it is mostly marked with -a (or in some cases, -ora), for example, in:

1 *"amigo" – "friend" – (masculine) vs "amiga" – "friend" – (feminine).*
2 *"professor" – "teacher" – (masculine) vs "professora" – "teacher" – (feminine).*

In mixed-gender human groups, or unknown individuals, or even groups in which the gender balance is unknown, the masculine is used as a default in the language. A quick search over Brazilian Portuguese textbooks and manuals, designed to teach the language to speakers of other languages, captures this phenomenon as a linguistic fact, as Figure 2.1 illustrates.

As can be seen in Figure 2.1, the so-called generic masculine is a feature to be learned in Portuguese as applying to a group of people "even if there is only one man!". The exclamation mark in the sentence reflects the potential weirdness of the rule for most speakers of other languages

The masculine form is usually considered the **"default"** form in Portuguese. This even applies to pronouns: we have both **eles** they *(masc.)* ··· for male groups and **elas** they *(fem)* ··· for female groups, but if it's a group of **both** males and females, you have to use ***eles***, even if there's only one man!

Figure 2.1 Gender Mark in Pronouns in Brazilian Portuguese.
Source: https://www.practiceportuguese.com/.

Most of these words pertain to **objects**, i.e. things that don't *actually* have a biological gender, so the gender just has to be learned. You can't say ✕ *o porta* or ✕ *a carro*, for example. In Portuguese, a door will *always* be feminine and a car will *always* be masculine. But like we said, even though it's much more common, it's not *always* as simple as adding an *o* for words ending in *o* and an *a* for words ending in *a*. For example:

- **A tribo** The tribe ··· - An example of a *feminine* word that ends in *-o*
- **O pijama** The pajamas ··· - An example of a *masculine* word that ends in *-a*

Figure 2.2 Only-gender words in Portuguese.
Source: https://www.practiceportuguese.com/.

and denounces its flagrant sexist orientation. Similarly, in Figure 2.2, also taken from a grammar book, the binary gender mark is explored.

It is thus possible to acknowledge that the gender mark is overt in the language even when the noun does not morphologically vary for gender. In these cases, gender is marked only with the article (-a/as for feminine and -o/os for masculine) and their corresponding adjective forms (if any). Figure 2.2 also calls attention to the fact that inanimate entities such as "porta" ("door") or collectives, such as "tribo" ("tribe"), also display grammatical genre in Brazilian Portuguese. The example with the term "tribo" is also interesting because it shows an additional layer of complexity in the system, occurring when the noun is marked as feminine, with the article "a" as the determiner, although it ends with -o, violating the general rule of -o endings for masculine and -a for feminine.

Apart from the grammatical prescriptions outlined in Figures 2.1 and 2.2, an inherent difficulty with a binary-oppositional grammatical gender system, like Brazilian Portuguese, arises when one considers people who fall outside the male–female social gender binary, such as non-binary individuals, who identify neither as male nor female. Using the genetic masculine also affects women, who can become underrepresented and are made invisible in the grammar of the language. From this perspective, it is possible to affirm that non-inclusive language renders women and LGBT+ people unable to communicate their gender identities adequately, causing social and psychological distress. Moreover, as speakers normalize patriarchal views through language, these practices endorse heteronormativity and contribute to the perpetuation of longstanding misconceptions about gender and sex, which may affect individuals and groups, restricting their basic rights.

In Brazilian Portuguese, gender-inclusive language, often referred to by some speakers as "neutral language", generally involves replacing traditional gender markers with elements that indicate "neutrality" (non-binary options) or simply omitting grammatical gender altogether. The phenomenon occurs, for example, in words like "meninx", "menin@", and "menine", to refer to girl/boy, instead of "menino" or "menina", which carry the -a/-o endings, as gender marks. This usage has been documented within the LGBT+ community and was formalized in 2015 through the Manifesto for Radically Inclusive Communication (Polido and Faria, 2024).[9] Forms kike "meninx", "menin@", and "menine", used to refer to girl/boy, are mostly designed for screen-based interactions and aim to include gender-fluid people.

In oral production, alunEs is the most common form used, particularly in the LGBT+ community, with the gender mark being completely suppressed from the plural form. In Spanish, another Romance language, speakers tend to substitute the generic masculine -o with other morphemes (-@, -x, or -e), as Tosi (2021) demonstrates. In data gathered from Twitter, the author found that, particularly from 2018 on, -@ emerged as the most frequently used gender-inclusive morpheme in the language, followed by -x, with -e being the least common. For many English speakers, "they" has been considered an adequate neutral pronoun, although some advocate for the introduction of a new gender-neutral option (Hekanaho, 2015). In a similar vein, in Sweden, the gender-neutral pronoun "hen" has been officially adopted and is commonly used across the country (Hekanaho, 2015). Discussions on inclusiveness were also proposed, for instance, in the works of French philosopher Monique Wittig (1935–2003) and the feminist debates since the 1970s. The debate has gained more traction among Generation Z, consisting of people born between the late 1990s and 2010. For this community, issues related to (self-)identity tend to occupy a significant space in the social debate, as Klein (2022) notes. Consequently, the topic of language inclusiveness has become widely debated, especially in digital communities.

As can be seen, although the debate surrounding gender-inclusive language has not been confined to the Brazilian context, it has gained momentum in the country due to the legal achievements of women and the LGBT+

community, regarding the recognition of their identity and rights. In 2023, the Brazilian Supreme Court supported gender-sensitive language in schools while overturning a state law banning such language in the public domain. Despite this, drawbacks often arise, for example, Brazilian lawmakers passed a bill in December 2023 prohibiting gender-inclusive language in the public sphere, which is still under consideration before the Senate. Other bill proposals in this direction have also been introduced, as we will show in the next section.

2.5 Recent Bill Proposals to Ban Gender-Inclusive Language in Brazil

In the context of legislative drafting, the default use of masculine terms in legal texts – such as "professor/teacher" (masculine) instead of "professor/a" (with both the masculine and feminine marks) – primarily impacts women. While the implications for the LGBT+ community may not be so salient, they still touch on gender expression and pluralism and represent a concern for Brazilian Feminist Constitutionalism and Critical Discourse Analysts. Hence, the intention to suppress initiatives aimed at introducing inclusive language in law-making and in public administration represents an important issue that touches on the technical aspects of law drafting and public policies at the same time. In this respect, since 2016, far-right leaders have introduced 34 bills aimed at banning inclusive language in the country. They were mostly devised by the Liberal Party (PL) or the Social Liberal Party (PSL), from the far-right spectrum. These bill proposals align with their characteristic approach of fostering enmity by curtailing the rights of vulnerable groups and sexual minorities, for example:

- Bill Proposal 180/2020 – by Congresswoman Bia Kicis (LP) – proposes a ban on gender-inclusive language in official documents and the promotion of traditional language aligned with binary gender norms.
- Bill Proposal 276/2020 – by Congressman Carlos Jordy (PSL) – seeks to mandate gender-specific language in government communications and educational materials, opposing gender-neutral forms.
- Bill proposal 2374/2020 – by Congresswoman Chris Tonietto (PSL) – suggests amendments to enforce gender-specific terms in official contexts, emphasizing binary language.
- Bill proposal 3/2021 – by Congressman Filipe Barros (PSL) – aims to revoke any decrees or regulations that permit gender-inclusive language, advocating for gender-specific norms in legislation.
- Bill Proposal 3171/2019 – by Congressman Junio Amaral (PSL) – supports the use of gender-specific language in both public and private

educational institutions, discouraging gender-neutral terms in teaching and communications.

The fixation with countering language inclusiveness is seen as a common feature of far-right leaders worldwide, although local differences can emerge. (Drinóczi and Bień-Kacała, 2022; Wodak, 2001). In Brazil, Jair Bolsonaro and his supporters have become popular for their outrageous statements about women and LGBT+ people, which have encouraged other political leaders to propose bills that combat language inclusiveness. The proposals can be viewed as a strategy to resonate with specific segments of society, where prejudicial practices are more readily accepted, especially when disguised as legitimate measures to protect a fictional majority, as noted by Oliveira et al. (2024) and Silva and Chueiri (2023).

The bill proposals described above reinforce at least two other relevant aspects deserving consideration. Firstly, the proposals reflect the effort to promote enmity, as described by Borba (2019). In this process, adopting gender-inclusive language in public schools will indoctrinate children and serve as fuel for moral transgression. This is particularly the case with PL 3171/2019 and PL 276/2020, which explicitly "reject gender-neutral or inclusive forms in government communications and educational materials". Secondly, the proposals also unravel the rise of the so-called gender ideology, a poorly defined but widely spread concept in the country, promoted by far-right politicians and their supporters. This debate is marked by misinformation and the false claim that the groups supporting the right of gender expression deny the biological differences between men and women. In most cases, there is a deliberate confusion between "sex" and "gender", intentionally stirred by the conservative agenda of the far-right to rally their supporters against a common enemy, in this case, women, the LGBT+ community, and human rights advocates (Oliveira et al., 2024; Silva and Chueiri, 2023).

The situation, though, is not restricted to far-right leaders; rather, it reflects a broader cultural and institutional inertia within Brazilian law-making or, putting it differently, the omissions in the country's legislative framework. As it stands, Brazil's legal system lacks specific guidelines for gender-inclusive language in legislative drafting. For instance, Supplementary Law 95/1998, which sets the standards for drafting laws, does not include directives on gender inclusiveness. This omission allows a traditional default masculine language to persist, which, legislators claim, encompasses all genders but lacks an informed interpretation or guidance to ensure this understanding. Additionally, Brazil's political landscape is marked by a range of views on this topic, with some groups pushing for modern, inclusive language practices, while others resist, citing merely prescriptive linguistic norms. Evidence of these views can be found in the excerpts below, which reflect traditional perspectives on language inclusiveness, as expressed by Internet users. The statements mirror the ongoing debate and resistance towards adopting more inclusive language practices in the country – a stance heavily supported by certain sectors of society, as we will demonstrate in the next section.

2.5.1 Public Reactions against Gender-Inclusive Language in Brazil

While traditional gender norms are hierarchical, they presuppose an unequal power structure related to them, which often works to the disadvantage of women and other vulnerable groups or sexual minorities. In what concerns LGTB+ people, most speakers simply rely on the standard form without considering other alternatives and their repercussions to social change and pluralism. Others deliberately endorse sexism and gender bias. They resist or even abominate gender-inclusive language because it is seen as a type of oppressive political correctness practice, which is believed to deprive a fictional majority of their rights. Not surprisingly, the most common argument against inclusive language in Brazil is the claim that it is superfluous because the generic masculine already includes both "women" and "men". The practice is often opposed through posts advocating for the "purity of the Portuguese language", which reject and strongly criticize any linguistic change based on gender inclusion. This view is consistent with the concept of nativism and patriarchal views, which is a prevailing feature of gender-biased discursive practices in different countries, as Zortolla and Borba (2022) have demonstrated, as can be seen in extracts I and II.

(I) *O pronome neutro, como "elu" ou "elx" nunca entraria em conformidade com a língua portuguesa, simplesmente porque a flexão de gênero nada tem a ver com a noção biológica de sexo. O pronome masculino não tem flexão de gênero, por isso é considerado neutro/A neutral pronoun, like "elu" or "elx"* (he/she with the gender mark removed and replaced by u or x), *would never align with the Portuguese language, simply because gender inflection has nothing to do with the biological notion of sex. The masculine pronoun has no gender inflection, which is why it's considered neutral.*

(II) *Não, não é problema real nenhum e, quando muito, o problema é delas (das mulheres) e não da língua ... Em português, o genérico masculino engloba todas as pessoas. É assim. É limitado? Talvez, mas é o que é/No, it's not a real problem at all, and if anything, the problem is theirs (the women), not the language's ... In Portuguese, the generic masculine encompasses all people. That's how it is. Is it limited? Maybe, but that's how it is.*

The nativist perspectives in excerpts (I) and (II) reinforce the idea that "that's just how it is", suggesting that women are inherently inferior and must accept not being properly addressed. This belief, among other implications, undermines women's right to self-expression while providing a flawed rationale to justify discriminatory language practices. Notably, women are portrayed as the ones responsible for stirring the debate on inclusive language ("No, it's not a real problem at all, and, if anything, the problem is theirs (the women), not the language's").

Other arguments commonly employed to reject gender inclusiveness are illustrated by the tweet in extract (III).

(III) *Linguagem neutra é uma aberração, é ilegal posto que a língua oficial no brasil é o português. Idiotas para promover uma linguagem que exclui a distancia da linguagem culta, completa e que lhe permite amplo esclarecimento daquilo que transmitido pela forma escrita correta. / Neutral language is an aberration; it is illegal since the official language in Brazil is Portuguese. Idiots promote a language that excludes distance from cultured, complete language and that allows broad clarification of what is transmitted in the correct written form.*

(Source:[10] Twitter/X)

As can be seen, the message in extract (III) relies on the allegedly fixed and permanent feature of linguistic structures and helps propagate this view. It also confirms that certain linguistic forms inherently carry more social prestige than others, which, in this example, also reflects a distinction strongly grounded on heteronormativity. In this line, the comment "neutral language is an aberration, it is illegal since the official language of Brazil is Portuguese" also indicates that, according to the user, language inclusiveness hurts the "purity" of the Portuguese language and violates its norms. The post portrays the practice as inferior and incorrect, labelling it as something used only by "an idiot lacking intelligence". It strongly promotes a strict distinction between right and wrong, overlooking the reality that language evolves through social influences and constantly adapts to them.

Similarly, in extract (IV), a user replies to the same post with an unmitigated attack on language inclusiveness, which is depicted as a "disgrace".

(IV) *Pode ser isso, ou … Os evangélicos são os únicos nesse país de merda que são contra o aborto, a liberação de drogas, ideologia de gênero, linguagem não binária e essas desgraças todas Se não fosse a bancada evangélica, esse país moralmente já tinha derretido / It could be that, or … Evangelicals are the only ones in this shitty country who are against abortion, the release of drugs, gender ideology, non-binary language, and all these disgraces If it weren't for the evangelical group, this country would have already morally melted.*

(Source: Twitter/X)

Political polarization is also highlighted in (IV), as it foregrounds the role that some sectors of the evangelical and catholic churches have played in countering gender-inclusive language. As Cesarino notes, these religious groups upheld the political divide in the country, by strongly supporting the far-right. At the same time, they also took advantage of the polarized scenario in the country to give vent to their previously marginalized views on gender and sex, used to create enemies and heighten the perceived need for protection. Fuelling enmity is a means to gain space in the market of ideas, as Borba (2019) notes. From this angle, extract (IV) recalls the strategy to divide the country between those who are "ensuring the country's morality" and "the rest of the nation, who are morally corrupted". This aspect is also underscored in the post by the term "disgraces", which adds emotional weight to it, contributing to its appealing tone. According to Wodak (2021), emotionalization is a crucial tool for spreading far-right rhetoric, especially because it is simple and easy to propagate online.

The opposition to language inclusiveness is also visible in extract (III), where impolite language (Culpeper, 2008; Wodak et al. 2021; Oliveira et al., 2024) is to undermine the practice.

(V) *Mlk eu assistindo esses desenhos modernos não da, caralho porra de linguagem neutra / Dude me watching these modern cartoons oh no it is fucking neutral language.*

(Source: Twitter/X)

As can be seen, language usages are often associated with stigma. In this sense, stigmatization reflects "a generalized negative evaluation of the habits, customs, and lifestyles of groups deemed socially inferior" (Kienpointner and Stopfner, 2017, p. 87). Although there is growing support for gender-inclusive practices, especially within younger and urban populations, this shift has yet to be fully embraced in the legislative and governmental spheres since, for many, gender-inclusive language is seen as unnecessary or ideologically motivated. As can be seen, in the political and legislative sphere, especially in polarized societies like Brazil, since 2016, the connection between language and stigma also involves framing the communicative behaviour of certain social groups as transgressive and immoral, while portraying their opponents as pure and respectable. These evaluations shape language practices and have driven the debate on gender inclusiveness in the country, both within and beyond the parliament, as we have attempted to illustrate in this section.

2.6 Final Remarks

The use of gender-inclusive language, especially the one characteristically of the LGBT+ community, is a controversial topic on social media, as Oliveira et al. (2024) have noted. In law-making, this lack of representation can be very consequential since it denounces the fact that open choices were made to reproduce and legitimate the invisibility of these groups, affecting their rights to equality and gender expression. In this line, we argued that the masculine default, widely used in Brazilian Portuguese, excludes the explicit representation of women and LGBT+ individuals, reinforcing a structural oversight rather than promoting intentional inclusiveness. We have also aimed to explore whether and how language inclusiveness in Brazil could be examined from the perspective of Critical Discourse Analysis and Brazilian Feminist Constitutionalism. To do that, we provided the reader with an outlook on grammar gender in Brazilian Portuguese against the backdrop of e advances and drawbacks in the struggle for the rights of the LGBT+ people and women in the country. To do that, we showed how Brazilian lawmakers, particularly from the far-right, oppose inclusiveness as a strategy to gain supporters, as the public reactions to language inclusiveness on social media showed.

Our efforts to address gender-inclusive language and law-making in Brazil also suggest at least two important implications. Firstly, it is not surprising that certain sectors of society reject inclusiveness and resist revising longstanding language practices. These views are cemented in the culture and reveal the role of heteronormativity and patriarchalism in the country (Silva and Chueiri, 2023). The approach is also deployed by the far-right under the pretext of defending so-called traditional family values, which are often used as a political platform to gain or maintain power. Secondly, although the history of languages teaches us that successful changes tend to emerge spontaneously, we believe it should always be in the purview of the State to promote inclusiveness, particularly in what concerns the language used in public administration. In this sense, in our view, the numerous attempts to combat or ban inclusive language, discussed in this chapter, represent a serious threat to democracy and equality that deserves scholarly attention.

In attempting to answer the question that has motivated the drafting of this chapter, we believe that the intersection of gender-inclusive language as a social practice and its incorporation into law-making faces several challenges in Brazil. While recent years have seen shifts towards inclusiveness in social and educational contexts, the legal and political adoption of gender-inclusive language has encountered significant resistance from lawmakers and conservative sectors of society. As such, Brazil's administrative and legal language remains mostly gendered, with "masculine generic" forms still being the standard in legal and official documents. While Brazil's Supreme Court and other judicial bodies have sometimes recognized women and LGBT+ rights, these decisions are not consistently reflected in the language of legislation, which often fails to adopt terminology that acknowledges gender diversity. That said, in this chapter, we reject the claim that the masculine form "implicitly" includes the feminine and the non-binary forms. We believe that this use undermines gender equality, as true inclusiveness primarily requires the explicit recognition of all groups within the language itself.

Lastly, with our work, we hope we have provided the reader with a vantage point of the stage of language inclusiveness in Brazil from the perspective of law-making, the protection of rights, and language as a social practice.

Notes

1 Source: Wilson Center (https://www.wilsoncenter.org).
2 Electoral Law, Article 10, Paragraph 3 of Law No. 9.504/1997. The bill requires that this bill requires that each party or coalition fill a minimum of 30% and a maximum of 70% of candidacies of each gender in the elections. https://www.tse.jus.br/legislacao/codigo-eleitoral/lei-das-eleicoes/lei-das-eleicoes-lei-nb0-9.504-de-30-de-setembro-de-1997
3 We chose to use LGBT+ because we understand that the "+" symbol includes the various identities encompassed by the acronym.
4 Bill proposal – Lei 5167/09 (Source: Agência Câmara de Notícias).
5 Bill proposal 1904/2024.
6 2024 National Report on Salary Transparency and Remuneration Criteria through the Labor Statistics Dissemination Program Platform – PDET.
7 Ministry of Health, 2013, Ordinance No. 2.836, December 1, 2011
8 The expression "neutral language" ("linguagem neutra") has been frequently employed in Brazilian Portuguese, followed by "non-binary language" and "inclusive language" ("linguagem não-binária" e "linguagem inclusiva", respectively). In our understanding, the three expressions refer to the same phenomenon, revolving around the attempt to promote gender inclusiveness through language usage. In this chapter, we use "inclusive language", as an umbrella-like term. We base our decision on the fact that choosing any other expression would bring about a semantic dispute that does not make a real contribution to the discussion we seek to propose.
9 The *Manifesto for Radically Inclusive Communication* (Bertucci: Zantella, 2015) is a guiding document aimed at fostering language that respects and represents all gender identities, sexual orientations, ethnic backgrounds, and other intersecting identities. It calls for moving away from traditional, often discriminatory, language practices and advocates for the inclusion of marginalized groups in what is termed "inclusive communication".

10 Extracts taken from a bigger Project, entitled "Digitally Mediated Language of Aggression", funded by the Brazilian Council of National Council for Scientific and Technological (CNPq), process n. 404672/2023-0.

Bibliography

Amaral, E. T. R. (2024). Preferred name in the Brazilian legal system: Creating an institution to combat prejudice and discrimination. *Comparative Law and Language*, 3(1), 35.

Borba, R. (2019). Gendered politics of enmity: Language ideologies and social polarisation in Brazil. *Gender and Language*, 13(4), 423–448.

Brazil Ministry of Health. (2011, December 1). Ordinance No. 2,836. Retrieved from https://bvsms.saude.gov.br/bvs/saudelegis/gm/2011/prt2836_01_12_2011.html

Brazil Ministry of Health. (2013). Ordinance No. 2,836, of December 1, 2011.

Brazil Presidency of the Republic. (2016, April 28). Decree No. 8,727. Retrieved from https://www2.camara.leg.br/legin/fed/decret/2016/decreto-8727-28-abril-2016-782951-publicacaooriginal-150197-pe.html

Brazil Presidency of the Republic. (2018, February 5). Decree No. 9,278. Retrieved from https://legislacao.presidencia.gov.br/atos/?tipo=DEC&numero=9278&ano=2018&ato=1a4g3Zq5UeZpWTd8a

Brazil Presidency of the Republic. (2022, February 23). Decree No. 10,977. Retrieved from https://www2.camara.leg.br/legin/fed/decret/2022/decreto-10977-23-fevereiro-2022-792318-norma-pe.html

Brazil Chamber of Deputies. (2023). Propostas legislativas. Retrieved from https://www.camara.leg.br/buscaProposicoesWeb/?wicket:interface

Brazil Presidency of the Republic. (2023, April 6). Resolution No. 11. Retrieved from https://pesquisa.in.gov.br/imprensa/jsp/visualiza/index.jsp?data=10/04/2023&jornal=515&pagina=4&totalArquivos=280

Culpeper, J. (2008). Reflections on impoliteness, relational work and power. In D. Bousfield & M. A. Locher (Eds.), *Impoliteness in language: Studies on its interplay with power in theory and practice* (pp. 17–44). Berlin: Mouton de Gruyter.

Drinóczi, T., & Bień-Kacała, A. (2022). *Illiberal constitutionalism in Poland and Hungary: The deterioration of democracy, misuse of human rights and abuse of the rule of law*. London: Routledge.

Fairclough, N. (1995). *Critical discourse analysis: The critical study of language*. London & New York: Longman.

Federal University of Amapá. (2009, October 19). Resolution No. 13. Retrieved from https://www2.unifap.br/consu/files/2011/07/Resolu%C3%A7%C3%A3o-013-09-Travestis-e-Transexuais.pdf

Flavinho. (2017, September 29). Bill No. 8.614. Retrieved from https://www.camara.leg.br/proposicoesWeb/prop_mostrarintegra?codteor=1599235&filename=PL%208614/2017

Hekanaho, L. (2015). *Man as his own worst enemy: Lexical and pronominal masculine generics - An online survey on language use and attitudes* (Master's thesis). University of Helsinki. Retrieved from the web.

Hellinger, M. (2001). English–Gender in a global language. In M. Hellinger & H. Bußmann (Eds.), *Gender across languages: The linguistic representation of women and men* (Vol. 1, pp. 105–113). John Benjamins Publishing Company.

Hord, L. C. R. (2016). Bucking the linguistic binary: Gender neutral language in English, Swedish, French, and German. *Western Papers in Linguistics/Cahiers linguistiques de Western*, 3(1), Article 4.

Kienpointner, M., & Stopfner, M. (2017). Ideology and (Im)politeness. In J. Culpeper, M. Haugh, & D. Z. Kádár (Eds.), *The Palgrave handbook of linguistic (im)politeness* (pp. 61–87). London: Palgrave Macmillan.

Klein, J. (2022, January 16). O pragmatismo da geração Z sobre amor e sexo. *BBC Worklife*. Retrieved from https://www.bbc.com/portuguese/vert-cap-59982142

Krzyżanowski, M., Wodak, R., Bradby, H., Gardell, M., Kallis, A., Krzyżanowska, N., & Rydgren, J. (2023). Discourses and practices of the 'new normal': Towards an interdisciplinary research agenda on crisis and the normalization of anti-and post-democratic action. *Journal of Language and Politics*. 22(4), 415–437.

Merkel, E. (2013). The two faces of gender-fair language. (Doctoral dissertation, Università degli Studi di Padova, 163 pages). Padua Research Archive.

National Council of Justice. (2018, December 11). Resolution No. 270. Retrieved from https://atos.cnj.jus.br/atos/detalhar/2779

Oliveira, A. L. A. M., & Drinóczi, T. (2025). *Ataques verbais a juízes, mulheres e pessoas LGBT+: A corrosão discursiva da democracia e dos direitos humanos no Brasil*. Belo Horizonte: Ed. UFMG.

Oliveira, A. L. A. M., Drinóczi, T., & Miranda, M. V. (2024). Far-right discourse in Brazil: Shameless language as a common practice? Journal of Language and Politics, 23(2). Advance online publication. https://doi.org/10.1075/jlp.23120.oli

Oliveira, A. L. A. M., & Marciano, L. W. O. (2022). #Edaí: um estudo sobre impolidez e tomada de postura no Twitter brasileiro. *Confluência: Revista do Instituto de Língua Portuguesa*, 63, 199–221.

Oliveira, A. L. A. M., & Miranda, M. V. (2022). 'Calling a spade, a spade': Impoliteness and shame on Twitter. *Journal of Research in Applied Linguistics*, 13(2), 22–32.

Polido, F. B. P., & de Faria, M. K. (2024). Direitos Lgbtq+ entre Estudos Internacionais Queer e a Jurisprudência da Corte Europeia de Direitos Humanos. *Revista Da Faculdade de Direito da UFMG*, 85, 65–88.

Prewitt-Freilino, J. L., Caswell, T. A., & Laakso, E. K. (2012). The gendering of language: A comparison of gender equality in countries with gendered, natural gender, and genderless languages. *Sex Roles*, 66(3), 268–281.

Sarrasin, O., Gabriel, U., & Gygax, P. (2012). Sexism and attitudes toward gender-neutral language: The case of English, French, and German. *Swiss Journal of Psychology/Schweizerische Zeitschrift für Psychologie/Revue Suisse de Psychologie*, 71(3), 113–124.

Sczesny, S., Moser, F., & Wood, W. (2015). Beyond sexist beliefs: How do people decide to use gender-inclusive language? *Personality and Social Psychology Bulletin*, 41(7), 943–954.

Severi, F. C., & de Jesus Filho, J. (2022). "Is there a gender pay gap in the Brazilian judiciary?." *Revista de Administração Pública*, 56, 208–225.

Silva, J. P., & Karam de Chueiri, V. (2023). Feminism for a future Brazilian constitutionalism. In I. Spigno, V. R. Scotti, & J. P. Silva (Eds.), *The rights of women in comparative constitutional law* (pp. 137–150). London: Routledge.

Spain. (2023, February 28). Law n. 4 for the real and effective equality of transgender persons and for the guarantee of the rights of LGBTQI+ individuals. Retrieved from https://www.boe.es/buscar/act.php?id=BOE-A-2023-5366

Stout, J. G., Dasgupta, N., Hunsinger, M., & McManus, M. A. (2011). STEMing the tide: Using ingroup experts to inoculate women's self-concept in science, technology, engineering, and mathematics (STEM). *Journal of Personality and Social Psychology*, 100(2), 255.

Tavits, M., & Pérez, Efrén O. (2019). "Language influences mass opinion toward gender and LGBT equality." *Proceedings of the National Academy of Sciences*, 116(34), 16781–16786.

Walters, M. A., Paterson, J., Brown, R., & McDonnell, L. (2020). Hate crimes against trans people: Assessing emotions, behaviors, and attitudes toward criminal justice agencies. *Journal of Interpersonal Violence*, 35, 4583–4613.

Wodak, R. (Ed.). (1997). *Gender and discourse.* London, Thousand Oaks, New Delhi: Sage Publications Ltd.

Wodak, R. (2021). *The politics of fear: The shameless normalization of far-right discourse* (2nd ed.). London: Sage.

Wodak, R., & Meyer, M. (Eds.). (2001). *Methods of critical discourse analysis.* London: Sage Publications.

3 Law, Language, and Legal Certainty

Transformation and Challenges of the Georgian Legal Language

Dimitry Gegenava

3.1 Introduction

The language of law is one of the most developed, specialized professional languages,[1] which is entirely logical, as law operates in and through language, fully utilizing hermeneutics, based on the linguistic content of terminology. The content of law is perceived and understood through legal language;[2] therefore, logically, what cannot be expressed in linguistic form cannot be regulated. Legal language is the language of actions; it conveys the content of rights and obligations, which should make it flexible and easily understandable for individuals, although, in practice, this is not the case. In reality, legal language is a collection of heavy, technical, and difficult-to-understand constructions, which is why it usually has quite a bad reputation in society, especially when it comes to a state and people who have gone through Soviet occupation and have a completely different conception of not only the linguistic expression of law but law as a whole.

The Georgian language historically performed the function of social integration at the legislative level. Rules written in Georgian were much more acceptable to Georgian society and perceived as their own. To some extent, this was also the reason that, despite the policy of Russification, Georgian legal statutes were used for almost half a century after Georgia's conquest, almost until the end of the 1860s.[3] This was precisely why imperial and Soviet legislation and law, in general, could not become part of the legal culture of the people. Numerous factors have influenced and left their mark on Georgian legal culture: various conquerors, political pressure, closed and isolated space during the Cold War period, social and economic issues, etc.[4] Moreover, it should be noted that lawmaking is an essential element of legal globalization,[5] as consideration of comparative legal factors is inevitable in this process. No matter how universally the legal order is perceived and attempts are made to present it as detached from the standards of the national legal system, locally,[6] it is impossible to completely abstract law and its value system.

DOI: 10.4324/9781003430308-5

The Georgian normative language is characterized by an abundance of passive forms. The preference for the passive voice is determined by the basic semantics of these forms, where attention shifts to the conceptual object and the fact of the action itself. The linguistic characteristics of the Georgian language, such as the polypersonal nature of the verb, the synthesis of forms, agglutinative nature, etc., are quite naturally reflected in the legal language, as the latter is based on and is an integral part of the basic, common language. The Georgian language is rich in verbal forms, making it possible to convey an entire sentence with one word, which also lends its individual characteristic to the normative language. Unlike literary language, Georgian legal language requires the use of auxiliary verbs and additional constructions, which may seem artificially produced. However, it is important for law that legal concepts and institutions are conveyed in precise terms, unambiguously.[7]

Georgian legal language has not been researched properly. There are only a few academic works that explore this topic from legal or linguistic perspectives. In lawmaking and judicial proceedings, linguistic correctness and terminological clarity are among the most pressing challenges, which are not adequately addressed at either academic or official, state levels. Problems are not analyzed in terms of cause and effect, so state language policy could be directed precisely at solving these issues rather than pursuing generally unattainable goals.

This chapter examines the main characteristics of the formation and development of the modern Georgian legal language and the circumstances that have had the greatest impact on this process and have determined the form of the language as it exists today. Special attention is paid to the problems of using legal Georgian in the process of lawmaking and justice, as well as its difficulties and challenges in the modern, globalized world. Since this is one of the first attempts in recent years to consider the issue interdisciplinarily, the work focuses on analyzing and studying the causes, with general indications of ways to solve them, which is a subject for independent research.

3.2 Georgian Legal Language: Development and Modern Tendencies

3.2.1 Formation of the Modern Georgian Legal Language

Georgia and Georgian law have never been confined to national values[8] but have always enthusiastically and openly accepted innovations and experiences from other legal cultures, including both institutions and specialized terminology. A clear example of this is the codifications of the first quarter of the 18th century, when the Book of Law by King Vakhtang VI separately accommodated the laws of the peoples living in the kingdom. For this purpose, Greek, Armenian, Persian, Syrian, and Jewish statutes and legal concepts were translated[9] and adapted as much as possible to the Georgian legal language.

Despite the attacks and repressions of powerful neighboring empires, Georgia and the Georgian language maintained their independence and identity,[10] which determined the special status of the Georgian language not only legally but also culturally and socially. It also bore the social mission and the burden of state unity. At the beginning of the 19th century, the Russian Empire conquered Georgia and began to pursue an aggressive policy.[11] This process proceeded relatively slowly in the direction of law and justice, as Russian laws and Georgian laws were very different from each other. Moreover, conducting legal proceedings in Russian initially precluded any kind of trust in the justice system. Law formulated in a language understandable to people and oriented to their traditions and character had a direct social effect; even the empire tried to avoid direct interruption in this.

Jurisprudence and legal studies were quite developed in the Russian Empire, which was mainly due to the empire's favorable attitude toward European culture, including law.[12] Georgian law benefited from this to some extent. Georgia maintained its identity and autonomy, on the one hand, due to the cultural differences of society and, on the other hand, due to linguistic uniqueness. At the beginning of the 20th century, professionals educated in European universities strengthened the liberational and educational movement in Georgia. In 1918, when the Democratic Republic of Georgia declared independence, among the most important reforms were legislative initiatives related to the state language: "Georgianization" of geographical toponyms, defining Georgian as the language of legal and administrative proceedings, gradual replacement of imposed terminology in legal acts and judicial practice, etc.[13] Particularly noteworthy is the work on Georgia's first constitution. The basic law introduced many new institutions and terms into the language. It's also worth noting that even the draft constitutions were published in advance with comments and explanations,[14] so that ordinary people could understand what the basic law was about, and the future legal order that would be established or developed based on this act would be predictable.

The Democratic Republic of Georgia was conquered by Soviet Russia in its third year of existence, and the first constitution was in effect for only a short time.[15] During the three years of independence, the Georgian language made significant progress, and the same can be said about the legal language. Independence necessitated word formation, translation, adaptation, and reception of foreign terms. Unfortunately, this process then continued artificially, disregarding the peculiarities of the Georgian language, with Soviet tendencies and forced calquing, as a result of which the Georgian legal language took on more or less its current modern form.

3.2.2 *Russification of the Legal Language and Soviet Linguistic Expansion in Georgia*

After the Soviet occupation in 1921, state policy regarding both the official language and the legal language changed radically. While the Russian Empire pursued direct Russification not only to eradicate the language but to destroy Georgian identity in general, the policy in the Soviet Union changed to some extent. On Stalin's personal orders, the translation of specialized terminology began, often using direct and crude methods. In law, even the pseudo-independence that was created as an illusion in some spheres did not exist. All levels of legal acts of the Soviet Republic of Georgia, from the constitution to ordinary subordinate normative acts, were translated from the central-level acts of the Soviet Union,[16] without any interpretation or linguistic adaptation. As a result, the Georgian legal language became cumbersome, clumsy, and inflexible. Positive law should adapt to the legal consciousness and culture of a specific people; otherwise, legal norms become completely alienated from the people, which was clearly happening in the case of the Soviet Union[17]: The law in content and the law in form, both linguistically and stylistically, did not at all sympathize with the psycho-emotional disposition of the law's addressees. Despite these challenges, some Georgian professors, both during and after the Soviet occupation, tried to maintain linguistic purity, promote the development of the legal Georgian, and guide it in the right direction. It is thanks to their efforts that, along with borrowed terms, many original, unique terms and adequate understandings of legal institutions were established[18] (for example, "მამკვიდრებელი" [Mamk'vidrebeli] – testator; "სამისდღეშიო რჩენა" [Samisdgheshio rchena] life annuity; "ბოჭვა" [boch'va] – limitation/binding).

The issue of protecting the state language and preserving the Georgian language was prominent during the work on the draft of the 1978 Constitution of Soviet Georgia.[19] The attempt to abolish the constitutional status of the Georgian language was met with mass protests and demonstrations.[20] After intense protests, the provision on language was still reflected in the final version of the constitution: Georgian remained as the state language, with the state undertaking obligations for its development and use. Additionally, the free use of Russian was ensured, without granting privileges to any particular language.[21] The 1978 Constitution is also notable because its updated version was in force in Georgia during the first years of the restoration of independence.[22] Even at the end of Soviet occupation, as a result of the victory of national liberation forces in parliamentary elections, the country's supreme legislative body changed the text of the basic law linguistically as well, removing Soviet designations, acronyms, and symbols from the constitution.[23] Formally, before the restoration of independence, it was necessary to eradicate the Soviet influence from the linguistic and terminological levels. Quite rightly, linguistic independence and the liberation of normative language from occupation were considered a priority as the foundation for legal independence. Such symbolism is extremely important for national consolidation.

3.2.3 Restoration of Independence and New Breath of the Legal Language

After the restoration of independence in 1991, numerous legislative reforms were implemented. The initial steps focused on creating basic laws and legal acts. However, against the backdrop of ongoing political processes in Georgia, temporary governments, and other challenges, unfortunately, terminological issues were not given proper attention, if any at all. Nevertheless, one thing was recognized at the normative level – the rejection of any form of Soviet heritage,[24] which, of course, implied the content and form of Soviet law.

The commissions working on Georgia's Civil, Criminal, and General Administrative Codes played an irreplaceable role in expanding the lexical stock of modern legal Georgian.[25] Their purpose was far greater than creating key laws for the newly independent country. Formal regulations existed before and operated to some extent even under Soviet occupation (naturally, in a completely deformed manner in the field of private law, but still). The codes were meant to fulfill a social integration function, which the 1995 Constitution failed to achieve. Moreover, political confrontation, party interests, and personal ambitions of politicians completely overshadowed substantive issues in the process of drafting the constitution,[26] not to mention the necessity of overcoming the textual coherence and heavy Soviet terminological heritage of the basic law.

The main task of the commission developing the Civil Code of Georgia was to make the Civil Code understandable to citizens, written in the simplest and most unambiguous language possible. It quite naturally gave preference to Greco-Roman terminology, which was organic for civil law, but did not reject those Oriental terms that had already been established in Georgian tradition for centuries and were accepted by the society ("სერვიტუტი" [servit'ut'i] – easement; "უზუფრუქტი" [uzuprukt'i] – usufruct; "იპოთეკა" [ipot'ek'a] – mortgage, etc.). In some cases, established foreign terms were deliberately replaced with Georgian equivalents to ensure that the content of the legal institution or relationships was perceived accurately and correctly by the ordinary people (for example, "ბეითალმანი" [beitalmani] to "უმკვიდრო ქონება" [umk'vidro koneba] – heirless estate). Many old Georgian legal terms began a new life; their reuse and establishment at the legislative level gradually limited and completely expelled from practice the artificial terms imposed during Soviet and Russian occupation (for example, "ნასყიდობა" [nasq`idoba] – sale). Ultimately, the language of the Civil Code of Georgia did not turn out to be entirely simple; in terms of legal language, it is between the French and German civil codes: neither simple nor very complex.[27]

The working commissions of the Criminal and General Administrative Codes worked with varying degrees of success. Rather than undertaking comprehensive terminological changes, these commissions maintained most of the existing official terms. This resulted in a significant qualitative difference between the codes in terms of linguistic coherence and terminology. It can be said that the main secret of the success of the Civil Code of Georgia is that it was well received by Georgian society both linguistically and substantively; in fact, it removed the alienation between legal consciousness and law.[28]

After the codifications of the 1990s, there has been virtually no systematic reform of legislation preceded by coordinated work of lawyers, linguists, and representatives of various academic fields, with serious research. The vast majority of changes, including constitutional reforms, were often approved thoughtlessly, in compressed timeframes, hastily, without in-depth analysis and discussion. This has had a severe effect and continues to cause irreparable damage to the understanding and practical operation of legal norms, as rules or regulations are created for people, for those people who need to know the content of the rule, to perceive it easily, so that they can elementarily live and act in accordance with the law.

3.3 Legal Language in Action

3.3.1 Legal Language and Passions of Lawmaking

Law is more than just a will of legislator, expressed through mere linguistic constructs,[29] yet the path to understanding law passes through normatively formulated texts. Legislation is a private and very peculiar form of communication,[30] its language expressing both the content of norms and related elements.[31] It is authentic, carries an exclusive meaning,[32] and should, to some extent, be of national character.[33] This by no means implies the pursuit of narrow nationalist views but rather the reflection of constitutional identity, common will, and public sentiment in legal texts. Active work in this direction in lawmaking took place after the restoration of independence, when historical documents and sources were researched, old terms were analyzed, and it became possible to adapt them to modern challenges so that specific words would not become alienated and could be used in practice.[34] The separation of legal language from the language of the people renders any norm ineffective. Communications carried out through legislative means aim to influence citizens' lives and frame their actions within certain normative processes.[35] Consequently, for legislation to have real power and fulfill its intended purpose – to bind and compel the addressee to follow established rules – legal technique and language should be structured in a way that allows individuals to grasp the content.

Both the legislator and the judge are representatives of a particular society; logically, their worldview cannot be radically different from that of the society itself.[36] The same applies to legal language and its use, as linguistic processes occurring in society directly reflect on the professional language of lawyers in one form or another. Unfortunately, the Georgian legislator is often detached from reality, including literary and colloquial language trends, which creates a gulf between the legislative body and the people. Cases are particularly frequent when the legislator is unaware of original Georgian terms or fails to use them properly, creating the impression that there is no equivalent for a specific word in Georgian. This, in turn, leads to the pollution and complication of legal language.

Statutory definitions are precisely the connecting chain between legal and ordinary languages.[37] Through such definitions, non-specialists navigate the extensive paths and labyrinths of legislation, which are often quite challenging even for professionals. However, it is also true that linguistic simplicity directly implies a greater number of norms, more descriptions, and more details.[38] Moreover, formulating legal norms in a way that is understandable and easily perceivable for absolutely all participants in civil relationships is practically impossible; often, logic and language knowledge alone are not sufficient to understand the content of the law.[39]

Legislative terms in Georgian legislation are often inconsistent, differing significantly from each other, caused by the multiplicity of legislative initiators and uncoordinated work. The substantive collision and overlap of terminologies completely remove deontic logic from Georgian legal acts. (According to the logic of the Civil Code, it is impossible to predict the content of the Law on Entrepreneurs; the Code of Administrative Offenses is a remnant of the Soviet past and completely deviates from modern legislative standards, and so forth.) This is compounded by the significant delegation of the lawmaking function characteristic of the parliamentary regime to the executive branch, which increases the mass of legal text by adopting subordinate normative acts. The uncontrolled granting of broad interpretation and freedom of action to the executive, unfortunately, negatively affects the language of lawmaking and legislation as a whole. Ultimately, such attitudes make the law completely unpredictable and unforeseeable, which negatively impacts the practical operation of the rule of law.

3.3.2 *Legal Georgian and Judicial Hermeneutics*

Legal practice often gives different interpretations to the content contained in normative acts. A broad interpretation can give a completely different meaning to a norm, and, in this sense, the court also becomes a lawmaker.[40] Constitutional Court and common courts in Georgia assume the function of the legislator to varying degrees, which in some cases is entirely justified from the perspective of human rights protection, while sometimes it may pose a threat to the rule of law, especially if the content given to the norm as a result of judicial hermeneutics differs sharply from the statutory definition.

The use of legal language in the practice of Georgian common courts is associated with formal and substantive problems caused by deficiencies in the personal qualifications of judges and the current form of the judiciary. Unfortunately, the vast majority of decisions are template-based, saturated with linguistic clichés, common constructions, professional jargon, calques (mainly influenced by the Russian language and to a lesser extent by English, considering modern sources of information), and severe grammatical errors. Moreover, the language of court decisions, rulings, and judgments is of a very low standard. The main source of problems is the lack of knowledge of the state language itself, and little attention is paid to its acquisition even at the stage of judges' training. Due to the system's overload, it is practically impossible to ensure the linguistic correctness of decisions and their accuracy even at an elementary level; they do not undergo philological expertise.

Along with the problems of the linguistic apparatus, there are noticeable challenges in the direction of terminological interpretation. When philosophical, anthropological, and social categories exist in legal norms, Georgian courts find it difficult to operate correctly in the flow of information. Interpretation in a narrow legal context results in giving different content to norms, which, in turn, creates a danger of unpredictability of law and damages the rule of law. Judicial hermeneutics is inconsistent when giving practical content to important legislative concepts such as "morality" and "ethics," "public order," "public interest," "best interest," "separation of powers," and others in law,[41] which is mainly due to incomplete possession of interdisciplinary knowledge and language.

The practice of using contra legem interpretation by common courts is noteworthy. This technique of legal methods requires special caution, as, in such cases, the judge may significantly exceed the limits set by positive law and change the meaning of the law in such a way that it actually gives the norm a new, opposite content to the original.[42] The separation of the judicial language and the legislator's will leads to the existence of contradictory normative texts, which is quite damaging. Georgian courts periodically resort to such practices,[43] often quite rightly and to protect human rights, but, even in this case, linguistic analysis of the norm, comparison of the legal and literary linguistic meanings of terms, and adding arguments in this direction for motivation are rarely used.

The Constitutional Court of Georgia uses legal language interestingly. Of course, the formal side of court acts is problematic in this case as well. The Constitutional Court helps the legislator to form the correct will by abolishing norms,[44] but often through its own interpretation and development of new terms, it also becomes a positive legislator.[45] According to the legislation, the Constitutional Court of Georgia does not have the authority of constitutional control over the decisions of common courts, so it had to resort to improvisation and legal technique when in 2011 the Court first abolished not the norm itself but the interpretation established as a result of its practical application.[46] For this, the Constitutional Court created the concept of "normative content of the norm," by which it distinguished the meaning established as a result of the application of the norm from its legislative content. Although this practice was quite high-risk, it was justified by the motive of protecting human rights. This technique was used many times in the future through precedental practice and is now an integral part of constitutional legal proceedings.

Unfortunately, such legal-linguistic experiments are not frequent; only in cases of extreme necessity does the Constitutional Court have to go beyond artificial frameworks, resort to methodological tools, and try innovative mechanisms of legal technique. Of course, law is a conservative phenomenon, and the court maximally supports this tendency, but the goal of protecting human rights justifies the risk, especially if it results in the creation of new constructions, institutions, and ideas in legal language, and word formation.

3.4 Sovietization, Foreign Words, and Linguistic Pressure on Legal Georgian

3.4.1 Sovietization of the Language and Results of Russification

In the process of forming the modern Georgian legal language, as with other specialized fields, new terms were often artificially created, directly translated from Russian, based on political rather than linguistic grounds. This process completely ignored the historical memory and inherited oral traditions that naturally existed among the people at the everyday level in a common language.[47] As a result, the Georgian legal language is distorted by Russian calques, and the influence of Russian terminology is still noticeable today.[48]

The codifications carried out after the restoration of independence were preceded by significant work on the drafting of the Georgian Constitution, which involved Georgia's legal elite.[49] Although the legal language was significantly refined during the work on the constitution, it most reflected the influence of "Russification" in terms of linguistic expressions. For professors educated in the Soviet Union, the main source of understanding law and jurisprudence was Russian-language academic literature, which led to significant distortion of legal language in both legislative and academic directions.[50] Nevertheless, the codification process had a tremendous impact on refining the Georgian legal language and shaping the prospects for its further development. The limited stock of legal vocabulary was somewhat processed, refreshed, and enriched as much as possible.

Despite many attempts, it remains difficult to cleanse the legal language of those impurities that were reflected in the language as a result of "Russification" and "Sovietization." In addition to numerous differences between Russian and Georgian legal languages, there is a significant expressive difference, which is conditioned by the individuality of the Georgian language and its unique belonging to its language family. Often, unjustified and completely unfounded calquing diminishes the already scarce Georgian legal language, whose resources are not even partially utilized, let alone fully studied. The offspring of forced and unjustified calquing have become ingrained in the modern Georgian language, which is why distorted forms of legal language are often more familiar to lawyers than the true Georgian ones.

3.4.2 *Foreign Words and Barbarisms in Georgina Legal Language*

No nation can escape the influx of foreign words, as modern trends compel them to resort to such means. In many languages, equivalent concepts may no longer be found. It's entirely inconceivable to devise different, national concepts for technical terms; this would lead to misunderstandings and hinder the development of intercultural relations.

In the process of foreign words becoming established in the Georgian language, several elements can be identified. Some of these are positive and entirely natural phenomena, while others, although also natural, are characterized as entirely negative. Positive aspects include legal and social innovations, translation practices, terminological harmonization, and adaptation. Negative aspects are barbarisms, artificial replacement of terms, the substitution of already-existing adequate concepts with foreign words, and unnaturally formed constructions.

Borrowing of foreign words is a natural phenomenon that enriches the language.[51] At different stages of language development, it is entirely natural for contact to occur with other languages, resulting in the reception and penetration of various terms from these languages. This process leads to changes in the language's inherent nature and the transformation of words and concepts.[52] But this should not destroy the process of term production and work on new words. One of the primary sources of legal reception in Georgia was the translation and adaptation of legal acts from other states and model systems, although the translation was always creative.[53] (The following terminology and designations were established through these and analogous processes: "ბათილი" [batili] – null/void; "დასტური" [dast'uri] – confirmation; "სათათბირო" [satatbiro] – advisory/consultative; "იჯარა" [ijara] – lease, etc.). Unfortunately, often thoughtless actions in the translation process and mechanical adoption of terms artificially burden the legal language.[54]

For centuries, the so-called linguistic pressure accustomed Georgian society to parasitism. Whether forced or voluntary, it was not possible to process new concepts, arrange legal institutions and relationships, or find their individual Georgian variations. Contrary to this, there was an automatic influx of terms from foreign languages and their direct adaptation to Georgian reality, no matter how painful this implementation was. This process intensified particularly in the 1990s when the agenda of the newly independent country included creating a modern legislative corpus. Disorganized and chaotic processes paved the way for many barbarisms. Their influx was mainly caused by direct translation of international acts, where the translator, often unfamiliar with the law and legal techniques, used the same term as in the original, not only in a modified form but by direct "Georgianization" or simply transliteration (for example, official translation of the Vienna Convention on International Treaties provided terminology directly from the original text or transliterated them, keeping their Latin or English forms).[55]

Modern Georgian legal language naturally adopts words and word combinations created and derived over many centuries of history, turning them into legal field belongings.[56] Both Greco-Roman and Eastern legal cultures have had a noticeable and significant influence on the Georgian legal language, resulting in legal terminology entering the language from both worlds and establishing itself with a peculiar, often national, Georgian meaning.[57] Words of Greco-Roman origin were reflected in the Georgian legal language both formally and substantively, with their authentic and original meanings, unlike Persian-Arabic and Turkish terminology, which were mainly given Georgian content and significance, as their initial understanding could not cover the content of legal relations themselves[58] (these terms are employed across public administration and state organization, as well as in various branches of private law, including the articulation of contractual relationships). As a result, numerous specific Oriental words have been integrated into various fields of Georgian law. Civil law is particularly rich in this regard[59] (as terminology received from Oriental languages over the centuries has been used to regulate usual, ordinary private legal relationships and convey their content).

3.4.3 Calquing

In the process of adapting terminology, the use of calques is quite frequent, as finding adequate forms during translation is sometimes not only challenging but also impossible. It is necessary to distinguish between two types of calquing: (1) when language distortion occurs and an existing version is replaced with a new, stylistically improper calque and (2) calquing as a necessary measure for diversifying the language.

Any calquing that threatens the integrity of the Georgian legal language, its uniqueness, and originality should be condemned. If such cases are systematically repeated, the very existence of the language might be called into question. In these instances, calquing is often the result of ignorance or a low level of knowledge of the language and linguistic forms. This is also influenced by the reduced involvement of professional editors in the process of reception and implementation of legal terms.

In some cases, calques are even necessary as they fill a void in the language, establishing a unique, individual, and exclusive meaning for a specific term.[60] Unfortunately, such situations often confront nations with ancient cultures and, consequently, those speaking ancient languages. The antiquity of a language, while a virtue, can also create complexities. Therefore, in some cases, calquing is precisely the necessary evil that legislators and society must resort to in order to keep the law modern and adapted to the reality that prevails in the state and the entire world.

After all, the essence of law is to ensure public and state security, order, and tranquility for the peaceful coexistence of individuals, which is entirely inconceivable without considering modernity and reality. The law must evolve linguistically to effectively address contemporary issues and maintain its relevance in a rapidly changing world.

When employing calques in legal language, it's crucial to strike a balance between preserving the linguistic integrity of Georgian and introducing necessary new concepts. This process should involve careful consideration by linguistic experts and legal professionals to ensure that new terms are both accurate in their legal meaning and consistent with the structural and stylistic norms of the Georgian language. Calquing can serve as a bridge between international legal concepts and domestic legal frameworks, facilitating legal harmonization and international cooperation. However, this process cannot be left to run its own course. Any such calquing, as a "necessary evil," must be comprehended by both lawyers and linguists, with active oversight and participation from the national agency responsible for protecting the state language.

3.4.4 Linguistics, Terminological Migration, and Jurisprudence

The relationship between linguistics and jurisprudence is diverse and multi-layered, which is due to the linguistic complexities of legislative terminologies and legal texts.[61] The migration of specific terms and words from the common language lexicon into the legal terminological system is characteristic of all languages, and Georgian is no exception.[62] Such migration requires special attention and supervision from field experts. This is especially important considering that, after the restoration of independence, Georgia intensely absorbed both new field-specific terminology and foreign words or barbarisms that entered the colloquial language. This was compounded by many qualitatively new institutions for both Georgian law and society, as well as objectively new concepts brought by technological progress. In such circumstances, the best solution is the collaborative work of linguists and legal scholars for processing and "inventing" concepts. However, this remains a significant challenge in Georgian reality. Introducing new legal terms is particularly delicate, as it's crucial to consider how civil life and participants in legal relations will accept them.[63] Without such acceptance, any regulation is doomed to "death," as a norm lives only as much as it is used in practice.

Legislation is not created only for educated people; the textual fabric of a legal act should be formulated in such a way that it is perceptible in terms of both values and language even to those with the lowest legal consciousness.[64] Despite this noble and grand goal, the language of law cannot mechanically fully approach colloquial language. The key is that their accuracy and understanding intensively interact with each other.[65] Among Georgian legislation, the Civil Code has been best received and practically used by the public. Of course, this has its rational basis, as it regulates civil relations, and, logically, practical necessity determines its popularity. However, it's essential to note the style and language of the Civil Code, which are clear, precise, and specific, largely due to the active involvement of linguists in the commission's composition.[66] Unfortunately, in creating modern legal acts, legislators and lawyers collaborate less and less with representatives of the humanities, paying less attention to the formal expression of content and linguistic correctness. This violates the harmonious interdependence and synergy of content and form, which ultimately should imply the law's acceptability and its function of social integration.

The difficulty in using legal Georgian additionally lies in the extremely low level of knowledge of the Georgian language itself, as specialized language is nourished by general language. If a person doesn't know the basics, they will never be able to properly use and benefit from what's derived from that foundation. Therefore, considering the level of knowledge in society, the existence of difficulties in using legal language and the gap not only between colloquial and legal languages but also between them and literary Georgian should not be surprising. This is a result of both the ineffectiveness of the education system and the inefficiency of the state language policy and uncoordinated work at the national level.

3.5 Researchers, Academia, and Legal Georgian

One of the main challenges of the Georgian legal language is related to the lack of interest in the issue from academia and the university community. This is not due to the irrelevance of the topic itself but rather to the general lack of interdisciplinarity in Georgian academic space and the scarcity of interdisciplinary collaboration. Issues of legal language cannot be considered the exclusive research domain of lawyers or linguists; it is complex in nature and naturally requires fundamental study from both the humanities and legal theory. Unfortunately, at the current stage of legal language development, Georgian language researchers are practically not involved in the processes of lawmaking, creation, and reception of terminology. This is due to many factors: (1) considering lawmaking and judiciary as the exclusive domain of lawyers, (2) low level of humanity and legal studies, (3) abstraction of linguists and Georgian language philologists from ongoing political–legal processes, and (4) locality of scientific fields and a minimal level of positive interaction.

The problem became particularly acute in the events related to the Georgian law "On Transparency of Foreign Influence." The discussion and adoption of a legal act containing numerous legal challenges took place against the backdrop of mass protests. The Venice Commission harshly criticized the draft law,[67] and the discriminatory nature of the act was repeatedly highlighted in problematic content issues. It stigmatizes civil activists and organizations by establishing the status of "foreign," "foreign power influence," and "agent" toward them.[68] The law has been challenged before the Constitutional Court, and linguists are actively participating in the discussions. For the first time in recent years, a linguistic analysis of the law was carried out, based on which the nature of the legal terminology used in the law, their linguistic aspect, and the perceptions and understandings of society about them were studied.[69] These analyses of law further highlighted the gulf that exists between language and law researchers, as well as the need for systematic and interdisciplinary analysis. Without this, it is impossible, on the one hand, for the law to carry content desirable for society and, on the other hand, for people themselves to adequately perceive the law and achieve legal security as a legitimate aim.

3.6 State Language Policy and Coordination of Legal Language Protection

The scope of state language use is quite broad: culture, politics, legal proceedings, lawmaking, science, etc.[70] It is one of the most important symbols and practical mechanisms of the state, through which the institutional will of the nation is expressed. The issue of the state language was reflected in the original version of the 1995 Constitution of Georgia, which declared that "The official language of Georgia shall be Georgian, and, in the Abkhazia, also Abkhazian,"[71] and despite subsequent fundamental constitutional reforms, it remains an integral part of the content of the basic law to this day.[72] As a result of the 2017–2018 constitutional reform, the Constitution established the obligation to regulate state language protection issues through an organic law.[73]

The State Language Department is responsible for protecting and developing the state language and ensuring proper inter-agency coordination.[74] While it develops the state language strategy, action plan, and policy, its effectiveness is very low:[75] there is virtually no synchronization of the legislative, executive, and judicial authorities' lawmaking activities, no research on normative language problems, and no systematic analysis of legal and literary Georgian language with the aim of bringing them closer and maximizing harmonization. Part of these problems is caused by the department's place among administrative bodies – it is an executive body, therefore, distanced from legislative activities. Moreover, its authority is not sufficiently high, and reports and proposals on language problems often bear only a recommendatory nature, while initiatives on literary norms are not sufficiently resonant.

Particularly noteworthy is the direction of expertise and linguistic analysis of legal acts, which is usually formal in nature. Under conditions of constantly accelerated reviews and unplanned legislative initiatives, proper philological expertise of acts cannot be achieved. The same can be said about subordinate normative acts, which substantively undergo only legal verification before publication and not serious linguistic expertise, which, unfortunately, leads to unharmonized, contradictory legislation and poorly structured normative material.

3.7 Conclusion

Legal Georgian has been greatly influenced by the languages of conquering empires as well as the cultural processes of neighboring nations. It's worth noting that these influences should not be viewed solely negatively, as such interactions and the introduction of globalization elements are often necessary. They enrich the language, refine professional terminology, and, most importantly, linguistic richness is accompanied by new legal institutions and the dissemination of information about them in society. Linguistic processes are reflected in law, which is ultimately a product expressed in language and does not exist independently of it. This is why the state of Georgian legal language has been largely determined by societal attitudes, as the development of specialized legal language has never been a priority for modern Georgian society, which is directly reflected in the state of the language.

Legal language has long since diverged from everyday, colloquial language and has essentially become a completely different tool, often unnaturally distanced from literary norms, over which lawyers have taken exclusive and complete monopoly. The artificial alienation of linguistics and jurisprudence, the lack of involvement and interest from the university community, and the absence of interdisciplinary research have turned legal Georgian into an object of unplanned experiments by lawyers.

Particularly problematic is the struggle against the consequences of language Sovietization and forced Russification, compounded by the active, powerful influx of foreign words and calques in the context of natural globalization. The antiquity of the Georgian language and the absence of certain forms must be taken into account, which is why the language naturally assimilates innovations, especially when no one is concerned with terminological adaptation and conceptual reception. Without coordinated work between linguists and lawyers, it is impossible to speak of any kind of progress. The lack of interdisciplinary research and coordination precludes the expression of law in such a way that form fully reflects content and both together harmoniously convey information to the individual, who is the sole and primary addressee of the law.

Uncoordinated national policy toward the state language and ineffective methods of its protection in the process of lawmaking and justice leave the language completely unprotected; it is left to its own devices, relying solely on the linguistic knowledge and conscientiousness of legislators or judges, which is certainly not reassuring. The State Language Department should conduct an effective policy and achieve the establishment of a philological–linguistic expertise requirement alongside legal expertise, at least at the level of legal and judicial acts. This mechanism will ensure not only the existence of well-formed legal texts but also the prevention of errors that are common in legal practice.

Notes

1 Bekauri, 2001, p. 22.
2 Bix, 2003, pp. 5–6.

3 See Gegenava, 2010, p. 9.
4 Maisuradze, 2006, p. 101
5 Maisuradze, 2006, p. 89.
6 See Teubner, 1997, pp. 3–28.
7 Tsnobiladze et al., 2000, pp. 268, 270, 284–285.
8 Zoidze, 2005, p. 20.
9 Surguladze, 2002, pp. 131–137; Metreveli, 2003, pp. 31–41.
10 Zoidze, 2005, p. 20.
11 See Act of Restoration of State Independence of Georgia, 19 April 1991.
12 Zoidze, 2003, p. 90.
13 See Kobakhidze et al., p. 2018.
14 See Gegenava et al., 2021, pp. 38–40.
15 Gegenava, 2021, pp. 84–85.
16 Gegenava et al., 2021, pp. 50–51.
17 Zoidze, 2003, p. 94.
18 Zoidze, 2005, 174.
19 Gegenava, Partsvania, and Tusashvili, 2024, p. 59.
20 Bolkvadze, 2023, pp. 209–211.
21 Constitution of the Socialist Republic of Georgia, 15 April 1978, Art. 75.
22 Demetrashvili, 2010, p. 9.
23 Gegenava et al., 2021, p. 52.
24 See Act of Restoration of State Independence of Georgia, 19 April 1991.
25 Gegenava, 2010, p. 13.
26 See Gegenava et al., 2021, p. 54.
27 See Zoidze, 2005, pp. 150, 157–159.
28 Zoidze, 2007, p. 94.
29 Zoidze, 2006, p. 43.
30 Hoecke, 2002, p. 130.
31 Tsnobiladze et al., 2000, p. 264.
32 Bekauri, 2001, p. 23.
33 Knipper, 1998, p. 75.
34 Zoidze, 2005, p. 155.
35 Hoecke, 2002, p. 131.
36 Maisuradze, 2006, pp. 91–92.
37 Hoecke, 2002, p. 132.
38 Zoidze, 2005, p. 153.
39 Zoidze, 2005, p. 153.
40 Dürr, 2011, p. 171.
41 See Gagoshidze, 2022.
42 See Khubua, 2018.
43 See Partsvania, 2019.
44 Zoidze, 2007, p. 61.
45 See Javakhishvili, 2017, p. 266.
46 *Public Defender of Georgia v. The Parliament of Georgia*, Decision No 1/1/477 of the Georgian Constitutional Court, 22 December 2011.
47 Tsnobiladze et al., 2000, p. 280.
48 Zoidze, 2005, p. 174.
49 Gegenava et al., 2021, p. 54.
50 Zoidze, 2005, p. 174.
51 Tsnobiladze et al., 2000, p. 281.
52 Bekauri, 2001, p. 23.

53 Zoidze, 2005, p. 173.
54 Tsnobiladze et al., 2000, p. 282.
55 Gegenava, 2010, p. 15.
56 Tsnobiladze et al., 2000, p. 156.
57 Zoidze, 2005, p. 156.
58 Zoidze, 2005, pp. 156–157.
59 Surguladze, 2005, pp. 4–5.
60 Tsnobiladze et al., 2000, p. 282.
61 Bekauri, 2001, p. 23.
62 Tsnobiladze et al., 2000, p. 277.
63 Zoidze, 2005, p. 161.
64 Zoidze, 2006, p. 45.
65 Bekauri, 2001, p. 23.
66 Zoidze, 2005, p. 152.
67 See Venice Commission, CDL-AD(2024)020, Urgent Opinion on the Law on Transparency of Foreign Influence, 24 June 2024.
68 See Kvintskhadze, 2024.
69 See Tabatadze et al., 2024.
70 Gorgoshadze and Jakeli, 2023, p. 86.
71 Constitution of Georgia, 24 August 1995, Art. 8 (Original Redaction).
72 Gegenava, Partsvania, and Tusashvili, 2024, p. 60.
73 Constitution of Georgia, 24 August 1995, Art. 2(3).
74 Organic Law N4084-რს of Georgia "On the State Language," 22 July 2015, Art. 36(1)(6).
75 Gegenava, Partsvania, and Tusashvili, 2024, pp. 62–63.

References

Bekauri, Irma. 2001. "Some Issues of Language and Style of Law," *Law*, no. 12: 22–23.

Bix, Brian. 2003. *Law, Language and Legal Determinacy,* New York: Clarendon Press.

Demetrashvili, Avtandil. 2010. "Review of the Georgian Constitutional History," in Avtandil Demetrashvili (ed.) *Constitution of Georgia and Constitutional Reform 2010*, 6–13. Tbilisi: Constitutional Law Research and Support Regional Center.

Dürr, Schnutz Rudolf. 2011. "Comparative Overview of European Systems of Constitutional Justice," *International Constitutional Law Journal,* vol. 5, no. 2: 159–179.

Gagoshidze, Mariam. 2022. "Moral" and "Ethics" in the Content of the Art. 54 of the Civil Code of Georgia (in the Light of One Decision of the Constitutional Court of Georgia)," in Dimitry Gegenava (ed.) *Giorgi Kverenchkhiladze 50*, 119–1931.

Gegenava, Dimitry. 2010. "Legal Language – Catalyst for Georgian Legal Culture," in *Collected Papers of the Winners of the 70th University Scientific Conference*, Tbilisi: Society of TSU Students and Young Scientists.

Gegenava, Dimitry. 2021. "The First Constitution of Georgia: Between Myths and Reality," *Journal of Constitutional Law*, no. 1–2: 79–86.

Gegenava, Dimitry and Goradze, Giorgi (eds.). 2021. *Introduction to Georgian Constitutional Law*, 2nd edition, Tbilisi: Sulkhan-Saba Orbeliani University Press.

Gegenava, Dimitry, Partsvania, Maka and Tusashvili, Tamar. 2024. "Legal Guarantees and Regulation of the State Language in Georgia," *Teka Komisji Prawniczej PAN Oddział w Lublinie,* vol. XVII, no. 1: 57–69.

Gorgoshadze, Murman and Jakeli, Levan. 2023. "Comparative Analyzes of the Laws on the State Language in the Countries of the South Caucasus," *Orbeliani*, no. 6: 81–101.

Hoecke, Mark van. 2002. *Law as Communication*, Oxford, Portland: Hart Publishing.

Javakhishvili, Paata. 2017. "Constitutional Court of Georgia and de facto Real Control," *Journal of Law*, no. 1: 264–275.

Khubua, Giorgi. 2018. "Interpretation Contra Legem," *Legal Methods*, no. 2: 1–20.

Knipper, Rolf. 1998. "Several Opinions of the Reforms of the Private Law in Georgia," *Herald of the National Academy of Sciences of Georgia (Law)*, no. 1, 73–81.

Kobakhidze, Rusiko, Silakadze, Dimitri, Khvadagiani, Davit and Khvadagiani, Irakli. 2018. *Democratic Republic of Georgia: 100 Years/100 Stories*, Tbilisi: Artanuji.

Kvintskhadze, Khatuna. 2024. *Why the Russian Law Contradicts to the European Convention of Human Rights and Rule of Law Principles?* Tbilisi: Social Justice Center.

Maisuradze, Natela. 2006. "Lawmaking: Issues of Legal Culture and Legal Pluralism," *Human and Constitution*, no. 3: 89–101.

Metreveli, Valerian. 2003. *History of the Georgian State and Law,* Tbilisi: Meridiani.

Partsvania, Maka. 2019. "Contra Legem Interpretation: One Interesting Decision from the Practice of Administrative Court Proceedings," *Legal Methods*, no. 3: 75–101.

Surguladze, Ivane. 2002. *Sources of the History of Georgian Law,* Tbilisi: Meridiani Publishing.

Surguladze, Nugzar. 2005. *Islamic Law*, vol. 1, Tbilisi: Meridiani Publishing.

Tabatadze, Shalva, Gabunia, Kakha, Beridze, Marina and Purtskhvanidze, Zakaria. 2024. *Law of Georgia on 'Transparency of Foreign Influence'*, Tbilisi: Sulkhan-Saba Orbelaini University Press.

Teubner, Gunther. 1997. "Global Bukowina: Legal Pluralism in the World Society," in Gunther Teubner (ed.), *Global Law Without a State*, Brookfield: Dartmouth.

Tsnobiladze, Paata, Khubua, Giorgi, Khmaladze, Vakhtang, Metreveli, Nana and Kapanadze, Otar. 2000. *Legislative Drafting*, Tbilisi: Azri Publishers.

Zoidze, Besarion. 2003. "From the History of Creation of the Civil Code of Georgia," *Georgian Law Review*, vol. 6, no. 1: 87–114.

Zoidze, Besarion. 2005. *Reception of the European Private Law in Georgia,* Tbilisi: Tinatin Tsereteli Institute for Law and State.

Zoidze, Besarion. 2006. "Science of Legislative Culture," *Human and Constitution*, no. 1, 30–51.

Zoidze, Besarion. 2007. *Constitutional Control and System of Values in Georgia*, Tbilisi: GTZ.

4 EU "Better Regulation"

The Role of the European Committee of the Regions

Gaetano Armao

> To make up for the defect of the laws, making them applicable to those cases that the legislator has not prevented, without uselessly multiplying their number. Thus the legislation, continually repaired, reformed and supplied in its parts, could acquire a certain degree of stability and perfection capable of guaranteeing it from the insults of time, and from the torrent of events that agitate political bodies, and that continually change the aspect of society. Thus one would no longer see so many exceptional laws for a single law of principle, so many interpretative laws for a single fundamental law, nor so many new laws that contradict the old ones; thus finally the codes of laws, which today are the books of disorder and confusion, could become the monuments of good order, and the aggregate of many uniform principles linked together, and directed to a common object.
>
> G. Filangieri, *La Scienza della legislazione e gli opuscoli scelti*, Firenze, Niccolò Conti, 1820, Cap. VIII

1 The regulatory requirement must be made more comprehensible both by operators of the different levels of government (citizens, businesses, bureaucrats, politicians) and by the operators called upon to implement it. This is a problem of substantial democracy.

The rule of law postulates the comprehensibility of itself, so methods and tools of legal drafting in the planning, development and formulation of legal regulations (e.g. challenges and opportunities of digitisation in the formulation of regulations, strategies for the development of regulatory concepts and for the drafting of regulations) become essential elements to ensure the practicability of legal norms.[1]

In other words, it is analysed as a module that considers the regulation as a circular process that goes from the ex-ante phase to the legislative drafting (i.e. the drafting of the texts of a law), up to the approval of the law itself and the subsequent ex-post monitoring, a particularly important phase from an evaluation point of view because it is here that the participation of citizens and stakeholders comes into play: the social partners and, in general, the so-called stakeholders.[2]

DOI: 10.4324/9781003430308-6

It seems appropriate to underline, without being able to illustrate in detail from its origins the path undertaken by the European institutions, that regulation principles originated from the

> desire for better European governance and for anchoring sustainable development in the Union's policymaking by looking at economic, social and environmental impacts together. Better regulation is about professionalising every aspect of our policy-making and keeping it fit for today's world,

for anchoring sustainable development in the Union's policymaking by looking at economic, social and environmental impacts together. It is not an obscure bureaucratic procedure. Better regulation is about legislating when this is needed to deliver on shared objectives, which can only be effectively achieved through common action at the European level. It is not a hidden deregulatory agenda.

But it must be remembered that *better regulation* is also about considering alternative ways to achieve results since legislation should never be an end in itself.[3] Actions at the EU level should always add value compared with what can be done at the national, regional or local levels.[4]

It must also be noted that the principles of subsidiarity and proportionality, enshrined in Art. 5 of the Treaty on the European Union (EU), do not only represent two fundamental moments in the decision-making process but also appear as the basic rules to guarantee the quality of regulation. On the one hand, the principle of subsidiarity obliges us to consider the so-called zero option; that is, it requires us to take into consideration the opportunity of not adopting any regulatory measures and in this sense contributes to containing the production of regulations; on the other hand, the reference to the principle of proportionality involves assessments and feasibility studies (so-called ex-ante analysis) and ex-post checks, i.e. constant monitoring of the impact of the legislation, contributing to, at least potentially, greater effectiveness of the legislation and the European policies connected to it.[5]

If well implemented, the evaluation cycle is an excellent tool for political decision-makers, making it possible to choose which one of a number of options is likely to produce the best results; manage processes through which ideas become actions and actions produce effects; report to interested parties; motivate beneficiaries; and learn about and enhance results based on experience.[6]

2 There are technical tools for drafting legal standards that must be strengthened through quality control in legislation[7] such as the "Better Regulation Guidelines" of the European Commission deal with "Better

Drafting of Legal Acts", highlighting the link between the writing of regulatory acts and the effectiveness of the rules: "If legislation is clear it can be implemented effectively, citizens and economic actors can know their rights and obligations and the courts can enforce them".[8]

In particular, the new EU Commission Communication on "better legislation" (*Joining forces to make better laws*)[9] creates the conditions for improving the legislative process and regulatory technology in the EU and strengthening the Commission's commitment to increasing the transparency, inclusiveness and efficiency of the policymaking process.[10]

After the "better regulation" Communication,[11] guidelines[12] explain what "better regulation" is and how it applies to the day-to-day practices of Commission officials preparing new initiatives and proposals or managing existing policies and legislation and the "better regulation" toolbox that provides operational and detailed guidance on specific aspects – in other words – practical, hands-on guidance and operational detail.[13]

What has been summarised so far makes it clear the Commission's aim that EU laws should deliver maximum benefits to citizens and businesses, in particular, small- and medium-sized enterprises (SMEs), and its intention to make the approach to better law-making more dynamic and adaptable to further developments. The commitment to making better use of strategic foresight, and calls for its integration into impact assessments and evaluations; underlines that the better regulation agenda should support the green transition of the Union's economy by allowing, inter alia, innovative and enabling technologies to be brought to market more efficiently. The intention is to improve the analysis and reporting of proposals' impacts, for example, on competitiveness and SMEs, territoriality, sustainability, equality, subsidiarity and proportionality,[14] which could also help identify gaps, needs and opportunities, as well as help discover existing risks and trends, and therefore contribute to defining policy priorities and devising strategic planning with a long-term perspective, especially in the least developed countries and with regard to achieving the sustainable development goals (SDGs).[15]

3 The European Committee of the Regions (CoR) approved an opinion by the plenary assembly on 1 December 2021 "Better regulation: joining forces to make better laws",[16] calling on the Commission not only to commit itself to more effectively involving local and regional authorities (LRAs) throughout the entire programmatic cycle but also to recognise the need to develop a legislative approach that is attentive to the specificities of the territories.

The EU Commission Communication recognises that LRAs are at the heart of better standardisation because it acknowledges the function and relevance of territorial impact assessments as valuable instruments for completing the Commission's ex-ante impact assessments. It also confirms the leading role of LRAs in the process of reviewing EU legislation, a role that had already been recognised with the establishment of the *Fit for Future* (F4F) platform in May 2020.

More specifically, it is particularly important in the light of the general strengthening of the role of assessments within the framework of the Commission's better regulation system. These positions recognise that LRAs play a crucial role not only in the implementation and enforcement of EU policies in the field but also in their final assessment.

The European CoR also appreciated the Commission's intention to systematically use the subsidiarity assessment grid developed by the European CoR to help assess whether or not EU legislative action is appropriate. Through its "better regulation" policy, the EU Commission has committed to designing, delivering and supporting the implementation of high-quality policies. "Better regulation" covers the whole EU policy cycle: planning, design, adoption, implementation, evaluation and revision. All EU interventions – legislative or non-legislative, policy initiatives or spending programmes – aim to achieve certain objectives through one or several means, in line with the goals and responsibilities set by the EU Treaty.[17]

The European CoR[18] was asked to express its opinion on the better regulation measures outlined by the European Commission, in the context of relations between Union bodies.[19]

Better legislation will play a crucial role in this endeavour, and the F4F platform will support efforts to simplify and better adapt EU legislation to the needs of tomorrow. Introduce a "one-in, one-out" approach, with the precise objective of increasing the focus of policymakers on the implications and costs of law enforcement, in particular, for SMEs.

The opinion highlights efforts to increase the quality of assessments through independent controls and welcomes the establishment of the *Regulatory Control Committee* (CCN); it reiterates the request to include in the CCN a permanent member designated by the CoR.

As regards the translation into practice of the new communication and its objectives, the Committee looks forward to the updated guidelines for better regulation and the appropriate toolkit, which are not only the main means of implementing the Commission's commitment to better standardisation but also the way forward to taking into account the principles of subsidiarity and proportionality in the development of EU policies.

With the opinion approved the Committee has undertaken to bring together its tools and methodologies of research and spatial data analysis in a single package for "better legislation", which also includes *RegHub* consultations, creating a better link with the toolbox for the theme "better legislation" of the EU Commission and with the tools of the *Research Service* of the European Parliament, encouraging the EU Commission and the Member States to extend their cooperation to LRAs. It is also recommended that local and regional autonomies, in line with what the *Subsidiarity Task Force*, has already pointed out to cooperate in the preparation of national implementation plans, which can have added value compared to those of the European Commission.

A final reference also concerns the request, in line with that articulated by the EU Commission, to raise awareness among Member States and regions of the phenomenon of gold-plating. Should it be considered essential to adopt additional rules at the national or regional level in the implementation of European legislation, it is recommended that their identification be made clear by means of transposition acts or related documents, in accordance with what is stated in the Inter-institutional Agreement. Furthermore, there is a recommendation not to resort to gold-plating, particularly during the implementation of programmes in the context of shared management and in national procurement rules.[20]

4 This is the contribution of the European CoR to the objective of improving regulation, which has underlined the emphasis taken on local and regional autonomy over other stakeholders, which follows the importance of involving the CoR in open consultations on legislative proposals that significantly affect subnational levels of government, as well as in a systematic and widespread information campaign on the annual work programmes of the EU Commission on the territories.

The Committee underscores that it is fundamental that the better regulation system incorporates "multi-level governance" in the EU since European legislation is implemented by the Member States, regions and local authorities: the involvement of levels of government which are responsible for implementing EU legislation is a prerequisite for high-quality legislation able to work towards common goals. Therefore, the Committee recommends that the EU Commission prioritise the collaboration with LRAs, particularly those with legislative powers, throughout the policy cycle, based on a multi-level governance working method.[21]

The impact on territories can be assessed using qualitative and quantitative methods, as well as specific tools developed to support impact assessments or the consultation process.

To understand the role that can be played in the implementation of better regulation initiatives an essential element of improving the quality of assessments of territorial impacts. LRAs should contribute to identifying potential impacts in their consultation responses and providing feedback on the "call for evidence". It seems appropriate to underline that the CoR and its network of regional hubs (*RegHub*) can help disseminate information about consultations by reaching out to its members, and the impact on territories can be assessed using qualitative and quantitative methods, as well as specific tools developed to support impact assessments or the consultation process.[22]

Furthermore, as has been rightly observed, the connection between better regulation and subsidiarity remains a delicate issue. It should clarify the principles of subsidiarity and proportionality and identify policy areas that should be returned to EU countries or re-delegated to the EU.[23]

Although it does not seem marginal to observe, in conclusion, better regulation has led to the creation of a procedural and organisational apparatus through which the decision-making process has certainly been burdened. Furthermore, better regulation, despite having, among its objectives, that of reducing burdens, leads, almost paradoxically, to an increase in costs.[24] It is not sufficient to implement an evaluation cycle for each statutory instrument to ensure a multi-level governance system of public policies; analyses, surveys and assessments carried out from time to time to make informed decisions and understand their impact on beneficiaries must be integrated.

What has been briefly described is the essence of the contribution that the "guardian of European subsidiarity" has given and through the entire system of LRAs can and must further give to better implement the European Commission Communication for better regulation with the aim of improving the EU's policymaking process, updating the better regulation agenda to mainstream SDGs and the digital and green transition and ensuring more foresight-based policymaking. In this area, too, the European CoR has demonstrated the most valuable contribution it can make to the future of the EU: strengthening European democracy by bringing it closer to the citizens but also accustoming them to a new way of conceiving democracy itself.[25]

It is possible to legislate "better", with the aim of giving quality to the normative texts and to rationalise, systematise, the rules governing the various sectors is possible. It is therefore necessary for the different levels of government to commit themselves to help make life easier for citizens, families, communities and productive sectors.

Notes

1 OECD (2022), *Better Regulation Practices across the European Union 2022*, Paris. In law doctrine, see for all R. Baldwin, M. Cave and M. Lodge, *Understanding Regulation: Theory, Strategy, and Practice*, Oxford, Oxford University Press, 2013 and F. Blanc, 'Regulation, Regulatory Delivery, Trust and Distrust: Avoiding Vicious Circles,' in M. De Benedetto, N. Lupo and N. Rangone (eds), *The Crisis of Confidence in Legislation,* Oxford, Nomos-Hart, 2020, pp. 307–335.

About the Italian legal system see N. Rangone, 'The Quality of Regulation: The Myth and Reality of Good Regulation Tools,' *Italian Journal of Public Law*, 2012, vol. 4, 1 ff.

2 The main thrust of better regulation policies is to bring novel ideas into the policymaking process that sectoral policymakers are unlikely to consider otherwise. This toolbox includes the consultation with multiple stakeholders during the policy development process, the increased use of evidence in policy design (e.g. by drawing on insights from experimental research) and the consideration of the regulative burden (compliance costs) for regulates; see for all C. M. Radaelli and A. C. M. Meuwese, 'Better Regulation in Europe: Between Public Management and Regulatory Reform,' *Public Administration,* 2009, Vol. 87, n. 3, 639 ff. recently C. Dunlop and C. M. Radaelli, 'Better Regulation in the European Union,' in M. Maggetti, F. Di Mascio and A. Natalini (eds), *Handbook of Regulatory Authorities*, Cheltenham, Northampton, Edward Elgar Publishing, 2022, pp. 302–312.

3 As specified by the most authoritative UK doctrine on regulation: "Smart regulation thus envisages a movement away from restrictive, rule-based, 'command and control' regimes towards those that place more emphasis on alternative, less coercive methods as applied by a variety of institutions – be they regulators, professional bodies, or companies/service providers themselves. The tension between better regulation and smart regulation is that better regulation gives centrality of place to regulatory impact assessment (RIA), whereas smart regulation advocates complex policy mixes and 'softer' styles of control that are extremely difficult to put through a RIA process. Such mixes are almost impossible to evaluate numerically in terms of costs and benefits because of their multi-instrumental and multi-institutional complexity. Any proponent of a new regulatory system who knows that a RIA process has to be negotiated will have a huge disincentive to put forward a smart regime and an almost irresistible imperative to opt for something closer to an old-fashioned command and control system. On the one hand, the Government advocates the use of more imaginative, 'alternative' and less restrictive approaches to regulation (Better Regulation Task Force, 2005), whilst, on the other hand, it evaluates regulatory proposals with a process that is almost wholly unsympathetic to such approaches". See R. Baldwin, 'Better Regulation in Troubled Times,' *Health Economics Policy and Law,* (2006), Vol. 1, n. 3, 203–207.

4 European Commission, *Secretariat-General, Better Regulation-Taking Stock and Sustaining Our Commitment*, 15 April 2019, to which reference is made for a reconstruction of the various interventions of the European institutions on the topic.

5 F. Simonelli and N. Jacob, 'Can We Better the European Union Better Regulation Agenda?,' *EJRR* (Dec. 2021), Vol. 12, n. 4, 849 ff. This essay points out that several proposals also have great potential to simplify the better regulation process and make it more transparent. By contrast, the envisaged simplification of the public consultation process may jeopardise its effectiveness and should be carefully reconsidered. In addition, a more cautious, stepwise approach to introducing, testing and adjusting the new EU one-in, one-out system is certainly needed.

6 In Italy, for example, use of these techniques – *impact analysis and assessment* (AIR and VIR), *measuring administrative burdens* (MOA) and *consultations* – is often undertaken merely as a bureaucratic exercise. A system of AIRs and VIRs integrated between the various levels of government is missing; the

evaluation cycle is essentially unfinished: only in very rare cases have approved acts undergone ex-post monitoring and assessment; Senato della Repubblica, *L'incompiuta. La valutazione degli atti normativi in Italia: criticità, prospettive e buone pratiche*, 2018, https://www.senato.it/service/PDF/PDFServer/BGT/01082849.pdf.

7 See E. Golberg, *'Better Regulation': European Union Style,* Harvard Kennedy School, 2018, https://www.hks.harvard.edu/sites/default/files/centers/mrcbg/files/98_final2.pdf.pdf.

8 Communication from the Commission, *EU Law: Better Results through Better Application* (2017/C 18/02). A detailed analysis of the objectives achieved by the Union institutions in the context of the so-called better regulation, is found in the broad doctrine that has examined the context, among which see A. Renda, 'European Union and Better Law-Making: Best Practices and Gaps,' in AA.VV., *Workshop on the Best Practices in Legislative and Regulatory Process in a Constitutional Perspective, Study for the AFCO Committee*, Brussels, 2015, 5 ff; M. Dawson, 'Better Regulation and the Future of EU Regulatory Law and Politics,' in *CMLR*, 2016, 1209 ff.; E. Griglio, 'Better Law-making and the Integration of Impact Assessment in the Decision-making Process: The Role of National Parliaments', in A. De Feo and B. Laffan (eds). *Scrutiny of EU Policies: Contributions to the Workshop Organised by the RSCAS February, 27–2017*, 2017, European University Institute, Robert Schuman Centre for Advanced Studies, 64–87; S. Garben and I. Govaere (eds), *The EU Better Regulation Agenda: A Critical Assessment*, Oxford, Bloomsbury Publishing, 2018; C. M. Radaelli, 'Halfway Through the Better Regulation Strategy of the Juncker Commission: What Does the Evidence Say?,' *JCMS*, 2018, Vol. 56, 85 ff.; G. Listorti, E. Basyte Ferrari, S. Acs, G. Munda, E. Rosenbaum, P. Paruolo and P. Smits, *The debate on the EU Better Regulation Agenda: A Literature Review*, Luxembourg, Publications Office of the European Union, 2019; S. Garben, 'A Taste of Its Own Medicine: Assessing the Impact of the EU Better Regulation Agenda,' *ELJ*, 2020, Vol. 26 (1–2) 83 ff., I. Schömann, 'Simplifying EU Law: The Mirage of the New European Commission Better Regulation Agenda?,' in *Lavoro e diritto*, 3/2020, 463 ff.; M. Picchi, *Legiferare meglio: a proposito della nuova Comunicazione della Commissione europea*, in Osservatoriosullefonti.it, XIV, 3/2021.

5 How Legal Translation Matters in Türkiye? Examination of International Agreements through the Lens of Private International Law

Belkis Vural Celenk and Aysun Bolaca

5.1 Introduction

Language is not only effective in the application of an international legal instrument, but the language used in those texts can even profoundly affect international relations. There have been conflicts in history, where translation inaccuracies have triggered. For instance, the first Italian–Ethiopian war precipitated due to a language matter. A mistranslation in a treaty of friendship signed between Italy and Ethiopia has led to such an incident. Indeed, in the official language of Ethiopia (Amharic language), Italy was designated as a facilitator for the relations of Ethiopia with other nations. However, the wording in the Italian version of the same provision had the meaning of Italy's claim of protectorate, and this was pointed to as one of the reasons behind the Italian–Ethiopian war in 1896.[1] As this example points out, the language used in international legal instruments is likely to have various consequences in practice.

International agreements have been constructed on the premise that (contracting) States fulfil their commitments and the motivation for States behind signing those agreements is to pursue common goals to improve their relations in various areas. They achieve the so-called goals through common standards – usually in the form of uniform rules and standardised practices. The subjects of the international agreement may cover a wide range of issues. It may be fundamental rights or freedoms, as well as matters such as climate and environmental protection, economic and military cooperation, or harmonisation and unification of international trade. This list can be expanded. However, depending on the subject, the preparation of international agreements entails different processes.[2] Recognising that all processes in the preparation of international agreements are important, the translation of the so-called agreement is one of the most critical stages.[3] Certain concepts applied in international agreements written in more than one language sometimes may not coincide with agreement texts in different languages, which can also lead to serious problems.

DOI: 10.4324/9781003430308-7

For example, the concept *bien* used in the French text and the concept *possessions* used in the English text of Article 1 of the Additional Protocol I to the European Convention on Human Rights[4] have caused hesitation as they do not have the same legal meaning in these two different languages.[5] The Convention itself states that both languages (English and French) are equally authentic.[6] Therefore, to eliminate the conceptual difference arising from English and French texts, the European Court of Human Rights has stated that autonomous meaning should be given to those concepts to determine their scope rather than relying on the official languages of the Member States. According to the decision (*Gasus Dosier und Fördertechnik Gmbh v. the Netherlands*) rendered by the European Court of Human Rights:

> The Court recalls that the notion "possessions" (in French: "biens") in Article 1 of Protocol No. 1 (P1-1) has an autonomous meaning which is certainly not limited to ownership of physical goods: certain other rights and interests constituting assets can also be regarded as "property rights," and thus as "possessions," for the purposes of this provision (P1-1).[7]

Not only are translation problems limited to the translation between authentic languages of international agreements, but such problems may also arise when translating the agreement text into the official language of contracting States, where the translation is not one of the authentic languages of the international agreement. If the written text has a translation problem, it is important to resolve it within the purposes of the agreement.

That's why, this chapter aims firstly to clarify how translation matters in a legal context and its vital role in the application of international legal instruments by national court judges. Then the study will illustrate how Türkiye translates an international agreement after its ratification process and will also refer to the lack of a specific unit that is devoted only to the translation activity. In this respect, it examines which kinds of situations arise out of translation-related problems in the country and what would its potential impact be on national jurisdiction as well as its international legal footprint. Lastly, the chapter will argue some target-oriented recommendations for countries that adopt foreign legal instruments into their legal systems to prevent translation-related problems. In this respect, both pro-active solutions (anticipating problems before they arise and taking preventive steps) and re-active solutions (reacting to problems as they arise) will be discussed.

5.2 International Agreements and Legal Translation in General

The sources of international law are listed under Article 38 of the International Court of Justice (ICJ) statute. As referred to in the related article, international conventions (agreements) are considered to have a superior position over the other sources of international law.[8] In the theory of international law, the reason why international agreements are considered superior to customary international law is that the rules are clearly written in these agreements and the participating States have explicitly consented to them.[9]

In some cases, due to their foreign characters, these written texts (international agreements) may contain various translation-related problems, especially for multilateral agreements. This is because the multilateral agreement is usually translated into numerous languages, and this potentially leads to discrepancies between different language versions. As for bilateral agreements, it is easier for parties to determine the original language of the agreement and the agreement can be concluded in accordance with the chosen language. However, in most of the cases, there is no such choice between the parties to the bilateral agreements. In principle, the agreement is written in the official languages of each party/State.[10] Although the agreement is written in the official languages of each party, a text in a third (neutral) language might also be added to resolve any problems arising from those two diverging texts.[11] The third language can be either one of the UN's official languages or another third language determined depending on the cultural and geographic position of parties to the bilateral agreement.[12]

Under international law, it has been a common practice that multilateral agreements are concluded under the auspices of international organisations.[13] And unlike bilateral agreements, multilateral agreements lead to problematic language-related instances. Indeed, the incongruity of different authentic texts poses certain difficulties of interpretation for contracting States.[14] If there is an ambiguity in the text prepared in the authentic languages of international agreement, it will lead to more inaccuracies in the process of international agreement translation into other (non-authentic) languages.

International agreements exhibit a limited multilingualism. It may be the desire of each State party to an international agreement that its own language should be the agreement's language. However, in practice, they firstly draft a text with a widely accepted language among participating States, and then they translate it into other languages.[15] After the first draft has been issued, this international agreement may also be translated into other authentic languages. Since the legal value attributed to all authentic languages is equal, consistency among those translations would be essential.[16]

If the official language of a contracting State is not one of the authentic languages of the agreement, the translation of the international agreement to its own language means a lot to that State.[17] To ensure legal certainty, the problems arising from this translation should be minimised. As previously mentioned, contracting States to multilateral international agreements usually translate the text into their languages. Taking their binding force into account, these agreements are not recognised as legal texts having legal validity under international law.[18]

The Vienna Convention on the Law of Treaties (VCLT) (1969) explicitly regulates the interpretation of agreements authenticated in two or more languages and gives priority to *authentic texts of the agreements* in case of a dispute arising from the translation of the different texts of an international agreement.[19] Articles 32 and 33 of the VCLT are complementary to each other, and it is accepted that different meanings arising from the authentic texts of an agreement can also be eliminated by additional methods of interpretation.[20] However, Article 33 (4) of the VCLT is specifically considering the object and purpose of the agreements to ascertain which text reconciles the best.[21]

As can be seen, translation problems are often experienced in international agreements, and an appropriate solution as regards authentic texts of the agreements in VCLT has been provided. On the contrary, the translation problems to be encountered while translating the international agreement from the authentic languages into the official languages (which are not authentic languages in terms of international agreement application) of the contracting States should be emphasised.

5.3 Translation and Transposition of International Agreements into Turkish Law and Specific Cases Illustrating Turkish Legal Translation Practice

Where problems arise from the differences between the authentic language of the international agreement and the text translated into the language of the contracting State, the national court judges thereof should eliminate these problems by applying the agreement in accordance with its purpose. In this sense, specific cases illustrating Turkish legal translation practice of international agreements and the courts' assessments will be evaluated below.

5.3.1 Translation of International Agreements under Auspice of Turkish Authorities

Translation of international agreements under auspice of Turkish authorities is not an easy issue to understand at first glance. Translation of the agreements, especially concluded with foreign States and international organisations, and translation of documents and texts required by the Foreign Affairs Ministry within the framework of the implementation of the policy or to review the translations already made are all assigned to the Department of Translation at Republic of Türkiye Ministry of Foreign Affairs. This can be found in Article 8 (e) of the Law on the Establishment and Duties of the Ministry of Foreign Affairs dated 2010 and numbered 6004.[22] However, in spite of the establishment of the Translation Department at the Ministry of Foreign Affairs and its task given by the specific Law (Law No. 6004), the practice shows that not all the international agreements are being translated by this department.

Under the Turkish legal system, it has also been observed that every other relevant Ministry would be involved in the process of translation of international agreements. However, there is no single central unit, devoted only to the translation of all international agreements within the system. As the usual practice indicates, depending on their own fields of activity, relevant ministries conduct the translation activities of international agreements. In this process, the Translation Department at the Ministry of Foreign Affairs also supports other ministries by reviewing the translations they have already made. To give an example, for agreements that fall within the duties of the Ministry of Justice, specialised translators and lawyers at this Ministry translate the relevant agreement, and then the Department of Translation of the Ministry of Foreign Affairs provides revision services for these translations.

5.3.2 *Transposition of International Agreements into Turkish Law*

Under Turkish law, international agreements are approved and ratified according to Article 90 and Article 114 of the 1982 Constitution of the Turkish Republic[23] as well as Presidential Decree (No. 9) on the Procedures and Principles Regarding the Ratification of International Treaties.[24]

Article 90 of the 1982 Constitution distinguishes between international agreements. The first group is international agreements, which require a law by the Grand National Assembly of Türkiye to approve ratification.[25] The second is international agreements, which do not require the Grand National Assembly of Türkiye's approval for ratification by law but directly the President of the Republic. Then the so-called international instrument is published. In relation to the transposition of international agreements into Turkish Law, Article 104 of the 1982 Constitution further states that the President of the Republic ratifies and promulgates these international agreements.

According to Article 90 (3) of the 1982 Constitution, with regard to agreements in connection with the implementation of an international agreement and economic, commercial, technical, or administrative agreements concluded on the basis of the authority granted by law and among the agreements that regulate economic, commercial, or technical relations and whose duration does not exceed one year, it has been regulated that the agreements that do not require any financial commitments by the State and do not affect the personal status and property rights of Turkish citizens in foreign countries are to be directly ratified by the President of the Republic and are not subject to the approval of a law by the Grand National Assembly of Türkiye.

Apart from these exceptional cases, Article 90 (4) of the 1982 Constitution regulates that the ratification or accession to any international agreement containing provisions amending Turkish Law is subject to the enactment of a law by the Grand National Assembly of Türkiye on the ratification or accession.

Article 3 (2) of the Decree (No. 9) stipulates that in addition to the Presidential Decree ratifying the international agreement, the Turkish text of the international agreement and the authentic (original) version of this agreement shall be published in the Official Gazette of the Republic of Türkiye.[26] As can be seen, within the context of Turkish domestic legal practice, both Turkish and one of the languages of the international agreement are published together in the Official Gazette. Thereinafter, this will be revisited for the evaluation of international agreements through the translation practice of Türkiye.

In relation to the application of international agreements, it would be good to refer some prominent legal provisions. For instance, according to Article 90 (5) of the 1982 Constitution, international agreements duly put into effect have the force of law. Additionally, Article 1 (2) of the Turkish Code on Private International Law and International Civil Procedure can also be referred to here: *The provisions of international conventions to which the Republic of Türkiye is a party shall be reserved.*[27] This provision leads us that if there is a dispute with a foreign element[28] before Turkish Courts, the courts will apply the provisions of the concerned international agreement instead of the provisions of this Code.[29]

As previously referred, Article 90 (5) of the 1982 Constitution also clarifies where international agreements have been placed under the hierarchy of norms – if an international agreement has been duly entered into force, this will be recognised as equivalent to codes of domestic law. In other words, provisions of international agreements are applicable in the same hierarchy as the provisions of codes in the Turkish legal system.[30]

5.4 Translation-Related Issues on the Application of International Agreements by Turkish Courts

Since international agreements and codes in Turkish law have the same legal force in principle, the translation-related issues arising from the application of the provisions of international agreements can be a serious matter before Turkish Courts. This will be concretised with selected examples of the application of international agreements having uniformity attempts through the lens of private international law below.

"The term '*international agreement*' in its generic sense consequently embraces the widest range of international instruments." However, under this part, it has specifically been referred to specific *conventions* as international agreements, which are "generally used for formal multilateral treaties with a broad number of parties. Conventions are normally open for participation by the international community as a whole, or by a large number of states. Usually, the instruments negotiated under the auspices of an international organization are entitled conventions."[31]

5.4.1 United Nations Convention on Contracts for the International Sale of Goods (1980)

With the purpose of unification in international law practice and through the UNCITRAL efforts, the United Nations Convention on Contracts for the International Sale of Goods (CISG) has been created.[32] In the course of time, it was adopted by many countries in the world and has become a quite successful legal instrument in international commerce. Türkiye[33] is also a contracting party to the Convention, and it has been brought to the agenda of Turkish domestic courts in some cases so far.[34] In the recent past, the Istanbul Regional Court of Justice[35] applied the Convention in a controversial manner to the dispute at hand, and this was also approved by the Court of Cassation (Yargıtay), 11th Civil Chamber.[36] The problem specifically revolves around an improper examination of Article 2 (the Convention's sphere of application), and the so-called impropriety is closely related to the mistranslation of the relevant provision.

The judges in this case took the Turkish-translated version of the CISG into account and, correspondingly, did not apply the Convention to the dispute.[37] To be more precise, Article 2 of the CISG illustrates the non-applicability of the Convention to sales of ships, vessels, hovercraft, or aircraft.[38] Within this context, it would be good to elaborate firstly on what we should understand from hovercraft.

"Hovercraft" has actually been defined as *a vehicle that travels quickly just the surface of water or land by producing a current of air under it to support it.*[39] As it is understood from the definition, the item hovercraft refers to a specific vehicle that travels on a cushion of air. However, in the Turkish-translated text of the CISG, this has been referred to as "hava yastıklı taşıt," which encompasses all types of vehicles having an airbag. In this case, the Istanbul Regional Court of Justice denied the Convention's applicability based on Article 2 (e). Since the dispute at hand related to sales of cars/automobiles between contracting parties, the Turkish Court here concluded that the subject of dispute was out of the Convention's scope; therefore, it would not be applicable to the case.[40]

As seen, incorrect translation has naturally an adverse impact on the application of international agreement by its Member States, and, through the above-mentioned case, this has been clearly unfolded: by applying the non-official language of the Convention (Turkish-translated text), the Turkish Court rendered an unexpected decision, which was not in compliance with the very key purpose of the CISG – the uniform application for substantive law within the field of international sale of goods.[41]

5.4.2 Convention on the Contract for the International Carriage of Goods by Road (1956)

This is another critical example that illustrates the translation-related issue while applying an international agreement by Turkish Courts. Türkiye has also been a contracting State to the Convention on the Contract for International Carriage of Goods by Road (CMR) since 1993.[42] According to Article 1 of the CMR, the carriage of goods by road shall be subject to the Convention in cases when the place of taking over of the goods and the place designated for delivery, as specified in the contract, are situated in two different countries, of which at least one is a contracting country, irrespective of the places of residence and the nationalities of the parties. Based on this, the CMR will be applicable to every carriage of goods by road that begins or ends in or passes through Türkiye.

In the exemplary case, the parties[43] agreed to transport various types of goods in accordance with the contract of carriage they already signed. However, the cost of the goods was not paid to the sender, because the carrier delivered the goods to the buyer contrary to the instructions written under the shipping document/bill of lading. As a consequence of this, the claimant argues that the carrier was liable for acting contrary to those instructions; therefore, he should pay the respective amount of compensation.[44] The carrier, as the respondent, objected to the claims by bringing a "lapse of time" (the period of limitation) argument as one year indicated in the Convention has already passed.[45] The respondent further added that the requested amount of compensation was too high, and the liability of the respondent should be limited since he acted in accordance with the order and delivered the respective goods to the buyer.[46] The first instance court did not render a decision in favour of the respondent; therefore, he appealed the case to the highest court – the Court of Cassation (Yargıtay) of Türkiye.[47]

The CMR's authentic/original languages are English and French. Both are equally valid for contracting States of the Convention. However, these States also translated the Convention to their own language (if not one of the authentic) for its application at the domestic level as Türkiye also did. In this regard, it would be good to remember that non-authentic language translation by a contracting State has not been accepted as a legally binding text in the context of international law.[48] In the case of Türkiye, once the ratification process of the CMR had been completed at the international level, it was adapted to domestic law through a law approving the ratification.[49] After a while, an official text (English version) of the Convention and its Turkish translation (non-official language of the Convention) were also published under the Official Gazette.[50]

The Court of Cassation (Yargıtay) highlighted the mistaken translation of the Turkish version and ignored this text while applying the Convention to resolve the matter at hand.[51] The specific issue in this case relates to "the period of limitation" and "when it will begin to run?" The Turkish Court in this case paid particular attention to "what the CMR literally states in its officially written text," rather than interpreting the matter through the Turkish translation as its published version in the Official Gazette. If the Court adhered to the Turkish-translated text of the Convention only, the respondent's "the period of limitation" defence would be accepted, and, in that case, the claimant would not be able to have the right to compensation.

Considering all the above mentioned, it would not be wrong to say that the Turkish Court/judges hereby contributed the justice of private international law by interpreting the Convention accurately – in strict compliance with its original letter and spirit.[52] Without a doubt, the attitude of the Turkish court here has also contributed to the primary aim of the Convention,[53] which is the uniform application of the law within the field of international carriage of goods by road.

5.4.3 Convention on the Recognition and Enforcement of Foreign Arbitral Awards (1958) (the New York Convention)

Convention on the Recognition and Enforcement of Foreign Arbitral Awards (the New York Convention) was ratified by Türkiye in 1992; since then, Türkiye has been a part of harmonisation process on recognising and enforcing international arbitral awards.[54] In relation to the translation of an international agreement, the New York Convention has also been at the very heart of heated debates. In the case of Türkiye, the mis(taken)-translation criticism becomes concrete at the application of Article V (1)(e) of the Convention by domestic courts of the contracting States.[55] To be more precise, this article clearly states that:

> Recognition and enforcement of the award may be refused, at the request of the party against whom it is invoked, only if that party furnishes

> to the competent authority where the recognition and enforcement is sought, proof that:
>
> ...
>
> (e) The award has not yet become binding on the parties, or has been set aside or suspended by a competent authority of the country in which, or under the law of which, that award was made.

Briefly stated, the wording of Article V (1) regulating that "Recognition and enforcement of the award may be refused ..." gives discretion to the court's judge on the recognition and enforcement of arbitral awards, which have been set aside in the country of origin.[56] In other words, even if any of the grounds for refusal are found in the case, the court does not necessarily have to refuse the enforcement and may exercise its discretion in favour of enforcement.[57]

However, the relevant article under the Turkish-translated text does not fully reflect the statement "Recognition and enforcement of the award *may be* refused ..." as prescribed in one of the authentic languages (English) of the New York Convention. Rather, the Turkish translation published under the Official Gazette indicates that "the request for recognition and enforcement of the arbitral award *cannot* be refused unless the existence of the enumerated enforcement obstacles is proven."[58]

As seen from the above-mentioned comparison, no discretionary power has been attributed to the enforcement authority (domestic courts of Türkiye) through the Turkish-translated Convention; therefore, if an award was set aside at the seat of arbitration, the Turkish Courts may likely not enforce it.[59] In that case, an incorrect translation of a modal verb ("may") here will have a significantly harsh impact on the applicability of the New York Convention. To put it differently, this will open the door to non-uniform approaches taken by domestic courts of contracting States (to the New York Convention) on the recognition and enforcement of awards, which have been set aside. Therefore, interpretation of the relevant article in accordance with the official language of the Convention should be encouraged to eliminate the potential problems that may arise from this mistranslation.

5.5 Conclusion and Recommendations

This study has tried to examine the application of international agreements by domestic courts from the perspective of Türkiye. It further illustrated the existing and potential issues emerging from the mistranslation of those agreements. To sum up, after completing the ratification process at the international level, an international agreement has been translated to Turkish and published under the Official Gazette of Türkiye. Even though

Turkish is not one of the original languages of the so-called international agreement, legal practitioners (law-appliers) would usually prefer the Turkish-translated text while applying and interpreting this agreement.

Although there has been a common motivation for uniformity of law through the provisions of international agreements, today it is not possible to fully guarantee such uniform application in the implementation of international agreements by the contracting (sovereign) States. While States may show a collective will to implement the uniform rules contained in the international agreements, the actual implementation of uniformity is a matter, especially for those who will apply these rules.[60] Indeed, non-compliance between the official language(s) of the international agreement and its Turkish-translated text usually leads to conflicts in terms of the accurate (and uniform) application of this agreement. Elimination of translation-related problems to a great extent will have significant consequences.[61] Most importantly, it will provide legal security both at the domestic and international levels and will eventually contribute to the justice of private international law.[62]

There are some reasons behind the problematic translation of international legal instruments into legal systems as also observed in the case of Türkiye. The first reason is translation process is usually decentralised and a completely separate stage from the preparation of the international agreements; in other words, after the ratification process has been completed, the international agreement written in a foreign language is translated into the official language of a State who signs this agreement. The second is a very short time devoted to this process. The third is competent persons/authority has not always been preferred through the translation process, and, relevant to this, the need for having legal knowledge along with translation skills is usually ignored by translators. Consequently, it would be important to bring some pro-active solutions, which anticipate problems before they arise and take preventive steps and re-active solutions that usually react to problems when they arise for translation-related problems in the application of international agreements by foreign State courts.

To prevent potential problems arising from the translation of international agreements within the domestic legal systems of contracting State parties (as well as in Türkiye), the translation process should be conducted in a more centralised manner. In this regard, a permanent and professionally designed unit, which is assigned only to translation activities, will be of very much use to eliminate translation-related problems beforehand. Furthermore, the qualification of translators should meet the important standards that legal translation requires. For instance, legal translation particularly needs to have a legal background along with linguistic knowledge.[63] Within this context, using legal terms consistently among the legal doctrine may also have a positive impact on the translation process of international legal instruments. As known, English has become the lingua franca in many fields (including science, technology, international relations, commerce, and law). For this reason, consistency awareness should be kept alive, while translating English terms (at least) to another language in academic sources. Hereby, translators can benefit from these sources in the translation process of international legal instruments.

Despite all efforts previously taken, if there have still been some problems in the translated international agreement text, as the re-active solution, the domestic courts' judges can play a significant role here to eliminate the negative consequences of this mistranslation. Firstly, the domestic court's judge should always pay regard to the very purpose of the international agreement (uniformity) and its original language(s). To do this, domestic court judges can be trained in foreign languages;[64] through this way, they will be able to understand the original languages of international agreements and compare them with their own languages and will not need to adhere to the non-authentic language translation of this text. Domestic court judges can also benefit from the rich jurisprudence of the other contracting States to the international agreement if any mistaken or ambiguous translation exists.

Notes

1 European Commission Final Report, 'Studies on Translation and Multilingualism – Language and Translation in International Law and EU Law' 6/2012, (Publications Office of the European Union (Luxembourg), 2012) p. 22.
2 European Commission Report, p. 5.
3 "It is not possible to expunge from international law 'the problem of interpretation-translation' ... Translation is one of the most promising aspects in the interpretation of international law since it guarantees the specific character of the international legal system: multilingualism." Constanza Margiotta Broglio and Federico Ortino, 'Treaty Interpretation, Multilingualism, and the WTO Dispute Settlement System: Towards the Comparative Translation Paradigm?' (2024) 15 (4) *Journal of International Dispute Settlement* 487, 494.
4 Protection of Property – Article 1 of Protocol No.1: "Everyone has the right to own property and use its possessions. No-one shall be deprived of his property unless public necessity so demands. If so, the State must guarantee fair compensation."
5 Rona Aybay and Elif Oral, *Kamusal Uluslararası Hukuk* (İstanbul: Bilgi Üniversitesi Yayınları, 2016), pp. 71–72.
6 "Authentic" means within this context the "original" language(s) of an international agreement. "The text of Treaty is 'equally authentic' in each of these languages, i.e. from a legal standpoint they are all considered original versions." European Parliament Briefing, 'Legal Aspects of EU Multilingualism' (January 2017), available at: https://www.europarl.europa.eu/RegData/etudes/BRIE/2017/595914/EPRS_BRI%282017%29595914_EN.pdf accessed 29 September 2024.

7 *Gasus Dosier-und Fördertechnik Gmbh v. the Netherlands,* European Court of Human Rights, Application No. 15375/89, Judgment, 23 February 1995, para. 53.
8 Apart from *international conventions*, Art. 38 of the ICJ Statute specifically refers *international custom*; *the general principles of law recognized by civilized nations*; *judicial decisions and the teachings of the most highly qualified publicists of the various nations* as sources of international law.
9 Serap Akipek, "Türk Mevzuatının Onaylanan Uluslararası Antlaşmalar ile Uyumlaştırılması Sorunu" (1999) 48 (1) *Ankara Üniversitesi Hukuk Fakültesi Dergisi*, pp. 15, 17.
10 Aybay and Oral, *Kamusal Uluslararası Hukuk*, p. 71.
11 European Commission Report, p. 17.
12 Aybay and Oral, *Kamusal Uluslararası Hukuk*, p. 71. "A boundary treaty concluded in 1897 between Great Britain and Ethiopia was written in English and Amharic and it was clear in the treaty that both texts were to be considered authentic, in addition to these two languages, a French version of the treaty was annexed, and it was stated to be authoritative in the event of a dispute. The given case has been shown in the Commentary as what Art. 33(2) of Vienna Convention on the Law of Treaties addresses." International Law Commission, 'Draft Articles on the Law of Treaties' (1966) *Yearbook of the International Law Commission*, Vol. II, Part 1. Art. 29 para. 5.
13 Aybay and Oral, *Kamusal Uluslararası Hukuk*, p. 71.
14 Christopher B. Kuner, 'The Interpretation of Multilingual Treaties: Comparison of Texts versus the Presumption of Similar Meaning' (1991) 40 *International and Comparative Law Quarterly*, p. 953.
15 European Commission Report, p. 5.
16 European Commission Report, p. 5.
17 European Commission Report, p. 5.
18 Yusuf Çalışkan, 'Milletlerarası Özel Hukukta Uluslararası Anlaşmaların Uygulanması: Tercüme ve Yorum Problemleri' in Doğan Vahit, Yılmaz Alper Çağrı, Ayhan İzmirli Lale, *Antalya Bilim Üniversitesi Hukuk Fakültesi Milletlerarası Özel Hukukta Güncel Meseleler Sempozyumu* (Savaş Kitabevi, 2019), p. 231.
19 Article 33 (2) of the VCLT states that "A version of the treaty in a language other than one of those in which the text was authenticated shall be considered an authentic text *only if* the treaty so provides or the parties so agree."
20 "Additional methods of interpretation" refers here to the Article 32 of the VCLT, more specifically "the preparatory work of the treaty" and "the circumstances of its conclusion." In other words, after applying the general rules of interpretation (Article 31 of the VCLT), if the resulting interpretation needs further support or if the meaning is ambiguous or leads to a manifestly absurd or unreasonable result, additional/supplementary interpretation methods can be applicable.
21 Zora Kızılyürek, 'The Significance and Utility of the Rules of Treaty Interpretation, as Encapsulated in the 1969 Vienna Convention on the Law of Treaties, for the Purpose of Ascertaining the Meaning of Treaty Provisions' (2021) 70 *Annales de la Faculté de Droit d'Istanbul* 243, pp. 248–249.
22 The Official Gazette of the Republic of Türkiye (No. 27640) on 13 July 2010.
23 *See* 1982 Constitution of the Republic of Türkiye (The official translation published by the Grand National Assembly of Türkiye, Department of Laws and

Resolutions, May 2019) available at: https://www.anayasa.gov.tr/media/7258/anayasa_eng.pdf accessed 29 September 2024.

24 Presidential Decree on the Procedures and Principles Regarding the Ratification of International Treaties Numbered 9, published in the Official Gazette of the Republic of Türkiye (No. 30479) on 15 July 2018.

25 A law approving the ratification is a short text and contains only the name of the international agreement, whose ratification has been approved.

26 Hüseyin Pazarcı, *Uluslararası Hukuk* (23rd eds. Turhan Kitabevi, 2023), p. 77.

27 *See* for non-official translation of the Code, Ayşe Odman Boztosun, 'The 2007 Turkish Code on Private International Law and International Civil Procedure' (2007) 9 *Yearbook of Private International Law*, p. 583.

28 The Code regulates the law applicable to private law transactions and relations that contain a foreign element. In this respect, a foreign element refers to private law relationships that are connected to a foreign legal system, personally, geographically, or by subject matter. *See* Cemal Şanlı, Emre Esen and İnci Ataman-Figanmeşe, *Milletlerarası Özel Hukuk – 10th Edition* (Beta, 2023), p. 5.

29 For instance, this article is also a basis for the applicability of Convention on the International Sale of Goods (1980) – one of the most comprehensive international agreements around the world.

30 Çalışkan, 'Milletlerarası Özel Hukukta Uluslararası Anlaşmaların Uygulanması', p. 228.

31 *See* United Nations Treaty Collection, Definition of Key Terms Used in UN Treaty Collection, available at: https://treaties.un.org/Pages/overview.aspx?path=overview/definition/page1_en.xml accessed 25 September 2024.

32 For more details, *see* Belkıs Vural Çelenk, *CISG ve Milletlerarası Özel Hukuk* (Yetkin Yayınları, 2023).

33 Türkiye has been a party to the CISG since July 2010, and the Convention has entered into force on 1 August 2011, and a Law Approving Ratification of the CISG (No. 5870) was published under the Official Gazette of the Turkish Republic (No. 27200) on 14 April 2009.

34 *See* for the *CISG case law from Türkiye*: https://cisg-online.org/CISG-by-jurisdiction?command=detail&detail=43, accessed 29 September 2024.

35 Istanbul Regional Court of Justice, Decision No. 2019/765 (24 May 2019).

36 The Court of Cassation (Yargıtay) of Türkiye, 11th Civil Chamber, Decision No. 2021/2836 (24 March 2021).

37 For more details with regard to the case mentioned, *see* Esra Kiraz, 'Türk Mahkemelerinde CISG'nin Uygulanma(ma)sı: Madde 2 (e) Bağlamında Bir Değerlendirme', (2023) 2 *Yildirim Beyazit Law Review* 565–585.

38 Art. 2 CISG – "This Convention does not apply to sales: (a) of goods bought for personal, family or household use, unless the seller, at any time before or at the conclusion of the contract, neither knew nor ought to have known that the goods were bought for any such use; (b) by auction; (c) on execution or otherwise by authority of law; (d) of stocks, shares, investment securities, negotiable instruments or money; (e) of ships, vessels, hovercraft or aircraft; (f) of electricity."

39 Cambridge Dictionary, "hovercraft", available at: https://dictionary.cambridge.org/dictionary/english/hovercraft accessed 29 September 2024.

40 Seemingly, Istanbul Regional Court of Justice grouped cars with airbag under "hovercraft" in the sense of Article 2 (e) of the CISG.

41 For more details translation matters within the context of CISG, *see* Claire M. Germain, 'CISG Translation Issues: Reducing Legal Babelism' (15 June 2012) available at: https://papers.ssrn.com/sol3/papers.cfm?abstract_id=2120620

42 The Convention has entered into force on 31 October 1995, and a Law Approving Ratification of the CMR (No. 3939) was published under the Official Gazette of the Turkish Republic (No. 21788) on 14 December 1993.

43 In this case, the CMR, as an international agreement, is applicable since both parties, Türkiye and the United Kingdom, are contracting States to the Convention. *See* status of the CMR at https://treaties.un.org/Pages/ViewDetails.aspx?src=TREATY&mtdsg_no=XI-B-11&chapter=11&clang=_en accessed 29 September 2024.

44 Istanbul 1st Commercial Court of First Instance, Decision No. 2001/965 – 2002/1065 (13 November 2002).

45 Article 32 (1) of the CMR: "The period of limitation for an action arising out of carriage under this Convention shall be **one year**. Nevertheless, in the case of wilful misconduct, or such default as in accordance with the law of the court or tribunal seized of the case, is considered as equivalent to wilful misconduct, the period of limitation shall be three years. The period of limitation shall begin to run: (a) In the case of partial loss, damage or delay in delivery, from the date of delivery; (b) In the case of total loss, from the thirtieth day after the expiry of the agreed time-limit or where there is no agreed time-limit from the sixtieth day from the date on which the goods were taken over by the carrier; (c) In all other cases, on the expiry of a period of three months after the making of the contract of carriage. The day on which the period of limitation begins to run shall not be included in the period."

46 Istanbul 1st Commercial Court of First Instance Decision.

47 11th Civil Chamber of Court of Cassation (Yargıtay), Decision No. 2003/12065 (19 December 2003).

48 Çalışkan, 'Milletlerarası Özel Hukukta Uluslararası Anlaşmaların Uygulanması', p. 231.

49 1982 Constitution of Türkiye, Art. 90.

50 The Official Gazette of the Turkish Republic (No. 22161) on 4 January 1995.

51 11th Civil Chamber of Court of Cassation Decision, para. 6: The Court highlighted here that the relevant article (Art. 32 of the CMR) has been regulated as a general phrase to include not only the beginning of the three-year period of limitation but also the beginning of the one-year period of imitation. In this case, the additional period (three months) must also be taken into account in the one-year period of limitation. Therefore, the Respondent's claim with regard to "the period of limitation" has passed would not have a ground under the Convention since it did not encompass so-called additional period.

52 Relevant to this context, Yeşilova states that: "The original text of the CMR has been prepared in English and French, with equivalent force. The difference in grammatical structure between these two languages becomes even more complicated in the translated texts of member states other than England and France, leading to different interpretations of the provisions of the Convention at the judicial stage. For this reason, in interpreting the provisions of the Convention during the court process, there is a need to benefit from the rich jurisprudence of Germany, which became a party to the Convention approximately thirty years before Türkiye." Ecehan Yeşilova, 'CMR Taşıma Senedinin İspat Kuvveti', (2005) 7 (1) *Dokuz Eylül Üniversitesi Hukuk Fakültesi Dergisi* 237–274.

53 *See* Preamble of the Convention: "THE CONTRACTING PARTIES, HAVING RECOGNIZED the desirability of standardizing the conditions governing the contract for the international carriage of goods by road, particularly with respect to the documents used for such carriage and to the carrier's liability, HAVE

AGREED as follows ..." available at: https://www.unidroit.org/instruments/transport/cmr-1956/ accessed 25 September 2024.

54 For more details, *see* Bihter Kaytaz Eker, *Harmonising Role of the New York Convention* (Yetkin Yayınları, 2020).

55 The authentic texts of "the New York Convention are provided in Chinese, English, French, Russian and Spanish languages." (Article XVI of the Convention), available at: https://www.newyorkconvention.org/text#:~:text=The%20authentic%20texts%20of%20%22The,(Article%20XVI%20sub%201), accessed 29 September 2024.

56 For more details, *see* Cemal Şanlı, *Uluslararası Ticari Akitlerin Hazırlanması ve Uyuşmazlıkların Çözüm Yolları – 8th Edition* (Beta, 2023), pp. 456–466; Esra Öğünç, 'Verildiği Ülkede İptal Edilen Hakem Kararlarının Tanınması ve Tenfizi – Recognition and Enforcement of Arbitral Awards Set Aside in the Country of Origin' (2021) 70 (3) *Ankara Üniversitesi Hukuk Fakültesi Dergisi* 801–839.

57 Apart from problematic translation of the relevant provision under the Turkish text of the Convention, there has been an ongoing discussion in international arbitration as to whether an arbitral award set aside at the seat of arbitration (the country of origin) can be enforced or not. However, the so-called discussion is not specifically an interest of this chapter.

58 The Convention has entered into force for Türkiye on 2 July 1992, and a Law Approving Ratification of the New York Convention (No. 3731) was published under the Official Gazette of the Turkish Republic (No. 20877) on 21 May 1991. The non-authentic Turkish translation of the Convention can also be found under the referred law.

59 For example, Article 62 of Private International Law and Procedural Law Code of Türkiye (No. 5718): "The court shall dismiss the enforcement request of a foreign arbitral award, if, ... (h) The arbitral award is not final, enforceable, or binding under the governing law or the governing procedure or the law of the country where it is rendered or it is annulled by the competent authority in the place where the award is rendered." As seen, in case of foreign arbitral award enforcement through, not the New York Convention, but Turkish Private International Law and Procedural Law Code, there is no discretionary power for Turkish Courts as well.

60 Vural Çelenk, *CISG ve Milletlerarası Özel Hukuk*, p. 101: Once the necessary conditions for the CISG to come into force in a contracting State are fulfilled, the Convention becomes a part of the domestic law of that State.

61 Ramos Fernando Prieto, 'International and Supranational Law in Translation: From Multilingual Lawmaking to Adjudication' (2014) 20 (3) *The Translator* 313, p. 326: "Translation remains an instrumental vehicle and a key quality filter for the creation of international (or supranational) multilingual law, and judicial interpretation emerges as a safety net to reinforce the overall coherence of the system as it is applied in different national jurisdictions."

62 As seen through the study, the exemplary international agreements have been specifically chosen from the field of Private International Law.

63 However, in some cases, the field that the international legal instrument relates may require technical knowledge as well (as in the CISG/hovercraft example previously given in this study). In such a case, the translation support from the specific field (engineering, medicine, agriculture, etc.) should also be provided.

64 For instance, today, as a promising development in Türkiye, law faculties aim to train lawyers, who are competent in linguistic. So that with the professionals, who have a good command of legal knowledge and can use foreign languages in their professional lives, it may be ensured that translation-related problems are eliminated, and international agreements by the courts are applied in accordance with the purpose and spirit of the agreements.

Bibliography

Akipek Serap, 'Türk Mevzuatının Onaylanan Uluslararası Antlaşmalar ile Uyumlaştırılması Sorunu' (1999) 48 (1) *Ankara Üniversitesi Hukuk Fakültesi Dergisi* 15–22.

Aybay Rona and Oral Elif, *Kamusal Uluslararası Hukuk* (Bilgi Üniversitesi Yayınları, 2016).

Çalışkan Yusuf, 'Milletlerarası Özel Hukukta Uluslararası Anlaşmaların Uygulanması: Tercüme ve Yorum Problemleri' in Doğan Vahit, Yılmaz Alper Çağrı, Ayhan İzmirli Lale, *Antalya Bilim Üniversitesi Hukuk Fakültesi Milletlerarası Özel Hukukta Güncel Meseleler Sempozyumu* (Savaş Kitabevi, 2019).

European Commission Final Report, 'Studies on Translation and Multilingualism – Language and Translation in International Law and EU Law' 6/2012. Luxembourg: Publications Office of the European Union.

European Parliament Briefing, 'Legal Aspects of EU Multilingualism' (January 2017), Available at: https://www.europarl.europa.eu/RegData/etudes/BRIE/2017/595914/EPRS_BRI%282017%29595914_EN.pdf

Germain Claire M., 'CISG Translation Issues: Reducing Legal Babelism' (15 June 2012) Available at: https://papers.ssrn.com/sol3/papers.cfm?abstract_id=2120620

Kaytaz Eker Bihter, *Harmonising Role of the New York Convention* (Yetkin Yayınları, 2020).

Kiraz Esra, 'Türk Mahkemelerinde CISG'nin Uygulanma (ma)sı: Madde 2 (e) Bağlamında Bir Değerlendirme' (2023) 2 *Yıldırım Beyazıt Hukuk Dergisi* 565–585.

Kızılyürek Zora, 'The Significance and Utility of the Rules of Treaty Interpretation, as Encapsulated in the 1969 Vienna Convention on the Law of Treaties, for the Purpose of Ascertaining the Meaning of Treaty Provisions' (2021) 70 *Annales de la Faculté de Droit d'Istanbul* 243–252.

Kuner Christopher B., 'The Interpretation of Multilingual Treaties: Comparison of Texts versus the Presumption of Similar Meaning' (1991) 40 *International and Comparative Law Quarterly* 953–964.

Margiotta Broglio Constanza and Ortino Federico, 'Treaty Interpretation, Multilingualism, and the WTO Dispute Settlement System: Towards the Comparative Translation Paradigm?' (2024) 15 (4) *Journal of International Dispute Settlement* 487–505. (in press)

Odman Boztosun Ayşe, 'The 2007 Turkish Code on Private International Law and International Civil Procedure' (2007) 9 *Yearbook of Private International Law* 583–604.

Öğünç Esra, 'Verildiği Ülkede İptal Edilen Hakem Kararlarının Tanınması ve Tenfizi – Recognition and Enforcement of Arbitral Awards Set Aside in the Country of Origin' (2021) 70 (3) *Ankara Üniversitesi Hukuk Fakültesi Dergisi* 801–839.

Pazarcı Hüseyin, *Uluslararası Hukuk* (23rd Edition, Turhan Kitabevi, 2023).

Ramos Fernando Prieto, 'International and Supranational Law in Translation: From Multilingual Lawmaking to Adjudication' (2014) 20 (3) *The Translator* 313–331.

Şanlı Cemal, Esen Emre and Ataman-Figanmeşe İnci, *Milletlerarası Özel Hukuk – 10th Edition* (Beta, 2023).

Şanlı Cemal, *Uluslararası Ticari Akitlerin Hazırlanması ve Uyuşmazlıkların Çözüm Yolları* (Beta, 2023).

Vural Çelenk Belkıs, *CISG ve Milletlerarası Özel Hukuk* (Yetkin Yayınları, 2023).

6 Institutional Translation

Balancing Multilingual Legal Discourse between EU and Switzerland

Annarita Felici

6.1 Introduction: Institutional Translation in Multilingual Settings

Translation ensures the functioning of many multilingual institutions, both nationally and internationally. This is the case of the EU, perhaps the largest and most emblematic multilingual institution in the world but also of other distinct international organisations and of many multilingual countries and regions (e.g., Switzerland, Canada, Belgium, South Africa). In its broad sense, institutional translation serves the communication needs of any multilingual administrative and governmental body, thus intersecting several technical disciplines. The variety of content dealt with within institutions is reflected in the abundance of text genres: legislation, reports, surveys, press releases, correspondence, minutes, information for the public, etc. The audience for these translated texts includes both experts and the lay public. Without delving into the conceptualisation of institutional translation,[1] multilingual institutions essentially "govern by translation" (Koskinen 2014, 483) and democratically ensure – despite the hierarchical point of view – their performing function. Primarily concerned with the translation of legal instruments, institutional translation falls outside of mainstream translation work and presents challenges related to (i) the context of production and (ii) the product, i.e., the institutional (legal) text. The first involves anonymous and collective work (Schäffner et al. 2014, 494) with texts being translated both in-house and outside the institutions. In addition, institutions may use a working language or lingua franca during drafting, as well as pivot languages[2] to overcome the problem of language combinations and poor resources. The second challenge is the translation itself, often lacking a true original because of the multiple drafts of the source text and their recycled content but in the end equally authentic to all the other language versions (Derlén 2015; Felici 2010; Šarčević 1997). Finally, institutional translation is highly standardised (Schäffner et al. 2014, 494), and this applies to both translation production and the final

DOI: 10.4324/9781003430308-8

product. Translations of legal instruments are meant to be linguistically consistent amongst themselves (in terms of lexis, grammar, and style) and with previous versions of similar or higher-ranking texts. In addition, they should sound natural and thus conform to the textual and linguistic convention of non-translated language (Biel 2017, 35).

This complex relation between the inter- and the intra-linguistic dimension goes to the very heart of quality and ensures by means of "standardised procedures" that the translation product meets the inherently required purposes. The link between the multilingual dimension (i.e. translation accuracy/multilingual concordance) and the monolingual dimension (i.e. the consistency with other institutional texts and with the non-translated language) is a distinctive mark of institutional translation, especially when it comes to legal texts. The matter has been particularly researched within the EU context and is known with different labels: "horizontal dimension" vs. "vertical dimension" (Robertson 2015, 41–44),[3] "concordance, continuity and fit" (Biel 2019, 32), and "inter-linguistic concordance and intra-linguistic consistency" (Prieto Ramos 2021, 176).

Drawing on these features and focusing exclusively on the translation product, this chapter attempts to depict how EU legal discourse interacts with institutional translation practices in multilingual Switzerland. Legal discourse is used here as an umbrella term to encompass any use of language in legal genres and contexts, both socio-political and cross-cultural (Bhatia and Bhatia 2011, 481; Kurzon 1997, 119), thus shifting the focus from linguistic features of legal language to its situational use.

Although it is not a Member State of the EU, Switzerland is an official trilingual country that incorporates a great deal of European legislation. Moreover, recent studies on language contact and EU translation have singled out the presence of an EU variety or Eurolect in many European languages (Mori 2018), which would be due to the implementation of EU directives in domestic legislation.

Through the lens of qualitative analysis, this contribution intends to answer the following questions: is it still possible to ensure translation equivalence and intra-linguistic concordance between two multilingual institutions? Does the EU language impact Swiss legal discourse and translations?

After describing the implementation procedure of EU law in Switzerland, the analysis of both macro-textual and micro-linguistic features follows. The macro-textual analysis is meant to highlight how the supranational legal discourse of the EU is recontextualised within the Swiss borders in terms of drafting conventions. The micro-textual analysis focuses on micro-linguistic aspects, more specifically modals and sentence structure, to highlight interlinguistic consistency and naturalness within every single language.

Data are drawn from CHEU-lex, a parallel and comparable corpus of Swiss and European Union legislation published in the three official languages of the Swiss Confederation (French, German, and Italian).[4] It comprises (1) bilateral agreements entered between Switzerland and the EU from 1972 to 2017 and (2) Swiss federal legislation including the reception of these agreements. As a further source of reference for EU law, the EUR-lex database was also consulted.

6.2 EU Law in Multilingual Switzerland: A Double Challenge

Despite not being part of the EU, Switzerland has close relations with the Union and is one of its major trading partners. The foundations for this economic cooperation date back to the Free Trade Agreement in 1972, followed by the Insurance Agreement (1989) and the Agreement on the Carriage of Goods (1990).

At the beginning of the 1990s, Switzerland applied for EU membership, but its rejection by popular referendum resulted in the continuation of its relations with Europe on another basis, i.e., sector-specific bilateral agreements and the "autonomous adaptation" (*autonomer Nachvollzug*) of Swiss Law to EU law. Based on mutual recognition of legislation, bilateral agreements are the best way for Switzerland to maintain relations with the EU without having to abide by the *acquis*.[5] Between 1999 and 2004, Switzerland and the EU signed 16 core agreements (Bilateral I and II) and over 100 secondary agreements. As regards the "autonomous adaptation", it refers to the intention of the Federal Council to enact laws compatible to the extent possible – with EU norms.[6] While safeguarding its sovereignty, Switzerland has therefore integrated a great bulk of European law over the years, thus resulting in a progressive Europeanisation of Swiss law (Amstutz 2005; De Rossa Gisimundo 2010; Jenni 2014; Lavenex 2009; Maiani 2008; Oesch 2020; Vahl and Grolimund 2006). However, in contrast to the implementation of directives in EU Member States, there is no direct linguistic correspondence between EU and Swiss law. The Confederation can produce a new act by means of references to the texts of the agreements or insert European provisions within annexes in pre-existing Swiss legislation. The transposition of EU law

> has [therefore] developed in a reactive, incremental, ad hoc fashion, and it has taken a great many legal forms [...] encompassing varying degrees of approximation, and always resulting in the creation of something new – more or less similar to, but still different from EU Law.
>
> (Maiani 2008, 1–2)

From a practical point of view, the transposition is documented in the *Règles d'or de la reprise du droit de l'UE dans le droit suisse* (2019, 6–7)[7] and takes place in three ways, depending on the size of the legislation: (1) reformulation of EU norms, (2) literal reproduction, and (3) express reference to EU provisions. While the first of these has the clear advantage of reformulating EU law in a Swiss manner, easily understandable to the Swiss citizen, the other two imply a minor investment of resources in terms of drafters and a clearer and intentional reference to the EU legislation. Overall, Swiss authorities have a great deal of freedom in implementing EU law and may choose to transpose only selected parts or the entirety of EU legislation.

However, when transposing EU legislation, Swiss drafters often refer to the German EU version and draft their own Swiss German version, which is later translated into French and Italian. This means that the Swiss French and Italian versions may be different from their respective EU versions, thus challenging the "inter-linguistic concordance and the intra-linguistic consistency" mentioned before. One may wonder whether the Swiss French and Italian versions should be consistent with the Swiss German "source" text or with the EU French and Italian versions. In both cases, the risk is to betray the EU institutional discourse or the Swiss domestic one. Moreover, Switzerland often uses its French version, or an English ad hoc translation, to check consistency with the EU law. Intra-linguistic aspects and language naturalness are also questioned because of double exposure to language contact and the inherent drafting and translation procedures of the two institutions. The EU German version used in Switzerland is itself a "pseudo-source text", because of the hybrid genesis of EU language versions and their linguistic equivalence.

Institutional translation results therefore in a multilingual legal patchwork, where the interlinguistic consistency of Swiss legislation intertwines with one of the EU languages at a supranational level, against a background of linguistic equivalence and language fit within each national legal frame and language. The next sections draw on these premises and attempt to illustrate this difficult balance with examples.

6.3 Intra-Linguistic Concordance: Macro-Textual Features

Although a great bulk of European legislation enters Switzerland through the bilateral agreements from a linguistic point of view, it does so in a very Swiss way. EU and Swiss instruments are not symmetrical; nor are the agreements with Swiss laws and ordinances. This is particularly evident in macro-textual features like the organisation of content, definitions, annexes, referencing, and even titles.

EU secondary legislation is generally dense in information and includes lengthy preambles, several detail-oriented articles, complex textual conventions, and long annexes. In contrast, Swiss legislation has almost no preambles, simpler enacting terms, and fewer annexes that regulate specific details. This can be seen partially in the Agreement on the Free Movement of Persons (AFMP) in Table 6.1. Since the Agreement is a *superpartes* instrument of diplomacy, its enacting terms only account for general provisions. Articles 4 and 5 of Directive 2004/38/EC[8] concerning the right of exit and entry are included in Annex 1 of the Agreement. It is worth noting that the two articles in the directive, both preceded by the same conditional clause (*without prejudice*), are integrated into a single article only, in Annex 1 of the AFMP. The Agreement does indeed reproduce some of the formulations and lexis of the directive; however, the two sub-paragraphs of the annex have the same subjects with the same semantic roles, thus contributing to a certain circularity within the frame of granting. If we look at Directive 2004/38/EC, the same sentence structure and frame are valid only for Article 5. In Article 4, the subject is the Union citizens and their family members, who are entitled to leave the territory[9] and hence trigger a more static frame. The reading is also different in terms of speech acts and illocutionary force. While Article 4 entails a declarative constitutive sentence (*shall have the right*), Article 5 of the same Directive and Article 1 of the Agreement's Annex allow for a deontic reading (*shall grant*).

Table 6.1 Example 1

Directive 2004/38/EC	*AFMP*
Article 4 Right of exit 1 Without prejudice to the provisions on travel documents applicable to national border controls, all Union citizens with a valid identity card or passport and their family members who are not nationals of a Member State and who hold a valid passport *shall have the right* to leave the territory of a Member State to travel to another Member State. Article 5 Right of entry 1 Without prejudice to the provisions on travel documents applicable to national border controls, Member States *shall grant* Union citizens leave to enter their territory with a valid identity card or passport and shall grant family members who are not nationals of a Member State leave to enter their territory with a valid passport.	Art. 3 Right of entry The right of entry of nationals of one Contracting Party into the territory of another Contracting Party *shall be guaranteed* in accordance with the provisions laid down in Annex I. *Annex I* Art. 1 Entry and Exit 1 The Contracting Parties *shall allow* nationals of the other Contracting Parties and members of their family within the meaning of Article 3 of this Annex and posted persons within the meaning of Article 17 of this Annex *to enter* their territory simply upon production of a valid identity card or passport. [...] 2 The Contracting Parties *shall grant* nationals of the Contracting Parties, and members of their family within the meaning of Article 3 of this Annex and posted workers within the meaning of Article 17 of this Annex, the right to leave their territory simply upon production of a valid identity card or passport.

A different density of information and an easier sentence layout are even more evident when comparing the Agreement and the Swiss law. Example 2 (Table 6.2) shows the transposition of Article 6, Annex 1 of the same Agreement (AFMP/ALCP[10]) in the Swiss Ordinance on the free movement of persons (OLCP).[11] The French version of the ordinance is provided and will be provided for other examples of Swiss legislation where there is no English version.

The ordinance clearly shows how the content of one sub-paragraph in the Agreement (AFMP/ALCP) is split into three sub-paragraphs in the Swiss domestic text (OLCP), to conform to the practice of the one-sentence rule.

Table 6.2 Example 2

AFMP	*ALCP*	*OLCP*
Article 6 Rules regarding residence 1 An employed person who is a national of a Contracting Party (hereinafter referred to as "employed person") and is employed for a period of one year or more by an employer in the host state shall receive a residence permit which is valid for at least five years from its date of issue. It shall be extended automatically for a period of at least five years. When renewed for the first time, its period of validity may be limited, but not to less than one year, where its holder has been involuntarily unemployed for more than 12 consecutive months.	Article 6 Réglementation du séjour 1 Le travailleur salarié ressortissant d'une partie contractante (ci-après nommé travailleur salarié) qui occupe un emploi d'une durée égale ou supérieure à un an au service d'un employeur de l'État d'accueil reçoit un titre de séjour d'une durée de cinq ans au moins à dater de sa délivrance. Il est automatiquement prolongé pour une durée de cinq ans au moins. Lors du premier renouvellement, sa durée de validité peut être limitée, sans pouvoir être inférieure à un an, lorsque son détenteur se trouve dans une situation de chômage involontaire depuis plus de douze mois consécutifs.	Art. 6. Titres pour étrangers 1 Les ressortissants de l'UE et de l'AELE, les membres de leur famille, ainsi que les prestataires de services visés à l'art. 2, al. 3, qui sont au bénéfice d'une autorisation en vertu de l'accord sur la libre circulation des personnes ou de la Convention instituant l'AELE reçoivent un titre pour étrangers. 2 Le titre pour étrangers attestant l'autorisation d'établissement UE/AELE est établi à des fins de contrôle pour une période de cinq ans. Son détenteur le remettra à l'autorité compétente en vue de sa prolongation deux semaines avant l'échéance de ce délai. 3 L'établissement et la présentation des titres pour étrangers sont régis par les art. 71 à 72 OASA.[12]

A similar strategy is also evident when specifying residence conditions and financial means for people not pursuing economic activity in Switzerland. The general scope of Article 24 (AFMP/ALCP) translates into a long article, where the contracting parties account for several conditions: the required financial means when UE/AELS citizens are not working, unemployment benefits in case of a previous job, student status, and breaks in residency. Although the ordinance draws heavily on the Agreement wording and contemplates an equally ad hoc section for people not pursuing an economic activity, it devotes a single article to their financial means (Article 16). The potential renewal of the residence permit (wave underline in Table 6.3) is addressed instead in a separate article (Article 17) at the end of the first sub-paragraph of the Agreement.

The references in the ordinance to other Swiss legislation also highlight a flexible – but no less precise – integration of EU law in an attempt to "adjust" to existing domestic norms (in this case, legislation from the 1960s).

Particular attention is devoted to the integration of definitions. Like many instruments of international law, they are indeed very popular in EU law and less so in Swiss law, but they are generally used in many civil law systems, like Italy or France. Their presence makes it possible to agree on common scopes and concepts that would be interpreted differently if we consider the cultural specificity and sometimes the indeterminacy of legal concepts.

Although each institution has its own guidelines for the drafting of definitions, they are either grouped in definition sections (in the general provisions or in the annexes) or can appear "in the main body of the instrument [and] usually take the form of 'real' provisions" (Šarčević 1997, 154). The Swiss legal drafting guidelines[13] advise inserting definitions only if they provide useful information for the purpose of the legal instrument. Overall, if not dealing with a highly technical topic, the use of plain language should not require definitions (Directives de la Confédération sur la technique legislative 2019, 25). The guidelines also recommend brevity, conciseness, and respect of logical relations, i.e., moving from the main general definitions to more specific ones.

Although definitions vary in form depending on their position in the legal instrument, the explanatory definition of "multi-manning"[14] in Article 4 of EC Regulation 561/2006[15] is completely restructured in the driver ordinance.[16] In the definition section, we have only a short definition of what multi-manning is; the details concerning its duration, which were part of the same definition in the EC Regulation, are inserted in a different article concerning weekly rests and multi-manning driving (Table 6.4).

Table 6.3 Example 3

AFMP	*ALCP*	*OLCP*
V. PERSONS NOT PURSUING AN ECONOMIC ACTIVITY	V. PERSONNES N'EXERÇANT PAS UNE ACTIVITÉ ÉCONOMIQUE	Section 6: Séjours sans exercice d'une activité lucrative
Article 24	Article 24	Art. 16 Moyen financiers
Rules regarding residence	Réglementation du séjour	(art. 24 de l'annexe I de l'Ac. sur la libre circulation des personnes)
1 A person who is a national of a Contracting Party not pursuing an economic activity in the state of residence and having no right of residence pursuant to other provisions of this Agreement shall receive a residence permit valid for at least five years provided he proves to the competent national authorities that he possesses for himself and the members of his family: (a) sufficient financial means not to have to apply for social assistance benefits during their stay; (b) all-risks sickness insurance cover.	1 Une personne ressortissante d'une partie contractante n'exerçant pas d'activité économique dans l'État de résidence et qui ne bénéficie pas d'un droit de séjour en vertu d'autres dispositions du présent accord reçoit un titre de séjour d'une durée de cinq ans au moins, à condition qu'elle prouve aux autorités nationales compétentes qu'elle dispose pour elle-même et les membres de sa famille: a) de moyens financiers suffisants pour ne devoir faire appel à l'aide sociale pendant leur séjour; b) d'une assurance-maladie couvrant l'ensemble des risques.	1 Les moyens financiers des ressortissants de l'UE et de l'AELE ainsi que des membres de leur famille sont réputés suffisants s'ils dépassent les prestations d'assistance qui seraient allouées en fonction des directives «Aide sociale: concepts et normes de calcul» (directives CSIAS), à un ressortissant suisse, éventuellement aux membres de sa famille, suite à la demande de l'intéressé et compte tenu de sa situation personnelle.
The Contracting Parties may, if they consider it necessary, require the residence permit to be revalidated at the end of the first two years of residence.	Les parties contractantes peuvent, quand elles l'estiment nécessaire, demander la revalidation du titre de séjour au terme des deux premières années de séjour.	2 Les moyens financiers d'un ayant droit à une rente, ressortissant de l'UE ou de l'AELE ainsi que les membres de sa famille, sont réputés suffisants s'ils dépassent le montant donnant droit à un ressortissant suisse qui en fait la demande, éventuellement aux membres de sa famille, à des prestations complémentaires au sens de la loi fédérale du 19 mars 1965 sur les prestations complémentaires à l'assurance-vieillesse, survivants et invalidité.
2 Financial means shall be considered sufficient if they exceed the amount below which nationals, having regard to their personal situation and, where appropriate, that of their family, can claim social security benefits. Where that condition cannot be applied, the applicant's financial means shall be regarded as sufficient if they are greater than the level of the minimum social security pension paid by the host state.	2 Sont considérés comme suffisants les moyens financiers nécessaires qui dépassent le montant en dessous duquel les nationaux, eu égard à leur situation personnelle et, le cas échéant, et à celle des membres de leur famille, peuvent prétendre à des prestations d'assistance. Lorsque cette condition ne peut s'appliquer, les moyens financiers du demandeur sont considérés comme suffisants lorsqu'ils sont supérieurs au niveau de la pension minimale de sécurité sociale versée par l'État d'accueil.	*Art. 17 Renouvellement de l'autorisation de séjour UE/AELE* En cas de séjour sans activité lucrative, les autorités compétentes peuvent, quand elles l'estiment nécessaire, demander la revalidation de l'autorisation de séjour UE/AELE au terme des deux premières années de séjour.

Table 6.4 Example 4

EC Regulation 561/2006	*Règlement CE 561/2006*	*OTR1*
Article 4 For the purposes of this Regulation the following definitions shall apply: [...] (o) "multi-manning" means the situation where, during each period of driving between any two consecutive daily rest periods, or between a daily rest period and a weekly rest period, there are at least two drivers in the vehicle to do the driving. For the first hour of multi-manning the presence of another driver or drivers is optional but for the remainder of the period it is compulsory;	Article 4 Aux fins du présent règlement, on entend par: [...] o) l «conduite en équipage»: la situation dans laquelle, pendant une période de conduite comprise entre deux temps de repos journaliers consécutifs, ou entre un temps de repos journalier et un temps de repos hebdomadaire, il y a au moins deux conducteurs à bord du véhicule pour assurer la relève. Au cours de la première heure de conduite en équipage, la présence d'un autre ou d'autres conducteurs est facultative, mais elle est obligatoire pour le reste de la période à courir;	Art. 2 Définitions Au sens de la présente ordonnance on entend par: ...... *k. équipage*, le cas où deux conducteurs ou plus sont engagés pour se relayer au volant d'un véhicule entre deux temps de repos; [...] Art. 11. Temps de repos hebdomadaire ... Art. 11c. Conduite en équipage 1 En cas de conduite en équipage, le temps passé pendant la marche du véhicule à côté du conducteur ou sur une couchette est réputé temps de disponibilité. 2 En cas de conduite en équipage, la présence d'un autre conducteur est facultative pendant la première heure et obligatoire le reste du temps.

The visual organisation of the content also increases its accessibility and allows the relevant definition to be easily found. Although the Swiss foodstuff legislation[17] reproduces literally the definitions of EC Regulation 178/2002,[18] the Swiss article is split into three sub-paragraphs (Table 6.5).

On the contrary, the explicit reference to EU instruments within the same Swiss legislation is not uncommon. This is the case of the referencing technique mentioned before, which is particularly used when regulating policy areas that are strongly oriented towards EU law, e.g., the manufacture of products governed by EU law. This is evident in the ordinance on machine safety.[19] Article 1 refers explicitly to Directive 2006/42/EC[20] for putting into service and placing on the market of the machines, its scope, and definitions (Table 6.6).

Table 6.5 Example 5

EC Regulation 178/2002	*Règlement CE 178/2002*	*LDAI*
Article 2 Definition of "food" For the purposes of this Regulation, "food" (or "foodstuff") means any substance or product, whether processed, partially processed or unprocessed, intended to be, or reasonably expected to be ingested by humans. "Food" includes drink, chewing gum and any substance, including water, intentionally incorporated into the food during its manufacture, preparation or treatment. It includes water [...] "Food" shall not include: feed; (b) live animals unless they are [...]	Article 2 Définition de «denrée alimentaire» Aux fins du présent règlement, on entend par «denrée alimentaire» (ou «aliment»), toute substance ou produit, transformé, partiellement transformé ou non transformé, destiné à être ingéré ou raisonnablement susceptible d'être ingéré par l'être humain. Ce terme recouvre les boissons, les gommes à mâcher et toute substance, y compris l'eau, [...] Le terme «denrée alimentaire» ne couvre pas: a les aliments pour animaux; b les animaux vivants à moins qu'ils ne soient [...]	**Section 2 Définitions** *Art. 4 Denrées alimentaires* 1 On entend par denrées alimentaires l'ensemble des substances ou des produits transformés, partiellement transformés ou non transformés qui sont destinés à être ingérés ou dont on peut raisonnablement s'attendre à ce qu'ils soient ingérés par l'être humain. 2 Sont également considérées comme des denrées alimentaires: a les boissons, y compris l'eau destinée à la consommation humaine; b les gommes à mâcher; c toute substance incorporée intentionnellement dans la denrée alimentaire au cours de sa fabrication, de sa transformation ou de son traitement. 3 Ne sont pas considérés comme des denrées alimentaires: a les aliments pour animaux; b les animaux vivants, à moins qu'ils n'aient été [...];

Table 6.6 Example 6

OMach
Art. 1 Objet, champ d'application, définitions et droit applicable 1 La présente ordonnance règle la mise sur le marché et la surveillance du marché des machines, telles que les entend la directive 2006/42/CE (directive UE relative aux machines). 2 Le champ d'application est régi par l'art. 1 de la directive UE relative aux machines. L'art. 3 de cette directive s'applique par analogie. 2bis Les définitions de l'art. 2 de la directive UE relative aux machines et de l'art. 3, ch. 8 à 13, du règlement (UE) 2019/1020 (règlement UE sur la surveillance du marché) s'appliquent. Les équivalences terminologiques figurant à l'annexe 1, ch. 1, s'appliquent également. [...]

The same reference is valid for Article 1 of the Ordinance on the Safety of Personal Protective Equipment,[21] which makes explicit reference to the scope and definitions of EU Regulation 2016/425 on personal protective equipment.[22]

Finally, titles also differentiate the two institutions and highlight two different needs. EU instruments are very well known for their long titles that often extensively qualify their content and sometimes also record their evolution, e.g., *Council Regulation EU 264/ 2012 of 23 March 2012 amending Regulation (EU) No. 359/2011 concerning restrictive measures directed against certain persons, entities, and bodies in view of the situation in Iran* in the previous example. *The Joint Practical Guide* (2016) explains that "short titles may create risks for the accuracy and coherence of legal acts of the Union" (2016, 8.4) and that in the context of the EU they are not very useful because the legal instrument can be easily identified by a system of letters and numbers, e.g., EU 264/2012. Short titles are, therefore, rare (e.g. Habitats Directive 92/43 EEC), and sometimes the abbreviation is put into parentheses as for Regulation EU 2016/429, also known as the "Animal Health Law". On the contrary, Swiss titles always include an abbreviation in parentheses as, for example, in "Ordonnance sur la sécurité des machines (Ordonnance sur les machines, OMach)" and tend to be very short. The abbreviation is in fact quite significant, because references in legal texts must be made with the abbreviated title and without parentheses.

6.4 Interlinguistic Concordance: Micro-Linguistic Features

Interlinguistic concordance is particularly challenged when it comes to implementing EU provisions. While the agreements are generally negotiated in French or English,[23] the Swiss legislator uses the German EU version as a basis to implement EU law, and this, in turn, becomes the Swiss source text for French and Italian. It is, however, a source text of a very particular type. Although the EU German version is *de jure* authentic, *de facto* it remains a translation subject to all the well-known constraints of EU multilingualism and is indeed influenced by German terminology, which may differ from the terminology used in Switzerland. Divergences are inevitable and can especially be seen at a micro-linguistic level in the choice of terminology, the use of modals, conjunctions, and sentence structure.

Table 6.7 highlights cross-linguistically several solutions for the noun phrase "residence card". Unlike the literal translation of the EU directive, if we also consider the Agreement, intra-linguistic consistency only applies to French (*titre de séjour*). Depending on the context of its use, it may be unclear whether we are always referring to the same thing. Articles 9 and 10 of Directive 2004/38/EC clearly refer to a card issued to family members of a Union citizen who are not nationals of a Member State and whose period of residence is more than three months. In the Agreement, the concept of a residence card or permit seems interchangeable with the generic permit required in Switzerland for foreign nationals, when the stay is more than three months (in the Italian version, it is explicitly used as a synonym[24]). This is confirmed in the Swiss legislation, such as in Article 41 of Lois étrangers and Article 4 of OLCP that refer to a permit or a residence authorisation of five years for foreign nationals. The ordinance, however, uses "residence and permit authorisation" as a generic title and then distinguishes among the different Swiss residence permits depending on the length and the conditions of stay. Here, the "residence card" is again mentioned, but it seems to be reserved this time for family members and other service providers employed by an EU/EFTA company.

The impact of language contact is not limited to terminology, and morpho-syntactical patterns provide several examples of interlinguistic concordance within the same institution or of intra-linguistic concordance across the two institutions. Example 8 in Table 6.8 concerns the reception of Regulation EU 305/2011, which lays down harmonised conditions for the marketing of construction products[25] within the ordinance on these same products.[26] The article focuses on the declaration of performance, which is required for each new product on the market either in paper form or by electronic means. Linguistically speaking, it allows us to reflect on several nuances in terms of modality, sentence structure, connectives, and genres, while highlighting different links across the three languages and between the two institutional legal discourses.

Although the two German versions look quite similar, the French ordinance shows a high degree of concordance with the EU French

Table 6.7 Example 7

<table>
<tr><th></th><th>English</th><th>French</th><th>German</th><th>Italian</th></tr>
<tr><td>Directive 2004/38/EC</td><td>Residence card</td><td>carte de séjour</td><td>Aufenthaltskarte</td><td>carta di soggiorno</td></tr>
<tr><td>Agreement (AFMP)</td><td>Residence permit</td><td>Titre de séjour</td><td>Aufenthaltserlaubnis</td><td>carta di soggiorno, permesso di soggiorno</td></tr>
<tr><td>Lois étrangers (LEI)</td><td>Identity card (official English translation)</td><td>Titre de séjour</td><td>Ausweis</td><td>carta di soggiorno</td></tr>
<tr><td>Ordinance free movement (OLCP)</td><td>Permit authorisation, residence permit</td><td>autorisations et titre de séjour {autorisation de séjour de courte durée UE/AELE| autorisation d'établissement UE/AELE| titre pour étranger }</td><td>Bewilligungskarte und Ausländerausweis {Kurzaufenthaltsbewilligung EU/EFTA| Aufenthaltsbewilligung UE/EFTA| Niederlassungsbewilligung UE/EFTA| Ausländerausweis}</td><td>permessi e carte di soggiorno {permesso di soggiorno di breve durata UE/AELS| permesso di dimora UE/AELS| carta di soggiorno per stranieri},</td></tr>
</table>

Regulation, especially with regard to sub-paragraphs 2 and 3, which are almost identical. Where a batch of the same product is supplied to a single user, both French versions (EU and CH) imply discretion (i.e. modal verb *peut*)[27] in the delivery of the declaration. On the contrary, in Swiss Italian, where we probably would expect a literal translation from French, the declaration "must" (*deve*) be supplied. The shift to the modal verb "must" focuses on a necessary requirement in Swiss German (*muss*). If we consider that the EU German version serves as a basis for the Swiss drafter, the discrepancy lies in the interpretation of the German EU text at least twice: (1) interlinguistically between the EU languages because *braucht* expresses a need or a requirement, (2) intra-linguistically in German because "must" has a different illocutionary force from

Table 6.8 Example 8

German	*French*	*Italian*
Regulation EU 305/2011		
Artikel 7 *Zurverfügungstellung der Leistungserklärung* (1) Eine Abschrift der Leistungserklärung jedes Produkts, das auf dem Markt bereitgestellt wird, *wird* entweder in gedruckter oder elektronischer Weise *zur Verfügung gestellt.* Wird jedoch einem einzigen Abnehmer ein Los gleicher Produkte geliefert, so *braucht* diesem lediglich eine einzige Abschrift der Leistungserklärung in gedruckter oder elektronischer Form beigefügt zu werden. (2) Eine Abschrift der Leistungserklärung in gedruckter Form wird zur Verfügung gestellt, sofern diese vom Abnehmer gefordert wird. [...]	*Article 7* *Fourniture de la déclaration des performance* 1 Une copie de la déclaration des performances de chaque produit mis à disposition sur le marché *est fournie* soit sous format papier, soit par voie électronique. Toutefois, lorsqu'un lot du même produit est livré à un même utilisateur, il *peut* être accompagné d'une seule copie de cette déclaration, soit sous format papier, soit par voie électronique. 2 Une copie papier de la déclaration des performances est fournie au destinataire s'il en fait la demande. [...]	Articolo 7 Fornitura della dichiarazione di prestazione 1 *È fornita* una copia della dichiarazione di prestazione di ciascun prodotto messo a disposizione sul mercato, in forma cartacea o su supporto elettronico. Se tuttavia un lotto dello stesso prodotto è fornito a un unico utilizzatore, esso *può* essere accompagnato da una sola copia della dichiarazione di prestazione in forma cartacea o su supporto elettronico. 2 Se il destinatario lo richiede, è fornita una copia cartacea della dichiarazione di prestazione. [...]

(*Continued*)

Table 6.8 (Continued)

Ordinance on construction products		
Art. 9 Zurverfügungstellung der Leistungserklärung	Art. 9 Mise à disposition de la déclaration de prestation	Art.9 Messa a disposizione della dichiarazione di prestazione
1 Für jedes Produkt, für das eine Leistungserklärung *zu erstellen ist, ist* diese entweder in gedruckter oder in elektronischer Form zur Verfügung *zu stellen.*	1 Pour tout produit *devant faire* l'objet d'une déclaration des performances, celle-ci *est à mettre à disposition* soit sous forme papier, soit sous forme électronique.	1 Per ciascun prodotto per il quale *occorre* redigere una dichiarazione di prestazione, quest'ultima *deve essere messa a disposizione* in forma cartacea o elettronica.
2 Wird einer Abnehmerin oder einem Abnehmer ein Los gleicher Produkte geliefert, so *muss* diesem Los lediglich ein Exemplar der Leistungserklärung beigefügt werden.	2 Lorsqu'un lot du même produit est livré à un utilisateur, il *peut* être accompagné d'un seul exemplaire de la déclaration des performances.	2 Se a un utilizzatore è fornito un lotto dello stesso prodotto, esso *deve* essere accompagnato soltanto da un esemplare della dichiarazione di prestazione.
3 Verlangt es eine Abnehmerin oder ein Abnehmer, so *muss* ihr oder ihm eine Leistungserklärung in gedruckter Form zur Verfügung gestellt werden.	3 Une déclaration des performances sous forme papier *est fournie* à l'utilisateur qui en fait la demande.	3 Se un utilizzatore lo esige, gli *deve* essere messa a disposizione una copia cartacea della dichiarazione di prestazione.

"needs". In terms of modality, the whole Swiss article is reformulated in imperative terms. The passive (*wird gestellt, est fournie, è fornita*) of the first sub-paragraph in the EU Regulation is correctly reformulated in imperative terms (*ist zu stellen, est à mettere à disposition, deve essere fornita*), because the declaration of performance serves as a warranty and is a necessary requirement imposed by the Union.

If we look at the sentence structure, the two texts (the EU Regulation and the Swiss Ordinance) show a semantic nuance in the layout of the information. Although both texts deal with the delivery of the declaration of performance – be it in paper or electronic form – in the EU Regulation this applies to every product on the market (double underline in Table 6.8). The Swiss Ordinance, on the contrary, seems to imply that only the products that require the declaration require it in paper or electronic form. The nuance in meaning is clearly due to the use of the modal (*zu erstellen ist, devant faire, occorre*) in the fact-situation but also to the "product" placed at the beginning of the sentence.

The last sub-paragraph is about the condition for the supply of the paper copy and highlights a different arrangement of fact-situation and statement of law (wave underline in the example). While the two French versions have the statement of law ("a paper copy must be provided") at the beginning of the sentence, Swiss German and Italian seem to conform with traditional drafting that places it at the end of the sentence, i.e., fact-situation followed by the statement of law ("if the user requests it, a paper copy must be provided"). In the EU version, this is only valid for Italian. Although the substance of the legal rule is the same, the focus of the sentence, in other words, the part of the utterance that brings new content and knowledge, is different, i.e., the user in French and the paper copy of the declaration in German and Italian.

Finally, gender inclusiveness (dashed underline in the example) only affects the Swiss German text (*Abnehmer, Abnehmerin*) and is not reproduced in French and Italian, thus in perfect agreement with local usage. At the institutional level, gender inclusiveness is a typical feature of Swiss German that is also gradually influencing the other two drafting languages.

6.5 Conclusions

Swiss law is indirectly affected by EU decisions and legislation, and in recent years many legal scholars have repeatedly pointed the finger at the Europeanisation of Swiss law. Focusing exclusively on linguistic features, the present chapter has tried to look exclusively at the European impact on language, thus bearing in mind the constraints of institutional legal translation. The fact that both institutions are multilingual potentially increases the dynamic of language contact and pushes the boundaries of linguistic equivalence and intra-linguistic concordance. Moreover, dealing in both cases with "authentic translations", equivalence and translation accuracy is sought between different languages and within the legal conventions of every single language. It follows multiple concordances across the different languages and at the intra-linguistic level but also between the two institutions, because Switzerland needs to prove concordance with EU law.

The analysis has considered macro-textual features like content disposition and some micro-linguistic aspects, e.g., terminology, modals, and sentence order.

The results have shown that language is indeed affected by contact with other EU languages but not in a massive way and that the weight of the specific Swiss legal discourse often overcomes the pitfalls of language contact in the case of Switzerland. In this regard, Maiani's observation (2008, 1–2) is also valid in linguistic terms, because the transposition results in "the creation of something new – more or less similar to, but still different from EU Law".

This is evident above all with reference to macro-textual features. The Swiss legal drafter adjusts the EU provisions time after time according to the subject, its scope, extent, and presence in Swiss legislation. The examples of the implementation of the Schengen Agreement – a topic heavily dependent on EU law – have given rise to new legislation, from a drafting point of view, which fits with other Swiss legal and drafting conventions. The same guidelines for the integration of EU law stress repeatedly that implementing EU law equates to drafting Swiss law (Directives de la Confédération sur la technique legislative 2019, 2). Although legislative texts share a standardised hierarchical partition, nowhere is to be found the long preambles and abundant definitions of EU texts. Paragraph divisions and short titles highlight a more synthetic and down-to-earth approach, which is at the heart of the long-standing Swiss tradition of clear writing. Switzerland's semi-direct democracy, with its popular rights of initiative and referendum, has a very concrete impact on legislation and is likely to be put to the vote by citizens.

The micro-linguistic level also shows a certain independence in the reformulation of EU content. Swiss drafters seem to be faithful to the one-sentence rule, and the result is shorter sentences and fewer chains of subordinate clauses. On the contrary, the double multilingual context, and the fact that the German EU version is used as a basis for the Swiss implementation of EU law is not devoid of ambiguities, as has been particularly shown in the translation of modals and in the way information is presented. More corpus-based studies are needed to take these features into account quantitatively and provide a more generalised picture.

Finally, when it comes to Swiss authentic translations, literal translation and visual equivalence are not as evident as in the EU texts. If we consider that German is always the source text, the French and Italian translations – although equivalent in terms of semantic meaning and legal effects – may show quite different patterns. Previous examples have shown that Italian may be translated directly from German, while the Swiss French version seemed to reproduce the EU text. On the contrary, one might have expected a greater closeness between Italian and French, given their common romance origin and similar linguistic structures. With reference to Italian, this linguistic independence has also been highlighted by Canavese (2023, 83). It is indeed an aspect which account for language naturalness and conformity to the linguistic convention of every single language. The concession to gender in the Swiss German version is further proof of this monolingual concordance with the inherent convention of every single language while ensuring semantic equivalence across the other languages.

Notes

1 For a thorough account of institutional translation, see Kang (2009), Koskinen (2011, 2014), and Schäffner et al. (2014).
2 A pivot language is a "bridge" language used as an intermediary language for translation between many different languages.
3 Robertson distinguishes between the "horizontal dimension", i.e., the relation between different language versions in terms of multilingual concordance and the "vertical dimension" that indicates consistency with previous EU versions in the same language and with national legislation in that same language (2015, 41–44).
4 https://transius.unige.ch/en/research/cheu-lex/
5 Each of the parties is responsible for implementing the agreement on its own territory, thus excluding the transferring of any legislative power to a supranational authority. Any change to the agreements requires in fact the consent of both parties, which are not subject to systematic judicial and political monitoring like in the European Economic Area (EEA) or in the European Neighbourhood Policy (ENP). On this subject, Lavenex highlights that "the consensus brought about by the negotiations may be referred to as the acquis helveto-communautaire" (2009, 551).
6 The *Rapport sur l'Intégration* (1999, 36) highlights that "depuis 1988, le Conseil fédéral a essayé, dans les domaines d'importance transfrontalière, d'assurer qu'aucune divergence ne soit créée de manière injustifiée entre l'ordre juridique suisse et le droit communautaire [...]. Dans la pratique, le Parlement et le Conseil fédéral n'adoptent qu'exceptionnellement des actes juridiques qui ne sont pas compatibles. Cependant, la compatibilité ne signifie pas nécessairement une reprise textuelle, mais plutôt l'effort de parvenir à une réglementation équivalente, les divergences formelles ne la compromettant pas".
7 The *Règles d'or de la reprise du droit de l'UE dans le droit suisse* (2019) is a publication of the Linguistic Service of the Federal Chancellery.
8 Directive 2004/38/EC on the right of citizens of the Union and their family members to move and reside freely within the territory of the Member States (https://eur-lex.europa.eu/legal-content/EN/TXT/?uri=celex:32004L0038R%2801%29)
9 In Article 1, Annex 1, AFMP the Contracting Parties (Agent) perform the (Action) of granting nationals of the other contracting parties (Theme involved in the Action) the right to leave (the Goal of the action). In Article 4 of the Directive, the Union citizen (Agent) shall have (Action) the right (Theme, the object of the Action) to travel to another Member State (the Goal of the Action).
10 French abbreviation of *Accord entre la Confédération suisse, d'une part, et la Communauté européenne et ses États membres, d'autre part, sur la libre circulation des personnes.*
11 https://www.fedlex.admin.ch/eli/cc/2002/261/fr
12 Ordinance on admission, residence, and gainful activity.
13 Directives de la Confédération sur la technique législative (DTL): https://www.bk.admin.ch/apps/gtr/fr/index.html
14 This example is also listed on page 9 of *Règles d'or de la reprise du droit de l'UE dans le droit suisse* (2019).
15 EC Regulation 561/2006 of the European Parliament and of the Council of 15 March 2006 on the harmonisation of certain social legislation

relating to road transport: https://eur-lex.europa.eu/legal-content/EN/ALL/?uri=CELEX%3A32006R0561
16 Ordonnance sur la durée du travail et du repos des conducteurs professionnels des véhicules automobiles (Ordonnance sur les chauffeurs, OTR 1): https://www.fedlex.admin.ch/eli/cc/1995/4031_4031_4031/fr
17 Lois fédérale sur les denrées alimentaires et les objets usuels (Lois sur les denrées alimentaires, LDAI): https://www.fedlex.admin.ch/eli/cc/2017/62/fr
18 EC No 178/2002 of the European Parliament and of the Council of 28 January 2002 laying down the general principles and requirements of food law, establishing the European Food Safety Authority and laying down procedures in matters of food safety: https://eur-lex.europa.eu/legal-content/EN/ALL/?uri=celex%3A32002R0178
19 Ordonnance sur la sécurité des machines (Ordonnance sur les machines, OMach): https://www.fedlex.admin.ch/eli/cc/2008/263/fr
20 Directive 2006/42/EC of the European Parliament and of the Council of 17 May 2006 on machinery: https://eur-lex.europa.eu/legal-content/EN/TXT/?uri=celex%3A32006L0042
21 Ordonnance sur la sécurité des équipements de protection individuelle (Ordonnance sur les EPI, OEPI): https://www.fedlex.admin.ch/eli/cc/2017/635/fr?manifestation=https:%2F%2Ffedlex.data.admin.ch%2Ffilestore%2Ffedlex.data.admin.ch%2Feli%2Fcc%2F2017%2F635%2F20180421%2Fde%2Fhtml%2Ffedlex-data-admin-ch-eli-cc-2017–635–20180421-de-html-4.html
22 Council Regulation EU 264/2012 of 23 March 2012 amending Regulation (EU) No 359/2011 concerning restrictive measures directed against certain persons, entities, and bodies in view of the situation in Iran: https://eur-lex.europa.eu/legal-content/EN/TXT/?uri=CELEX%3A32016R0425
23 French is a common language between the two contracting parties, and English has become more and more the universal lingua franca of many international institutions.
24 In Article 2, Section 10, in General and final provisions: "I titolari di *una carta di soggiorno* di durata inferiore a un anno hanno diritto al rinnovo del proprio *permesso di soggiorno* senza che possa essere contestato loro l'esaurimento dei contingenti". This is not the case of French and German that look consistent with the previous term.
25 Regulation EU 305/2011 laying down harmonised conditions for the marketing of construction products and repealing Council Directive 89/106/EEC Text with EEA relevance: https://eur-lex.europa.eu/legal-content/EN/TXT/?uri=celex%3A32011R0305
26 Ordonannce sur les produits de construction (OPCo): https://www.fedlex.admin.ch/eli/cc/2014/496/fr
27 The English version also mentions *may*.

References

Amstutz, Marc. "Evolutorische Rechstsmethodik im europäischen Privatrecht - Zur richtlinienkonformen Auslegung und ihren Folgen für den autonomen Nachvollzug des Gemeinschaftsprivatrechts in der Schweiz". In *Le droit privé Suisse face au droit communautaire européen*, edited by Franz Werro & Thomas Probst, 105–144. Bern: Stampfli, 2005.

Bhatia, Vijay K. and Aditi Bhatia. "Legal discourse across cultures and socio-pragmatic contexts", *World Englishes*, 30, no.4 (2011): 481–495.

Biel, Łucja. "Quality in institutional EU translation: Parameters, policies and practices". In *Quality aspects in institutional translation* edited by Tomáš Svoboda, Łucja Biel & Krzysztof Łoboda, 31–57. Berlin: Language Science Press, 2017.

Biel, Łucja. "Theoretical and methodological challenges in researching EU legal translation". In *Legal translation: Current issues and challenges in research; Methods and applications*, edited by Ingrid Simonnaes & Marita Kristiansen, 25–39. Berlin: Frank &Timme, 2019.

Canavese, Paolo. "Translation and clarity in Swiss multilingual legislation: A qualitative study on textuality", *The International Journal for Translation & Interpreting*, 15, no.2 (2023): 77–95.

De Rossa Gisimundo, Federica. "Interpretazione del diritto svizzero secondo il diritto europeo recepito autonomamente?", *RtiD* (2010): 329–356.

Derlén, Mattias. "A single text or a single meaning: Multilingual interpretation of EU legislation and CJEU case law in national courts". In *Language and culture in EU law: Multidisciplinary perspectives*, edited by Susan Šarčević, 53–72. Farnham: Ashgate, 2015.

European Union. *Joint practical guide of the European parliament, the council, and the commission for persons involved in the drafting of European Union legislation.* Luxembourg: Publication Office of the European Union, 2016. https://op.europa.eu/en/publication-detail/-/publication/3879747d-7a3c-411b-a3a0-55c14e2ba732

Federal Chancellery. *Directives de la Confédération sur la technique législative (DTL).* Bern: Federal Chancellery, 2019. https://www.bk.admin.ch/apps/gtr/fr/index.html?_toc348089268.html.

Federal Chancellery, Central Language Services. *Règles d'or de la reprise du droit de l'UE dans le droit suisse.* Bern: Federal Chancellery, 2019. https://www.bk.admin.ch/bk/fr/home/documentation/accompagnement-legislatif/reprise-du-droit-de-lue--aspects-formels/instruments.html#-373759508.

Federal Council. *Suisse-Union européenne: Rapport sur l'intégration*, 1999, https://www.fedlex.admin.ch/eli/fga/1999/4__3600_/fr.

Felici, Annarita. "Translating EU law: Legal issues and multiple dynamics", *Perspectives: Studies in Translatology*, 18, no.2 (2010): 95–108.

ISO. *ISO 17100: translation services- requirements for translation services*, 2015, https://www.iso.org/standard/59149.html.

Jenni, Sabine, "Europeanization of Swiss law-making: Empirics and rhetoric are drifting apart", *Swiss Political Science Review*, 20, no.2 (2014): 208–215.

Kang, Jie-Hae. "Institutional translation". In *Routledge encyclopaedia of translation studies*, edited by Mona Baker & Gabriela Saldanha, 141–144. London and New York: Routledge, 2009.

Koskinen, Kaisa. "Institutional translation". In *Handbook of translation studies*, Vol. 2, edited by Yves Gambier, 54–60. Philadelphia: Johns Benjamins, 2011.

Koskinen, Kaisa, "Institutional translation: The art of government by translation", *Perspectives: Studies in Translatology*, 22, no.4 (2014): 479–492.

Kurzon, Dennis, "Legal language': Varieties, genres, registers, discourses", *International Journal of Applied Linguistics*, 7, no. 2. (1997): 119–139.

Lavenex, Sandra. "Switzerland's flexible integration in the EU: A conceptual framework", *Swiss Political Science Review*, 15, no.4 (2009): 547–575.

Maiani, Francesco. "Legal Europeanization as legal transformation: Some insights from Swiss "Outer Europe", *EUI Working Papers MWP* 2008/32 (2008): 1–18.

Mori, Laura. *Observing Eurolects: corpus analysis of linguistic variation in EU Law*. Amsterdam: John Benjamins Publishing House, 2018.

Oesch, Matthias, "Switzerland- EU bilateral agreements, the incorporation of EU law and the continuous erosion of democratic rights", *Yearbook of European Law*, 39, no.1 (2020): 602–639.

Prieto Ramos, Fernando, "Translating legal terminology and phraseology: Between inter-systemic incongruity and multilingual harmonization", *Perspectives: Studies in Translatology*, 29, no.2 (2021): 175–183.

Robertson, Colin. "EU multilingual law: Interfaces of law, language and culture". In *Language and culture in EU law: Multidisciplinary perspectives*, edited by Susan Šarčević, 33–52. Farnham: Ashgate, 2015.

Šarčević, Susan. *New approach to legal translation*. The Hague: Kluwer Law International, 1997.

Schäffner, Christina, Luciana Sabina Tcaciuc & Wine Tesseur, "Translation practices in political institutions: A comparison of national, supranational, and non-governmental organisations", *Perspectives: Studies in Translatology*, 22, no.4 (2014): 493–510.

Vahl, Marius and Nina Grolimund. *Integration without membership: Switzerland's bilateral agreements with the European Union*. Brussels: Centre for European Policy Studies, 2006.

7 Simplification of Legal Language and Turkishization of the Turkish Constitutions of 1924, 1961, and 1982

Ömer Faruk Gençkaya and Şeref İba

The paramount criterion in the Venice Commission of the Council of Europe's Rule of Law Checklist is the predictability of law (Venice Commission 2016). Consequently, it is imperative to prepare legislation in a language that is accessible to everyone, and it is vital for new regulations to explicitly amend current ones. The criterion of legal stability and consistency is of considerable significance in this context. Consequently, any requisite modifications to legislation must encompass the public's knowledge. The necessity for simplification in legal terminology arises from the concept that the language employed must be unambiguous and comprehensible.

Modern law is not an aim in itself but rather a means to achieve social fairness. While Hobbes and Locke believed that the law should safeguard liberty, Kant defined a balance between individual liberty and the rights of others, and Bentham believed that the law should aim to maximize the happiness of as many people as possible (Brunner 2007; Watkins 2019). The legal framework and judicial systems are essential for societal functioning (Funk 1972). Normative law prescribes actions to take or avoid, while social law promotes desirable behavior and prevents undesirable behavior. However, due to their antiquated and intricate vocabulary, protracted phrases, and numerous clauses, legal documents can often be difficult for the general populace to comprehend (Cemri, Çukur, and Koç 2022). In almost all countries, legal practitioners employ legal language, a specialized sublanguage characterized by intricate terminology, to enhance precision and clarity in written documents. As a result, simplifying legal texts is critical to improving the comprehensibility of legal documents for the general public and legal professionals and crucial for ensuring access to and effective exercise of fundamental rights for all citizens (Mendes et al. 2021). The use of old and challenging-to-understand words and phrases, like "witnesseth," "hereinafter," and "injunction," along with Latin and French phrases like "*mens rea*" (criminal intent), "*prima facie*" (at first appearance), and "*actus reus*" (guilty act), makes legal texts challenging to understand. Another reason is that legal texts have long sentences and

DOI: 10.4324/9781003430308-9

lots of clauses (Garimella et al. 2022; Collantes et al. 2015). As technology advances and globalizes today, native languages continue to absorb the influence of other languages through various interactions among nations (Heyd 1954; Miller 2012) or the legal terminology of the dominant languages throughout history (Baker 1998; Martin 2018).

The concept of law definitely arose in antiquity for both the Turks and other civilizations. Legal interpretation of Turkish society, initially recorded during the Uyghur period (Özyetgin 2011), has evolved in response to social and cultural transformations (Şen 2014). The Seljuk era (10th century) adopted Islamic law, primarily customary law, to reconcile ancient Turkish customs with unwritten law based on kut and custom. After the disintegration of the Anatolian Seljuk State, Karamanoğlu Mehmet Bey declared Turkish as the official language in 1277 in all Anatolian principalities (Yılmaz 2020, 147). However, during the Ottoman period, Arabic and Persian emerged as influential administrative languages. Thus, language duality emerged: the palace language and the public language.

Arabic terminology supplanted them at the advent of Islam and remained unchanged during the *Tanzimat* period (1839–1876), when the orientation toward Westernization commenced (Davison 1963). Until the late Ottoman Empire, the primary language for education in the *madrasahs*, jurisprudence books, and the Ottoman legal system was Arabic. However, due to the widespread use of Turkish in daily life, the courts adopted it as their primary language, with the majority of court records, *fatwas* (decrees), and the Sultan's code of laws written in Turkish. The search for simplification in the language in the Ottoman Empire began after the *Tanzimat Edict* (Yılmaz 2020, 71–81). Mecelle[1] was an important step in the development of the legal language. During the First Ottoman Constitutional Period, the *Kanun-u Esasi*, the 1876 Constitution, ended the use of long sentences and the text-less system in law writing and instead adopted a more precise expression with short and clear provisions (Seyit 2020, 51). The Constitution (Article 18) required knowledge of Turkish, the official language of the state, to enter public service in the Ottoman Empire. Thus, the Turkish language gained constitutional status as an official language. Furthermore, Article 68 of the KE mandated knowledge of Turkish as a prerequisite for a deputy election.

Early Republican reforms challenged the influence of Arabic and Persian terminology in the early years of the Republic (Heyd 1954). Subsequently, the ideals and reforms of Mustafa Kemal Atatürk, the founder of the present Turkish Republic, spurred alterations and advancements in the language, influencing all segments of society. On December 19, 1923, the Commission of Interior Affairs presented the Draft Village Law, a pioneering example of using the Turkish language in a plain manner and writing it in a simple and short sentence that the villagers could understand.

This law introduced and established words such as "köy derneği" (village association), "köy sınırı" (village border), "köy orta malı" (village common property), and "sulama" (irrigation) into the legal language for the first time (TBMM 1340). The reform of the alphabet and the elimination of Arabic and Persian courses from the national education curriculum intensified this trend in legal terminology. Besim Atalay Bey, a deputy of Aksaray province, specifically addressed the language of the law on March 19, 1924, and proposed the establishment of a language commission in the parliament to ensure the clear and plain writing of the laws (Seyit 2020, 62). The enactment of the Law of Obligations in 1926 demonstrated the importance of language simplicity. During the legal reforms, there was a conscious effort to focus on language. Meanwhile, the draft bill initiated the amendment of some Persian phrases and terminology in the Rules of Procedure of the GNAT in 1929 (TBMM 1929). However, a brief debate over the proposal resulted in its postponement until the completion of the new Turkish Dictionary, to ensure linguistic unity (Seyit 2020, 69–73). With the adoption of the Law on the Acceptance and Application of Turkish Alphabets in 1928, the tendencies toward purification and simplification in the language accelerated. Out of the two laws that were adopted in 1934, the "Surname Law" played a significant role in the process of Turkishizing the legal language. Instead of old family names (e.g., *Osmanzade*) and nicknames, the Turkish expression (Osmanoğulları) was adopted (Seyit 2020, 78). Adopted earlier in the same year, the Settlement Law of 1934 is considered the first radical purification attempt in the field of legal language. The Temporary Commission of the Settlement Law made modifications to the draft to improve its simplification. For instance, the Commission renamed the draft of the "İskan Kanunu Layihası" as the "Yerleştirme Kanunu" and made numerous revisions to the articles in this respect (Seyit 2020, 80–83). Under Atatürk's leadership, the old words and "pure" Turkish words started to coexist in legal regulations, official correspondence, and official speeches, particularly after 1935 (Seyit 2020, 83–94).

The 1924 Constitution's simplification of language marked the first manifestation of advancements in legal terminology (Seyit 2020; Yılmaz 2020; Lewis 2000). However, in 1952, the newly elected Democrat Party government turned the constitutional text into old Turkish (Lewis 2000, 156). Notwithstanding this alteration, the 1961 Constitution preserved the reduced legal vernacular that had been established in 1945 (Lewis 2000, 128–132). The 1982 Constitution primarily mirrored the text of its predecessor (Lewis 2000, 133). In other words, since then, republicans and conservatives have been engaged in a political dispute over language reform or the simplification of language and legal language, specifically the distinction between new Turkish and old Turkish-Ottoman script. The governments have utilized the Constitution's clarity as a benchmark for other legislation. In the 2000s, legislation in Turkey transitioned from Arabic to Turkish, eliminating most old terms. Books, articles, and court decisions began to use words of Turkish origin, marking the beginning of this change in daily life.

The Justice and Development Party (AK Parti) governments since 2002, known for their conservative approach, have largely embraced this change, over and above the Turkish Civil Code of 2001 (Gözler 2021, 10). Modifications and simplifications in legal terminology have consistently influenced other statutes. Regulations and directives reflect the *Turkishization* of legal language, implicitly associating it with Turkish social life and progressively improving its comprehensibility (Özdemir 2006). However, both the current 1982 Constitution, which has undergone 19 amendments, and the current legislation, particularly the Penal Code adopted in 2005, lack uniformity in terms of vocabulary, grammar, and meaning (Selçuk 2019). Instead of approaching pure *Turkishization* or simplification of the language as merely teaching new words and concepts instead of old ones, it is appropriate to follow a holistic approach that includes semantic and spelling rules. In particular, it is emphasized that simplification of legal language should be done by legal experts as well as linguists (Gözler 2021, 20).

Constitutional texts serve as a crucial record of the language's evolution over a century, revealing its characteristics in terms of sound, spelling, structure, and vocabulary. This study aims to evaluate the simplification of the Turkish legal language and *Turkishization* through selected articles from three Republican constitutions, namely, the 1924, the 1961, and the 1982. As previously noted, the process of Turkishizing the language has accelerated since the Republican era, particularly in the legal domain. State elites initially initiated this process, which later evolved due to the intricate social, economic, and political dynamics of organizations; legal practitioners; and particularly the rulings of the Supreme Court (Constitutional Court). This process has also enhanced the people's comprehension of legal regulations and their access to justice. Several studies have analyzed the Constitution, the law, and court decisions that have to do with it. These have included the history of constitutional language (Aksoy 1964; Eroğul 1995); how words, concepts, phrases, and syntax are organized (Aydemir 2010 and 2014; Gaddar 2020; Gözler 2021; Özdemir 2003 and 2006); the role of mother tongue in writing legal texts (Selçuk 2019); how legal language is simplified, transformed, and adapted (Arslan 2019; Yılmaz 2022; Seyit 2020); the gender perspective (Bora-Çınar 2023); and comparative perspectives (Altay-Akansel 2002). This study is unique in its examination of the evolution of language use across the three constitutions. After briefly introducing the background of *Turkishization* in the language and legal system, we will examine the simplification, vocabulary, and syntax of the original and amended texts of the 1924, 1961, and 1982 constitutions.

7.1 Simplification of Language: The Late Ottoman State and the Republic of Turkey

The need for simplification in language is the expectation of being able to "explain" and "understand" spoken varieties of language (phonology, morphology/lexicon, syntax, and semantics) as well as written forms of language. Various aspects, such as common vocabulary, minimal compound words, idiomatic expressions, and fewer inflectional morphemes, reflect language simplicity (Tweissi 2007). This is due to the reduced number of subordinate clauses, the significance of the present tense in comprehending time, the absence of embeddings and S-nodes, and the frequent use of the topic-comment structure. At the semantic level, the use of hyponyms and the avoidance of ambiguous words further enhance the clarity of meaning in language. Language simplification involves various modifications to a language's sound system, inflectional and lexical aspects, syntactic structure, and semantic features. Such modifications are reportedly efficient in rendering a language easier to perceive, use, and learn. Keeping other factors constant (Crystal 2003), while a language with simpler linguistic features (easier to perceive, use, and learn) and a flexible orthographic system will facilitate the transmission of knowledge, it also may become a global language.

In particular, the Ottoman intellectuals of the 19th century held expectations of linguistic simplification as they reorganized their lives. They imagined that language serves as a tool not only for communication but also for the development of thought, its transmission to others, its nationalization, and the creation of the necessary conditions for the establishment of a political freedom regime. The Tanzimat Era faced a resurgence of legal language through the implementation of new laws and legal institutions derived from France. However, since some terms that entered Turkish law through codifications inspired by French law did not have Turkish equivalents, the use of Arabic and Persian terms continued (Ejder 2022, 76). During this period, the legal procedures incorporated phrases such as "mukavelat muharriri" (later known as "katibiadl," notary), "muhami" (trust), and "müddeiumumi" (prosecutor) and created their equivalents to accurately represent these concepts. The Court of Appeals, the Court of Cassation, the Council of State, and the Court of Accounts were established (Berkes 1964, 160–172). In the late Ottoman Empire, Mehmet Emin Ali Pasha, the Minister of Foreign Affairs, directed his clerks, who had trouble with clear communication, to initially write documents in French and then translate them into Turkish, highlighting issues in administrative language and the urgent need for simplification (Levend 1960, 142). During this period, literary authors, periodicals, and newspapers led the way in modernizing language; however, the administration's initiatives in this area lasted until the establishment of the Republic in 1923.

Concerns about the possibility of using a dual script, particularly in state administration, delayed the language reform's transition to the Latin alphabet during the Republican era (Lewis 2000, 31–32). After the GNAT adopted the international numerals on May 20, 1928, the Council of Ministers established the Language Commission ("Dil Encümeni") to explore the feasibility of incorporating Latin letters into the Turkish language. On August 9, 1928, Mustafa Kemal Atatürk introduced the Turkish alphabet to the Republican People's Party meeting. Following a heated debate, the meeting unanimously adopted a resolution to abandon Arabic letters and adopt Turkish letters based on Latin, with the aim of rescuing the nation from ignorance and ensuring the adoption of the Turkish alphabet. Following Atatürk's historic statement, the focus shifted to the alphabet issue, leading to the Law on the Acceptance and Application of the Turkish Alphabet on November 3, 1928. This law mandated the use of the new alphabet for transactions in all state departments, companies, societies, and private institutions. The state opened training courses to teach the new alphabet throughout Anatolia and conducted inspections to expedite the abandonment of the old alphabet. This situation laid the foundation for the anticipated language revolution in a short span of time. Establishing the Turkish Language Research Society on July 12, 1932, led to the 1st Turkish Language Congress on September 26, 1932, and the 2nd Turkish Language Congress on August 18–23, 1934. Held on August 24–31, 1936, the 3rd Turkish Language Congress focused on discussions around the Sun-Language theory, aiming to prove that many foreign words were Turkish and enrich the Turkish vocabulary.

The language of key legislation, including the Civil Code, Code of Obligations, Penal Code, and Enforcement and Bankruptcy Code drafted during the 1920s, exhibited a modest propensity toward purification (Ejder 2022, 90–106, 109–110). The transformation of constitutional language to pure Turkish in 1945 was a significant milestone in legal terminology. The removal of Arabic-derived terms from fundamental legislation culminated at the turn of this century. Adopted in 1988 (Law No. 3488) and 2007 (Law No. 5637), the codifications of the "Repeal of Laws That Are No Longer Implementable" significantly reduced the influence of old languages, such as Ottoman, Persian, and Arabic, on the Turkish legal system (İba 2009). However, the Presidential Legislation Information System indicates that some legislation formerly known as Ottoman Laws is still in effect (Ejder 2022, 75).

7.2 The Language of the Turkish Constitutions of 1924, 1961, and 1982

According to a study on the vocabulary and syntax in the Turkish Constitutions (Özdemir 2003, 76–82), the 1982 Constitution consists of 60% Turkish, 37% Arabic and Persian, and 3% words from other languages (French, Italian, Russian, and Greek); the 1961 Constitution consists of 62% Turkish, 36% Arabic and Persian, and 2% words from other languages (French, Italian, Russian, and Greek); the 1952 Constitution consists of the 1924 Constitution, which consists of 75% Arabic, 21% Turkish, and 4% Persian. The 1945 Constitution consists of 62% Turkish, 31% Arabic, 6% Persian, and 1% words from other languages (French, Italian, and Greek). The 1921 Constitution consists of 78% Arabic, 21% Turkish, and 1% Persian and Italian, and the 1876 Constitution consists of 72% Arabic, 24% Turkish, and 4% Persian words. The vocabulary of Turkish Constitutions consists of, on average, 65% Arabic, 29% Turkish, 3% Persian, and 3% other languages (French, Italian, Russian, and Greek).

Ottoman law consisted of Arabic-based religious law (Sharia), which originated primarily in *fiqh* (İpşirli 2003), and customary law (*Kanunname*), generally written in Turkish, which was based on the legislative authority of the sultans (İnalcık 2001). The *Kanun-i Esasi*, the first Ottoman Constitution of 1876, is one of the most important legal texts of the pre-Republican period. The *Kanun-i Esasi* did not contribute any innovations to the grammar or vocabulary of the Turkish legal language. The *Kanun-i Esasi*, like the laws of that era, penned this Constitution in Turkish with an eloquent style, incorporating 75% Arabic words and extensive Persian and Arabic phrases.

A radical change occurred in 1945, which shaped the legal terms in the Constitution. The new education system, which had removed Arabic and Persian courses from the curriculum in the early years of the Republic, laid the foundation for this change. The constitutional text removed most Ottoman terms and replaced them with Turkish equivalents. Despite the swift adoption of most of these terms, political reasons led to the translation of the Constitution into the old language in 1952. Most of the new terms used in the 1945 text of the 1924 Constitution, along with new ones, found their way into the later adopted 1961 and 1982 constitutions. Turkish rules replaced Arabic and Persian rule-based phrases, adapting them to the logic of the language. For example, instead of *mürur-u zaman* (zamanaşımı, statute of limitations) or *fevka'l-ade hal'* (olağanüstü hal, state of emergency), new terms such as "salt çoğunluk" (absolute majority) were used.

In 1945, the Turkish Constitution underwent a significant change in legal terms due to the removal of Arabic and Persian courses from the formal education system (Ejder 2022, 112–119). Turkish words now make up 60% and 70% of the texts, with Turkish equivalents replacing most Ottoman (old Turkish) terms. Turkish adapts rule-based phrases from Arabic and Persian to the logic of the language. While the constitutions of 1876, 1921, and 1924 followed traditional spelling, there were traces of phonetic spelling in 1876 and possibly earlier. Terms like "bağıt" (contract), "salt çokluk" (absolute majority), and "kamutay" (assembly), which do not appear in subsequent documents, represent the failure aspect of the proposals put out in 1945. Certain phrases either remained unused or experienced structural modifications.

The Turkish constitutional language underwent simplifications. Words and phrases in the Ottoman (old Turkish) such as *divani muhasebat*, *başvekil*, *divanı ali*, *idarei örfiye*, *icra*, *idare*, *kaza*, *teşri*, *hakim*, *ademi devam*, *adedi mürettep*, *hazar*, *ıskat etmek*, *istihkak*, *istimlak*, *itimat*, *mahremiyet*, *meccani*, *murakabe*, *müruruzaman*, *saldhiyet*, *takyidat*, *vekalet*, and *müttehem* were replaced by new terms "sayıştay"(court of accounts), "başbakan" (prime minister), "yüce divan" (supreme court), "sıkıyönetim" (martial law), "yürütme" (executive), "yönetim" (administration), "yargı" (judiciary), "yasama" (legislative), "yargıç" (judge), "devamsızlık" (absence), "tamsayı" (total number), "barış" (peace), "düşürmek" (bring down the government), "hak ediş" (entitlement), "kamulaştırma" (expropriation), "güven" (confidence), "gizlilik" (confidentiality), "parasız" (gratuitous), "denetleme" (audit), "zaman aşımı" (statute of limitations), "yetki" (authority), "kısıntı" (restriction), "bakanlık" (ministry), and "sanık" (defendant) (Özdemir 2003, 96).

The 1921 Constitution (*Teşkilat-Esasiye Kanunu*) is a succinct document consisting of 24 articles, accompanied by a miscellaneous article that functions as a transitional provision. Compared to earlier times, the language used in the three-article introductory provisions is pretty simple. However, it is still clear that they contain words, ideas, compound verbs, phrases, and foreign suffixes that come from Arabic. The 1921 Constitutional Law comprises 633 words. One hundred and forty-four of these words originate in Turkish. The proportion of words of Turkish origin in the overall text is 23%. Of the word suffixes, 82% are derived from Turkish, whereas 18% originate from foreign sources (Özdemir 2006, 53–55). These percentages closely resemble those in the 1876 Constitution. This example illustrates that the syntax adheres to Turkish conventions and aligns with Turkish cognitive frameworks. We analyzed 73 terms in the texts of the 1921 and 1982 constitutions. The comparison of phrases created according to foreign norms to the total quantity of words yields a result of 9.63%. This rate ranks as the second highest among constitutional documents. Conversely, there has been a notable rise in the development of word groupings in conformity with Turkish regulations. Turkish inflectional suffixes link the aforementioned words to sentences that follow Turkish grammatical standards, such as "election to the Grand National Assembly" and "the terms of membership."

The 1924 Constitution ((*Teşkilat-Esasiye Kanunu*) comprises 106 articles, including one temporary article. This language is far more elaborate and comprehensive than the 1921 Constitutional Law. This text also encompassed novel notions that emerged in Turkish social life following the proclamation of the Republic. As a result, there were minor differences in terminology compared to the previous period. The 1924 Constitution comprises a total of 2,587 words. Six hundred and twenty-four of these words originate in Turkish. The proportion of words of Turkish origin in the overall text is 24% (Özdemir 2006, 63). In the analysis of the selected articles, 80% of the additions are of Turkish provenance, while 20% are of foreign origin. The frequency of Turkish suffixes in these articles is six (6) points lower than that in the 1876 Kanun-Esasi. This circumstance neither impedes nor facilitates the processing of syntax in accordance with Turkish norms. Similar to the 1921 Constitution, Turkish principles conceptualize the underlying logic. Conversely, despite the decrease in Turkish regular phrases since 1921, Turkish rules prevail throughout the book. The text contains 1,587 words and includes 250 sentences composed utilizing foreign rules or elements. The comparison of the percentage of phrases formed with foreign rules or constituents to the total word count yields 9.66%. This rate is the highest among constitutional documents (Özdemir 2006, 66–68).

There are 2,423 words in the 1945 version of the 1924 Constitution; more than two-thirds (66%) of them are of Turkish origin (Ejder 2022, 119). Examining these three selected articles in relation to their annexes yields the following results: Of the 158 annexes in the text, 157 (almost 100%) are of Turkish origin. This data further demonstrates that Turkish grammar rules triggered the formation of syntax in the Constitution. One can conclude from this that the main logic follows Turkish rules, as stated in the 1921 Constitution. For instance, a 96% Turkishization rate in the three examined articles is observed (Özdemir 2006, 78). Despite the absence of foreign syntax rules, this text contained seven foreign phrases totaling 2,423 words. The ratio of phrases formed with foreign suffixes to the total number of words is 0.3%. This is the lowest rate among all Turkish constitutional texts. Legislation and legislative amendments adopted during this period reflected the simplification efforts in the Constitution. Among these, notable examples include the Law on Changing the Names of Certain Months; the Law on Judges; the Law on Labour and Employer Unions and Trade Union Associations; the General Accounting Law; the Provincial Administration Law; and the efforts to harmonize the terms used in the Law of Obligations, the Civil Code, and the Commercial Code (Seyit 2020, 121–131).

The Republican era's language simplification attempts, coupled with the shift in political power during the 1950 elections, politicized the language issue. The Democrat Party defined the Turkishification attempts as the creation of a fake language (seyit 2020, 131–145). The 1952 revisions restored the 1924 Constitution to its original form, which includes the amendments made to it until 1937 (Ejder 2022, 119–127; Seyit 2020, 145–158).[2] One can categorize these changes into three areas: phrase formation, word structure, and inflectional suffixes (Özdemir 2006, 88–90). The Court of Cassation, also known as Mahkeme-i Temyiz (or later printed as "Temyiz Mahkemesi" in Turkish), is an exception to this rule, and all other institution names remain unchanged. The goal was to Turkishize phrases, abandoning Persian rules and applying Turkish ones. The main element, the complement, was placed at the end of phrases, and auxiliary elements were listed before the main element, resulting in phrases that aligned with the logic of the Turkish language (Özdemir 2006, 88). For instance, the phrase "Âdâb-ı mu'âşeret-i umûmiye," which was made according to the Persian rule, was adapted to the Turkish phrase rule and changed to "umumi muaşeret âdabı" (general etiquette). Moreover, the word "kavânîn" (legislation) was transformed into the form of "kanunlar hükümleri." Thus, the plural form formed according to the Arabic rule was made compatible with the rule by adding the Turkish plural suffix. Furthermore, the verb "mugayyir olmamak" (not to be contrary) was replaced with a Turkish verb "aykırı bulunmamak." This change is an intriguing example of taking two steps forward and one step back in the simplification of legal language.

While preparing the 1961 Constitution, it was taken as a principle to preserve and not change the words that had become established in the public language, regardless of their origin, and to use new Turkish equivalents as much as possible instead of those that were not adopted Velidedeoğlu (1972, 21), Seyit (2020, 163–171), and Ejder (2022, 128). The 1961 Constitution comprised 179 provisions, 22 of which were provisional, primarily specifying the procedures to be followed until the inaugural elections. A study (Özdemir 2006, 93–96) that evaluated the vocabulary of the 1961 Constitution in three selected articles (Article 20 Freedom of Thought; Article 62 Right to Petition; and Article 130 Exploration and Operation of Natural Resources) shows that there is a significant increase in the number of words and phrases of Turkish origin. The text includes foreign-origin words like authority ("makam"), assembly ("meclis"), nation ("millet"), owner ("sahip"), complaint ("şikâyet"), homeland ("vatan"), law ("kanun"), judgment ("hüküm"), and permission ("izin"), which are still in use today, despite a noticeable decrease in the number of foreign elements. There are 9,316 words in the 1961 Constitution, of which 5,833 are of Turkish origin (63%). Of the 117 prefixes or suffixes in the text, 115 (98%) are of Turkish origin, and only the remaining 2% are of foreign origin, indicating the fact that word syntax is made in accordance with Turkish rules. The language of the 1961 Constitution and subsequent scholarly studies, high court decisions, and published legal dictionaries were influential in simplifying the laws made in the following period (Seyit 2020, 177–1999), such as the preliminary draft of the 1971 Civil Code and the legal language, and they also influenced the language of the new Civil Code of 2001 (Ejder 2022, 130–131). Throughout the 1970s, political polarization led to the emergence of a duality regarding legal terminology (Seyit 2020, 211–214).

Despite the preceding developments and general approach to the military coup on September 12, 1980, the language of the 1982 Constitution appears to have followed the path of previous constitutions (Seyit 2020, 221). The 1982 Constitution is the most comprehensive document regarding terminology and content among all Turkish Constitutions. It comprises 193 articles, of which 16 are provisional ones. The aforementioned source (Özdemir 2006, 102–106) analyzes the counterparts of articles from the 1961 Constitution in the 1982 Constitution. It cannot be representative of the entire constitutional text; 62 of the 136 words in the three relevant articles (46%) come from Arabic or Persian, while the remaining 74 words (54%) come from Turkish. Of the total 16,752 words in the 1982 Constitution, 12,211 words (73%) are of Turkish origin. Examining these three articles in terms of their prefixes or suffixes reveals that 149 (98%) of the text's 152 are Turkish, while the remaining three (3) are of foreign origin. In summary, the syntax followed Turkish rules, similar to the 1961 Constitution, and the principal logic followed Turkish standards, just like previous constitutional documents.

7.3 A General Assessment

The founders of the Turkish Republic recognized the importance of language reform in nation-building. First, the language reform initiatives, supported by laic education and legal reforms, focused on the nation-state and nationalism as non-linguistic elements (Güven-Kılıçarslan 2022, 1670–1671). A formal education system and legal reforms standardized the official language, solidifying the Turkish language's identity and empowering the nation to embrace modernization and European civilization's ideals. Moreover, the language committee, a politically authoritative decision-making body, emphasized participation and published books to facilitate the use of pure Turkish. The Turkish Language Society played a crucial role in this process and developed a dictionary to standardize corpus planning, removing foreign elements and elevating the language's status.

Starting in the multiparty era, opposition to these developments politicized the language issue, affecting the language of the Constitution and various legal regulations. The societal division of the 1970s into political factions reinstated linguistic duality, rendering language purification institutions useless ideologically. The post-1980 military coup period highlighted the "living language" perspective, which further obstructed the processes of simplification and purification of legal language. Tracing its roots to the Ottoman Empire, the current political power in Turkey primarily advocates for language simplification and the use of public-friendly legal terminology. The president's direct or indirect influence on appointments in the higher judiciary will intensify the trend toward outdated and vague language, thereby transforming it into "a language of political power." This trend aligns with the concentration of power in a single individual who can approach law as an objective, method, or obstacle. The rigid dichotomy between law and politics, defined as "ours" and "yours" or ally and adversary, has the potential to undermine the rule of law. The sensitivities of the courts that interpret the laws in force also vary regarding the issue of pure Turkish. The political power cannot consider the advocates of pure Turkish, who represent a progressive political understanding, and the opponents, who present the discourse of "the language that the people can understand" in isolation.

Similar to how French, Latin, and old English interacted to shape the evolution of legal English and link it to political developments and legal professionals' language use (Durant and Leung 2016), among other factors, political conjuncture appears to have a significant influence on the future of Turkish legal language. The evolution of legal language in Turkey is open to the positive and negative effects of globalization, technological developments such as artificial intelligence and the internet, as well as its close political, economic, and social relations with the European Union and the Council of Europe. Realistically, legal documents need to maintain consistency, withstand adversarial attacks, be anti-discriminatory, and decontextualize for future interpretation by legal experts, academics, and legal practitioners.

Notes

1 *Mecelle-i Ahkam-ı Adliye*, or simply *Mecelle*, was a codex of Islamic private law rules compiled by a commission headed by Ahmet Cevdet Pasha between 1868 and 1876 and used in sharia courts. Şerif Arif Mardin, "Some Explanatory Notes on the Origins of the 'Mecelle' (Medjelle)," *Muslim World*, 51(4), 1968: 274–279.

2 The intriguing aspect of this amendment proposal is the signature of Democratic Party Prime Minister Adnan Menderes, who also signed the 1945 simplification proposal.

References

Aksoy, Ö. A. 1964. "Anayasanın Dili." *Türk Dili Araştırmaları Yıllığı - Belleten* 11: 39–62.

Altay-Akansel, A. 2002. "İngilizce ve Türkçe hukuk dillerinin özellikleri: karşılaştırmalı bir çalışma." *Hacettepe Üniversitesi Edebiyat Fakültesi Dergisi* 19(2): 13–32.

Arslan, Serhat. 2019. "Diliçi Çeviri: Hukuk Metinlerinin Günümüz Türkçesine Uyarlanması Örneği ve Hukuk Terminolojisine Bağlı Sorunlar." In *Terminoloji ve Çeviri*, edited by Fadime Çoban, 123–140. İstanbul: Aktif yayınevi.

Aydemir, İ. A. 2010. "Türk Hukuk Dili Üzerine Araştırmalar I." *Türk Dili Araştırmaları Yıllığı-Belleten* 58(2): 19–36.

Aydemir, İ. A. 2014. "Türk Hukuk Dili Üzerine Araştırmalar II." In *Prof. Dr. Mehmet Özmen Armağanı*, 47–60. Adana: Çukurova Üniversitesi.

Baker, J. H. 1998. "The Three Languages of the Common Law." *Revue de droit de McGill/ McGill Law Journal* 43: 5–24.

Berkes, N. 1964. *The Development of Secularism in Turkey*. Montreal: McGill-Queen's University Press.

Bora-Çınar, S. 2023. "Kadına Karşı Her Türlü Ayrımcılığın Önlenmesi Sözleşmesi (CEDAW) m 2/f Işığında 6102 sayılı Türk Ticaret Kanunu'ndaki Cinsiyetçi İfadelerin Değiştirilmesi Gerekliliği Üzerine Bir Değerlendirme." *İstanbul Hukuk Mecmuası* 81(2): 349–376. https://doi.org/10.26650/mecmua.2023.81.2.0002

Brunner, J. 2007. "Modern Times: Law, Temporality and Happiness in Hobbes, Locke and Bentham." *Theoretical Inquiries in Law* 8(1): 277–310.

Cemri, M., Çukur, T., and Koç, A. 2022. "Unsupervised Simplification of Legal Texts." arXiv.org, 1 September, https://doi.org/10.48550/arXiv.2209.00557

Collantes, M., Hipe, M., Sorilla, J., Tolentino, L., and Samson, B. P. 2015. "Simpatico: A Text Simplification System for Senate and House Bills." *11th National Natural Language Processing Research Symposium*. https://www.researchgate.net/publication/277925965_Simpatico_A_Text_Simplification_System_for_Senate_and_House_Bills.

Crystal, D. 2003. *English as a Global Language*. Cambridge: Cambridge University Press.

Davison, R. H. 1963. *Reform in the Ottoman Empire: 1856–1876*. Princeton: Princeton University Press.

Durant, A. and J. Leung. 2016. Language and Law: A Resource Book for Students. London and New York: Routledge.

Eroğul, C. 1995. "Anayasa ve Tüze Dilinin Türkçeleştirilmesi." *A.Ü. Siyasal Bilgiler Fakültesi Dergisi* 49(3–4): 119–148.

Funk, D. A. 1972. "Major Functions of Law in Modern Society Featured." *Case Western Reserve University Law Review* 23(2): 257–306.

Gaddar, Z. 2020. "Hukuk Dili ve Belirsizlik." *Toplum Bilimleri Dergisi* 28: 261–272.

Garimella, A., Sancheti, A., Aggarwal, V., Ganesh, A., Chhaya, N., and Kambhatla, N. 2022. "Text Simplification for Legal Domain: Insights and Challenges." *Proceedings of the Natural Legal Language Processing Workshop*, V.1: 296–304.

Gözler, K. 2021. *Hukuk Dilinin Öz Türkçeleşmesi Üzerine*. Bursa: Ekin.

Güven Kılıçarslan, Z. 2022. "Language Policy in Turkey and Azerbaijan: A Comparative Approach to the Two Language Reforms". *Littera Turca, Littera Turca Journal of Turkish Language and Literature* 8(2): 1660–1672.

Heyd, U. 1954. *Language Reform in Modern Turkey*. Jerusalem: The Israel Oriental Society.
İba, Ş. 2009. "Hukuk Tarihimizde Mevzuat Ayıklama ve Süpürge Kanular Geleneği Oluşturmak." *Terazi Hukuk Dergisi* 4(29): 185–190.
İnalcık, H. 2001. "Kanunnâme", *TDV İslâm Ansiklopedisi*, https://islamansiklopedisi.org.tr/kanunname
İpşirli, M. 2003. "Medrese", *TDV İslâm Ansiklopedisi*, https://islamansiklopedisi.org.tr/medrese#2-osmanli-donemi
Levend, A. S. 1960. *Türk Dilinde Gelişme ve Sâdeleşme Evreleri*. Ankara, Türk Dil Kurumu Yayınları.
Lewis, G. 2000. *The Turkish Language Reform: A Catastrophic Success*. Oxford: Oxford University Press, 2000.
Malheiros Mendes, M. J., Schmitz Mendes, A. K., de Souza, A. E., Junges, F. C., Mendes, A. C., and Zimmermann de Souza, L. 2021. "Simplification of Legal Language as a Way to Expand Society's Access to Justice." *International Journal for Innovation Education and Research*, 9(10): 454–464.
Mardin, Ş. A. 1968. "Some Explanatory Notes on the Origins of the 'Mecelle' (Medjelle)." *Muslim World* 51(4): 274–279.
Martin, I. P. 2018. "Linguistic Challenges of an English-Dominant Legal System in the Philippines." *Asian Englishes* 20(2): 134–146. https://doi.org/10.1080/13488678.2017.1418716
Miller, D. G. 2012. *External Influences on English: From Its Beginnings to the Renaissance*. Oxford: Oxford University Press.
Özdemir, H. 2003. Türkçenin Sadeleşme Tarihinde Anayasaların Dili. MA Thesis, Ankara University Institute of Social Sciences.
Özdemir, H. 2006. Cumhuriyet tarihinde Hukuk dilindeki değişmeler ve gelişmeler. Ph.D. dissertation. Ankara University Institute of Social Sciences.
Özyetgin, A. M. 2011. "Turfan Uygurlarında Ceza Hukukuyla İlgili Uygulamalar." *Belleten* 75(273): 337–360.
Selçuk, S. 2019. "Ana Dili Bilinci, Türkçe ve Hukuk Dilimiz." D.E.Ü. Hukuk Fakültesi Dergisi, Prof. Dr. Durmuş Tezcan'a Armağan, 21: 3013–3023.
Şen, M. 2014. "The Historical Development of Turkish Law." *HUFS Global Law Review*, 6(2): 65–76.
Seyit, G. 2020. *Türkiye'de Hukuk Dilinin Dönüşümü*. İstanbul: Oniki Levha Yayınları, 2. Baskı.
TBMM Zabıt Ceridesi, D.3, Y.3, C.X, B.59, 29.4.1929.
TBMM Zabıt Ceridesi, Devre 2, Y.1, C VI, B.108, O.2, 21.2.1340, s. 236–238.
Tweissi, A. I. 2007. "Language Simplification and Language Globalization." *International Journal of Arabic-English Studies (IJAES)* 8: 141–150.
Velidedeoğlu, H. V. 1972. *1961 Anayasasının Dili*. Ankara: TDK yayını.
Venice Commission (European Commission For Democracy Through Law). 2016. *Rule of Law Checklist*. Strasbourg: Council of Europe.
Watkins, E. 2019. *Kant on Laws*. Cambridge: Cambridge University Press. https://doi.org/10.1017/9781316683026
Yılmaz, E. 2020. *Hukuk Dilinin Gelişmesi ve Sadeleşmesi*. Ankara: Yetkin Hukuk Yayınları.

8 The Quest for Legislative Reform in Kosovo

Bridging Regulatory Governance with Legal Drafting and Legislative Language Discourses

Novitet Nezaj

8.1 Introduction

> All those which have written of laws, have written either as philosophers or as lawyers, and none as statesmen. As for the philosophers, they make imaginary laws for imaginary commonwealths: and their discourses are as the stars, which give little light because they are so high. For the lawyers, they write according to the states where they live, what is received law, and not what ought to be law.
>
> (Francis Bacon, *Of the Proficience and Advancement of Learning, Divine and Human,* 1605)

What qualities should it have, and in which direction should it evolve? remains a valid question today for language and legislation, especially as artificial intelligence and human interaction grow across societies. This chapter examines the interaction between language and legislation, drawing on interdisciplinary legal analysis and Kosovo case law outcomes. Kosovo serves as a key example, where limited legal scrutiny has negatively impacted legislative development. Despite efforts to align its laws with European Union standards, Kosovo remains in the early stages of achieving successful outcomes. Constitutional challenges persist, with several laws declared unconstitutional due to imprecise drafting and linguistic barriers. The chapter illustrates how rushed legislative processes and vague language have undermined legal clarity, conciseness, and precision.

Language plays a pivotal role in shaping legislation, impacting its clarity, interpretation, and accessibility. In multilingual jurisdictions like the European Union, legislative drafting must account for linguistic diversity to ensure that laws are applied consistently across member states. The use of precise and unambiguous language reduces the risk of misinterpretation, while translation can introduce challenges, as subtle legal nuances may be lost or altered. Effective legislation depends on drafting techniques that incorporate linguistic clarity, fostering a balance between legal precision

DOI: 10.4324/9781003430308-10

and the need for broader comprehension across different linguistic groups. For example, the EU prioritizes drafting in multiple official languages and uses simplified language for consistency across legal systems, ensuring uniformity in implementation.[1]

The conventional history of language and legislation in Kosovo is evolving. When analyzing the background, it is apparent that the language and legislation came from various transitional legal systems. Scholars emphasize the importance of precise language in legislation to prevent legal ambiguities and misinterpretations. Smith argued that national law development always encounters a certain tension between laymen and lawyers.[2] According to Hart, the distinctive characteristics of legal language are to explain the discourse of the law with special features in a simpler model.[3] Lawyers use operative words to differentiate functional language from descriptive language.[4] The diversity of laws appears in many languages and forms, evolving within societies with varied organizations.[5] According to Xanthaki, the normative language used by lawyers and others to describe the content of law should be precise, clear, and consistent, ensuring it effectively conveys legal principles, obligations, and rights, fostering a comprehensive understanding and adherence.[6] Therefore, Kosovo's legislative reform for sustainability is vital for EU accession, requiring alignment with EU standards, strengthening legal frameworks, and addressing implementation deficits. This chapter analyzes Europeanization, explores legal reform dynamics, and recommends regulatory, drafting, and language changes for EU integration.

8.2 Historical Baseline

The language and legislation, as means of communication, serve as tools for common regulation, as highlighted by Roscoe Pound's rules of "social engineering."[7] The relationship between law and language, and vice versa, has been the subject of study by influential schools of thought and scholars since ancient times.[8] Linguistics and legal thought are connected across legal cultures.[9] The European tradition is emphasized for its historical influence on the development of legal language, which continues to play a central role in shaping legislative expressions.[10] In 1958, a key development in shaping legislation and language within the rule of law and the judiciary, conducted in four official languages—French, German, Dutch, and Italian—emerged under European integration.[11] For more than half a century, the European integration process has included a system of 24 official languages, making it the most linguistically diverse legal system in the world. In the context of European integration, it should be noted that the language, structure, and genesis of the treaties reflect a blend of diverse and ever-growing legal cultures.[12] In this regard, the extent and mode of

European integration's impact on domestic policies and administrative structures depend on the specific country's existing policy practices and political and institutional structures.[13]

However, policy practices and institutional structures vary significantly across countries. Although part of Europe, efforts to transplant and codify language and legislation to shape Kosovo's society have led to diverse outcomes. Before declaring independence in 2008, Kosovo's legal landscape was shaped by deeply embedded compromises stemming from past communist struggles and internationally supervised administration. These compromises influenced legislation and language layers, levels, or categories. Influenced by unique historical, cultural, and socio-economic contexts, shaping language for legislation and legislation through language was very challenging. The most critical challenges were establishing institutional and structural principles for drafting legislation and developing legal language based on European best-established practices. These challenges in legislation and language stem from the legacy of former communist rule and transitional administration.

An important step in legislation and language development occurred after Kosovo declared independence in 2008. The principles and provisions of the legislation and language are fundamentally enshrined in the Constitution. The Constitution ensures the application of best legislative practices and consistent use of international standards in both legislation and language. All these theoretical constitutional provisions and principles, intended for practical use, lacked practical application. The practical application has always been a challenging issue for Kosovo's young institutional structures. They faced difficulties in clarifying legislation and language, leading to inconsistencies in legislative characteristics across different subject matters. Foreign projects, along with modern administration and management perspectives, are employed to guide Kosovo's institutional structures in the implementation of practical and productive knowledge.[14]

The historical baseline highlighted key elements essential to understanding the evolution of legislative and language practices. The European integration example shows that significant outcomes in legislation and language can be achieved through a shared purpose and objective. A brief examination of Kosovo's historical baseline reveals that its modern legal frameworks are still evolving. In its journey toward European integration, Kosovo's case highlights the presence of opportunity, meaning its young institutional structures will need to determine actions and anticipate progress gradually. In sum, the historical baseline reveals that Kosovo's legislation and language development are deeply influenced by its past, with challenges rooted in its communist legacy and transitional administration. While European integration offers a model for progress, Kosovo's evolving legal frameworks highlight the need for gradual adaptation of institutional structures to ensure effective legislation and language development. We may conclude that the European integration model, with its principles and provisions on legislation and language, is unquestionably relevant for Kosovo's approach moving forward.

8.3 Law and Legislative Duty between Multiple Streams

Law is traditionally viewed as an "ought," requiring individuals to align their conduct with specific postulates.[15] A strong synthesis between law and legislative duty may combine tradition, data, and inclusiveness.[16] In parallel, they strengthen the country's legal order and advance the law in society. A country's legal order is closely tied to its experience of legal certainty, which is directly influenced shaped by legal language. Many scholars on contemporary legal issues highlight the importance of promoting an effective system of law and legislative duty.[17] The relationship between language and legislative drafting is foundational in creating accessible, clear, and effective laws. By applying linguistic principles, legislative drafters can avoid terms that may obscure meaning or exclude groups. For example, gender-neutral language and simplified sentence structures improve readability and legal understanding, which is especially important for cross-cultural applications. Legal drafters must balance these techniques with legal precision to ensure consistency across jurisdictions. This interdisciplinary approach underscores how linguistics and law combine to serve both legal standards and public comprehension, resulting in legislative texts that are socially relevant and legally enforceable across diverse legal environments.[18]

The traditional roots of preserving and enforcing justice in one country serve as a model for guiding other legal systems. This is because the past practices of preserving and enforcing justice can serve as an imperative model for the present and future. In this context, the imperative includes the objective of promoting societal good through the proper reciprocal use of legislation and language. When evaluating legislation and language aimed at preserving and enforcing justice, one must consider the jurisprudential cases that arise from attempts to establish the validity of ultimate goals.[19]

Data on law and legislative duties require evaluating the value objectives inherent in regulation through legal language. Particularly relevant is the clear record of legislative evolution expressed in legal terms. In Kosovo's case, the data has been somewhat ambiguous, as prior to 2008, legislative developments were often partial and at times contradictory. This complexity arose from multifaceted causes. However, after 2008, Kosovo's institutions began to achieve broader consensus by reviewing legislation from diverse perspectives, including language considerations, using various benchmarks and standards.

In transitional countries, legislative attempts to address or regulate issues often rely on abstract, broad formulas and legal jargon. An over-inclusive use of a word or provision violates the first law of semantics, which requires that dissimilar phenomena should be denominated by different concepts.[20] Complicated language and a lack of clarity in provisions can push legal development in divergent, potentially contradictory, directions. The pursuit of constancy seeks to preserve the status quo, while the drive to eliminate complexity aims to renew the law toward greater equality. The dynamic forces in social and legal life boost the law toward reform, though this progress can sometimes appear misleading due to the legal culture of emancipation in achieving social and legal change. In Kosovo's case, to ensure legislative success, decision-makers must foster a new state of affairs, using legal consolidations based on clear language and coherent legislative principles. At this critical juncture, a new legal language should apply in Kosovo's drafting practice. It balances two approaches: the first seeks to remove conservative and inertial legislative tendencies, while the second focuses on maintaining and aligning Kosovo's legislation with European standards. When the legal system is transformed by removing conservative and inertial legislative tendencies, while aligning Kosovo's legislation with European standards through the actions of politically empowered bodies, the dynamism of the legal and legislative process is enhanced. This results in a legal order characterized by detailed language, significantly contributing to legal certainty within the country.

Freeing the legal order from the conservative and inertial weight of the past allows for its fundamental regeneration. Since 2016, under favorable circumstances brought by the Europeanization process,[21] Kosovo has been able to implement necessary large-scale reforms.[22] The table below provides an overview of Kosovo's legislative progress from 2016 to 2024. It highlights institutional development, focusing on reforms and alignment with EU standards (Table 8.1).

From 2016 to 2024, a recurring concern in Kosovo's legislative landscape has been the inefficiency of the judicial system, compounded by political interference and corruption. Despite efforts to align with European Union standards, the slow pace of judicial reforms, backlog of cases, and non-merit-based public administration appointments have undermined legal and institutional progress. The frequent use of fast-tracking procedures, bypassing thorough legislative debate, has further weakened legal development. Corruption remains a pervasive issue, with inconsistent enforcement of anti-corruption laws and inadequate accountability mechanisms. Political instability and polarization have also hindered the effective implementation of reforms, particularly in ensuring judicial independence and transparency in public administration. However, despite these

Table 8.1 EU Assessment of Kosovo's Scale Reform

Year	*Summary of Legislative Process*	*Weakest Indicators of Legislation*	*Strongest Indicators of Legislation*
2016	The year marks the implementation of the Stabilization and Association Agreement between Kosovo and the EU. The legislative process is influenced by EU norms, with the Assembly playing a critical role in lawmaking.	Major concerns in 2016 include weak political stability, with frequent parliamentary disruptions. Transparency in public administration remains poor.	Kosovo made strides in rule of law reforms, with progress in judicial appointments and meeting requirements for Schengen visa liberalization. The Europeanization process was further integrated into the legal framework.
2018	By 2018, institutional development focused on aligning with EU legal norms. Public financial management reforms and improvements in administrative procedures were key legislative focuses.	Political interference in the judiciary persisted, and public administration remained inefficient. Accountability mechanisms were weak, and the backlog of court cases grew.	Efforts to strengthen the judiciary and public procurement were more visible. Kosovo enhanced anti-corruption measures, establishing investigation teams and prosecuting high-level cases.
2019	Legislative processes became more focused on administrative accountability. Greater emphasis was placed on aligning Kosovo's legal framework with EU standards, particularly in public finance management and anti-corruption efforts.	The judiciary still faced challenges with inefficiency and political interference. Anti-corruption efforts, although initiated, faced roadblocks in implementation. Political and ethnic divisions also created a barrier to progress.	Progress in judicial reform and law enforcement, particularly in customs, public procurement, and financial transparency, provided a solid foundation for future reforms. The adoption of anti-corruption tracking mechanisms boosted confidence.
2020	The institutional focus in 2020 was on solidifying the reforms of previous years, especially in public administration and judicial efficiency. Legislative processes began to stabilize, though challenges remained.	Legislative fast-tracking and lack of parliamentary debate weakened the process. The judicial backlog remained a significant issue, alongside persistent corruption and non-merit-based recruitment in public administration.	Strengthened public financial management reforms and increased transparency in customs were notable successes. Kosovo's international agreements began to yield results, strengthening legal reforms and international cooperation.

(*Continued*)

Table 8.1 (Continued)

Year	*Summary of Legislative Process*	*Weakest Indicators of Legislation*	*Strongest Indicators of Legislation*
2021	Kosovo's institutional reforms continued, with specific attention to judicial independence and accountability. Legislative changes aimed at aligning with EU legal standards were pursued, focusing on the rule of law and anti-corruption.	Despite progress, judicial independence was hampered by political influence. Public sector appointments were still influenced by political factors, and the fight against organized crime remained slow.	The judiciary showed improvements in clearing backlogs, and public procurement reforms helped to reduce corruption. Legal reforms aligned more closely with EU norms, boosting the credibility of Kosovo's institutions.
2022	In 2022, institutional reforms focused on strengthening judicial accountability and reducing political influence. Legislative efforts included further aligning Kosovo's legal system with EU frameworks, particularly in anti-corruption laws.	Political polarization continued to impede reforms. Corruption, inefficiency in the judiciary, and the lack of transparency in political appointments remained key concerns.	The introduction of more transparent procurement processes and international cooperation in law enforcement improved Kosovo's legal infrastructure. Judicial independence saw incremental improvements.
2023	The focus of 2023 was on solidifying rule of law reforms and ensuring legislative alignment with EU standards. Judicial reform and public sector accountability remained legislative priorities.	Challenges remained in implementing reforms in practice, with political influence and corruption continuing to weaken progress. The backlog of judicial cases persisted, and political instability affected governance.	Significant progress was made in anti-corruption measures, with increased international cooperation and enforcement of legal standards. Public financial management reforms were consolidated, contributing to greater transparency and governance.
2024	Kosovo's legislative process struggles with low participation and opposition boycotts, impeding legislation adoption. Strengthening cooperation, transparency, and oversight is essential to stabilize the legislative process, enhance accountability, and improve the Assembly's legislative output efficiency.	Challenges include insufficient public consultations, delayed regulatory impact assessments, and poorly integrated strategic and budget planning processes. Weak inter-ministerial coordination and limited administrative capacity slow down reforms, further affecting the legislative environment and its alignment with EU standards.	Key progress includes updated public administration policies and gender equality initiatives. Enhanced transparency in legislative bodies and targeted strategic reforms support a more robust legislative framework, aiming for gradual EU compliance and public service improvements.

Source: European Commission.

challenges, there has been some significant progress in aligning legislation with EU standards, particularly in public procurement, customs, and anti-corruption measures. Kosovo's legal framework continues to evolve, but the core challenges of judicial inefficiency, corruption, and political influence persist as central issues.

Furthermore, based on the European Commission's remarks, we can argue that the designed system still shows the interplay between reform and stability in legislation and legal language. The failure to maintain coherent reform and stability led to increased complexity. This complexity may be the primary force opposing legislative change and could serve to maintain the status quo. Complex language has hindered accessibility and legal consistency, making legislative texts difficult to interpret and apply uniformly over the years.[23] Thus, law and legislative duty in Kosovo are prompted by multiple streams at varying strengths. To this aim, the interpenetrations between reform and stability in the life of the law in Kosovo should be primarily a living instrument because this will press upon favorable circumstances when law and legislative duty are sufficiently strong to prevent stagnation and a disadvantageous prevalence of regressive tendencies in legislation and language and vice versa.

In sum, the major negative influence impacting the law and legislative duty in Kosovo revolves around the lack of proper implementation and enforcement of existing laws. This issue is compounded by institutional weaknesses, including political influence in appointments, delays in enacting crucial reforms, and a general lack of capacity within legislative and regulatory bodies to ensure compliance with EU standards. These factors hinder legislative progress and obstruct the necessary structural reforms essential for aligning Kosovo's legal framework with EU norms. The integration of linguistic principles in legislative drafting is crucial for Kosovo to ensure accessible, inclusive, and precise laws aligned with EU standards. Addressing linguistic diversity and simplifying legal language will enhance clarity, consistency, and enforceability within the context of EU integration.

8.4 Layers of Constitutional Design

Layers of constitutional design relate to law and legislative duty between multiple streams by structuring lawmaking authority, ensuring legal harmonization, balancing governance priorities, and addressing diverse cultural, linguistic, and political dynamics. The constitutional language of EU member states embodies a form of language constitutionalism, intertwining diverse cultural and linguistic traditions with legal and legislative duties. This dynamic reflects the interplay between national constitutions and EU law, where legislative drafting must align domestic laws with EU standards while preserving local linguistic and cultural identities.[24]

This requires clear, accessible drafting that balances inclusivity and legal precision, fostering effective governance and legal clarity within the multilingual and multicultural framework of the European Union.[25]

Kosovo's constitutional history, the youngest in Europe since 2008, remains an evolving process of legal development.[26] The Constitution upholds strict hierarchical structures and fundamental rights in the development of Kosovo law by subjecting provisions to uniform norms of international law, thereby establishing the principles and conditions of justice. The Constitution of Kosovo is organized along the lines of a hierarchical legal order.

At the top are provisions that establish the fundamental principles, forming the foundation for the entire legislative system. The Constitution of the Republic of Kosovo outlines the fundamental principles of statehood, governance, and the legal system. Articles 1 to 20 set the foundation for Kosovo as a sovereign, democratic, and indivisible state (Article 1), with sovereignty derived from the people (Article 2). It ensures equality before the law and the rule of law in a multi-ethnic society (Article 3). Immediately below them are ranked the provisions on fundamental rights, freedoms, and state powers. The separation of powers defines the Republic of Kosovo's form of government, with distinct roles for the legislative, executive, and judicial branches (Article 4). The official languages are Albanian and Serbian (Article 5), and Kosovo is described as a secular state (Article 8), with protections for its cultural and religious heritage (Article 9).

Various provisions specify principles of international law. The Constitution acknowledges the supremacy of its provisions (Article 16), ensuring that all laws and international agreements conform to its principles. International law is integrated into Kosovo's legal system, with ratified international agreements taking precedence over national laws (Article 19). Kosovo also participates in international organizations and may delegate state powers in specific matters through such agreements (Article 20). At the bottom, there are provisions on state powers. The constitutional system emphasizes clarity and alignment with international norms, ensuring a balance between reform and stability. Legislative initiative, according to Article 79, can be proposed by the president, the government, Assembly deputies, or citizen petition. This structure allows for dynamic legal development while maintaining consistency with both domestic and international legal obligations.

Kosovo's legal framework ensures dual compliance by embedding international obligations (Article 19) and aligning its structure with EU legal supremacy to support future EU accession.[27] In sum, significant elements of Kosovo's constitutional provisions are designed to guide policymakers and decision-makers in their practical application. Thus, it can be argued that Kosovo's constitutional framework enables the pragmatic realization of key principles of the rule of law.

8.5 The Way We Are Governed Now

Establishing an institutional and legal structure for the legislative and regulatory framework is evolving.[28] Kosovo's basic structure and legislative and regulatory framework principles are incorporated within the Constitution, law, regulation, and administrative instructions. They together aim to structure the roles, responsibilities, and procedures of governance, ensuring legal clarity and operational efficiency. For example, the Constitution of Kosovo establishes the fundamental legal structure, focusing on human rights, state institutions, and the rule of law.[29] Meanwhile, the *Law on Government of the Republic of Kosovo* outlines the organization and functioning of the government, particularly defining its relationship with the legislative branch and other state entities, emphasizing accountability and constitutional compliance.[30] Additionally, the *Law on Legislative Initiatives* provides a procedural framework for initiating laws, involving various actors, including the president, government members, parliamentarians, and citizens.[31] This law ensures democratic participation in lawmaking by establishing clear guidelines for proposing and debating legislation. *Regulation on Rules of Procedure of the Government* provides detailed rules for the government's procedural conduct, decision-making, and legislative drafting, with a specific focus on consistency, transparency, and compliance with EU standards.[32] Furthermore, *Administrative Instruction on Standards for the Drafting of Normative Acts* sets out the standards for drafting normative acts, focusing on legal precision, language clarity, and coherence with broader legal frameworks.[33] Mutually, these laws and regulations aim to create a robust, transparent, and legally sound framework for governance, ensuring legislative clarity and consistency across the Kosovo government (Table 8.2).

As an interconnected set of guidelines to ensure the drafting of clear, concise, and unambiguous legislation, they put into effect a set of obligatory procedures regarding legislation and language in lawmaking. Starting with *Law on the Government of Kosovo*, it establishes a solid foundation for how the government should operate within the legal framework of the Constitution and other relevant laws. This law emphasizes principles such as legality, transparency, and professionalism (Article 3) to ensure that all governmental actions are aligned with constitutional and legal mandates (Article 22). These principles also inform the decision-making process, where proposals for legislation must adhere to procedural and constitutional consistency. Further reinforcing this structure, the *Regulation on Rules of Procedure* provides detailed instructions on how to draft, evaluate, and finalize legislative texts. The regulation emphasizes the need for drafting legislation that aligns with EU standards and Kosovo's national development strategies (Article 13), ensuring consistency with the broader

Table 8.2 Key Points on Legal Drafting

Phase	*Processes*	*Requirements for Drafting Legislation*	*Usage of Legal Drafting Language*
Initiation of Legislation	Proposal of legislative initiatives by authorized entities	Legislative initiatives can be taken by:	Clearly state the purpose and scope of the legislative initiative.
	Notification to relevant bodies	President of the Republic (from their scope). Government. Members of Parliament (at least six MPs). At least 10,000 citizens with the right to vote. Initiatives must comply with the Constitution and laws.	Use precise legal terminology to define the intent. Ensure language is consistent with constitutional principles and existing legislation.
Planning and Preparation	Inclusion in Government's Work Plan	The Government's Work Plan must align with:	Use terminology consistent with EU standards when applicable.
	Strategic planning	Government Program.	Align language with strategic objectives and national priorities.
	Coordination with EU integration plans and national strategies	Statement of Government's Medium-Term Priorities. National Program for European Integration. Strategic documents must be consistent with EU *Acquis* and national development strategies.	Ensure clarity in articulating goals and actions.
Drafting of Legislation	Establishment of working groups	Draft laws must adhere to standards set by the Government.	Use clear, concise, and unambiguous language.
	Drafting of concept documents	Concept documents are required to explore policy options.	Ensure legal coherence and consistency with existing legislation.

(*Continued*)

Table 8.2 (Continued)

Phase	*Processes*	*Requirements for Drafting Legislation*	*Usage of Legal Drafting Language*
	Preparation of draft laws and sub-legal acts	Working groups must include representatives from relevant units, other ministries, and stakeholders.	Apply standard legal drafting techniques and structures.
	Compliance checks with existing laws and policies	Alignment with EU *Acquis* when applicable.	Use definitions to clarify terms where necessary.
Consultation and Review	Preliminary consultations	Mandatory public consultation according to established standards.	Present drafts in language understandable to stakeholders.
	Public consultations	Drafts must be reviewed by relevant units in the OPM for compliance with laws and policies.	Incorporate feedback coherently and transparently.
	Inter-ministerial consultations	Incorporate feedback from consultations.	Maintain consistency in terminology across documents.
	Review by relevant units in the Office of the Prime Minister (OPM)	Ensure no conflict with existing or proposed documents.	Use plain language where possible while retaining legal accuracy.
Approval Process	Submission to Government	Proposals must include all required accompanying documents.	Ensure the legal text is precise and aligns with existing laws.
	Government meetings and decision-making	Government decisions are taken by majority vote.	Avoid contradictions and redundancies.
	Submission to Assembly (Parliament) for enactment	Draft laws submitted to the Assembly must meet the conditions set by the Rules of Procedure of the Assembly.	Use formal legislative language appropriate for enactment.
			Draft clear explanatory memoranda to accompany the legislation.

(*Continued*)

Table 8.2 (Continued)

Phase	*Processes*	*Requirements for Drafting Legislation*	*Usage of Legal Drafting Language*
Enactment	Approval by Assembly	Laws must be in accordance with the Constitution.	The final legal text must be clear, coherent, and unambiguous.
	Promulgation by the President	Final texts must adhere to legislative drafting standards.	Use standard legal formulations for enactment clauses and provisions.
	Publication in the Official Gazette	Sub-legal acts must be sent to the OPM and published accordingly.	Ensure all necessary definitions and references are accurate.
		Entry into force as specified in the law.	Language should facilitate effective implementation and enforcement.

Source: Law No. 08/L-117, Law No. 04/L–025, Regulation (GRK) No. 17/2024, Administrative Instruction No. 03/2013.

legal framework (Article 23). Articles 16 to 21 specifically outline the importance of strategic planning and the procedural steps to draft laws, involving cross-ministerial coordination and the use of working groups (Article 23). This fosters coherence across different sectors of the government and mitigates the risk of legal and policy contradictions. *Law on Legislative Initiatives* complements these provisions by enabling various actors—including citizens, parliamentarians, and the government—to initiate legislation in an inclusive, democratic manner. Articles 7–10 of this law are particularly significant in maintaining the integrity of the legislative process, requiring that legislative initiatives comply with constitutional norms and relevant laws (Article 21). Additionally, it introduces mechanisms for reviewing and improving draft laws to ensure they meet legal clarity and policy objectives (Article 21). *Administrative Instruction on Standards for the Drafting of Normative Acts* plays a fundamental role in ensuring consistency and clarity in legislative drafting by defining strict standards for normative acts. It outlines clear rules for how laws and regulations should be formulated, focusing on linguistic accuracy, legal precision, and avoidance of ambiguity (Article 23). The instruction emphasizes that all legal documents must be clear, coherent, and aligned with existing legal norms to prevent contradictions or misinterpretations in their application (Article 23).

Together, these regulatory frameworks form a comprehensive guide to drafting legislation in Kosovo. They provide explicit provisions for ensuring consistency in legal language, avoiding vagueness or ambiguity, and ensuring that all legal texts are coherent with both national and international legal frameworks. By focusing on procedural consistency and cross-sectoral coordination, these regulations and laws aim to produce well-structured, unambiguous legislation that upholds the principles of the rule of law. Obligatory procedures, however, regarding legislation and language in lawmaking, are overridden.[34] We may argue that these overridden procedures resulted from inadequate planning, improper time management, and unclear policy processes. In sum, Kosovo's distorted regulatory enforcement has specifically impacted legislation's linguistic dimension and legal development's unsystematic nature.

8.6 Evolving and Recent Development

Although Kosovo's constitutional framework supports the pragmatic realization of key principles of the rule of law, much of the legislation is marked by indeterminacy, vagueness, ambiguity, or incompleteness. Misconceptions about language use can undermine a clear understanding of the legislation's purpose.[35] This section addresses these potential obstacles. In recent years, Kosovo Constitutional Court cases have documented ruled that the discursive lawmaking processes against the rule of law. As noted in the previous section, procedural inconsistencies, lack of cross-sectoral coordination, unstructured and ambiguous legislation, and overridden procedures because of inadequate planning, poor time management, and unclear policy processes have impacted the linguistic dimension of Kosovo's legislation and the unsystematic nature of legal development.

The following cases from Kosovo's Constitutional Court show an inconsistent focus of proposed legislation on the compatibility with international standards, respectively, the European Convention on Human Rights.[36] These cases highlight the Court's approach to addressing conflicts between domestic laws with constitutional and international legal standards. These cases primarily focus on constitutional articles concerning the form of government, separation of powers, equality before the law, the right to legal remedies, judicial protection of rights, and the right to liberty and security. Furthermore, they highlight concerns over procedural fairness, the wording of legal provisions, and fundamental values.

The main findings in the joint cases KO100-22 and KO101-22, decided by the Constitutional Court, refer to the constitutional review of Law No. 08/L-136 on amending the Kosovo Prosecutorial Council (KPC). The Court found several provisions unconstitutional, particularly regarding the composition of the KPC and the involvement of non-prosecutor members in decision-making processes. The Court emphasized that these provisions violated the principle of separation of powers, judicial independence, and equality before the law, necessitating changes to align with constitutional standards.[37]

In addition, in the joint cases KO216-22 and KO220-22, the Constitutional Court reviewed the constitutionality of various articles of Law No. 08/L-197 on Public Officials. The Court found that several provisions, such as those concerning the general requirements for admission of public officials and the transitional provisions, violated constitutional principles of equality before the law, separation of powers, and the protection of acquired rights. The Court emphasized the need for laws to align with international standards and Kosovo's constitutional values, particularly in relation to public officials' rights and employment stability.[38]

In Case No. KO79-23, the Constitutional Court reviewed the constitutionality of Law No. 08/L-196 on Salaries in the Public Sector. The Ombudsperson challenged several provisions, arguing they violated constitutional principles such as the separation of powers, the rule of law, and equality before the law. The Court found some provisions unconstitutional, specifically regarding salary reductions, transitional allowances, and the scope of public sector salaries. The decision emphasized the need for legal clarity, proportionality, and protection of public sector employees' rights.[39]

In joint cases No. KO232-23 and KO233-23, the Constitutional Court reviewed the constitutionality of Law No. 08/L-180, which amended the Law on the Independent Oversight Board for Civil Service of Kosovo. The Court found that several provisions of the contested law were unconstitutional, particularly those relating to the exclusion of senior management-level civil servants from the Board's oversight, the composition of the Board, and the removal of immunity for Board members. The Court ruled these provisions violated the principles of equality before the law, fair trial, and legal remedies.[40]

In Case No. KO46-23, the Constitutional Court reviewed the constitutionality of Law No. 08/L-121 on the State Bureau for Verification and Confiscation of Unjustified Assets. The applicants, members of the Assembly, challenged several provisions, arguing that they violated key constitutional principles such as equality before the law, the protection of property, and the separation of powers. Specifically, they opposed that the law's provisions concerning the scope of asset verification, the independence and status of the Bureau, and the composition of the oversight committee lacked legal certainty and were arbitrary. The Court found several articles unconstitutional, particularly those relating to the Bureau's asset verification procedures and oversight mechanisms, emphasizing the need for clearer legal standards to protect property rights and ensure judicial transparency.[41]

In Case No. KO158-23, the Constitutional Court reviewed the constitutionality of Law No. 08/L-142, which amended laws concerning the minimum wage and pension benefits for war veterans, blind persons, and individuals with paraplegia and tetraplegia. The applicants, members of the Assembly, argued that the law violated constitutional principles such as equality before the law, protection of property, and social justice by removing the link between the minimum wage and these pensions. They claimed this change would reduce economic security for vulnerable groups and undermine their legitimate expectations. The Court upheld the constitutionality of certain provisions but stressed the importance of legal clarity to protect vulnerable social categories and ensure that their pensions are determined in a fair and equitable manner.[42]

The developments in the above court cases highlight that the legislative drafting process, including the use of clear legal language, is fundamental to ensuring justice and the proper functioning of the legal system. Language principles such as clarity, coherence, and consistency of legal provisions are essential to avoid ambiguities that can lead to misinterpretation.[43] When these principles are not followed by lawmakers, legislation may be unclear or inconsistent with constitutional norms and international standards. In sum, Constitutional Court findings provide crucial feedback for lawmakers, identifying shortcomings in the drafting process. Incorporating these findings ensures that future laws are corrected, robust, and aligned with constitutional and international standards, reducing legal challenges and strengthening public trust in Kosovo's legal system.

8.7 The Scope of Regulatory Conditions

Legal scholars and international institutions remain dynamically involved in drafting and adopting lawmaking guidelines. Their scope of regulatory conditions in the legislative process is vast, requiring a delicate balance between clarity, consistency, and adherence to constitutional norms.[44] Regulatory frameworks are designed to shape behavior, set boundaries, and establish guidelines across various sectors.[45] The drafting process must incorporate fundamental principles to ensure that laws are functional and equitable.[46] Regardless of the form or volume of legislative guidelines, their use will help ensure legal provisions are preserved with clear, plain language. Legislative guidelines come in various forms, through books, case law, or codified versions.[47]

Regarding the scope of regulatory conditions, Kosovo's approach should focus on Europeanization and domestic change, reflecting shifts in internal preferences. Although national institutions play a critical role in establishing regulatory monitoring principles, policy changes often prioritize the volume of laws over quality-driven legislation. This results in tensions and inconsistencies between the initial goals and the practical implementation within Kosovo's integration process, creating adaptation pressure. The nature and extent of this pressure depend on ongoing changes within domestic institutions. Properly aligning domestic structures and preferences with clear, concise, and comprehensive legislative drafting can foster a more effective approximation process.

European integration creates pressure for uniform positive outcomes at both the policy and institutional levels in aspirant countries. However, these countries tend to have a homogeneous institutional response to European adaptation requirements, moving toward alignment for reasons of efficiency, adoption of best practices, or overall harmonization with the EU *acquis*. The European Union recently established the Reform and Growth Facility for the Western Balkans, setting objectives, financing, and budget for 2024–2027 to support EU-related reforms.[48] This includes inclusive and sustainable socio-economic reforms, fundamental reforms in the enlargement process, and investments aligned with EU values to implement their respective reform agendas. One objective of the facility is to "support the enlargement process by accelerating alignment with Union values, laws, rules, standards, policies, and practices (the '*acquis*') through the adoption and implementation of reforms aimed at future Union membership."[49]

In the context of language and legislation management for Kosovo's EU integration, this involves a structured approach to reforming national frameworks to comply with EU norms. This entails conducting assessments and gap analyses to identify discrepancies between Kosovo's current systems and the EU *acquis*, followed by legislative drafting and harmonization to amend or develop laws accordingly. Additionally, it includes building institutional capacity to ensure effective implementation and enforcement, along with establishing mechanisms to synchronize national policies with EU standards in areas such as the rule of law, human rights, and market regulation. Monitoring and evaluation frameworks are then put in place to assess compliance and progress, ensuring transparency and accountability. The ultimate goal is to create a legal and institutional environment that meets EU requirements, thereby facilitating Kosovo's pathway toward future membership.

Thus, to enhance the effectiveness and stability of Kosovo's administrative operations, it is crucial to develop a regulatory framework that is both coherent and specifically tailored to local dynamics. This approach should encompass Kosovo's unique problem-solving strategies, organizational practices, and stakeholder relationships. Establishing clear, consistent legislative language aligned with the broader principles of legal certainty and transparency is essential. Such language ensures that laws not only are implementable but also facilitate compliance, addressing ambiguities and reducing enforcement issues. By adapting the legislative framework to fit local conditions, Kosovo can achieve more effective governance and significantly improve institutional operations across various sectors.

8.8 Running into the Future

In 2023, the European Union created the new Growth Plan for the Western Balkans with the objective of fostering economic growth and expediting the region with the EU, ahead of full EU membership. The plan involves a €6 billion financial instrument known as the Reform and Growth Facility (the reform plan), allocated for the period 2024–2027.[50] The reform plan includes preparing individual reform agendas by each Western Balkan country, based on existing EU recommendations.[51] In 2024, the European Commission's communication outlined its assessment of Kosovo's Reform Agenda under the Reform and Growth Facility, highlighting its alignment with EU policies.[52] The reform agenda details Kosovo's commitment to socio-economic reforms focusing on the rule of law, anti-corruption, and environmental and digital transformations. The reform agenda aims to bridge the socio-economic gap between Kosovo and the EU, enhancing Kosovo's development and facilitating its EU integration process. The alignment with *acquis* is critical for Kosovo to meet the EU's accession requirements and benefit from related EU funding and support.

However, the evolving regulatory landscape in Kosovo, as previously noted, encounters challenges from legislative frameworks that are often incoherent or ambiguous.[53] To overcome these challenges, it's essential that Kosovo's legislative language be carefully crafted to reflect its unique administrative requirements and stakeholder dynamics. Based on a rule of law claim, effective legislation should be clear, consistent, and aligned with established principles of legal certainty and transparency.[54] Such alignment, according to Xanthaki, not only helps in implementation and compliance but also enhances governance, ensuring institutional stability and improving the effectiveness of administrative operations across multiple sectors.[55] This approach is crucial for addressing current gaps and fostering a stable administrative environment in Kosovo. Based on Xanthaki's recommendation, Table 8.3 outlines the roadmap for aligning third countries' legislation with EU standards, in particular Kosovo.

The table presents a structured roadmap for aligning third countries' legislation with the EU integration process.[56] It starts by establishing foundational techniques for sustainable EU legislation and progresses through understanding and analyzing transposition tasks. The focus shifts to crafting and refining laws to ensure they are clear, robust, and EU compliant. The process concludes with a thorough review to verify that the laws align with EU principles, prepare legal frameworks for EU accession, and ensure comprehensive and strategic legislative development.

Table 8.3 Harmonizing European Legislative Enhancements and Norms (HELEN)

Objectives	*Focus Area*	*Key Outcomes*
Transposition techniques for EU legislative reform	Establishing foundational techniques for sustainable legislation	Foundation set for long-term legislative sustainability within the EU framework
Understanding the transposition task	Detailing complexities and initial steps in transposition	Clear understanding of transposition tasks and initial preparations
Analyzing the transposition task	Examining requirements and methodologies in transposition	Detailed analysis of transposition requirements and strategic approaches
Designing the transposition law	Crafting laws for effective integration into EU standards	Robust legislative drafts aligned with EU standards
Composing and developing the transposition law	Writing and refining laws for clarity and EU compatibility	High-quality legislative texts ready for EU compatibility assessment
Verifying the transposition draft law and completing the transposition task	Final review and adjustments to align with EU principles	Completed and verified laws ready for implementation
Legislating for EU accession and approximation	Focusing on legal preparations for EU accession and meeting criteria	Legal frameworks prepared for EU accession

Source: Helen Xanthaki, *Legislative Drafting for the EU: Transposition Techniques as a Roadmap for Better Legislation and a Sustainable EU* 1–3 (Edward Elgar Publishing, 2024).

Based on Table 8.3, in the gray zones covering objectives, focus areas, and outcomes, Kosovo is still developing its transposition techniques for EU legislative reform to establish foundational techniques for sustainable legislation, aiming to achieve a foundation for long-term legislative sustainability within the EU framework. This indicates that Kosovo is still in the early stages of developing the necessary legislation and language requirements for European integration.

Therefore, to effectively align with the EU's legislative framework, Kosovo should strategically focus on developing its legislative and language capacities through the following threefold key areas.

First, Kosovo's primary objective should be to adopt *transposition techniques* that are compatible with the EU legislative framework. This involves understanding and implementing EU regulations and directives into Kosovo's national legislation in a manner that aligns with EU standards while addressing the country's specific needs. Kosovo must prioritize these techniques to ensure sustainable legal development that is compatible with future EU accession goals.

Second, in line with its objective, Kosovo must focus on establishing a *solid legislative foundation* that ensures the consistent application of EU norms across all sectors. This requires investing in capacity-building for legislative drafting, emphasizing clarity, precision, and consistency in legal language. Kosovo's legislative bodies should work to ensure that the laws are clear, unambiguous, and aligned with EU principles of transparency and legal certainty. Stakeholder consultations, including government officials and civil society, should be part of this foundation to enhance participatory lawmaking.

And, third, the ultimate outcome of Kosovo's efforts should be the creation of a *sustainable legislative system* that facilitates long-term governance, ensuring compliance with EU laws. This will not only enhance Kosovo's legal and institutional stability but also improve its prospects for EU integration. By focusing on long-term sustainability, Kosovo will ensure its laws remain adaptable, clear, and aligned with the evolving legal requirements of the EU, setting the stage for successful accession and full compliance with EU standards. In conclusion, Kosovo must prioritize developing transposition techniques and a solid legislative foundation to ensure long-term sustainability, legal clarity, and alignment with EU standards, paving the way for future EU integration. By focusing on these key areas, Kosovo will improve its chances for successful EU integration, setting a strong foundation for compliance with evolving EU requirements and ensuring that its legal framework remains adaptable and enforceable.

8.9 Conclusions

The pursuit of legislative reform in Kosovo is a vital part of the country's efforts to achieve EU accession. This reform is not merely a procedural requirement but a transformative opportunity to embed sustainability and the rule of law into Kosovo's governance framework. As highlighted in this chapter, the alignment with EU standards requires the adoption and implementation of legislation that promotes sustainable development, strengthens legal certainty, and enhances institutional capacities. However, the challenge for Kosovo lies in overcoming its unique organizational and policymaking culture, which has historically experienced implementation deficits and a lack of key reform drivers. As Kosovo endeavors to meet the EU's acquis, it must recognize that legislative reform goes beyond passing new laws—it necessitates a thorough integration of reform into the broader governance and institutional structures. This chapter has shown that legislative reform must be seen as part of a cohesive process that includes regulatory governance, legal drafting, and legislative language.

Three key contributions have been made throughout this chapter. First, the analysis of Europeanization within Kosovo's domestic institutional structures underscores the importance of adapting governance frameworks to internalize EU norms effectively. Second, the exploration of the dynamics of legal reform highlights the critical role of precise legal drafting and clear legislative language in ensuring the effectiveness of these reforms. Finally, the recommendations for changes in regulatory governance provide a clear roadmap for the reforms Kosovo must undertake on its path to EU accession.

In sum, while Kosovo's legislative reform challenges are substantial, the potential for transformation is equally significant. By adopting a comprehensive approach that integrates regulatory governance with legal drafting and legislative language improvements, Kosovo can strengthen its legal framework, align with EU standards, and advance its aspirations for EU membership. Legislative reform, therefore, stands as both a critical step and an opportunity for Kosovo to prepare for its future within the European legal and political landscape. As the ancient Latins wisely observed, "Cessante ratione legis cessat et ipsa lex," which translates to the principle that when the reasoning behind a law ceases, the law itself should cease—or, more pragmatically, when a law has outlived its usefulness, it must be reformed to reflect evolving societal needs. This maxim resonates deeply with Kosovo's quest for legislative reform, underscoring the imperative to bridge regulatory governance, legal drafting, and legislative language in pursuit of EU integration and a more adaptive legal framework.

Notes

1 *See* Helen Xanthaki, *Drafting Legislation: Art and Technology of Rules for Regulation* 57 (Bloomsbury Professional, 2014), Ulrich Karpen and Helen Xanthaki, *Legislation in Europe: A Comprehensive Guide for Scholars and Practitioners* 1–3 (Hart Publishing, 2017), Patricia Popelier et al., *Lawmaking in Multi-Level Settings: Legislative Challenges in Federal Systems and the European Union* 1, 17 (Nomos, 2019), Ulrich Karpen and Helen Xanthaki, *Legislation in Europe: A Country-by-Country Guide* 2–4 (Hart Publishing, 2020), Helen Xanthaki, *Thornton's Legislative Drafting* 5–6 (5th edn, Bloomsbury Professional, 2022), Helen Xanthaki, *Legislative Drafting for the EU: Transposition Techniques as a Roadmap for Better Legislation and a Sustainable EU* 1–3 (Edward Elgar Publishing, 2024).

2 Munroe Smith, *The Development of European Law* 286 (Columbia University Press, 1920).

3 Hart H. L. A., *The Essay on Jurisprudence and Philosophy* 26 (Oxford Academic, 1983).

4 Hart, *The Essay on Jurisprudence and Philosophy*, at 94.

5 Rene David and John E. C. Brierley, *Major Legal Systems in the World Today* 18 (3rd ed., Stevens & Sons: London, 1983).

6 Xanthaki, *Legislative Drafting for the EU*.
7 See Roscoe Pound, *An Introduction to the Philosophy of Law* 17 (Yale University Press, 1930). *See also* Roscoe Pound, Interpretations of Legal History 15 (Harvard University Press, 1946).
8 See Huntington Cairns, *Legal Philosophy from Plato to Hegel* (The Johns Hopkins Press, Baltimore, 1956). *See also* Donald R. Kelley, *The Human Measure: Social Thought in the Western Legal Tradition* (Harvard University Press, 1990). For more on legal transplants, see Alan Watson, *Legal Transplants: An Approach to Comparative Law* 21 (2nd ed., The University of Georgia Press, 1993) (*arguing that legal transplants—the transfer of laws or legal systems from one country or culture to another—have been common since the earliest recorded history*). *See, generally*, Gunnar Folke Schuppert, *A Global History of Ideas in the Language of Law* 1–31 (Rhodes Barrett, trans., Max Planck Institute for Legal History and Legal Theory, Frankfurt am Main, 2021) (ebook) (*analyzing the history of ideas in the language of law, where the history of ideas aligns with languages, exploring five key functions: legitimacy of political authority, political change, rights, justice, and the foundation of a new global order*).
9 Peter Goodrich, *Legal Discourse: Studies in Linguistics, Rhetoric and Legal Analysis* 125–157 (Palgrave Macmillan, 1987).
10 Goodrich, *Legal Discourse*, pp. 205–208.
11 Stuart A. Scheingold, *The Rule of Law in European Integration: The Path of the Schuman Plan* 35 (Yale University Press, New Haven and London, 1965).
12 Roland Bieber and Cesla Amarelle, "Simplification of European Law," *The Europeanisation of Law: The Legal Effects of European Integration*, 223 (Francis Snyder, ed., Hart Publishing, 2000).
13 Adrienne Héritier, "Differential Europe: National Administrative Responses to Community Policy," *Transforming Europe: Europeanization and Domestic Change*, 44 (Maria Green Cowles, James Caporaso, and Thomas Risse eds., Cornell University Press, 2001).
14 *See* Zane Ratniece, "Engagement of Kosovo's Domestic (Internationalized) Courts with International Law," in *The Practice of Shared Responsibility in International Law* 245–269 (André Nollkaemper and Ilias Plakokefalos eds., Cambridge University Press, 2017).
15 *See* Hans Kelsen, *Pure Theory of Law* 4–10 (M. Knight, transl., Berkeley, 1967).
16 Kelsen, *Pure Theory of Law*.
17 *See* Karpen and Helen Xanthaki, *Legislation in Europe*, pp. 265–296, Karpen and Xanthaki, *Legislation in Europe: A Country-by-Country Guide*, pp. 1–34, Xanthaki, *Legislative Drafting for the EU*, pp. 348–357.
18 *See* Giulia Adriana Pennisi, "Introduction: Special Issue on Legislative Drafting and Linguistics—Strategies to Communicate the Law," *The Theory and Practice of Legislation*, vol. 2, issue 2, 109–113 (Taylor and Francis online, 2014). *See also* Giulia Adriana Pennisi, "A Linguistic Insight into the Legislative Drafting of English-Speaking Jurisdictions: The Use of 'Singular They'," issue 1, 3–19 (*European Journal of Law Reform*, 2020). For additional background on plain English style in legislative drafting, see generally Louis J. Sirico, Jr., and Nancy L. Schults, *Persuasive Writing for Lawyers and the Legal Profession* 27–36 (Matthew Bender Publishers, 1995), Jean Stefancic and Richard Delgado, *How Lawyers Lose Their Way: A Profession Fails Its Creative Minds* 82–83 (Duke University Press, Durham and London, 2005) (*describing approaches by lawyers and judges involving strategic justifications, often reinforced by posturing*

or polite critique when countered), Richard C. Wydick, *Plain English for Lawyers* 69–75 (5th ed., Carolina Academic Press, North Durham, 2005) (*analyzing methods to eliminate unnecessary words in legal writing by avoiding language quirks, elegant variation, noun chains, multiple negatives, cosmic detachment, and sexist language*), Matthias Klatt, *Making the Law Explicit: The Normativity of Legal Argumentation* 33–44 (Hart Publishing, 2005) (*analyzing the doctrine of wording limits, hermeneutics legal theory, ontological hermeneutics in law, and their significance for law application, wording boundaries, typology, linguistic analogy, and legal interpretation), Bryan A. Garner,* The Redbook: Manual of the Legal Style 173–336 (3rd ed., West Group Publishing, 2013), Antonio Gidi and Henry Weihofen, *Legal Writing Style*, ch. 5 (3rd ed., West Academic Publishing, 2018), Peter Butt, *Legal Usage: A Modern Style Guide* (LexisNexis, 2018) (ebook) (*summarizing legal terms and concepts*), Richard C. Wydick and Amy E. Sloan, *Plain English for Lawyers*, ch. 7 (6th ed., Carolina Academic Press, 2019), Laurel Currie Oates et al., *The Legal Writing Handbook: Analysis, Research, and Writing* pt. II, pt.VII–VIII (8th ed., Aspen Publishing, 2021) (ebook).

19 *See* CJEU Case C-106/89, *Marleasing SA v. La Comercial Internacional de Alimentación* SA, 1990 E.C.R. I-4135 (*requiring Member States to interpret national law in light of the wording and purpose of the directive*); CJEU Case C-41/74, *Van Duyn v. Home Office*, 1974 E.C.R. 1337 (*establishing that treaty provisions have direct effect in Member States' legal orders, conferring rights on individuals that national courts must protect*); CJEU Case C-129/96, *Inter-Environnement Wallonie ASBL v. Région wallonne*, 1997 E.C.R. I-7411 (*requiring Member States to refrain, during the directive's transposition period, from adopting measures liable to seriously compromise the directive's prescribed result*).

20 Edgan Bodenbeimer, *Power, Law and Society* 138 (Crane, Russak & Company, 1972).

21 Law on Ratification of the Stabilization and Association Agreement between the Republic of Kosovo of the one part and the European Union and the European Atomic Energy Community of the other part, December 1, 2015, No. 05/L-069, art. 74 (Kos.). *See also* Council Decision (EU) 2016/342, of February 12, 2016, on the conclusion, on behalf of the union, of the stabilization and association agreement between the European Union and the European Atomic Energy Community, of the one part, and Kosovo, of the other part, 2016 O.J. (L 71/1) 1.

22 *See* Progress Reports on Kosovo, https://ec.europa.eu/neighbourhood-enlargement/enlargement-policy_en, (follow "Negotiations status" hyperlink; then search starting point field for "Kosovo" and search destination field for "Key documents") (last visited August 25, 2024).

23 From 2016 to 2024, EU progress reports on Kosovo consistently highlight the need for enhanced legislative drafting to improve legal clarity and accessibility. The reports emphasize the importance of aligning laws with EU standards and ensuring effective implementation to strengthen the rule of law and governance.

24 *See* Ulrich Karpen and Helen Xanthaki, *Legislation in Europe: A Comprehensive Guide for Scholars and Practitioners* pp. 1–19, 275–296 (Hart Publishing, 2017). *See also* Ulrich Karpen and Helen Xanthaki, *Legislation in Europe: A Country-by-Country Guide* pp. 1–34 (Hart Publishing, 2020).

25 See Stefan Griller and Lina Papadopoulou, "Squaring the Circle—How National Constitutions and EU Law Interact," in *National Constitutions and EU Integration* 795–839 (Stefan Griller at al., eds., Hart Publishing, 2022).

26 The official languages in Kosovo are Albanian and Serbian. Turkish, Bosnian, and Roma languages have the status of official languages at the municipal level. *See* Constitution of the Republic of Kosovo, April 9, 2008, K-09042008, Art. 5 (Kos).

27 Provisions supporting the legal foundation of EU supremacy include Article 4(3) TEU, which establishes the principle of sincere cooperation, obligating member states to ensure compliance with EU law; Article 288 TFEU, affirming the binding nature of EU regulations, directives, and decisions over conflicting national laws; and Article 267 TFEU, allowing national courts to seek preliminary rulings from the CJEU, ensuring uniform interpretation and application of EU law. For additional information, *see generally* Hermann-Josef Blanke, "Article 4. The Relations Between the EU and the Member States," in *The Treaty on European Union (TEU): A Commentary* 185–244 (Hermann-Josef Blanke and Stelio Mangiameli, eds., Springer-Verlag Berlin Heidelberg, 2013), Markus Kotzur, "Article 288 Legal Acts; Catalogue," in *European Union Treaties: A Commentary, Treaty on European Union, Treaty of Functioning of the European Union, Charter of Fundamental Rights of the European Union* 937–943 (Rudolf Geiger et al., eds., Bloomsbury Publishing, 2015), Bernhard Schima, "Article 267 TFEU," in *Commentary on the EU Treaties and the Charter of Fundamental Rights* 1822–1840 (Manuel Kellerbauer et al., Oxford University Press, Oxford, 2019).

28 Jean-Louis Halpérin, *Five Legal Revolutions Since the 17th Century: An Analysis of a Global Legal History* 125–140 (Springer, 2014). However, legislative drafting and regulatory frameworks can significantly influence corruption by creating opportunities for misuse or fostering clarity and transparency. According to Maria De Benedetto's analysis, overly complex or poorly designed regulations can increase corruption risks by making it harder for individuals and businesses to understand and comply with the rules. This complexity often creates discretionary spaces for public officials, which can be exploited for corrupt purposes. On the contrary, clear, well-structured, and transparent regulations reduce opportunities for corruption by minimizing discretion and ensuring that rules are uniformly applied and enforced. *See* Maria De Benedetto, *Corruption from a Regulatory Perspective* 96–100 (Hart Publishing, 2021).

29 *See* analysis on Layers of constitutional design. *See also* Ronan Cormacain, *The Form of Legislation and the Rule of Law* 232–268 (Hart Publishing, 2022) (discussing the principle of equality before the law as a cornerstone of good legislation, addressing how non-discriminatory language, gender-neutral drafting, and equality impact assessments are crucial in legislative practices, exploring the legal treatment of specific groups, and discussing accessibility to ensure equal access to justice).

30 Law No. 08/L-117 on Government of the Republic of Kosovo, Published: 18.11.2022, Official Gazette: 34/2022, Art. 1 (Kos.).

31 Law No. 04/L-025 on Legislative Initiatives, Published: 26.10.2011, Official Gazette: 23/2011, Art. 1 (Kos.).

32 Regulation (GRK)—No. 17/2024 on rules of procedure of the Government of the Republic of Kosovo, Published: 21.06.2024, Official Gazette: QRK-17/2024-RR, Art. 1 (Kos.).

33 Administrative Instruction No. 03/2013 on Standards for the Drafting of Normative Acts, Published: 16.05.2013, Official Gazette: QRK-03/2013, Art. 1 (Kos.).

34 *See* data on Table 1: EU assessment of Kosovo's scale reform (*Weakest Indicators of Legislation*).

35 *See* Mario Hernández Ramos and Volker Heydt (eds, Karpen and Xanthaki, 2017), pp. 129–142, 229–255. *See also* Xanthaki (2024), *Legislative Drafting for the EU*, pp. 96–137.

36 *See* analysis on Layers of constitutional design. Article 22 of the Kosovo Constitution establishes that certain international agreements and instruments related to human rights and fundamental freedoms are directly applicable in Kosovo. These international instruments take precedence over national laws and acts of public institutions in case of conflict. The specific agreements mentioned include Universal Declaration of Human Rights (United Nations General Assembly, 1948), European Convention on Human Rights (ECHR) and its Protocols (Council of Europe, 1950), International Covenant on Civil and Political Rights (ICCPR) and its Protocols (United Nations General Assembly, 1966), Council of Europe Framework Convention for the Protection of National Minorities (Council of Europe, 1976), Convention on the Elimination of All Forms of Racial Discrimination (United Nations General Assembly, 1969), Convention on the Elimination of All Forms of Discrimination Against Women (United Nations General Assembly, 1981), Convention on the Rights of the Child (United Nations General Assembly, 1989), Convention against Torture and Other Cruel, Inhumane or Degrading Treatment or Punishment (United Nations General Assembly, 1984) This provision ensures that Kosovo adheres to these key international human rights standards, giving them supremacy over conflicting national legislation.

37 Kosovo Constitutional Court, April 5, 2023, Joint Cases No. KO100/22 and KO101/22, *Constitutional review of law no. 08/L-136 on amending and supplementing Law no.06/L-056 on Kosovo Prosecutorial Council*, 1–5, II–VII (Kos.).

38 Kosovo Constitutional Court, September 12, 2023, Joint Cases No. KO216–22 and KO220–22, *Constitutional review of articles 9, 12, 46 and 99 of law no. 08/L-197 on Public Officials*, 1–5, III–VI, VIII–X (Kos.).

39 Kosovo Constitutional Court, January 23, 2024, Case No. KO79/23, *Constitutional review of law no. 08/L-196 on Salaries in the Public Sector*, 1–4, II–VI (Kos.).

40 Kosovo Constitutional Court, July 23, 2024, Joint Cases No. KO232/23 and KO233/23, *Constitutional review of law no. 08/L-180 on amending and supplementing law no. 06/L-048 on Independent Oversight Board for Civil Service of Kosovo*, 1–6, II–IV (Kos.).

41 Kosovo Constitutional Court, July 29, 2024, Case No. KO46/23, *Constitutional review of law no. 08/L-121 on the state bureau for verification and confiscation of unjustified assets*, 1–4, II–VI (Kos.).

42 Kosovo Constitutional Court, July 31, 2024, Case No. KO158/23, *Constitutional review of law no. 08/L-142 on amending and supplementing the laws that determine the amount of the benefit in the amount of the minimum wage, procedures on setting of minimum wage and tax rates on annual personal income*, 1–4, II–VI (Kos.).

43 David Lowe and Charlie Potter, *Understanding Legislation: A Practical Guide to Statutory Interpretation* 15–25 (Hart Publishing, 2018).

44 *See* Neil Duxbury, *Elements of Legislation* 66, 81–99 (Cambridge University Press, 2013). *See also* Karpen and Xanthaki, *Legislation in Europe: A Country-by-Country Guide* (Hart Publishing, 2017). For the importance of clarity and consistency in legislative drafting is emphasized, *see also* Xanthaki, *Thornton's Legislative Drafting*, pp. 232–268 (5th edn, Bloomsbury Professional, 2022)

(emphasizing that legislation must be clear, precise, and organized logically to ensure comprehensibility, suggesting that drafters are encouraged to revise texts frequently with simplicity in mind and to test their comprehensibility, recommending that consistency is necessary at various levels, such as word choice, stylistic practices, and harmony with common law and statutory contexts and suggesting that the balance between simplicity and precision is vital to avoid vagueness or complexity, ensuring the legislative text communicates effectively to diverse audiences and avoids ambiguity).

45 *See* Felix Uhlmann and Stefan Höfler, "Professional Legislative Drafters – New Ideas for Switzerland?" *Professional Legislative Drafters: Status, Roles, Education* 137–148 (Felix Uhlmann and Stefan Höfler, eds., Dike Verlag AG, Zürich/St. Gallen, 2016).

46 In CJEU Case C-110/03 *Belgium v Commission* 2005, the Court emphasized that the principle of legal certainty is a fundamental aspect of EU law, requiring that rules be clear and precise so individuals can unequivocally understand their rights and obligations and act accordingly.

47 For example, legal books come in various forms, each serving a distinct purpose. *Textbooks* provide comprehensive coverage of a specific area of law and are often recommended by lecturers. *Cases and materials* offer key excerpts from cases, legislation, and journal articles relevant to particular legal fields. *Statute books* compile statutes in different legal areas and are updated annually. *Monographs* delve into the complexities and debates of a specific subject, ideal for those seeking a deeper understanding. Finally, *practitioner texts* are detailed, authoritative references used by practitioners, offering concise guidance and key legal authorities, often accessible through legal databases. For additional information on writing clear, concise, and accessible to legal writing, *see* Martin Cutts, *Oxford Guide to Plain English* (Oxford University Press, 2013) (ebook) (*offering practical guidelines for short sentences, active voice, plain vocabulary, and coherent organization, advocating plain language for legal, technical, and public texts to enhance understanding, reduce errors, and build trust*).

48 *See* Regulation (EU) 2024/1449, of the European Parliament and of the Council of May 14, 2024, on Establishing the Reform and Growth Facility for the Western Balkans, 2024/1449 O.J. (L 8/29) 1.

49 Regulation (EU) 2024/1449, Art. 3 para (a).

50 Regulation (EU) 2024/1449, Art. 1.

51 These reform agendas will guide the disbursement of funds, with payments made twice a year following the verification of achievement of set conditions. If conditions are not met, funds may be suspended or deducted, with a possibility of redistribution if conditions are fulfilled within one to two years. The ultimate goal is to double the size of Western Balkan economies within the next decade, enhancing regional stability and integration into the EU's single market.

52 *See* Commission Staff Working Document Kosovo* Accompanying the document commission implementing decision approving the reform agendas and the multiannual work program under the Reform and Growth Facility for the Western Balkans of October 23, 2024, SWD (2024) 243 final, pp. 8–24. *Note*: The asterisk (*) regarding Kosovo indicates that any designation or reference to Kosovo in official documents is made without prejudice to international positions on its status. This neutrality aligns with United Nations Security Council Resolution 1244 from 1999 and the International Court of Justice's opinion on Kosovo's declaration of independence.

53 *See* analysis on Evolving and recent development.

54 *See* CJEU Case C-310/99, *Italy v Commission.* In *Italy v Commission*, the European Court of Justice ruled against Italy, which had contested a decision by the European Commission. The case revolved around Italy's failure to meet certain EU directives, where the Commission had imposed penalties for non-compliance. The Court upheld the Commission's decision, emphasizing the importance of Member States adhering to EU laws and the Commission's role in ensuring compliance to maintain the uniform application of EU law across all Member States. *See also* Case C-231/03, Coname. The Coname case involved a dispute regarding public service contracts and the principles of free competition within the EU. The European Court of Justice held that municipal authorities awarding public service contracts must adhere to EU competition laws. This case highlighted that local entities, when acting as contracting authorities, are bound by the same rules on public contracts as state-level bodies, thereby ensuring that all public contracts within the EU are subject to the principles of transparency and non-discrimination. For additional CJEU cases of legal certainty on rule of law, *see* Case C-90/95, De Compte, EU:C:1999:158, para 35; Case 120/86, Mulder, EU:C:1988:213, para 24; Case 98/78, Racke, EU:C:1979:14, para 20; Case 169/80, Gondrand Freres, EU:C:1981:171, para 17; Case 222/86, Unectef/Heylens, EU:C:1987:442, para 15; Case T-461/08, Evropaïki Dynamiki/ EIB, EU: T:2011:494, para 118.

55 *See* Xanthaki (2024), *Legislative Drafting for the EU*, p. 24 *et seq* (discussing the basis of EU legislative reform, focusing on transposition techniques for enhancing sustainability and integration of third countries with the EU). The book's sections collectively offer a comprehensive roadmap for third countries aiming to align their legislation with EU standards, emphasizing the meticulous crafting of laws that support effective and sustainable integration into the EU.

56 The acronym HELEN encapsulates the idea of aligning and improving legislative processes and standards within a European context, which is quite fitting for discussions involving EU legislation and language clarity in Kosovo.

Bibliography

Administrative Instruction No. 03/2013 on Standards for the Drafting of Normative Acts, Published: 16.05.2013, Official Gazette: QRK-03/2013, art. 1 (Kos.).

Adrienne Héritier, "Differential Europe: National Administrative Responses to Community Policy," in *Transforming Europe: Europeanization and Domestic Change*, 44 (Maria Green Cowles, James Caporaso, and Thomas Risse eds., Cornell University Press, 2001).

Alan Watson, *Legal Transplants: An Approach to Comparative Law*, 21 (2nd ed., The University of Georgia Press, 1993).

Antonio Gidi & Henry Weihofen, *Legal Writing Style*, ch. 5 (3rd ed., West Academic Publishing, 2018).

Bernhard Schima, "Article 267 TFEU," in *Commentary on the EU Treaties and the Charter of Fundamental Rights 1822–1840* (Manuel Kellerbauer et al., Oxford University Press, Oxford, 2019).

Bryan A. Garner, *The Redbook: Manual of the Legal Style*, 173–336 (3rd ed., West Group Publishing, 2013).

CJEU Case C-106/89, Marleasing SA v. La Comercial Internacional de Alimentación SA, 1990 E.C.R. I-4135, ECLI:EU:C:1990:395.
CJEU Case C-110/03 Belgium v Commission 2005, ECLI:EU:C:2005:223.
CJEU Case C-129/96, Inter-Environnement Wallonie ASBL v. Région wallonne, 1997 E.C.R. I-7411, ECLI:EU:C:1997:628.
CJEU Case C-231/03, Coname, ECLI:EU:C:2005:487.
CJEU Case C-310/99, Italy v Commission, ECLI:EU:C:2002:143.
CJEU Case C-41/74, Van Duyn v. Home Office, 1974 E.C.R. 1337, ECLI:EU:C:1974:133.
Commission Staff Working Document Kosovo* Accompanying the document commission implementing decision approving the reform agendas and the multiannual work programme under the reform and growth facility for the Western Balkans of 23 October 2024, SWD (2024) 243 final, pp. 8–24.
Council Decision (EU) 2016/342, of 12 February 2016 on the conclusion, on behalf of the union, of the stabilization and association agreement between the European Union and the European Atomic Energy Community, of the one part, and Kosovo, of the other part, 2016 O.J. (L 71/1) 1.
David Lowe & Charlie Potter, *Understanding Legislation: A Practical Guide to Statutory Interpretation*, 15–25 (Hart Publishing, 2018).
Donald R. Kelley, *The Human Measure: Social Thought in the Western Legal Tradition* (Harvard University Press, 1990).
Edgan Bodenbeimer, Power, *Law and Society*, 138 (Crane, Russak & Company, 1972).
Felix Uhlmann & Stefan Höfler, "Professional Legislative Drafters – New Ideas for Switzerland?," in *Professional Legislative Drafters: Status, Roles, Education*, 137–148 (Felix Uhlmann & Stefan Höfler, eds., Dike Verlag AG, Zürich/St. Gallen, 2016).
Giulia Adriana Pennisi, "A Linguistic Insight into the Legislative Drafting of English-Speaking Jurisdictions: The Use of 'Singular They'," issue 1, 3–19 (*European Journal of Law Reform*, 2020).
Giulia Adriana Pennisi, "Introduction: Special Issue on Legislative Drafting and Linguistics—Strategies to Communicate the Law," in *The Theory and Practice of Legislation*, vol. 2, issue 2, 109–113 (Taylor and Francis online, 2014).
Gunnar Folke Schuppert, *A Global History of Ideas in the Language of Law*, 1–31 (Rhodes Barrett trans., Max Planck Institute for Legal History and Legal Theory, Frankfurt am Main, 2021) (ebook).
Hans Kelsen, *Pure Theory of Law*, 4–10 (M. Knight, transl., Berkeley, 1967).
Hart, H. L. A., *The Essay on Jurisprudence and Philosophy*, 26 (Oxford Academic, 1983).
Helen Xanthaki, *Drafting Legislation: Art and Technology of Rules for Regulation*, 57 (Bloomsbury Professional, 2014).
Helen Xanthaki, *Legislative Drafting for the EU: Transposition Techniques as a Roadmap for Better Legislation and a Sustainable EU*, 1–3 (Edward Elgar Publishing, 2024).
Helen Xanthaki, *Thornton's Legislative Drafting*, 5–6 (5th edn, Bloomsbury Professional, 2022).

Hermann-Josef Blanke, "Article 4. The Relations Between the EU and the Member States," in *The Treaty on European Union (TEU): A Commentary*, 185–244 (Hermann-Josef Blanke & Stelio Mangiameli, eds., Springer-Verlag Berlin Heidelberg, 2013).

Huntington Cairns, *Legal Philosophy from Plato to Hegel* (The Johns Hopkins Press, Baltimore, 1956).

Jean-Louis Halpérin, *Five Legal Revolutions Since the 17th Century: An Analysis of a Global Legal History*, 125–140 (Springer, 2014).

Jean Stefancic & Richard Delgado, *How Lawyers Lose Their Way: A Profession Fails Its Creative Minds*, 82–83 (Duke University Press, Durham and London, 2005).

Kosovo Constitutional Court, Apr. 5, 2023, Joint Cases No. KO100/22 and KO101/22, *Constitutional review of law No. 08/L-136 on amending and supplementing law no. 06/L-056 on Kosovo Prosecutorial Council*, 1–5, II-VII (Kos.).

Kosovo Constitutional Court, Sept. 12, 2023, Joint Cases No. KO216–22 and KO220–22, *Constitutional review of articles 9, 12, 46 and 99 of law no. 08/L-197 on public officials*, 1–5, III-VI, VIII-X (Kos.).

Kosovo Constitutional Court, Jan. 23, 2024, Case No. KO79/23, *Constitutional review of law no. 08/L-196 on salaries in the public sector*, 1–4, II-VI (Kos.).

Kosovo Constitutional Court, July 23, 2024, Joint Cases No. KO232-23 and KO233-23, *Constitutional review of law no. 08/L-180 on amending and supplementing law no. 06/L-048 on independent oversight board for Civil Service of Kosovo*, 1–6, II-IV (Kos.).

Kosovo Constitutional Court, July 29, 2024, Case No. KO46/23, *Constitutional review of law no. 08/L-121 on the State Bureau for Verification and Confiscation of Unjustified Assets*, 1–4, II-VI (Kos.).

Kosovo Constitutional Court, July 31, 2024, Case No. KO158-23, *Constitutional review of law no. 08/L-142 on amending and supplementing the laws that determine the amount of the benefit in the amount of the minimum wage, procedures on setting of minimum wage and tax rates on annual personal income*, 1–4, II-VI (Kos.).

Laurel Currie Oates et al., *The Legal Writing Handbook: Analysis, Research, and Writing*, pt. II, pt.VII-VIII (8th ed., Aspen Publishing, 2021) (ebook).

Law No. 04/L–025 on Legislative initiatives, Published: 26.10.2011, Official Gazette: 23/2011, art. 1 (Kos.).

Law No. 08/L-117 on Government of the Republic of Kosovo, Published: 18.11.2022, Official Gazette: 34/2022, art. 1 (Kos.).

Law on ratification of the stabilization and association agreement between the Republic of Kosovo of the one part and the European Union and the European Atomic Energy Community of the other part] Dec. 1, 2015, No. 05/L-069, art. 74 (Kos.).

Louis J. Sirico, Jr., & Nancy L. Schults, *Persuasive Writing for Lawyers and the Legal Profession*, 27–36 (Matthew Bender Publishers, 1995).

Maria De Benedetto, *Corruption from a Regulatory Perspective*, 96–100 (Hart Publishing, 2021).

Markus Kotzur, "Article 288 Legal Acts; Catalogue," in *European Union Treaties: A Commentary, Treaty on European Union, Treaty of Functioning of the*

European Union, Charter of Fundamental Rights of the European Union, 937–943 (Rudolf Geiger et al., eds., Bloomsbury Publishing, 2015).

Matthias Klatt, *Making the Law Explicit: The Normativity of Legal Argumentation*, 33–44 (Hart Publishing, 2005).

Munroe Smith, *The Development of European Law*, 286 (Columbia University Press, 1920).

Neil Duxbury, *Elements of Legislation*, 66, 81–99 (Cambridge University Press, 2013).

Patricia Popelier et al., *Lawmaking in Multi-Level Settings: Legislative Challenges in Federal Systems and the European Union*, 1, 17 (Nomos, 2019).

Peter Butt, *Legal Usage: A Modern Style Guide* (LexisNexis, 2018) (ebook).

Peter Goodrich, *Legal Discourse: Studies in Linguistics, Rhetoric and Legal Analysis*, 125–157 (Palgrave Macmillan, 1987).

Regulation (EU) 2024/1449, of the European Parliament and of the Council of 14 May 2024 on Establishing the Reform and Growth Facility for the Western Balkans, 2024/1449 O.J. (L 8/29) 1.

Regulation (GRK) - No. 17/2024 on Rules of Procedure of the Government of the Republic of Kosovo, Published: 21.06.2024, Official Gazette: QRK-17/2024-RR, art. 1 (Kos.).

Rene David & John E. C. Brierley, *Major Legal Systems in the World Today*, 18 (3rd ed., Stevens & Sons: London, 1983).

Richard C. Wydick, *Plain English for Lawyers*, 69–75 (5th ed., Carolina Academic Press, North Durham, 2005).

Richard C. Wydick & Amy E. Sloan, *Plain English for Lawyers*, ch. 7 (6th ed., Carolina Academic Press, 2019).

Roland Bieber & Cesla Amarelle, "Simplification of European Law," in *The Europeanisation of Law: The Legal Effects of European Integration*, 223 (Francis Snyder, ed., Hart Publishing, 2000).

Ronan Cormacain, *The Form of Legislation and the Rule of Law*, 232–268 (Hart Publishing, 2022).

Roscoe Pound, *An Introduction to the Philosophy of Law*, 17 (Yale University Press, 1930).

See also Roscoe Pound, *Interpretations of Legal History*, 15 (Harvard University Press, 1946).

Stefan Griller & Lina Papadopoulou, "Squaring the Circle – How National Constitutions and EU Law Interact," in *National Constitutions and EU Integration*, 795–839 (Stefan Griller et al., eds., Hart Publishing, 2022).

Stuart A Scheingold, *The Rule of Law in European Integration: The Path of the Schuman Plan*, 35 (Yale University Press, New Haven and London, 1965).

Ulrich Karpen & Helen Xanthaki, *Legislation in Europe: A Comprehensive Guide for Scholars and Practitioners*, 1–3 (Hart Publishing, 2017).

Ulrich Karpen & Helen Xanthaki, *Legislation in Europe: A Country-by-Country Guide*, 2–4 (Hart Publishing, 2020).

Zane Ratniece, "Engagement of Kosovo's Domestic (Internationalized) Courts with International Law," in *The Practice of Shared Responsibility in International Law*, 245–269 (André Nollkaemper & Ilias Plakokefalos eds., Cambridge University Press, 2017).

Part Two

Tools

Terminology, Language Processing, and Technology

9 Terminology Management and Better Understanding of Legislative Intent for Citizens in the Age of Technological Disruption

Ágota Fóris

9.1 Introduction

The objective of this chapter is to underscore the significance of dynamic and adaptable terminology resources and tools for legislation, with the aim of facilitating effective and comprehensible communication and ensuring the clarity and comprehensibility of legal and other documents. This study will first examine the features of clear, comprehensible, and accessible communication. Second, it will investigate the comprehensibility of terminology. Third, it will analyze the impact of the technical disruption, specifically digitization, and artificial intelligence (AI), on the creation of texts, with a particular focus on legislation. Finally, it will examine the importance of legal corpora and terminology databases (termbases).

Several initiatives have been launched to enhance the clarity and comprehensibility of legal and administrative language. In the English-speaking world, the Plain Language Movement (https://www.plainlanguage.gov/) was initiated in the United States in the 1940s focusing on readability, and, later, in the 1970s, it had the primary objective of enhancing the accessibility of official language through the formulation of stylistic, syntactic, and lexical recommendations. The first iteration of what later became the Federal Plain Language Guidelines was developed in the mid-1990s, and, since then, they have been revised on a regular basis, typically every few years (Adler 2012; Schriver 2017). A detailed study of the history of the Plain Language Movement revealed three significant findings (Schriver 2017, 2):

1. Plain language has evolved significantly over the past 75 years – from a focus on crafting clear sentences to creating effective multimedia, electronic, or paper communications.
2. Research tells us that most readability formulas are outdated methods for assessing text quality. Usability testing is the best benchmark for assessing text quality and plain language.

DOI: 10.4324/9781003430308-12

3 The growing empirical evidence suggests that plain language works for everyone – young and old, experts and novices, first-language readers and second-language readers.

These movements were launched and subsequently strengthened as a result of social pressure and the growing importance of consumer protection and started out as citizens' initiatives that were subsequently taken up by the government and public administration and implemented into legislation (see Adler 2012; Biel 2023).

In several other countries, a similar campaign or language movement has been initiated to introduce plain administrative language, and the necessary staff training has been provided. For example, in the UK, a commercial organization was founded: the Plain English Campaign (https://www.plainenglish.co.uk/) in 1979, for the use of clear and concise language.

In Europe, the European Commission launched the Clear Writing for Europe campaign in 2010 to promote clarity, in line with the ambition to bring EU citizens closer to legislation and to ensure that legislation is written in a language that is understandable to the average citizen. The Commission regularly convenes conferences on this topic, offering practical guidance for translators. It has also published a booklet, *How to Write Clearly* (2011), in 24 official languages. This booklet assists individuals in drafting and writing EU documents, providing simple advice on wording, grammar, and punctuation. It summarizes the ten conditions ("hints") for clear drafting in a concise manner for the staff. The "hints" are on topics including planning, formatting, layout, and avoiding excessive noun phrases, and there are some terminological considerations as well (see Fóris and Faludi 2021).

The creation of legal texts in English and the drafting of the texts in an understandable way are covered in several legal handbooks, including Xanthaki (2023) and Garner (2023). Additionally, there has been a proliferation of books and articles about language and law (e.g., Karpen and Xanthaki 2017; Solan and Tiersma 2021; Biel and Kockaert 2023; Engberg 2023).

The movements and recommendations encompass a comprehensive range of linguistic elements, including readability, sentence structure and length, style, word usage or terminology, and textual features such as the use of synonyms in text, text structure, and the creation of effective electronic, multimedia, or paper communications. However, there are no universally applicable guidelines for the comprehensibility of legal texts. Furthermore, the use of simplified language (e.g., shorter sentences and the use of colloquialisms) does not necessarily result in increased comprehensibility. Additionally, content accuracy and comprehensibility are often in conflict. It is also crucial to consider the target audience and their legal and linguistic background. In recent years, some legal scholars (e.g., Simonnas 2016; Ződi 2018; Pázmándi 2018; Corpas Pastor and Sánchez Rodas 2023) have highlighted the necessity of incorporating semantic and pragmatic analysis methods alongside morphological, syntactic, and word use analysis, in alignment with the findings of the terminological literature (Cabré 1998; Zauberga 2005; L'Homme 2020). In consequence, it is not feasible to devise a set of concise and comprehensive rules for effective language use, given that it is contingent upon a multitude of variables, including the requirements of the target audience.

Text linguistics research indicates that textual communication adheres to at least three fundamental principles: efficiency, effectiveness, and appropriateness. A text is efficient if it meets the standards of textuality and requires the least amount of effort for processing. The effectiveness of a text can be defined as the extent to which the communicative aim is fulfilled and the impact it has on the receiver. The appropriateness of a text is contingent on its relationship with the surrounding context. It is determined by whether the text is suitable for the context in which it is situated, as well as for the individuals involved in communication (Beaugrande and Dressler 1981; Fóris 2011; Fóris and Faludi 2021). Among the factors that make texts difficult to understand, some highlight the use of terminology and the characteristics of syntax and text. In her article Vincze (2018), for example, lists the following syntactic factors (with reference to the psycholinguistics literature: Pléh and Lukács 2014) that make legal texts difficult to understand: sentence and word length, non-traditional word order, sentences without verbs, text structure, embedded sentences, and the use of impersonal structures. It is evident that there are numerous factors that contribute to the comprehensibility of legal texts, and terminology is merely one of these elements.

There are two principal methods (or a combination of them) for ensuring that terminology is readily comprehensible. One method is to replace technical terms that are more complex or unfamiliar to the recipient with more accessible (potentially colloquial) terms within the texts. This is referred to as intralingual translation. The other solution, which is set forth in the technical standards, is to facilitate comprehension of technical texts – for lawyers and other professionals as well as for laypersons – by publishing the definitions of the terms and their positions within the technical terminology in a glossary or database. Creating terminology databases is a crucial component in the implementation of this recommendation (see Fóris 2023).

There are many ways to translate within a language, one of which is to use colloquial words instead of technical terms (Jakobson 1958; Dobos 2022, 2023). It is not always clear, however, whether the form or the meaning of the terms should be colloquial or both. In a recent article, Mouritsen

(2023) discussed the concept of "ordinary meaning", a term that is frequently used by judges in the United States. He observed that "Yet judges have appealed to ordinary meaning without a shared understanding of what ordinary meaning actually means, and without effective methods for evaluating claims of ordinary meaning", and he suggests that the meaning of words should be decided on the basis of language use from linguistic corpora (Mouritsen 2023, 86–87). In the Hungarian-language legal literature, the issue of accessibility, i.e., ordinary meaning, is also addressed in several writings. Tóth (2023), for instance, observes that Hungarian legislation does not define the concept of accessibility (i.e., ordinary meaning) or its criteria.

Based on the standard IEC/IEEE 82079-1:2019, it is essential to consider the six principles of information quality when preparing documentation. These are completeness, minimalism, correctness, conciseness, consistency, comprehensibility, and accessibility. The comprehensibility of information refers to the fact that the text must be understandable for the target audience. This also means that you need to define your target audience and choose text features and terms accordingly. In the case of text intended for lay audience, it is essential to employ clear and unambiguous language, terminology, and illustrations. Additionally, safety signs and graphic symbols must be utilized with clear and concise representation. Furthermore, the orientation methods and medium must be clearly delineated for optimal comprehension. Plain language, in this context, encompasses both clarity and comprehensibility. It is also necessary to consider additional rules related to terminology. Particular attention should be paid to terms that may be challenging for the target audience, and these should be listed and explained in detail.

The significance of plain language is underscored by the recent publication of a new standard on the subject: ISO 24495-1:2023 *Plain language – Part 1: Governing principles and guidelines*. This standard will be followed by two others: a second part on legal communication and a third on science writing. Based on this standard, the definition of plain language is: "communication in which wording, structure and design are so clear that intended readers can easily find what they need, understand what they find, and use that information". The most prevalent application of plain language is in documents designed for the general public. This standard highlights the fact that the principles of plain language can also be applied to other contexts, including technical writing, legislative drafting, and the use of controlled languages.

Based on the BSI (BSI web1), "a standard is an agreed way of doing something". It can cover a wide range of activities, from making products to managing processes and supplying materials. Standards are the knowledge of experts in their field and the needs of the organizations they represent. They can drive innovation, increase productivity, and make organizations and people's lives easier, safer, and healthier. Governments often use standards when making laws or guidance documents. Standards are used to establish technical details, allowing laws to focus on long-term policy objectives. Following the standard means following the relevant law, but there are usually ways of following the law without using a standard. However, it is important to distinguish between standards and regulations. While following a standard may be a useful practice, it does not necessarily guarantee that one is operating within the bounds of relevant legislation. Furthermore, it is rare for standards to cite specific legislation, since legislation can and often does change over time (BSI web2). Standards are an instrument of deregulation. The use of standards is voluntary. They become mandatory only if referenced in contracts, laws, or regulations. They are also beneficial in liability cases, as they provide a framework for demonstrating that one has followed best practices (DIN web).

9.2 Clear, Comprehensible, and Accessible Communication

The drafting of documents in an understandable way presents a legal, ethical, linguistic, and financial issue. In the following section, an examination of the general factors affecting the clarity and comprehensibility of official documents will be undertaken, after which the comprehensibility of legal documents will be addressed.

9.2.1 Clarity and Comprehensibility in Technical Documentation

It is essential for all technical texts to incorporate legal and regulatory frameworks, which are invariably produced within them. Technical texts encompass a wide range of text types, each of which is subject to a distinct set of standards, laws, and other regulations. The imperative for clarity and comprehensibility, as well as the necessity for regulatory oversight, is especially pronounced in text types designed to disseminate professional information to non-professional audiences.

The documentation and publication of technical data (i.e., technical specifications) are subject to legal regulations. Consequently, companies and manufacturers operating within the global market are obliged to prepare these materials. This is governed by the 2006/42/EC directive in the European Union, as well as by national-level legal acts. In the context of technical documentation, user documentation, and instructions for use, a special role is ascribed to these texts, which the manufacturer, importer, or distributor is legally obliged to publish in the target language. The regulations stipulate that the instructions for use must be comprehensible and unambiguous, containing all the information in the official language of the country published by the manufacturer in the manual and operating instructions written in the relevant language (B. Papp 2021, 42).

In the field of technical documentation, documents intended for the public are typically referred to as "instructions for use" (see B. Papp 2021; Csontos 2021b; Fóris and Faludi 2021). In the field of medical documentation, documents are typically referred to as "patient information" documents (see Fogarasi and Patonai 2021). Finally, in the field of legal documentation, documents are known as "legal acts" (see Drinóczi and Petrétei 2004; Németh 2022; Tóth 2023). The preparation of documentation is subject to regulation by legislation, standards, and editorial guidelines or style sheets (Czinkóczki and Fehér 2021). It is primarily a legal obligation that these documents and associated legislation must be readily comprehensible and free of ambiguity. In other words, in a wide range of fields, if the texts are not produced for professionals but for lay users, there is a legal obligation to ensure that they are clear and understandable.

The question at hand is to determine what is meant by the term "specialized text" (or technical text) and to identify the characteristics that should be taken into account when producing texts for readers having varying degrees of prior knowledge. The results of various studies indicate that the comprehensibility of a text is not solely dependent on the terms used in it. Therefore, it is essential to examine the criteria for comprehensibility at multiple linguistic levels, including the lexical, sentence, textual, and pragmatic levels. In her 2021 study, Csontos used a functional cognitive approach (see Langacker 1987) to highlight the regulated nature of technical text production and the language users' concept of specialized text. In this approach the concept of specialized text has two basic components: experience-based knowledge and institutionalized knowledge. The latter has a very important component:

> The creation of specialized texts takes place along the lines of institutionalized knowledge: documentation, standards and legal regulations can regulate the content and form of texts. The style guides of scientific texts and the marketing of commercial products can also be rated here. (Csontos 2021a, 273)

Csontos also highlights that the accessibility and shareability of knowledge contained in texts are not solely determined by the author of the text:

> The common components of specialized texts include the KNOWLEDGE and the sharing of this KNOWLEDGE. *Sharing* means this is not about a simple *handing over* from the creator of the text, but dialogue between the creator of the text and the recipient also occurs. The recipient creates the understanding of the text, this way actively participates in

> creating the text, and simultaneously creates the opportunity for sharing KNOWLEDGE.
>
> (Csontos 2021a, 284)

Temmerman (2007) indicates that the use of metaphors and metonymies enhances comprehension of texts and that conceptual metaphors and metonymies can contribute to a better understanding of technical texts. However, their significance in technical texts and legislation has only recently been more thoroughly examined. For instance, cognitive semantic studies of the types of meaning expansion (conceptual metaphors and metonymies and related processes of making meaning, e.g., metaphorical and metonymical expressions and personifications) have been studied in the Hungarian version of the quality management system standard known as MSZ EN ISO 9001: 2009 (Sólyom 2021), as well as in the text of the Fundamental Law of Hungary, and Act C of 2012 the Criminal Code of Hungary (Sólyom 2024). Sólyom stated that metaphorical and metonymical language use is common and frequent in technical and legal texts:

> The use of metaphors (which are in many cases personifications) and metonymies does not make understanding of the text more difficult, but on the contrary: they help the reader to comprehend the text. They also provide more precise meaning, help to avoid misunderstandings, and specify or extend the meaning of words.
>
> (Sólyom 2021, 371)

9.2.2 *Clarity and Comprehensibility in Legal Documentation*

Establishing a standard for the drafting of legal texts can be challenging. But there may be certain standardized elements that are commonly included across different texts (Duprat and Xanthaki 2017). However, there are several fundamental requirements that all such texts must meet. The process of drafting is contingent upon several factors, including the specific type of text, the subject matter, the intended audience, and the social and professional context. Xanthaki (2011) has created a "pyramid of virtues" in which she establishes a hierarchy of qualities for drafting texts: efficacy, effectiveness, efficiency (clarity, precision, ambiguity), simplicity/plain language, and gender-neutral language. In the view of Hernández Ramos and Heydt (2017, 130), the most crucial criteria for normative language are clarity and precision, followed by brevity, coherence, consistency, simplicity, and certainty. It is possible to produce legal texts in a single language or multiple languages, with the latter option being particularly relevant in the context of translation.

Fuglinszky and Somssich (2020) confirm that the legal translation field is significantly shaped by the system-bound nature of law and language, as well as their cultural and social influence. Furthermore, a language can be used in multiple legal systems simultaneously. This results in a multitude of legal languages expressed through the same natural language. "Thus, legal languages still remain system-bound, but bound to not only a single but more than one system" (Fuglinszky and Somssich 2020, 751).

In the Hungarian legal literature, some authors consider accessible, barrier-free communication to be primarily an ethical requirement, although one that is subject to legal constraints (Tóth 2022). Tóth highlights the diverse range of expectations and requirements that the heterogeneous legal community must meet, including considerations of economy, rational financial burden, good faith, impartiality, legality, and the application of scientific or other expertise appropriate to the specific case. In addition, Németh (2022) draws attention to the fact that comprehensibility is an ethical requirement not only for legislative documents but also for other legal and judicial content.

Both Drinóczi (2010, 2015) and Xanthaki (2011) include the comprehensibility and accessibility of legislation within the quality of legislation. Drinóczi and Novák (2015) confirm that effective management of legal terminology is essential for the quality of legislation. By sharing terminological expertise and utilizing terminological tools, it is possible to enhance the legislative process and ensure that future laws and statutes are linguistically accurate. Novák (2018) emphasizes that the primary objective of the study of legislation is the maintenance of legal certainty, as well as the adequacy and comprehensibility of the content of legislation. He also stresses that the comprehensibility of legislation and the correctness of terminology are essential elements of both quality legislation and law enforcement. Ződi (2018) situates the issue of the comprehensibility of legal texts within the broader context of "access to justice".

As previously stated, standardization represents a significant advancement in the implementation of effective practices. It can standardize processes and the terminology used in those processes. The process and details of creating legal documents can be regulated by legislation or supported by other codes, such as standards or style guides. Terminology may be standardized through the use of terminology standards or included in glossaries, dictionaries, and databases. With regard to the legislative process, Drinóczi and Petrétei (2004) maintain that the current regulatory framework in Hungary is sufficiently regulated but believes that greater regulation is necessary, particularly with respect to the drafting phase. In another study, Drinóczi (2017) examined the feasibility of adapting the principles of quality management systems to the legislative process. Her findings indicate that it is possible to adapt the fundamental concepts of quality management systems without standardizing the legislative process.

Comprehensible communication is in fact communication without barriers. Thus, the comprehensibility of documentation – including legislation, technical documents, and patient information leaflets – serves as the foundation for effective official communication. A clear understanding of the rules makes them easier to follow, and this becomes even more important in the digital space. Nevertheless, the question of what is meant by "comprehensibility" remains unanswered. What communication and linguistic features can be employed to objectively describe it, and under what circumstances does a text or a term meet the requirements of comprehensibility? There are general, language-independent tips (e.g., *How to Write Clearly*, 2011), but there are also language-specific requirements that must be compiled for each language. Clarity also depends on the audience, the type of text, the terminology, and the context.

In several studies, Tóth has examined how the requirement of comprehensibility is included in Hungarian legal norms. Her findings revealed that "Act CXXX of 2010 on Legislation" establishes a general requirement that the regulatory content must be defined in a manner that it is clear (unambiguous) to the addressees of the legislation. Consequently, the requirement of comprehensibility is not explicitly stated in the legislation itself (Tóth 2022, 20). She examined the form in which the requirement of comprehensibility is incorporated into laws in effect and into norms regulating public law organizations, either for further legislation or for the application of the law. Her findings revealed that the incorporation of the requirement of comprehensibility into legislation remained formalistic. To date, no developed and applied method for implementing and measuring comprehensibility in Hungarian legislation has been established (Tóth 2023, 164).

In the field of public administration in Hungary, for instance, Szoták (2021, 99) identifies the simplification of the use of the Hungarian administrative language as a strategic task that is impracticable without the will of the governing bodies. Furthermore, she highlights the lack of a coherently developed communication strategy and action plan for achieving public accessibility that permeates the entire public administration. Additionally, she notes the absence of continuous and developed academic training and further training on simplifying the use of administrative language. She provides several examples of agencies that have produced and are implementing strategy documents on administrative communication. Nevertheless, it remains unclear whether and to what extent these strategies and programs result in enhanced clarity and accessibility.

In today's globalized world, where English is the dominant language for communication, the necessity for bilingual terminology is becoming increasingly apparent. While public administration is undoubtedly associated with a particular state and linguistically anchored to the official language of that state, public administration is also one of the domains where bilingual communication is of paramount importance. In 2011, the Hungarian public administration underwent a radical transformation with the support of "The Magyary Programme for Public Service" (web1). Subsequently, a number of publications have been released in both Hungarian and English regarding Hungarian public administration. With regard to the English terminology utilized in these publications, Rixer (2013) observed that there is an exceptional diversity in the terminology used to describe the same subject, the use of synonyms, or the use of terms that are related but not identical in meaning. Clearly, one challenge in English-language publications on Hungarian public administration is the lack of uniform English terminology corresponding to the Hungarian conceptual system, despite the precision and clarity of the terminology used in Hungarian. The system of public administration varies from country to country, resulting in differences in conceptual systems and terminology. A solution to this issue would be to harmonize the terminology of Hungarian public administration in English. One potential solution would be to create a public bilingual terminology dictionary or database.

9.3 Comprehensibility of Terminology

From a terminological standpoint, language can be defined as a communication system whose function is to convey knowledge abstracted in concepts and summarized in conceptual systems. The primary objective of terminology is to delineate the characteristics of terms and terminological systems, concepts and conceptual systems, and their interrelationships within a given domain. This is typically achieved through definitions and an examination of the semantic networks that underpin them. Additionally, terminology work entails the study of the linguistic and pragmatic features associated with terms. In essence, it is a discipline that bridges the gap between concepts and linguistic signs, interpreting the complex relationships between them (Fóris 2022, 38).

The advent of modern technological tools in recent decades has not only facilitated and accelerated work but also enabled the development of new principles and methodologies. Terminology work is primarily descriptive in nature, with the objective of mapping the terminological system of a given domain. However, prescriptive work, which is oriented toward teaching and standardization, is also prevalent, to provide guidance and advice on the use of terms. Traditionally, terminology work can be classified as domain-oriented, text-oriented, or ad hoc (see, e.g., Fóris 2022, 36–37). Many publications on comprehensibility reflect the principles of text-oriented terminology work. Typically, and understandably, writings on the comprehensibility of legal texts also look at terminology from a text-oriented view. This includes the importance of using the same terms consistently within a text, as using synonyms is not recommended. This approach promotes coherence of the text (see, e.g., Jopek-Bosiacka 2023).

As a solution to problems of terminological comprehensibility, the use of common words, as opposed to technical terms, is often suggested (particularly, in plain language recommendations). However, this approach is viable only for specific text types, intended for a defined target audience, and at a basic level of abstraction within the context of technical texts. The opposite is also advocated: that the meaning of terms in technical texts and their position within the terminology system should be provided in a glossary or database, with the aim of facilitating comprehension. The latter approach prioritizes the creation of terminology databases (termbases). It serves the purpose of this discussion to examine the various standards in this respect.

It is essential to consider the principles of information quality when preparing documentation in accordance with the IEC/IEEE 82079-1:2019 standard (see Introduction). Regarding terminology, it is crucial that it is accessible. Clarity and comprehensibility are both critical elements of effective communication. Furthermore, additional rules on terminology should be considered, such as the avoidance of colloquial terms and non-standard, regional versions of names and product descriptions. When the target audience is non-specialist, it is advisable to explain the terms in question, whether through definitions, references, or glossaries. In accordance with this standard, unavoidable acronyms, abbreviations, and technical terms that are not readily comprehensible to the intended audience should also be enumerated and clarified. In the event of uncertainty regarding the comprehensibility of the terminology to the target audience, empirical testing should be conducted (e.g., interviews, focus group discussions, usability testing, peer review, feedback from complaint handling).

The activities typically involved in terminology work can be broadly classified into the following categories: identifying, collecting, analyzing, and describing terms; classifying and representing terms; creating and filling in any missing terms; standardizing and validating terms in the terminology system; and finally, managing, recording, and publishing them. The translation and documentation project process usually requires multilingual, text-oriented terminology work (ISO 1087:2019, Fóris 2022).

The creation of terminology databases is a central task in terminology work and terminology strategy. A terminology database is comprised of terminological entries. In accordance with ISO 12616-1:2021, the fundamental components of a terminological entry are as follows: term, definition or explanation or context, part of speech, date of entry, source or source identifier, and concept identifier. (In translation practice, however, regardless of the wording of this standard, bilingual glossaries are frequently referred to as terminology databases.)

Given that professional texts are constructed with multiple layers and their comprehension necessitates a certain degree of prior knowledge on the part of the recipient, the literature on professional translation has led to the emergence of what is known as intralingual translation (Dobos 2022, 2023). As terms are the carriers of professional content, the professional is also necessarily engaged in the process of translating terms in the context of expert-to-lay communication. The extent of the "translation" required depends on the prior knowledge of the target audience, which may range from passive to fully competent in understanding the terms. Passive understanding can be defined as having an approximate idea of where a concept is located within a given domain. In contrast, full understanding can be described as having a precise understanding of a concept's relationship with other concepts within the same domain (Baker and Saldanha 2019). For instance, Fóris and Faludi (2021) consider the work of technical writers as a form of translation within a language. This is because they act as intermediaries in the communication between actors with disparate knowledge bases and also because their own knowledge differs from that of other individuals involved in the communication process. In their view, the use of appropriate concepts and terms ensures clarity, while the appropriate translation of technical terms ensures comprehensibility. This is achieved by using terms that match the reader's background knowledge and level of education.

Drinóczi and Novák (2015) have shown that terminology services have at least three uses in drafting. First, it makes sure that the same concepts are expressed in the same way in different languages. Second, it makes sure that the same words are used to express the same concepts in different languages. Third, terminology makes sure that laws and public administration are transparent, consistent, and clear. They also highlight that when translation is required during the drafting process, it is essential to have a solid understanding of the relevant legal system. In addition to the obvious need for familiarity with translation studies, a thorough knowledge of comparative law is crucial. This will ensure the quality of the translated text and the efficiency of the legal process. Drinóczi and Novák (2025) observe that the impact of the legal system on legal language and terminology manifests in different ways when we examine a single legal system within a single language or multiple legal systems across multiple languages.

While the drafting process is text-oriented, writers of legal texts can benefit from domain-oriented terminology work in both monolingual and multilingual work, i.e., the drafting of texts (writing any type of documentation or legislation) and in the translation process. Legal terminology databases are usually created by terminologists and/or lawyer-linguists. The creation and use of legal terminology databases is widespread and well known, such as *IATE* at European level, and national-level legal terminology databases such as *TERMDAT* in Switzerland (see Drinóczi and Novák 2025), the Lithuanian term bank (*Lietuvos Respublikos terminų bankas*, LRTB) (Umbrasas 2023), or the Hungarian legal terminology database *Termin* (Gáspár and Somssich 2019). The creation of terminology databases in both monolingual and multilingual environments is a useful and practical method, as they can contain definitions, context, and hierarchical relationships. Including English equivalents in national terminology databases is a common solution, as harmonization of English terms is essential in international contexts. In the absence of an adequate terminology database or a glossary of terms, there is an increased probability that quality issues will arise in the creation and translation of texts due to inconsistent term usage. The lack of terminological consistency impedes text comprehension, diminishes the effectiveness of language technology tools, and increases costs and time requirements for translation. Moreover, issues may emerge that, while not inherently terminological in nature, can be readily mitigated through the utilization of a comprehensive terminology database.

9.4 Technological Disruption: Digitization, Automation, and AI

There are already several legal terminology databases in existence at both national and supranational levels (Fóris and Bölcskei 2019). However, the necessity for further databases is becoming increasingly apparent, particularly in light of the impending rise of large language models (LLMs) as a significant user group. This section will examine the relationship between technological disruption and terminology management.

Terminology management issues are partly simplified and partly complicated by the increasing use of digitization, automation, and AI. For example, the digitization of texts and databases has enabled more convenient and expedient access to information, and the increasing reliance on machines and AI for data processing and decision making. However, these systems require accurate data, instructions, suitable questions (prompts), and access to relevant back-end corpora and databases for effective operation. It is crucial to ensure the clarity and comprehensibility of textual content prior to its processing by machine learning (ML) algorithms. Consequently, clarity, comprehensibility, and accessibility are not merely ethical necessities in the analysis and machine processing of legal documents but also fundamental prerequisites.

The rise of new technologies thus results in a constant stream of innovation. AI is a broad field that includes different techniques and approaches.

ML is a part of AI that helps systems learn from data. Generative AI is a broad concept that includes various forms of content generation. LLMs are a specific type of generative AI. LLMs are used for a wide range of natural language processing tasks. Generative AI can be used for more than just language generation; it can also be used for image and video generation, music composition, and more. LLMs are a specific application of generative AI: they are designed for tasks revolving around natural language generation and comprehension (toloka.ai).

Among the most relevant topics in the current context are the impact of digitization, ML, and AI, including the potential applications of LLMs such as ChatGPT or Microsoft Copilot, and other AI tools, like the language AI platform DeepL, for tasks such as lexicography, terminology, translation, language teaching, among other areas. In practice, the creation of digital content involves the transformation of information (e.g., documentation) into a machine-readable format. In this process, AI operates as a user, extracting content (information and metadata) from databases and human-generated (written or spoken) texts and creating new content based on these extracted elements. However, rapid advances in language technology and its applications in everyday life raise questions not only about how a database works for human users but also about how various AI and ML systems can make use of the data. In fact, terminology databases not only represent and transfer purely lexical knowledge to human users but also explore and capture the relationships between concepts through extensive analysis of different domains (Iantosca 2023; Lew 2024; Nesi 2024).

Terminology databases represent a modern tool for the dissemination of knowledge. The incorporation of linguistic data (terms), definitions, and contextual information within these databases facilitates the management of information in a more efficacious manner. Furthermore, hierarchical relationships between terms are also accounted for, thus providing a comprehensive and structured repository of linguistic data. Therefore, terminology databases can also be a good starting point for building taxonomies, ontologies, and knowledge graphs, where the development of a terminology database and the knowledge and experience accumulated there can be directly linked to other emerging areas of research. This also has implications for the technological environment in which both terminology experts and human and machine users operate, as ideally, they should all work, collaborate, and use the knowledge captured in the same architecture.

In the context of terminology work and databases, the source of the information is of crucial importance. One of the key challenges associated with AI-generated texts is the limited knowledge available about their origin, particularly in terms of their source on the internet. This lack of transparency makes it difficult to trace the origin of the texts, such as whether it was generated by ChatGPT. The source of the data, information, and knowledge remains uncertain.

As anticipated by Iantosca (2023), the future of Web3 will be characterized by a proliferation of knowledge sources, including taxonomies, ontologies, and knowledge graphs. However, some authors have already begun to explore the potential of ChatGPT and other AI-generated tools. San Martín (2024) investigated the writing process of terminological definitions, and he concluded that "the integration of AI into terminology work appears inevitable" and that "the gap in quality between AI-generated and human-created content is likely to diminish". In terms of the reliability of the sources, he believes that the use of ChatGPT in terminology work has both advantages and disadvantages. The principal advantage of a terminological definition incorporated into a resource is its reliability. However, this is accompanied by certain limitations. First, the responses may contain factual, logical, and linguistic errors. Second, they can also be biased and discriminatory. Third, ChatGPT is capable of fabricating incorrect information, which is often referred to as hallucinating. San Martín believes that the definitions contained within standards, patents, legislation, and terminology databases that reflect the terminology utilized by an organization will "not probably be replaced by AI because they intend to reflect a consensus among human beings" (San Martín 2024).

As Iantosca (2023) indicates, it seems probable that, in domains where reliable technical knowledge is required, such as in the field of law, LLMs will only be able to function effectively if they can rely on accurate semantic information. It is the terminology databases, taxonomies, ontologies, and knowledge graphs that will provide reliable semantic information for LLMs such as ChatGPT. The future is the combination of LLMs with knowledge graphs and terminology databases. In consequence, the creation of legal terminology databases and knowledge graphs is both imperative and increasingly critical, given the imminent rise of LLMs as a significant user group.

9.5 Legal Corpora and Terminology Databases

This section will present an overview of text corpora that contain and process legal texts. The category of legal texts can include an extensive range of text types, and, as a consequence, the databases of legal texts typically comprise multiple sub-corpora. It should be noted that both texts, corpora and databases, can be monolingual or multilingual. This section will present a brief overview of Hungarian examples in this field.

The current scientific and technological evolution is leading to the expansion of knowledge in specific domains, the acceleration of its dissemination, and the emergence of cross-disciplinary collaboration. Additionally, the use of information and communication technology tools is becoming increasingly vital in this evolving landscape. In their article, Drinóczi and Novák (2015) present the potential correlations between terminology and legislation. They also highlight the role of information technologies in facilitating the drafting process. In addition to their use in parliamentary procedures and interdepartmental cooperation, information technologies are employed for the circulation and discussion of drafts among ministers, government meetings, and during drafting. They also serve as tools for terminology, taking the form of databases and software.

On legal definitions, Jopek-Bosiacka (2023, 37) points out that "In law, a prescriptive approach predominates – legal definitions are the basic interpretative directives, as opposed to the discipline of terminology, where a descriptive approach applies". She indicates also that in the field of law, definitions serve as the fundamental interpretive guidelines for legal texts. Consequently, the definitions of legal terms are constrained by a set of rigorous criteria. The function of legal definitions is to organize the world of legal texts. They create new legal concepts, clarify the meaning of existing concepts that are also used in general language, and strive to bring maximum clarity and precision to legal texts.

The terminology utilized in the process of translation encompasses a multitude of elements, including termbases, which can potentially contribute to the canonization of a singular, accepted variant form while simultaneously eliminating the existence of other forms. Additionally, there are databases of legal texts and CAT (computer-assisted translation) tools, which facilitate the work with multilingual legal texts (Chiocchetti et al. 2017; Biel 2023).

In her article, Fóris (2024) affirmed that Hungary was a monolingual country for the majority of the 20th century, which shaped the landscape of monolingual terminology work. However, the geopolitical dynamics of the 21st century, including globalization, the rise of English-language research and publications, and membership in the European Union, as well as closer links with Hungarian communities beyond the borders, have served as a catalyst for the rise of Hungarian and English bilingual terminology work and in some cases multilingual terminology work and building termbases. This has made it necessary to study and describe more precisely the terminological systems of the domains influenced by these processes. It is evident that the most active areas of terminology work and research are those fields of science that have become of direct practical importance, namely law and public administration. Moreover, it seems that, particularly within the legal and administrative domain, terminology research and work are closely intertwined with translation. The advent of large linguistic models and the widespread use of AI has created a need for larger, more accurate, and more complex corpora of specialized language and terminology databases and knowledge bases than ever before. It is also the case that the legal field is subject to the same constraints as other professional domains.

Following Hungary's accession to the European Union at the turn of the millennium, the field of multilingual terminology work underwent a period of significant expansion. This development also saw the prominence of research into Hungarian terminology. In addition to studies of terminology, research into the linguistic characteristics of texts, including those of a legal nature, has been intensified. One of the first corpus-based research has been conducted to examine the comprehensibility of Hungarian legal texts. The *Miskolc Legal Corpus* was created with the objective of employing corpus linguistic methods to examine the characteristics of legal texts, comprising 2.4 million words (tokens) and 150,000 sentences. In this large-scale project, lawyers and linguists collaborated to ascertain whether there are features of Hungarian legal terminology that impede its comprehensibility (Vinnai 2017; Szabó and Vinnai 2018; Vincze 2018). This is a text corpus of written and spoken language texts and transcripts of legal texts in Hungarian. The corpus was constructed using a variety of legal texts, including code law and other legislation, court judgments, ministerial justifications of legislation, university coursebooks on law, and online legal forum discourses. Additionally, transcripts of audio recordings of trials and police interrogations were incorporated (see also Katona and Bódi 2024). In one part of this research project, an analysis was conducted on sentence structure and spelling features, including predicate structures, subject structures, coordination and subordination, and punctuation. Furthermore, the conceptual and terminological structure, as well as the meaning structure of the texts, were analyzed (grammatical, semantic, and pragmatic elements were captured). The findings indicate that comprehensibility varies according to the type of text. For instance, the texts that are easiest to understand are forum texts and transcripts, followed by pieces of legislation. In contrast, the texts that are most difficult to understand are court decisions and explanatory texts, such as explanatory memorandum to a bill or teaching materials. The significance of semantic and pragmatic features in the analysis, coupled with the tendency of law to adopt the language of the regulated reality, indicates that the challenge often arises not from the legal terminology itself but from the unfamiliar terminology, schemas, and scripts prevalent within the profession (Szabó and Vinnai 2018, 33; Ződi 2018, 260). The findings of the studies indicate that comprehensibility is a distinctive attribute of texts. This attribute is particularly evident in texts authored by professionals for a lay audience in general language, as evidenced by the analysis of Hungarian texts.

Several publications on the subject of translation and terminology in multilingual contexts have appeared in recent years. The field of legal and administrative document translation encompasses the processes of translating documents from foreign languages into Hungarian and of translating Hungarian documents into foreign languages. The majority of these publications share useful practices in day-to-day operations by institutional actors, namely state-funded entities, who are involved in this work. A number of these publications address terminology-related issues. The objective of these publications is to standardize terminology in the EU's legal translation program and map legal terms for the everyday work of the Hungarian Office for Translation and Attestation. Additionally, they provide guidance to translators about legal terms in the official languages of Hungary's neighboring countries (Tamás and Szoták 2021).

Prior to Hungary's accession in 2004, the Ministry of Justice commissioned the translation of EU legislation. The Hungarian terminology was subsequently published in the *Termin* database (https://termin.im.gov.hu/), which is maintained by the Ministry of Justice. A supranational layer of official languages has been established at the EU level, comprising a variety of specialized languages, including those utilized in legal and administrative contexts, in all national languages of the EU (see, e.g., Somssich 2014; Fischer 2023). Following Hungary's accession, the terminology was uploaded to the EU's interinstitutional terminology database, *IATE*. The *Termin* database remains operational to this day, containing typical terms of Hungarian legislation in both Hungarian and English. In 2017, the Ministry of Justice initiated a comprehensive program for translating Hungarian legislation into English. The English translations of Hungarian legislation have been published in a digital repository called *Nemzeti Jogszabálytár* (www.njt.hu), and the terms generated during the translation process have been recorded in the *Termin* database. Additionally, a guide on how to translate legislation has been published, which contains general guidelines on form, methodology, spelling, punctuation, and layout (Gáspár and Somssich 2019; Fuglinszky and Somssich 2020; Somssich 2023).

In Hungary, the administration started to go digital commenced in the beginning of the millennium and has affected all areas of administration, with a particularly substantial impact on public administration. From both a terminological and a comprehensibility standpoint, it is crucial that customers and administrations utilize an identical lexicon, conceptual framework, and terminology. The advent of e-government and e-public administration also necessitated a significant investment of time and resources by developers tasked with the digitization process, particularly in terms of terminology. The objective of the developers was not to construct an entirely novel terminology system; rather, it was to integrate the established terminology systems of administration and information technology (IT) into an electronic information system that would facilitate multi-level communication between administrators and customers. One aspect of this undertaking was the classification of terminology by experts through the harmonization of linguistic signs. Additionally, the standardization of concepts was conducted. Consequently, the developers have undertaken both terminology planning and terminology work, employing IT methods to delineate a hierarchical system of administrative terms based on their denotative and connotative meanings. They were tasked with integrating the management of the databases into the operational framework of the sectoral systems, thereby facilitating interoperability – that is, technical, organizational, and semantic interoperability between the systems (Majzikné Bausz 2008, see also Fóris 2024).

9.6 Conclusion

In the field of legislation, language and terminology issues are frequently addressed in legal publications in relation to the necessity of clear, comprehensible, and accessible communication. These issues are linked to concerns regarding efficiency and ethical conduct. In the legal field, the necessity for the use of clear and concise language is of particular importance when drafting and translating legislation. In the administrative domain, this requirement is primarily pertinent when communicating with citizens (who are often not versed in legal terminology) and when drafting official documents. Several initiatives have been launched globally with the objective of enhancing the clarity of official language use. These initiatives primarily focus on providing stylistic, syntactic, and lexical recommendations. The comprehensibility of legal documents is a multifaceted phenomenon, encompassing both linguistic and legal dimensions. It can be assessed along a range of variables. The comprehensibility of texts is influenced by numerous factors, including terminology. Ensuring the comprehensibility of terminology entails two main approaches: intralingual translation and the creation of terminology databases, which can be supported by terminology recommendations and standards.

The advent of digitization, automation, and AI – especially LLMs – has introduced both simplifications and complications to the field of terminology management. The availability of dynamic and adaptable terminology resources and tools for legislation is important, particularly given the role of AI in this process. AI operates as a user, extracting content (information and metadata) from databases and human-generated (written or spoken) texts and subsequently creating new content based on these extracted elements.

Acknowledgements

This research was supported by the project titled "Hungarian Terminology Strategy: Plans and Feasibility" by the Károli Gáspár University of the Reformed Church in Hungary, between 2025 and 2026.

References

Adler, Mark. 2012. "The plain language movement." In *The Oxford Handbook of Language and Law,* edited by Lawrence M. Solan and Peter M. Tiersma. Oxford Handbooks Online.

B. Papp, Eszter. 2021. "Professional documentation in the 21st century." In *Linguistic Research in the Fields of Content Development and Documentation,* edited by Ágota Fóris and Andrea Bölcskei. KRE. L'Harmattan. 41–57.

Baker, Mona, and Saldanha, Gabriela. 2019. "Terminology, theory." In *Routledge Encyclopedia of Translation Studies.* Routledge (3rd ed.).

Beaugrande, Robert-Alain de, and Dressler, Wolfgang U. 1981. *Introduction to Text Linguistics.* Longman.

Biel, Łucja. 2023. "Variation of legal terms in monolingual and multilingual contexts: Types, distribution, attitudes and causes." In *Handbook of Terminology. Volume 3. Legal Terminology,* edited by Łucja Biel and Hendrik J. Kockaert. John Benjamins. 90–123. https://doi.org/10.1075/hot.3.var1

Biel, Łucja, and Kockaert, Hendrik J. 2023. *Handbook of Terminology. Volume 3. Legal Terminology.* John Benjamins. https://doi.org/10.1075/hot.3

Cabré, Maria Teresa. 1998. *Terminology: Theory, Methods and Applications.* John Benjamins.

Chiocchetti, Elena, Wissik, Tanja, Lušicky, Vesna, and Wetzel, Michael. 2017. "Quality assurance in multilingual legal databases." *The Journal of Specialised Translation* 27: 164–188.

Corpas Pastor, Gloria, and Sánchez Rodas, Fernando. 2023. "EU phraseological verbal patterns in the PETIMOD 2.0 corpus: A NER-enhanced approach." In *Handbook of Terminology. Volume 3. Legal Terminology,* edited by Łucja Biel and Hendrik J. Kockaert. John Benjamins. 397–430.

Csontos, Nóra. 2021a. "Means of sharing knowledge in technical texts." In *Linguistic Research in the Fields of Content Development and Documentation,* edited by Ágota Fóris and Andrea Bölcskei. KRE. L'Harmattan. 269–292.

Csontos, Nóra. 2021b. "Technical texts from the perspective of text typology: Text typology analysis of instructions for use." In *Linguistic Research in the Fields of Content Development and Documentation,* edited by Ágota Fóris and Andrea Bölcskei. KRE. L'Harmattan. 293–312.

Czinkóczki, Ágnes, and Fehér, Ildikó. 2021. "How is technical content created? The lifecycle of technical documentation." In *Linguistic Research in the Fields of Content Development and Documentation,* edited by Ágota Fóris and Andrea Bölcskei. KRE. L'Harmattan. 119–137.

Dobos, Csilla. 2022. "A szaknyelvről köznyelvre történő intralingvális fordítás szerepe a tudásmegosztásban." *Alkalmazott Nyelvészeti Közlemények* 15 (2): 38–64.

Dobos, Csilla. 2023. "Az intralingvális fordítás jogi aspektusa: Fordítástudományi szempontok a jogi-közigazgatási területen." *Glossa Iuridica* 10 (3): 105–132. https://doi.org/10.55194/GI.2023.3.6

Drinóczi, Tímea. 2010. *Minőségi jogalkotás és adminisztratív terhek csökkentése Európában.* HVG ORAC.

Drinóczi, Tímea. 2015. "Concept of quality in legislation – revisited: Matter of perspective and a general overview." 3 *Statute Law Review* 36 (3): 211–227. https://doi.org/10.1093/slr/hmv008

Drinóczi, Tímea. 2017. "Quality control and management in legislation: A theoretical framework." *KLRI Journal of Law and Legislation* 7 (1): 57–85.

Drinóczi, Tímea, and Petrétei, József. 2004. *Jogalkotástan*. Dialóg Campus.

Drinóczi, Tímea, and Novák, Barnabás. 2015. "Linguistic approach in legisprudence – Terminology, translation studies and databases." *Theory and Practice of Legislation* 3 (1): 113–129. https://doi.org/10.1080/20508840.2015.1041707

Drinóczi, Tímea, and Novák, Barnabás. 2025. "Making drafting clearer and more accessible in a multilingual context: The role of contrastive terminology and comparative law." In *Language for Legislation and Legislation through Language* [this book].

Duprat, Jean-Pierre, and Xanthaki, Helen. 2017. "Legislative drafting techniques/formal logistics." In *Legislation in Europe: A Comprehensive Guide for Scholars and Practitioners*, edited by Ulrich Karpen and Helen Xanthaki. Hart Publishing. 109–126.

Engberg, Jan, ed., 2023. *Between Text, Meaning and Legal Languages: Linguistic Approaches to Legal Interpretation.* (Foundations in Language and Law [FLL] Book 8) De Gruyter Mouton.

Fischer, Márta. 2023. *Eurolektusok. Az Európai Unió hatása a nyelvekre, különös tekintettel a jogi nyelvre.* Akadémiai Kiadó.

Fogarasi, Katalin, and Patonai, Zoltán. 2021. "Az egészségügyi dokumentáció szerepe és jelentősége." In *Tartalomfejlesztés és dokumentáció. Nyelvészeti vonatkozások*, edited by Ágota Fóris and Andrea Bölcskei. KRE. L'Harmattan. 265–288.

Fóris, Ágota. 2011. "Terminology and text linguistics." *Terminologija* 18: 51–65. https://lki.lt/wp-content/uploads/2017/06/Terminologija-18-ilovepdf-compressed-ilovepdf-compressed.pdf

Fóris, Ágota. 2022. *Translation and Terminology: Theory and Practice in Hungary*. KRE. L'Harmattan.

Fóris, Ágota. 2023. "A terminológiastratégia szempontjai a jogi-közigazgatási területen." *Glossa Iuridica* 10 (3): 35–64. https://doi.org/10.55194/GI.2023.3.2

Fóris, Ágota. 2024. "The history and recent trends of terminology in Hungary in the 21st century." *Terminologija* 31: 53–74. https://doi.org/10.35321/term31-03

Fóris, Ágota, and Bölcskei, Andrea. 2019. "Ajánlások a magyar terminológiastratégiához." In *Terminológiastratégiai kihívások a magyar nyelvterületen*, edited by Ágota Fóris and Andrea Bölcskei. L'Harmattan. OFFI Zrt. 140–164.

Fóris, Ágota, and Faludi, Andrea. 2021. "Technical writing and documentation as intralingual technical translation." In *Linguistic Research in the Fields of Content Development and Documentation*, edited by Ágota Fóris and Andrea Bölcskei. KRE. L'Harmattan. 157–176.

Fuglinszky, Ádám, and Somssich, Réka. 2020. "Language-bound terms – term-bound languages: The difficulties of translating a national civil code into a lingua franca." *International Journal for the Semiotics of Law* 33: 749–770. https://doi.org/10.1007/s11196-020-09704-x

Garner, Bryan A. 2023. *Legal Writing in Plain English*. (Chicago Guides to Writing, Editing, and Publishing). University of Chicago Press (3rd ed.).

Gáspár, Endre, and Somssich, Réka. 2019. "A magyar jog fordítva: Az Igazságügyi Minisztérium átfogó fordítási projektje a magyar joganyag angol nyelvű elérhetőségének biztosítására." *Fontes Iuris* 1: 55–60.

Hernández Ramos, Mario, and Heydt, Völker 2017. "Legislative language and style." In *Legislation in Europe: A Comprehensive Guide for Scholars and Practitioners*, edited by Ulrich Karpen and Helen Xanthaki. Hart Publishing. 129–144.

Iantosca, Michael J. 2023. "Intelligence in, knowledge out: Augmenting large language models with knowledge graphs for effective, responsible and explainable AI (XAI)." https://thinkingdocumentation.com/downloads

Jakobson, Roman. 1958. "On linguistic aspects of translation." In *On Translation*, edited by Reuben Brower. OUP. 232–239.

Jopek-Bosiacka, Anna. 2023. "Definitions in law across legal cultures and jurisdictions." In *Handbook of Terminology. Volume 3. Legal Terminology*, edited by Łucja Biel and Hendrik J. Kockaert. John Benjamins. 37–71. https://doi.org/10.1075/hot.3.def1

Karpen, Ulrich, and Xanthaki, Helen, eds., 2017. *Legislation in Europe: A Comprehensive Guide for Scholars and Practitioners*. Hart Publishing.

Katona, József Álmos, and Bódi, Zoltán. 2024. "Language planning issues of Hungarian legal language and the clear writing programme as a possible solution." *Current Issues in Language Planning* 26(1): 1–18. https://doi.org/10.1080/14664208.2023.2283653

L'Homme, Marie-Claude. 2020. *Lexical Semantics for Terminology*. John Benjamins.

Langacker, Ronald W. 1987. *Foundations of Cognitive Grammar*. Science.

Lew, Robert. 2024. "Dictionaries and lexicography in the AI era." *Humanities and Social Sciences Communications* 11: Article No. 426. https://doi.org/10.1057/s41599-024-02889-7

Majzikné Bausz, Ágota. 2008. "Az e-kormányzat, e-közigazgatás problémái és terminológiai vonatkozásai Magyarországon." *Magyar Terminológia* 1 (1): 59–76. https://doi.org/10.1556/mterm.1.2008.1.5

Mouritsen, Stephen. 2023. "Ordinary meaning in common law legal interpretation." In *Handbook of Terminology. Volume 3. Legal Terminology*, edited by Łucja Biel and Hendrik J. Kockaert. John Benjamins. 72–89. https://doi.org/10.1075/hot.3.ord1

Németh, Gabriella. 2022. "Közérthető, tisztességes, hatékony és kompetens – Etikai minőségbiztosításra tett kísérletek az igazságügyi szakértői közreműködésben." *Jog – Állam – Politika* 14 (1): 161–176.

Nesi, Hilary. 2024. "Are we witnessing the death of dictionaries?" *Iberica* 47: 7–14. https://doi.org/10.17398/2340-2784.47.7

Novák, Barnabás. 2018. "A terminológiai munkafolyamat a minőségi jogalkotásban. Magyar–olasz összehasonlító vizsgálat az alkotmányjogi terminológia területén." PhD diss., University of Pécs.

Pázmándi, Kinga. 2018. "A jog nyelvi dimenziói és a fogyasztóvédelem 'devizahiteles' perek szereplőinél azonosítható nyelvi attitűdök." In *A törvény szavai*, edited by Miklós Szabó and Edina Vinnai. Bíbor Kiadó. 261–280.

Pléh, Csaba, and Lukács, Ágnes. 2014. *Pszicolingvisztika 1–2*. Akadémiai Kiadó.

Rixer, Ádám. 2013. "A magyar közigazgatás idegen nyelvű irodalmának egyes jellegzetességei az elmúlt negyedszáz esztendőben." *Pro Publico Bono – Magyar Közigazgatás* 3 (3): 4–22.

San Martín, Antonio. 2024. "What generative artificial intelligence means for terminological definitions." In *Proceedings of the 3rd International Conference on Multilingual Digital Terminology Today (MDTT 2024)*. https://doi.org/10.48550/arXiv.2402.16139

Schriver, Karen A. 2017. "Plain language in the US gains momentum: 1940–2015." *IEEE Transactions in Professional Communication* 60 (4): 343–383. https://ieeexplore.ieee.org/document/8115322/, https://doi.org/10.1109/TPC.2017.2765118

Simonnas, Ingrid. 2016. "Legal language: Pragmatic approaches to its interconnectivity with legal interpretation and legal translation." *Meta* 61 (2): 421–438.

Solan, Lawrence M., and Tiersma, Peter M., eds., 2021. *The Oxford Handbook of Language and Law*. Oxford University Press. https://doi.org/10.1093/oxfordhb/9780199572120.001.0001

Sólyom, Réka. 2021. "Conceptual metaphors and metonymies in a technical text." In *Linguistic Research in the Fields of Content Development and Documentation,* edited by Ágota Fóris and Andrea Bölcskei. KRE. L'Harmattan. 353–373.

Sólyom, Réka. 2024. "Movements and directions, constructions and forces: Prevalent metaphorical source domains in Hungarian legal texts." *Terminologija* 31: 155–167. https://doi.org/10.35321/term31-08

Somssich, Réka. 2014. "The process and methodology of coordinating the transposition of EU law in Hungary." In *The Law of the European Union in Hungary: Institutions, Processes and the Law*, edited by Márton Varju and Ernő Várnay. HVG-ORAC. 112–150.

Somssich, Réka. 2023. "Translation hindrances and linguistic (im)possibilities to challenge the Hungarian legal language." In *Research Handbook on Jurilinguistics,* edited by Anne Wagner and Aleksandra Matulewska. Edward Elgar. 360–373.

Szabó, Miklós, and Vinnai, Edina. eds., 2018. *A törvény szavai*. Bíbor Kiadó.

Szoták, Szilvia. 2021. "Társadalmi különbségek, közérthetőségi dilemmák – A közérthetőségről szociolingvisztikai megközelítésben." *Jog – Állam – Politika* XIII (1): 89–101.

Tamás, Dóra Mária, and Szoták, Szilvia, eds., 2021. *Magyar jogi alapterminusok a szomszédos országok nyelvén*. OFFI Zrt.

Temmerman, Rita. 2007. "Les métaphores dans les sciences de la vie et le situé sociocultural." *Cahiers du Rifal* XXVI: 72–83.

Tóth, Judit. 2022. "A közérthetőség úgy, ahogy a jogalkotó elképzeli." *Közjogi Szemle* 4: 20–27.

Tóth, Judit. 2023. "A közérthetőség kutathatósága és a jogi nyelv reformja?" *Glossa Iuridica* X (3): 153–166.

Umbrasas, Alvydas. 2023. "Lietuvos Respublikos terminų bankas: 20 metų po įstatymo priėmimo." *Terminologija* 30: 142–167. https://doi.org/10.35321/term30-7

Vincze, Veronika. 2018. "A Miskolci Jogi Korpusz nyelvi jellemzői." In *A törvény szavai,* edited by Miklós Szabó and Edina Vinnai. Bíbor Kiadó. 9–36.

Vinnai, Edina. 2017. *Jog és nyelv határán. A jogi nyelvhasználat nemzetközi és hazai kutatása.* Gondolat.
Xanthaki, Helen. 2011. "Quality of legislation: An achievable universal concept or a Utopian pursuit?" In *Quality of Legislation,* edited by Marta Travares Almeida. Nomos. 75–85.
Xanthaki, Helen. 2023. *Thornton's Legislative Drafting.* Bloomsbury Professional (6th ed.).
Zauberga, Ieva. 2005. "Handling terminology in translation." In *New Trends in Translation Studies: In Honour of Kinga Klaudy*, edited by Krisztina Károly and Ágota Fóris. Akadémiai Kiadó. 107–116.
Ződi, Zsolt. 2018. "A jog érthetőségének határai: Meg tudják-e oldani a nyelvészek a jogi szövegek érthetetlenségének problémáját?" In *A törvény szavai,* edited by Miklós Szabó and Edina Vinnai. Bíbor Kiadó. 241–260.

Sources

BSI web1 = The British Standard Institution (BSI). What is a standard? https://www.bsigroup.com/en-IN/Standards-and-Publications/Information-about-standards/What-is-a-standard/
BSI web2 = The British Standard Institution (BSI). Standards and regulation. https://www.bsigroup.com/en-IN/Standards-and-Publications/Information-about-standards/Standards-and-regulation/
Clear writing for Europe. https://commission.europa.eu/about-european-commission/departments-and-executive-agencies/translation/clear-writing-europe_en
DIN web = Deutsches Institut für Normung e. V. (DIN). Standards and the law. https://www.din.de/en/about-standards/standards-and-the-law
Directive 2006/42/EC of the European Parliament and of the Council
How to write clearly, Luxembourg, Publications Office of the European Union, 2011, available in 24 languages. https://op.europa.eu/en/publication-detail/-/publication/c2dab20c-0414-408d-87b5-dd3c6e5dd9a5
IATE (Interactive Terminology for Europe). (https://iate.europa.eu/)
IEC/IEEE 82079-1:2019 Preparation of information for use (instructions for use) of products — Part 1: Principles and general requirements.
ISO 24495-1:2023 Plain language – Part 1: Governing principles and guidelines.
Lietuvos Respublikos terminų bankas (LRTB). (https://terminai.vlkk.lt/)
Plain English Campaign. (https://www.plainenglish.co.uk/)
Plain Language Movement. (https://www.plainlanguage.gov/)
Termin. (https://termin.im.gov.hu/)
Toloka.ai. Difference between AI, ML, LLM, and Generative AI. https://toloka.ai/blog/difference-between-ai-ml-llm-and-generative-ai/
web1= The Magyary Programme for Public Service. https://2010-2014.kormany.hu/en/ministry-of-public-administration-and-justice/news/the-magyary-programme-for-public-service

10 Making Drafting Clearer and More Accessible in a Multilingual Context

The Role of Contrastive Terminology and Comparative Law

Barnabás Novák and Tímea Drinóczi

10.1 Introduction

Literature at the crossroads of language and law has theorized how laws can be intelligible while unequivocally expressing the needed legal content. It has been established that laws need to be drafted in a way that respects several principles, such as efficiency, economy, unambiguity, accessibility, and intelligibility (see Xanthaki 2013; Xanthaki 2014; Cormacain 2022; Mosmouti 2019). It has also been reaffirmed that linguistics, terminology, the science of translation, and the tools they apply can play a crucial role in legislation (Drinóczi and Novák 2015; Tamás 2021). The effectiveness of national legislation depends, among other factors (Mosmouti 2019), on its ability to create a clear and consistent legal terminology system – from the perspective of law (e.g., criminal legal dogmatics) and linguistics (e.g., versions of laws in multilingual jurisdictions). Clarity in the legal and linguistic framework demands, for instance, that lawmakers adopt simple and consistent legal measures that the addresses of the law can easily understand. Thus, the observance of the requirement of clarity in lawmaking, supported by its proper management and verification mechanisms, can contribute to the adoption of better law, i.e., the quality of legislation can increase in terms of having a more democratic lawmaking process and effective laws (Xanthaki 2014; Drinóczi 2015; OSCE ODIHR 2023). These result in more compliance, legal certainty, and less problematic implementation practices. As law works through language, and as neither law nor language is a static phenomenon but prone to changes, complying with these principles has always been challenging. This challenge is most evident in jurisdictions constitutionally mandated to multilingualism. Multilingualism relies on the collaboration of many actors in drafting, adopting, publishing, and consolidating the laws in more than one language in the context of each language's origin state in which legal terminology and dogmatics might differ. Thus, finding equivalents in the source and

DOI: 10.4324/9781003430308-13

target language can be complicated. It is not only because, in normative systems, using synonyms or deviating from the conventional use of specific terms is advised against but also because any disagreement on the translation and drafting can be (over)politicized, especially in the relationship between the European Union (EU) and its Member States. We will highlight these issues with some salient examples from Hungary. During the translation and drafting process, "functional equivalents" are thus recommended to be found and consistently used. Understanding another state's legal system and legal terminology requires knowledge of comparative law and comparative terminology. These fields have evolved significantly, and technological developments have enabled rapid progress to facilitate, categorize, and classify legal knowledge (Tamás 2019). The digital revolution, open-source terminology databases, and the new type of institutional cooperation also energized the growth of interdisciplinary research (Hellwege and Soniewicka 2024; Fóris 2009). Both terminologists and legal comparatists have always searched for the best solutions in analyzing legal problems interrelated with the law and language (Michaels 2011; Olsen 2019). The spread of IT tools and legal terminology databases has enabled us to learn faster about other legal systems, traditions, and cultures and the relations between them. This progressive development of the collection and storage of legal information in the virtual world today reaches, speeds up, and transforms its foundations into the basis of legal and terminological comparisons (Chiocchetti, Lušicky, and Wissik 2023, 460–461).

There are already some practical implementations of the abovementioned theoretical demands and technological possibilities, for instance, in Italy, Switzerland, and the EU. For this chapter, we have chosen to showcase the Swiss and EU drafting experiences, more precisely, how the Swiss Federal Administration's terminology database (TERMDAT) and the EU's terminology management system (IATE; Interactive Terminology for Europe) contribute to the quality of the drafting process in terms of clarity and accessibility. This chapter compares these extensive multilingual databases, which provide a versatile aid for communication, legislation, and specialized translation, and examines the challenges they have faced. It also highlights the potential commonalities they have developed in addressing them. Drawing on, among others (see Section 10.2), our previous research in which we presented the correlation between terminology, translation studies, and drafting and highlighted the technical aspects of terminology databases and translation (Drinóczi and Novák 2015), in this chapter, we provide a more law-oriented and less technical approach to address the multilingual challenges the drafting process faces. Based on this approach and the lessons learned from some salient Hungarian experiences with translation, the overview of the Swiss and the EU translation and drafting processes, and the use of databases, we argue that the drafting process in multilingual jurisdictions could benefit from contrastive terminology, comparative law, and terminology databases created on these bases. It also supports the view that precise language contributes to an increased quality of the lawmaking process (Osnabrügge and Vannoni 2024).

The remainder of the chapter discusses the intersection of law and language, explaining why and how they are interlinked, especially in a multilingual environment. Section 10.3 contains the case studies on Switzerland and the EU, and based on these, Section 10.4 collects the lessons learned. The last section concludes by reflecting concisely on the central thesis of this chapter, the importance of contrastive terminology, comparative law, and terminology databases, and offers two additional observations.

10.2 Law and Language

10.2.1 Law, Terminology, and Translation

The lawmaking process is fundamentally related to both law and language (see, for more details, Danet 1980; Lind and Tyler 1988; Levi and Walker 1990; Tiersma 2008; Nussbaumer 1997; Haß-Zumkehr 2002; Galdia 2021). It is linked to the former by its content and to language by its unique expression. The content of the law follows the changes in the socio-economic relations and conditions on which it is based, and its language evolves and develops together with the law. As the law evolves, new concepts are born that require new terminology and, in a multilingual state, translation services. The speeding up of information exchange and the need to avoid any possible misunderstandings or create unintentional loopholes with ambiguous legal terms go hand in hand with the increased demand for linguistic services (Drinóczi and Novák 2015). Most recently, the ODIHR Guidelines for Democratic Lawmaking for Better Laws[1] appreciate the interconnectedness and interdependence of law and language when naming clarity and intelligibility, foreseeability, publication, and accessibility as principles of democratic lawmaking, and emphasize the importance of language choices, consistency in terminology (Fóris 2026), and the benefits of using technology in drafting. After all, legal terminology, embracing legal dogmatics, drafting, and linguistic principles, facilitates democratic lawmaking and creates a simplified, understandable, and user-friendly regulatory environment.

As we have established in our previous research, terminology services (and, generally, terminology studies) serve at least three purposes in the drafting process (Drinóczi and Novák 2015). First, it aims to create perfect compliance between the concepts available in two (or more) different languages and simultaneously ensure a uniform legal interpretation of the official versions of the two (or more) languages. It also reduces the use of synonymous expressions of these languages, thus eliminating potential legal confusion and the possibility of inconsistent interpretations. Third, terminology promotes transparency, consistency, and clarity in law and public administration, ensuring equal access of different native speakers (citizens) to authorized texts.

Terminology services, to function properly, rely on translation services. Translation studies examine subject-matters' reconciliation in source and target languages (Crystal 1987, 344). This reconciliation necessitates considering the languages' cultural, social, and historical fixities. It should carry the same professional values and credibility in the target language and text as the source language and text (Magris and Musacchio 1999, 150). Therefore, traditional translations require the knowledge of two linguistic systems (in the case of multiple target languages, the number consequently varies) and all the belonging fixities. The translator's task is to bridge the gaps between these compound systems (Lécrivain 1998, 349). Therefore, knowledge of relevant legal systems and comparative law is also essential when translation is needed in the drafting process and when creating and feeding a terminology database.

Compliance with the mentioned basic legal, terminological, and translation principles (Magris and Musacchio 1999; Nielsen 2023; Machuska et al. 2023) will most likely lead to better lawmaking. At least three preconditions exist for this: political commitment to uphold and implement these principles, adequate training and the necessary resources and capacity for those who deal with lawmaking daily, and consistency, i.e., the consistent use of the same technical terms for all possible occurrences. As we have indicated in the Introduction, this chapter emphasizes the latter.

10.2.2 Legal Terminology and Its Culturally Bound Aspects

Legal terminology, including and requiring translation, is essentially characterized by its technical and cultural boundness. Legal terminology is often considered a specialized part of terminology studies, a more formal and technical discipline concerning law. However, precisely because it is legal terminology, with emphasis on the adjective, it is difficult to draw a sharp division between law, culture, and terminology, as the legal language itself is culturally bound (Terral 2004, 876).

In monolingual states, translating any legal term from one language to another can be identified as an exercise of legal research during the policy-making process, thus preceding or occurring during drafting. Even in this case, accuracy is essential, but it could be seen as a requirement of decent research and, occasionally, legal certainty. In contrast, in multilingual states, having an accurate translation of legal texts with authoritative force can be considered a human right (see De Luca

2017; Arzoz 2007). Nevertheless, the influence of the legal system on the legal language and terminology is particularly apparent if we distinguish between two different occurrences of legal translation. It can be based on a single legal system but in several languages. It is the case, for example, in the multilingual laws of countries such as Switzerland, where the same legal system is transcribed into several languages. In Switzerland, where the objective is to have a coherent national legal system in all the official languages, legal and terminological comparison and research may be conducted without external comparison. Besides fulfilling translation and terminology-related tasks and harmonization, the official documents are characterized by consistency and exactitude in each national language.

The influence of the legal system on the legal language and terminology appears in a different way when we consider several legal systems in several languages. For instance, this is when international law and EU law are incorporated into the domestic legal systems. In these cases, it might happen that the drafters of the text to be translated into national law (literally and metaphorically) do not have practical experience in applying the law in the target language and legal system. Nevertheless, international and supranational commitments require observance, followed by less and more scrutiny. During this scrutiny, many languages are expected to describe the same legal reality (appearing in international and EU law). It is also expected that the conceptual system be carried out within one single conceptual system, which is quite challenging (Kjaer 2015, 94), as states seldom share the same conceptual systems, especially in law. Yet, those guarding the proper implementation of, for instance, EU law might also want to see literal translations also in cases in which it is incompatible with the domestic legal system. Reasons for the possible incompatibility can be manifold: common law vs. civil law traditions and institutions; established legal practice on the legal meaning of a concept/legal terms; structure of the domestic branch of law, etc. It does not mean that national drafters do not offer alternatives, as they might provide worse or better textual variations. Still, the resistance might also (or predominantly) come from political and not only legal and drafting motivations. As further requirements might be needed to achieve the full effectiveness of the EU directives in the national law, meeting these might raise difficulties for Member States. EU supranational terms are a special category of legal terms as they are required to "travel" from a supranational context to national ones, where they are confronted with and need to co-exist with domestic law variants (Biel and Doczekalska 2020, 185). As per the general statement, EU legislation helps achieve the objectives of the EU and puts EU policies into practice. However, even when monitoring Member States' compliance, EU requirements must be carefully formulated and applied to avoid terminological clashes with domestic legal principles and conventional interpretations of national laws' structure and phrases.

There might be inconsistencies between what one language (e.g., English) means under a particular word and what another language (e.g., Hungarian), culturally and legally, means under the same word. These differences might result in terminology conflicts between the EU and the Member States, causing lengthy and cumbersome negotiations and reconciliation sessions between drafters of EU and national laws. For example, when the policy of how to fight bribery was on the agenda of the EU, the notion of active bribery in the Criminal Code of Hungary (CC), i.e., what precisely the criminalized behavior is and which verb best expresses this criminal act, has given rise to a severe interpretative controversy. It was because of the cultural and linguistic boundaries of the Hungarian term "promise" ["ígér"], which has a considerable added value compared to the English equivalent ("promise"). Behaviors, i.e., verbs describing active bribery of public domestic officials are "ad vagy ígér" (in Hungarian – "give or promise" in English), are established in Section 253 CC, which reads:

> (1) *Any person who – in connection with the duties of the public official –* ***gives or promises*** *undue advantage to a public official or to another person on account of such public official, is guilty of a felony punishable by imprisonment of up to three years.*

The content and meaning of the Hungarian word "ígér" ["promises"], which appears in the original text, covers both the action of "promise" and "offer" ["ajánl"] in both ordinary language and in the Hungarian criminal justice system as well. The GRECO considered that the wording of Section 253 CC (active bribery in the public sector[2]) in its English translation contained only the elements "gives" or "promises" of undue advantage. Thus, it seemed that it does not criminalize the behavior meant by the English "offer". Therefore, the request was to include an additional verb, "offer" ["ajánl"], to the CC as a criminalized behavior in this context. However, following the Hungarian authorities' explanations, supported by references to the continued judicial practice on the interpretation of the verb "ígér" in the Hungarian criminal justice system and other interlocutors with whom the GRECO Evaluation Team for Theme I (GET) met on-site, the GET accepted that the Hungarian expression "ígér" ["promises"], as a verb, includes in its meaning both "promises" and "offers" (see Evaluation Report on Hungary on Incriminations 2010).

These short examples from Switzerland and Hungary demonstrate two aspects of the connection between translation and drafting quality. The first is that legal translation always involves both a legal and a linguistic operation. The only difference between the EU–Hungarian scenario and the one occurring in a multilingual nation-state (Switzerland) is the type of translation difficulty involved. Even though they go hand in hand, this difficulty may, in some cases, lean more toward linguistic issues (Swiss case) and, in other cases, lean more toward legal ones. The problems arising from transposing EU directives into national law can be viewed more as a legal issue having a linguistic basis.

The second aspect highlights the importance of appreciating the context in which this legal and linguistic operation appears. The experience shown in the bribery case on how legal translation can happen might lead to two extreme conclusions drawn in the 2020s. The first is that adequate legal and terminological unification and harmonization, especially in the EU, are not feasible and desirable. The second is that resistance to this kind of compliance can always be justified by recalling the constitutional identity and constitutional heritage of the Member States' legal systems. However, we would be very cautious with these arguments not only because a certain extent of unification is the essence of the EU but also because of the most recent emergence and abuse of the concept of constitutional identity (see de Poorter et al. 2023; Drinóczi 2020). We would warn against using the arguments of constitutional identity and constitutional heritage of the Member States' legal systems to oppose meaningful considerations of translation variations. It would also be equally misleading to suspect ulterior motives behind insisting on a particular legal institution or wording practice.

Finding balance would be a good compromise, but the habitual abuse of the concept of constitutional identity makes it difficult. To avoid the suspicion of the Hungarian intention of circumventing the joint effort to fight corruption by hiding behind "traditions of criminal dogmatics", we used an example above from a GRECO report published in June 2010,[3] i.e., before the illiberal remodeling that took place in the country in an accelerated manner after the entering into force of the new Constitution (Fundamental Law, FL) in 2012 (see Drinóczi and Bień-Kacała 2022). Finding this balance can be supported by what we suggest as the central thesis of this chapter: comparative and/or contrastive terminology and comparative law should be prioritized because the examination of legal concepts for translation and drafting purposes is better based on a system-comparative rather than a system-independent basis. To further support this statement, we explain why comparison matters before exploring the two case studies on translation and drafting in multilingual contexts.

10.2.3 The Use of Comparison

Comparative terminological analysis could resolve possible linguistic differences between the conceptual systems of the respective legal systems by reducing the number of potential legal interpretations. A linguistic interpretation of legislation in a descriptive way does not in itself constitute a comparison of the legal systems. However, legal comparatists can use this linguistic interpretation as a source of legal ideas to solve a domestic legal issue. The language of law is determined by its own context and can only be perfectly understood and interpreted in that context. Differences in legal cultures are reflected in legal concepts specific to each legal system and the use of legal concepts and terms common to legal systems but with slightly different meanings (see Somssich 2007). The latter poses a real challenge in terms of conceptual correspondence, like in the example of the Hungarian *Kúria* ("Curia" in the official English translation of the Hungarian authorities). The Hungarian Fundamental Law introduced the concept of the *Kúria*, which is the name of the body that replaces the Supreme Court. The legal status, procedure, and functions of the *Kúria* are regulated by Article 25 (1) and (3) of the Fundamental Law and by Act CLXI of 2011 on the Organization and Administration of Courts. When examining the possible English equivalent of the *Kúria*, we must be aware that this term has historical roots in Hungary: from the 16th century until 1949, this was the name given to the highest judicial forum. In 1949, the name was altered to *Supreme Court*, referring to the restructuring of the judicial organization. Although the FL clarifies the legal status and the new functions of the *Kúria* and the definition of the term *Kúria* is clear when looking at the conceptual system of the Hungarian court system, in any foreign language equivalence, we find a kind of circumscription as the adequate translation. For example, both the English and the Italian translations use the "place" of the *Kúria* in the Hungarian court system by naming it *Supreme Court* (in English) and *Corte Suprema* (in Italian) to describe its name (*Kúria*, Curia) instead of using this proper name. This choice expresses the "content", and it also seems to be a more straightforward and comprehensible phrase than a more foreign concept used by Hungarian translators (Curia).

The reason behind this use of expressions is that the character of a legal system lies in the concepts it has developed over its historical evolution. While rules may vary over time, concepts remain because they are closely linked to a particular legal tradition. The relationship between language and law is studied here in reverse, considering the legal system's influence on legal language (Terral 2004, 881). As with all types of terminology, legal terminology is dynamic and subject to change over time. This change can be to the great advantage of lawmakers if the terms are selected based on objective considerations such as national legal requirements or expected performance. Variants in terminology can be synchronic or diachronic (Freixa 2006, 59). Both synchronic and diachronic variants share many theoretical concepts and methodological concerns. Synchronic variants co-exist in time and are frequent in new emerging domains where terminology is under formation and hence unstable. For example, *legal heir*, *heir at law*, and *heir by operation of law*. Under such circumstances and the co-existence of so many variants, it is necessary to inquire whether legal comparison today is apt to uncover other than linguistically relevant features of law. Diachronic variants were used in the past; thus, they usually do not compete with newer variants. For example, the abbreviation of BIC, *Bank Identifier Code*, which is now called the *Business Identifier Code* (ISO 9362:2022), consists of 8 or 11 alphanumeric characters, comprising a business party prefix for financial and non-financial institutions for which such an international identifier is required to facilitate the automated processing of information for financial services. The BIC addresses messages, routes business transactions, and identifies parties. The international standard under ISO 9362:2014 defines the BIC Code structure, which allows no misunderstandings and unclarity regarding the use and meaning of a particular abbreviation, such as BIC, in this example.

Knowledge of foreign laws can inform reflection on one's own legal system and laws; exposure to foreign experiences may assist in developing a more profound and potentially more critical perspective of domestic (and foreign or different) law (Siems 2018). Consequently, comparative law broadens the understanding of how legal rules work in context and the embeddedness of legal rules in other societies and legal traditions. In the field of (national/non-comparative) terminology, the aim is to consider and, if needed, adopt and adapt well-developed and well-supported practices, thereby continuously improving and building up the national legal terminology system. Foreign laws can provide models of how (well) different sets of legal rules work in addressing a particular problem or pursuing a particular policy, which comparative and contrastive terminology can use mostly to understand and explain the different systems. Understanding different legal approaches can be fundamental to providing appropriate legal concepts. We often hear about the rule of "best solution" (Jopek-Bosiacka 2023, 44, EPA 2014), especially in contemporary terminology studies. Suppose a decision is made to unify the terminology system of a particular field of law. In that case, comparing the existing domestic laws is essential to choosing the most common approach or a general solution comprising the existing models. However, the comparative terminology analysis, and thus the translation, may lead to the recommendation not to unify the terms, because, for instance, different legal terms are irreconcilable or because unification outweighs its benefits. The Hungarian case suggests a halfway "solution", which got stuck in the expression of the appropriate terminologies in the opinion of the Hungarian authorities and foreign translators. Even though this example is not EU multilingualism-related, it highlights the importance of the collaborative efforts of experts, such as lawyers, translators, and terminologists, in finding the "best solution".

The above shows that the suggested combined comparative methodology is valuable and can even be supported by technology, which is particularly pertinent in today's globalized world. The next section provides examples in the form of case studies (Scarciglia 2015).

10.3 Case Studies

Modern constitutions and constitutional systems typically contain a variety of provisions on language for diverse considerations. They may designate one or more official languages with different legal statuses. They may also create language rights, usually held by minority language speakers, granting groups and individuals the right to communicate with and receive services from the government in their native tongue. In multi-level governance, constitutions may vest the authority to designate official language(s) for each level of the government (Choudhry and Houlihan 2021, 21). There are 24 languages in the EU, each with equal status, and the EU must respect this diversity as stated in the Charter of Fundamental Rights of the European Union (see Faingold 2020; Skorupa Wulczynska 2019; van der Jeught 2015). Generally, the official language (or state language) is defined and used as the government's language (or languages) to conduct official, day-to-day business. By contrast, a national language is defined as the language shared among the people(s) of the state or its particular territory, and it does not imply anything regarding its legal status (Choudhry and Houlihan 2021, 6). States certainly have the right to express preferences for the state/national/official language(s), whose choice usually depends on their individual history, like in Switzerland. Therefore, in many ways, Switzerland and also the EU provide a unique case study for exploring the connection between law and language.

10.3.1 The Swiss Legal Environment

Switzerland has specific features that have made and continue to make the Swiss legal and linguistic system unique, sustainable, and functional. This country is a multi-ethnic, multi-confessional, and multilingual nation. Since 1848, it has been a federal republic under a three-level structure: the Confederation, the cantons, and the communes. The Swiss Constitution, adopted in 1999 through a referendum, establishes the legal framework for the use of language by distinguishing between national and official languages, emphasizing mutual understanding and equality, decentralization, and firm protection of the interests of linguistics communities.

The relationship between the Swiss concept of nationhood and language is based on mutual understanding and equality. The Swiss Constitution guarantees the freedom to use any language (Art. 18). The national language is determined as German, French, Italian, and Romansh (Art. 4). The first three, i.e., German, French, and Italian, serve as official languages of the Confederation. In Switzerland, there is a third category, i.e., the official national language, which deserves special consideration, as its use at the cantonal level is often synonymous with the official language. Since the official language is a concept specifically linked explicitly to the states, it is natural that each state should define what it means by national and official language in its own legal systems (Choudhry and Houlihan 2021, 7), as this is the case in Switzerland. The Constitution expresses that "the cantons shall determine their own official language", with a further explanation that "in order to preserve harmony between linguistic communities, the cantons shall respect the traditional boundaries of languages and shall take account of Indigenous linguistic minorities" (Art. 70 (2)).

In the Swiss legal system, the symbolic, state-political functions of the official language are decisive in the state language classification of the four national languages. In addition to the political and symbolic functions of the national languages, particular importance is attached to the legally guaranteed freedom of the language spoken by the majority nation (Koopmans and Orgad 2020, 104), its unhindered use, freedom of cultivation and teaching, and the provision of institutional conditions (Grünert 2018, 18). This approach emphasizes the historically evolved, community-building, and value-carrying role of the languages of the nation-states, eclipsing the linguistic roots of assimilationist language policies (Kużelewska 2016, 45) that seek national, linguistic exclusivity. According to the Federal Act on National Languages and Understanding between the linguistic communities, known as the Language Act and abbreviated LLC, the Swiss language system is based on the principle that everyone has the right to use their own mother tongue. Therefore, this right does not introduce privileges or positive discrimination but is based on the principle of equal rights. Switzerland's approaches to the use of the mother tongue are based on a legal intervention that allows linguistic minorities to preserve their (linguistic) identity and avoid linguistic assimilation and the relationship between the official national language and the (official) minority language in terms of individual and collective rights. In other words, Switzerland is a federal country where linguistic sovereignty historically belongs to the cantons. It also means that all federal legislation is published in German, French, and Italian, and, based on the Publications Act of 18 June 2004 (*Federal Act on the Compilations of Federal Legislation* and the *Federal Gazette*), the three versions are equally binding. The LLC determines that the local language is used alone at all levels of administration, except within the Federal Administration itself for its internal operations. The principle of territoriality also applies within bilingual and trilingual cantons, where responsibility for defining the official language has been entrusted to the communes.

The LLC implements the mentioned constitutional provisions. It came into force on the 1st of January 2010, and the Federal Council adopted its implementing ordinance on the 4th of June 2010. The LLC clearly distinguishes between the concepts of national and official languages. In the case of official language, the LLC determines it either without reservation (German, Italian, and French), implying that all official acts are to be published in these languages, or with a reservation. It means that Romansh is an official language in dealing with the people who speak it (LLC Art. 5). The LLC gives everyone the possibility to use the official language of their own choice when dealing with federal authority (Art. 6). To facilitate language use, the LLC also supports non-profit organizations in their efforts to provide translation and plurilingual cantons to provide services. This support takes the form of adopting specific measures to assist non-profit-making organizations and institutions active in Switzerland for written translations from one official Swiss language into others (Art. 19) and support multilingual cantons in the operation of political authorities, law enforcement, justice system, and administrative authorities (Art. 21).

In a broader sense, the whole legislative and decision-making process, which, of course, has a significant impact on the correctness of language and terminology, can be summarized as follows. Before any item of business is placed before the Federal Council, it goes through various stages, all under the watchful eye of the Federal Chancellery. After a draft from a department goes through the office consultation procedure, the departmental head responsible signs the final proposal. Federal Council colleagues can comment on it in a joint report procedure. Only when this procedure (*decision-taking at meetings of the Federal Council*) is completed and the Federal Council has checked the formal and legal aspects is the matter placed on the agenda of the Federal Council. It is the legal, social, and linguistic environment in which Swiss laws should be made. It has posed a challenge to the lawmaking design, especially regarding how best to ensure coherency and consistency in the multilanguage state.

10.3.2 EU and Its Multilingualism

The legal framework of the EU has created a specific multilingual situation on the continent, which is essentially rooted in the international conventions that govern it. Here, we cannot discuss the EU's key regulations on language and their use; therefore, we will focus on the *Charter of Fundamental Rights of the European Union* (Charter). The Charter makes two critical statements on languages. It ensures linguistic diversity and prohibits all forms of linguistic discrimination. On this basis, it is fair to assume that the 24 official languages of the EU, in all their forms, enjoy equal status. Equal use of 24 languages would complicate the EU's legislative, organizational, operational, and overall decision-making procedures. For this reason, three languages (English, French, and German) enjoy a higher standing. They are considered procedural languages of the European Commission, complemented by two other languages (Spanish and Italian), giving them a special status as support languages. It is legitimate to ask why these five languages have such a status. As with national language policies, the answer is to be found in the political and economic power of the countries, as these are the languages of the strongest economies in the EU. When examining the documents and the language policy of the EU, we often come across the concepts of linguistic diversity and multilingual language policy (multilingualism). As per Article 3 of the Treaty on European Union, "Linguistic diversity is a reality, observance of which is a fundamental value of the EU". So, EU language policy is based on respect for linguistic diversity in all Member States and creating an intercultural dialogue throughout the EU. As a preliminary point, the European Parliament (EP) has adopted a multilingual language policy in its own communication strategy, clarifying that every Member of the EP has the right to speak in their EU language of choice and prescribing the basic criteria for the translation of official documents. The question often arises whether it would not be more cost-effective from all procedural points of view if the EU were to use only English as an official language instead of multilingualism. However, translation and interpretation, though not free of charge, remain an effective solution for the EU as the EU can strengthen its commitment to the idea of a multilingual Europe through these methods. At the same time, it is also fairer than a monolingual regime, which unavoidably privileges native speakers (Michele Gazzola and François Grin 2013, 93).

The Directorate-General for Interpretation (also known as SCIC for its former French name: Service Commun Interprétation-Conférences) and the Directorate-General for Translation provide cross-language services. The SCIC runs interpretation services[4] for the Commission, European Council, Committee of the Regions, European Economic and Social Committee, European Investment Bank, and agencies and offices in EU countries. The Directorate-General for Translation is responsible for, among others, the translation of laws, policy papers, reports, and correspondence drafted by or sent to the Commission, and it also assists the Commission in communicating with the public. In this way, it contributes to helping citizens understand EU policies. It also advises the Commission departments on language and managing multilingual websites, ensuring the correct terminology in all official EU languages, as documented in the interinstitutional database IATE.

European countries and the EU have always spoken through translation, and today's translation is more than ever an active process. The multiple levels at which translation plays a role in the framework of the EU's multilingualism policy clearly show that the language issue today has also acquired a dimension that concerns rights and not just languages (Benedetti 2011, 133).

Legal terminology within the EU and at the national level constantly follows socio-cultural changes, which causes concepts and terms to change, disappear, emerge, and reappear (see Tamás 2019). Now, let us explore the drafting processes through the lenses of multilingualism and terminology databases of Switzerland (TERMDAT) and the EU (IATE).

10.3.3 The Swiss Multilingual Drafting Process and TERMDAT

The Swiss drafting process observes the multilingual nature of constitutionalism and implements mechanisms that enforce this commitment. Three mechanisms need to be emphasized: the drafting process in general, the creation, maintenance, and use of the TREMDAT, and the work of the responsible federal unit, i.e., Federal Chancellery's Central Language Services.

An Internal Drafting Committee (*IDC – Verwaltungsinterne Redaktionskommission*, VIRK) of four people is created when drafting a law. For each draft, the IDC will be composed of a German-speaking and a French-speaking linguist from the Federal Chancellery and a German-speaking and French-speaking lawyer from the Federal Office of Justice. In this bilingual setting, the Committee reviews all drafts for constitutional amendments, acts of Parliament, and important secondary legislation. The German Section of the IDC ensures that legislative texts are precise, clear, non-contradictory, and formulated as simply as possible. Texts must also be identical in the three official languages. The section also checks the clarity and linguistic quality of other official texts, such as the reports and statements of the Federal Council. The German and French versions of the text (the original and the translation) are revised and further developed in parallel. Because text versions are being drafted in parallel, that is, independent from one another, at the end of this process, neither language version can be considered the original or the translation anymore (Höfler, Nussbaumer, and Uhlmann 2020, 491).

A similar approach is used in the case of popular initiatives, which are usually submitted in just one language. The text is then translated and co-revised between the languages by the administration. At the end of this process, the Federal Administration certifies that the three language[5] versions of the text are equivalent (Höfler, Nussbaumer, and Uhlmann 2020, 65). This text can thus no longer be changed, and the collection of the required signatures may begin.

Whether parallel work using different languages to draft the same content or translation from one language to another, interdisciplinary collaborative work is the cornerstone and an enshrined practice of the Swiss drafting process. It has led to institutional improvements and the development and use of TERMDAT.

Due to the rapid growth in the volume of official texts, the acceleration and expansion of translation and terminology workflows, the development of working tools, and the need to meet communication needs as quickly as possible, the Federal Chancellery's Central Language Services (*Zentrale Sprachdienste, Servizi linguistici centrali, Les services linguistique centraux*) have undergone major developments in recent years. Currently, the Federal Chancellery's Central Language Services has six main responsibilities. It participates in the parallel drafting of legislative acts, which, as mentioned, consists of small multidisciplinary and multilingual teams; translates texts (legislative acts, messages, reports, speeches, parliamentary interventions, press releases, etc.) for the Federal Chancellery, the Federal Council, and Parliament; edits texts (legislative acts, messages, reports, Federal Council opinions, etc.) for the Official Compendium of Federal Law; participates in the work of various national and international bodies (*Délégation à la langue française, Conférence des services de traduction des Etats européens*, etc.); serves the multilingual public; and must, therefore, provide publications in German, French, and Italian. Its most important task, we consider for this chapter, is ensuring that all laws and other official texts are clear and legally correct in the given language, with careful attention, as the French, German, and Italian language versions of all laws are equal and legally binding.

In addition, the Federal Chancellery's Terminology Section provides relevant and up-to-date terminology in the four national languages and English for the entire Federal Administration. It also supports the terminology work of federal offices and other agencies by recording, publishing, and distributing its specialist vocabulary. The Terminology Section's work helps ensure the quality of multilingual communication and information distribution in the Federal Administration. It facilitates national and cantonal cooperation and harmonization of legislation by collaborating closely and systematically on terminology with all the involved parties. For this purpose, the Terminology Section coordinates terminology work throughout the whole administration, manages data stocks, and makes them available to departments in a suitable form.

The quality of terminology used in a text, whether originally written or translated, greatly influences its clarity and readability. The results of the terminology work, particularly of systematic terminology work, are made available to the users through lists of specialized terms, glossaries, or technical dictionaries, or these can be accessed in terminological databases. The Swiss Terminology Section operates in all four national languages and English and ensures that the terminology it processes is made publicly available via TERMDAT.

The use of TERMDAT in drafting ensures that particular terminology variations are examined and discussed and that unnecessary, misleading, and unclear regulations and legal terms are identified in time. A broader goal and an essential requirement are to demonstrate transparency[6] of this process to all target groups and legal actors. A reliable and uniform legal language can be created and employed only in this way. The TERMDAT terminology database, resulting from a merger with the European database EURODICAUTOM,[7] currently comprises around 1,600,000 records, including 380,000 Swiss records and 400,000 abbreviations in two to five languages. The data recorded are primarily derived from legislation, but the database also covers other areas, with a clear focus on managing the federal legal and administrative terminology. TERMDAT uses linguistic, professional, formal, methodological, and content validation. Content validation is conducted with a legal expert by consulting a terminologist. Terminology work is carried out at the Federal Chancellery's quarters in Bern and the cantons. The cantonal entries and records are marked separately in the database. It naturally raises the issue of synonyms and duplicates, but the aim here is to systematize the terms and to unify and organize the cantonal terminology. TERMDAT is the only database in Switzerland that is truly open to a broad audience. It is a platform for exchange and dissemination between administrations and public or private organizations. Nevertheless, data can only be visible to external users to ensure reliability after a multi-level validation.

10.3.4 EU Drafting Process in Light of IATE

The uniqueness of the EU and its legal system is due to its 24 official languages, co-existing in 27 different national legal systems. When translating and implementing EU law, national terms are often preferred for two reasons. First, to avoid linguistic and terminological interference with national legislation and, second, to ensure that national sectors and domains using specific terminology can maintain their national best practice (see Šarčević 2015). Therefore, sometimes we can find formal correspondence between EU and national terms, and, other times, finding this equivalence is more challenging (Várnai, Bérczi, and Somssich 2010, 132). This complexity and dynamics of the – to some extent – converging and diverging use of language have led to a co-existence between existing national legislation and the legal terminology created by the EU. IATE was created to manage and organize terminology for the EU to resolve this situation. The IATE, the EU's terminology database, contributes to the legal harmonization in the EU legislative processes. The need to build a terminology database generally arises in multilingual contexts to meet the needs of public administration. In the European context, the need to standardize terms was born simultaneously with the development of the EU. The design of IATE has led to the establishment of a database containing terms used in legislative and administrative texts published by the various EU institutions. IATE is a fundamentally important tool for professionals. It gives access to controlled terminological content, places the term and the concept in its European context, and provides considerable information on its translation and correspondence in other languages of the EU. As we can read in the *Joint Handbook for the Presentation and Drafting*, throughout the drafting process, drafts shall be framed in terms and sentence structure that respect the multilingual nature of EU legislation, and concepts or terminology of any national legal system are to be used with care.

Of course, there is a legal need for consistency in the use of terminology by all language versions of EU texts. It is often overlooked, but it should be borne in mind that the transfer of information from an EU text to a national context is not only a political and legal task but also a linguistic activity. It is a parallel process for each EU language. To make appropriate decisions when confronted with equivalence issues in any databases, be it at the national (TERMDAT) or the EU level (IATE), the following basic information is necessary: detailed information relating to the domain of the legal term, its definition, the context of its use, and the degree of equivalence. However, as the EU's multilingual drafting system is not based on co-drafting but on a system of drafting, translating, and legal linguistic revision, the drafting language (source language) can significantly influence the final terminology. To understand it, we should study the terminology dimension, which would take us to the linguistic and legal interpretation and application of the legislative texts in all languages and Member States. It is important to note that, while there may be a divergence between linguistic meanings of individual language versions, the law requires a single meaning. IATE is an excellent solution to this, as it allows us to find the legal and linguistic meanings, the linguistic versions, and the legal interpretations. All this leads us to appreciate the descriptive terminological approach in the case of IATE, which examines terms and concepts in context, paying attention to the dynamic aspects of language and understanding, the recurrent theme of variation, and the relationship between languages (Temmerman 2020, 122).

10.4 Lessons Learned

Considering the case studies on the Swiss and the EU drafting process in a multilinguistic context and the mentioned Hungarian experiences, we can summarize the identified lessons learned in five points. If the goal is achieving a high-quality, clear, transparent, and accessible draft, (i) linguistic and legal considerations are inseparable, (ii) collaboration is essential;

therefore, (iii) the process might be time-consuming, but these will ensure (iv) consistency, which (v) might be best achieved using a methodology prioritizing contrastive and comparative approaches. Let us briefly explain each.

Inseparable. The basic conditions for creating a harmonized legal language include considering legal and linguistic aspects of the use of language in drafting. The consistency of legal terminology and language is essentially linked to the following aspects: coherent and predictable legislation, uniform application of the law, and the use of the same language. Switzerland's multilingual and multilayered legal system creates specific challenges for legislative drafting. In contrast, with its 27 Member States, the EU has to cope with the specific situation of national and European legal terminology that transcends the Member States but is reflected in their languages. In the case of Switzerland, from a legal perspective, it is fundamental that any new laws accurately implement all relevant higher-level legislation and that they are amenable to implementation at the next lower level of government (Uhlmann 2017, 2). The EU has faced a different challenge, one driven by valuing the much wider language diversity than the one in Switzerland and looking for the best tools for realizing this commitment. Innovations in legislative procedures have been partly a practical necessity, as new approaches had to be found to guide policy-making in the context of a growing number of official texts and to ensure transparency between official languages. From a linguistic viewpoint, the realization of the benefit of combining legal and linguistic aspects of the use of language in drafting has also created opportunities for both Switzerland and the EU.

Collaboration. Based on the Recommendations for Terminology Work by the Conference of Translation Services of European States, one can assert that if high-quality terminology work is carried out from the outset when new legislation is being drafted, this will provide the regulatory area with a clear conceptual structure. It will make dialogue between the disciplines and interest groups involved in the process considerably more manageable, and the regulatory goal will be reached more quickly. Terminology work is also an essential condition for conceptually coherent legislation. Conceptual coherence facilitates the application of the law and strengthens legal certainty (see CST 2003). In the context of EU legislation, certain elements are built into the system to ensure, in formal and informal ways, that the final legal text adopted is of the appropriate quality, including its terminology. It can guarantee the same legal effect in all official languages. The efforts made by Switzerland to study and understand the status and the importance of the official/national language have drawn attention to different profiles of the terminological and linguistically structured national juridical phenomenon. Multilingual legislation is based on a mixed system. In such a system, planning, drafting, and translation and legal terminology activities alternate, and each phase is supported by procedural guarantees and collaborative works to achieve high-quality and equivalent legal texts.

Time-consuming. We often hear the criticism that the lawmaking process in Switzerland is slow, overregulated, and over-detailed. However, the slowness, combined with a great quality of legislation in all the national languages, has yielded good results. In general, the EU has not been failing to produce high-quality legislative texts in all official languages by the end of the lawmaking process. The autonomy of EU legal acts, just like that of the national ones, is unquestionable, even if this autonomy means lengthy and complex interactions between drafters of EU law and national law, which sometimes leads to some terminological clashes. Accepting that perfect equivalence and one-to-one conceptual correspondence do not or only partially exist, EU law-related translations are, at the end of the day, basically a chain of compromise. The evolution of TERMDAT shows that thanks to the state's involvement and cooperation between institutions, terminology can be considered a prerequisite for legal certainty and successful legislation. In Switzerland, both the drafting process and the actual texts generated through this process exhibit high levels of transparency and coherence, and are generally well accepted. This achievement has been accomplished under pressure from an increasingly activist political environment, amid the co-existence of four national languages and the growing influence of English on legal terminology more broadly. Similar considerations have influenced the creation of IATE, alongside even greater institutional complexity, international and EU legal frameworks and commitments, and the fast pace at which legislation happens everywhere.

Consistency. The terminology database can be used not only for terminology and translation work but also to provide answers to questions of legal interpretation, legal comparison, and other issues related to legal language. Legal dogmatics, whose primary role is to explore the objective meaning and systematic understanding of the legal terms of a specific legal system, can be significantly assisted by terminology databases. By focusing on legislation, terminology can help examine the fitness of newly created terms in the legal system and their relationship to existing legal institutions. It can also support understanding the disruption of the legal system and legal order caused by the changes. Terminology databases, i.e., TERMDAT and IATE, even if their purpose and reliability are different, provide a tool for lawmakers to draft and publish legislation free of inconsistencies in its wording and correct and coherent in its linguistic formulation. They ensure an accurate understanding between citizens and the state, and their theoretical basis contributes considerably to the development of terminology as a discipline.

Methodology. Today, the complexity of modern infrastructure, society, and the economy makes cooperation necessary. The multilingualism of the EU legal system represents both a challenge and an opportunity. On the one hand, having 24 official languages unavoidably requires an additional safeguard to ensure that all language versions of a legislative text have the same content and legal interpretation. Of course, this demands a firm commitment from the Member State, extra time, and the involvement of additional language and legal experts. It poses a severe challenge to the whole lawmaking process for multilingual systems, as the legal quality should be achieved and ensured by comparing different language versions of a legislative text. On the other hand, it can also be an advantage. Legal and terminological uncertainties may be identified that might otherwise remain undetected during the drafting and translation process. The confusion caused in the application of the law due to some ambiguous terms in one of its language versions can be resolved when consulting the other language versions and the context, i.e., the drafting process. While in the case of Switzerland (and TERMDAT), a well-functioning legislative process, essentially based on a contrastive approach, ensures appropriate and coherent linguistic representation, in the case of the EU (and IATE), the contrastive approach plays only a secondary role. The primary challenge lies in ensuring internal compliance within each language and integrating the terminology into the respective legal systems.

10.5 Conclusion

This chapter has aimed to discuss how to best observe the principles of efficiency, economy, unambiguity, and intelligibility when drafting in different multilingual contexts, such as the EU and Switzerland. Here, we can briefly conclude that the presented examples, case studies, and lessons learned support the thesis of this chapter, which suggests that the drafting process in multilingual jurisdictions could benefit from contrastive terminology, comparative law, and terminology databases created on these bases. We can also make two additional observations.

The first is that terminology databases and their development and use embedded in the drafting process play a vital role in the management of multilingual (legal) knowledge in the production of any (legal and specialized) documents, in facilitating and accelerating information interchange, and in the integration of language resources for a knowledge-based society. This well-organized and coordinated interdisciplinary work between law and terminology can encourage and result in a comprehensible terminology database of the highest level and quality. This interdisciplinary framework facilitates addressing the challenges of merely seeking the meaning of EU law solely from the perspective of EU legal language as a purely supranational language. While the meanings of the national languages in the case of Switzerland are anchored in the authority of national languages and legislation, in the case of the EU, the real meaning is more present in the implementing laws. Translations and terminology databases are a benefit to the legislative process, but only if adequately embedded in the process and if there is a genuine exchange between the involved parties.

The second is that the Swiss TERMDAT could serve as a best practice for those working with language and law, even for the IATE. This latter could be viewed as a shared supranational polycentric institution, producing norms according to the institutional interaction between the national and European level in 24 different languages. Through different methods and drafting mechanisms in which they are involved, both TERMDAT and IATE contribute to producing clearer, more precise, more transparent, and more accessible laws.

Notes

1 The Guidelines draw on international commitments and scholarly works, however, seem to shy away from mentioning terminological databases as best practices.
2 To ensure clarity and consistency in domestic criminal law, Section 254 CC on active bribery in the private sector used the same wording to express the criminalized behavior, which was also criticized for the same reason.
3 In 2010, the first year of the reign of the Orbán regime, Hungary was much less corrupt than in 2024, when Hungary managed to be the most corrupt Hungary in the EU, according to the Transparency International. See the decrease from 2012 in Graph 1 here: https://transparency.hu/en/news/cpi-2023-results-annual-report/.
4 The European Parliament and the Court of Justice of the European Communities each have their own, separate interpreting service.
5 As per the *Brochure attestion de la qualité d'électeur:* "Romansh is considered an official language of the Confederation, it is therefore possible to collect signatures for popular initiatives in Romansh. The committee can also request that an initiative be translated into this language. If necessary, which is rare, the Romansh text of the initiative is published in the German version of the Federal Gazette. If, for linguistic reasons, it is difficult to determine which initiative is being discussed, the Federal Chancellery website allows the text of the initiatives to be displayed in the various languages".
6 Transparency is regulated by "*Loi sur la Transparence de l'administration*" or Law on Transparency (LTrans), which came into effect in July 2006.
7 Eurodicautom was the European Commission's pioneering terminology database created in 1975. It was initially for use by translators and other Commission staff. Later, it was available to the general public with free access to multilingual terminology in the EU's fields of activity. It was replaced by IATE in 2007.

References

Arzoz, Xabier. 2007. "The nature of language rights." *Journal on Ethnopolitics and Minority Issues in Europe*. 6 (2): 1–35.

Benedetti, Marco. 2011. "Interpreting in the European commission" *Gramma: Journal of Theory and Criticism* 19 (1): 133–138, www.enl.auth.gr/gramma/gramma11/Benedetti.pdf

Biel, Łucja, and Doczekalska, Agnieszka. 2020. "How do supranational terms transfer into national legal systems? A corpus-informed study of EU English terminology in consumer protection directives and UK, Irish and Maltese transposing acts." *Terminology. International Journal of Theoretical and Applied Issues in Specialized Communication* 26 (2): 184–212. DOI: 10.1075/term.00050.bie

Chiocchetti, Elena, Lušicky, Vesna, and Wissik, Tanja. 2023. "Multilingual legal terminology databases: Workflows and roles." *Handbook of Terminology Online* 3: 458–484. DOI: 10.1075/hot.3.mul1

Choudhry, Sujit, and Houlihan, Erin C. 2021. *Official Language Designation.* International IDEA. DOI: 10.31752/idea.2021.40

Cormacain, Ronan. 2022. *The Form of Legislation and the Rule of Law.* Hart.

COTSOES, 2002, Recommendations for Terminology Work, MediaCenter of the Confederation CH-3003 Berne, https://cotsoes.org/sites/default/files/public_files/COTSOES_Recommendations_for_Terminology_Work.pdf

Crystal, David. 1987. *The Cambrigde Encyclopedia of Language.* Cambridge UP.

Danet, Brenda. 1980. "Language in the legal process." *Law & Society Review* 14 (3): 445–564.

De Luca, Christine. 2017. "Mother tongue as a universal human right." *International Journal of Speech-Language Pathology* 20 (1): 1–5. DOI: 10.1080/17549507.2017.1392606

De Poorter, J., van der Schyff, G., Stremler, M., de Visser, M., Leijten, I. and van Oirsouw, C. 2023. European Yearbook of Constitutional Law 2002. A Constitutional Identity for the EU?, The Hague, Asser Press.

Drinóczi, Tímea. 2015. "Concept of quality in legislation – revisited: Matter of perspective and a general overview." *Statute Law Review* 36 (3): 211–227.

Drinóczi, Tímea. 2020. "Constitutional identity in Europe: The identity of the constitution. A regional approach." *German Law Journal* 21: 105–130.

Drinóczi, Tímea, and Bień-Kacała, Agnieszka. 2022. *Illiberal Constitutionalism in Poland and Hungary: The Deterioration of Democracy, Misuse of Human Rights and Abuse of the Rule of Law.* Routledge.

Drinóczi, Tímea, and Novák, Barnabás. 2015. "Linguistic approach in legisprudence – Terminology, translation studies and databases." *Theory and Practice of Legislation* 3 (1): 113–129. DOI: 10.1080/20508840.2015.1041707

Faingold, Eduardo D. 2020. *Language Rights and the Law in the European Union.* Palgrave Pivot.

Fóris, Ágota. 2009. "A terminológia interkulturális vonatkozásai a szakmai kommunikációban." In *Hatékony nyelvi, idegen nyelvi és szakmai kommunikáció interkulturális környezetben.* Dunaújvárosi Főiskola, 18–26.

Fóris, Ágota. 2026. How can terminology management support bridging the gap between legislative language and better understanding of legislative intent for citizens?, In *Language for Legislation and Legislation through Language.*

Freixa, Judit. 2006. "Causes of denominative variation in terminology: A typology proposal." *Terminology: International Journal of Theoretical and Applied Issues in Specialized Communication* 12 (1): 51–77. DOI:10.1075/term.12.1.04fre

Galdia, Marcus. 2021. "Conceptual origins of legal linguistics." *Comparative Legilinguistics* 47 (1): 17–56. DOI: 10.2478/cl-2021-0011

Gazzola, Michele, and Grin, François. 2013. "Is ELF more effective and fair than translation? An evaluation of the EU's multilingual regime." *International Journal of Applied Linguistics*, 23 (1): 93–107. DOI: 10.1111/ijal.12014

Grünert, Matthias. 2018. "Multilingualism in Switzerland." *Manual of Romance Sociolinguistics* 19: 526–548. DOI: 10.1515/9783110365955-020.

Haß-Zumkehr, Ulrike. 2002. *Sprache und Recht*. de Gruyter.

Hellwege, Phillip, and Soniewicka, Marta. 2024. *Law and Interdisciplinarity*. Mohr Siebek.

Höfler, Stefan, Nussbaumer, Markus, and Felix, Uhlmann. 2020. "Legislation in Switzerland." In *Legislation in Europe: A Country by Country Guide*. Hart Publishing.

Jopek-Bosiacka, Anna. 2023. "Definitions in law across legal cultures and jurisdictions." *Handbook of Terminology Online* 1 (3): 37–71.

Kjaer, Anne Lise. 2015. "Theoretical aspects of legal translation: The paradoxical relationship between language, translation and the autonomy of EU law." In *Language and Culture in EU Law: Multidisciplinary Perspectives. Law, Language and Communication series*, Routledge (London). 91–109.

Koopmans, Ruud, and Orgad, Liav. 2020. "Majority-Minority Constellations: Towards A Group-Differentiated Approach", *WZB Discussion Paper*. https://bibliothek.wzb.eu/pdf/2020/vi20-104.pdf

Kużelewska, Elżbieta. 2016. "Language policy in Switzerland." In *Studies in Logic: Grammar and Rhetoric* 45 (1): 125–140. DOI: 10.1515/slgr-2016-0020.

Lécrivain, Claudine. 1998. "Europe, Traduction et Spécificités Culturelles." *Europe et Traduction*, 1: 345–358.

Levi, Judith, and Walker, Anne Graffam. 1990. *Language in the Judicial Process*. Plenum Press.

Lind, Allan, and Tyler, Tom. 1988. *The Social Psychology of Procedural Justice*. Plenum.

Machuska, Iryna, Machusky, Volodymyr, Gulyar, Tatyana, and Leshchenko, Inna. 2024. "Legal terminology in environmental and land law: Theoretical-legal analysis." *Visegrad Journal on Human Rights* 1: 45–50. DOI: 10.61345/1339-7915.2024.1.7.

Magris, Marella, and Musacchio, Maria Teresa. 1999. "La Terminografia Orientata Alla Traduzione Tra Pragmatismo E Armonizzazione." *Terminologie Et Traduction* 1: 150–151.

Michaels, Ralf. 2011. *Comparative Law*. Duke Law School. https://scholarship.law.duke.edu/faculty_scholarship/2388/ https://scholarship.law.duke.edu/cgi/viewcontent.cgi?article=3014&context=faculty_scholarship

Mosmouti, Maria. 2019. *Designing Effective Legislation*. Edward Elgar.

Nielsen, Sandro. 2023. "Legal lexicography and legal information tools." *Handbook of Terminology* 1 (3): 432–457. DOI: 10.1075/hot.3.leg4.

Nussbaumer, Markus. 1997. *Sprache und Recht*. Julius Groos.

Olsen, Frances. 2019. "Law, language and justice." *Legal Linguistics Beyond Borders: Language and Law in a World of Media, Globalisation and Social Conflicts* 2: 253–290. https://www.duncker-humblot.de/_files_media/leseproben/9783428554232.pdf

Osnabrügge, Moritz, and Matia, Vannoni. 2024. "Quality of legislation and compliance: A natural language processing approach." *Political Science Research and Methods* 1 1–9. DOI: 10.1017/psrm.2024.21

Šarčević, Susan. 2015. "Basic principles of term formation in the multilingual and multicultural context of EU law." In *Language and Culture in EU Law*. Routledge.

Scarciglia, Roberto. 2015. "Methodological pluralism and legal comparison: Challenges in a post-global age." *Beijing Law Review* 6 (1): 42–48. DIO: 10.4236/blr.2015.61006

Siems, Mathias. 2018. *Comparative Law*. Cambridge University Press.

Skorupa Wulczynska, Aneta. 2019. "Legal aspects of the European Union language policy." *The Review of European Affairs* 3 (5): 123–144.

Somssich, Réka. 2007. *Az európai közösségi jog fogalmainak nyelvi megjelenítése, különös tekintettel az európai magánjogra*. https://www.ajk.elte.hu/file/AJKDI_SomssichReka_dis.pdf

Tamás, Dóra Mária. 2019. *Bevezetés a jogi terminológiába a terminológus szemüvegén át*. ELTE Eötvös Kiadó. OFFI Zrt.

Tamás, Dóra Mária. 2021. "Terminology and documentation in terminology databases." In Fóris, Ágota and Bölcskei, Andrea (eds.) *Linguistic Research in the Fields of Content Development and Documentation*. L'Harmattan Kiadó, 227–238.

Temmerman, Rita. 2020. "Terminology across languages: Researching neologisms and terminological variation in multilingual settings". In *Svijet od riječi. Terminološki i leksikografski*, John Benjamins, 119–135.

Terral, Florence. 2004. "L'empreinte culturelle des termes juridiques" *Meta* 49 (4): 876–890. DOI: 10.7202/009787ar

Tiersma, Peter. 2008. "What is language and law? and does anyone care?' In *Law and Language: Theory and Society*. Düsseldorf University Press.

Uhlmann, Felix. 2017. "Wer hat und wer macht wie viel? – Rechtsbestand und Rechtsetzungsaktivität in den Schweizer Kantonen" *Leges* 28 (2): 371–378 https://leges.weblaw.ch/dam/jcr:69b0eaaf-9488-4cd9-953b-d5c0869408da/LeGes_2017_2_371-378.pdf

Van der Jeught, Stefaan. 2015. *EU Language Law*. Europa Law Publishing.

Várnai, Judit, Bérczi, Anna, and Somssich, Réka. 2010. *European Commission, Directorate – General for Translation, Lawmaking in the EU multilingual environment*. Publications Office of the European Union.

Xanthaki, Helen. 2013. *Thornton's Legislative Drafting*. Bloomsbury.

Xanthaki, Helen. 2014. *Drafting Legislation: Art and Technology of Rules for Regulation*. Hart.

Sources

Central Language Services Terminology Section, https://www.bk.admin.ch/bk/en/home/regierungsunterstuetzung/languages/terminologie.html

Charter of Fundamental Rights of the European Union, https://www.europarl.europa.eu/charter/pdf/text_en.pdf

COTSOES / CST Recommendations for Terminology Work, https://cotsoes.org/sites/default/files/public_files/COTSOES_Recommendations_for_Terminology_Work.pdf

EPA. 2014. *Proposed Outline for Terminology Development and Management Manual: A Guide for Editors*. https://sor.epa.gov/sor_internet/registry/termreg/outreachandeducation/educationalresources/referencematerials/Terminology_Development_and_Governance_(Best%20Practices)_April_2014_Final.pdf

European Public Law. 2021, 27 (3).

European Yearbook of Constitutional Law. 2022.

Evaluation Report on Hungary on Incriminations (ETS 173 and 191, GPC 2) Adopted by GRECO at Its 47th Plenary Meeting (Strasbourg, 7–11 June 2010). https://rm.coe.int/CoERMPublicCommonSearchServices/DisplayDCTMContent?documentId=09000016806c6b2d

German Law Journal. 2017, 18 (7).

IATE. About IATE. https://iate.europa.eu/home

IATE and IATE Handbook. https://iate.europa.eu/assets/handbook.pdf.

Joint Handbook for the Presentation and Drafting of Acts Subject to the Ordinary Legislative Procedure. https://www.consilium.europa.eu/media/67390/joint_handbook_en_01-october-2023_clean_def_final.pdf

Language Policy in the EU. www.europarl.europa.eu/factsheets/en/sheet/142/language-policy

Official translation of the Hungarian Fundamental Law. https://njt.hu/jogszabaly/en/2011-4301-02-00

Ordinance on the Federal Administration Language Services. https://www.fedlex.admin.ch/eli/cc/2012/771/en

OSCE ODIHR. 2023. *Guidelines of Democratic Lawmaking for Better Laws*.

Popular initiatives in Switzerland. https://www.ch.ch/en/political-system/political-rights/initiatives/what-is-a-federal-popular-initiative/

The Commission's Use of Languages. https://commission.europa.eu/about-european-commission/service-standards-and-principles/commissions-use-languages_en

The Directorate-General for Translation. https://commission.europa.eu/about-european-commission/departments-and-executive-agencies/translation_en

11 Analyzing the Language of Legislation Using Natural Language Processing

Xiao Lu, Moritz Osnabrügge and Gerrit Quaremba

11.1 Introduction

Legal scholars and social scientists have a long-standing interest in studying the language of legislation. Legal drafting experts, for instance, have developed standards to guide legislative drafting practices (e.g., Butt 2013; Xanthaki 2014, 2022; Garner 2002, 2016). Meanwhile, social scientists increasingly rely on natural language processing (NLP) techniques to address descriptive or causal research questions related to legislation (e.g., Coupette et al. 2023; Katz et al. 2021; Wilkerson et al. 2015; Gratton et al. 2021). This growing body of literature typically measures variables of interest based on legislative texts. For example, previous studies have applied NLP techniques to measure delegation patterns and to analyze the contingency, indeterminacy and complexity of legislation (e.g., Anastasopoulos and Bertelli 2020; Vannoni et al. 2020; Ash et al. 2024; Osnabrügge and Vannoni 2025; Hurka 2024; Williams 2022). However, notwithstanding their utility and recent advancements in analyzing legislative documents, legal scholars have not widely used these techniques.

In this chapter, we provide an overview of major techniques that can be used to study legislative texts (Jurafsky and Martin 2024; Eisenstein 2019; Hastie et al. 2009; Grimmer et al. 2022). We outline regular expressions, dictionary-based methods, supervised and unsupervised text classification, part-of-speech (POS) tagging and dependency parsing. These techniques serve to pre-process textual data, classify texts and analyze lexical and syntactic elements of texts. Our focus lies on explaining key concepts and how these techniques can be used to study legislative texts. We also provide examples from political science and political economy to present these methods in practice.

Following an overview of the techniques, we illustrate the usefulness of NLP techniques by analyzing a corpus of European Union (EU) legislation, which encompasses all secondary legislation adopted from 2014 until 2019. This corpus is based on Lu et al. (2024) and includes 421 legislative

DOI: 10.4324/9781003430308-14

acts, encompassing 41 decisions, 106 directives and 274 regulations. In our analysis, we focus on two relevant features of legislative texts as highlighted in the legislative drafting literature: the prevalence of passive voice and negations. Legislative drafting experts and guidelines recommend using active instead of passive voice and positive expressions rather than negations (Xanthaki 2014, 2022; Garner 2016; European Commission 2015).[1] To our knowledge, quantitative research on legislative texts in the EU has not yet studied these language features systematically (e.g., Hurka 2024; Cross and Hermansson 2017; Rauh 2021; Osnabrügge and Vannoni 2025).

We find that passive voice and negations are frequently used in EU legislation. In legislative acts, 41.0% of sentences use the passive voice and 9.7% use negations. Our descriptive analysis reveals that the usage of passive voice and negations does not change within a legislative period. Passive voice and negations are used more frequently in directives than in decisions and regulations. Also, patterns of passive voice and negations vary significantly across areas. Passive voice is especially prevalent in legislation on taxation and financial stability but appears less frequently in texts on employment and communications networks. Legislation on internal markets and taxation uses negations more frequently than texts on employment and home affairs.

The chapter is structured as follows. Section 11.2 introduces basic concepts and provides an overview of various NLP techniques available for examining the language of legislation. Subsequently, Section 11.3 outlines the data and methods used in our analysis. Then our analysis demonstrates the application of these techniques by exploring the prevalence of passive voice and negations as an example. Section 11.4 concludes.

11.2 NLP Techniques

This section outlines several NLP techniques that enable large-scale, automatic analysis of legislative texts. We focus on explaining the core concepts and their application, omitting technical details of the methods. We aim to offer insights into a selection of commonly used approaches. For a comprehensive introduction to NLP methods, we refer the reader to Jurafsky and Martin (2024) or Eisenstein (2019). Another useful resource is Grimmer et al. (2022), who focus on the research design of NLP projects.

We start by explaining multiple key concepts. The collection of all texts compiled for analysis, such as those of legislative acts, is referred to as the *corpus*. The unit of analysis, or observation, in the corpus is a *document*, which can be an entire text, a single paragraph, a sentence or any other unit of text defined by the researcher. Each document can be segmented into smaller parts, called *tokens*, through the process of *tokenization*.

In English, a document is typically tokenized by whitespace such that a token corresponds to a word. Still, other tokenization methods tokenize by character or sub-word level (e.g., byte-pair encoding). n-*grams* refer to a sequence of tokens, where *n* defines the number of tokens (Grimmer et al. 2022, chapter 5).

11.2.1 Regular Expressions

In the initial stage of text cleaning or analysis, researchers typically focus on identifying patterns within the texts. A regular expression, or *regex*, is a language used to identify, extract or manipulate specific combinations of strings. Regular expressions are processed by a character-search algorithm that sifts through the corpus to return all instances matching the pattern. For example, in a corpus of legislative acts, regex can be used to identify the date of publication, the number of recitals or the occurrence of certain keywords. Also, regular expressions are useful for removing text from a corpus, such as titles, headers, page numbers or footnotes. Regular expressions can also be applied to match any word, which can subsequently be used to compute the total number of words in legislation, a proxy for the complexity or quality of legislation in some studies (e.g., Gratton et al. 2021). Regular expressions are implemented in almost all computer languages (Jurafsky and Martin 2024, chapter 2).

A useful application of regular expression is to pre-process the textual data. This step involves reducing the complexity of the textual data before the analysis. For example, regular expressions can be used to remove punctuation, stopwords or numbers from texts.[2] We exemplify a regular expression focusing on removing numbers from the following sentence: "The criteria for the identification of the operators of essential services, as referred to in point (4) of Article 4, shall be as follows".[3] The regex pattern that matches the characters of interest is "[0–9]+". "[0–9]" is a regex notation that matches any digit (0–9). The "+" is a quantifier that identifies patterns of at least one or more digits.[4]

11.2.2 Dictionary-Based Approach

A *dictionary-based approach* is a simple quantitative method for classifying each document in a corpus into categories or for measuring the extent to which texts belong to categories. The dictionary-based approach involves using an existing or creating a new list of words indicative of the categories of interest. These lists of words can then be used to classify the texts based on word frequencies or weighted word frequencies, as some dictionaries assign a weight to each word to capture how strongly the word is associated with a category. In classification tasks, decision rules determine when a document is classified into a category. For example, a simple rule is to classify a text into a category if it includes at least one word related to a category. Another rule is to assign a document to a category based on relative frequencies (Grimmer et al. 2022, chapter 16).

Dictionaries enable large-scale, automated text analysis with the benefits of ease of use and high interpretability. The accuracy of dictionaries depends on how well the words map to the categories. Researchers commonly use customized or generic dictionaries. Customized dictionaries are dictionaries created for one specific use case or context. Creating such a dictionary can be time-consuming and requires profound domain expertise. Generic dictionaries aim at analyzing textual data across different contexts (Quinn et al. 2010; Osnabrügge et al. 2023). An example of a generic dictionary is the Linguistic Inquiry Word Count, which includes categories related to psychological processes, such as affect and cognition (Pennebaker et al. 2022). The validity of a dictionary can vary significantly across domains as the usage and meaning of words may differ (Grimmer et al. 2022, chapter 16). Hence, it is important to validate dictionary-based methods.[5]

A recent application of the dictionary-based method to legislative texts is by Ash et al. (2024), who, focusing on the legislation adopted in US states from 1965 until 2012, show that legislative detail increases economic growth. The rationale behind this finding is that legislative detail reduces legal uncertainty and thus facilitates economic activities and businesses. To measure legislative detail, the authors use data on the number of provisions and the contingency of these provisions. The authors develop a customized dictionary to identify whether clauses in US state legislation are contingent. They identify a clause as contingent if it includes at least one of the following words: as long as, could, in case, if, otherwise, provided that, so long as, should, supposing, unless, where, would. In the analysis, Ash et al. (2024) demonstrate that the effect on legislative detail is causally driven by contingent provisions.

11.2.3 Supervised Text Classification

Supervised text classification is a technique in which researchers train a statistical model to automatically classify text into categories using a sample of labeled documents. The first step is to either find an existing labeled corpus or manually label a subset of the documents in the corpus. The documents to be labeled are usually randomly selected from the corpus. The labeled data is then divided into three sets. The training set is used to train the model, and the development set to tune the model's hyperparameters. Finally, the test set serves to evaluate the model's final predictions (Jurafsky and Martin 2024, chapter 4).[6]

Next, researchers select a machine learning model, which learns a mathematical function that describes how the text relates to the categories, identifying which features (e.g., words or n-grams) are most effective in distinguishing between categories (Hastie et al. 2009, chapter 2). A standard machine learning model is, for example, the regularized multinomial logistic regression model (James et al. 2013, chapter 4). The training, development and test sets are subsequently used to select the best model and evaluate its performance. A common evaluation metric is the accuracy score, defined as the proportion of correct predictions in the test data (James et al. 2013, chapter 2).

Supervised text classification usually outperforms dictionary-based methods in classifying textual data, especially in complex tasks. To achieve good classification results, high-quality training data are crucial. At the same time, generating this labeled data is costly as it requires generating codebooks, recruiting multiple annotators and assessing reliability (Barberá et al. 2021). Recently, researchers have used pre-trained language models, such as BERT (Devlin et al. 2019), for text classification, which significantly reduces the required size of the training data.

An example of supervised text classification is Anastasopoulos and Bertelli (2020), who use supervised learning to identify articles in EU legislation that delegate authority to Member States or the Commission or constrain these actors. The authors use a humanly annotated sample from Franchino (2007) including 8,417 provisions from 158 major EU acts. Then they use these data to train multiple models to automatically classify the articles from 59,423 regulations and directives adopted from 1959 until 2017 in the EU. To assess the method's validity, Anastasopoulos and Bertelli (2020) replicate the results of Franchino (2007) focusing on a subset. They show that acts decided under unanimity grant more discretion to Member States than acts decided under qualified majority voting.

11.2.4 *Unsupervised Text Classification*

Unsupervised text classification involves classifying text with unlabeled text data. Rather than learning how to predict predefined categories, the model uncovers underlying patterns and relationships in texts (James et al. 2013, chapter 12). Two common methods for unsupervised text classification are clustering and topic modeling. The underlying objective is to map document features—specifically, the words that represent them—to a significantly smaller number of groups or topics that are previously unknown.

Clustering aims to identify natural and coherent groups among all documents in the corpus. A common method for clustering is the k-means algorithm, which groups documents into k clusters based on the similarity of their features (Hartigan and Wong 1979). However, clustering assumes that each document belongs to only one distinct cluster (Grimmer et al. 2022, chapter 12).

Topic models soften this assumption by suggesting that a document is a mixture of topics. As a result, they are also referred to as mixed-membership models. Latent Dirichlet Allocation (LDA) is a popular topic modeling technique that treats each document as a mixture of topics, and each topic is a probability distribution over words (Blei et al. 2003). This model can be used to estimate the share of topics in each document and the probability that words are associated with the topics. The researcher needs to define the number of topics ex-ante. The content of the topics can be labeled manually by reading documents or inspecting the words associated with topics. The words provide an intuitive understanding of the topic's content. For example, if the top words in a topic are "tax", "GDP" and "growth", the topic might be labeled "economics". The LDA model has been extended to incorporate document-level variables in the estimation, which can help to estimate better topics or to discover relationships between these variables and topics (Grimmer et al. 2022, chapter 13). A prominent example of an extension is the structural topic model (Roberts et al. 2013).

Unsupervised topic classification is a powerful tool for exploring topics in textual data and requires no labeled training data, which reduces the costs of applying the method. At the same time, evaluating unsupervised models is more challenging because there are no gold standard labels (Denny and Spirling 2018). Approaches for validating topic models include manual inspection of words, reading documents, inspecting fit statistics, bespoke validation and crowd-sourced coding of model outputs (Ying et al. 2022).

An example of applying an unsupervised learning method to legislation is Hagemann et al. (2017). This paper shows that governments are more likely to vote against and abstain from voting on legislative proposals affecting EU authority if their domestic public opinion is Eurosceptic. As part of the analysis, the authors apply LDA to summaries of 1,793 EU legislation and then study the variation of the effect of public opinion by topics. They estimate 45 topics and validate the topics by inspecting the words highly related to the topics. Hagemann et al. (2017) find that the effect is especially strong in acts on topics such as environment, migration and border control.

11.2.5 POS Tagging

POS tagging involves assigning grammatical roles to each word in a sentence, commonly known as tagging (Jurafsky and Martin 2024, chapter 17). Each tag represents the grammatical classification of a word, such as common English parts of speech like nouns, verbs, adjectives, prepositions and others.[7] In the following, we illustrate an example sentence with the corresponding tags, which we computed with the tagger implemented in the spaCy Python module (Honnibal et al. 2020):[8]

> They *(pronoun)* shall *(auxiliary)* immediately *(adverb)* communicate *(verb)* the *(determiner)* text *(noun)* of *(adposition)* those *(determiner)* measures *(noun)* to *(adposition)* the *(determiner)* Commission *(proper noun)*. *(punctuation)*

Beginning with rule-based algorithms, which tagged words based on linguistic rules, leading POS models are now based on artificial neural networks (e.g., Ma and Hovy 2016). An artificial neural network is a machine learning model that forms the foundation of deep learning. Inspired by the human brain, the model consists of deep, interconnected neurons that learn abstract patterns from large amounts of data (Hastie et al. 2009, chapter 11). Neural network-based POS tagging models are trained using a large dataset including text and the annotated POS tags. In the training process, the model learns patterns and relationships between tokens and their corresponding POS tags. For example, at a low level, a model may learn that "the" is likely to be followed by a noun or that words ending in "-tion" are more likely to be nouns. For each word in a sentence, the model produces a probability distribution over all POS tags and assigns the most probable tag.

11.2.6 Dependency Parsing

Dependency parsing goes beyond the role of individual words by analyzing the syntactic structure of sentences. This technique assigns a grammatical relation to pairs of words, where one word is the *head*, or the so-called central organizing word, and the other the *dependent* (Jurafsky and Martin 2024, chapter 19). The Universal Dependencies Project has created a standardized list of grammatical relations (de Marneffe et al. 2021). For example, in the phrase "the law" the token "the" is the dependent, "law" is the head and the grammatical relation is "determiner", as the dependent "the" is the head's article.

These grammatical relationships of words in a sentence can be illustrated using a directed graph (Jurafsky and Martin 2024, 392), as Figure 11.1 exemplifies. We computed this dependency parsing tree using spaCy (Honnibal et al. 2020). The directed, typed arcs represent head-dependent pairs. Besides illustrating the dependencies, the graph includes the POS tags below the words. For example, the pronoun "They" is a nominal subject and dependent on the verb "communicate". Similarly, the graph reveals that "immediately" is the adverbial modifier of "communicate". The root node of the tree is "communicate" as it exhibits no incoming arcs.

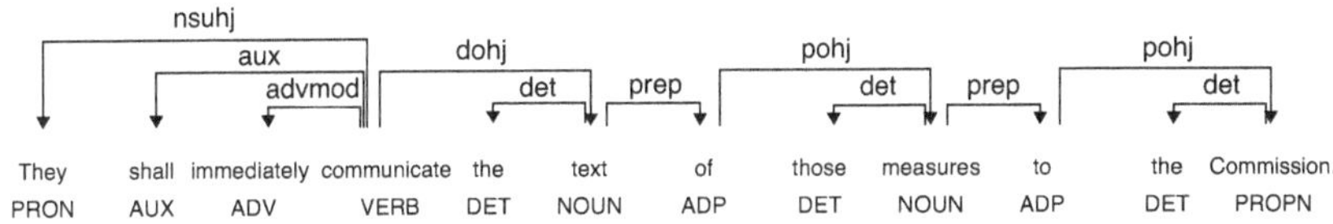

Figure 11.1 Dependency Parsing Tree.

Note: We summarize in the following spaCy acronyms. POS acronyms—AUX: auxiliary, ADP: adposition, ADV: adverb, DET: determiner, NOUN: noun, PROPN: proper noun, PRON: pronoun, VERB: verb. Dependencies—advmod: adverbial modifier, aux: auxiliary, prep: prepositional modifier, det: determiner, dobj: direct object, nsubj: nominal subject, pobj: object of preposition.

The best-performing dependency parsers are also based on neural networks (e.g., Dozat and Manning 2017). Dependency parsers are trained on large datasets with annotated syntactic dependencies. These structured data are called treebanks (Goldberg and Nivre 2012; Honnibal and Johnson 2015). A prominent project for building treebanks is the Universal Dependencies Project, an open community project that has created more than 200 treebanks in more than 150 languages (de Marneffe et al. 2021).

A recent application of dependency parsing is Osnabrügge and Vannoni (2025), who study the effect of legislative quality on compliance with EU legislation at the national level. They expand the data of König and Mäder (2014) on 299 compliance cases from 21 directives adopted between 1999 and 2003 in the EU. As an indicator of legislative quality, the authors focus on syntactic complexity measured with the percentage of adjectival modifiers in a legislative text. They find that syntactic complexity is negatively related to compliance. However, this finding is not robust to controlling for the length of legislation since this variable is correlated with syntactic complexity.

11.3 Application

To illustrate the usefulness of NLP techniques, we apply them in this section to all EU legislation adopted between the 2014 and 2019 European elections. This section first outlines the data and provides descriptive statistics. Then, we explain the measurement strategy and study variation in the usage of passive voice and negations, with a special focus on patterns by type of legislation, legislative procedure, year and area.

We contribute to previous quantitative research on EU legislative texts by studying two new aspects of the language that drafting experts identify as important: passive voice and negations. Previous work examined, among others, the changes in legislative texts in the decision-making process (Cross and Hermansson 2017; Rauh 2021), the policy complexity (e.g., Hurka 2024; Senninger 2023) and the quality of legislation as measured with indicators on syntactic complexity and vagueness (Osnabrügge and Vannoni 2025).

11.3.1 Data

We rely on data from Lu et al. (2024), which are based on the HTML files of the legislation as available via the EUR-Lex database.[9] We take into account all acts adopted in the period between the 2014 and the 2019 European elections. To keep only the text of the legal provisions, we pre-process the textual data by removing the recitals and appendices using regular expressions. We only focus on directives, decisions and regulations adopted via three main legislative procedures, excluding corrigenda.

As shown in Table 11.1, the resulting data contains 421 legislative acts, where 41 acts are decisions, 106 acts are directives and 274 acts are regulations. The number of acts also varies over the years of the term. While there were only 31 acts recorded in the first year (2014) of the term, the number of acts increased to 88 in 2018. Among the three types of acts, the regulations have the highest increase from the beginning to the end of the period, accounting for 74% of all acts in 2019.

Table 11.2 further illustrates the breakdown of legislative acts by procedure. Predominantly, the EU institutions adopted the three types of legislative acts through the ordinary legislative procedure, the primary method of EU lawmaking. The sample includes eight decisions and seven regulations

Table 11.1 Number of Adopted Legislation by Type and Year

	Decision	*Directive*	*Regulation*	*Total*
2014	6	9	16	31
2015	4	18	46	68
2016	6	23	53	82
2017	10	17	56	83
2018	12	24	52	88
2019	3	15	51	69
Total	41	106	274	421

Table 11.2 Number of Adopted Legislation by Type and Procedure

	Consent	*Consultation*	*Ordinary*	*Total*
Decision	8	10	23	41
Directive	0	21	85	106
Regulation	7	7	260	274
Total	15	38	368	421

adopted using the consent procedure. Additionally, 10 decisions, 21 directives and 7 regulations were adopted through the consultation procedure.

To better understand the corpus of legislative acts, we plot the distribution of the number of words and the percentage of sentences above 20 words. We use this limit of 20 words following Garner (2016, 5) as he recommends this maximum for "general expository prose in law". We treat dots, semicolons and double colons as delimiters of sentences. As Figure 11.2 shows, each legislative act contains, on average, about 6,254 words, and 52.1% of all sentences in an average act are longer than 20 words. However, extreme cases with more than 30,000 words influence the average length of acts. After excluding these extreme cases, the average is reduced to 4,646 words. According to the figure, the variable on the percentage of sentences above 20 words exhibits considerable variation. In 12 acts, fewer than 25% of the sentences are longer than 20 words. But, for six acts, the percentage of sentences above 20 is larger than 75%.

Different services in the European Commission prepared the legislation used in this chapter before being formally introduced into the legislative decision-making process. Overall, 33 different services were involved. The most frequent ones were the Directorate-General (DG) for the Internal Market (38 acts); Legal Service (36 acts); DG Taxation and Customs Union (35 acts); DG Migration and Home Affairs (34 acts); DG Mobility and Transport (34 acts); DG for Justice (25 acts); DG for Financial Stability, Financial Services and Capital Markets Union (21 acts); DG for Maritime Affairs and Fisheries (20 acts); DG for Communications Networks, Content and Technology (18 acts); DG Trade (17 acts); and DG

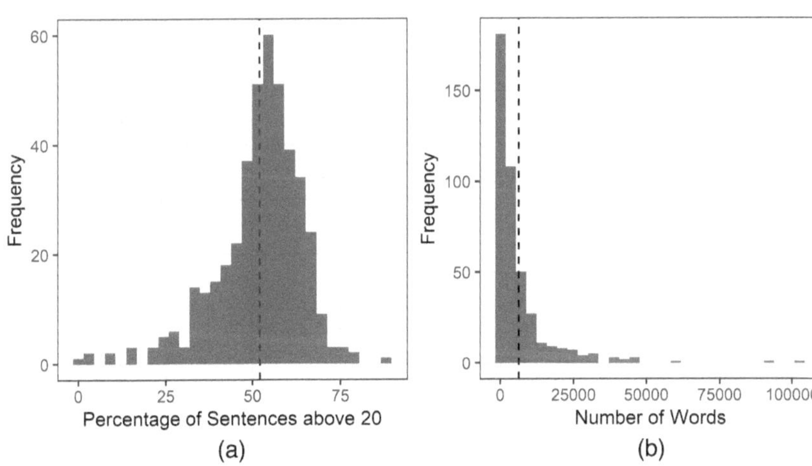

Figure 11.2 Number of Words and Percentage of Sentences above 20 Words.

Note: The vertical dashed lines indicate the mean values.

for Employment, Social Affairs and Inclusion (14 acts). Note that the legal service is the leading service for recast legislation.

11.3.2 Measurement

We utilize the Python module spaCy to measure the presence of passive voice and negations in EU legislation. To this end, we rely on the previously introduced NLP techniques of POS tagging and dependency parsing.

To detect passive voice constructions, we develop a rule-based matcher using spaCy's Matcher functionality (see also Sepehri et al. 2023).[10] Our pattern matches a range of passive forms using POS and dependency tags, including those containing negations and adverbs. Specifically, our pattern targets combinations of tokens in a sentence that start with an auxiliary verb—optionally followed by a negation and various optional adverbs—succeeded by a main verb in its past participle form. By accommodating optional negations and adverbs, our pattern captures more passive voice constructions, such as "was not completed" or "has been thoroughly analyzed". We quantify passive voice usage by computing the percentage of sentences with passive voice by legislation.

For negations, we use spaCy's dependency parsing model that tags each negation, such as "never" or "not", with the dependency tag "negation" ("neg"). We build a function that takes a sentence as input and iterates over all its tokens and outputs whether any token is a negation. We apply this function to all sentences in an act and calculate the percentage of sentences, including a negation by legislative act.

Table 11.3 presents examples for both sentences with passive voice and negations. We selected these sentences randomly from the corpus.

Table 11.3 Examples of Passive Voice and Negations

Category	*Example Sentence*
Passive Voice	The quantities for which a renunciation has been made shall immediately be added to the quantities to be allocated under paragraph 6.
	In paragraph 5, the words "the Community Fisheries Control Agency established in accordance with Regulation (EC) No 768/2005" are replaced by "EFCA".
	A product covered by this Regulation shall not be placed on the market unless ....
Negations	However, generic terms shall not be registered.
	This Directive shall not apply to take over bids for securities issued by the Member States' central banks.
	If no penalties were imposed in a given year, Member States shall not be required to report to the Commission.

11.3.3 Patterns of Passive Voice and Negations

To quantify the usage of passive voice and negations, we compute the percentage of sentences using passive voice and negations for each act. According to legal drafting experts and guidelines (Xanthaki 2014, 2022; Garner 2016; European Commission 2015), legislative texts should be drafted in plain language, avoiding, if possible, the usage of negations and passive voice. Therefore, the amount of passive voice and negations in a legislative act provides valuable information to measure how far legislation is drafted in line with these standards.

As shown in Figure 11.3, on average, about 41.0% of the sentences in each bill contain passive voice, and about 9.7% of the sentences contain negations. However, as demonstrated by the wide distribution of the measures, there is significant variation among legislative acts. The measure of the percentage of passive voice sentences is close to a normal distribution with the lower and upper limits equal to 0% and 80%. The measure of the percentage of negations exhibits a more right-skewed distribution, meaning that, while most acts have a lower percentage of negations, there are acts with an exceptionally high percentage of negations. In fact, among all acts, there are about 65 acts that contain no negations. At the same time, however, there is an act where almost half of the sentences contain negations. Overall, the results indicate that passive voice is used more frequently than negations in EU legislation.

Figure 11.4 illustrates the variation of our variables on the percentage of passive voice and the percentage of negations over time. Both the usage of passive voice and negations remain relatively stable over time (about 40%

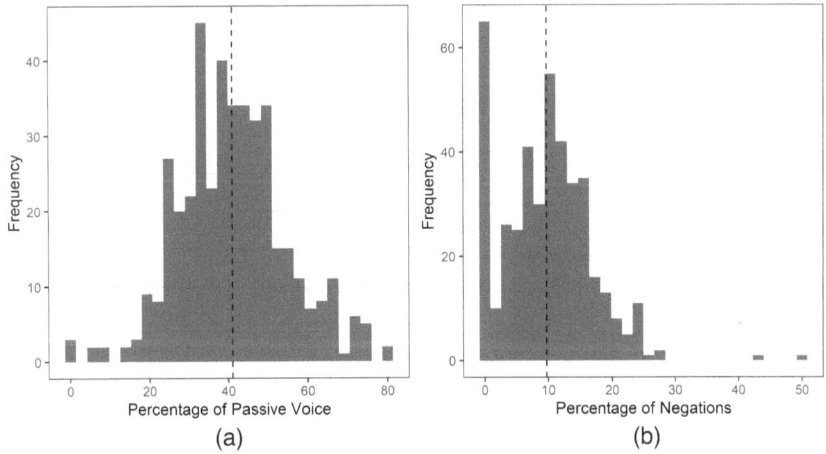

Figure 11.3 Distribution of the Percentage of Passive Voice and Negations.

Note: The vertical dashed lines indicate the mean values.

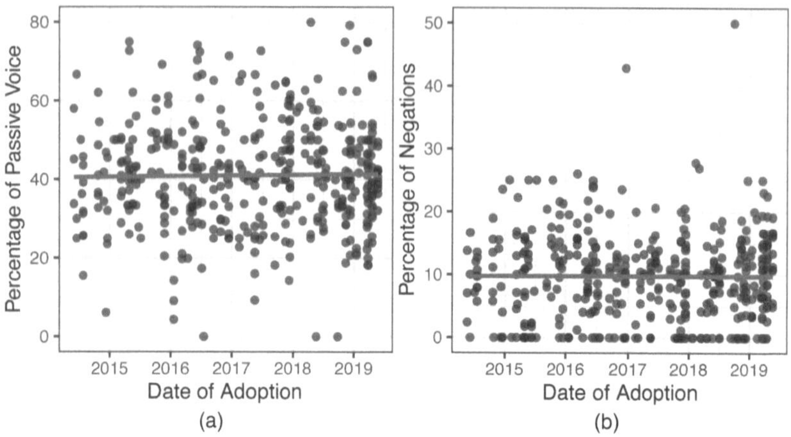

Figure 11.4 Distribution of Percentage of Passive Voice and Negations over Time.
Note: The solid line represents the trend predicted by linear regression.

and 10%, respectively). Hence, we do not find evidence for an electoral cycle in using passive voice and negations in EU legislation.

Although the use of passive voice and negations remains temporally stable, it is reasonable to expect variations in drafting styles across various types of legislation and procedures. Figure 11.5 presents the average percentages of sentences with passive voice and negations for three types of legislative texts: decisions, directives and regulations (the upper panels of the figure). It also evaluates the two criteria across three procedures: the consent, the consultation and the ordinary legislative procedures (the lower panels of the figure).

The top-left panel of Figure 11.5 illustrates the average percentages of passive voice sentences across the three types. Directives exhibit the highest passive voice usage at 43.5%, decisions have the lowest at 37.3%, and regulations fall in between at 40.6%. The variable on negations has a similar pattern: directives have the highest average at 11.3%, decisions the lowest at 7.9% and regulations occupy the middle ground at 9.4%. However, the pattern is less clear when inspecting the variation across different procedures. The acts issued through the consultation procedure appear to use passive voice and negations more frequently than acts adopted via the consent procedure (see bottom-left and bottom-right panels). However, the acts adopted under the ordinary procedure have the lowest average percentage in passive voice (40.4%) and the highest in negations (9.9%).

To better understand the variation of passive voice and negations in legislation, we continue by exploring variation in language by area.

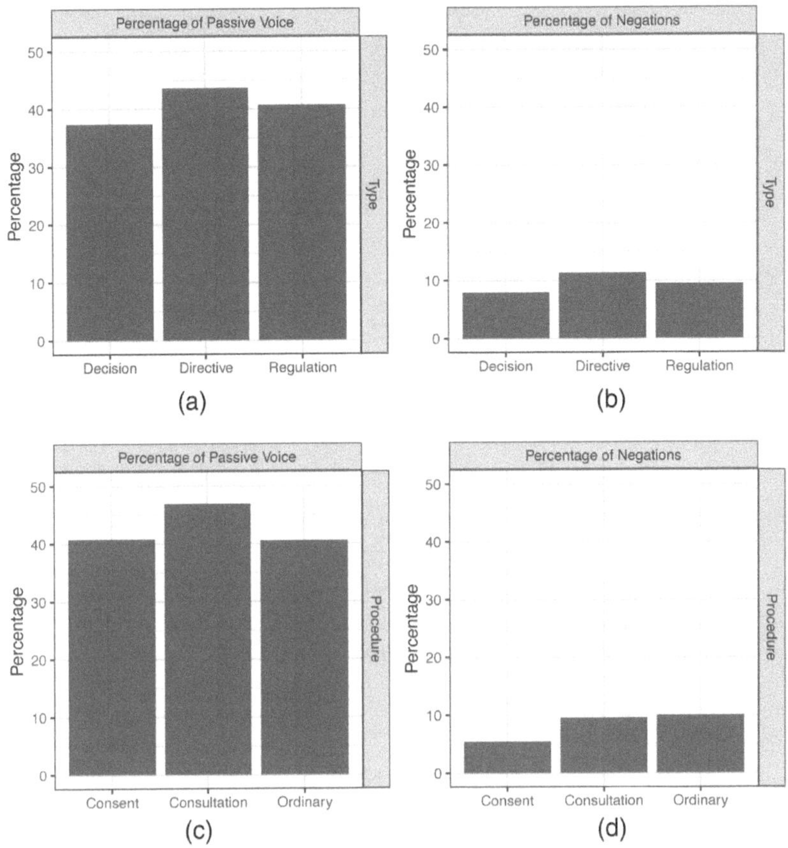

Figure 11.5 Average Percentage of Passive Voice and Negations across Types and Procedures.

Figure 11.6 illustrates the percentage of sentences with passive voice and negations in different areas. We identify these areas based on the DGs responsible for initiating the legislation and focus on the ten most frequent DGs. The left panel of Figure 11.6 illustrates that passive voice appears frequently in legislation on taxation and customs union. For example, legislation on taxation includes, on average, 49.2% of sentences with passive voice constructions. On the contrary, legislation initiated by DG Communications Networks and Employment tends to use passive voice less frequently. As the right panel of Figure 11.6 shows, negations are particularly frequent in the internal market and taxation areas and less frequent in legislation on employment and home affairs. Interestingly, legislation on financial stability uses passive voice often,

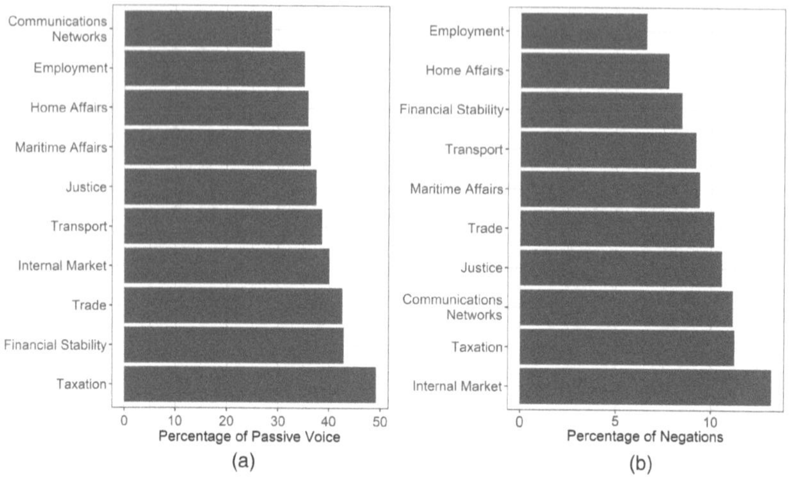

Figure 11.6 Average Percentage of Passive Voice and Negations by Area.

but negations are less common. Overall, we find that the variation in the usage of passive voice and negations across areas is larger than across time, type of legislation and procedure.

11.4 Concluding Remarks

This chapter provides an overview of NLP techniques, highlighting examples of how these methods can be used to analyze legislative texts. These techniques allow for the automatic analysis of large corpora of legislative texts and thus are promising tools to complement traditional linguistic analyses. Despite their benefits, legal scholars have not yet widely adopted these techniques.

To promote greater use of NLP in legal studies, this chapter outlines a selection of techniques, including regular expressions, dictionary-based approaches, supervised and unsupervised text classification, POS tagging and dependency parsing (Jurafsky and Martin 2024; Grimmer et al. 2022). We also present examples of how these methods are used in recent work focusing on political science and political economy research.

Furthermore, we demonstrate the value of NLP using an application. We use a corpus of all secondary legislation adopted in the legislative period from 2014 to 2019 in the EU (Lu et al. 2024). After presenting descriptive statistics, we focus on the usage of passive voice and negations over time and across types of legislation, legislative procedures and areas. This analysis is relevant as drafting experts recommend using active instead of passive voice and positive over negative language (Garner 2016; Xanthaki 2014, 2022; European Commission 2015).

Our findings show that passive voice is used more frequently than negative language. While on average 41.0% of sentences include passive voice, 9.7% of sentences on legislation include negations. The usage of passive voice and negations is relatively constant over time. Also, directives tend to contain more passive voice and negations than other types of legislation. We also document variation across areas, which is larger than the variation over time or across types and procedures. The examination of EU legislation underscores the practical value of such methods as they can quantify how language is used.

Future research may expand our analyses by studying a more extended period and the causal effect of using passive voice and negations. Another promising avenue for future research would be identifying the subset of sentences using passive voice and negations that are especially problematic for textual clarity. Finally, practitioners at the EU institutions may consider using NLP to monitor the drafting quality before introducing a legislative proposal and during the legislative process.

Acknowledgments

We gratefully acknowledge funding from the British Academy/Leverhulme Small Research Grants scheme (SRG22/220129). Xiao Lu acknowledges funding from the Fundamental Research Funds for the Central Universities, Peking University. For helpful comments and suggestions, we thank Helen Xanthaki. We thank William Cooke, Chilufya Mumba and Saskia Poulter for excellent research assistance.

Notes

1 Note that there are some exceptions in which passive voice and negations are seen as acceptable (see, e.g., Garner 2016, 60–62).

2 Other common pre-processing steps are the removal of infrequent words, stemming and lowercasing the letters (e.g., Denny and Spirling 2018).

3 Directive (EU) 2016/1148 of the European Parliament and of the Council of 6 July 2016 concerning measures for a high common level of security of network and information systems across the Union. *Official Journal of the European Union* L194: 1–30.

4 A useful website for testing regular expressions is https://regex101.com/, and for an overview of regex metacharacters, see https://www.w3schools.com/python/python_regex.asp (last accessed: September 24, 2024).

5 Recent research combines dictionary-based method with word-embedding techniques to improve the measurement of standard dictionaries (e.g., Rice and Zorn 2021; Osnabrügge et al. 2021).

6 An alternative strategy is to use k-fold cross-validation (James et al. 2013, chapter 5).

7 See the full tag list at https://universaldependencies.org/u/pos/ (last accessed: September 24, 2024).
8 The sentence comes from the following source: Directive (EU) 2020/2184 of the European Parliament and of the Council of 16December 2020 on the quality of water intended for human consumption (recast). *Official Journal of the European Union* L535: 1–58.
9 https://eur-lex.europa.eu/homepage.html (last accessed: September 24, 2024).
10 https://spacy.io/api/matcher (last accessed: September 24, 2024).

References

Anastasopoulos, J. L. and A. Bertelli (2020). Understanding Delegation through Machine Learning: A Method and Application to the European Union. *American Political Science Review* 114 (1), 291–301.

Ash, E., M. Morelli, and M. Vannoni (2024). More Laws, More Growth? Evidence from U.S. States. *Journal of Political Economy.* https://www.journals.uchicago.edu/doi/abs/10.1086/734874

Barberá, P., A. E. Boydstun, S. Linn, R. McMahon, and J. Nagler (2021). Automated Text Classification of News Articles: A Practical Guide. *Political Analysis* 29 (1), 19–42.

Blei, D. M., A. Y. Ng, and M. I. Jordan (2003). Latent Dirichlet Allocation. *Journal of Machine Learning Research* 3, 993–1022.

Butt, P. (2013). *Modern Legal Drafting.* Cambridge: Cambridge University Press.

Coupette, C., D. Hartung, J. Beckedorf, M. Böther, and D. M. Katz (2023). Law Smells: Defining and Detecting Problematic Patterns in Legal Drafting. *Artificial Intelligence and Law* 31 (2), 335–368.

Cross, J. P. and H. Hermansson (2017). Legislative Amendments and Informal Politics in the European Union: A Text Reuse Approach. *European Union Politics* 18 (4), 581–602.

de Marneffe, M.-C., C. D. Manning, J. Nivre, and D. Zeman (2021). Universal Dependencies. *Computational Linguistics* 47 (2), 255–308.

Denny, M. J. and A. Spirling (2018). Text Preprocessing for Unsupervised Learning: Why It Matters, When It Misleads, and What to Do about It. *Political Analysis* 26 (2), 168–189.

Devlin, J., M.-W. Chang, K. Lee, and K. Toutanova (2019). BERT: Pre-training of Deep Bidirectional Transformers for Language Understanding. In *Proceedings of the 2019 Conference of the North American Chapter of the Association for Computational Linguistics: Human Language Technologies*, Minneapolis, Minnesota. Association for Computational Linguistics, pp. 4171–4186.

Dozat, T. and C. D. Manning (2017). Deep Biaffine Attention for Neural Dependency Parsing. https://arxiv.org/abs/1611.01734.

Eisenstein, J. (2019). *Introduction to Natural Language Processing.* Cambridge, MA: MIT Press.

European Commission (2015). *How to Write Clearly.* Publications Office of the European Union. https://data.europa.eu/doi/10.2782/022405.

Franchino, F. (2007). *The Powers of the Union: Delegation in the EU.* Cambridge: Cambridge University Press.

Garner, B. (2016). *Guidelines for Drafting and Editing Legislation*. Dallas, TX: RosePen Book.
Garner, B. A. (2002). *The Elements of Legal Style*. Oxford: Oxford University Press.
Goldberg, Y. and J. Nivre (2012). A Dynamic Oracle for Arc-Eager Dependency Parsing. In *Proceedings of COLING 2012: Technical Papers, COLING 2012*, Mumbai, India. The COLING 2012 Organizing Committee, pp. 959–976.
Gratton, G., L. Guiso, C. Michelacci, and M. Morelli (2021). From Weber to Kafka: Political Instability and the Overproduction of Laws. *American Economic Review* 111 (9), 2964–3003.
Grimmer, J., M. E. Roberts, and B. M. Stewart (2022). *Text as Data: A New Framework for Machine Learning and the Social Sciences*. Princeton, NJ: Princeton University Press.
Hagemann, S., S. B. Hobolt, and C. Wratil (2017). Government Responsiveness in the European Union: Evidence from Council Voting. *Comparative Political Studies* 50 (6), 850–876.
Hartigan, J. A. and M. A. Wong (1979). Algorithm AS 136: A k-means Clustering Algorithm. *Journal of the Royal Statistical Society Series C: Applied Statistics* 18 (1), 100–108.
Hastie, T., R. Tibshirani, J. H. Friedman, and J. H. Friedman (2009). *The Elements of Statistical Learning: Data Mining, Inference, and Prediction*. New York, NY: Springer.
Honnibal, M. and M. Johnson (2015). An Improved Non-monotonic Transition System for Dependency Parsing. *Proceedings of the 2015 Conference on Empirical Methods in Natural Language Processing*, Lisbon, Portugal, 17–21 September 2015, pp. 1373–1378.
Honnibal, M., Montani, I., Van Landeghem, S. and Boyd, A. (2020). spaCy: Industrial-strength Natural Language Processing in Python. https://doi.org/10.5281/zenodo.1212303.
Hurka, S. (2024). The Institutional and Political Roots of Complex Policies: Evidence from the European Union. *European Journal of Political Research* 62 (4), 1168–1190.
James, G., D. Witten, T. Hastie, and R. Tibshirani (2013). *An Introduction to Statistical Learning*. New York, NY: Springer.
Jurafsky, D. and J. H. Martin (2024). Speech and Language Processing: An Introduction to Natural Language Processing, Computational Linguistics, and Speech Recognition. https://web.stanford.edu/~jurafsky/slp3/.
Katz, D. M., D. Ron, and M. J. Bommarito (2021). *Legal Informatics*. Cambridge: Cambridge University Press.
König, T. and L. Mäder (2014). The Strategic Nature of Compliance: An Empirical Evaluation of Law Implementation in the Central Monitoring System of the European Union. *American Journal of Political Science* 58 (1), 246–263.
Lu, X., M. Osnabrügge, G. Quaremba, and M. Vannoni (2024). Measuring Ambiguity in Legislative Texts. Working Paper.
Ma, X. and E. Hovy (2016). End-to-end Sequence Labeling via Bi-directional LSTM-CNNs-CRF. In *Proceedings of the 54th Annual Meeting of the Association*

for Computational Linguistics (Volume 1: Long Papers), 1064–1074, Berlin, Germany. Association for Computational Linguistics.

Osnabrügge, M., E. Ash, and M. Morelli (2023). Cross-Domain Topic Classification for Political Texts. *Political Analysis* 31 (1), 59–80.

Osnabrügge, M., S. B. Hobolt, and T. Rodon (2021). Playing to the Gallery: Emotive Rhetoric in Parliaments. *American Political Science Review* 115 (3), 885–899.

Osnabrügge, M. and M. Vannoni (2025). Quality of Legislation and Compliance: A Natural Language Processing Approach. *Political Science Research and Methods*, 13 (3), 736–744.

Pennebaker, J., R. L. Boyd, R. J. Booth, A. Ashokkumar, and M. E. Francis (2022). *Linguistic Inquiry and Word Count: LIWC2022*. Austin, TX: Pennebaker Conglomerates (www.LIWC.net).

Quinn, K. M., B. Monroe, M. Colaresi, M. H. Crespin, and D. R. Radev (2010). How to Analyze Political Attention with Minimal Assumptions and Costs. *American Journal of Political Science* 54 (1), 209–228.

Rauh, C. (2021). One Agenda-setter or Many? The Varying Success of Policy Initiatives by Individual Directorates-General of the European Commission 1994–2016. *European Union Politics* 22 (1), 3–24.

Rice, D. R. and C. Zorn (2021). Corpus-based Dictionaries for Sentiment Analysis of Specialized Vocabularies. *Political Science Research and Methods* 9 (1), 20–35.

Roberts, M. E., B. M. Stewart, D. Tingley, and E. M. Airoldi (2013). The Structural Topic Model and Applied Social Science. In *Advances in Neural Information Processing Systems Workshop on Topic Models: Computation, Application, and Evaluation*.

Senninger, R. (2023). What Makes Policy Complex? *Political Science Research and Methods* 11 (4), 913–920.

Sepehri, A., M. S. Mirshafiee, and D. M. Markowitz (2023). PassivePy: A Tool to Automatically Identify Passive Voice in Big Text Data. *Journal of Consumer Psychology* 33 (4), 714–727.

Vannoni, M., E. Ash, and M. Morelli (2020). Measuring Discretion and Delegation in Legislative Texts: Methods and Application to US States. *Political Analysis* 29 (1), 43–57.

Wilkerson, J., D. Smith, and N. Stramp (2015). Tracing the Flow of Policy Ideas in Legislatures: A Text Reuse Approach. *American Journal of Political Science* 59 (4), 943–956.

Williams, M. (2022). *Judges and the Language of Law*. Cham: Palgrave Macmillan.

Xanthaki, H. (2014). *Drafting Legislation: Art and Technology of Rules and Regulation*. London: Bloomsbury.

Xanthaki, H. (2022). *Thornton's Legislative Drafting*. London: Bloomsbury.

Ying, L., J. M. Montgomery, and B. M. Stewart (2022). Topics, Concepts, and Measurement: A Crowdsourced Procedure for Validating Topics as Measures. *Political Analysis* 30 (4), 100–108.

12 An Empirical Approach of Multimodality and Legal Language Reform in Brazil

Thiago B. V. Hermont,
Fabiana de Menezes Soares,
and Mônica Sette Lopes

12.1 Introduction

Language plays a crucial role in law, functioning both as a tool for communication and as a mechanism of power. Legal language, often referred to as "legalese," is characterized by its complexity, formality, and reliance on technical jargon. While this specialized form of language serves to ensure precision and consistency within the legal system, it also has the effect of creating barriers for those without legal training. In Brazil, these barriers are particularly pronounced, as the legal system has historically been rooted in archaic terminology and convoluted sentence structures that make it difficult for the average citizen to understand their rights and obligations.

This complexity is not merely a linguistic issue; it has profound implications for access to justice. When legal texts are difficult to understand, they effectively limit the public's ability to engage with the legal system, thereby perpetuating inequalities. Citizens who are unable to comprehend legal documents are often left reliant on legal professionals, which can be a costly endeavor, particularly for marginalized groups. This creates a system in which legal information, and by extension justice, is accessible only to those with the resources to navigate the complexities of legal language. As Riner (2023) stresses:

> Experts are often called upon to try to resolve such conflict, essentially translating legal language into "everyday language" and back again. Such a process, while it ostensibly (and sometimes practically) helps lay people attempting to use the legal system, also reinforces the insider/outsider distinction that maintain law as an autonomous institution and contributes to its aura of impenetrability.
>
> (2023, p. 519)

DOI: 10.4324/9781003430308-15

Tiersma (1999), under the same perspective, also highlights that legal language can be seen as a gatekeeper that either facilitates or hinders access to legal rights, depending on its level of accessibility. When average Brazilian citizens and their lack of formal education, let alone legal formation, are taken into the equation, mastering the content and its meaning becomes a herculean mission.

One of the earliest examples of legal treatment concerning the simplification of legal language emerged in 1998 with the enactment of Complementary Law No. 95, which governs the drafting, editing, amending, and consolidation of laws. There are several innovations in this law that direct the interpretation and application of plain language. The first is the legislator's duty to consider the public's real ability to understand the new law. As such, the enactment of a new law must be explicitly indicated and allow a reasonable period to ensure its widespread understanding. In other words, laws with significant social impact – either due to their novelty or due to the number of normative and situational changes – require enhanced publicity. In this sense, Complementary Law No. 95 reserves the clause "shall take effect on the date of its publication" solely for laws with limited impact. It also establishes specific rules for the clarity and precision of the legal text, aimed at increasing the readability of normative texts and avoiding ambiguities, expressly mentioning the duty to ensure "the understanding of the law's purpose and to ensure that its text clearly expresses the content and scope intended by the legislator" (Lei Complementar No. 95, 1998).

Another impactful example is Brazil's Access to Information Law, published in 2011, which applies to the entire public administration of the executive, legislative, and judicial branches, at all levels of the Brazilian federation. It emerged within the global Open Data context and lays the foundation for managing official publicity, transparency (both active and passive), and the treatment of secrecy as an exception. The most notable innovation regarding the understanding and legal regulation of plain language concerns the wording of Article 5: "It is the State's duty to guarantee the right of access to information, which shall be provided through objective and swift procedures, in a transparent, clear, and easily understandable language" (Lei No. 12.527, 2011).

The use of the terms "clear" and "easy" as attributes of official information is combined with the idea of a technical procedure aligned with impersonality, a guiding principle of Brazilian public administration found in Article 37 of the Federal Constitution. Another term linked to the efficiency of producing official information is speed, which is also present in the Administrative Procedure Law published in 1999 (Lei No. 9.784, 1999). Although it applies to federal public administration, this law is used by other entities of the federation and has become the general norm for procedures in Brazilian public administration.

Another example arises with the Public Service User Protection Code, Federal Law No. 13.460/2017, which regulates the participation, protection, and defense of the rights of public service users across all branches (executive, legislative, judiciary) at all levels of the federation (municipal, state, and federal). The law governs the relation between the user and the government, clearly addressing aspects of communication between the two poles, highlighting the correlation between the idea of an efficient government and the use of technology. One of the public administration's expressed duties is to use "technological solutions aimed at simplifying processes and procedures for user service and providing better conditions for sharing information" (Lei No. 13.460, 2017). In other words, information must be legible when extracted and treated, notably in its content. The law also emphasizes the use of "simple and understandable language, avoiding the use of acronyms, jargon, and foreign terms" (Lei No. 13.460, 2017).

Finally, another perspective on language simplification appears in the regulations for broadcasting (audio and audiovisual) found in the Accessibility Law for People with Disabilities (Lei No. 10.098, 2000). The law establishes a technical plan aimed at enabling the use of sign language or other forms of subtitling as a guarantee of the right of access to information for people with hearing disabilities. Thus, the legal system governing the right to public information considers various levels for implementing clarity and language simplification, making it a condition for the exercise of rights and accountability.

Under such premises, the Brazilian Chamber of Deputies introduced Bill 6.256/2019, which mandates the simplification of legal language across the country. This legislative effort is grounded in the belief that legal texts should be comprehensible to all citizens, not just those with formal legal education. The bill requires that all legal documents, including laws, regulations, and court decisions, be written in plain language, which is defined as language that is clear, concise, and easily understandable. This move toward simplification is expected to have a transformative effect on the Brazilian legal system by making legal information more accessible to the general public, thus promoting greater transparency and inclusivity.

The introduction of Bill 6.256/2019 aligns with global movements toward plain language in law, which have gained momentum in recent decades. Countries such as Sweden, the United Kingdom, Canada, and Australia have already implemented comprehensive plain language policies to ensure that legal texts are accessible to their citizens (Williams, 2004). These reforms have demonstrated that simplifying legal language does not necessarily mean sacrificing precision. Rather, it involves rethinking how legal information is communicated to ensure that it serves the needs of the public. In Brazil, the success of Bill 6.256/2019 will depend on its implementation,[1] including the willingness of legal professionals to embrace these changes and the development of educational programs to train lawyers, judges, and other legal professionals in the use of plain language.

The shift toward plain language must be accompanied by changes in how legal information is presented, particularly in digital formats. It goes without saying, especially in the era of social media, that the power of images and videos surpasses the importance attributed to texts. Such media play an extremely important role in conveying messages that are intended for broader audiences, which should take into consideration the addressees of public policies and acts of the government. In this regard, official websites, such as the Ministry of Environment's homepage,[2] are increasingly becoming the primary means through which citizens access legal and regulatory information, not to mention accounts on social media, which provide direct and instantaneous information in simple and accurate ways. The Ministry of Environment's homepage, for instance, provides an example of how multimodal communication – using a combination of text, images, videos, and interactive elements – can enhance the accessibility of complex information. By combining the principles of plain language with multimodal design, government websites, and social media can serve as powerful tools for democratizing access to legal information, overcoming some of the barriers when documents rely solely on texts to convey meaning and divulge information.

Bill 6.256/2019, as previously stressed, represents a significant step toward simplifying legal language in Brazil, with the potential to make the legal system more accessible and inclusive. When coupled with multimodal communication strategies, such as those employed by the Ministry of Environment's homepage – which will be further detailed in its own section – the impact of this reform can be further amplified, ensuring that all citizens, regardless of their legal expertise and background, can engage with and understand the laws and regulations that govern them.

12.2 The Role of Legal Language and Multimodality

Legal language has long been regarded as a specialized form of communication, designed to convey complex legal principles and ensure precision in legal proceedings. However, this specificity often results in texts that are inaccessible to individuals without formal legal training, excluding a large segment of the population from fully understanding their rights and obligations. As mentioned at the very beginning of this chapter, legal documents are typically characterized by dense jargon, convoluted sentence structures, and formalistic expressions. As a result, many citizens struggle to engage with legal information, creating a gap between the law and those it is designed to serve. Such discrepancy, far from being merely unintentional, allows for the maintenance of a certain status quo, guaranteeing that access to justice is restricted to very few groups, since language confers legal power, turning into the power itself (Conley, O'Barr, & Riner, 2019). In a reference to the American system, which finds parallels in many other countries, Brazil included, Riner (2023) states that

> [t]he dominant view of legal language as simply "fixing" the meaning of a word, however, elides this process of linguistic-cultural construction, thereby erasing the cultural, indexical meanings of signs and reinforcing the insularity of law. The obscurity and impenetrability of US legal language is well-recognized. This impenetrability is in fact strategic – by (purportedly) creating a semantic world to which only legal language refers, the law attempts to control the ways in which events and experiences are classified in order to be dealt with.
>
> (2023, p. 518)

And she continues highlighting that

> [c]onceptualizing law as an autonomous, self-referential system requires professionals who can facilitate the process of translation of everyday events into legal categories, and of legal categories into terms that a non-professional can understand. This is difficult to achieve because language ideologies held by legal professionals do not often correspond with those held by witnesses, victims, or other non-professionals who call on the law in situation of trouble. This can cause conflict when these groups meet and use language in disparate ways within legal processes. Lay people who need to "navigate legal contexts" are often at an "ideological and semantic disadvantage."
>
> (Andrus, 2015, p. 53; Riner, 2023, pp. 518–519)

This has raised concerns about the ability of legal systems to provide equitable access to justice, particularly for marginalized communities who may not have the financial means to hire legal representation. Brazil, as previously mentioned, is no exception to this global issue, with its legal system historically relying on archaic and complex legal language rooted in its Portuguese colonial past, even though such connection has been diluted over the centuries. Legal texts, from statutes to court rulings, especially after the massive use of computers and their copy-and-paste functionalities, are often laden with formal, technical language that is difficult for the average citizen to comprehend. This complexity creates barriers to justice, as individuals are unable to navigate the legal system without professional assistance, which is often costly. The impact of inaccessible legal language is particularly evident in cases where understanding legal documents is crucial, such as disputes involving property rights, environmental regulations, or criminal proceedings.

12.3 The Global Context of Plain Language Initiatives

Bill 6.256/2019 is part of a larger international trend toward plain language in legal communication. Countries such as the United Kingdom, Sweden, and Canada, referred to in the first part of this chapter, have long recognized the importance of making legal texts more accessible to their citizens.

In the UK, the Plain English Campaign[3] has been a leading force in advocating for clear and simple language in legal and governmental documents. This campaign has been instrumental in introducing plain language reforms in the legal sector, leading to the publication of numerous legal texts in easy-to-understand English. In 1971, Chrissie Maher, the founder of the campaign, introduced the Tuebrook Bugle, the first community newspaper in Britain, crafted by local residents, which motivated other communities to create their own publications. In 1979, Maher formally started the Plain English Campaign by publicly shredding complex jargon in Parliament Square and translating the outdated Metropolitan Police Act into clear language. The campaign quickly gained traction, leading to government revisions of 58,000 forms and notable cost savings. Throughout the 1980s and 1990s, the Plain English Campaign broadened its scope, establishing the Crystal Mark, which recognizes clear communication, and advocates for plain language in legal documents. By 2006, the campaign had solidified its global influence, engaging in public surveys and events to further its mission of promoting clear and understandable communication (Plain English Campaign, n.d.).

Similarly, the Swedish reforms have resulted in legal texts that are more accessible to the public, allowing citizens to better understand their rights and obligations without needing legal representation (Williams, 2004). Sweden has implemented comprehensive plain language policies across its government agencies, including legal documents, having a Language Act aimed at the public sector since 2009. According to Jonas Carlquist, Professor of Nordic Languages at the University of Umeå,

> Plain language is important in a democracy because everyone has the right to understand their own rights – for example, how to appeal a court decision or how to access social security benefits. [...] Authorities should express themselves in a comprehensible way, while not simplifying anything by removing information – everyone who is affected by what is communicated has the right to understand. The importance of

> this is particularly evident in crisis situations, such as during the pandemic, when people must act for their own safety and the safety of others.
>
> (Umeå University, 2023)

Canada's plain language movement also provides a valuable example. In the 1990s, the Canadian government implemented plain language reforms in several sectors, including law. One of the most notable initiatives was the simplification of tax forms and other legal documents to make them easier for citizens to understand. The use of plain language in Canadian legal documents has been credited with improving transparency and reducing the number of legal disputes arising from misunderstandings of legal obligations.

According to the Government of Canada's Directive on the Management of Communications, the use of plain language is mandatory when communicating with the public. *Canada.ca Content Style Guide* clarifies the importance of using language that is direct, transparent, and relatable:

> Writing in plain language doesn't mean over-simplifying or leaving out critical information. Using plain language actually makes critical information accessible and readable for everyone. By writing plainly and simply, you: increase the chances that people will find, read and understand your information from any device; make your information more accessible to people with disabilities; allow people who are reading your information on a small screen to see essential information first; save resources when editing and translating your text; improve task completion and cuts costs by, for example, reducing enquiries.
>
> (Government of Canada, n.d.)

Australia has also been a significant proponent of the Plain Language movement, aiming to make legal and government communications more accessible. The country has implemented reforms across various sectors, including law, health, and public services, to enhance clarity and reduce complexity in written documents. Some interesting examples include courts in Queensland which have introduced plain language initiatives aimed at simplifying court orders and directions. The reforms focus on self-represented litigants, many of whom struggle with legalese. These documents now include clear, concise instructions that allow individuals to better navigate court proceedings (Queensland Government, n.d.). In addition to that, Australia has implemented the Style Manual, which provides guidelines for everyone involved in content production within the government. It has been widely adopted by various departments to improve public-facing communications, focusing on how people read documents and the design for accessibility and inclusion, which goes hand in hand with the concepts of multimodality (Digital Transformation Agency, n.d.).

In conjunction with the previous countries' examples, the use of plain language has been advocated throughout the world, covering all continents, which is proof of its urgency and necessity when it comes to the dialogue between governments and citizens. These international examples highlight the potential benefits of simplifying legal language, in terms of both improving access to justice and reducing legal costs, which is sought by legislators in the Brazilian context as highlighted in the following sections.

12.4 Multimodal Communication and Government Websites

While legal language reform is crucial, it is equally important to consider how legal and governmental information is presented, particularly in the digital age. Government websites, such as the Ministry of Environment's homepage, have become essential platforms for disseminating information to the public. These websites use a combination of text, images, videos, and interactive elements to create a multimodal experience for users. Multimodality, as defined by Bateman (2008), refers to the use of multiple semiotic modes to convey meaning, which can significantly enhance the accessibility of information.

In short, as it is not the scope of this chapter, the GeM (Genre and Multimodality) model provides a framework for analyzing multimodal documents, particularly how different modes (like text, images, and layout) work together to create meaning. Methodologically, it integrates insights from linguistics, semiotics, and communication studies.

A brief overview of its key components is demonstrated below (Bateman, 2008):

1. **Genre:** The model starts with the concept of genre, recognizing that different types of documents (e.g., news articles and advertisements) follow specific conventions that influence how modes are used and combined.
2. **Linguistic and Semiotic Resources:** It analyzes not only the textual content but also visual elements (such as images, diagrams, and page layout). These elements are studied in relation to their semiotic function (Halliday, 2004) and the meaning conveyed.
3. **Four Layers of Analysis:**
    - **Content Structure:** Focuses on what is being communicated: the informational content.
    - **Rhetorical Structure:** Examines how the content is organized to achieve specific communicative purposes (e.g., to inform, persuade).

- **Layout Structure:** Deals with the physical organization of elements on the page or screen, analyzing their spatial arrangement.
- **Navigation Structure:** Investigates how users interact with the document, particularly how the document guides the reader's movement through it.

4 **Integration of Modes:** The model emphasizes the interplay between modes (verbal, visual, spatial) and examines how their combination affects interpretation. Each mode is analyzed based on its contribution to the overall meaning and the way it complements or contrasts with other modes.

The GeM model is designed to systematically break down and categorize elements within multimodal texts, offering a comprehensive understanding of how various semiotic resources work together to shape meaning. For example, the Ministry of Environment's homepage illustrates how multimodal communication enhances the dissemination of complex information. Through interactive maps that allow users to explore protected areas and environmental regulations, the Ministry uses visual elements to make environmental policies more accessible. This approach simplifies content that might otherwise be conveyed through dense legal texts, encouraging greater user engagement and understanding.

This multimodal approach, whose features will be further discussed, aligns with the principles of plain language, as it seeks to present information in a way that is both clear and engaging. In this regard, by implementing more than one mode of communication (multimodality) – by using images, colors, audio, etc. – the language of laws enhances its reach and becomes more accessible, especially when we consider a country like Brazil in which the levels of illiteracy are still high, as approximately 30% of the population lacks full literacy control (G1, 2021).

Real-life examples of effective multimodal communication on government websites can also be found internationally. For instance, the Australian government's *MyGov* website provides citizens with access to a range of services, from tax filings to health records, using a multimodal interface that combines text, visuals, and interactive features. The website is designed with accessibility in mind, ensuring that citizens of all ages and educational backgrounds can easily navigate and use its services (Digital Transformation Agency, n.d.). This model of communication demonstrates how multimodality can complement plain language reforms, making complex legal and governmental information more accessible to a broader audience.

The combination of legal language reform under Bill 6.256/2019 and multimodal communication strategies presents a promising opportunity to improve access to justice and governmental information in Brazil. By simplifying legal language, the bill will empower citizens to engage with the legal system more effectively, particularly those who have been historically marginalized by the complexity of legal texts. At the same time, the use of multimodal communication on digital platforms can further enhance accessibility, ensuring that official information is presented in a way that is both clear and enticing. Together, these reforms have the potential to democratize access to justice and information in Brazil, promoting greater transparency and inclusivity in the legal system.

12.5 Brazil's Legal Language and Multimodal Communication: Historical Context

Brazil's legal language has deep historical roots in Portuguese colonial law, which has traditionally favored complexity and formality. The transplantation of Portuguese legal traditions to Brazil in the colonial period included the adoption of legal terminology and structures that prioritized formality over accessibility. This emphasis on complexity was designed to maintain the authority of the legal profession and ensure that only those with formal legal training could fully understand and interpret the law, which is in accordance with Riner's (2023) statement:

> Conceiving of legal language as an autonomous entity and requiring experts to act as gatekeepers to its insular world of meaning serves as a bastion of law's power. Not only does law purport to control meaning, but the process of legal translation takes away control from legal outsiders in understanding and navigating their own experiences.
>
> (2023, p. 520)

As a result, legal language in Brazil, as well as in other countries, has become increasingly dense and formalized over time, making legal texts difficult not only for the average citizen to comprehend but for anyone without a legal background, regardless of their level of education.

The persistence of this legal tradition has had significant consequences for access to justice. Citizens are often unable to engage with legal documents, including laws, contracts, and court decisions, without the assistance of legal professionals. This inaccessibility has created a legal system that is inherently exclusionary, limiting the ability of individuals to understand their rights and obligations.

A genuine yet painful example of that is the case of the 2015 Mariana dam disaster, in which a Brazilian dam owned by the mining company Samarco collapsed, causing widespread environmental damage and loss of life[4] (Assembleia Legislativa de Minas Gerais, 2020). The legal proceedings that followed were marked by the complexity of environmental regulations and legal arguments, which were difficult for the affected communities to comprehend. Many of the residents who sought compensation struggled to understand the legal documentation related to their claims and, as a result, were unable to effectively advocate for their rights (Assembleia Legislativa de Minas Gerais, 2024). Simplifying the language used in legal documents related to such environmental disasters could have a profound impact on the ability of affected communities to seek justice.

In cases like the previous one, in which legal representation is not affordable or accessible, individuals are left at a disadvantage, unable to navigate the complexities of the system. As Bhatia (1993) notes, in agreement with Riner's (2023) excerpt in the beginning of this section, legal language often functions as a gatekeeper, separating those who have legal knowledge from those who do not, thereby perpetuating inequalities in access to justice.

The complexity of Brazil's legal language is compounded by the fact that many legal texts continue to use archaic terminology and Latin phrases to create verbose narratives, further distancing the law from ordinary citizens. For example, the widespread use of the term *periculum in mora* (referring to the risk of harm in legal delays) or *fumus boni iuris* (the appearance or presumption of good law) may be familiar to legal professionals but are often incomprehensible to the general public. This reliance on outdated legal concepts creates confusion and limits the public's ability to engage meaningfully with the legal system. In this regard, the Brazilian law on legislative drafting, Complementary Law No. 95 of 1998, established general rules applicable to all legislative drafting processes across the federation, explicitly defining a drafting model that prioritizes clarity, precision, and logical order, aiming to enhance the level of certainty in legal texts and to minimize opportunities for interpretative manipulation and the chances of including unfamiliar vocabulary, such as the previous Latin examples.[5] However, despite the legislative attempts to facilitate the construction of sentences in the formal structure of legal texts, since the promulgation of CL 95/1998, legal texts still carry lengthy sentences and complex clauses, which contributes to the inaccessibility of legal documents.[6] Fighting centuries of convoluted legal writing tradition takes more than a few decades of approved laws on the matter: it is important to reeducate Law students and monitor professionals by setting standards and accreditations, for instance.

Similarly, governmental websites in Brazil used to follow formal structures in their communication. Historically, these websites have mirrored the complexity of legal texts, often lacking the flexibility that modern communication tools, such as multimodality, offer. Government websites have primarily relied on static text to convey information, making it difficult for users to find and understand the information they need. This approach has failed to take advantage of the potential that digital platforms offer for enhancing communication through a combination of text, images, videos, and interactive elements.

However, recent developments, including the approval of Bill 6.256/2019, suggest a shift toward simplification. The bill is a response to growing concerns about the accessibility of legal information in Brazil and aims to make the legal system more inclusive by ensuring that legal documents are written in clear, straightforward language. The adoption of plain language standards is expected to have a transformative effect on the Brazilian legal system, reducing barriers to justice and empowering citizens to better understand their rights.

One of the key provisions of Bill 6.256/2019 is the requirement that legal texts be written in language that is both concise and logical, avoiding the use of unnecessary technical jargon. By simplifying legal language, the bill aims to eliminate the confusion caused by outdated and complex terminology. Having the previous example and the bill's spirit in mind, it is possible to assume that terms such as *periculum in mora* would be replaced by simpler phrases like "risk of harm" to ensure that legal documents are understandable to all citizens, regardless of their level of legal education.

In addition to simplifying legal language, Bill 6.256/2019 recognizes the importance of how legal information is presented, which is crucially connected with the idea of multimodality. The bill calls for the use of multimodal elements in government communications, including text, images, and interactive features, to make legal information more accessible to a broader audience. By incorporating multimodal communication strategies, government websites can provide a more engaging and user-friendly experience, ensuring that citizens can easily access and understand legal and regulatory information.

An interesting illustration that highlights the importance of multimodality in government communication is the case of the Rural Environmental Registry (*Cadastro Ambiental Rural* – CAR, in Portuguese), an environmental registry used to monitor land use in rural areas of Brazil. Initially, the CAR system was criticized for its complexity, as the registration process required landowners to navigate dense legal language and submit detailed environmental data through a text-heavy online platform. However, following complaints from landowners and environmental groups, the Ministry of Environment revised the CAR platform to include visual aids, step-by-step guides, and interactive tools that simplify the registration process. These improvements, which incorporate multimodal elements, have made the CAR system more accessible and easier to use, resulting in higher compliance rates and greater transparency in land management (Ministério do Meio Ambiente, n.d.a).

12.6 The Ministry of Environment's Homepage: A Case Study in Multimodal Design

The homepage of the Ministry of Environment in Brazil is a prime example of how multimodal communication can enhance access to government information, employing a combination of text, images, videos, and interactive links to communicate complex environmental policies and regulations. By doing so, the homepage ensures that a wide range of users – regardless of their legal or technical knowledge – can easily find and understand the information they need.

Multimodal communication, previously referred to in several sections of this chapter and as outlined in the GeM model developed by Bateman (2008), discusses the integration of different semiotic resources (such as text, visuals, and interactive elements) to convey meaning. When applied to a website, the GeM model helps analyze how these different modes work together to create a cohesive and engaging user experience. In the case of the Ministry of Environment's homepage, the use of multimodal elements ensures that users are not overwhelmed by dense blocks of text. Instead, the information is broken down into manageable units, often accompanied by visual aids such as images or infographics that help to clarify the content.

One section of the homepage, for instance, provides an interactive map of Brazil's conservation units. This map allows users to click on specific regions to access detailed information about the environmental regulations and protected areas in that location. By presenting this information visually, the Ministry makes it easier for users to understand environmental policies, as well as the specific regulations that apply to different regions. This interactive feature not only engages users but also helps them navigate complex legal frameworks without needing to read lengthy legal documents.

The Ministry's use of video content is another effective multimodal strategy.[7] Videos explaining recent environmental initiatives or summarizing key policies are featured prominently on the homepage. These videos provide an accessible way for users to learn about environmental laws and regulations, particularly for those who may struggle with reading long texts or complex legal language, as they are presented by ordinary people using everyday language. By incorporating such multimedia elements, the Ministry broadens the reach of its communication, ensuring that more citizens can access and understand environmental policies. This approach is particularly beneficial in a country like Brazil, where digital literacy levels vary significantly across different regions and socioeconomic groups.

When analyzed using the GeM model, the homepage of the Ministry of Environment reveals a sophisticated structure in which base units (such as text, images, and videos) are grouped into coherent layouts. These layouts are designed not only to present information but to guide the user through the site in a logical and intuitive manner. For instance, the homepage is organized into sections that focus on different areas of environmental policy, such as biodiversity, climate change, and water resources. Each section includes links to further resources, such as legal documents, policy reports, and interactive tools, allowing users to explore topics in greater depth if they choose.

The GeM model's focus on the interaction between different modes of communication is evident in how the Ministry's homepage integrates text and visuals to convey information. In one example, a section of the site dedicated to explaining Brazil's Forest Code – a set of laws regulating land use and environmental protection – combines textual explanations with diagrams that visually represent the legal requirements for rural landowners. By presenting the legal information alongside visual aids, the Ministry makes it easier for users to grasp complex regulations, such as those governing deforestation and reforestation efforts, which is crucial in a year that has witnessed huge and devastating fires across the country. This multimodal approach helps bridge the gap between the legal language of the Forest Code and the practical implications for landowners, ensuring that more citizens can comply with environmental laws. The integration of interactive links that direct users to these external platforms demonstrates the multimodal nature of the website, as it combines static information with dynamic, user-driven content. It goes without saying that this structure aligns with the goals of Bill 6.256/2019, which reinforces the use of plain language in legal and governmental communication to make information more accessible to a broader audience.

Another real-life example of how this approach benefits users can be seen in the aftermath of the Amazon rainforest fires, which drew international attention to Brazil's environmental policies. In response to widespread concern, the Ministry of Environment updated its homepage to provide real-time information on fire hotspots, deforestation rates, and the government's response to the crisis. The information on the Ministry's homepage was presented through a combination of interactive maps, data visualizations, and textual updates, which ensured that users could easily access the latest developments. The multimodal presentation of this data allows citizens, environmental organizations, and the international community to stay informed about the situation, demonstrating how effective multimodal communication can enhance transparency in government operations. Nevertheless, it is important to stress that, despite the changes mentioned above, the actions of the Ministry were not sufficient to improve the handling of wildfires in Brazil, as proven by images from the Copernicus system and air quality index measurements in major cities (Copernicus, n.d.; AQI, n.d.).

All in all, the Ministry of Environment's homepage exemplifies how multimodal communication can be used to improve access to government information. When analyzed using the GeM model, the homepage reveals a carefully structured layout that guides users through the site, making information both accessible and engaging. As previously and continuously stressed throughout this chapter, this approach aligns with the goals of Bill 6.256/2019, which seeks to simplify legal communication and make government information more intelligible. By integrating multimodal communication strategies with plain language reforms, the Ministry of Environment is helping to promote transparency, inclusivity, and citizen engagement in environmental policy.

12.7 Understanding Bill 6.256/2019

Bill 6.256/2019 represents a pivotal initiative within the Brazilian legal framework, aiming to transform how legal language is used in official documents, judicial decisions, and public communications. At its core, as previously referred to, the bill advocates for the adoption of plain language in legal proceedings, seeking to dismantle barriers that obscure understanding and hinder access to justice for the broader population. The bill also emphasizes that legal terminology, traditionally laden with complex jargon, should be simplified to facilitate comprehension by non-specialists, which is especially relevant given the historical challenges posed by convoluted legal discourse as they often exclude marginalized communities and impede their ability to effectively engage with legal processes.

In addition, the bill aligns with the principles of multimodal formats, which work hand in hand with the contemporary strategies that focus on accessibility, aiming to ensure that individuals with varying levels of literacy and legal knowledge can navigate legal systems more effectively. As demonstrated in the previous section, which analyzed the multimodal composition of the Ministry of Environment's homepage, the use of diverse communication channels can significantly enhance the public's understanding of complex subjects, including legal and environmental policies.

By promoting these principles, Bill 6.256/2019 aims not only to democratize access to legal resources but also to foster greater transparency and inclusivity within Brazil's legal frameworks. The bill's inclusive language policies[8] are poised to create a more equitable legal system, particularly benefiting vulnerable groups such as indigenous communities, rural populations, and individuals with disabilities. In support of its promulgation, the Senate issued a favorable opinion, which can be found in full in the annex, reflecting the legislative body's endorsement of this critical reform.

In short, the bill aims to improve communication between public authorities and citizens by promoting clear, accessible language in official documents, outlining specific language techniques to be used, such as short sentences, and avoiding complex terms. It also emphasizes the need for accessibility, including versions of documents in indigenous languages when necessary. Some amendments were proposed to refine the bill, including the removal of Article 8, which exempted municipalities with fewer than 50,000 inhabitants from compliance, as it was deemed unnecessary. The Commission on Communication and Digital Law (CCDD)[9] also endorsed the bill's alignment with constitutional guarantees, such as the right to information, and existing legislation, including the Access to Information Law and the Law on the Rights of Public Service Users, both of which emphasize the use of clear language. The bill's requirement for public bodies to designate officials responsible for managing simple language communications was seen as a key measure to ensure compliance. However, the CCDD recommended removing some elements, such as the requirement to adhere to the Orthographic Vocabulary of the Portuguese Language, due to its slow updates, and the obligation to prepare two versions of official documents.

Overall, the CCDD suggested additional techniques to improve the clarity of official texts and proposed changes to ensure the bill's constitutionality and practicality, supporting its approval with the previously mentioned adjustments.

12.8 Conclusion

The combination of multimodality and simplified legal language holds immense potential for improving access to justice, particularly for underserved populations. Multimodal documents integrate various forms of communication, such as text, images, icons, and even audiovisual elements, to convey information more effectively. A clear example is the homepage of the Ministry of Environment, which uses both visual and textual components to present important information about environmental policies and programs. By presenting data in multiple formats, multimodal approaches can help bridge communication gaps and provide users with a clearer understanding of complex issues (Kress & van Leeuwen, 2001). This is especially important for those who may struggle with traditional, text-heavy documents, such as people with low literacy levels, disabilities, or non-native speakers.

When multimodality is paired with legal language reform, the effect on access to justice becomes even more profound. Legal language is notoriously complex, often filled with jargon, archaic terms, and intricate sentence structures that make it difficult for laypeople to fully grasp their rights and obligations (Mattila, 2006). Bill 6.256/2019, proposed in Brazil, seeks to address this by promoting the use of plain language in official documents across all levels of government. This bill aims to make legal and administrative communication clearer, more concise, and more accessible to the average citizen. Combining this initiative with multimodal strategies creates a powerful tool for enhancing public understanding of legal and governmental information, thus facilitating a more inclusive legal system.

The Ministry of Environment's homepage, the example referred to throughout this chapter, serves as a practical model for how governmental websites can integrate both multimodal communication and simplified legal language to improve accessibility. By using a combination of images, easy-to-understand language, and clear organization of information, the Ministry provides users with a streamlined experience, allowing them to navigate complex legal and environmental policies more easily. This model could be replicated across other governmental agencies, including those dealing with critical issues like healthcare, social services, and justice, where understanding one's rights and responsibilities is essential. Simplifying the way information is both written and presented can reduce the reliance on intermediaries, such as lawyers or public officials, allowing individuals to interact more directly with the legal system (Mattila, 2006).

The democratization of information through the use of plain language and multimodal elements also promotes greater transparency within the government. Transparency is a cornerstone of democratic governance, and when citizens can easily access and comprehend legal documents or government policies, they are more empowered to engage in public oversight and hold authorities accountable (Fox, 2007). Plain language reforms, like those suggested in Bill 6.256/2019, are crucial for ensuring that public administration does not obscure vital information behind the convoluted language. When this is coupled with user-friendly design principles seen in multimodal platforms, governmental agencies can foster a culture of openness and trust between the state and its citizens (Kress & van Leeuwen, 2001).

In conclusion, the integration of multimodal communication and simplified legal language, as outlined in Brazil's Bill 6.256/2019, represents a critical advancement in improving access to justice. Governmental platforms, such as the Ministry of Environment's homepage, demonstrate the effectiveness of combining visual and textual elements to make complex information more accessible to a broader audience. Obviously, official information, such as laws and normative acts, is essential, but the real reach of plain language in legal texts depends on various factors. Among these, the effective implementation of the reconstruction of the sources of law and the translation of these actions into concrete government policies stand out. Even though simplifying the language can help reduce the number of lawsuits triggered by ambiguities, lack of precision, and obscurity in legal texts, it is crucial to ensure proper oversight of the authorities responsible for implementing the norms, so that they fulfill their duties efficiently. By implementing these strategies across different sectors, Brazil has the potential to pave the way for a more transparent and inclusive legal system. This approach would empower citizens and enhance democracy, equipping everyone with the necessary tools to comprehend and actively participate in the law and government (Fox, 2007).

Notes

1 The process of approving bills in Brazil is complex and lengthy: on average, it takes 1,263 days for that to happen, and only 1 out of 284 actually turn into laws (JOTA, n.d.). The chances, however, of having Bill 6256 approved are higher considering that there is a significant interest and momentum from the Judicial spheres with the adoption of programs that enable courts to simply language (Câmara dos Deputados, 2023).

2 For more information about the Brazilian Ministry of the Environment, visit the official website at https://www.gov.br/mma

3 The website provides accreditations to demonstrate that the documents that bear their stamps – Crystal Mark, Internet Crystal Mark, and Approved By – are easy to understand and convey meaning in a simplified form. https://www.plainenglish.co.uk/

4 This article discusses the five-year anniversary of the Mariana tragedy, a significant environmental disaster in Brazil, and outlines actions taken since the event.

5 Important references on the matter: TEPEDINO, Gustavo. Crise de fontes normativas e técnica legislativa na parte geral do Código Civil de 2002 (Crisis of Normative Sources and Legislative Technique in the General Part of the Civil Code of 2002). In: A parte geral do novo código civil: estudos na perspectiva civil constitucional. Rio de Janeiro: Renovar, 2002. CARVALHO, Kildare Gonçalves. Técnica legislativa (Legislative Technique). Carvalho, (2007). CASTRO, Marcílio França. A técnica legislativa além da regra (Legislative Technique Beyond the Rule). Cadernos da escola do legislativo, v. 4, n. 7, pp. 120–179, 1998. CRUZ, Francisco Carvalho de Brito. Direito, democracia e cultura digital: a experiência de elaboração legislativa do Marco Civil da Internet (Law, Democracy, and Digital Culture: The Legislative Drafting Experience of the Civil Rights Framework for the Internet). 2015. PhD thesis. Universidade de São Paulo. ALEIXO, Leticia Soares Peixoto. Efetividade dos direitos humanos e a necessária elaboração legislativa em matéria de implementação das sentenças interamericanas no Brasil (Effectiveness of Human Rights and the Necessary Legislative Drafting Regarding the Implementation of Inter-American Court Rulings in Brazil). Master's dissertation. Universidade Federal de Minas Gerais, 2017. GUASTINI, Riccardo. Interpretare e argomentare (Interpret and Argue). Giuffrè Editore, 2011. DICIOTTI, Enrico. Norme espresse e norme inespresse. Sulla teoria dell'interpretazione di Riccardo Guastini (Expressed Norms and Unexpressed Norms: On Riccardo Guastini's Theory of Interpretation). Rivista di Filosofia del Diritto, v. 2, n. 1, pp. 103–124, 2013. GUASTINI, Riccardo. Conoscere il diritto. Un inventario di problemi (Knowing the Law: An Inventory of Problems). Diritto & Questioni Pubbliche, v. 13, pp. 513–536, 2013. SOARES, Fabiana de Menezes. Teoria da legislação: formação e conhecimento

da lei na idade tecnológica (Theory of Legislation: Formation and Understanding of the Law in the Technological Age). SA Fabris Editor, 2004. MENDES, Gilmar Ferreira. Teoria da legislação e controle de constitucionalidade: algumas notas (Theory of Legislation and Constitutional Control: Some Notes). Revista Jurídica da Presidência, v. 1, n. 1, 1999. NASCIMENTO, Roberta Simões. Teoria da legislação e argumentação legislativa na Espanha e no Brasil: análise dos cenários das leis sobre a violência contra a mulher (Theory of Legislation and Legislative Argumentation in Spain and Brazil: Analysis of the Laws on Violence Against Women), 2019.

6 An interesting example provided by the British Plain English campaign demonstrates how a 630-word sentence was used by a local council to advise citizens on the removal of a path to a different location. The same happens quite often in Brazilian contexts. To ease comprehension, we cite the English one: "A path from a point approximately 330 metres east of the most south westerly corner of 17 Batherton Close, Widnes and approximately 208 metres east-south-east of the most southerly corner of Unit 3 Foundry Industrial Estate, Victoria Street, Widnes, proceeding in a generally east-north-easterly direction for approximately 28 metres to a point approximately 202 metres east-south-east of the most south-easterly corner of Unit 4 Foundry Industrial Estate, Victoria Street, and approximately 347 metres east of the most south-easterly corner of 17 Batherton Close, then proceeding in a generally northerly direction for approximately 21 metres to a point approximately 210 metres east of the most south-easterly corner of Unit 5 Foundry Industrial Estate, Victoria Street, and approximately 202 metres east-south-east of the most north-easterly corner of Unit 4 Foundry Industrial Estate, Victoria Street, then proceeding in a generally east-north-east direction for approximately 64 metres to a point approximately 282 metres east-south-east of the most easterly corner of Unit 2 Foundry Industrial Estate, Victoria Street, Widnes and approximately 259 metres east of the most southerly corner of Unit 4 Foundry Industrial Estate, Victoria Street, then proceeding in a generally east-north-east direction for approximately 350 metres to a point approximately 3 metres west-north-west of the most north westerly corner of the boundary fence of the scrap metal yard on the south side of Cornubia Road, Widnes, and approximately 47 metres west-south-west of the stub end of Cornubia Road be diverted to a 3 metre wide path from a point approximately 183 metres east-south-east of the most easterly corner of Unit 5 Foundry Industrial Estate, Victoria Street and approximately 272 metres east of the most north-easterly corner of 26 Ann Street West, Widnes, then proceeding in a generally north easterly direction for approximately 58 metres to a point approximately 216 metres east-south-east of the most easterly corner of Unit 4 Foundry Industrial Estate, Victoria Street and approximately 221 metres east of the most southerly corner of Unit 5 Foundry Industrial Estate, Victoria Street, then proceeding in a generally easterly direction for approximately 45 metres to a point approximately 265 metres east-south-east of the most north-easterly corner of Unit 3 Foundry Industrial Estate, Victoria Street and approximately 265 metres east of the most southerly corner of Unit 5 Foundry Industrial Estate, Victoria Street, then proceeding in a generally east-south-east direction for approximately 102 metres to a point approximately 366 metres east-south-east of the most easterly corner of Unit 3 Foundry Industrial Estate, Victoria Street and approximately 463 metres east of the most north easterly corner of 22 Ann Street West, Widnes, then proceeding in a generally north-north-easterly direction for approximately 19 metres to a point

approximately 368 metres east-south-east of the most easterly corner of Unit 3 Foundry Industrial Estate, Victoria Street and approximately 512 metres east of the most south easterly corner of 17 Batherton Close, Widnes then proceeding in a generally east-south, easterly direction for approximately 16 metres to a point approximately 420 metres east-south-east of the most southerly corner of Unit 2 Foundry Industrial Estate, Victoria Street and approximately 533 metres east of the most south-easterly corner of 17 Batherton Close, then proceeding in a generally east-north-easterly direction for approximately 240 metres to a point approximately 606 metres east of the most northerly corner of Unit 4 Foundry Industrial Estate, Victoria Street and approximately 23 metres south of the most south westerly corner of the boundary fencing of the scrap metal yard on the south side of Cornubia Road, Widnes, then proceeding in a generally northern direction for approximately 44 metres to a point approximately 3 metres west-north-west of the most north westerly corner of the boundary fence of the scrap metal yard on the south side of Cornubia Road and approximately 47 metres west-south-west of the stub end of Cornubia Road" (Plain English Campaign, n.d.).

7 For more information about the Brazilian Ministry of the Environment, visit the official website at https://www.gov.br/mma

8 The policies include the following: to ensure clear communication, it is important to write sentences in direct order and keep them short, developing one idea per paragraph. Using common, easily understandable words is essential, along with employing synonyms for technical terms and jargon or explaining them within the text itself. Avoiding foreign words that are not in common use and refraining from using derogatory terms enhances clarity. Additionally, always write the full name before using acronyms and organize the text in a schematic way, when applicable, using lists, tables, and charts. It is also crucial to arrange the text so that the most important information appears first. Finally, do not use new forms of gender and number inflection of Portuguese words that contradict established grammatical rules, the Vocabulário Ortográfico da Língua Portuguesa (Volp), or the Portuguese Language Orthographic Agreement, enacted by Decree No. 6,583, of September 29, 2008.

9 To briefly understand the latest steps of the lawmaking process, on February 7, 2024, the CCDD noted that the matter was awaiting the designation of a rapporteur, having been received by the commission on that date. On May 22, 2024, the matter was distributed to Senator Alessandro Vieira for him to issue a report. Then, on September 12, 2024, the CCDD reported that the matter was ready for analysis after receiving a report from Senator Alessandro Vieira with a favorable vote on the project, which included four amendments (available in the annex of the chapter). On October 11, 2024, the matter was included in the agenda for the meeting scheduled for October 16, 2024. However, on October 16, 2024, the commission stated that the matter was ready for the agenda but was not considered due to the cancellation of the 24th meeting of the Commission.

Bibliography

Andrus, J. (2015). *Entextualizing Domestic Violence: Language Ideology and Violence against Women in the Anglo-American Hearsay Principle*. Oxford University Press.

AQI. (n.d.). *Air quality index dashboard: Brazil.* https://www.aqi.in/pt/dashboard/brazil

Assembleia Legislativa de Minas Gerais. (2020, November 5). Cinco anos da tragédia de Mariana: o que foi feito até agora? *Assembleia Legislativa de Minas Gerais.* https://www.almg.gov.br/acompanhe/noticias/arquivos/2020/11/05_direitos_humanos_cinco_anos_tragedia_mariana.html

Assembleia Legislativa de Minas Gerais. (n.d.). Comissão vai discutir atuação da Samarco em Ouro Preto e Mariana [Commission will discuss Samarco's actions in Ouro Preto and Mariana]. *Assembleia Legislativa de Minas Gerais.* https://www.almg.gov.br/comunicacao/noticias/arquivos/Comissao-vai-discutir-atuacao-da-Samarco-em-Ouro-Preto-e-Mariana/

Bateman, J. A. (2008). *Multimodality and genre: A foundation for the systematic analysis of multimodal documents.* Palgrave Macmillan.

Bhatia, V. K. (1993). *Analyzing genre: Language use in professional settings.* Longman.

Brasil. (2019). Projeto de Lei No. 6.256 de 2019. *Câmara dos Deputados.* https://www.camara.leg.br

Câmara dos Deputados. (2023, October 18). Especialistas destacam importância da linguagem simples para comunicação efetiva com cidadão. *Câmara dos Deputados.* https://www.camara.leg.br/noticias/1103909-especialistas-destacam-importancia-da-linguagem-simples-para-comunicacao-efetiva-com-cidadao/

Cane, P., & Kritzer, H. M. (Eds.). (2010). *The Oxford handbook of empirical legal research* (online edn, Oxford Academic, September 18, 2012). Oxford University Press. https://doi.org/10.1093/oxfordhb/9780199542475.001.0001

Carvalho, K. G. (2007). *Técnica legislativa (Legislative technique).* Editora Del Rey.

Conley, J. M., O'Barr, W. M., & Riner, R. C. (2019). *Just words: Law, language, and power* (3rd ed.). University of Chicago Press.

Copernicus. (n.d.). *Copernicus: The European Union Earth observation programme.* https://www.copernicus.eu/en

Digital Transformation Agency. (n.d.). *myGov.* Australian Government. https://my.gov.au/

Digital Transformation Agency. (n.d.). *Style manual.* Australian Government. Retrieved October 23, 2024, from https://www.stylemanual.gov.au/

Fox, J. (2007). The uncertain relationship between transparency and accountability. *Development in Practice*, 17(4–5), 663–671.

G1. (2021, November 12). *Analfabetismo funcional atinge 29% da população brasileira.* G1. https://g1.globo.com/sc/santa-catarina/especial-publicitario/prefeitura-municipal-de-jaragua-do-sul/viver-jaragua/noticia/2021/11/12/analfabetismo-funcional-atinge-29percent-da-populacao-brasileira.ghtml

Government of Canada. (n.d.). *Design style guide.* https://design.canada.ca/style-guide/

Halliday, M. (2004). *An introduction to functional grammar* (3rd ed.). Hodder Education and Hachette UK Company.

JOTA. (n.d.). Congresso – Tramitômetro. *JOTA.* Retrieved October 23, 2024, from https://www.jota.info/legislativo/aprovometro-projetos-previsao

Kress, G., & van Leeuwen, T. (2001). *Multimodal discourse: The modes and media of contemporary communication.* Arnold.

Lei Complementar No. 95, de 26 de fevereiro de 1998 [Complementary Law No. 95, of February 26, 1998]. Estabelece normas para a elaboração, a redação, a alteração e a consolidação das leis conforme o disposto no parágrafo único do art. 59 da Constituição Federal [Establishes norms for the drafting, writing, amendment, and consolidation of laws in accordance with the sole paragraph of art. 59 of the Federal Constitution]. *Presidência da República.* https://www.planalto.gov.br/ccivil_03/leis/lcp/lcp95.htm

Lei No. 9.784, de 29 de janeiro de 1999 [Law No. 9.784, of January 29, 1999]. Regula o processo administrativo no âmbito da Administração Pública Federal [Regulates the administrative process within the scope of the Federal Public Administration]. *Presidência da República.* https://www.planalto.gov.br/ccivil_03/leis/l9784.htm

Lei No. 10.098, de 19 de dezembro de 2000 [Law No. 10.098, of December 19, 2000]. Estabelece normas gerais e critérios básicos para a promoção da acessibilidade das pessoas portadoras de deficiência ou com mobilidade reduzida [Establishes general norms and basic criteria for promoting accessibility for people with disabilities or reduced mobility]. *Presidência da República.* https://www.planalto.gov.br/ccivil_03/leis/l10098.htm

Lei No. 12.527, de 18 de novembro de 2011 [Law No. 12.527, of November 18, 2011]. Regula o acesso a informações previsto no inciso XXXIII do art. 5°, no inciso II do § 3° do art. 37 e no § 2° do art. 216 da Constituição Federal [Regulates access to information provided in item XXXIII of art. 5, item II of § 3 of art. 37, and § 2 of art. 216 of the Federal Constitution]. *Presidência da República.* https://www.planalto.gov.br/ccivil_03/_ato2011-2014/2011/lei/l12527.htm

Lei No. 13.460, de 26 de junho de 2017 [Law No. 13.460, of June 26, 2017]. Dispõe sobre participação, proteção e defesa dos direitos do usuário dos serviços públicos da administração pública [Provides for the participation, protection, and defense of the rights of users of public administration services]. *Presidência da República.* https://www.planalto.gov.br/ccivil_03/_ato2015-2018/2017/lei/l13460.htm

Mattila, H. (2006). *Comparative legal linguistics: Language of law, Latin and modern languages.* Ashgate Publishing.

Ministério do Meio Ambiente. (n.d.a). *Cadastro Ambiental Rural.* https://www.car.gov.br/

Ministério do Meio Ambiente. (n.d.b). *Ministério do Meio Ambiente.* https://www.gov.br/mma

Plain English Campaign. (n.d.). Long sentences. *Plain English Campaign.* https://www.plainenglish.co.uk/campaigning/legal/drafting-in-plain-english

Plain English Campaign. (n.d.). *Plain English Campaign.* https://www.plainenglish.co.uk/

Queensland Government. (n.d.). *A plain language guide to the Human Rights Act 2019.* Queensland Government. Retrieved October 23, 2024, from https://www.publications.qld.gov.au/dataset/a-plain-language-guide-to-the-human-rights-act-2019/resource/9ff883e6-afa9-4934-a153-7c9d42d4926d

Riner, R. C. (2023). Legal language and its ideologies. In A. Duranti, R. George, & R. C. Riner (Eds.), *A new companion to linguistic anthropology* (pp. 509–524). Wiley Blackwell. https://onlinelibrary.wiley.com/doi/10.1002/9781119780830.ch28

Tiersma, P. M. (1999). *Legal language*. University of Chicago Press.

Umeå University. (2023, September 15). *Everyone has the right to understand their rights*. https://www.umu.se/en/news/everyone-has-the-right-to-understand-their-rights_11840796

Williams, C. (2004). Legal English and plain language. In M. Gotti & C. Candlin (Eds.), *Legal discourse in multilingual and multicultural contexts: Arbitration texts in Europe* (pp. 139–158). Peter Lang.

Annex: Senate Favorable Opinion of Bill 6.256/2019

Opinion No. __ of 2024

From the Commission of Communication and Digital Law on Bill No. 6.256 of 2019, proposed by Deputy Erika Kokay, which establishes the National Policy for Simple Language in the public administration bodies and entities, both direct and indirect, at all federative levels.

Rapporteur: Senator Alessandro Vieira

REPORT

This Commission has been presented with Bill No. 6.256 of 2019, authored by Federal Deputies Erika Kokay and Pedro Augusto Bezerra, which "establishes the National Policy for Simple Language in public administration bodies and entities, both direct and indirect, at all federative levels."

The project consists of ten articles.

Article 1 of the bill defines its objective and scope of application – it addresses the goals, principles, and procedures for communication between public administration bodies and entities at all levels of government and the population.

Article 2, items I to VII, outlines the objectives of the National Policy for Simple Language, including enabling citizens to find, understand, and use public information; reducing the need for intermediaries in communication between public authorities and citizens; reducing administrative costs and time spent in serving citizens; promoting active transparency and clear access to public information; facilitating public participation and social oversight; and improving comprehension by people with intellectual disabilities.

Article 3, items I to VI, sets the principles of the National Policy for Simple Language: citizen focus, transparency, facilitating citizens' access to public services, promoting public participation and social oversight, enhancing communication between public authorities and citizens, and enabling the exercise of citizens' rights.

Article 4 provides a legal definition of simple language as a set of techniques aimed at clearly and objectively transmitting information so that the words, structure, and layout of the message allow citizens to easily find, understand, and use the information.

The main section of Article 5 states that public administration, when drafting texts directed at citizens, must comply with the Orthographic Vocabulary of the Portuguese Language (Volp), provided by the Brazilian Academy of Letters (ABL), and employ simple language techniques.

The items in Article 5 list several techniques for simple language: using direct word order in sentences, employing short sentences, presenting only one idea per paragraph, using common and easily understood words, organizing the text schematically, among others.

The sole paragraph of Article 5 stipulates that whenever possible, official documents directed at the population should have a version in simple language, in addition to the original version.

Article 6 of the bill suggests that in the case of official communication directed at indigenous communities, a version of the text in indigenous languages, in addition to the Portuguese version, should be provided whenever possible.

Article 7 states that the public administration must define, within 90 days of the law's publication, the entity responsible for managing information in simple language.

Paragraph 1 of Article 7 requires that the contact information of the official in charge of managing simple language information be made publicly available in a clear and objective manner, preferably on the entity's website.

Paragraph 2 of Article 7 assigns two responsibilities to the person in charge of managing simple language information: (i) to promote training of the organization's communicators in the use of simple language techniques, and (ii) to supervise compliance with the law within the organization.

Article 8 exempts municipalities with fewer than 50,000 inhabitants from complying with the law's requirements if it would result in an increase in costs.

Article 9 states that each level of government must define complementary guidelines and implementation strategies for complying with the law.

Finally, Article 10 establishes that the law will come into effect upon its publication.

In the Chamber of Deputies, the bill was first sent to the Committee on Labor, Public Administration, and Public Service (CTASP), where it received a favorable opinion in the form of a substitute presented by the rapporteur, Deputy Vicentinho.

The bill was then forwarded to the Committee on Constitution, Justice, and Citizenship (CCJC), where a request for urgency was approved. This meant that the committee's report was delivered in plenary by rapporteur Deputy Pedro Campos.

The report concluded that the bill, as well as the CTASP's substitute, were constitutional, lawful, and adhered to good legislative technique. It recommended the bill's approval in the form of a global substitute amendment.

This substitute amendment, among other changes, transformed the list of simple language techniques from an exhaustive to an exemplary one, removed some techniques mentioned in the previous text, and changed the scope of the project to mandate the use of simple language only in official communications directed at citizens, rather than all acts of public administration.

Plenary Amendment No. 1, proposed by Deputy Junio Amaral and others, was approved, prohibiting public administration from using "new forms of gender and number flexion in Portuguese words contrary to established grammatical rules."

Plenary Amendment No. 2, proposed by Deputy Bia Kicis, aimed at removing the exemplary list of simple language techniques, was rejected.

The bill was approved by the Plenary of the Chamber of Deputies in the form of the global substitute amendment, with Plenary Amendment No. 1.

In the Federal Senate, the bill was registered, published, and referred by the Presidency to this Commission of Communication and Digital Law (CCDD). It will next be considered by the Commission on Transparency, Governance, Inspection, and Consumer Defense (CTFC) and then deliberated by the Plenary.

ANALYSIS

In accordance with Article 104-G of the Internal Regulations of the Federal Senate, it is the duty of this Commission to issue opinions on matters related to communication innovations, the national communication policy, social communication media, ethical issues related to communication, and other related matters (items I, II, V, VII, and VIII).

The bill, which aims to establish the National Policy for Simple Language, falls within the Union's competence to pass ordinary legislation that regulates public participation, particularly regarding access to information about government actions (Article 37, Paragraph 3, item II of the Federal Constitution).

Facilitating the comprehension of communications from public bodies and entities through the adoption of simple language techniques upholds the fundamental individual right of access to information, guaranteed by Article 5, item XIV of the Federal Constitution.

The Federal Constitution ensures that everyone has the right to receive information from public bodies that is of personal or public interest, provided within the timeframe established by law under the penalty of accountability (Article 5, item XXXIII of the Constitution).

We understand that the "receipt" of information and "access" to it presupposes the information's understanding and comprehension by the recipients. The mere formal availability of information is manifestly insufficient to fulfill the constitutional objectives.

In this context, the bill is meritorious because it aims to strengthen the full and integral exercise of citizenship by facilitating citizens' understanding through the use of simple, clear, direct, and objective language in official communications.

Moreover, the project aligns with other laws addressing this subject that are already part of the legal framework, serving to reinforce the need for simple language use in public communication with citizens.

For instance, the Access to Information Law – LAI (Law No. 12.527 of November 18, 2011), in Article 5, stipulates the use of "easy-to-understand language."

Similarly, the Law on the Rights of Public Service Users (Law No. 13.460 of June 26, 2017), in Article 5, item XIV, mandates that public officials and public service providers use "simple and comprehensible language, avoiding acronyms, jargon, and foreign words." This legislation also ensures that the "User Service Charter" contains clear and precise information about each of the services provided (Article 7, Paragraph 2).

Given this, we conclude that the bill satisfies the legal requirement for constitutionality, fitting harmoniously and coherently into the legal system.

As for regulatory aspects, we find that the bill complies with the rules of the Internal Regulations of this Legislative House.

Finally, we consider it appropriate and convenient to propose several amendments to the project aimed at improving and refining it.

First, we amend the wording of Article 5 to remove the requirement to adhere to the Orthographic Vocabulary of the Portuguese Language (Volp). While we understand the intent to use officially cataloged terms, the slow pace of updates to this vocabulary does not keep up with the evolution of language. Its last update was in 2021, with the previous update occurring in 2009. Terms like "telemedicine" and "judicialization," for example, were not included in the 2009 update. Requiring Volp would hamper administrative activity, and it is not regarded as a technique of simple language.

Additionally, we removed the provision in the sole paragraph that required the preparation of two versions of official documents – one in the original form and another in simple language – when directed to the citizen. At the same time, we incorporated new techniques into the list outlined in Article 5.

We modified the wording of Article 6 to require that versions of the text in indigenous languages for official communications directed at indigenous communities be prepared "whenever possible."

In Article 7, we removed the time limit imposed for public bodies and entities to designate the official responsible for managing simple language information, as we find this provision to be unconstitutional. We also refined the text of this article.

Lastly, we seek the removal of Article 8 from the bill because we believe that using simple language in official documents does not necessarily increase costs, and the criterion used to exclude certain municipalities from complying with the law lacks clarity.

VOTE

Based on the above, we express our opinion in favor of the constitutionality, legality, and adherence to regulations of Bill No. 6.256 of 2019, and, on the merits, recommend its approval, subject to the following amendments:

AMENDMENT No. __ - CCDD

Amend the main section and item IX of Article 5, delete the sole paragraph of Article 5, and add items XII to XVIII to the main section of Article 5 of the Bill, as follows:

> Article 5 Public administration shall comply with the techniques of simple language in drafting texts directed at the citizen, including:
>
> ...
>
> IX – Organizing the text schematically, where applicable, using lists, tables, and graphic resources;...

- Writing sentences, preferably in the active voice;
- Avoiding intercalated sentences;
- Avoiding the use of nouns in place of verbs;
- Avoiding redundancies and unnecessary words;
- Avoiding vague words;
- Using language accessible to people with disabilities, in accordance with the accessibility requirements established in Law No. 13.146 of July 6, 2015 (Statute of the Person with Disabilities);
- Testing with the target audience to ensure the message is understandable.

(Sole paragraph deleted).

AMENDMENT No. __ - CCDD

Amend Article 6 of the Bill as follows:

"Article 6 In cases where official communication is directed to indigenous communities, in addition to the Portuguese version, a version in the language of the recipients should be published whenever possible." (NR)

AMENDMENT No. __ - CCDD

Amend the main section and Paragraphs 1 and 2 of Article 7 of the Bill as follows:

> Article 7 The bodies and entities of the public administration, both direct and indirect, shall designate the official responsible for managing simple language information.
>
> Paragraph 1 The contact information of the official responsible for managing simple language information should be made publicly available in a clear and objective manner, preferably on the website of the respective body or entity.
>
> Paragraph 2 The responsibilities of the official responsible for managing simple language information include:
>
> ...
>
> II – Supervising compliance and taking appropriate administrative measures to ensure this law is enforced within the body or entity.
>
> (NR)

AMENDMENT No. __ - CCDD

Delete Article 8 of the Bill, and renumber the subsequent articles.

Committee Room

President

Rapporteur

Part Three

Interconnection in Praxis

Language for Effectiveness and Legal Certainty for Language

13 Translation as a Lens through Which to View Legislation's Effectiveness

John O'Shea and Daniel Webber

13.1 Introduction

Over the course of several decades in her ground-breaking work on legislative drafting, Xanthaki has persuasively argued that clarity, precision and unambiguity[1] are essential elements of effective legislation, though Mousmouti (2018) has argued legislative effectiveness is a vague concept, hard to pin down. In the pyramid of legislative drafting virtues Xanthaki has proposed (2018), these elements are presented as three tools for achieving effectiveness. Her work foregrounds effectiveness as an essential step on the path to achieving efficacy (Xanthaki, 2014, 2018, 2019, 2024b). She has argued that "what makes a law a good law therefore is the ability of the drafter to use the criterion of effectiveness consciously and correctly" (Xanthaki, 2011). Effectiveness is equated with quality in her view:

> If one attempts to use all of the elements of these enlightened definitions of effectiveness, one could suggest that effectiveness of legislation is the ultimate measure of quality in legislation, which reflects the extent to which the legislation manages to introduce adequate mechanisms capable of producing the desired regulatory results.
>
> (Xanthaki, 2020)

The purpose of legislation is to convey a regulatory message to ensure understanding of the law and promote compliance, thereby facilitating implementation. While Xanthaki (2018) has written "effectiveness is not about words, and neither is drafting and scrutinising legislation", that seems more like a passing remark; one that does not truly reflect her real argument. Elsewhere in her work she explicitly acknowledges the vital importance of words for legislation. Indeed, it is generally recognised that law operates through words (Mellinkoff, 1963); words are therefore powerful players in the field of legislation. She has, in fact, developed specific

DOI: 10.4324/9781003430308-17

tests and questions highlighting the importance of words and language. She has proposed that the effectiveness of legislative expression be tested by asking the question, "Does the language of each provision communicate its message to each of the intended user groups in a manner that they can understand?" (2018), clearly recognising this key interface between regulation and words. As a discipline, translation studies, too, in recent decades has seen the emergence of a broad body of work on the relationship in general between law, language and words, on the importance—and difficulty—of legal translation, its relationship to comparative law, and has also seen the emergence of disciplines such as legilinguistics and jurilinguistics (see, for example, the contributions made by academics such as McAuliffe and Trklja (2018), Gémar (2005), Šarčević (1997) and Husa (2017)). This present book stands as a further piece in that puzzle and is strongly in that vein. In this chapter, we come not from a legislative drafting background but from a legal translation one and argue that legal translators can – even in monolingual states – provide valuable input that can be instrumentalised by legislative drafters in their effort to achieve effectiveness.

Another key factor in reaching that goal is that legislation be subject to scrutiny. Xanthaki (2018) has argued that legislative scrutiny:

> invites inter-disciplinarity in its conceptualisation and conduct: it invites the contribution of policy officers, who can assess the extent of achievement of regulatory goals; finance officers who can measure cost efficiency; lawyers who can assess the effects of the legislation to the legal system as a whole; and drafters who can use all the above data, and assess the effectiveness of the text.

We would add legal translators here, who can identify all the shortcomings in the text as currently worded, especially in relation to clarity, precision and unambiguity. This concords with something else Xanthaki (2018) has argued for:

> At a post-legislative scrutiny exercise, effectiveness demands answers to the following questions in a consecutive order: ... Were there any issues arising from the choice of legislative expression and how can these be addressed?

This builds too on the argument made by Pennisi (2016) that linguistics can provide a method by which drafters can assess the effectiveness of their draft.[2] This also builds on Thornton's conceptualisation of the drafting process, introduced in 1970, which consists of five stages: (i) understanding the proposal, (ii) analysing the proposal, (iii) designing the law, (iv) composing and developing the draft and (v) verifying the draft (Xanthaki, 2022). We posit that legal translators have a strong role to play in stages (iv) and (v), especially in stage (v), where their careful and nuanced reading of the text for the purposes of the translation will have identified a wide number of issues relating to clarity, precision and unambiguity, which may not have been picked up by others.[3]

So what do clarity, precision and unambiguity mean in this context? A text (and a legislative text in particular) is clear if readers and users can easily grasp what is being said. When a poorly drafted segment has the reader wondering "Who is doing this/to whom is this being done?", the problem is lack of clarity. Precision relates to exactness of expression or detail. When a poorly drafted segment has the reader wondering "Does this also cover situation X?" the problem is lack of precision. Unambiguity refers to certain or exact meaning though can be divided into two types: semantic and syntactic. Where there is semantic unambiguity, each word used in a text signifies one single meaning, often referred to as monoreferentiality, which is to say different words are not used to refer to the same concept (Valeontis and Krimpas, 2014).[4] Where there is syntactic unambiguity, phrases or clauses within a sentence are in the proper place, there are no dangling particles and no interruptions in the flow of meaning because of poor syntax. Our work in translating Greece's codes into English provides an opportunity to explore these concepts.

13.1.1 *The Lex Graeca Project*

Over the decades, there have been haphazard and piecemeal attempts to translate various pieces of important Greek laws into foreign languages. In terms of civil law, the first 20th-century translation of a Greek code appears to have been a German translation of the Greek Civil Code of 1940 (Gogos, 1951). This was followed by a French translation of the same Code (Mamopoulos, 1956) and a German translation of the Greek Code of Civil Procedure (Baumgärtel and Rammos, 1969). Roughly a decade later, an English translation of the Greek Civil Code was published (Taliadoros, 1982). In terms of criminal law, the Penal Code has been translated into English twice, once in 1973 (Lolis) and once in 2017 (Billis). Prior to the efforts of the Lex Graeca team, the Greek Codes of Criminal and Civil Procedure had never been translated into English. In any case, it is important to note that all the aforementioned translations constituted private—rather than state-sponsored—initiatives, mostly from academic institutions established in countries other than Greece. To the authors' knowledge, there are no official (or at least state-sanctioned) translations of any major Greek legal documents save the Hellenic Constitution.

In the age of the internet, however, we observe an increasing number of individual pieces of legislation provided online in translation. Many of these translations suffer from various defects. As with the previous translations of the codes referred to above, none of these were done as part of a dedicated effort at translating the texts. No effort was made to cross-reference the translations or employ successful solutions adopted in previous translations. Often the texts were done by non-native speakers resulting in unusual, non-English syntax or strange word choices. There is also a considerable amount of inconsistent terminology, despite the recognised importance of consistent terminology in legal documents (Prieto-Ramos and Guzman, 2017; Peruzzo, 2012). Some of the past translations of the codes are also replete with spelling mistakes, partly explainable by the fact that many were done prior to the advent of computer spell-checking. While the aim may have been to provide non-Greeks with access to the functioning of aspects of the Greek legal system, which is a praiseworthy policy aim, the issues outlined above meant that they often fall short of achieving that objective.

It was against this backdrop of legislative translations of doubtful quality and utility that Lex Graeca was founded. Its purpose is to translate Greece's key legislation into English, the primary focus of the project in the initial phase being to translate the core Codes of this continental legal system: the Penal Code and Code of Criminal Procedure, the Civil Code and the Code of Civil Procedure. At the time of writing in early 2025 all those codes have been translated, though only the Code of Criminal Procedure and Code of Civil Procedure have been published; the others are being edited and nearing publication. The philosophy underpinning the project is very different from the situation described above. Lex Graeca seeks to ensure that the translation of each Code takes account of previously employed translation solutions; that terminology is consistent across the entire range of texts; and that there is a consistent style. Legislative drafters certainly have such objectives in mind when formulating new legislative texts. The project draws inspiration from their practices.

13.1.2 Why Translated Law Matters

In an increasingly globalised world, such translations are important. Just as Xanthaki (2013) has identified various "audiences" for legislation, the users of translated legislation fall into various categories: comparativists seeking insights into how the Greek legal system operates for research, practical and comparative law purposes; Greek lawyers seeking an easy way to explain the complexities of Greek procedural and substantive law to clients; foreign lawyers handling cases involving Greece, seeking an understanding of the Greek system; foreign journalists interested in correctly reporting legal proceedings in Greece when they involve foreigners; individual citizens interested in learning more about their rights and obligations within the Greek legal system (particularly relevant in an age of freedom of movement, work, establishment and capital within Europe); translators in search of well-researched solutions to their translation queries; law students in preparing their dissertations and so on.

While other European countries have long had translations of their codes easily available and accessible (Arnaud, 1973; Cachard, 2005), Greece has until now never had all its codes translated. This has impacted the ability of legal academics to look to Greece as a source of interesting legal solutions to common problems (Zweigert and Kötz, 1998; Husa, 2017). Having legislative texts (and in particular codes) available in translation, we argue, plays a vital role in making the Greek legal world and Greek legal thinking accessible to a wider audience.

13.1.3 Aim of This Chapter

The corpus of translations done as part of the Lex Graeca project provides us with important insights into Greek legislative drafting practices and the quality of Greek laws. The purpose of this chapter is thus to explore whether the Xanthakian elements of effectiveness are actually being applied in practice, as evidenced by the corpus.

The simple answer is not always and there is much room for improvement.

Through detailed examples from the translated codes, we demonstrate how issues such as unclear phrasing in the legislative provisions, lack of precision and the existence of ambiguity (or put differently the lack of semantic unambiguity) hinder the translation process. We further describe specific strategies developed by Lex Graeca to overcome these challenges in the translation process. We note too that these Codes are regularly updated and that numerous amendments have been made to each of the Codes in recent years (Dianeosis, 2017). While Schlesinger asserts that codes are "to the civilian [lawyer] what the common law is to the common law lawyer ... the very core of the legal order" (1998: 552), we ought not to forget that they have no special status and can be amended by ordinary law following normal parliamentary procedure. This onslaught of amendments comes at a time when Greece was also engaging in efforts to promote better drafting practices. By exploring this rich dataset in more detail, we seek to ascertain, albeit on a preliminary basis, whether those better practices are seeping through. This chapter concludes with recommendations for improving the legislative drafting of codes in Greece, suggesting that these enhancements could have broader applications to the drafting of legislation in the Greek system given that codes do not have any special status.

Table 13.1 Size of Corpus

Name of Code	*Size*
Civil Code	~101,000 words, including Introd. Law
Code of Civil Procedure	~108,000 words, including Introd. Law
Penal Code	~45,000 words
Code of Criminal Procedure	~91,000 words
Total	~345,000 words

13.2 A Taxonomy of Issues

For the purposes of our chapter, the corpus consists of our translations of the Greek Civil Code, Code of Civil Procedure, Penal Code and Code of Criminal Procedure.[5] The total number of words in Greek is roughly 345,000 (Table 13.1).

While translating the codes, we began to see similar types of language-related issues in the source text of each code that hampered the process of translation and required a specific translational strategy to be employed. As an initial foray into classifying these, we grouped them into seven broad categories. The taxonomy as presented here is based on the one in the published versions of the Codes of Civil and Criminal Procedure.[6] We acknowledge that there may be certain overlaps between those categories and that the boundaries are fuzzy. We further acknowledge that the taxonomy requires improvement. We also accept that a larger corpus may yield additional clarity on the nodes comprising the taxonomy and that the taxonomy may not be complete. The nodes in our working taxonomy are:

- Citation/typographic/capitalisation errors[7]
- Vague terms[8]/outdated language[9]
- Problematic syntax/inconsistent word choices[10]
- Polysemic terms/ambiguous language[11]
- Acronyms/official translations and names of entities[12]
- Elegant variation/euphemisms[13]
- Discrepancy between article headings and text[14]

Table 13.2 presents the number of items per taxonomic category per code.[15]

13.2.1 Exploring the Issues

This section explores those categories in the order set out above not by order of severity. We set out examples of the types of issues identified during the translation process which reflect various aspects of problematic drafting of the Greek source text that hampered the translation process (Molnár, 2013). The examples are accompanied by a discussion of the strategies developed to enable translation to take place.

Table 13.2 Quantification of Issues Identified in the Source Text

	Code				
Taxonomic Issues	*Civil Code*	*Code of Civil Procedure*	*Penal Code*	*Code of Criminal Procedure*	*Issue Total*
Citation/typographic/ capitalisation errors	36	63	24	15	**138**
Vague terms/outdated language	42	42	24	36	**144**
Problematic syntax/ inconsistent word choice	78	57	39	30	**204**
Polysemic terms/ ambiguous language.	45	21	3	27	**96**
Acronyms/official names	0	12	0	6	**18**
Elegant variation/ euphemism	39	33	45	39	**156**
Article heading/text discrepancy	60	3	24	3	**90**
Total for code	**300**	**231**	**159**	**156**	

13.2.1.1 *Citation/Typographic/Capitalisation Errors*

13.2.1.1.1 CITATION ERRORS

Citation errors occur when the source text cites a provision but does so incorrectly. Throughout our translations of the codes, where citation errors were identified in the source text, we decided not to alter the Greek but to use explicitation brackets to correct the error in the translation. This strategy is clearly explained in the Forewords to the published translations to ensure readers/users understand what the brackets mean.

For example in Article 571(2) of the Greek Code of Civil Procedure, the source text reads:

> Η αίτηση υποβάλλεται μέσα σε προθεσμία εξήντα (60) ημερών από την επίδοση της διάταξης και κατατίθεται στη γραμματεία του Αρείου Πάγου, η οποία συντάσσει σχετική έκθεση στο βιβλίο της παραγράφου 3.[16]

In our translation the text reads:

> The application shall be submitted within a deadline of 60 days from the date the order was served, and shall be filed with the registry of the Supreme Court, which shall enter a relevant report in the [special] register referred to in paragraph [4].

While paragraph 3 of Article 571 makes no reference to any register, paragraph 4 makes reference to special registers for the entry of council orders and applications. This is a clear citation error and the legislator must have meant paragraph 4 rather than 3.

A further example can be found in the very first sentence of the First Article of Law 4620/2019 containing the Greek Code of Criminal Procedure, where reference is made to "Law 4193/2013" on narcotics. This is clearly a mistake, as the law in question is actually numbered 4139, not 4193, and we have provided a correct translation using explicitation brackets around the proper number.

13.2.1.1.2 TYPOGRAPHIC ERRORS

Typographic errors occur when the source text contains an error that is clearly typographical in nature and was not intentional. For example, Article 410 of the Greek Code of Criminal Procedure reads as follows:

> Άρθρο 410. - Παραπομπή της αίτησης στην τακτική διαδικασία ή έκδοση **<u>απόφαση</u>**.

The final word is in the nominative when it should clearly be in the genitive ("*απόφασης*"), and there is a combination of full stop and hyphen that is a mainstay of Greek typography in the text which we omitted in our translation. The former is moot in translational terms, given that it does not impact the English translation, but it was still picked up during the translation process and was therefore considered worthy of highlighting. Thus the translation reads as follows:

> Article 410—Referral of the application to ordinary procedure or <u>rendering of judgment</u>.

13.2.1.1.3 CAPITALISATION ERRORS

Capitalisation errors occur when the source text arbitrarily (and often inconsistently) capitalises the first letter of a word. For example, in Article 6 of the Greek Code of Criminal Procedure, the source text reads:

> Το μονομελές δικαστήριο ανηλίκων συγκροτείται από έναν πρόεδρο πρωτοδικών σε κάθε **<u>πρωτοδικείο</u>**, ο οποίος ορίζεται ως δικαστής ανηλίκων και αναπληρώνεται σύμφωνα με τις διατάξεις του κώδικα οργανισμού δικαστηρίων και κατάστασης δικαστικών λειτουργών.

and Article 11 of the same Code reads:

> Στα εφετεία και πρωτοδικεία Αθηνών, Θεσσαλονίκης και Πειραιά καθορίζονται από την **ολομέλεια** των δικαστηρίων αυτών ιδιαίτερα ποινικά τμήματα σύμφωνα με τις διατάξεις του κώδικα οργανισμού δικαστηρίων και κατάστασης δικαστικών λειτουργών.

This example concerns the terms "*πρωτοδικείο*" (court of first instance) and "*ολομέλεια*" (full court). In these examples, we see that they appear in lower case. However, in Article 142(4), we see the following:

> Με απόφαση του Υπουργού Δικαιοσύνης, Διαφάνειας και Ανθρωπίνων Δικαιωμάτων, που εκδίδεται ύστερα από γνώμη της **Ολομέλειας** του οικείου **Πρωτοδικείου**, μπορεί να καθορίζεται για ποιες αποφάσεις δεν είναι αναγκαία η καθαρογραφή.

In this case we see both terms appearing in upper case. The solution we decided on was to disregard the unnecessary capitalisation and to translate the text as we would normally expect to see it in English. Thus our translation of Article 142(4) reads as follows:

> A decision issued by the Minister of Justice following an opinion issued by the competent court of first instance sitting in full court may stipulate which other judgments need not be engrossed.

13.2.1.2 Vague Terms/Outdated Language

13.2.1.2.1 VAGUE TERMS

Vague term issues occur when the source text employs a term for which no definition[17] is provided and which, absent any contextual clues, could have broader implications in the source language, in the sense that it may carry one or more connotations that need to be borne in mind by readers, in source text terms, and which could raise issues in the target text if mistranslated and without regard for context, on the other. For example, Article 23 of the Greek Code of Criminal Procedure states that:

> Τα δικαστικά πρόσωπα που αναφέρονται στην προηγούμενη παράγραφο οφείλουν να δηλώσουν με τον ίδιο τρόπο τυχόν σοβαρούς λόγους **ευπρέπειας** που επιβάλλουν την αποχή τους από την άσκηση των καθηκόντων τους, ακόμη και αν δεν υπάρχουν οι λόγοι της παρ 1.

In our translation we rendered that word as propriety:

> The court officials referred to in the preceding paragraph must declare any serious grounds of **propriety** that require their recusal in the same manner, even where the grounds of paragraph 1 do not apply.

In source text terms, upon reading the text, the most reasonable question a reader would have would be what these unspecified grounds of propriety might be. Following consultation of article-by-article interpretations of the Code, monographs and scholarly articles, as well as discussion with legal practitioners, we determined that this provision almost always concerns conflicts of interest, e.g., when a court official involved in the proceedings (public prosecutor or judge) is related to a party in the proceedings, thus going hand-in-hand with the grounds for exclusion provided for in Article 14(1) of the Code and, in rarer cases, for reasons of conscience, e.g., when judicial officers feel that they have become emotionally invested in a case over the course of the proceedings and wish to recuse themselves for reasons of objectivity.

"*Ευπρέπεια*" could also be rendered as "decorum" or "civility" in English. Were a translator to understand and translate this vague source text term as such, this could lead to a skewed understanding of the intended meaning and therefore a mistranslation.

In another example, Article 495 of the Greek Code of Civil Procedure states:

> Σε περίπτωση ολικής ή μερικής νίκης του καταθέσαντος, το δικαστήριο με την απόφασή του διατάσσει να επιστραφεί το παράβολο σε αυτόν, αλλιώς διατάσσει να εισαχθεί στο **δημόσιο ταμείο**.

Our translation reads:

> If the person who filed the legal remedy is successful in whole or in part, the court shall order reimbursement of the procedural fee to the said person in the judgment it hands down, otherwise it shall order that it be paid to the **tax office**.

A context-blind, literal translation of the Greek term in question would be "public/state fund". However, this would have no meaning for either Greek or English speakers, nor would it reflect the actuality of life in Greece. Having consulted legal practitioners, we were assured that this means the tax office with which persons, both natural and legal, are registered and must pay their debts and taxes to.

At the same time, a top priority of the Lex Graeca project was to produce a streamlined, annotation-free, flowing English text (cf. Legrand,

2021). We consciously decided to highlight such issues in the Foreword to our translations and, where necessary, provide citations for readers to further explore such thorny issues pertaining to connotation and context. Furthermore, we heavily advise readers of the translation to consult the foreword before reading the translations so as to stand forewarned.

13.2.1.2.2 OUTDATED LANGUAGE

Legislators frequently opt to change the terms they employ for specific things to reflect societal or attitudinal views. New terms are introduced in law by saying henceforth X shall be known as Y. In our corpus we identified cases where such terminological changes have been adopted but these have not been consistently and uniformly applied throughout the Codes. Similarly, institutions that once existed no longer exist, yet references to them are retained in the legislation even though best drafting practice would suggest they ought to be updated. We have dubbed this phenomenon when the source text employs a term which has become obsolete or is antiquated "outdated language".

For example, Article 828 of the Greek Code of Civil Procedure states:

> αν τη σφράγιση την ενεργεί συμβολαιογράφος, υπάλληλος της γραμματείας, διοικητής του σταθμού **χωροφυλακής** ή πρόεδρος της κοινότητας, την παραλαμβάνει και την παραδίδει.

Our translation reads:

> if the sealing is being effected by a notary public, registry clerk, commander of the ***gendarmerie*** station or president of a community, the person in question shall collect it and deliver it without delay to the court of the peace.

There has been no gendarmerie in Greece for 40 years, as the corps was merged with the City Police before both were abolished pursuant to Law 1481/1984. Nevertheless, we have chosen to render the Greek term accordingly and consider it an oversight on the part of the legislator. In another example, Article 75 of the Law Introducing the Code of Civil Procedure (1968) states:

> Με **β.δ.** που εκδίδεται ύστερα από πρόταση του υπουργού δικαιοσύνης, θα κωδικοποιηθούν σε ενιαίο κείμενο οι διατάξεις του κώδικα πολιτικής δικονομίας και του εισαγωγικού του νόμου, όπως ισχύουν τώρα και όπως τροποποιούνται και συμπληρώνονται από το νόμο αυτόν και θα μεταβληθεί και η αρίθμηση των άρθρων τους.

Our translation reads as follows:

> The provisions of the Code of Civil Procedure and the Law Introducing the Code, as currently in force and as amended and supplemented by this Law, shall be codified into a single text and the numbering of their Articles shall be changed pursuant to a ***Royal Decree*** issued on a proposal from the Minister of Justice.

The abbreviation "*β.δ.*" stands for "*βασιλικό διάταγμα*" (Royal Decree). However, the monarchy was abolished pursuant to the referenda of 1973 and 1974, and therefore any reference to a Royal Decree and requirement for such a Royal Decree, in the present, to change the numbering of Articles cannot but be a failure on the part of the legislator to update the text. As above, we chose to render the term accordingly despite the error. We consider this to be the soundest way to address the issue to keep the text streamlined but still highlight the issue, as we have done in the Foreword to forewarn readers of this and numerous other such problems.

13.2.1.3 Problematic Syntax/Inconsistent Word Choices

13.2.1.3.1 PROBLEMATIC SYNTAX

Problematic syntax issues arise when the source text uses a syntax which is either confusing or inaccurate. By "confusing" we mean the use of syntax that leaves a reader questioning what is actually occurring among several possibilities or who is the one doing something among several possible candidates. By "inaccurate" we mean the use of syntax that does not reflect the actual reality of what the text is saying (or trying to say).

As an example of the former, problematic syntax leading to confusion, Article 965(3) of the Code of Civil Procedure states:

> Ο υπερθεματιστής έχει υποχρέωση να καταβάλει στον υπάλληλο του πλειστηριασμού το πλειστηρίασμα σε μετρητά ή με μεταφορά πίστωσης στον ειδικό τραπεζικό επαγγελματικό λογαριασμό του υπαλλήλου του πλειστηριασμού ή με επιταγή έκδοσης τράπεζας που λειτουργεί νόμιμα στην Ελλάδα, **την τρίτη εργάσιμη μέρα** από τον πλειστηριασμό και αμέσως μετά του παραδίδεται το κατακυρωμένο πράγμα.

The text quite unequivocally says "on the third day", and an incautious translator might translate it as such. However, it seemed odd to us that the legislator would set so exact a date, where something has to happen exactly three days after something else, especially in a text riddled with deadlines and abstract time periods. Having consulted lawyers, we are confident that the intended meaning is "by the third day" and have rendered it as such in our translation using explicitation brackets:

> The highest bidder is obligated to pay the auction price to the auctioneer in cash or by transferring that amount into the special business account held by the auctioneer or by providing a letter of guarantee issued by a bank lawfully operating in Greece **[by]** the third working day after the auction, and the awarded thing shall then be immediately handed over to the highest bidder.

As an example of problematic syntax which is inaccurate, Article 495(3) of the Greek Code of Civil Procedure states:

> Εκείνος που ασκεί το ένδικο μέσο της έφεσης, της αναίρεσης **και** της αναψηλάφησης, υποχρεούται να καταθέσει παράβολο, που επισυνάπτεται στην έκθεση που συντάσσει ο γραμματέας, ως εξής.

This is an issue arising frequently both within that specific Code (and in Articles 114(4), 539(1) and 553(1) among others) and in Greek law in general, where the legislator uses the Greek conjunction "*και*" ("and") instead of "*ή*" ("or") even though the intended meaning is definitely disjunctive. Thus, in the example presented above, the meaning is certainly not that a person has filed all three legal remedies but that they have filed any one of them. We therefore rendered it as follows using explicitation brackets.

> The person filing the legal remedy of appeal, cassation *[or]* application for re-opening proceedings is obligated to pay the following procedural fee, the receipt for which shall be appended to the report prepared by the registrar.

Problematic syntax also manifests in the extensive use of latent hypotheticals, by which we mean the case where the source text contains an ostensibly declarative sentence which is (or could be better expressed as) a conditional ("if X then Y") sentence. An example can be found in the final subparagraph of Article 2023 of the Civil Code:

> Στην εκπλήρωση των υποχρεώσεών του ο εκτελεστής ευθύνεται απέναντι στον κληρονόμο κατά τους κανόνες της εντολής για κάθε ζημία της κληρονομίας από πταίσμα του. Σε περίπτωση διαχείρισης έχει υποχρέωση και να λογοδοτήσει. **Περισσότεροι εκτελεστές ευθύνονται για κοινό πταίσμα τους εις ολόκληρον**.

The source text contains a declaratory sentence which, translated literally, would read "*Several executors are severally liable for joint fault*". However, there being "several executors" in the first place is an exception, not the rule, as Article 2023 concerns the normal course of events, where there is a single executor and how liability will arise. The final sentence introduces a hypothetical and explains what would occur in a situation where there happens to be more than one executor. Our translation solution was to tease out the hypothetical ("*Where there are several executors, they are severally liable for joint fault*") rather than use a literal translation which would not flow naturally in English and would seem incongruous to what had preceded that sentence.

13.2.1.3.2 INCONSISTENT WORD CHOICE

Inconsistent word choice issues arise when the source text uses a term which appears to be out of place, given the usual wording used by the Greek legislator either in the immediate vicinity of the term or in a broader context. This is a matter of failed referentiality. For example, Article 349(1) of the Greek Code of Criminal Procedure states:

> Το δικαστήριο μπορεί, μετά από πρόταση του εισαγγελέα ή και αυτεπαγγέλτως, να διατάξει την αναβολή της δίκης για λόγους ανώτερης βίας, με αίτημα δε κάποιου από τους διαδίκους, για **σοβαρούς λόγους** υγείας ή λόγους ανώτερης βίας.
>
> Το **σημαντικό αίτιο** μπορεί να προβληθεί από οποιονδήποτε ακόμη και όταν αφορά το πρόσωπο του διορισμένου κατ' άρθρο 340 παρ. 3 πληρεξουσίου δικηγόρου.
>
> Ο **σοβαρός λόγος** υγείας αποδεικνύεται με ιατρική πιστοποίηση.

The second subparagraph curiously pivots away from the term used in the first and third subparagraphs, using the term "*σημαντικό αίτιο*" (literally "important cause") where one would expect the repeated use of the term "*σοβαρός λόγος*" ("serious reason"). Given that these phrases are linguistically and factually synonymous for all intents and purposes, we decided to use a single term throughout our translation of Article 349(1), which reads as follows:

> The court may, at the proposal of the public prosecutor or *ex officio*, order the adjournment of the trial for reasons of force majeure and at the request of any party in the proceedings for ***serious reasons*** of health or force majeure.
>
> The ***serious reason*** may be pleaded by any party, even where it concerns the authorised lawyer appointed under Article 340(3).
>
> The ***serious reason*** of health shall be proven by medical certificate.

13.2.1.4 Polysemic Terms/Ambiguous Language

13.2.1.4.1 POLYSEMIC TERMS

A common problem facing translators from Greek into English is the plethora of polysemic terms used in the Codes. Moving beyond taxonomies of polysemy established by other researchers, such as internal–external (Baghici, 2021) or equivocal–unequivocal (Chromá, 2011), and focusing instead on the phenomenon peculiar to the Greek codes, we identify within the corpus several distinct categories of polysemy: (i) the same Greek term used within the same legal context (for instance, criminal law) but referring to two distinct situations; (ii) the same Greek term used in different legal contexts (say, criminal law and civil law) for concepts which may or may not be related conceptually; and (iii) a catch-all category of generally polysemous terms that do not fall into the other distinct categories.

An example of the first taken from the criminal codes is the Greek term "*κατηγορούμενος*", which does not have a single meaning. It is highly context dependent, and its meaning shifts depending on the stage of the criminal procedure, with the result that it can either be rendered as "accused person" (i.e., after an accusation has been made, whether by a victim or the prosecution authorities or following an arrest) or as "defendant" (after a charge sheet has been issued and it has been decided to commit the individual in question to trial). There is also the possibility that both senses are intended at one and the same time, when there is no indication of the stage of the proceedings and both are distinct possibilities, which would require this term to be rendered as "accused person/defendant". Another similar example is the Greek term "*διακοπή*". Depending on the context, this noun can mean "suspension", "interruption", "stay of proceedings", "termination", and "adjournment"—not to mention "vacations" when used in the plural form ("*διακοπές*").

As an example of the second category, consider the term "*απάτη*", which means "deceit" or "deception" when used in Articles 147–149, 1204, 1576 and others of the Civil Code. However, the same term means "fraud" and constitutes the crime of the same name when defined in Article 386 of the Penal Code and used throughout that code. Similarly, the term "*κατάσχεση*" means "seizure" in a criminal law setting but "attachment" in a civil law setting—except when referring to aircraft or ships, in which case it would be best rendered as "arrest".

In the third category, we can take as an example the term "*παραγραφή*" used to denote both the concept of time-barring/statute of limitations (Article 1032 of the Civil Code) and the period during which such time-barring runs (Article 634 of the Code of Civil Procedure). Likewise, the term "*αναγνώριση*" is used to denote "recognition" of a child (as used in the European Convention on the Legal Status of Children Born out of Wedlock and Article 1475 of the Civil Code) but is better rendered as "acknowledgement" when concerning debts and obligations (Article 260 of the Civil Code).

In all the above cases, in-depth discussions between the translators and legal practitioners were required to fully grasp the intended meaning of each appearance of the term and to feel confident in the accuracy of the translation and determine the appropriate rendering, which is to say the expert advice was needed to be sure of the meaning (Peruzzo, 2017).

13.2.1.4.2 AMBIGUOUS LANGUAGE

The problem of polysemic terms, i.e., terms having a finite number of possible meanings based on context, is aggravated by the occurrence of ambiguous language[18] where an entire phrase is worded ambiguously, leaving the reader to wonder what actually occurs in the context of litigation. Context often provides no aid, if there even is context to speak of; nor does the syntax allow for unequivocal interpretation. One example can be found in Article 535(2) of the Code of Civil Procedure, which reads as follows:

> 2 Αν η προσβαλλόμενη απόφαση εξαφανίζεται για αναρμοδιότητα του πρωτοβάθμιου δικαστηρίου, η υπόθεση παραπέμπεται στο αρμόδιο δικαστήριο και εφαρμόζονται οι διατάξεις του άρθρου 46. Αν πρόκειται για κατά τόπον αναρμοδιότητα και κριθεί αρμόδιο άλλο πρωτοβάθμιο δικαστήριο που υπάγεται στην περιφέρεια του δευτεροβάθμιου δικαστηρίου το οποίο δικάζει την έφεση, **αυτό** μπορεί ή να παραπέμψει την υπόθεση στο αρμόδιο δικαστήριο ή να την κρατήσει και να τη δικάσει κατ' ουσίαν.

The second sentence of the paragraph in question states, translated literally, that where there is lack of jurisdiction *ratione loci* and where a different first-instance court belonging to the district of the second-instance court trying the appeal is found to have jurisdiction, "it" may either remit the case to the competent court or stand seised of it and try it on its merits. The use of the neuter pronoun "*αυτό*", literally translated as "it" in the preceding sentence, to refer to a court makes it impossible to immediately tell which court is being referred to. Is the different first-instance court belonging to the district of a second-instance court empowered to either remit a case or hold it over and try it? Or is it the second-instance court in question? This is a case of prima facie ambiguity that cannot be picked apart through context clues and requires consultation with legal practitioners to resolve. Our theory, which was corroborated by legal practitioners and law professors, was that the latter is the case, i.e., that the pronoun indeed refers to the second-instance court.

Another example can be found in Article 586(1) of the Code of Civil Procedure, which reads as follows:

1 Με τις προϋποθέσεις του άρθρου 583 μπορεί να ασκηθεί τριτανακοπή κατά της οριστικής απόφασης που εκδόθηκε **μεταξύ άλλων**.

The highlighted phrase "*μεταξύ άλλων*" (literally translated as "between others") is confusing. One would usually expect to see the phrase preceding a list and used in the sense of "inter alia", or "among other things", as it is used, for example, in the final paragraph of Article 307 of the same Code. Its placement at the end of the sentence is an indication that this is not the case, and one would wonder whether it means "between other parties" and, if so, whom, the parties involved in the litigation in question, a party in a different set of proceedings or a third party in general. Having consulted analyses of the Code of Civil Procedure and confirmed the issue with lawyers, we are confident that this is the Greek version of the concept of "*tierce-opposition*", where a party may initiate third-party proceedings against a judgement handed down in proceedings involving two (or more) other parties. We have thus rendered the above paragraph as follows:

1 Third-party proceedings may be brought against the final judgment handed down with regard to **other parties** under the conditions laid down in Article 583.

13.2.1.5 Acronyms/Official Translations and Names of Entities

Whenever we encountered acronyms such as "*ΦΕΚ*" ("Government Gazette Issue"), "*Σ.Δ.Ο.Ε.*" ("Financial and Economic Crime Unit"), and "*ΠΚ*" ("Penal Code"), we chose not to use existing acronyms or create new ones in English but rather to type out the full translation of the abbreviated term. This was done to save readers from having to consult a table of abbreviations and acronyms and to achieve clarity in our texts. In any event, it should be noted that the number of acronyms used in the codes is rather low compared to other genres of Greek legal documents.

A more ponderous question, which is also discussed in James Brannan's introduction to our translation of the Greek Code of Criminal Procedure,[19] is the use of official names of entities. The most characteristic example of this issue concerns the *Άρειος Πάγος*, the Greek court of cassation and Supreme Court. According to its official website and the official English translation of the Hellenic Constitution,[20] the full name of the court in English is the unwieldy "Supreme Civil and Criminal Court [of Greece]". Taking a number of factors into account, such as the fact that transliterating the Ancient Greek name as "Areios Pagos" would be nonsensical to English-speaking readers not familiar with the Greek legal system, especially those presented with a contextless extract of our translations, or the fact that, as intimated above, the "official" name is lengthy, especially when repeated often in the same sentence, we chose to abbreviate it to "Supreme Court", as a more readily recognisable term. We opted not to use the term "court of cassation" (whether or not capitalised) as that is more a descriptor of its function, as clearly indicated in Article 10 of the Greek Code of Criminal Procedure.

Another example concerns the name of the Ministry of Justice. At times it appears as the *Υπουργείο "Δικαιοσύνης"* (Ministry of Justice) (Articles 5(1) and 689 of the Greek Code of Civil Procedure), at times as Υπουργείο "*Δικαιοσύνης, Διαφάνειας και Ανθρωπίνων Δικαιωμάτων*" (Ministry of Justice, Transparency and Human Rights) (Articles 53(2), 505(2) and 571(1) of that same Code). We consider this an oversight on the part of the legislator, failing to keep up with the ever-changing name of Greek Ministries, a separate problem unto itself, as discussed in our Foreword to the translation of the Greek Code of Private Maritime Law.[21]

13.2.1.6 Elegant Variation/Euphemisms

13.2.1.6.1 ELEGANT VARIATION

The first part of this category stands in contrast to the category of polysemic terms. Whereas before we were facing a single term having several possible meanings, we now have to consider the problem of several terms being used interchangeably, often within the same article of a code, but the referent remaining unaltered. Dubbed elegant variation by the brothers Fowler in the early 20th century,[22] in legal texts, in particular, one cannot but wonder if employing this strategy could cause more harm than good. From a Xanthakian viewpoint, its use is to be decried. There are numerous examples to be found in all the codes in the corpus:

- "*άσκηση*", "*κίνηση*" and "*έναρξη*"—all meaning initiation/institution of proceedings
- "*διαδικασία*" and "*δίκη*"—both meaning trial/proceedings
- "*πραγματικά γεγονότα*" and "*πραγματικά περιστατικά*"—both meaning actual facts
- "*παθών*", "*εγκαλών*" and "*θύμα*"—all meaning victim
- "*τέλεση*" and "*διάπραξη*"—both meaning commission (of a crime)
- "*κύηση*" and "*εγκυμοσύνη*"—both meaning pregnancy

- "*εξ αίματος γονείς*" and "*φυσικοί γονείς*"—both meaning biological parents
- "*αντισυμβαλλόμενος*" and "*άλλο μέρος*"—both meaning counterparty

Our solution was to use a single term in English when faced with such synonymous usage in Greek, so as to streamline both our translation and the glossaries found at the end of all our translations of the codes.

13.2.1.6.2 EUPHEMISM

The second part of this category concerns the use of euphemism, defined as "a word or phrase that is considered a more polite manner of referring to a topic than its literal designation" (McGlone, 2006: 266). Examples from all the codes include:

- "*χωρισμός από τραπέζης και κοίτης*" ("*a mensa et thoro*", "from bed and board"): this term euphemistically refers to legal separation of spouses.
- "*προσκαλώ*" ("to invite", most commonly in Modern Greek): this verb is often used when one is "invited" by an authority to do something, e.g., in Article 686(4) of the Greek Code of Civil Procedure. Depending on context, though, this "invitation" may be a euphemism and the intended meaning is far stricter: this is a command issued that compels one to do something, e.g., in the Code of Criminal Procedure, summoned by the court registrar to appear in court (Article 686(4)) or instructed by the judge to give precise testimony (Article 225), and in the Code of Civil Procedure, ordered by a Court of the Peace judge to attend a settlement intervention (Article 209), notified by the court to lodge a claim (Article 843) or notified by an auctioneer to pay the auction price (Article 965).
- "*αποβιώνω*" ("to pass away"); however, it should be noted that "πεθαίνω" ("to die") is also used—in fact, the latter appears far more frequently than the former.
- "*απομάκρυνση*" ("removal"): this term is a euphemistic reference to deportation and curiously appears in paragraph 4(b) of Article 72, which actually has the heading "*Απέλαση αλλοδαπού*" ("Deportation of an alien").
- "*μεταβολή οικογενειακής τάξης ανηλίκου*" ("altering the family status of a juvenile"): this term is a vague and euphemistic reference to illegally placing a child for adoption.[23]
- "*σπουδαίος λόγος*" ("serious reason"): this term is used in Article 1350 of the Civil Code in the context of a marriage necessarily going forward "due to a serious reason". This "serious reason" is a vague and euphemistic reference to several circumstances that could lead the court

to allow the marriage to proceed, such as pregnancy, a long-standing relationship, and the creation of a potential scandal.[24]

13.2.1.7 Discrepancy between Article Headings and Text

Another issue observed in the codes is the discrepancy between a term used in the heading of an article and the actual text of the article in question. One example can be found in Article 366 of the Greek Code of Criminal Procedure, where the heading uses the phrase "*Συμπληρωματικές έρευνες*" ("follow-up questions"), but the term is nowhere to be found in the actual text of the Article in question, which uses the term "*Συμπληρωματική εξέταση*" ("follow-up examination") instead. "*Έρευνες*" is employed in the Greek Code of Criminal Procedure in the context of the pre-trial procedure, which is to say when collecting information about the crime and evidence (Article 251), ordering anyone at the home not to leave (Article 252), undercover operations (Articles 254–255), searching a suspect's home (Article 256), etc., and its general sense is "inquiry". In Article 366, however, we are at the trial stage, and the judge simply asks the public prosecutor and the parties in the proceedings whether they need (a) any follow-up examination (of a witness) or (b) a clarification (presumably concerning a testimony given). There is therefore a mismatch between the word "*έρευνες*" being used in the sense of "inquiry" (or "investigation") throughout the text in a pre-trial context, yet suddenly appearing in a trial context and using an established (by that point) pre-trial term in a trial setting, which creates a discrepancy.

A final example is Article 1936 of the Civil Code, which uses the term "*τιμώμενο πρόσωπο*" (literally "person honoured", as in the person on whom benefits are bestowed) in the heading but the term "*καταπιστευματοδόχος*" ("beneficiary of the trust") in the text. Our translation solution in such cases was, bearing in mind the place the provisions hold within the system created by the code, to translate according to common sense, e.g., if the two different terms in the source could be translated using the same word in English, then to do so (as in the case of Article 1936 of the Civil Code mentioned above) and, as always, point out the incongruity between heading and text in the Foreword.

13.3 Discussion

The process of translating Greece's core codes into English reinforces the picture of well-known pathogenies in the law-making process (Dianeosis, 2017; KEFIM Research Paper, 2023; Petrakis, 2024), revealing that the legislator stumbles in consistently meeting the requirements of clarity, precision and unambiguity in the core codes of the Greek legal system. In Table 13.3, we map Xanthaki's tripartite schema onto our more fine-grained taxonomy.

Table 13.4 shows the order of frequency of occurrence of the items in our taxonomy within the corpus plus an indication of which element of the Xanthakian tripartite schema they relate to.

Unclear legal provisions are the most common category of issue in the codes, accounting for 41.13% of the problems identified in our taxonomy, followed by ambiguous provisions which account for 29.79% of the issues we identified, and then imprecise provisions accounting for 29.08% of cases. Nonetheless, we see scope for enriching Xanthaki's schema to make it more fine-grained by incorporating other considerations; while the tools for achieving legislative effectiveness she suggests are useful as broad categories, the ways in which drafters fail in Greece reveal more specific issues they need to focus on. We make no claims as to the comprehensiveness of our taxonomy. Undoubtedly a wider corpus that includes other codes and other pieces of legislation translated into English could bring up differing considerations. An interesting avenue for future exploration would be to examine what else to include at this level to ensure a more robust and encompassing taxonomy.

We posit too that there may have been some improvement in the drafting of the codes in recent years, especially in light of governmental efforts to make the legislative drafting system better (Xanthaki, 2024). We note that the Penal Code, radically overhauled in 2019 and then again in 2024, contained fewer of the issues in our taxonomy than the other codes. Exploring the causes and scale of this is outside the scope of this chapter and is a matter for future research. Another interesting avenue to pursue is whether provisions frequently amended reveal a greater frequency of issues than those amended less frequently; we posit they do but that hypothesis too remains to be tested. Yet another interesting avenue for exploration is whether taxonomic issues in the codes relate to the incorporation into national law of provisions derived from EU legislation.

Table 13.3 Mapping of Issues Identified onto Xanthakian Requirements

Clarity	*Precision*	*Unambiguity*
Vague/outdated language	Citation/typographic/ capitalisation errors	Elegant variation/ euphemism
Problematic syntax/ inconsistent word choices	Acronyms/official names	Polysemic terms/ ambiguous Language
	Article heading/text discrepancy	

Table 13.4 Issues Ordered by Frequency of Occurrence across All Codes in the Corpus

Ranking	*Taxonomic Issue*	*Aspect of Xanthakian Schema*
1st	Problematic syntax/inconsistent word choice	Clarity issue
2nd	Elegant variation/euphemism	Unambiguity issue
3rd	Vague terms/outdated language	Clarity issue
4th	Citation/typography/capitalisation	Precision issue
5th	Polysemic terms/ambiguous language	Unambiguity issue
6th	Article heading/text discrepancy	Precision issue
7th	Acronyms/official names	Precision issue

Drafters of the codes do not consistently check cross-references with other laws, letting wrong citations slip through into the final text; they do not check if the names of ministries or organisations have been updated or changed, nor do they always ensure that defined terms are consistently used throughout a code or that new terms introduced are consistently used in replacement of older terms. Older euphemistic formulations are retained in newer versions of the codes. Elegant variation is commonplace. Too many provisions are vague or ambiguously worded. The heading of a provision does not always employ the same term as the actual body of the provision. One issue on which drafters appear to be performing well is their relatively infrequent use of acronyms within the codes.

To rectify this we make the following recommendations (some general in thrust, some specific to the topics discussed in this chapter):

General:

- A way to report errors (ranging from simple typos or misplaced commas to points of law that need to be clarified/corrected). This could take the form of a platform accessible to all citizens—but perhaps more realistically lawyers in particular—enabling them to immediately point out errors/inconsistencies they have identified, plus a fast-track procedure for rectifying them.
- An official governmental platform hosting all (major) Greek legislation, along the lines of the EU's EUR-Lex platform, is required. It should be kept completely up to date and offer both past versions of legislation for historical/legal research purposes and the latest up-to-date consolidated versions, instead of having to rely on the plethora of private websites which currently exist.
- In future endeavours to amend codes a stronger plain language approach (along the lines of those seen in the English-speaking world) to syntax and terminology should be adopted. This would help resolve issues such

as odd word choice, problematic syntax and elegant variation, which we have identified as commonplace in the current versions of the codes.[25]

Specific:

- Greek legislative drafters should undergo training on the specific issues identified in our taxonomy. Such training could/should involve translators, enabling drafters to see how translating the provisions they propose (and the difficulties the process of translation brings us) can help them formulate clearer laws. Intralingual translation (reformulating wordings in the same language) would also be a useful skill to teach.
- Modules on legal/legislative drafting could also be usefully added to law degrees in Greece.
- Translation should be used as an extra layer in scrutinising the provisions of codes. Translators should be viewed as sense-makers, spotters of inconsistencies and vagueness in the source text provisions, and unblinkered editors whose insights can be utilised in the service of achieving clarity, precision and unambiguity. This will necessitate translators being in perpetual interaction with the drafting teams to discuss, explain and eliminate these issues.[26] Once the issues identified during the translation process are resolved, translations of the consolidated versions of the codes should be available on the publicly accessible repository referred to above to help promote understanding of and access to Greek law.

While we see these changes as important for codes given their central position within the legal system, we see no reason not to extend these recommendations to Greek legislation in general as part of the drive to boost the quality of legislation overall.

13.4 Conclusion

Translation can serve as a lens through which to view legislative effectiveness. Meticulous translation of Greece's core codes has shown that Xanthaki's schema is useful but may not be fine-grained enough to capture all the drafting problems the codes contain. We have identified concrete problems in the wording of the Greek text of Greece's core codes and proposed various avenues for improvement which foreground the expertise of legal translators and the insights they can bring. We assert that modern machine-based approaches to translation are unlikely, at the present time and given their current state of development, to be of assistance in capturing issues relation to clarity, precision and unambiguity, given their well-reported propensity to "hallucinate", generalise, utilise elegant variation in terminology (Wiesmann, 2019), create fluid-sounding yet incorrect legal texts (Schumacher, 2021) and omit key parts of the text (Wiesmann, 2019). The objective in translating codes (or any legal document for that matter) is not to have "any old" translation, but to have one that makes sense and is useful to its intended audience. As Appleby et al. have recently asserted, "[i]n order to achieve effectiveness, the constancy of how the words of law are wielded is paramount" (2024); machine-based approaches fail with constancy. Drafters, it appears, also fail, as Xanthaki has observed (2011, 2013). Expert translators versed in law and legal nuance are, we argue, well-positioned to help fix this problem: to identify source text issues, propose linguistic solutions and engage with drafters to resolve them.

Notes

1 The existence of ambiguity in legal writing is well known. Xanthaki argues that to make legislative provisions "effective" such ambiguity ought to be avoided. Of course, such ambiguity may be deliberate on the legislator's part.
2 Pennisi has also explicitly acknowledged that "the need to produce a better legislation cannot be reached without the help of other disciplines such as linguistics", to which we would add "translation".
3 Indeed multilingual institutions such as the Commission and Court of Justice of the European Union utilise the skills of lawyer linguists/law revisers/legal translators in drafting multilingual versions of legislation or court judgments. Our argument here is slightly different because the context is slightly different; the setting here is not multilingual. We posit, though, that, even in a monolingual country, such as Greece, skilled legal translators can provide useful and actionable insights to improve the quality of the national legislation. Much can be learned from how the EU handles such matters. An in-depth exploration of how the multilingual model could be applied to a monolingual setting is outside the scope of this chapter but could be a useful avenue of future exploration.
4 This is a prescription to not employ elegant variation.
5 Note that other codes have also been translated as part of the project, such as the Code of Private Maritime Law, but we have elected to focus on the core ones for the purposes of this chapter.
6 In future publications certain nodes in the taxonomy (such as problematic syntax/inconsistent word choices) will be separated out into distinct nodes rather than being grouped together.
7 These three nodes were grouped together because they do not affect the legibility of the text, nor do they raise (major) legal certainty issues. They are surface-level errors but still need to be pointed out, if nothing else, to stress the fact that even a legislature—and even when faced with statutes as important as the four codes—make such mistakes.
8 Inclusion in the category of vague terms does not take into account whether the vagueness is deliberate or not. In future publications this node will be renamed "fuzzy concepts".
9 These two nodes have been grouped together as both issues give the reader pause, leading one to ask "what does this term mean"—the former in the sense

that the term in question is vague, the latter in the sense that the reader might have never encountered the term in either theory or practice (especially if they are younger).

10 We view inconsistent word choices as situations where a term is repeated several terms in the same paragraph or section of text but suddenly a different term is used. In that sense, it differs from elegant variation where different terms for the same concept are used interchangeably and frequently throughout the text. These two nodes in the taxonomy have been placed together because both issues disrupt the flow of the text and force a reader to pause, ask "what is going on here" and question what they are reading, either because a) they cannot tell who is being referred to because of the pronouns) or b) they have seen one word being used for a concept and suddenly see a completely different word is being used and have to wonder whether these denote the same concept.

11 These two nodes have been grouped together as both issues again give the reader pause, leading one to ask "which possible meaning does this have", the former from within a finite list of candidate definitions, the latter in the context of an entire sentence where the intended meaning is unclear.

12 These two nodes have been grouped together as both constitute conventions on the part of Greek legal drafters which might not raise issues in the source text, but do when one is called to translate them into a different language.

13 These two nodes have been grouped together because *the phenomenon referred to add complexity*. Although elegant variation is employed, the drafters could have just used the same word rather than opting for a different one. This requires more mental gymnastics for the reader without good reason. With euphemism, the drafter could have said the thing plainly rather than hiding behind the euphemism. Obfuscation of meaning is what links the two nodes together entailing an undermining of precision.

14 We have included this because the discrepancy may give the reader pause for thought; having read the heading they may expect to see the same term used within the article but suddenly see another term being used. It may be jarring and, if nothing else, raises the question of why should there be a different term used in the first place? Of course there may be reasons for the discrepancy, such as, inter alia, the heading containing a hypernym and the text containing a hyponym, but that rationale may not be immediately apparent to readers/users of the text.

15 Individual issues when identified once were not counted upon any subsequent recurrence in the text. The overall number of issues is therefore in fact higher.

16 In all examples from the Codes, we have marked the relevant phrase our discussion relates to with bold and underlining in both the original Greek and its English translation.

17 A recurring problem we have identified in the codes which hampers the translation process is the lack of definitions when legal terms are employed. While the penal code and civil code do employ definitions to a certain degree, the procedural codes contain very few definitions of terms.

18 Defined as occurring "where there is lack of clarity or when there is uncertainty about the application of a term" (Schane 2002: 167).

19 Brannan, James. "Introduction—Some Observations from the Perspective of the European Court of Human Rights" pp. 9–14 in Webber, Daniel A. & O'Shea, J.A. *The Greek Code of Criminal Procedure*. Lex Graeca, 2022.

20 https://www.hellenicparliament.gr/en/Vouli-ton-Ellinon/To-Politevma/Syntagma/

21 Webber, Daniel A. & John A. O'Shea. *The Greek Code of Private Maritime Law*. Lex Graeca, 2023.

22 Fowler, H.W., & F.G. Fowler. *The King's English*. Clarendon Press, 1908.
23 See, for example, Supreme Court Judgment No 1362/2020 (5th Chamber), available at https://www.areiospagos.gr/nomologia/apofaseis_DISPLAY.asp?cd=3CJMXBIBGFILY0JBJ7A9GK7VVWTCRJ&apof=1363_2020&info=%D0%CF%C9%CD%C9%CA%C5%D3%20-%20%20%C5 (in Greek).
24 Vathrakokoilis, Vasilis Ant. *Detailed Interpretation—Case-law of the Civil Code. Vol. II*. s.n., 1992 (in Greek).
25 Another additional layer, more from the perspective of plain language, could be to poll ordinary people to determine which part of the codes they do not understand or find confusing so that efforts can be directed at reformulating those parts. We note that there is currently a platform that allows public consultation on proposed legislation but no such platform for laws once enacted.
26 As already indicated, such approaches are widely used within the EU institutions in multilingual settings. There is clear utility is employing such approaches even in monolingual countries.

References

Appleby, Thomas, Scott, Juliette, Flannery, Wesley and Donelan, Edward. "Making Sense of Interlinkages in EU Marine Environment Legislation: Unearthing Effectiveness." *International Journal for the Semiotics of Law—Revue Internationale de Sémiotique Juridique*, 37 (September 2024): 2287–2341. https://doi.org/10.1007/s11196-024-10182-8.

Arnaud, André-Jean. *Essai d'Analyse Structurale Du Code Civil Français* (Librairie générale de droit et de jurisprudence, 1973).

Baghici, Nicoleta. "The Polysemy of Legal Terms." *National Law Journal*, 1, no. 243 (July 2021): 162–167. https://doi.org/10.52388/1811-0770.2021.1(243).15.

Baumgärtel, Gottfried and Rammos, Georgios. *Das griechische Zivilprozeß-Gesetzbuch mit Einführungsgesetz* (C. Heymanns, 1969).

Billis, Emmanouil (ed.) and Vassiliki Chalkiadaki, *The Greek Penal Code* (Duncker & Humblot, 2017).

Cachard, Olivier. "Translating the French Civil Code: Politics, Linguistics and Legislation." *Connecticut Journal of International Law* 21, no. 1 (Fall 2005): 41–66.

Chromá, Marta. "Synonymy and Polysemy in Legal Terminology and Their Applications to Bilingual and Bijural Translation." *Research in Language*, 9, no. 1 (2011): 31–50. https://doi.org/10.2478/v10015-011-0004-2

Fowler, Henry Watson and Fowler, Francis George. *The King's English* (Clarendon Press, 1908).

Gémar, Jean-Claude. "De la traduction (juridique) à la jurilinguistique: Fonctions proactives du traductologue." *Meta* 50, no. 4 (2005). https://doi.org/10.7202/019840ar.

Gogos, Dimitrios. *Das Zivilgesetzbuch von Griechenland* (De Gruyter, 1951).

Husa, Jaakko. "Translating Legal Language and Comparative Law". *International Journal for the Semiotics of Law - Revue Internationale de Sémiotique Juridique* 30, no. 2 (2017): 261–272.

Legrand, Pierre. "Mind the Gap! Translation of Foreign Law Is Not What You Think." *Revista de Investigações Constitucionais* 8 (2021): 601.

Lolis, Nicholas. *The Greek Penal Code* (Fred B. Rothman & Co., 1973).
Mamopoulos, Pierre, *Code Civil Hellenique* (Institut français d'Athènes, 1956).
McAuliffe, Karen and Trklja, Alexandar. "Superdiversity and the Relationship Between Law, Language and Translation in a Supranational Legal Order" in *The Routledge Handbook of Language and Superdiversity* (Routledge Press, 2018).
McGlone, Matthew S., Beck, Gary, and Pfiester, Abigail. "Contamination and Camouflage in Euphemisms." *Communication Monographs*. Informa UK Limited (2006) https://doi.org/10.1080/03637750600794296.
Mellinkoff, David. *The Language of the Law* (Little, Brown & Co., 1963).
Molnár, Ondřej. "Source Text Quality in the Translation Process" in Jitka Zehnalová, Ondřej Molnár, a Michal Kubánek (eds.), *Trends and Tradition in Translanguage Communication* (Olomouc: Univerzita Palackého, 2013), pp. 59–86.
Mousmouti, Maria. "Making Legislative Effectiveness an Operational Concept: Unfolding the Effectiveness Test as a Conceptual Tool for Lawmaking." *European Journal of Risk Regulation* 9 (2018): 445.
Pennisi, Giulia Adriana. "Legislative Drafting and Language: Legal Language in Context." *Statute Law Review* 37, no. 2 (June 2016): 97–100. https://doi.org/10.1093/slr/hmw024.
Pennisi, Giulia Adriana. "Legislative Provisions in Context: A Linguistic Approach." *Statute Law Review* 37, no. 2 (June 2016): 101–115. https://doi.org/10.1093/slr/hmw023.
Peruzzo, Katia. "European English and the Challenges Faced by the Interdisciplinary Team Involved in the Translation of the Italian Code of Criminal Procedure. In Dullion, Valérie, ed. Between Specialised Texts and Institutional Contexts—Competence and Choice in Legal Translation." Special issue of *Translation and Translanguaging in Multilingual Contexts* 3, no. 1 (2017): 5–19.
Peruzzo, Katia. "Quality in Terminology: A Question of Consistency? A Case Study on EU Victim-related Texts" in Lew N. Zybatow, Alena Petrova, and Michael Ustaszewski (eds.), *Translationswissenschaft: Alte und neue Arten der Translation in Theorie und Praxis, Tagungsband der 1. Internationalen Konferenz TRANSLATA «Translationswissenschaft: gestern - heute - morgen»* (Frankfurt am Main: Peter Lang, 2012).
Petrakis, Panagiotis E. "The Legislative Process and Regulatory Interventions in the Greek Democracy: Deep-Rooted Weaknesses and Recommendations for Improvement." *Statute Law Review* 45, no. 1 (April 2024), https://doi.org/10.1093/slr/hmae001.
Prieto-Ramos, Fernando and Guzmán, Diego. "Legal Terminology Consistency and Adequacy as Quality Indicators in Institutional Translation: A Mixed-Method Comparative Study" in F. Ramos (ed.), *Institutional Translation for International Governance: Enhancing Quality in Multilingual Legal Communication* (London: Bloomsbury Methuen Drama, 2017), pp. 81–101. Retrieved February 7, 2025, from https://doi.org/10.5040/9781474292320.0015.
Šarčević, Susan. *New Approach to Legal Translation* (Kluwer Law International, 1997).
Schane, Sanford. "Ambiguity and Misunderstanding in the Law." *Thomas Jefferson Law Review* 25, no. 1 (2002): 167–193.

Schlesinger, Rudolf B., Baade, Hans W., Damaska, Mirjan R. and Herzog, Peter E. *Comparative Law, Cases—Texts—Materials*, 5th ed. (Foundation Press Mineola, 1988).
Schumacher, Perinne. La TA neuronale et ses défis: compte-rendu d'une expérience pédagogique en traduction économique. *Presented at IVe Colloque International sur la Traduction Économique, Commerciale, Financière et Institutionnelle*, Université Française d'Égypte, Cairo (6–7 December 2021).
Taliadoros, Constantine. *The Greek Civil Code*. Ant. N. Sakkoulas Publishers (s.n., 1982).
Valeontis, Kostas and Panagiotis, Krimpas. *Νομική γλώσσα, νομική ορολογία: θεωρία και πράξη [Legal Language, Legal Terminology: Theory and Practice]* (Nomiki Viviliothiki - Hellenic Society for Terminology, 2014).
Vathrakokoilis, Vasilis Ant. *Detailed Interpretation—Case-law of the Civil Code*. Vol. II. (s.n., 1992) Sakkoulas Press (in Greek).
Webber, Daniel A. and O'Shea, John A. *The Greek Code of Private Maritime Law* (Lex Graeca, 2023).
Webber, Daniel A. and O'Shea, John A. *The Greek Code of Criminal Procedure* (Lex Graeca, 2022).
Wiesmann, Elizabeth. "Machine Translation in the Field of Law: A Study of the Translation of Italian Legal Texts into German." *Comparative Legilinguistics* 37 (2019): 117–153. https://doi.org/10.14746/cl.2019.37.4.
Xanthaki, Helen, "The Greek Executive State Model: A Paradigm for Better Legislation." *Statute Law Review* 45, no. 2 (August 2024a). https://doi.org/10.1093/slr/hmae025.
Xanthaki, Helen, *Legislative Drafting for the EU: Transposition Techniques as a Roadmap for Better Legislation and a Sustainable EU* (Elgar Publishers, 2024b).
Xanthaki, Helen. *Thornton's Legislative Drafting* (Bloomsbury Publishing, 2022).
Xanthaki, Helen, "Gender Inclusive Legislative Drafting in English: A Drafter's Response to Emily Grabham" *feminists@law* 10, no. 2, 23–49 (2020).
Xanthaki, Helen, "Misconceptions on Legislative Quality: An Enlightened Approach to the Drafting of Legislation" in Daniel Oliver (ed.), *Conceptions and Misconceptions of Legislation* (Springer, 2019).
Xanthaki, Helen, "An Enlightened Approach to Legislative Scrutiny: Focusing on Effectiveness." *European Journal of Risk Regulation* 9, no. 3, 431–434 (2018).
Xanthaki, Helen, "The limits of legislation as a product." *Hukim-Journal on Legislation* (2017).
Xanthaki, Helen, *Drafting Legislation: Art and Technology of Rules for Regulation* (Hart Publishers, 2014).
Xanthaki, Helen, "Legislative Drafting: The Birth of a New Sub-discipline of Law." *1 IALS Student Review* 1, no. 1, 57–70 (2013).
Xanthaki, Helen, "Quality of Legislation: An Achievable Universal Concept or a Utopian Pursuit?" in Marta Travares Almeida (ed.), *Quality of Legislation* (Nomos, 2011), pp.75–85.
Xanthaki, Helen and Pennisi, Giulia. "Crossing the Borders Between Legislative Drafting and Linguistics: Linguists to the Aid of Legislative Drafters" in *Explorations in Language and Law* (Novalogos, 2012).

Zweigert, Konrad and Kötz, Hein. *An Introduction to Comparative Law*, 3rd ed., trans. by Tony Weir (Oxford University Press, 1998).

Δείκτης Ποιότητας Νομοθέτησης [Legislative Quality Index] KEFIM, Research Paper, December 2023. Available at https://kefim.org/deiktis-poiotitas-nomothetisis-2023-arnitiki-i-fetini-proeklogiki-chronia-gia-tin-poiotita-tis-nomothetisis/.

Πολυνομία, Κακονομία και Γραφειοκρατία στην Ελλάδα Ανάλυση Αποτυχιών του Παρελθόντος και Προτάσεις Βελτιωτικών Παρεμβάσεων Δημήτρης Α. Σωτηρόπουλος Λεωνίδας Χριστόπουλος Νοέμβριος 2017 Dianeosis, available at https://www.dianeosis.org/wp-content/uploads/2017/12/Polynomia_Main_UPD_41217.pdf

14 Tense Aspects of Legislative Drafting

*Martin David Kelly**

14.1 Introduction

When legislative drafters are determining which words to use in a Bill, they must make several choices related to time. Perhaps the most obvious of them is the choice of tense, and, here, the near-universal mantra is: use the present tense! Even though legislation is typically designed to operate into the indefinite *future,* it is generally preferred to draft it in the present, rather than the future, tense: as it is 'always speaking' (in the authentic sense of that metaphor).[1] A less well-known, but also important, choice about time for drafters concerns what linguists call 'aspect'. This term of art may be unfamiliar to many readers, though some of the words used to label different aspects—such as the 'progressive' and 'perfect'—might well be more familiar. Aspect reflects the fact that, although some events and actions are effectively instantaneous, others (such as drafting legislation) extend over a period of time, and therefore—at any given moment—they might be ongoing (i.e. progressing) or might instead be finished (i.e. perfected). Choosing tense and aspect in legislative drafting raises several important issues that have been unduly neglected in the academic literature.[2] These issues are pervasive; as Lord Rodger put it:

> For the most part when you are simply applying the law in a routine fashion, you scarcely think of matters of time. But when something draws the question to your attention, all of a sudden you see the issue everywhere you look.[3]

In this chapter, I highlight some of these issues and—through analysing several reported cases—seek to assist drafters in making their choices.[4] I begin, in Section 14.2, by explaining the key concepts of tense and aspect. Next, in Section 14.3, I turn to the choice of *tense* and briefly explore the origins of the notion that legislation is (at least presumptively) 'always speaking' in the work of George Coode in the 1840s. I then examine, in

DOI: 10.4324/9781003430308-18

Section 14.4, Coode's arguments in favour of using the present (and past) tense in legislative drafting, and I put some pressure on those arguments. In Section 14.5, I chart the influence of Coode's recommendations, not least in the enactment of 'Always Speaking' Provisions across the common-law world. I examine, in Section 14.6, suggestions that there was an English common-law principle that legislation is presumptively 'always speaking'—based on an oft-quoted *dictum* regarding 'the present tense of logic'—and show that this is not so. In Section 14.7 I conclude, and I also highlight the dangers of using the 'bare' *progressive aspect* in legislation, i.e. using the progressive without specifying the part(s) of the ongoing activity that it is to cover (e.g. when it begins and when it ends).

14.2 Explaining Tense and Aspect

Choosing which tense to use is a very familiar experience for all of us. It is by no means confined to drafting legislation, drafting legal instruments, or even the use of formal documents: we all use different tenses, all the time, in our ordinary conversations. The three English tenses that we often use are the past, the present, and the future tense, and our verbs (at least in English) typically also have a form that is neutral as to time (the 'infinitive'). For example, when I am talking about someone driving, I might use the *past* tense ('she was driving'), the *present* tense ('she is driving'), or the *future* tense ('she will be driving') to show her temporal relationship to that activity, and 'to drive' is the verb form that is unmarked as to that temporal relationship, i.e. the *infinitive*.

The examples just given adopt the same *aspect* of the activity: they all use the '–ing' form of the verb to indicate the ongoing nature of the activity (the *progressive* aspect). We could, instead, indicate the completion of this activity by using the *perfect* aspect: past ('she had driven'), present ('she has driven'), and future tense ('she will have driven'). In addition to the progressive and perfect, there is also the *simple* aspect, which is neutral as to where we stand in the life of the event or action (e.g. 'she drove'). This gives us these nine types of phrasing:[5]

Table 14.1 The Nine Main Combinations of Tense and Aspect

	Simple Aspect	*Progressive Aspect*	*Perfect Aspect*
Past tense	Past simple 'drove'	Past progressive 'was driving'	Past perfect 'had driven'
Present tense	Present simple 'drives'	Present progressive 'is driving'	Present perfect 'has driven'
Future tense	Future simple 'will drive'	Future progressive 'will be driving'	Future perfect 'will have driven'

Legislation frequently seeks to govern events or actions that extend across time, and the drafter's choice of *aspect* has given rise to many disputes (not least in relation to driving). But, first, we will focus on how drafters should approach the choice of *tense*.

14.3 Tense and Types of Utterance

In previous work, I distinguished types of language use (which I call 'utterances')—including uses of language in enacting legislation ('legislative utterances')—that are 'momentary', 'extended', and '"always speaking"'.[6] A momentary utterance is directed only to a particular moment in time. When you see a baby and comment that it just gave a beautiful smile, you would do so by making a momentary utterance.[7] Some legislative provisions are momentary: ones effecting a divorce, for example, or ones repealing a statute.[8] Where a momentary utterance concerns only the time at which it is made, we inevitably make it by using the present tense ('that **is** a beautiful smile!'); where a momentary utterance is directed only to a moment *before* it is made, we naturally use the past tense ('that **was** a beautiful smile!'), and where the utterance pertains to some moment *after* it is made—if, when speaking to my friend about their newborn, I say that their first smile will be beautiful—we inevitably make it using the future tense ('that **will be** a beautiful smile!').[9]

We can capture this with some simple rules. Let's use 't_1' for the time at which an utterance is made; 't_0' for a time before t_1 (such as the time when the relevant facts obtained); and 't_2' for a time after t_1 (such as the time that a future-directed utterance is directed to). Our rules are then (a) if the relevant moment is at t_0 then use the past tense; (b) if the relevant moment is at t_1 then use the present tense; and (c) if the relevant moment is at t_2 then use the future tense.

Things get more complicated when we turn to 'extended' and 'always speaking' utterances. Extended utterances are those that are to operate for an extended period of time: not just at the time it is made (t_1) but additionally, and principally, at *later* times—t_2, t_3, t_4, and so forth until t_n (the time when it will cease to be operative). And the same is true of 'always speaking' utterances: those which are to operate from t_1 onwards, indefinitely—up to t_∞—unless and until 'repealed'. Because both extended and 'always speaking' utterances are overwhelmingly future-directed—technically they are operative also at the moment when made, but that is typically dwarfed by their future operation—I will use 'future-directed utterances' as an umbrella term for them.

It seems natural to make future-directed utterances using the *future* tense, and that was how future-directed legislative provisions were typically drafted. But George Coode, in his pioneering 1842 treatise *On*

Legislative Expression, argued influentially that such provisions should instead be drafted using the present and past tenses. I now turn to Coode's argument for this claim.

14.4 Coode on Using the Present and Past Tenses

For Coode, the fact that legislation is mainly to govern situations that arise in the *future* creates two issues for drafters. First, because the future is uncertain—the conduct that the legislation seeks to regulate might never arise—'the proper language to express' future-directed legislation is '*subjunctive* language' such as 'if any person be'.[10] Coode argued that, as this is similar to the conditional form ('if p then q'), it is better to reserve the word 'if' for expressing the conditions that must be satisfied for the legislation to apply, and so Coode recommended that drafters use 'the *indicative* mood' for future situations, e.g. 'Where any person is ...'.[11] This part of Coode's work has been less influential: legislation is still frequently drafted in the subjunctive mood.

The second issue for drafters, highlighted by Coode, is that using the present and past tenses in future-directed legislation might lead us to draw false inferences about its temporal operation. Coode's response to this issue quickly became—and continues to be—highly influential. Coode noted that it was frequently considered 'necessary' to draft legislation using:

> the future or perfect future, for fear that if it were expressed in the present tense, as, "when any person *is* aggrieved", the law would operate only upon cases existing at the moment of the passing of the Act; or that if it were expressed [in the past tense], "when any person *has been* convicted", the law would ... apply only to convictions previous to the passing of the Act.[12]

Here, Coode diagnosed two related concerns. One was that drafting future-directed legislation using the present tense would make that legislation *momentary*; i.e. it would be operative only at t_1. Coode noted that drafters were seeking to block this inference by using the future simple: typically by using the word 'shall', as in the phrase 'when any person *shall be* aggrieved ...'.

The other concern was that drafting future-directed legislation by using the past tense would make that legislation *retrospective* only; that is, it would make it operative only at times t_0. Drafters were trying to block this inference by using the future *perfect*, e.g. 'shall have been...'. Why, we might ask, would drafters use the past tense in future-directed legislation? The answer is that some legislation—indeed, more generally, some of our utterances (whether legislative or not)—deal with *more than one* future events or actions. Here's a simple (non-legal) example:

> **Resit:** I tell my students that those who fail the forthcoming exam must take the resit.[13]

This envisages at least two events or actions that may take place after the time of my utterance (i.e. after t_1). Where a question arises as to whether a specific student must take the resit (at t_3), the answer turns on what happened at t_2 i.e. whether or not that student failed the exam. Let's call an action or event that will be after the making of an utterance—but will be before that utterance comes to be applied—a 'future intermediate'. It is natural to speak of a future intermediate (here, failing the exam at t_2) using the past tense, even though it is a future event, because it will have become a past event by the time that my utterance comes to be applied (at t_3). That is, in **Resit** I can just use the past simple—'if you **failed** the exam then you must take the resit'—rather than using the (more 'proper', for Coode) future perfect: 'if you **will have failed** the exam then…'.[14]

For Coode, these concerns were 'entirely founded on a mistake'.[15] It is not clear, however, what Coode took this mistake to be. He addressed only the second concern, and claimed that statutes are given retrospective effect only 'when a retrospective intention is manifested by clear words'. Leaving aside that words of past tense may manifest just such an intention, Coode did not clearly explain why the first concern—that using the present tense would make its operation momentary—was mistaken. He simply noted that we regard the law 'while it remains in force as constantly speaking' and he claimed that, 'assuming the law to be always speaking', we can draft it to recite 'facts concurrent with its operation, as if they were present facts, and facts precedent to its operation, as if they were past facts'.[16] That is, if we treat legislation (when it is in force) as being continuously re-spoken—over and over again, indefinitely—then it is always being spoken at the time when the relevant facts arise, and so it is natural for it to speak of them in the present tense. This may well counter the inference that the drafter used the present tense to *make* the legislation momentary, although it is difficult to imagine scenarios in which that inference would have force.[17] But if Coode was right about this then it removes an obstacle to drafting future-directed legislation in the present tense: as it blocks an inference that the legislation is momentary only.

That, in itself, does not yet give us any positive reason to draft in the present tense, but Coode argued that doing so 'has two very considerable advantages'.[18] The first is that it avoids drafters having to use 'very complicated grammatical constructions', which Coode illustrated with this example:

> if a person *shall be* convicted of ...; and if he *shall have been* before convicted of the same offence; and if he *shall not have* undergone the punishment which he *should have* undergone for the offence of which he *shall have been so before* convicted.[19]

This is certainly awkwardly phrased. But note the temporal complexity of the situations that it seeks to regulate. It involves *three* future events, *two* of which are future intermediates: the earlier conviction (at t_2) and the punishment due for that earlier conviction (at t_3) post-date the legislation (t_1) but pre-date the later conviction (at t_4). The provision speaks of all three future events using the future tense, using the future simple ('shall be') for the later conviction (at t_4) and then using the future perfect ('shall have been' and 'shall not have undergone') for the two future intermediaries, adding the tongue-twisting 'shall have been so before' to show that one of them (the earlier conviction at t_2) comes before the other (the punishment due for the earlier conviction at t_3). Coode did not himself say how this provision could have been drafted less awkwardly than this. But if we use the *present simple* for the later conviction (at t_4), the *past perfect* for the earlier conviction (at t_2), and the *past simple* for the due punishment for the conviction (at t_3) then we get:

> If a person *is* convicted of... and if he *had been* convicted of the same offence; and if he *has not* undergone the punishment which he should have undergone for the offence of which he *had been* convicted ...

We therefore make some gains in readability by adopting Coode's recommendations, partly vindicating his claim that the 'attempt to express every action referred to in a statute in a future tense renders the language complicate [sic], anomalous, and difficult to be understood'.[20] But the provision remains somewhat difficult to read, and this seems partly due simply to the temporal complexity of the situations that it speaks to. In this regard, it would benefit from tabulation, e.g.:

> If a person—
>
> (i) is convicted of ...;
> (ii) had been convicted of the same offence; and
> (iii) has not undergone the punishment he should have undergone for that conviction, ...

It would also benefit from using more explicitly temporal language, such as '(ii) had been *previously* convicted'. Coode is right, therefore, that drafting legislation on the basis that it is 'always' (or 'constantly') speaking can improve readability, but query whether any such advantage is 'very considerable'. In any event, this provision does not seem to be a good candidate for being drafted solely in the present tense. If so drafted, it would read:

> If a person *is* convicted of ... and if he *is* convicted of the same offence; and if he *does not undergo* the punishment which he should *undergo* for the offence of which he *is* convicted.

What we gain here in less-awkward phrasing is outweighed by what we lose in clarity of content. Thus, although we can probably infer the temporal order of these events from the context, it is not a strong candidate for just using the present tense throughout and leaving the rest to the reader. It will often be advantageous not to use the future tense, at least where the legislation does not speak to events that may occur after the time when it falls to be applied.[21] But it is important not to lose sight of Coode's recommendation that we should use the present *and the past* tenses.[22]

Coode's second claimed advantage of present-tense drafting is that it enables us to reserve the word 'shall' for *imperative* (or modal) uses. Coode noted that 'shall' can be used *modally* (for 'the compulsion, the obligation to act') and also *temporally* (as a 'prediction' or 'prophesy that the party will or will not at some future time do the act') and that, in saying 'Thou *shalt* do no murder', 'the "shalt" is obligatory in the present tense, continuously through all the time of the operation of the law'.[23] Coode illustrated this ambiguity with: 'if the said commissioners *shall*, by any order, ...'; does it apply if the commissioners (a) make the order, or (b) have a duty to make the order? However, there are two reasons why this is not as great an advantage as Coode claimed. First, the word 'shall' has many other usages, and so eliminating its temporal use does not allow us to reserve it for obligations.[24] Second, we can—and legislative drafters typically now do—use other words (especially 'must') to impose obligations.

The force of Coode's argument—for using the present and past tenses, rather than the future tense, in future-directed legislation—is thus largely limited to improving readability. Even then, the advantage arises only for temporally-complex legislation. For example, section 1(4) of the Scotland Act 1998—'The validity of any proceedings of the Parliament is not affected by any vacancy in its membership'—could equally well have read '... shall not be affected by...', just as sub-section (5)—'Schedule 1 ... shall have effect'—could equally well have used the present tense: 'Schedule 1 ... has effect'. No readability concerns appear to arise here; the choice seems to be one of style.[25]

So Coode's claimed advantages of drafting future-directed legislation in the present and past tenses (rather than the future tense) are largely limited to the readability of provisions that regulate events and actions with complex temporal structures (and where tabulation, or explicitly temporal terms—such as 'before' and 'after'—may also help with clarity). Despite these doubts about the strength of the arguments for Coode's recommendation, it has been enormously influential with legislative drafters across the English-speaking world.

14.5 Coode's Influence

The influence of Coode's recommendation is perhaps most clearly seen in the Interpretation Acts of various jurisdictions. Starting in 'Canada' in the 1850s, two types of new provisions appeared: an 'Always Speaking' Provision (or ASP) and a 'Shall' Provision. A typical example is:

> Unless otherwise provided, or there be something in the context or other provisions of the act indicating a different meaning or calling for a different construction:—
>
> (1) The law in [any] Acts is to be considered as always speaking, and whenever any matter or thing is expressed in the present tense, the same is to be applied to the circumstances as they arise so that effect may be given to each Act and every part thereof according to its spirit, true intent, and meaning;
> (2) The word "shall" is to be construed as imperative ...[26]

The 'Always Speaking' Provision (sub-section (1)) is designed to block an inference from the use of the present tense to momentary operation: Acts are 'to be applied to the circumstances as they arise' into the indefinite future. And the 'Shall' Provision (sub-section (2)) is designed to discourage legislative drafters from using the future tense: by presuming that 'shall' is used to impose a duty.

Such provisions are found in Interpretation Acts across Canada—in fact, the very first Act of the new Parliament of the Dominion of Canada contains almost identically worded provisions.[27] They were then imported by other common-law jurisdictions, starting with New Zealand in 1888.[28] As far as I am aware, no legislature that is based in the United States has ever enacted the phrase 'always speaking'. But §1 of the US Code has (at least since 25 June 1948) stated that 'In determining the meaning of any Act of Congress, unless the context indicates otherwise ... words used in the present tense include the future as well as the present'.[29] This has a similar function to an 'Always Speaking' Provision, and it is cited in the legislative drafting manuals for the US House of Representatives and the US Senate:

> STAY IN THE PRESENT.—Whenever possible, use the present tense (rather than the past or future). Your draft should be a movable feast—that is, it speaks as of whatever time it is being read (rather than as of when drafted, enacted, or put into effect).[30]

There are at least two ways in which this drafting advice is sub-optimal. First, the important times at which legislation 'speaks' are the times at which it is operative, not the time when it is 'read' (or when someone 'hears' what it is 'speaking'). When judges are determining whether a provision has been complied with, the time that matters is the time when the relevant facts obtained, not when the judges 'read' that provision (or when they make their decision).[31] A moment's reflection on reading legislation that has been repealed, or legislation of a defunct jurisdiction (like ancient Rome), shows that the claim that legislation 'speaks as of whatever time it is being read' is infelicitous.

Second, as we saw in Section 14.4, drafters may want to use the *past* tense—and perhaps the past simple and/or the past perfect—in legislation that regulates temporally complex events (involving future intermediates). The US House Manual goes on to address this explicitly: after stating the 'general rule'—that 'Whenever possible, use the present tense and avoid the future and past tense'—it says (in a passage redolent of Coode's work):

> EXCEPTION.—When expressing time relationships, there may be cases in which it may be appropriate to use the present tense for facts contemporary with the law's operation and then the past (or future) tense for facts that must precede (or follow) its operation. However, even in such cases, it is preferable to remain in the present tense throughout and express the temporal relationships explicitly rather than by means of the verb tense.[32]

But the US House Manual gives no argument for this preference—nor gives any example provision drafted on this basis—and it is not obvious what this would look like, or why it would be preferable. It will often help to express temporal relationships explicitly (e.g. by using 'before' and 'after') but, where this requires the use of tense, the past tense is much more natural than the present tense (e.g. 'was previously' rather than 'is previously').

The UK Parliament has never enacted an 'Always Speaking' Provision (or a 'Shall' Provision). But the Parliament of Northern Ireland did so, in 1954, in wording almost identical to the original Canadian provisions.[33]

Commenting on the Northern Ireland ASP, Leitch and Donaldson (who drafted it) said that it:

> embodies a rule which has usually been accepted as one of existing law, although the authority on the point is scanty. But in *ex parte Pratt* ... Bowen LJ pointed out, in relation to the bankruptcy code that '... when the present tense is used, it is used, not in relation to time, but as the present tense of logic'. (For a discussion on the use of words referring to the present and the future, see the remarks of Somervell LJ in *Roppel v. Bennett*).[34]

This suggests that Leitch and Donaldson considered that the ASP codified a pre-existing (English) common-law rule. It is not entirely clear whether they took *Pratt* to be the authority for this rule, but it is instructive to examine both of the cases that they cited here.

14.6 The Present Tense of Logic?

The *Pratt* case concerned a question, about the temporal operation of legislation, that is entirely different from those that we have encountered so far. It concerned section 5 of the Bankruptcy Act 1883:

> Subject to the conditions hereinafter specified, if a debtor commits an act of bankruptcy the Court may, on a bankruptcy petition being presented either by a creditor or by the debtor, make an order, in this Act called a 'receiving order', for the protection of the estate.

This provision was clearly 'always speaking': it granted the court an ongoing (conditional) power to make a receiving order. It is also temporally complex: the power arose only if 'a debtor commits an act of bankruptcy' (using the present simple) and only on 'a bankruptcy petition being presented' (using the present progressive). The natural way to understand this provision, temporally, is as follows:

t_1: section 5 of the 1883 Act comes into force
t_2: debtor commits an act of bankruptcy
t_3: bankruptcy petition is presented
t_4: court makes (or declines to make) a receiving order

The issue in *Pratt* was that the act of bankruptcy was committed *before* section 5 came into force (i.e. at some t_0).[35] The debtor's act *would have counted* as an act of bankruptcy under section 5, if it had been committed after section 5 came into force, and the debtor's conduct *did count* as an act of bankruptcy under the previous legislation (the Bankruptcy Act 1869). So what the court had to decide in *Pratt* was not whether the use of the present tense in section 5 ('commits') prevented it from having a *prospective* effect but, instead, whether section 5 could have *retrospective* effect.

The Court of Appeal judges were unanimous that it was retrospective (in this limited sense). Cotton LJ, giving the leading judgment, read the provision as if—instead of 'commits'—it had said 'has committed'.[36] This sufficed to solve the problem in the *Pratt* case, but it is sub-optimal as a general solution: because it does not specify *when* the act of bankruptcy needs to have been committed (is the Act retrospective without limit?) or whether it is sufficient (or necessary) that the debtor's conduct counts as an act of bankruptcy under the 1883 Act (cf. the 1869 Act or earlier legislation). These questions could, of course, have been resolved via the drafting, for example, by enacting: 'if a debtor has committed (after [date]) an act of bankruptcy under this Act [or [earlier Act(s)]]...'.

But Leitch and Donaldson quoted not from Cotton LJ but from the concurring judgment of Bowen LJ:

> [T]he [1883] Act ... is framed in a very peculiar way. I think it is framed on the idea that a bankruptcy code is being constructed, and when the present tense is used, it is used, not in relation to time, but as the present tense of logic.[37]

Whatever principle of retroactivity Bowen LJ was endorsing here, it was clearly not a *general* one: it is explicitly limited to the 'very peculiar' situations where Parliament constructs a 'code'. And, in any event, it is not obvious how this could be taken to concern the notion that legislation is 'always speaking'.

The specific phrase that Leitch and Donaldson focused on—'the present tense of logic'—is one of these eminently-quotable judicial *dicta* (and it has indeed been much-quoted). The phrase appears to have been a coinage of Bowen LJ, and, other than in discussing Bowen LJ's judgment, I have found no other trace of its use. The problem is that it is not clear what this *dictum* is supposed to mean. The concept of tense always relates to time, and, while there is a branch of philosophical logic called 'tense logic', this concerns the logic of time. In *Pratt*, Fry LJ ventured an explanation:

> I entirely agree with Bowen LJ, as to the meaning of the present tense in this section; it is used, I think, to express a hypothesis, without regard to time, just as in stating the proposition 'if A is B, then B is C'. It is equivalent to saying, 'if at the time when the petition is presented the debtor shall have committed an act of bankruptcy'.[38]

Fry LJ was right that we use the word 'is' not only as the present simple of the (infinitive) verb 'to be' but also as a copula, in asserting logical relations: saying that 'Pluto is a planet' asserts an entailment between the concepts PLUTO and PLANET. Let's call this use of 'is' the 'present form', to distinguish it from uses of 'is' to indicate a particular time, i.e. to distinguish it from the present *tense* usages. Even using 'is' to assert a logical relation may rely on the time of the assertion: Pluto counted as a planet before 24 August 2006, when the International Astronomical Union changed its definition of 'planet', but Pluto has not counted as a planet since that change was made.[39] However, section 5 does not use the present form: the key legislative word ('commits') is used to indicate the present tense. And, in any event, Fry LJ's rewording does not work: it uses the future perfect ('shall have committed'), and its natural reading would mean that section 5 applied only to acts of bankruptcy committed *after* it came into force (and so section 5 would not have applied to Pratt's conduct).[40]

In fact, the 'present form' is also used for claims that A is typically, habitually, or generically—rather than necessarily—B.[41] The statement 'Martin David Kelly walks his dog Preston in the early evening' uses the present form of the verb 'to walk' to make a claim about what I *habitually* do, not to refer to a particular time. And the statement 'Colliedoodles are smart' uses the present form of the verb 'to be' to make a claim about what is typically true and not one indexed to a specific time. Similarly, we use the present form to make other types of generic claims: the statement 'ticks carry Lyme disease' uses the present form of the verb 'to carry' to state which creatures are the carriers of Lyme disease and, again, not to make an explicitly temporal claim.[42]

The *past* form can also be (and often is) used in making such claims, including in legislation. For example, *Albert* concerned a legislative provision imposing a motor insurance requirement for 'a vehicle in which passengers **are carried** for hire'.[43] For Lord Donovan, in giving the leading opinion of a unanimous House of Lords, this required that 'one of the vehicle's normal functions' is carrying passengers, and so it was immaterial whether 'passengers were in fact being carried for hire or reward at the time of the occurrence of an event giving rise to a claim'.[44] That is, the Act used the past form of the verb 'to carry' to make a claim of habitual use, not one of time.

Even the *future* form may be used in making claims about logical or generic relations. For example, under section 1(2) of the Scotland Act 1998 one member of the Scottish Parliament 'shall be returned for each constituency'—which stipulates that the relation between members and constituencies is one-to-one (it could have been written 'Each constituency has' one member). Similarly, section 1(3) concerns how regional members of the Scottish Parliament 'shall be returned at a general election'.

This unfortunate phrase—'the present tense of logic'—was nonetheless then appropriated in works on legislation, and explicitly connected to the notion that legislation is 'always speaking'. The precise way that this happened is worth charting, in some detail, as it is a striking example of what *not* to do when writing a treatise on legislation (or indeed on any other topic, for that matter) and, in particular, of how not to cite authority for a claim that one is making (whether that claim is unfortunate or not). Henry Thring—who was appointed as the UK's inaugural First Parliamentary Counsel in 1869—had popularised the present-tense drafting style pioneered by Coode and wrote in the first edition of his treatise *Practical Legislation* (1877) that 'An Act of Parliament should be deemed to be always speaking and therefore the present or past tense should be adopted, and "shall" should be used as an *imperative* only, and not as a *future*'.[45] William Craies then claimed, in 1892, that the 'practice' of using the present tense 'not in relation to time, but as the present tense of logic' is 'based on the rule of Lord Thring that an Act is always speaking'.[46] Next, Courtenay Ilbert—who was then First Parliamentary Counsel—wrote in 1901, referring to *Pratt* but not Craies, that:

> An Act of Parliament should be treated as always speaking. The idea on which this rule is based, according to Lord Bowen, is that a code on some particular subject is being constructed, and so, when the present tense used, it is used, not in relation to time, but as the present tense of logic.[47]

Finally, in 1907 Craies repeated his claim that the practice of using the present tense as that 'of logic' is based on the rule that 'an Act is always speaking' but—rather magnanimously, given that Ilbert had failed to attribute this claim to him—cited Ilbert (1901) as the authority for this (despite Ilbert apparently having followed Craies on this point).[48] This unfortunate claim thereby gained the appearance of weighty authority, enough to mislead Leitch and Donaldson (around 50 years later) to suggest that *Pratt* is authority for a rule that Acts are presumed to be 'always speaking' (despite the fact that it is clearly *not* authority for this).[49]

The second case mentioned by Leitch and Donaldson—*Roppel v Bennett*—concerned legislation which had used the present and future tenses but which did not use the past tense. In this case, however, the issue was not whether the legislation applied to facts arising *before* it came into force, but whether the use of the present tense required that the relevant facts must also obtain at the time of making a *claim* under the legislation. The relevant provision stated that:

> Where any person lets ... any dwelling-house ... and it is proved to the ... county court on the application of the lessee that the rent charged

is yielding or will yield to the lessor a profit in excess of the normal profit ... the court may order that the excess rent shall be irrecoverable, and that any such excess paid ... shall be repaid to the tenant.[50]

The key fact, in *Roppel*, was that before the lessee applied to the county court under this provision he had sought and obtained from the Rent Tribunal a reduction in the rent (to an acceptable level). So there was no question of the county court ordering that 'the excess rent shall be irrecoverable', and the sole issue was whether the county court should order the repayment of the 'excess paid'. We can use our schema to display the timeline of the relevant facts as follows:

t_1: section 9(1) of the 1920 Act comes into force
t_2: the dwelling-house is let at rent of 25s per week (19 August 1946)
t_3: the Rent Tribunal reduces (prospectively only) the rent payable to 14s per week (17 April 1947)
t_4: the tenant applies for repayment of the excess rent paid between t_2 and t_3 (5 September 1947)

The landlord argued that it was a condition precedent of the court's power to order repayment of the excess rent that at the time of the application to the court (at t_4) the rent charged 'is yielding' excess profit, and, thus, as the rent was not excessive at that time (although it *had been* excessive), the court had no power to order repayment. The county court rejected this argument, and its decision was upheld unanimously by the Court of Appeal – with Somervell LJ commenting:

> It is true that the words "has yielded" are absent. I could not follow [the landlord's] submission that "is yielding" has a different meaning from "yields"; but he was quite right in drawing our attention to the fact that words are not used referring to the past and that there are words referring to the future. I think that the explanation is simple: it is normally the case that people can by legal proceedings initiated on a certain date claim in respect of any relief to which they may be entitled over a past period, whereas it is less usual, or unusual, that a person can resort to a court before the injury complained of has actually descended upon him.[51]

This seems to have been the passage that Leitch and Donaldson had in mind in their commentary on Northern Ireland's ASP. Leaving aside that Somervell LJ appears to have denied that there is any difference between the progressive and the simple aspects, this was clearly the right decision: it would have been absurd if this legislation were read in such a way that a tenant could end up in a worse financial position as a result of having obtained a reduction in their rent (from an excessive level). It is also clear that this section could have been drafted so that this issue would not have arisen. But, leaving aside the merits of the decision (and of the legislative drafting), the *Roppel* case—like the *Pratt* case—simply did not concern the notion that legislation is 'always speaking'.

14.7 Conclusion

We have seen that the tools which drafters can use to indicate the temporal structure of the actions and events that their legislation seeks to regulate include aspect as well as tense. In particular, we've seen that two events or actions in the future—relative to when the legislation comes into force—can be distinguished, temporally, by using the perfect and the simple aspects. But what of the progressive aspect? Although the legislation contested in *Roppel* used the present progressive—'is yielding'—nothing turned on this choice of aspect. But many reported UK cases illustrate the potential dangers of using the 'bare' progressive aspect—i.e. just referring to an ongoing event or action, without specifying what is included in its scope (e.g. when it begins and when it ends)—in legislative drafting.[52]

The influence of Coode's work on tense is apparent in the statute books of jurisdictions across the common-law world: our legislative provisions are overwhelmingly drafted in the continuous present tense. However, the reasons for drafting future-directed legislation to reflect that it is 'always speaking' largely reduce to promoting readability, and, at least for provisions that regulate actions and events that are temporally simple, using the future tense (e.g. 'shall be ...') is just as readable (so this is primarily a matter of style).

For those legislative provisions which are directed to temporally complex actions and events, aspects may be used to mark the order in time of 'future intermediaries': actions and events which occur after the legislation comes into force but before the time by reference to which it is applied. But legislative drafters may find that a range of techniques—including tense and words such as 'before' and 'after', as well as tabulation—can be used in combination to show this temporal order more clearly than just by using aspect.

Notes

* I'm grateful to Ross Carter, Chris Cummings, Tímea Drinóczi, Fraser Gough, and the participants in workshops held at the legislative drafting offices of Scotland, the United Kingdom, Singapore, Western Australia, the Commonwealth of Australia, Queensland, New Zealand, Victoria, New South Wales, and Ontario, for their helpful comments on drafts of this chapter.

1 For the four main ways in which the 'always speaking' metaphor has been used, and the reasons why it is important to distinguish them from each other, see Martin D. Kelly, 'Applying Laws Across Time: Disentangling the "Always Speaking" Principles' (2024) 44 *Oxford Journal of Legal Studies* 563.
2 The most extensive treatment of the topic is Frederick Bowers, *Linguistic Aspects of Legislative Expression* (University of British Columbia Press, 1989), 232–249. See also Helen Xanthaki, *Thornton's Legislative Drafting* (6th edn, Bloomsbury Professional, 2022), 68, 114, 121, 125–126, 428; and Neil Goldfarb, '"Always Speaking"? Interpreting the Present Tense in Statutes' (2013) 58 *Canadian Journal of Linguistics* 63.
3 Alan Rodger, 'A Time for Everything Under the Law: Some Reflections on Retrospectivity' (2005) 121 *Law Quarterly Review* 57, 57.
4 This chapter focuses on *legislative* drafting, but these issues arise in drafting other types of legal instrument (such as constitutions, treaties, contracts, wills, trusts, and judgments) as well as non-legal instruments.
5 This table uses the third-person singular throughout (I am grateful to Chris Cummins for suggesting this). For completeness, I should note here that there are more aspects than these three principal ones.
6 See Kelly, 'Applying Laws Across Time'.
7 Virtually all actions and events are, of course, extended across time to some degree: the baby will likely have smiled for a second or two (at least). I am, therefore, using the word 'momentary' here slightly loosely. The key point is to distinguish those actions and events that are merely fleeting from those that are ongoing.
8 For other examples, see Kelly, 'Applying Laws Across Time', 567–568.
9 Such future-directed utterances typically play a different role in our discourse: past- and present-directed momentary utterances are (at least partly) descriptive of a set of facts, whereas future-directed ones typically function as a *prediction* (or, perhaps, as an *expressive* i.e. used to express an emotion or feeling).
10 George Coode, *On Legislative Expression: or, The Language of the Written Law* (1st edn, William Benning and Co., 1845), 23. This was published in 1845 but is dated 'July 25, 1842' (Coode, *On Legislative Expression*, 69).
11 Coode, *On Legislative Expression*.
12 Coode, *On Legislative Expression*, 63.
13 I first used this example in Kelly, 'Applying Laws Across Time', 565.
14 Coode, *On Legislative Expression*, 23. In reality, I would probably use the present simple for both of these future events—'if you fail the exam then you must take the resit'—because their temporal order is obvious from the context.
15 Coode, *On Legislative Expression*, 63.
16 Coode, *On Legislative Expression*, 63, 66.
17 Whether a legislative provision is momentary will turn on what it is designed to do, rather than the tense with which it is drafted. Coode did not, however, examine when legislation is (and is not) 'always speaking', nor even did he explicitly state that legislation is generally (or typically, or presumptively) 'always speaking'.
18 Coode, *On Legislative Expression*, 66.
19 Coode, *On Legislative Expression*, 66.
20 Coode, *On Legislative Expression*, 61–62.
21 For example, the Summary Proceedings Act 1957 (New Zealand), s 198(1) permits a search warrant to be granted if 'there is ... in any place' a specified type of thing

related to suspected offending. In *Hunt v R* [2011] 2 NZLR 499 (CA) the New Zealand Court of Appeal held that s 198(1) permitted a warrant to be granted anticipatorily i.e. when the relevant thing is not believed to be in the place in question at the time when granting a warrant is being considered. But in *Hamed v R* [2012] 2 NZLR 305 (SCNZ) the New Zealand Supreme Court held unanimously that, as s 198(1) was worded using 'is' rather than 'is or will be', anticipatory warrants are not permitted. I am grateful to Ross Carter for this example.

22 Reported English cases on disputes which arose because legislation used the present tense to speak about two or more different times include *Jackson v Hall* [1980] AC 854 and *In Re D (A Minor)* [1987] AC 317.

23 Coode, *On Legislative Expression*, 62.

24 For these other uses, see Martin D. Kelly, 'Shall We Will Must' (2024), https://ssrn.com/abstract=5040031.

25 On claims that 'shall' is 'pompous', see Editorial, 'In Honour of the Moribund "Shall"' (2014) 35 *Statute Law Review* v.

26 Consolidated Statues of Upper Canada 1859, s 18. For a history of these provisions, see Martin D. Kelly, '"Always Speaking" Provisions: Legal Transplants Gone Awry' (2024), https://ssrn.com/abstract=4738797.

27 Interpretation Act 1867 (Canada), s 6(1) ('Always Speaking' Provision) and s 6(3) ('Shall' Provision).

28 Interpretation Act 1888 (NZ), s 5(3) (ASP). New Zealand did not enact a 'Shall' Provision.

29 1 USC 1; June 25, 1948, ch 645, §6, 62 Stat 859.

30 Anthony J. Sciascia (ed.), 'House Legislative Counsel's Manual on Drafting Style' (3rd edn, December 2022) available at https://legcounsel.house.gov/sites/evo-subsites/legcounsel-evo.house.gov/files/documents/ManualDraftStyle_2022.pdf, 5 (the 'US House Manual').

31 For the reasons why, see Martin D. Kelly, 'The Loquacious Legislature: Are Statutes "Always Speaking"?' (PhD thesis, University of Edinburgh 2021), https://ssrn.com/abstract=4738764, 14–22.

32 Sciascia, 'House Legislative Counsel's Manual on Drafting Style', 46.

33 Interpretation Act 1954 (Northern Ireland), s 31.

34 W. A. Leitch and A. G. Donaldson, 'A Commentary on the Interpretation Act (Northern Ireland) 1954' (1955) 11 *Northern Ireland Law Quarterly* 66, 121.

35 Pratt (the debtor) had filed a liquidation petition on 30 November 1883, which was an 'act of bankruptcy' under the 1869 Act, but the power to make a receiving order did not come into force until 1 January 1884.

36 *Re Pratt; ex p Pratt* (1884) 12 QBD 334, 340.

37 Leitch and Donaldson, 'A Commentary on the Interpretation Act (Northern Ireland) 1954', 337.

38 Leitch and Donaldson, 'A Commentary on the Interpretation Act (Northern Ireland) 1954', 341.

39 This connects with a philosophical debate about the relation between propositions and time: according to temporalism, the truth-value of propositions can change over time; according to its rival position, eternalism, propositions have a truth-value timelessly. Under temporalism, the proposition PLUTO IS A PLANET was true prior to 24 August 2006 but is false from that date onwards; under eternalism, propositions are indexed to a specified time (and thus the proposition PLUTO IS A PLANET ON 23 AUGUST 2006 is eternally true and the proposition PLUTO IS A PLANET ON 24 AUGUST 2006 is eternally false). Either way, the question of time matters.

40 Merely using the future perfect does not, of course, *entail* that a provision is not retrospective in this sense. But it is natural to infer this from choosing the future perfect over the present perfect ('has committed').

41 Patrick Griffiths and Chris Cummins, *An Introduction to English Semantics and Pragmatics* (2nd edn, Edinburgh University Press, 2017), 64.

42 I borrow this example from Sarah-Jane Leslie and Adam Lerner, 'Generic Generalizations' in Edward N. Zalta and Uri Nodelman (eds.), *The Stanford Encyclopedia of Philosophy* (Fall 2022 Edition) 1. They continue 'we accept [this] even though very few ticks (approximately 1%) actually have the property': Leslie and Lerner, 'Generic Generalizations'.

43 The Road Traffic Act 1960, s 203(4) (my **emphasis**).

44 *Albert v Motor Insurers' Bureau* [1972] AC 301, 318.

45 Henry Thring, *Practical Legislation* (1st edn, John Murray, 1877), 83. This is all that Thring wrote about the notion that legislation is 'always speaking', and he made no reference to Coode's work. This may explain why Lord Steyn, in a leading opinion, claimed that 'the drafting technique of Lord Thring and his successors have brought about the situation that statutes will generally be found to be of the "always speaking" variety': *R v Burstow; R v Ireland* [1998] AC 147, 158. For criticism of this, see Kelly, 'Applying Laws Across Time', 583.

46 William F. Craies (ed.), *Hardcastle on Statute Law* (2nd edn, Stevens and Haynes, 1892), 33.

47 Courtenay P. Ilbert, *Legislative Methods and Forms* (Stevens & Sons, 1901), 248.

48 William F. Craies, *Statute Law* (1st edn, Stevens and Haynes, 1907), 29.

49 For further confusion on this, see Elmer A. Driedger, 'Legislative Drafting' (1949) 27 *Canadian Bar Review* 291, 303: '... the law must be construed as always speaking. This was the rule at common law [citation of *Pratt*]'.

50 The Increase of Rent and Mortgage Interest (Restrictions) Act 1920, s 9(1) (as amended) (my **emphasis**).

51 *Roppel v Bennett* [1949] 1 KB 115, 126.

52 See Martin D. Kelly, 'Progressives in Legislation' https://ssrn.com/abstract=5040037.

15 Terminological Controversies over a Legal Hendiadys

The “True and Fair” Case

Annalisa Zanola

15.1 Introduction

It is widely acknowledged that legislation has an impact on all areas of professional and everyday life (Corbett 2019; Durant and Leung 2016; Friedrich and Gomes de Matos 2016; Gadbin-George et al. 2014; Garner 2001, 2002, 2004; Tessuto 2023; Zanola 2023). In the following pages, we will examine an example from the financial sector to illustrate the difficulties arising from the legal interpretation of the expression “true and fair”, which is typical of the accounting sector and guarantees the validity of any corporate annual report: this hendiadys, which originated in English, is mostly adopted in all countries of the world and is rarely translated into other languages. However, this can lead to legal misinterpretations as the expression may not be fully understood in countries with legal, cultural, and linguistic backgrounds different from those of the United Kingdom, where it originated.

This contribution aims to review the history of the concept, from its origins to its current specific use in the field of accounting, to shed light on its authentic meaning and possible interpretations in international and global contexts. In doing so, we are convinced that the translation of the concept into different languages does not do justice to the wide and varied semantic layering of the original expression (Bhatia 1997).

Finance professionals rely on accounting information provided in annual reports, which are drawn up in accordance with the International Financial Reporting Standards (IFRS) (Piotti 2009). The adoption of IFRS, developed in English and translated into other languages, aims to enhance the comparability of financial statements across countries (Brockington 1996; Hellmann and Patel 2021). It is generally assumed that all translated IFRS convey consistent information, and the use of different languages does not compromise the comparability of financial information. However, there may be differences among the language versions of IFRS. Our discussion on the relevant linguistic effects in interpreting and applying IFRS

DOI: 10.4324/9781003430308-19

may help future research to systematically analyse why equally qualified professionals exercise their judgement differently.

Although IFRS were originally promulgated in English, they are often translated into the local language of each country. In the EU, for instance, the endorsement process necessitates the translation of IFRS from English into several official languages (IFRS Foundation 2024b; Nobes 2021). While there are benefits to translating IFRS, extensive translation of IFRS into many languages can also hinder the claimed advantage that IFRS improves global comparability. Hellmann (2016) noted that this could lead to translation and interpretation issues, which could undermine the consistent application of IFRS. Differences in the meanings of IFRS across languages may impact the decision usefulness and comparability of accounting information across countries, as well as result in legal disputes and court actions (Pan and Patel 2018). It is important to consider that accountants in different countries may interpret the meaning of IFRS differently from the intended meaning by the International Accounting Standards Board (IASB) due to the fact that the accounting standards are originally published in English and then translated into various languages globally (IFRS Foundation 2024a).

This contribution emphasizes the importance of having a comprehensive understanding of legal concepts, their origins, and the context in which they are used, before embarking on the process of translating them. The focus of this research is not on translation but rather on the more authentic meaning of legal terminology as applied to a legal text. Attention will be focused not only on the act of establishing the concept of "true and fair" but also on its definition: the latter completes the process of codification of the new expression, which fits into the sphere under consideration and finds its semantic space within the conceptual network in which the new notion appears. Terms are created through various means, such as chance, necessity, adaptation from other languages, or complete freedom (Zanola 2018: 20). These stories can be fascinating, taking the terms on a journey through usages, texts, discourses, styles, and variations. However, each term is linked to a specific domain, sector, or discipline, as it represents its own concept and the domain to which it pertains.

15.2 From "Ordinary" to Specialized Contexts

In English, it is not usual to describe something as both *true* and *fair*. However, in the domain of accountancy, the two adjectives are strictly connected. The use of these terms raises old problems regarding rhetoric. The pair originated in literary contexts in the 16th century, soon became a hendiadys in the following centuries, and then a codified formula in the specialized field of finance.

There has been a lengthy debate in the accounting literature about the need to clarify the interpretation of these terms (Canziani 1993; Chastney 1975; Kirk 2006). Nonetheless, this does not alter the inherent and long-standing vagueness and ambiguity of the undefined phrase "true and fair", which has been used since its introduction in the UK Companies Act 1948 (Financial Reporting Council 2014: 1). The item's legal origin dates back to the 18th century in the UK, and it appears to have been translated into a legal context related to corporate accountability in the 20th century. In other words, the term originated in non-specialized contexts and evolved later on into a technically relevant formula. In the following paragraphs, the analysis of this hendiadys in both non-financial and financial contexts, using etymological and lexical research methods, will be carried out to provide support for a more complete definition of this complex concept and aid in its correct interpretation. Hopefully, this will help in converting or transferring accurately the concept from English into any other language.

15.2.1 The Context

English has become the global language of business and accounting in the 20th century. Therefore, in the last century, the terminology used by English-speaking accountants to discuss accounting concepts has grown to be more than mere local interest. In his paper on English accounting words and concepts, Robert Parker (1994) discussed the challenges that English-speaking accountants encountered in finding appropriate terms to express some concepts that they attempted to formulate, notably in relation to the components of the annual financial statement: in his paper, Parker examined the sources of English accounting words and, in particular, their interactions with legal and economic terms and concepts, paying close attention to changes in meaning over time. The author emphasized the challenge of defining the relationships between accounting terms and their usage and meaning: given that it is debatable whether a concept can exist independently of words, he acknowledged the complexity of guaranteeing a relationship between a concept and the word used to express it. Developing a concept can certainly be delayed by a lack of appropriate words, and confusion can be resolved when appropriate words are found. Recognition of the need for new words should ideally be followed by agreement on what those words should be.

The meaning of accounting terms may only be agreed upon *ideally* (Gray et al. 1993), which could explain the lengthy debate surrounding two seemingly simple yet significant words: *true* and *fair*. These words have a long and independent history dating back to the origins of the English language. They were combined as a unique hendiadys in the first translations of the Bible and have been used in literary contexts since Shakespeare's time. They suddenly appeared as a legal formula in financial statements. As previously mentioned, the meaning of this formula is a subject of controversy, both in its country of origin, Britain, and in the international contexts where it has been adopted.

To provide clarity in this highly complex area, the phrase "true and fair" should first be defined as a concept with a legal nature. Therefore, it must be placed in the specialized context of jurisprudence. Since it is impossible to refer to jurisprudence in the broadest sense without addressing the specific features of some terminological subfields (such as commercial law, administrative law, criminal law, civil law, etc.), we will first try to define an aspect that is crucial to the definition of the concept, namely, the context in which the term was born and has developed.

Following Mariateresa Zanola (2018: 83), by *context* we mean:

> The part of a text or statement that surrounds a particular word and determines its meaning. A type of textual support (...) that provides information about the semantic features of a concept or the use of a term. (Our translation)

The use of a particular set of terms, such as "true and fair", presupposes a specialized context, that is, a common ground in terms of the specific area within the discipline and the parameters identified within the community of reference. The appropriate use and interpretation of this concept depends on its contextual application, its historical evolution, and the cultural milieu that informs it. As the definition of "true and fair" is derived from the Fourth Directive (Financial Reporting Council 2014: 1, n. 1) and applies to any context in which the *formula* is used in an explanatory text related to finance or law, all sources may be relevant to any potential analysis. These sources may include any organization providing information or any written work used to record the two combined terms or to formulate their definition.

The subject field for our research must be related to the specific sphere of human activity in which this research is carried out, namely financial accounting. These seemingly obvious considerations imply the following significant remarks. Firstly, the terms *true* and *fair* originate from common usage but are currently used only in specialized financial and accounting contexts. Secondly, their specialized usage is characterized by limited frequency compared to the high frequency of the single adjectives *true* and *fair* both in common and specialized English. Finally, the strong monosemantic character of the hendiadys joining the two adjectives must be considered: the special combination of the two adjectives cannot be synonymized due to the specific nature of the contexts of use and the related sources.

The following paragraphs describe the terminological evolution of the complex lexeme composed of *true* and *fair*, from common adjectives to specialized terms that have been combined in a hendiadys. These words have a unique polyrhematic function, which appears to contradict the monorhematic usage of other specialized terms in the same field. Following De Mauro (2000: 1177), the term "polyrhematic expression" is used to describe compound words consisting of multiple elements that comprise a unified whole, with the overall meaning of the word independent of the individual constituents. Instead, "monorhematic" words should be defined as

> dictionary entries consisting of a single word (...) or simple lexemes (units of the lexicon, in general a simple word coinciding with the lemma of a dictionary, which can also be a radical thematic basis that cannot be analysed further),

as from Monteleone (2023: 3). Most complex lexemes have a specialized or technical use and meaning. Moreover, in most of them, the secondary meaning of at least one constituent leads to an opaqueness, as in "true and fair", which is practically impossible to understand outside its typical context of use: at the same time, in many cases, the specialized use is determined by the context, as it happens in the context of the use of the expression that is the subject of this research. In this sense, the complex lexeme under consideration only allows for a "polyrhematic" interpretation of its meaning. It has a non-literal or a very specialized/technical meaning; it has a meaning which is not a hyponym of any other expression. It is not susceptible to insertions, inflections, or alterations to its word order (Nuccorini 2007).

15.2.2 The Background of the Adjectives "True" and "Fair"

The original meanings of these adjectives do not have a direct relationship with their contemporary usage in financial accounting. However, the combination of the two terms remains difficult to define in this field. Moreover, it is no longer regarded as an English formula but as an international one.

The combination of the two adjectives originated in a culturally and linguistically bound British oral tradition, possibly linked to the British literary tradition. It was later applied to the British legal system, where the idea of fairness and truth aligned with the requirements of the law. The focus of our research is not on discovering new or unpublished meanings of these terms. Quite the contrary, our aim is to show how important it is to look for the local cultural and linguistic roots of a legal concept before approaching it at an international level. As Kischel (2009: 7) puts it:

> Linguistically equivalent legal notions will frequently have different contents in different jurisdictions. The legal significance of notions can

differ vastly in their direction and extent. Also, the interconnections within each legal system as well as the legal culture in general influence the meaning and practical impact of legal concepts.

The question of understanding the authentic meaning of the expression *true and fair* is primarily a matter of correct translation rather than making it understandable to British accountants. The challenge lies in the way the concept was transferred or translated into other European languages. The equivalent of the phrase may be interpreted differently across different realities and cultures of the source language system. In legal translations, the question is often not which translation is right, but rather which one is less wrong (Olsen et al. 2009; Parker 1994; Prieto 2021; Rock et al. 2013). Although accountants worldwide understand the meaning of *true and fair*, the formula still requires interpretation rather than translation (Soriano Barabino 2020). This polyrematic expression combines two concepts into a single term with a unique global meaning. The following paragraphs will explore this concept further.

The complexity of the subject is reflected in the massive and impressive bibliographical production on the subject since the 1980s. Books, articles, and contributions on the topic have proliferated worldwide, starting from the original British sources and expanding to European and extra-European sources. As a result, the true and fair view concept can now be approached from a global perspective, as follows:

1 The British perspective (Harris 1987; Houghton 1987; Nobes and Parker 1988/89; Ryan 1967; Stewart 1998)
2 The European perspective (Alexander and Archer 2000; Flint 1982; Incollingo 1999)
3 The extra-European perspective (Karan 2002; Kirk 2001, 2006; Olsen et al. 2009)

We shall, however, leave aside the details which are more akin to accounting studies and turn instead to the terminological considerations that fall within our remit.

15.2.3 The "True and Fair" Travel

The two words first appeared in the Bible in *Revelation* 19:2, translated from the Greek words ἀληθιναὶ (true) and δίκαιαι (righteous, fair), as follows:

> Hallelujah!
> Salvation and glory and power belong to our God,
> for *true and fair* are his judgments.

> He has condemned the great prostitute
> who corrupted the earth by her adulteries.
> He has avenged on her the blood of his servants.
> (Zanola 2014: 113. Our italics)

The items are sometimes translated as: *True and Just, True and Righteous, True and Upright.* They appear also in *Revelation* 16:7 (quoted in Zanola 2014: 114. Our italics)

> Then I heard the altar answer, "Yes, Lord God Almighty,
> Your judgments are *true and fair*".

The strict link between fairness and justice is common in the English translation from the Greek version of the Bible, where *fairness* is often used as the English translation of the Greek word ἰσότητα, as in *Colossians* 4:1:

> Masters, provide your slaves with what is *right and fair,* because you know that you also have a Master in heaven (...). Masters, be *just and fair* to your slaves (...).
> (Quoted in Zanola 2015: 6)

Similar examples may be found in *Proverbs* 2: 9:

> Then you will understand what is *right and just and fair* (Our italics).

And in *Proverbs* 1: 3:

> (...) for acquiring a disciplined and prudent life, doing what is *right and just and fair.*
> (Quoted in Zanola 2015: 6)

The concept of justice and righteousness would appear to be the common ground for the birth of the hendiadys, centuries before it became a formula in the legal and financial fields. Nevertheless, the combination of the word *true* with the word *fair* in financial accounting seems to have been accidental rather than the result of a deliberate process (Van Hulle 1993: 100), although the message behind the words seems to be more important than the words used (Walton 1993: 51). Following Söderblom (2009: 10):

> There is a difference between the signifier, here TFV [True and Fair View], and the signified, here the message that TFV is communicating. Looking at TFV in that way, the underlying meaning instead of the actual words should be considered. The practical difficulty only seems

to be that there is no mutual understanding on the real meaning of TFV, the signified.

Söderblom, following Walton (1993: 51), argues on the basis of Ferdinand De Saussure (1922)'s distinction between the concept (what is *signified*) and the word used to express it (the *signifier*). However, the signified is defined by the current accounting practice. This implies that (a) true and fair is what the accountants declare it to be, (b) its meaning is related to a particular group and context, and (c) its meaning may change over time.

15.3 "True" and "Fair": Etymology and Meanings

In the following section, the focus will be on the etymology and the meaning of the two words. The result of the two signifiers and signified items will be much richer than expected, but the results of their mixture in a hendiadys, which has finally become a truly fair and fairly true formula in financial accounting, will be even more fascinating.

15.3.1 The Word "True"

The term has its origins in the Proto-Germanic **trewwjaz*, meaning "having or characterized by good faith". This term is related to the Old High German *gatriuwu*, or German *treu*, meaning *faithful* or *trustworthy*. The term may ultimately derive from the Indo-European root **dru-*, which means *tree*, with the connotation of being *steadfast as an oak*. This root is also present in the Lithuanian *drutas* (that is, *firm*), the Welsh *drud* or the Old Irish *dron*, meaning *strong*, and the Welsh *derw*, that is to say *true*. The Latin adjective *firmus* is also related to this etymological path (Zanola 2014: 118).

The word *true* has multiple meanings. Its sense of "consistent with fact" dates back to 1205. The meaning of "real, genuine, not counterfeit" comes for the first time in 1398, and the meaning of "conforming to a fixed standard" (as the true north) dates from around 1550. The expression *self-evident truth* dates from 1708, first recorded in the writings of Swift. The term "true-false" as a type of test question was first used in 1923.

Its basic meaning is that of *certainty* and *honesty*. Contemporary English dictionaries[1] provide multiple definitions of the word, though no reference to any specialized use in the field of accounting has yet been recorded. In the next few lines, some of the most widely recognized meanings and examples of usage of the adjective in common English contexts are listed:

- Not fictional, or illusory; factual or factually accurate; conforming with reality
- Being in accordance with the actual state or conditions; conforming to reality or fact; not false: *a true story*

- Being of real or natural origin; genuine; not synthetic: *true leather*
- Authentic: *true gold; true feelings*
- Sincere; not deceitful: *a true interest in someone's welfare*
- Firm in allegiance; loyal; faithful; steadfast: *a true friend*
- Being or reflecting the essential or genuine character of something: *the true meaning of his statement*
- Conforming to or consistent with a standard, law, or pattern: *a true copy, a true aim, a true fit*
- Exact; precise; accurate; correct: *a true balance*
- Of the right kind; proper: *to arrange things in their true order*
- Properly so called; rightly answering to a description: *true statesmanship*
- Legitimate or rightful: *the true heir*
- Reliable, unfailing, or sure: *a true sign*
- Exactly or accurately shaped, formed, fitted, or placed, as a surface, instrument, or part of a mechanism
- Honest; honourable; upright
- In music, exactly in tune: *a true note*

The most commonly used alternatives to the word are *factual*, *veracious*, *honest*, *trustworthy*, *firm*, *constant*, *steady*, *unwavering*, and *faithful.*

15.3.1 The Word "Fair"

The adjective comes from the Old English *fæger*, meaning "beautiful" or "pleasant". The etymology of the word is closely linked to the general idea of beauty and harmony. The root of the word dates back to the Old High German adjective *fagar, fagari* (765), which means *beautiful*, *splendid*, *pretty*, and *bright* and is related to the Latin adjective *pulcher*. The root *fagar-* is also behind contemporary English words such as *beauty* and *glory* (Latin: *claritas, pulchritudo*). The etymology of the word "fag" in Gothic suggests the concept of happiness and pleasure in appearance for any field related to it (Zanola 2014: 115).

By the end of the first millennium, the word had acquired an identity that was more related to aesthetics than to any moral or ethical field. The meaning in reference to weather (c. 1205) still preserves this original sense (opposed to foul). Around the 13th century (c. 1175), it evolved to mean "morally pure, unblemished", but the majority of attestations are still related to its original connotations. The sporting senses (fair ball, fair catch, etc.) only began in 1856, even though "fair play" dates back to 1595.

Contemporary English dictionaries provide multiple definitions of the word, but no reference to any specialized use in the field of accounting has yet been recorded. These are some of the most widely recognized meanings and examples of usage of the adjective in common English contexts:[2]

- Free from bias, dishonesty, or injustice: *a fair decision; a fair judge*
- Legitimately sought, pursued, done, given, etc.; proper under the rules: *a fair fight*
- Moderately large; ample: *a fair income*
- Neither excellent nor poor; moderately or tolerably good: *fair health*
- Marked by favouring conditions; likely; promising: *in a fair way to succeed*
- Unobstructed; not blocked up: *The way was fair for our advance*
- Without irregularity or unevenness: *a fair surface*
- Free from blemish, imperfection, or anything that impairs the appearance, quality, or character: *Her fair reputation was ruined by gossip*
- Easy to read; clear: *fair handwriting*
- Of a light hue; not dark: *fair skin*
- Pleasing in appearance; attractive: *a fair young maiden*
- Seemingly good or sincere but not really so: *The suitor beguiled his mistress with fair speeches*
- Courteous; civil: *fair words*

Its use as an adverb is also recorded in dictionaries, as follows:

- In a fair manner: *He doesn't play fair.*
- Straight; directly, as in aiming or hitting: *He threw the ball fair to the goal.*
- Favourably; auspiciously.

Finally, the term is used as a verb or appears in idiomatic forms, as in the following specific cases:

- *Shipbuilding*, (a.) to draw and adjust (the lines of a hull being designed) to produce regular surfaces of the correct form. (b.) to adjust the form of (a frame or template) in accordance with a design, or cause it to conform to the general form of a hull. (c.) to restore (a bent plate or structural member) to its original form. (d.) to align (the frames of a vessel under construction) in a proper position.
- To bring (rivet holes in connecting structural members) into perfect alignment.
- *(Obsolete)* to make fair.
- *Bid fair*, to seem likely: *This entry bids fair to win first prize.*
- *Fair and square*, (a.) honestly; justly; straightforwardly: *He won the race fair and square.* (b.) honest; just; straightforward: *He was admired for being fair and square in all his dealings.*

- *(Informal) a fair crack of the whip, a fair shake of the dice, a fair go*, a fair opportunity; fair chance.
- *Fair do's,* (a.) equal shares or treatment; (b.) an expression of appeal for equal shares or treatment.
- *Fair enough*, expression of agreement.

The definitions of the term in a legal English dictionary are also worth noting:

> *Some specialised meanings are attested in legal dictionaries of English, such as the where the adjective fair is defined as follows*[3]*:*
>
> *Fair:* characterized by honesty and justice, free from self-interest, deception, injustice, or favoritism; reasonable as a basis for exchange (*fair* wage, *fair* valuation); consistent with merit or importance (*fair* and just compensation for the injuries); conforming with established laws or standards (*fair* judicial process). *Merriam-Webster's Dictionary of Law.*

Regarding synonyms of the term, the most common alternatives pertain to both the ethical and physical connotations of fairness, as follows:

1 *Ethical meaning.* It implies the treating of all sides equally, justly, and equitably (i.e. *a fair compromise).* The terms *impartial, disinterested,* and *unprejudiced* are commonly used as synonyms to describe a lack of bias in opinions and judgments. *Impartial* and *fair* both suggest showing no more favour to one side than another, but *impartial* specifically implies a judicial consideration of a case, as in the case of an impartial judge. *Disinterested* suggests fairness arising from a lack of desire to obtain a selfish advantage, as in the case of the motives of a guardian being entirely disinterested. Unprejudiced means not influenced or swayed by bias or prejudice caused by irrelevant considerations, resulting in an impartial decision. Other possible synonyms include *passable, tolerable, average, middling, open, clear*, or *unencumbered.*
2 *Physical meaning.* The term may refer to both individuals and objects. Therefore, various synonyms may be appropriate depending on the context, such as *clean, spotless, pure, untarnished, unsullied, unstained; blond, pale; pretty, lovely; polite, gracious.*

The word's dual nature, encompassing both beauty and goodness, appears to reflect the Latin adjective *pulcher* or the Greek καλός καί αγαθός, where beauty is intrinsically linked to moral and ethical goodness and happiness. This presents a challenge in defining the true nature of the word, not least in a specialized field such as accounting.

Contemporary dictionaries of legal and financial terms describe the adjective *fair* in accounting without reference to its ethical origin. The following terms are used in this regard:

1 *Fair market value.* What a qualified buyer will pay for goods, services, or property (Scott 1997: 140).
2 *Fair presentation.* The IFRS and US regulations require that financial statements be presented in a non-misleading manner. In the US, financial statements that are fully audited and prepared in accordance with Generally Accepted Accounting Principles (GAAP) must *fairly present* the position and results of a company. To a great extent, this involves following GAAP regulations. However, the notion of impartiality may go beyond that to encompass an evaluation of the complete picture presented by the financial statements. In non-US contexts, the phrase *true and fair view* may have a comparable meaning. A related principle is that financial statements should reflect the substance of transactions rather than just their form (Nobes and Parker 1988/89: 134).
3 *Fair price amendment.* A provision in a company's statute that prevents an acquiring company or investor from offering different prices for the shares held by different shareholders during a takeover attempt. This amendment aims to deter takeover attempts by increasing their cost (Scott 1997: 141).
4 *Fair trade.* Fair trade is a term used by social justice, peace, ecology, and Green Movement groups to contrast with "unfair" trade practices, and sometimes with free trade as promoted by the World Trade Organization and by the North American Free Trade Agreement. The term is also used to refer to corporate governance and reforming anti-competitive trade principles (Mohan 2010).
5 *Fair value.* Fair value is the amount at which an asset could be exchanged or a liability settled between knowledgeable and willing parties at arm's length. It is different from *net realizable* value as it does not include any selling costs. Nowadays, investments and other assets with an observable fair value are commonly valued at fair value. In a business combination accounted for as an acquisition, the assets and liabilities of the new subsidiary are brought into the consolidated financial statement at their fair values, rather than their previous book values. In this context, fair value typically refers to *current replacement costs* (Nobes and Parker 1988/89: 134–135).
6 *True and fair view.* The presentation of financial statements for companies in the UK, the rest of the EU, and most of the Commonwealth is subject to overriding legal requirements. The exact meaning of this expression is difficult to determine and would ultimately have to be

interpreted in a court of law. However, most laws require *a* true and fair view, rather than *the* true and fair view. Therefore, it is obvious that the instruction must be interpreted in the context of normal accounting practice at the time of the financial statements. One interpretation of the phrase could be that it means "in accordance with the facts, and not misleading". The requirement under IFRS to show a fair presentation can be seen as equivalent (Nobes and Parker 1988/89: 299).

15.4 "Fair" and "True": The Hendiadys Was Born

One of the earliest meanings of the word *fair*, recorded in *The Oxford English Dictionary*,[4] is *beautiful to the eye; of pleasing form and appearance; good looking*. However, according to the dictionary, this meaning is "no longer in colloquial use; very common in literature, but somewhat archaic or rhetorical". Based on these premises, *fair* was interpreted as aesthetically or culturally desirable and referred to:

a people, referring mainly to the face and mostly used to describe women,
b personified abstractions, as in *fair rhetoric, fair science, fair freedom*, and
c inanimate things.

In English literature, the concept of beauty and elegance conveyed by the word *fair* was enriched by the addition of *true* through the Shakespearean hendiadys *fair and true*. This phrase was first used in 1596 in the "Merchant of Venice", Act II, Scene VI, where Lorenzo declares his love for Jessica, stating that he will love her in his "constant soul" because she is *wise, fair, and true*. This is the passage we are considering in our research:

> Beshrew me but I love her heartily;
> For she is wise, if I can judge of her,
> And fair she is, if that mine eyes be true,
> And true she is, as she hath proved herself,
> And therefore, like herself, *wise, fair and true*
> Shall she be placed in my constant soul.
>
> (Shakespeare, *The Merchant of Venice, II, vi.* Our italics)[5]

In this context, the second adjective reinforces the first, following a common tradition in Shakespearean literature. Following Wright (1981: 190–191),

> We frequently join adjectives on the pattern of *nice and warm, good and loud, big and fat, sick and tired, long and leggy*. Each of these pairs

> represents a single concept in which the general idea contained in the first adjective is explained or specified or opened up by the second; and, insofar as such expressions may be continually invented, the pattern seems the closest thing to adjectival *hendiadys* in English. Formulaic phrases such as *nice and* and *good and* may be completed by virtually any adjective (or at least any pithy one) in the language (Willis 1997). Being formulaic, however, they lack the elements of surprise, or improvisation, and of eccentric coordination that we find in classical hendiadys (Van Lancker-Sidtis and Rallon 2004).

The two words *fair and true* are turned into the well-known order *true and fair*, only for rhythmical reasons, in *The Holy Sonnets* by John Donne (Gardner 1965: 29).

> If thou best borne to strange sights,
> Things invisible to see...
> And sweare
> No where
> Lives a woman *true, and faire.*

This is one of the most celebrated early poems composed by John Donne dealing with female nature. The poem "Song: Go, and Catch a Falling Star" describes the metaphysical conceit of the unnaturally small number of beautiful and virtuous women in the world. Drawing on the fantastic and impossible examples of catching falling stars, the poet described how difficult it is to find a beautiful woman who will remain true and faithful to her husband.

In the following century, the expression was no longer used for mere physical description. On the contrary, from the 18th century on it was associated with the word *statement* to describe someone's way of thinking, as in Boswell's writings (1763, in Wilson Crocker 1832: 356):

> Here it is proper, once for all, to give a *true and fair* statement of Johnson's way of thinking upon the question, whether departed spirits are ever permitted to appear in this world, or in any way to operate upon human life.

From the 18th century onwards, there was a shift from the physical to the moral and ethical context of usage. It was from this century that the moral value of the hendiadys was established and given a legal foundation.

15.5 Hendiadys or Tautology?

The most obvious first consideration about the phrase *true and fair* seems to be that it should be seen as having a different meaning from that suggested by the two words taken in isolation. As a result, as McDonald et al. (2003: 44) put it:

> the NCSC (*The National Companies and Securities Commission)* in a green paper published in 1984 acknowledged the strength of the argument in favour of treating the words "true and fair" as a hendiadys.

Hendiadys refers to the expression of an idea using two nouns connected by *and* instead of a noun and its qualifier (Lanham 1991, s.v. *hendiadys*): for instance, "by length of time and siege" is the hendiadys of "by a long siege". Further examples:

> *He came despite the rain and weather.* Instead of "He came despite the rainy weather".
>
> *The distinction and presence of the dignitary moved his audience.* By separating the term "distinctive presence" into "distinction and presence", the speaker accentuates the adjective by transforming it into a noun. Were the separation not made, the modifier would be combined with its object and lose some of its potency.
>
> (Source: http://rhetoric.byu.edu/Figures/H/hendiadys.htm)

In law, the concept of "just and equitable", which has been generally interpreted as denoting a single concept, is also an example of hendiadys. Following Callaway (1978: 44),

> The expression "just and equitable" may be regarded as an example of a statutory hendiadys, the reference to equity being not by way of an additional test but for the purpose of ensuring that the justice to be applied will be equitable justice. Accordingly, justice and equity are referred to herein as one criterion, not two criteria.

Contemporary studies on *true and fair view* confirm this attitude towards considering the two words as an only concept. Parker et al. (1996: 57) refer to it as *the true and fair hendiadys*, and so does Bennion (2001: 210), who lists the couple "true and fair" as an example of typical hendiadys in statutes.

The two words are no longer considered distinct concepts, nor are they a form of tautology, which is a needless repetition of the same idea in different words (pleonasm). Instead, in accordance with the etymology of the word hendiadys, the couple "true and fair" is a single concept through two words, so that it becomes an authentic figure of speech, also called a figure of twins. Higson and Blake (1993: 104) define the concept of "true and fair view" as a formula. However, they argue that it is an inappropriate basis for international accounting harmonization due to its strong ambiguity and cultural dependence, which can lead to international disharmony. The formulaic component of the expression must, therefore, be recognized. From the linguistic perspective, the knowledge of formulas, better known as lexical phrases or idioms (Ashby 2006; Kavka and Zibert 2004; Kuiper 2000), is central to the communicative competence of any language user, even more so in specialized contexts of use. In a wider context, Widdowson (1989: 135) argues that

> communicative competence is not a matter of knowing rules for the composition of sentences. It is much more a matter of knowing a stock of partially pre-assembled patterns, *formulaic frameworks*, and a kit of rules, so to speak, and being able to apply the rules to make whatever adjustments are necessary according to contextual demands. Communicative competence in this view is essentially a matter of adaptation, and rules are not generative but regulative and subservient.

It appears that the complexity of financial discourse is not primarily due to sentence structure but rather to the complex phrases within sentences. Many of these phrases are recurrent and predictable, such as *true and fair*. Therefore, when interpreting and translating legal and financial texts, it is important to carefully consider these recurring phrases, also known as "the idiom principle", as identified by Sinclair (1991). Speech genres are believed to consist of situations that require the use of formulaic language, which contains fixed expressions on its content level. These expressions have unique meanings and restrict the selection of possible meanings for a given polysemous dictionary entry. Moreover, they are stable because there is a high probability that one constituent predicts the appearance of another related constituent, as is the case with *true* and *fair.*

15.6 Conclusions

The expression *true and fair* originated and developed within the British literary and legal/financial context. Its definition became problematic once it was adopted outside the Anglo-Saxon context for interpretative reasons.

Fairness in Great Britain has traditionally been defined as honesty, equity, and reasonableness (Crabb 1826: 532). Similarly, truth has always been understood as a synonym for honesty, sincerity, and simplicity (Crabb 1826:

535). These two concepts are inseparable and represent the British notion of justice and equity. Although the use of such terms has posed some rhetorical challenges, as anticipated at the beginning of this paper, history shows that ultimately the phrase has been restricted by its statutory context and purpose. In other words, the phrase has a clear and consistent meaning that does not rely on subjective or unregulated discretion.

The translation of these two words has resulted in a variety of choices, when viewed beyond the Anglo-Saxon context. Over the decades, international accounting standards have raised a number of important terminological translation issues, as well as wide-ranging debates about the translator's intercultural skills in accounting and law, and have brought to the fore what is at the heart of the problem par excellence: variation in the conceptual frame of reference (Maldussi 2009). Due to the significance of accounting in shaping a company's relationship with its investors, it is essential for accounting translations to be objective, clear, and accurate. This implies a high level of responsibility and attention to detail, particularly in press releases, investor relations, and financial reports (Giordano 2022). It is essential to maintain a formal and balanced tone, avoid biased or emotional language, and use precise technical vocabulary where appropriate. Translation, as a mediation tool, is expected to assist financial statement drafters in producing summary documents that comply with the regulations, while at the same time preventing them from introducing dangerous and misleading semantic interpretations. In this regard, Articles 9 and 10 of the *Vademecum for users of legal translations* issued by the European Legal Interpreters and Translators Association (AISBL, https://www.eulita.eu/en/) state that:

> (9) The legal systems of EU member states are very different. There is therefore never full concordance of legal concepts. Legal Translators are aware of these differences and should therefore be free to take account of this fact and provide readers with terminological comments, if necessary.
> (10) The authors of legal texts that are eventually translated should be aware of the fact that the legal systems of other countries are different from their own system and therefore use straightforward language that will enable translators and readers to more readily understand the text.
> (EULITA 2014)

To put it another way, it is crucial for common words to be approached and treated as "technical terms" as soon as they shift from common to specialized usage. Terms follow the same formation processes as natural language. The more they are used for scientific and professional purposes, the clearer and more precise they are required to be, and the more they need to be fully integrated into the language system. Their form does not change, but their meaning does, especially if they are combined with other pre-existing terminological units. This is the case of the phrase *true and fair*, which originated in the original English version of the Bible, was later adopted by Shakespeare, and eventually entered the accounting context as a formula of legal significance. The phrase has a long history of use in British literary contexts. However, recent studies on semantic change (Sandow et al. 2024) reveal that the phrase has undergone transformation and adaptation from English common usage to an internationally specialized one. Over the centuries, the polysemous meanings of the two separate adjectives have merged into the monosemantic character of the hendiadys, based on established statutory, legal, and equitable principles.

Nowadays, understanding the hendiadys "true and fair" is essential for selecting the most suitable equivalent in translation. The translation of specialized texts must be faithful to the meaning, terminology, and stylistic, cultural, and scientific specificities of the fields concerned. This contribution provides only an example of the terminological disputes that can arise from the complex combination of skills and knowledge inherent in any text having legal value. Dictionaries and glossaries may be useful, but only a thorough analysis of the context of use can ensure the effectiveness and efficiency of the resulting text.

Notes

1 The selection is based on *Collins English Dictionary – Complete & Unabridged Edition*, at https://www.collinsdictionary.com/dictionary/english/fair; *Oxford English Dictionary (Online)* at https://www.oed.com/search/dictionary/?scope=Entries&q=fair.
2 The selection is based on the following online dictionaries: *Dictionary.com Unabridged*, at http://www.dictionary.com/browse/fair; *Collins English Dictionary – Complete & Unabridged 10th Edition*, at https://www.collinsdictionary.com/dictionary/english/fair; *Online Etymology Dictionary* https://www.etymonline.com/search?q=fair; *Oxford English Dictionary (Online)* at https://www.oed.com/search/dictionary/?scope=Entries&q=fair.
3 *Merriam-Webster's Dictionary of Law*, at https://www.merriam-webster.com/dictionary/fair.
4 *Oxford English Dictionary (Online)*, at https://www.oed.com/search/dictionary/?scope=Entries&q=fair.
5 Quoted in Zanola (2015: 4).

References

Alexander, David and Simon Archer. 2000. "On the Myth of 'Anglo-Saxon' Financial Accounting." *The International Journal of Accounting* 35, no. 4: 539–557. https://doi.org/10.1016/S0020-7063(00)00078-9.

Ashby, Michael. 2006. "Prosody and Idioms in English." *Journal of Pragmatics* 32, no 10: 1580–1597. https://doi.org/10.1016/j.pragma.2005.03.018.
Bennion, Francis. 2001. *Understanding Common Law Legislation: Drafting and Interpretation*. Oxford: Oxford University Press.
Bhatia, Vijay. 1997. "Translating Legal Genres." In *Text Typology and Translation*, edited by Anna Trosborg, 203–221. Amsterdam and Philadelphia: John Benjamins. https://doi.org/10.1075/btl.26.15bha.
Brockington, Raymond. 1996. *Accounting for Intangible Assets: A New Perspective on the True and Fair View*. Wokingham: Addison-Wesley.
Callaway, Frank Hortin. 1978. *Winding up on the Just and Equitable Ground*. Sidney: Law Book Company.
Canziani, Arnaldo. 1993. "Group Accounting in Italy." In *International Group Accounting: Issues in European Harmonization*, edited by S. J. Gray, Adolf Gerhard Coenenberg, and Paul D. Gordon, 152–169. London: Routledge.
Chastney, John. 1975. *True and fair view: a study of the history and meaning of true and fair and a consideration of the impact of the fourth directive: a report prepared for the Research Committee of the Institute of Chartered Accountants in England and Wales*. Research Committee Occasional Paper, 6. London: ICAEW.
Corbett, Charlie. 2019. *The Art of Plain Speaking: How to Write and Speak in a Way that Will Impress the People that Matter*. London and New York: Routledge.
Crabb, George. 1826. *English Synonyms, with Copious Illustrations and Explanations*. London: Baldwin.
De Mauro, Tullio. 2000. "Introduzione". In *Grande Dizionario Italiano dell'uso (GRADIT 1999–2007)*, 1: VII–XLII, Torino: UTET.
De Saussure, Ferdinand. 1922. *Cours de linguistique générale*. Paris: Payot.
Durant, Alan and Janny H. C. Leung. 2016. *Language and Law: A Resource Book for Students*. London and New York: Routledge.
EULITA. 2014. *Vademecum for Users of Legal Translations*. QUALETRA-Vademecum_final: https://eulita.eu/wp-content/uploads/files/QUALETRA-Vademecum_final_0.pdf
Financial Reporting Council (FRC). 2014. *True and Fair*. London: The Financial Reporting Council.
Flint, David. 1982. *A True and Fair View in Company Accounts*. London and Reading: Gee & Co.
Friedrich, Patricia and Francisco Gomes de Matos. 2016. "Toward a Nonkilling Linguistics." In *English for Diplomatic Purposes*, edited by Patricia Friedrich, 1–19. Bristol: Multilingual Matters.
Gadbin-George, Géraldine, Anne Brunon-Ernst, Armelle Sabatier, Suhasini Vincent, and Justin Beplate. 2014. *Glossaire de droit anglais, méthode, traduction et approche comparative*. Paris: Dalloz.
Garner, Bryan A. 2001. *Legal Writing in Plain English: A Text with Exercises*. Chicago and London: The University of Chicago Press.
Garner, Bryan A. 2002. *The Elements of Legal Style*, 2nd ed. Oxford: Oxford University Press.
Garner, Bryan A. 2004. *The Winning Brief: 100 Tips for Persuasive Briefing in Trial and Appellate Courts*. Oxford: Oxford University Press.

Gardner, Helen (ed.). 1965. *The Elegies and the Songs and Sonnets of John Donne.* Oxford: Oxford at the Clarendon Press.
Giordano, Walter. 2022. "Translating Financial Statements from Italian into English: Strategies, Issues and Semantic Aspects". *Lingue e Linguaggi* 52: 111–136. https://doi.org/10.1285/i22390359v52p111.
Gray, Sidney J., Adolf Gerhard Coenenberg, and Paul D. Gordon (eds.). 1993. *International Group Accounting: Issues in European Harmonization.* London: Routledge.
Harris, N. G. E. 1987. "Fairness in Financial Reporting." *Journal of Applied Philosophy* 4, no 1: 77–88. https://doi.org/10.1111/j.1468-5930.1987.tb00205.x.
Hellmann, Andreas. 2016. "The Role of Accounting in Behavioral Finance". *Journal of Behavioral and Experimental Finance* 9: 39–42. https://doi.org/10.1016/j.jbef.2015.11.004.
Hellmann, Andreas and Chris Patel. 2021. "Translation of International Financial Reporting Standards and Implications for Judgments and Decision-making". *Journal of Behavioral and Experimental Finance* 30: 1–4. https://doi.org/10.1016/j.jbef.2021.100479.
Higson, Andrew and John Blake. 1993. "The True and Fair View Concept – A Formula for International Disharmony: Some Empirical Evidence." *The International Journal of Accounting* 28: 104–115. https://doi.org/10.1080/09638180902784405.
Houghton, Keith A. 1987. "True and Fair View: An Empirical Study of Connotative Meaning." *Accounting, Organizations and Society* 12, no 2: 143–152. https://doi.org/10.1016/0361-3682(87)90003-1.
IFRS Foundation. 2024a. *IFRS – The Use of IFRS Accounting Standards around the World.* Retrieved from: https://www.ifrs.org/use-around-the-world/ (Accessed 11 February 2024).
IFRS Foundation. 2024b. *IFRS Translations.* Retrieved from: https://www.ifrs.org/issued-standards/ifrs-translations/#other-available-translations (Accessed 11 February 2024).
Incollingo, Alberto. 1999. *L'applicazione del principio di "True and Fair View" nel bilancio di esercizio. L'impatto sull'informazione societaria nei principali paesi europei.* Milan: Giuffré.
Karan, Ram. 2002. *Irreconcilable Legal and Accounting Views of 'A True and Fair View': An Emerging Alternative from Australian Reforms.* Victoria (Australia): University of Ballarat. https://www.austlii.edu.au/au/journals/JlLawFinMgmt/2002/5.html.
Kavka, Stanislav and Jerzy Zibert. 2004. "Glympses on the History of Idiomaticity Issues." *Skase Journal of Theoretical Linguistics* 1, no 1: 54–66. http://www.skase.sk/Volumes/JTL01/kavka.pdf.
Kirk, Ngaire. 2001. *'True and Fair View' Versus 'Present Fairly in Conformity with Generally Accepted Accounting Principles'.* Discussion Paper Series 208. Palmerston North (New Zealand): Massey University.
Kirk, Ngaire. 2006. "Perceptions of the True and Fair View Concept: An Empirical Investigation." *Abacus* 2: 205–235. https://doi.org/10.1111/j.1467-6281.2006.00198.x.
Kischel, Uwe. 2009. "Legal Cultures – Legal Languages." In *Translation Issues in Language and Law,* edited by Frances Olsen, Alexander Lorz, and Dieter Stein, 7–17. London: Palgrave/Macmillan.

Kuiper, Koenraad. 2000. "On the Linguistic Properties of Formulaic Speech." *Oral Tradition* 15, no 2: 279–305. https://hdl.handle.net/10355/64812.

Lanham, Richard. 1991. *A Handlist of Rhetorical Terms.* Stanford: University of California Press.

Maldussi, Danio. 2009. "I concetti di *fair value* e *costo storico* nel diritto contabile francese e italiano: riorganizzazione concettuale, implicazioni semantiche e problematiche traduttivo-terminologiche." *mediAzioni* 7: 1–33. https://mediazioni.sitlec.unibo.it.

McDonald, Laurie, Grant Moodie, Ian Ramsay, and Jon Webster. 2003. *Experts' Reports in Corporate Transactions.* Sidney: The Federation Press.

Mohan, Sushil. 2010. *Fair Trade Without the Froth – a Dispassionate Economic Analysis of 'Fair Trade'.* London: Institute of Economic Affairs. https://ssrn.com/abstract=3922149 or https://doi.org/10.2139/ssrn.3922149.

Monteleone, Mario. 2023. "The Terminological Tagging of the NooJ Italian Compound Word Dictionary". *Aprendo con NooJ* 3. https://doi.org/10.35305/an.vi3.20.

Nobes, Christopher. 2021. "On Translating Goodwill." *Accounting in Europe* 18, no 3: 407–418. https://doi.org/10.1080/17449480.2021.1952284.

Nobes, Christopher and Robert Henry Parker. 1988/89. "'True and Fair': A Survey of UK Financial Directors." In *Discussion Papers in Accounting and Finance (Series D, vol. 1. Reading: University of Reading - Department of Economics). Truth in Accounting: The Ordeal of Kenneth Macneal*, edited by Stephen A. Zeff, 359–375. Houston: Rice University. https://doi.org/10.1111/j.1468-5957.1991.tb00600.x.

Nuccorini, Stefania. 2007. "Italian Phraseology." In *Ein internationales Handbuch der zeitgenössischen Forschung*, edited by Harald Burger, Dmitrij Dobrovol'skij, Peter Kühn, and Neal R. Norrick, 691–703. Berlin/New York: De Gruyter Mouton. https://doi.org/10.1515/9783110190762.691.

Olsen, Frances, Alexander Lorz, and Dieter Stein. 2009. *Translation Issues in Language and Law.* London: Palgrave/Macmillan.

Pan, Peipei and Chris Patel. 2018. "The Influence of Native Versus Foreign Language on Chinese Subjects' Aggressive Financial Reporting Judgments". *Journal of Business Ethics* 150: 863–878. https://doi.org/10.1007/s10551-016-3165-z.

Parker, Robert Henry. 1994. "Finding English Words to Talk about Accounting Concepts." *Accounting, Auditing & Accountability Journal* 7, no. 2: 70–85. https://doi.org/10.1108/09513579410058193.

Parker, Robert Henry, C. W. Wolnizer, and Christopher Nobes. 1996. *Readings in True and Fair.* New York: Garland Pub.

Piotti, Sonia Rachele. 2009. *Exploring Corporate Rhetoric in English: Hedging in Company Annual Reports. A Corpus-assisted Analysis.* Milan: EDUCatt. https://hdl.handle.net/10807/36096.

Prieto Ramos, Fernando. 2021. "Translating Legal Terminology and Phraseology: Between Inter-systemic Incongruity and Multilingual Harmonization". *Perspectives* 29, no 2: 175–183. https://doi.org/10.1080/0907676X.2021.1849940.

Rock, Frances, Chris Heffer, and John Conley. 2013. "Textual Travel in Legal-Lay Communication". In *Legal-Lay Communication: Textual Travels in the Law*, edited by Chris Heffer, Frances Rock, and John Conley, 3–32. New York-Oxford: Oxford University Press.

Ryan, F. J. O. 1967. "A True and Fair View." *Abacus* 3, no 2: 95–108. https://doi.org/10.1111/j.1467-6281.1967.tb00374.x.

Sandow, Rhys J., George Bailey, and Natalie Braber. 2024. "Language Change Is 'Wicked': Semantic and Social Meaning of a Polysemous Adjective." *English Language and Linguistics* 28, no 1: 135–156. https://doi.org/10.1017/S1360674323000515.

Scott, David Logan. 1997. *Wall Street Words. An Essential A to Z Guide for Today's Investor*. Boston/New York: Houghton Mifflin.

Sinclair, John. 1991. *Corpus, Concordance, Collocation*. Oxford: Oxford University Press.

Söderblom, Tryggve. 2009. "Language as a Barrier for Accounting Harmonization in Europe." In *Interne Kommunikation von Unternehmen, 2. Auflage Psychologische, kommunicationswissenschaftliche und kulturvergleichende Studien*, edited by Rogier Crijns and Nina Janich, 171–202. Berlin: VS Verlag.

Soriano Barabino, Guadalupe. 2020. "Cultural, Textual and Linguistic Aspects of Legal Translation: A Model of Text Analysis for Training Legal Translators." *International Journal of Legal Discourse* 5, no. 2: 285–300. https://doi.org/10.1515/ijld-2020-2037.

Stewart, Ian C. 1998. "The Explication of the True and Fair View Doctrine: A Comment." *Journal of Business Finance & Accounting* 15, no 1: 116–127. https://doi.org/10.1111/j.1468-5957.1988.tb00124.x.

Tessuto, Girolamo. 2023. "Introduction." In *Professional Discourse across Medicine, Law, and Other Disciplines: Issues and Perspectives*, edited by Girolamo Tessuto, Richard Ashcroft, and Vijay K. Bhatia, xiii–xxxiv. Newcastle upon Tyne: Cambridge Scholars Publishing.

Van Hulle, Karel. 1993. "Truth and Untruth about True and Fair: A Commentary on 'A European True and Fair View' Comment." *European Accounting Review* 2, no 1: 99–104. https://doi.org/10.1080/09638189300000008.

Van Lancker-Sidtis, Diana and Gail Rallon. 2004. "Tracking the Incidence of Formulaic Expressions in Everyday Speech: Methods for Classification and Verification." *Language and Communication* 24, no 3: 207–240. https://doi.org/10.1016/j.langcom.2004.02.003.

Walton, Peter. 1993. "Introduction: The True and Fair View in British Accounting." *European Accounting Review* 2, no 1: 49–58. https://doi.org/10.1080/09638189300000003.

Widdowson, Henry G. 1989. "Knowledge of Language and Ability for Use." *Applied Linguistics* 10: 128–137. https://doi.org/10.1093/applin/10.2.128.

Willis, Dave. 1997. Lexical Phrases in Syllabus and Materials Designs. *The Language Teacher (online)* 21, no. 9. https://www.jalt-publications.org/tlt/files/97/sep/willis.html.

Wilson Croker, John (ed.). 1832. *The Life of Samuel Johnson, Including a Journal of a Tour of the Hebrides (1763)*. Boston: Carter, Handel & Co.

Wright, George T. 1981. "Hendiadys and Hamlet." *PMLA* 96, no. 2: 168–193. https://doi.org/10.2307/461987.

Zanola, Annalisa. 2014. "Linguistic and Cross-Cultural Complexities of a Specialized Legal Item: The 'True and Fair' Case." *Journal of Arts and Humanities* 3, no 1: 110–125.

Zanola, Annalisa. 2015. "True and Fair: A Truly Fair Hendiadys or a Fairly True Tautology? Considerations on a Specialized Formulaic Item." *Iperstoria – Testi Letterature Linguaggi* 5 (Spring): 1–15. https://doi.org/10.13136/2281-4582/2015.i5.265.

Zanola, Annalisa. 2023. *La lingua inglese per la comunicazione scientifica e professionale*. Rome: Carocci.

Zanola, Maria Teresa. 2018. *Che cos'è la terminologia*. Rome: Carocci.

16 Drafting EU Soft Law Instruments as Persuasive Governance Tools

Corina Andone and Florin Coman-Kund

16.1 Introduction

Recommendations, opinions, communications, notices, guidelines, codes of conduct, resolutions, conclusions, press releases, statements, memoranda, white papers, green papers and non-papers are some of the numerous apparently non-binding legal instruments that have been enacted in the past decades at an extraordinary pace by EU institutions, agencies and bodies. They feature varying aims, functions, structures and practical, as well as arguably possible legal effects, depending on the policy area in which they are enacted, the relevant legal framework and the institutional practice within which they operate. Praised and much criticized at the same time, few legal instruments are as heterogeneous as these non-binding instruments commonly referred to as 'soft law instruments.'

The alleged blurred legal nature of these instruments has prompted us before to propose a new legal-argumentative perspective to address the many challenges and problems they raise (Coman-Kund and Andone 2019; Andone and Coman-Kund 2022, 2023). We have maintained that these instruments need to be strictly construed as legally non-binding, but in practice potentially effective instruments not least due to their persuasive force (Andone and Coman-Kund 2022, 2023). By conceiving these governance tools as non-binding argumentative instruments, we argued that their added value and effectiveness should not so much depend on their alleged ambiguous status in-between binding and non-binding instruments. In our view, they should be mainly judged on their persuasive power to convince addressees to adopt the desired course of action. Our legal-argumentative framework has been designed with a view to reinterpreting and reassessing EU soft law instruments in a way that finds solid grounding in the Union's legal framework and jurisprudence (Andone and Coman-Kund 2022). At the same time, it allows us to assess and improve the intrinsic quality and design of these EU governance tools in order to

DOI: 10.4324/9781003430308-20

ensure their effectiveness. It is with this last idea in mind that in this chapter we propose to tackle the drafting of EU soft law instruments.

The drafting of EU soft law instruments has not attracted significant attention so far, despite their common usage and influence in a wide area of policies and despite a core preoccupation with the quality of EU legal acts in general, most prominently in the context of the 'better lawmaking' initiatives (cf. SWD (2017) 350 final; SWD (2021) 305 final). The many drafting manuals (cf. European Commission 1997, 2015, 2022, Interinstitutional style guide 2022, European Parliament, Council of the European Union, European Commission, 1998, 2018, OJ L 2016) hardly ever mention these non-binding instruments, if at all. The Court of Justice of the European Union (CJEU) referred previously in its jurisprudence to the formal (drafting) quality of non-binding acts in close relationship with their substantive quality (see in particular Case C-322/88 *Grimaldi* para. 14, Case 22/70 *ERTA* para. 42, Case C-16/16P *Belgium v Commission* paras. 28–31). Yet so far the need for clearer, simpler and more accessible non-binding legal acts remains an ideal that is still to be fulfilled.

The added value of our enterprise lies in its focus on identifying, defining and operationalizing clear drafting criteria and guidelines for the creation and evaluation of these instruments, emphasizing their persuasive force, distinctively from legally binding acts. This chapter highlights the unique attributes of EU soft law instruments as persuasive governance tools (Section 16.2) before discussing the need to pay increased attention to a proper drafting of these instruments and the challenges this entails (Section 16.3). Next, concrete guidelines for a proper drafting of EU soft law instruments are put forward against the background of several argumentative and legal parameters used to assess the persuasive force of these governance tools (Section 16.4). Section 16.5 concludes our study.

16.2 Persuasive EU Non-Binding Legal Acts

For more than a decade, scholars in the legal field have both acclaimed and heavily denounced EU soft law instruments. The supporters of soft law (among others, Abbott and Snidal 2000; Scott and Trubek 2002; Trubek and Trubek 2005; Schäfer 2006; di Robilant 2013) underlined the instruments' flexibility and adaptability and particularly their capacity to enable effective cooperation between various actors, especially when their values and interests differ significantly. The critics of soft law (among others, Klabbers 1996, 1998; Andone and Coman-Kund 2022, 2023; Láncos 2019; Stefan 2020; Eliantino, Korkea-Aho and Stefan 2021) emphasized the instruments' legal fuzziness, bringing about potential confusion, uncertainty and adverse legal and practical consequences. In this respect, the unexpected 'hard' legal effects that these instruments may arguably entail affect the very principles of legality, legal certainty, institutional balance and distribution of powers between EU institutions and also the limits set on the scope and exercise of EU competences. As we explained before, 'the very effectiveness, legality and legitimacy of EU action' come under threat (Andone and Coman-Kund 2022, 28).

While we may easily conclude from the extensive existent literature that soft law is a contested category (cf. Stefan 2013), EU practice repeatedly demonstrated in the last years a clear preference for such instruments. There are more than 25 different types/labels (see Cappellina et al. 2022) used to refer to such instruments, only a few of which are formally enshrined in the EU Founding Treaties. To be sure, however, while instruments such as recommendations and opinions (Article 288 TFEU), guidelines (e.g. Article 148 (2) TFEU), conclusions (e.g., Articles 121 (2) and 148 (1) TFEU) and interinstitutional agreements (Article 295 TFEU) are explicitly mentioned in the EU Founding Treaties, the very concept of 'soft law' is not. Nor is it ever used as such in CJEU jurisprudence (cf. Andone and Coman-Kund 2023, 149–155). Instead, EU Courts continue to rely on the dichotomy between binding and non-binding legal acts, and consideration is given as to whether these acts are intended to produce genuine legal effects or not (see Case 22/70 *ERTA* para. 42). An instrument such as a recommendation, opinion, communication or any other such act is assessed as a genuine legally binding or non-binding act (e.g., Case C-16/16P *Belgium v Commission* paras. 28–30) but not as an 'in-between' category as proposed by some (cf. Terpan 2015).

This fundamental feature does not imply, however, that despite their legally non-binding nature, these instruments are not legal acts. On the contrary, they are legal acts through which EU institutions exercise their competences, and they are subject to the confines of the EU constitutional framework and potentially effective in practice (see Senden 2004, 482–501). This last feature is not problematic as long as such legal instruments entail 'purely *de facto* effects' (Senden 2004, 269) and voluntary compliance (Andone and Coman-Kund 2023, 153); i.e., there is no (overt) obligation to comply with them neither by the addressees nor by the courts.

Similarly to Snyder's (1993) definition of soft law, we see these instruments, as 'legally non-binding norms which may entail effects in practice' (Andone and Coman-Kund 2023, 148). We argue for conceiving of EU soft law instruments as legally non-binding acts, but we view their power to persuade as a distinctive feature and as key to their effectiveness. This idea aligns with CJEU's stance according to which 'Article 288 TFEU intended to confer on the institutions which usually adopt recommendations *a power to exhort and persuade* (our italics), distinct from the power to adopt acts having binding force' (Case C-16/16P *Belgium v Commission* para. 26). The CJEU further confirmed this approach with regard to the recommendations and guidelines of the European Banking Authority (see Case C-501/18 *BT v Balgarska Narodna Banka* para. 79 and Case C-911/19 *FBF v ACPR* para. 48). We maintain that such a stance holds, beyond the specific category of recommendations and guidelines, for EU soft law instruments in general (Andone and Coman-Kund 2023, 155). We prefer to use the term 'soft law,' instead of 'legally non-binding instrument' or 'non-binding act' because of its richer descriptive and analytical value, capturing the normative richness of such tools as a matter of voluntary compliance and de facto effectiveness.

The idea that EU soft law instruments are non-binding but persuasive prompts us to underline that they 'need to be clearer and more convincing about their intended effects as a way to foster [voluntary] compliance' (Andone and Coman-Kund 2022, 31). To do so, 'the duty to state reasons' as a legal parameter is notably pertinent. As enshrined in Article 296 (2) TFEU: 'Legal acts shall state the reasons on which they are based.' Upon closer reading, this provision covers both legally binding and legally non-binding acts, at least the recommendations and opinions formally enshrined in Article 288 TFEU. The legal parameters for assessing compliance with the duty to state reasons enshrined in the EU Founding Treaties were shaped and applied mainly by the CJEU in a varying though overall restricted fashion (limited to CJEU's judicial review function, see Mendes 2020).[1]

Yet the criteria and intensity of the duty to state reasons with regard to soft law acts remain rather obscure in current legal scholarship and practice, not least probably also because of the rather limited possibilities for judicial review of such instruments (see Andone and Coman-Kund 2023, 157). We suggested more concretely that under Article 296 (2) TFEU, EU soft law instruments in general, just like any EU legal act, need to provide clear, appropriate and sufficient reasons and explanations regarding the selected legal basis, the legal-factual background prompting the adoption of the instrument, including the scrutiny of the subsidiarity and proportionality principles, and not least, the intended aims of the instrument (Andone and Coman-Kund 2023, 157). Moreover, we argued that precisely their specific nature as exhortative and persuasive legal instruments would justify observance of the higher rather than the lower denominator in terms of clarity, consistency and adequacy of the legal parameters of the duty to state reasons applied by CJEU (Andone and Coman-Kund 2023, 157). The concrete judicial review of EU soft law instruments' compliance with the legal parameters of the duty to state reasons, resulting eventually in a finding of a breach of an essential procedural requirement, remains knotty in view of the non-binding nature of these legal acts. Yet in the past the CJEU had, on very rare occasions, declared a non-binding opinion inexistent because of the lack of a statement of reasons, seen as an essential element of the act (see Joined Cases 1–57 and 14–57 *Société des usines à tubes de la Sarre v High Authority of the European Coal and Steel Community* para. 112) and is increasingly reviewing EU non-binding acts especially under Article 267 TFEU (e.g. Case C-322/88 *Grimaldi*, Case C-501/18 *BT v Balgarska Narodna Banka* para. 79 and Case C-911/19 *FBF v ACPR* para. 48).

Next, we maintain that, beyond its legal dimension engraved by the CJEU, the duty to state reasons, as a multifaceted procedural principle, has a richer content as a normative parameter or as a 'norm of conduct.' As such, it may guarantee, even outside the boundaries of judicial review, the good functioning of the EU administration, and it may prevent arbitrary use of public power (see Mendes 2020). The duty to state reasons is most relevant for increasing the quality and effectiveness of EU soft law instruments by enhancing understanding of the leading factors/causes, content and aims of the rules of conduct envisaged; by persuading addressees to follow them; and by improving their public acceptance. Hence the more comprehensive normative dimension of the duty to state reasons as a self-imposed norm of conduct on EU institutions and bodies, while constitutionally justified in view of the ongoing unprecedented concentration of executive powers at the EU level (Mendes 2020, 316–319), becomes particularly important for construing and assessing persuasive EU soft law tools. Understood in this way, the duty to state reasons is essential to bring to light the validity, soundness and completeness of the reasoning employed in these instruments. This is relevant not only to foster legality but also to obtain effectiveness, without ignoring the design and format of these instruments in a way that they are easily distinguishable from legally binding acts (see Andone and Coman-Kund 2023, 158).

Against this background, we have proposed a novel *legal-argumentative framework* serving three closely interrelated functions. In its *analytical function*, the framework offers the tools to understand and interpret EU soft law instruments in a 'closer-to-reality' fashion. It enables analyzing the extent to which persuasive justificatory reasons are employed in the instrument and whether its effectiveness (i.e., level of voluntary compliance) is likely to be affected. In its *evaluative function*, the framework enables the assessment of the clarity, sufficiency, consistency and soundness of the arguments employed by the enactor of the instrument with a view to establish whether and to what extent arguments fall short on these grounds. In its *practical/design function*, the framework serves to better draft EU soft law instruments in line with their non-binding legal nature and their argumentative style.

The proposed legal-argumentative framework outlined in the table below (taken from Andone and Coman-Kund 2023, 160) encompasses and links up two main components: (i) the legal dimension of the duty to state reasons and (ii) the more far-reaching normative dimension thereof, focusing on the persuasive quality of EU soft law instruments from an argumentative perspective. The first component includes the *legal parameters* pertaining to the duty to state reasons – i.e., legal basis, legal-factual background and aims of the instrument – assessed in light of the judicially forged criteria 'clarity,' 'consistency' and 'adequacy.' The second component includes four interconnected *argumentative parameters*. First, the *argumentative content* of EU soft law instruments should address the legal parameters of the duty to state reasons, as well as any other aspects that might foster voluntary compliance, and it should reflect the distinctive non-binding nature of the instrument. Second, we call for particular attention to be paid to the *argumentative design* of EU soft law instruments in such a way that their formally non-binding nature is matched by persuasive suggestions inviting addressees to follow a course of action. Third, we point out that the *argumentative effectiveness* of EU soft law instruments plays a significant role in fostering voluntary compliance in the absence of legal coercion. Finally, we emphasize that *argumentative soundness* is vital to obtain compliance with EU soft law instruments through valid (non-fallacious) reasoning. The framework connects the legal parameters of the duty to state reasons with the argumentative parameters by paying attention at the same time to the form and the substance of the instruments. It should be noted that the distinction between the four argumentative parameters is merely analytic. In practice, they go together and therefore entail some degree of overlap (Table 16.1).[2]

The legal and argumentative components of the framework, though conceptually and functionally delineated, are closely interlinked in a complementary and mutually reinforcing fashion. The legal parameters of the duty to state reasons guide and set the floor for the application of the argumentative parameters. This is done with a view to assessing and enhancing compliance of the instrument with the duty to state reasons, seen as a norm of control that ensures observance of the principle of legality (see on duty to state reasons as a norm of control, Mendes 2020). From this vantage point, arguments and reasoning judged as sound and effective from an argumentative perspective will likely increase the chances that the instrument meets the legal parameters of the duty to state reasons and legality requirements more broadly. Yet the argumentative parameters examined here go one step further. Meeting the more restricted legal parameters of the duty to state reasons (even through adequate, clear and consistent reasoning) does not guarantee per se that EU soft law instruments as legally non-binding acts will be effectively complied with by addressees in practice. Therefore, embedded within the broader normative dimension of the duty to state reasons, the argumentative parameters are intended to assess and enhance the persuasive intrinsic quality of EU soft law instruments beyond minimum legality requirements. This could arguably increase the

Table 16.1 Legal-Argumentative Framework

Form	
• Argumentative style • Non-binding/inviting language • Intertwining arguments with suggestive rules of conduct throughout the instrument	
Substance	
Legal parameters (duty to state reasons)	*Argumentative parameters* (normative dimension of duty to state reasons)
Legal basis ***Legal-factual background*** ***Aims of the instrument***	***Argumentative content*** Criteria/requirements • The arguments should reflect the specificities of the situation and the policy area. • The argumentative patterns should be distinguishable from their counterparts in legally binding instruments. • Arguments should be provided in support of the legal basis as well as the necessity and desirability for enacting the instrument. • Argumentation should as much as possible integrate relevant evidence and information.
abiding by standards of clarity consistency adequacy	***Argumentative design*** Criteria/requirements • Arguments should be designed to reflect consistency between their legally non-binding nature and their verbal presentation. • Arguments should feature non-binding formulations merely inviting addressees to adopt the proposed measures. • Arguments should be employed throughout the instrument. ***Argumentative effectiveness*** Criteria/requirements • Argumentation should be employed to increase the chances that the instruments are complied with in the absence of legal coercion. • Argument types should be adapted to the preferences and values of the addressees depending on the specific goal that is aimed to be achieved by means of the instrument and the relevant policy area. ***Argumentative soundness*** Criteria/requirements • Argumentation should be encompassing and complete by enabling the addressees to judge whether to accept or not accept the proposed measures. • Arguments should be reasonable, logically valid and accurately reflecting the objectives and legal nature of the instrument, as well as the legal-institutional-policy context within which the instrument is enacted. • Fallacious arguments should be avoided.

likelihood of voluntary compliance by addressees and improve overall public trust in such governance tools.

16.3 Current Drafting of EU Soft Law Instruments

16.3.1 The Importance of Good Drafting

The drafting quality of EU soft law instruments is of acute importance for at least three reasons. First, a well-drafted legal act enables identifying its genuine legal nature. CJEU commonly tries to determine the genuine legal nature of EU legal instruments by examining primarily the wording and substance of their provisions, which constitute two key drafting components (see Case C-16/16P *Belgium v Commission*, paras. 31–37, Opinion AG Bobek in Case C-16/16P *Belgium v Commission* para. 63, Case T-496/11 *United Kingdom v ECB* paras. 31–32, Case C-911/19 *FBF v ACPR* paras. 38–49). Admittedly, for a comprehensive assessment of the intention of the author of the act, the Court considers also contextual elements, such as the legal-policy framework to which the act belongs, the powers of the institution enacting the act, the publication of the legal instrument, among others. These other aspects play generally a confirmatory function for the interpretation based on wording and substance, depending on each case. As Lenaerts and Gutiérrez-Fons (2013, 7) maintain:

> where the wording of an EU law provision is clear and precise, its contextual [...] interpretation may not call into question the literal meaning of that provision, as this would run counter to the principle of legal certainty and to the principle of inter-institutional balance enshrined in Article 13(2) TEU. Stated simply, the ECJ [CJEU] will never ignore the clear and precise wording of an EU law provision.

Second, a well-drafted legal act enables smooth and quick compliance, making the application of provisions foreseeable. Currently, soft law instruments are enacted more than ever before, especially in crisis situations, with national authorities, businesses and citizens being requested to comply with them in the short term. In this context, the quality of the drafting of these instruments is essential to comply with the principles of legal certainty and legitimate expectations, as well as to enable the national authorities to adopt and implement domestic measures in an effective and timely manner. Very recently, the CJEU reconfirmed that 'the principle of legal certainty requires, on the one hand, that the rules of law be *clear and precise* and, on the other, that their *application* be *foreseeable* (our italics) for those subject to the law' and that '*inter alia* (...) legislation must enable those concerned to know precisely the extent of the obligations imposed on them, and those persons must be able to ascertain unequivocally their rights and obligations and take steps accordingly' (Case C-156/21 *Hungary v Parliament and Council* para. 223). These judicial standards were made in the context of the application and effects of legally binding acts, but, in our view, they are applicable, at least *qua* leading drafting criteria, to soft law instruments as well.

Third, a well-drafted non-binding legal act will contribute to enhancing its persuasive value with a view to convincing addressees and the public at large of the added value of complying with these instruments. In this sense, we agree with Xanthaki (2001, 652) when she points out that badly drafted legal acts lead to 'vague, conflicting, inaccurate provisions, [...] which damages the credibility of the EU legislature and wounds public support for the cause of European integration.'

16.3.2 EU Drafting Manuals

The numerous EU drafting manuals and guidelines we mentioned in the introduction are not particularly informative about the drafting of EU non-binding legal acts. At best, they make minor observations and sometimes hardly observable and inconsistent distinctions regarding soft law instruments. To start with, the form and content of EU non-binding instruments are extremely flexible and do not seem constrained by a consistent pre-determined format. As explained to us by Commission experts in 2019,[3] they are drafted by any of the Directorates General responsible for a particular policy area, and, sometimes, though not always, checked by the Legal Service of the Commission. The Commission's *Legislative Drafting Manual* confirms explicitly that 'the form of the non-binding legal acts [...] is not prescribed and can vary according to circumstances,' pointing at a barely observable feature that 'in non-binding acts [...], the basic unit is not the article but the point' (6.3.1 (c)). The *Joint Practical Guide for Persons Involved in the Drafting of European Union Legislation* (JPG) specifies that 'in non-binding acts, [...] a structure or presentation too close to that of a binding act, must not be used' (2.3.3). This guideline is, however, apparently contradicted by the *Legislative Drafting Manual* when it points out that 'recommendations and resolutions should, however, be drawn up in a form modelled on that of binding acts' (I(1)).

Apart from these formal aspects, the manuals touch very briefly on the specific wording of non-binding legal acts. Drafting guidelines are limited to specifying that '[they] should not be worded too close to binding instruments and should include only provisions having no binding force" (JPG 2.2.4, 2.3.3). In the most recent guideline document of the Commission (2022), the same idea is reinforced: 'If the draft act being checked does not aim to be binding, this has various consequences for its wording, the main purpose of which is to avoid confusion with a binding act' (3.1.3). More concretely, 'non-binding acts should avoid using mandatory verbal forms and structures similar to those used in binding acts, but should also avoid including dates of entry into force or application' (3.1.3).

16.3.3 Concrete Drafting Challenges

Arguably, in the exercise of their regulatory powers, EU drafters aim at enacting non-binding legal acts as fast and as flexibly as possible, particularly when the intensity of EU competence is rather low and where various factors preclude the adoption of EU binding legal acts. The imbalance between the intended meaning of the norms of conduct and their expression seems to have been of little, if any, concern for those producing EU soft law instruments. This situation persists despite the risks of producing legal uncertainty, potential breaches of institutional balance or trespassing of the boundaries of EU competences and ultimately uncertainty for those applying EU law in the Member States, including national courts.

We point at some drafting challenges in the current practice of EU soft law instruments concerning the substance, as well as the form of EU soft law instruments, in light of the legal and argumentative parameters discussed earlier. In this way, we attempt to do justice both to the *substantial quality* of these instruments and to their *formal quality*, both of which are pertinent to drafting (cf. European Commission 2022, 331–333). We point at breaches of formal legal requirements, defective argumentation concerning the subsidiarity and proportionality principles, hardening language and format increasing the fuzziness of soft law instruments and lack of sufficient persuasive force for these instruments.

A close look at EU soft law instruments reveals that non-binding acts often fail to mention explicitly a *legal basis* (e.g., Commission Communication 91/C 273/02[4]), and, when they do so, the (sometimes questionable) choice of legal basis is not further justified (e.g., Commission Recommendation (EU) 2020/518). The latter is, for example, the case of the non-binding instruments in which Article 292 TFEU is doubtfully mentioned as a legal basis, without further explanation of the specific Treaty provision enabling the enacting institution to adopt it. Moreover, the preamble of such instruments, which should always concern the *legal-factual background* supporting the adoption of the legal instrument and its content, sometimes poses great challenges. While this background is usually quite detailed and refers to EU legal acts relevant to various aspects covered by the instrument, it is often built on the premise that measures already taken by the Member States necessarily lead to fragmentation and subsequently hamper their effectiveness, while harming the single market and fundamental rights. A further legal challenge resides with the *aim of the instrument* which may go beyond mere coordination and sometimes attempts to openly achieve harmonization among the Member States. Such is the case of the same Commission Recommendation (EU) 2020/518 which aims at creating a toolbox entailing a 'pan-European approach for the use of mobile applications' and a 'common scheme for using anonymized and aggregated data on mobility of populations.' As we explained in a previous more detailed analysis of this Commission Recommendation, such an approach

> raises questions about the suitability of a recommendation for reaching such ambitious aims, and about the 'orthodoxy' of the Commission's practice to use such an instrument in order to nudge Member States into things that do not normally belong to the EU competence, or, if they did, they should normally be regulated via an EU binding act.
>
> (Andone and Coman-Kund 2023, 164)

It has been shown that some EU soft law instruments, such as recommendations of the European Commission, commonly resemble legally binding instruments, in particular directives (Andone and Greco 2018; Láncos and Tauschinsky 2023). Such instruments are structured in such a way that their *argumentative pattern* is practically identical to directives (Andone and Greco 2018). The main standpoint adopted by the enactor of the instrument is a practical claim for action requesting addressees to adopt a certain measure ('Action X should be taken'). The main arguments supporting this standpoint point to the effectiveness of that measure at the Member State level and help remove the variations in the way in which Member States deal with the existing issues. Such variations are seen as a problem which can only be solved at the EU level. Two other coordinative arguments can be reconstructed from the preamble of the act, namely that Member States cannot effectively deal with the matter on their own, and adopting the proposed common measure will yield advantages. Such similarities are not per se legally problematic if they properly address (but they rarely do, as is shown below) the two-fold requirements of the subsidiarity test that both directives and recommendations need to meet when they are adopted in the areas of non-exclusive EU competence. However, the similarity with legally binding instruments such as directives goes further. Thus, the prescriptive part of the instrument is strikingly detailed in the way in which the objective is explained, alongside specific and precise guidelines to be followed. AG Bobek (Case C-16/16P: paras 89 and 119) argued that such details create 'a legitimate expectation that is analogous to legally binding acts by misleading the addressee in thinking that they *must* comply with the instrument' (our italics).

A challenge is at issue when the *argument types do not match the standpoint.* The argument according to which Member States cannot effectively deal with a matter on their own contains a descriptive proposition which stands in sharp contrast with the prescriptive standpoint ('Action X should be taken'), normally supported by a causal and an evaluative proposition. What is more, *important arguments* are sometimes *omitted*, as happened in many of the EU soft law instruments enacted during the recent COVID-19 crisis in which arguments about the urgency of the situation, threats and correlated risks are simply left aside. In a detailed case study (Andone and Coman-Kund 2023) we show that Commission Recommendation (EU) 2020/518 mentions the urgency of the situation (Point 2: 'Member States should take these actions as a matter of urgency'), but no arguments to support it, while the risk is only acknowledged in connection with 'a fragmented and uncoordinated approach' (Recital 2). Moreover, the omission of the positive effects of the actions taken by the Member States makes it look as if should the addressee not want to implement the recommended measures, it would act against 'a genuine spirit of solidarity,' especially, in times of crisis. This arguably amounts to a disguised *ad hominem* fallacy in the form of some sort of 'comply or be blamed' approach, by trying to undermine the legitimacy and credibility of addressees reluctant to implement the recommendation. It also makes it look as if just by acknowledging the same problems, the EU institution and the Member States also need to share the same solution. Closely connected to the mentioned challenges is the *evasion of the burden of proof* regarding the principle of subsidiarity. In numerous cases, the European Commission argues for action to be taken at the EU level, but instead of arguing why the different approaches taken at the national level do not and cannot solve a certain issue, it brings to the foreground the necessity for common standards at the European level. *False dichotomies* are created when erroneously limiting the available options and dismissing those already in existence. By presenting just one option, it is suggested that other options (such as the measures already taken by the Member States) are suboptimal by not discussing their advantages at all. All this points to a superficial and defective argumentation supporting the requirements of the subsidiarity test, raising serious questions as to the full compliance of the legal instrument with the principle of subsidiarity.

What is more, the legal fuzziness of EU soft law instruments is increased when *hardened formulations* are at issue. Such is the case when a structural compliance mechanism of reporting and reviewing is mentioned, and addressees are requested to report on actions taken pursuant to the legal act by a certain deadline and on a periodic basis thereafter (reporting and 'comply or explain' mechanisms). The use of these techniques, nudging into compliance and creating a more demanding situation for addressees in case of non-compliance, makes it quite clear that the act has not been enacted with the intention of being disregarded by the addressee

(Commission Recommendation 2014/478/EU, (EU) 2018/951). Moreover, by threatening to make use of its formal authority, including the power to adopt formal sanctions, combined sometimes with the publication of the legal instrument in the Official Journal, the drafter creates an impression of obligation on the addressee to comply in the same way as in the case of a legally binding act (Opinion AG Bobek in Case C-16/16P *Belgium v Commission* para. 126).

16.4 Guidelines for Good Drafting of EU Soft Law Instruments

All drafting manuals limit themselves to explaining legislative technique rules applied to legally binding acts. Although in the titles discussing such techniques, reference is made to 'legal acts' in general, which arguably include not only binding legal acts but also non-binding legal acts, at least the recommendations and opinions mentioned explicitly in Article 288 TFEU, all guidelines barely make any reference to the category of non-binding legal acts. In our view, there is no obvious reason not to provide ground rules for drafting such acts, especially in the context in which their wording and content are becoming the reason of discontent for the addressees and oftentimes subject to litigation. In what follows, we suggest a set of basic guidelines for drafting EU soft law instruments in light of the argumentative and legal parameters put forward for designing and assessing the quality of such instruments.

16.4.1 Drafting of EU Soft Law Instruments from a Legal-Argumentative Perspective

16.4.1.1 Clarifying Legal and Practical Effects of EU Soft Law Instruments

EU drafting guidelines mention the distinction between binding and non-binding legal acts and the importance of ensuring that 'in non-binding acts, imperative forms or a structure or presentation too close to that of a binding act, must not be used' (JPG, 12). This negative piece of advice is not of much use to the drafters in the absence of any concrete guidelines of what should actually be used to ensure a proper distinction between legally binding and non-binding acts. Most recently, the Commission (2022, 337) added that

> when drafting non-binding acts, it should be kept in mind that the Court of Justice has made it clear that their non-binding nature does not prevent them from producing certain legal effects or even from being binding on their authors.

This statement, however, instead of clarifying the category of non-binding acts and how they should be drafted accordingly, rather emphasizes the blurring of the lines between binding and non-binding acts and endorses the legal fuzziness of the latter.

In our view, a clear distinction should be maintained and plainly mentioned in the drafting guidelines between the legal and practical effects of soft law. We argued in earlier studies for practical effects as entailing voluntary compliance by the addressees of the act (Coman-Kund and Andone 2019; Andone and Coman-Kund 2022, 2023). In doing so, the ambiguity as to what is intended with these instruments is no longer questioned both by the addressees and by courts. As to the potential legal effects, we suggest providing more guidance to the drafter as to what that means in practice. Mentioning only that the drafter should 'keep in mind' their non-binding nature and possible legal effects is not informative enough and even ambiguous. What is expected from the drafter more particularly and how should they draft the legal act to do justice to this 'guideline'? The often mentioned 'duty to take into account' enshrined in the *Grimaldi* jurisprudence, arguably emanating from the principle of loyal cooperation and applicable in the case of recommendations, does not amount to a duty to comply with the instrument at issue by the addressee. In the best case, it entails self-binding effects on the EU enactor resulting from the principles of legitimate expectations, equal treatment or legal certainty (Andone and Coman-Kund 2023, 154). It should also be noted that the self-binding effect has been enshrined by the CJEU in the case of 'atypical' acts, not formally enshrined as non-binding acts in the Founding Treaties. It is for these reasons that we suggest making it clear that non-binding acts do not impose an overt legal obligation to comply with them either by the addressees or by the courts (Andone and Coman-Kund 2023, 155). A good example is European Commission notice 2021/C 305/01 on state aid, which in its final provisions (141) states: 'This notice aims to provide *guidance* to national courts in the application of the State aid rules. It *does not bind* the national courts or affect their independence' (our emphasis).

16.4.1.2 Increasing the Persuasive Force of EU Soft Law Instruments

Drafting manuals always build their guidelines around a general rule according to which 'the drafting of EU legal acts must be **clear** and therefore easy to understand, without ambiguity; **simple** and therefore concise, without unnecessary information or detail; and **precise**, thus leaving no uncertainty in the reader's mind' (emphasis in original) (European Commission 2022, 335). This general principle is viewed as 'commonsense' (JPG, 10) and connected to the principles of accessibility and comprehensibility for everyone and to the principle of legal certainty. We fully acknowledge the vital importance of this general principle, but we argue for the envisaged clarity, simplicity and preciseness to be defined specifically for the case of the legal acts at issue. In view of the important persuasive dimension of EU soft law instruments, we furthermore suggest reading clarity, simplicity and preciseness in light of the four argumentative parameters (design, content, effectiveness and soundness) discussed earlier. This entails additionally, persuading addresses to follow voluntarily a non-binding course of action through sufficient argumentation and evidence supporting that course of action.

16.4.1.3 The Legal and Normative Dimensions of the Duty to State Reasons

We contended already that the duty to state reasons is of key relevance to increase the quality and effectiveness of legally non-binding instruments. This duty needs to be fulfilled by observing the rule of law with its reflection in the principles of legality, proportionality and subsidiarity. Moreover, the persuasive dimension of EU soft law makes it all the more important to observe the requirements of the duty to state reasons, both as a legal and as a normative parameter to obtain a higher degree of voluntary compliance.

Accordingly, we argued that under Article 296 (2) TFEU, soft law instruments should provide clear and adequate reasons regarding the chosen legal basis, the legal-factual background prompting the adoption of the instrument, including considerations of subsidiarity and proportionality, as well as the intended aims of the instrument. Ideally, the statement of reasons should set out valid and sufficient arguments and evidence as to (i) why Union action is required and (ii) the conclusion that it is therefore necessary and desirable to adopt the proposed measures. The explicit statement of reasons in the legal act and whether it is well founded are distinct aspects that need to be mentioned. While each one is necessary for the fulfillment of the duty to state reasons, they are only cumulatively sufficient. By stating these aspects 'clearly and unequivocally,' the drafter makes explicit the reasoning upon which that act is based so that the addressees can ascertain the reasons for the measures and courts can eventually exercise their power of review (see Case C-493/17 Weiss paras. 31 and 33). According to CJEU, the fulfillment of the duty to state reasons as a norm of control must be assessed by reference to the wording, context of the measure and the whole body of legal rules governing the relevant matter (Case C-493/17 Weiss para. 33).

Moving beyond the legal floor laid down by CJEU, we maintained that the duty to state reasons as a more normative parameter is particularly useful for drafting effective soft law instruments. From this perspective, the duty to state reasons requires using sound, valid, sufficient arguments and reasoning to improve the persuasiveness of soft law instruments with a view to enhancing their effectiveness through increased levels of compliance by addresses. Thus, convincingly arguing for the proper legal basis of the instrument should persuade addressees of the legality of the soft law instrument. Arguing properly for the principle of subsidiarity is pertinent in this context to convince addressees at the Member State level that action taken by the Union is preferable. Arguing properly for the principle of proportionality is pertinent to convince the addressees that the selected non-binding instrument is the optimal tool for an existing problem and, therefore, desirable to be complied with. Explaining in an open and balanced manner, by relying on valid arguments and evidence, all the foreseeable consequences of the instrument, should contribute to an enhanced level of trust by addressees in the author of the measure. In this way, the drafter's burden of proof is appropriately fulfilled, not only by explaining why the chosen measure is the best solution to a problem from a legal perspective but also by effectively convincing addresses to comply with the instrument.

16.4.4 *Toward a Set of Guidelines for EU Soft Law Instruments*

Based on the previous analysis, we put forward and further explain more concrete guidelines for drafting EU soft law instruments.

1 *The form and the content of soft law instruments should properly and consistently reflect their non-binding nature.*

Being 'clear and therefore easy to understand' could be given substance *by making it explicit in the legal act that its aim is to be legally non-binding*, thus clarifying the intention of the drafter to invite rather than compel the addressees to adopt the proposed measures. In this way, the *argumentative design* of the legal act would be in line with its legal nature as a non-binding instrument. It would also avoid the traditional preference for assessment merely at the level of modality (shall/will/would, etc.) which EU courts and scholars alike favor (cf. Petropoulou and Eliantonio 2023), despite the fact that such modals provide only a partial indication of the strength of the obligations expressed in the legal acts (Andone and Coman-Kund 2023, 167). Moreover, non-binding rules of conduct should be drafted and structured in such a way that they are sufficiently comprehensible to the addressees and the public at large.

Being 'simple and therefore concise' should mean in the case of legally non-binding acts that *details about the course of action to be taken and the means to do so should be kept at a minimum and much leeway should be provided to the addressee. Similarly, details about comprehensive supervision and reporting, as well as requests for notification or other such 'enforcement' mechanisms should be avoided.* In this way, the *argumentative content* of non-binding legal acts would be specific to these instruments and would diminish any impression of the instrument being a binding legal act.

In line with recent views of the Quality of Legislation Team at the European Commission regarding binding legal acts (European Commission 2022, 338) and, by extension, legally non-binding acts, *the title of the instrument '(...) needs to be worded in a way that makes it possible to identify the subject matter of the act in a succinct, precise and consistent manner.'* This guideline is important with a view to creating clear expectations from the addressee. 'Subject matter' needs to be understood beyond its literal sense of making clear the topic and should make obvious that the act concerns a recommendation, communication, notice, opinion or any other such legally non-binding act. 'Precise manner' should mean that not only is the subject matter in the title unambiguous and fully consistent with the content of the instrument but also that the title is accurate by giving an indication of the type of act at issue. The European Commission notice 2021/C 305/01 is, for example, a case in point of an instrument that is titled 'Communication from the Commission' and confusingly subtitled 'Commission Notice on the enforcement of State aid rules by national courts.'

2 *The legal basis of soft law instruments needs to be clearly specified and properly explained.*

For reasons which we touched upon when discussing drafting challenges, we argue for *a clear indication of the legal basis supported by adequate and sufficient explanations of the specific Treaty provision enabling the enacting institution to adopt the act at issue.* After all, EU non-binding acts are subject to the confines of the EU competences and institutional framework (Andone and Coman-Kund 2023, 152) as reflected in the principle of conferral and the principle of institutional balance. Additionally, if addressees are persuaded about the legality of the measure adopted, they might be more inclined to comply with it.

3 *Soft law instruments should be accurate and explicit about the relevant legal-factual context, compliance with principles of subsidiarity and proportionality, and the envisaged aims.*

Being 'precise, thus leaving no uncertainty in the reader's mind' should amount *to being accurate and explicit about the goals which are envisaged with the legal act at issue. In these instruments, the drafter needs to convince through proper legal and persuasive arguments:* (1) that the measures Member States already have in place need to be coordinated with those of other Member States and (2) that new measures as proposed in the instruments in question need to be taken by the addressees. To devise EU soft law instruments that achieve these goals not as prescriptive tools but rather as effective persuasive tools, particular attention needs to be paid to *argumentative effectiveness* obtained in the absence of legal coercion. What is more, a precisely drafted instrument is a legal act that does not leave room for inconsistencies, invalid arguments, ambiguity, false dichotomies, evasions of the burden of proof and suchlike fallacies. In other words, *each measure or course of action proposed to the addressees needs to be matched by sound arguments.* In this way, drafting would take into account *argumentative soundness* as a key component of the argumentative style of these instruments.

4 *Soft law instruments should display overall particular persuasive force in order to foster compliance.*

Persuading addressees to follow a non-binding course of action requires sufficient argumentation supporting that course of action. In this respect, *simple, clear and precise rules of conduct in soft law instruments should be complemented, beyond the legal floor of the duty to state reasons, by sufficiently elaborated argumentation and explanations.* These should concern the legal-policy context justifying the proposed course of action, the reasons and aims of such measures, their added value and benefits for addressees, as incentives for voluntary compliance. Such explanations could be included in the preamble of the legal instruments. However, to mark a neater delineation from binding legal acts and emphasize the distinctive value of soft law instruments as persuasive tools, argumentation could be intertwined with the relevant rules of conduct throughout the instrument. For instance, each rule of conduct or a specific set of rules of conduct could come along in the instrument with the relevant arguments supporting them.

16.5 Conclusion

This chapter has made clear that general principles and guidelines for the drafting of EU soft law instruments are highly needed to do justice to the specific nature of these legal acts. We are aware that 'black-and-white' guidelines are difficult to design for these instruments in view of their persuasive force rather than legally binding force. This might explain the scarcity of any such rules in the current drafting manuals. Yet we also agree with Xanthaki (2001, 72), when discussing the quality of EU legislation in general, that 'accepting that drafting cannot be regulated by rigid rules cannot be taken to the extreme of negating rules of drafting altogether: general principles form a theoretical background against which legislative drafting develops.' The proposed guidelines are meant to underline that what is called a non-binding legal instrument should be drafted as a non-binding legal instrument and nothing else. The constant need to reassess these instruments to determine their genuine legal nature effects is arguably a good indicator of the need for better drafting of effective EU soft law instruments that are capable of achieving the desired objective, i.e., convincing addressees to comply with the proposed course of action in the absence of legal coercion.

Notes

1 This is dependent on the type of legal act and other factors; see Andone and Coman-Kund (2023, 156–157).

2 We made a small change to the original table (Andone and Coman-Kund 2023, 160) by placing the requirement that 'Arguments should be employed throughout the instrument' under argumentative design rather than argumentative content as originally the case. We believe that this aspect is predominantly a matter of design, while it remains at the same time a content-related aspect to a lesser degree.

3 Interviews with Commission experts from the Legal Service and Secretariat General, January 25, 2019.

4 This act concerns a Commission communication intended to have legal effects, as specified in Case C-325/91. The communication sets out to specify the manner of application of Article 5(2) of Directive 80/723 on the transparency of financial relations between Member States and public undertakings and was published in the C Series of the Official Journal and notified to each Member State. The Court (para. 23) argued that the act, because it required Member States annually to report to the Commission, on a general, systematic basis about data relating to the financial relations of a particular category of undertaking achieving a specified turnover, constitutes 'an act intended to have legal effects of its own distinct from those of Article 5(2) of the directive and adds new obligations to those provided for by that provision.' Zucchermaglio (2022, 111) contends that 'remarkably the Court, instead of holding that the communication lacked binding effects and declaring the appeal inadmissible, found that the act, as formulated, contributed to create new obligations on member states that did not stem from the directive, therefore implying a binding effect of it.'

References

Abbott, Kenneth W., and Duncan Snidal. 2000. "Hard and Soft Law in International Governance." *International Organization* 54(3): 421–456.

Andone, Corina, and Florin Coman-Kund. 2022. "Persuasive Rather Than 'Binding' EU Soft Law? An Argumentative Perspective on the European Commission's Soft Law Instruments in Times of Crisis." *The Theory and Practice of Legislation* 10(1): 22–47.

Andone, Corina, and Florin Coman-Kund. 2023. "A Legal-argumentative Framework for Persuasive EU Soft Law: The Case of the European Commission's Recommendations." In *The Legal Effects of EU Soft Law Theory, Language and Sectoral Insights*, edited by Petra L. Láncos, Napoleon Xanthoulis and Luis Arroyo Jiménez, 142–174. UK: Edward Elgar Publishing.

Andone, Corina, and Sara Greco. 2018. "Evading the Burden of Proof in European Union Soft Law Instruments: The Case of Commission Recommendations." *International Journal for the Semiotics of Law* 31(1): 79–99.

Cappellina, Bartolomeo, Anne Ausfelder, Adam Eick, Romain Mespoulet, Miriam Hartlapp, Sabine Saurugger, and Fabien Terpan. 2022. "Ever More Soft Law? A Dataset to Compare Binding and Non-binding EU Law across Policy Areas and Over Time (2004–2019)." *European Union Politics* 23(4): 741–757.

Coman-Kund, Florin, and Corina Andone. 2019. "European Commission's Soft Law Instruments: In-between Legally Binding and Non-binding Norms." In *Lawmaking in Multi-level Settings: Legislative Challenges in Federal Systems and the European Union*, edited by Patricia Popelier, Helen Xanthaki, William Robinson, João Tiago Siveira and Felix Uhlmann, 173–197. Oxford: Hart-Nomos Publishing.

Di Robilant, Anna. 2013. "Genealogies of Soft Law." *Scandinavian Studies in Law* 58: 217–268.

Eliantonio, Mariolina, Emilia Korkea-Aho, and Oana Stefan. 2021. "Introduction." In *EU Soft Law in the Member States: Theoretical Findings and Empirical Evidence,* edited by Mariolina Eliantonio, Emilia Korkea-aho and Oana Stefan, 1–18. Oxford: Hart Publishing.

Fabien, Terpan. 2015. "Soft Law in the European Union – the Changing Nature of EU Law." *European Law Journal* 21(1): 68–96.

Klabbers, Jan. 1996. "The Redundancy of Soft Law." *Nordic Journal of International Law* 65(2): 167–182.

Klabbers, Jan. 1998. "The Undesirability of Soft Law." *Nordic Journal of International Law* 67: 381–391.

Láncos, Petra Lea. 2019. "The Phenomenon of 'Directive-like Recommendations' and Their Implementation: Lessons from Hungarian Legislative Practice." In *Lawmaking in Multi-level Settings. Legislative Challenges in Federal Systems and the European Union*, edited by Patricia Popelier, Helen Xanthaki, William Robinson, João Tiago Siveira and Felix Uhlmann, 199–218. Oxford: Hart-Nomos Publishing.

Láncos, Petra Lea, and Eljalill Tauschinsky. 2023. "Verbal Markers of 'Softness' in EU Law? A Computer-based Analysis to Delimit Soft Law and Hard Law on Directive-like Recommendations." In *The Legal Effects of EU Soft Law Theory, Language and Sectoral Insights*, edited by Petra L. Láncos, Napoleon Xanthoulis and Luis Arroyo Jiménez, 111–141. UK: Edward Elgar Publishing.

Lenaerts, Koen, and José A. Gutiérrez-Fons. 2013. "To Say What the Law of the EU Is: Methods of Interpretation and the European Court of Justice." *EUI Working Paper AEL* 9: 1–48.

Mendes, J. 2020. "The Foundation of the Duty to Give Reasons and a Normative Reconstruction." In *The Foundations and Future of Public Law: Essays in Honour of Paul Craig*, edited by Elisabeth Fischer, Jeff King and Alison L. Young, 299–322. Oxford: Oxford University Press.

Petropoulou Ionescu, Danai, and Mariolina Eliantonio. 2023. "Words Are Stone: Constructing Bindingness through Language in EU Environmental Soft Law." In *The Legal Effects of EU Soft Law Theory, Language and Sectoral Insights*, edited by Petra L. Láncos, Napoleon Xanthoulis and Luis Arroyo Jiménez, 76–110. UK: Edward Elgar Publishing.

Schäfer, Armin. 2006. "Resolving Deadlock: Why International Organisations Introduce Soft Law." *European Law Journal* 12(2): 194–208.

Scott, Joanne, and David M. Trubek. 2002. "Mind the Gap: Law and New Approaches to Governance in the European Union." *European Law Journal* 8(1): 1–18.

Senden, Linda. 2004. *Soft Law in European Community Law*. Bloomsbury: Hart Publishing.

Snyder, Francis. 1993. "The Effectiveness of European Community Law: Institutions, Processes, Tools and Techniques." *Modern Law Review* 56(1): 19–54.

Stefan, Oana. 2013. *Soft Law in Court: Competition Law, State Aid and the Court of Justice of the European Union*. Dordrecht: Wolters Kluwer.

Stefan, Oana. 2020. "The Future of European Union Soft Law: A Research and Policy Agenda for the Aftermath of COVID-19." *Journal of International and Comparative Law* 7(2): 329–350.

Trubek, David M., and Louise G. Trubek. 2005. "Hard and Soft Law in the Construction of Social Europe: The Role of the Open Method of Co-ordination." *European Law Journal* 11(3): 343–364.

Xanthaki, Helen. 2001. "The Problem of Quality in EU Legislation: What on Earth Is Really Wrong?" *Common Market Law Review* 38: 651–676.

Zucchermaglio, Sergio. 2022. "The Use of Soft Law in EU Banking Regulation." PHD Diss., Luiss University Rome.

CJEU Jurisprudence

Case 22/70. *Commission v Council. European Agreement on Road Transport (ERTA)* ECLI:EU:C:1971:32.

Case C-156/21 *Hungary* v *Parliament and Council* ECLI:EU:C:2022:97.

Case C-16/16 P *Belgium v Commission* ECLI:EU:C:2018:79.

Case C-322/88 *Salvatore Grimaldi v Fonds des maladies professionnelles* ECLI:EU:C:1989:646.

Case C-325/91 French Republic v Commission of the European Communities. ECLI:EU:C:1993:245.

Case C-493/17 *Weiss and Others* ECLI: EU:C:2018:1000.

Case C-501/18 BT v Balgarska Narodna Banka ECLI:EU:C:2021:249.

Case C-911/19 *Fédération bancaire française (FBF) v Autorité de contrôle prudentiel et de résolution* (ACPR) ECLI:EU:C:2021:599.

Case T-496/11 Judgment of the General Court (Fourth Chamber), 4 March 2015 *United Kingdom of Great Britain and Northern Ireland v European Central Bank (ECB)* ECLI:EU:T:2015:133.

Joined Cases 1–57 and 14–57 *Société des usines à tubes de la Sarre v High Authority of the European Coal and Steel Community* ECLI:EU:C:1957:13.
Opinion of Advocate-General Bobek in *Case C-16/16P Belgium v Commission.* ECLI:EU:C:2017:959.

Other Sources

Commission Recommendation (EU) 2018/951 on standards for equality bodies [2018] OJ L167/28.
Commission Recommendation (EU) 2020/518 of 8 April 2020 on a common Union toolbox for the use of technology and data to combat and exit from the COVID-19 crisis, in particular concerning mobile applications and the use of anonymised mobility data [2020] OJ L114/7.
Commission Recommendation 2014/478/EU on principles for the protection of consumers and players of online gambling services and for the prevention of minors from gambling online [2014] OJ L214/38.
European Commission. 1997. *Legislative Drafting: A Commission Manual.*
European Commission. 2015. *Joint Practical Guide of the European Parliament, the Council and the Commission for Persons Involved in the Drafting of European Union Legislation.* https://op.europa.eu/en/publication-detail/-/publication/3879747d-7a3c-411b-a3a0-55c14e2ba732
European Commission. 2017. Commission Staff Working Document: Better Regulation Guidelines. SWD(2017) 350 final: https://www.europarl.europa.eu/RegData/docs_autres_institutions/commission_europeenne/swd/2017/0350/COM_SWD(2017)0350_EN.pdf.
European Commission. 2021. Commission Staff Working Document: Better Regulation Guidelines. SWD(2017) 305 final: https://commission.europa.eu/document/download/d0bbd77f-bee5-4ee5-b5c4-6110c7605476_en?filename=swd2021_305_en.pdf.
European Commission. 2022. *70 Years of EU Law: A Union for Its Citizens.* Luxembourg: Publications Office of the European Union.
European Commission, Communication. Notice on the enforcement of State aid rules by national courts (2021/C 305/01).
European Commission, Communication to the Member States. Application of Articles 92 and 93 of the EEC Treaty and of Article 5 of Commission Directive 80/723/EEC to public undertakings in the manufacturing sector (91/C 273/02).
European Parliament, Council of the European Union, and European Commission. 1998. Interinstitutional Agreement of 22 December 1998 on Common Guidelines for the Quality of Drafting of Community Legislation. [1999] OJ C 73/1.
European Parliament, Council of the European Union, and European Commission. 2018. Joint Handbook for the Presentation and Drafting of Acts Subject to the Ordinary Legislative Procedure. 2018. JHOLP 31.01.2018 ENv01.
Interinstitutional Agreement between the European Parliament, the Council of the European Union and the European Commission on Better Law-Making. 2016. OJ L123/1.
Publications Office of the European Union. 2022. *Interinstitutional Style Guide of the Publications Office of the European Union.* https://op.europa.eu/en/publication-detail/-/publication/01ed788a-d266-11ec-a95f-01aa75ed71a1.

17 A Linguistic Approach to Drafting Legislative Provisions

Giulia A. Pennisi

17.1 Introduction

The challenge in the construction of legislative norms is the nature and extent of specification of legal scope in the expression of legislative intentions. Largely owing to the new linguistic outlook on legal language, recent studies of language have demonstrated that drafters often miss the focus of the policy concepts that they wish to communicate, and aim to identify a method by which drafters may achieve their conceptual focus (Mousmouti 2019; Xanthaki 2022). Legislative drafters deal with a universe of human behaviour which is unlimited, in the sense that it is impossible to predict exactly what may happen within the human universe. This is particularly true within the common law jurisdictions. Not only are legislative expressions required to be clear, precise, and unambiguous, on the one hand, and all-inclusive, on the other (Bhatia 1993, 2014), but also the essence of the craftsmanship of legislative intent plays a clever balance between the two.

Modern legislative drafting theory urges legislative drafters to bare the text from preliminary provisions and to start as early as possible with the regulatory message that the government wants to convey to the final receivers. And so, the pursuit of modern drafters is to share that message with the users of the legislation in a manner that allows them to be heard loud and clear (Stefanou 2011; Xanthaki 2014). Linguistics can certainly provide a method by which drafters can improve legislative norms in terms of lexico-grammatical and textual structures and better assess the effectiveness of their draft.

As a matter of fact, there are inherent difficulties in the drafting of legislation. Complex societies make increasing political demands to produce legislation quickly and efficiently, whereas the lack of effective consultations between policy makers and drafters certainly affects the language used and the underlying function of the text. During the Sir William Dale Memorial Lecture for 2005, Geoffrey Bowman (2006: 3–4) said:

> It is not the drafter's job to make up the policy, and that it should not be his job. At the same time, it is part of his job to offer workable solutions

DOI: 10.4324/9781003430308-21

> when possible. The line between offering workable solutions (on the one hand) and making up the policy (on the other hand) is often a fine one. [...] the drafter has to express them. I think it is generally accepted that legal concepts and legal documents are often difficult to understand. In the case of legislative drafting the position is complicated by other factors. There is the audience. [...] In fact the drafter has several audiences. There will be administrative and legal civil servants, ministers, members of both Houses of Parliament, practising barristers and solicitors, and judges. There will also be the people the legislation affects. They may range over a wide area, and a lot depends on the nature of the Bill. At one extreme there may be specialists (such as tax accountants or pension experts or scientists). At the other extreme there may be laymen (perhaps lay members of a board established to promote the arts). [...]
>
> And then there is the peculiar nature of legislation. [...] An Act has a precise and narrow object, which is to change the law—no more and no less. It is not designed to offer the things that other forms of writing offer (such as entertainment, information, explanation, argument or stimulation).

The consequence of all this is that the language of Acts is tight and spare, and every word will be assumed to have a purpose. Therefore, Acts can be approached only with effort.

In this regard, a few considerations of leading scholars in the field of law, legislative drafting and language provide remarkable insight into the complex relationship between legislation and drafting. Indeed, legislation is the product of a dialogue between the actors of the drafting process (e.g., politicians, legal, and drafting experts), the discipline involved in the process (e.g., politics, substantive law), and the language used by the experts in their own discipline (e.g., policy, law, and drafting) (Stefanou 2011; Xanthaki 2014). In fact, the actors involved in the legislative process can constrain, adapt, and modify the intentions and policies that may have motivated the passage of legislation in the first place (Barnes 2006). For this reason, the legislative process should be considered in terms of its context or sites of engagement (Fairclough 2003; Scollon 2001; van Dijk 2005, 2007).

If lawmakers wish to test how the law in question has been drafted and the extent to which the goals of legislation have been met, the investigation will benefit from the adoption of a broadly scientific approach (Galdia 2009; Solan 2004; Tiersma and Solan 2012). This chapter takes into consideration legislative provisions from a linguistic point of view. It applies tests of language in a number of texts belonging to the current common law drafting practice to ascertain a loss of conceptual focus by legislative drafters and concludes that linguistics provides a method by which drafters can assess the effectiveness of their draft.

17.2 Legal Provisions and the Search for Specificity

The need for legislative provisions to be all-inclusive, precise, and clear (Bhatia 1993, 2004; Campbell 1996; Tiersma 1999) has usually resulted in an increase in sentence length, the great number of inserted parts, detailed terminological explanations, and the use of past-participle clauses to state clearly the source of the qualification of a term. In the case of common law systems, their adversarial nature is reflected in the drafters' stylistic choices featuring very long sentences traditionally consisting of three (or more) main clauses, each modified by many subordinate clauses (Gotti 2011). For instance, the intention to cover as many specific cases and interpretations as possible is evident in the number of definitions and explanations normally present, combined with the explicit indication of the limits of applicability of the norm. Reference, for instance, is typically facilitated by simple prepositions or complex prepositional phrases such as *under*, *in accordance with,* and *on the premises that* (Examples 1 and 2).

Example 1

(1) A person meets the condition of eligibility in this section if the person is in qualifying paid work on the date of the declaration.
(2) Regulations may—
  (a) make provision as to what is, or is not, qualifying paid work, and
  (b) specify circumstances in which a person is, or is not, to be regarded as in such work.
(3) Regulations *under* subsection (2) may, in particular—
  (a) make provision for calculating a person's expected income from any work for a period specified in the regulations,
  (b) provide that a person is in qualifying paid work only if the person's expected income from the work for the period, taken together with the person's expected income from any other work for the period, is greater than or equal to an amount specified in, or determined *in accordance with,* the regulations, and [...]
  (c) specify cases in which the condition mentioned in paragraph (b) does not need to be met.

(Childcare Payments Act 2014)[1] (emphasis mine)

Common law legislation is usually associated with particular emphasis on explicit textual schematisation (Driedger 1982) with recurrent alternative/complementary options and punctuation organised in such a way as to make the provisions more semantically transparent. In many jurisdictions, '*or*' is commonly taken to mean the same as '*and*' (Example 2). In this regard, Solan observes that 'generally, the words "*or*" and "*and*" in a statute may be construed as interchangeable when necessary to effectuate legislative intent' (1993: 45).

Example 2

(4) A police *or* customs officer who has boarded a vessel *or* aircraft may, for the purposes of disembarking from the vessel *or* aircraft, require that *or* any other vessel *or* aircraft—
   (a) to stop, *or*
   (b) to do anything else that would enable the officer to disembark from the vessel *or* aircraft.
(5) A police *or* customs officer may require any person on board a vessel *or* aircraft to provide any help *and* facilities, with respect to matters under that person's control, that the officer considers would facilitate the exercise of a power conferred by this section.
(6) The powers conferred by this section may be exercised in any place to which the officer lawfully has access (whether *or* not it is a place to which the public has access).

(Ivory Act 2018)[2]

The number of relative clauses inserted to minimise ambiguity and misunderstandings is at the origin of the considerable sentence length of legislative provisions, each of them supported also by specifications to clarify the meaning[3] (Examples 3 and 4).

Example 3

(3) A requirement has an adverse market effect if, *because it*—
   (a) puts at a disadvantage the incoming goods *(and any comparable goods that also have a relevant connection with the originating part and are also put at that disadvantage), but*
   (b) does not put at disadvantage (at all or to the same extent) some or all comparable goods *that have a relevant connection with the destination part and no other part of the United Kingdom,*

   it causes a significant adverse effect on competition in the market for such goods in the United Kingdom.

(Internal Market Act 2020)[4]

Example 4

If, *in view of a relevant change of circumstances*, a national fisheries authority takes a decision in the exercise of its functions relating to fisheries, fishing, or aquaculture *otherwise than in accordance with the policies contained in a JFS, SSFS, or fisheries management plan that are applicable to the authority*, the authority must prepare and publish a document—

(a) describing the decision and the relevant change of circumstances, and
(b) explaining how the relevant change in circumstances affected the decision (Fisheries Act 2020).[5]

This need contrasts with the high potential for ambiguity which arises from nominal attributes and other words, especially an adjective or a noun that is placed before a noun, and describes (or limits) its meaning in some way (i.e., premodifiers).[6] This is the case of 'a written notice *informing the employer*' that might be interpreted as 'a written notice that *informs the employer*' and 'a written notice that *has informed the employer*' (Example 5).

Example 5

Childcare account notice, in relation to a person who is an eligible employee in relation to a relevant childcare scheme, means *a written notice informing the employer* that the employee wishes to leave the scheme in order to be able to open a childcare account or enable the employee's partner to do so (Childcare Payments Act 2020).[7]

The frequent use of adverbials *hereby, herewith, thereafter,* and *thereof*, a practice that Bhatia (1987) defines as textual-mapping, is prompted by the quest for precision and is reflected in the frequent references to other parts of the text itself that specify the textual element being referred to (Example 6).

Example 6

(a) details of leases, charges, and any other interests which adversely affect the registered estate subsisting at the time of first registration of the estate or created *thereafter*, [...]

that the [disposition or specify type of disposition] is in accordance with [specify the disposition creating the trust] or some variation *thereof* referred to in the declaration, statement or certificate [...]

Pursuant to a trust deed of even date *herewith*, [made between A.B. (name of tenant for life) and C.D. and E.F. (names of trustees of the Settlement)], I, the said A.B., *hereby* declare as follows.

(The Land Registration Rules 2003)[8]

Another important aspect worth mentioning is the recurrent use of expressions, or linguistic units, that link two other constituents together and have a function similar to that of conjunction (i.e., copulas, conjunctive adverbs)[9] such as *and*, *or*, *but*, *whereas*, *for*. This technique makes meaning more transparent through inclusion in the surface form of minimal units of language (Example 7). These units of language, called lexemes in linguistics, possess a semantic interpretation and indicate their particular illocutionary force (i.e., statement, command, directive).[10]

Example 7

In subsection (3) 'the relevant period' means the period of two years ending with the day on which the order is made, *but* an event may be taken into account for the purposes of that subsection *only if* it occurred after the coming into force of this section.

(5) Without prejudice to the generality of subsection (3), a person has good reason for having a bladed article with them in a place mentioned in that subsection *if* the person has the article with them in that place—
  (a) *for* use at work,
  (b) *for* educational purposes,
  (c) *for* religious reasons, *or*
  (d) as part of any national costume. (Offensive Weapons Act 2019)[11]

Apart from words/expressions that have flexible meanings and indefinite adjectives that might be purposefully used because they are particularly gradable and vague,[12] the indeterminacy of interpretation may also be caused by the use of certain modality markers (Example 8), due to their polysemy, as in the case of *shall*, which has become extremely rare in legislative provisions.

Example 8

(2) In section 9F (Assistant Commissioners of Police of the Metropolis) for subsection (2) substitute—
'(2) Any appointment of an Assistant Commissioner *shall* be made, in accordance with regulations under section 50, by the Metropolitan Police Authority.
  (2A) Before appointing an Assistant Commissioner the Metropolitan Police Authority *shall*—
  (a) consult the Commissioner of Police of the Metropolis, and (b) obtain the approval of the Secretary of State'.
(Policing and Crime Act 2009)[13]

Legislative drafters need to consider carefully the lexico-grammatical structures of the provisions that are going to confer powers and impose duties. For instance, the use of *should* rather than *shall* (in Example 8, substituting '*shall* be made' with '*should* be made') could be construed as conveying a weaker degree of the obligation expressed (as if some sort of advice were implied by the text) and might allow greater discretionality of interpretation and application on the part of the final reader (Garzone 2013). Overall, an adequate use of modals (*should*, *will*, *must*, *may*, *might*, etc.) needs to be based on a consideration of the relation between linguistic semantic values and the social pragmatic setting of the legal provisions (Gotti and Dossena 2001). In line with the modal revolution in legal writing and the growing tendency of 'shall-free legislation' (Garzone 2013: 69), *shall* has been increasingly replaced by the modals *may* and *must*.

Particularly in the past few decades, the Plain Language Movement has strongly influenced legislation in common law systems (Williams 2004), as can be seen in the formulation of norms and regulations instructing legislative drafters how to adopt simpler and clearer writing.[14] Thanks to criteria such as a smaller number of words per sentence, the extensive use of simple and compound sentences, and the adoption of a common lexis to name just a few, laws have become more accessible to laypeople. However, the adoption of these practices is not in itself a guarantee of a completely successful result.

17.3 Linguistics to the Aid of Legislative Drafters

According to traditional legal drafting, sentences in common law legislative texts generally take a direct or indirect form of the legal reasoning formula:

- If A (*case*), then B (*legal subject*) shall be/shall do C (*legal action*).
- The structure of a rule should be *case* + *condition* + *sub-condition* + *legal subject* + *legal action*.[15]

Scholars working in the field of legal language (Fung and Watson-Brown 1994; Langton 2005) recommend that:

- *legal subjects* be highlighted with an active voice verb in the first principal clause,
- the *action rule* be placed after *(pre-)conditions* and *case descriptors*,
- main clauses be expressed in the active voice,
- everything that comes after this main verb be an expression of the *legal action* of the section/subsection, and
- the *legal subject(s)* or *action(s)* be identified by the *cases*, *pre-conditions*, or *conditions*.

As far as linguistics is concerned, scholars have extensively analysed specialised discourse and the different communicative purposes of specialised texts that have public implications (Bhatia 1987, 1993, 2014; Campbell 1996; Driedger 1982; Engberg 2013; Galdia 2009; Goddard 2009; Gotti 2011). In linguistic analysis, discourse means the construction and organisation of the segments of language above and below the sentence.[16] The elements of grammar, lexis, and phonology play a fundamental role, but they are reconsidered as a part of a multilayered cognitive, social, and cultural phenomenon (Fairclough 1989, 1995, 2003; Langacker 1991; van Dijk 1985, 1997; Wodak and Meyer 2001). Legislative provisions represent an example of specialised discourse, where the propositions of specialised information, or knowledge of the actors participating in the legislative process, is translated into meanings. In the case of legislation, as well as in any other specialised discourse(s) with public implications, two versions of specialised texts might be produced: (i) one for specialists and (ii) one for ordinary citizens. The two versions will have two different communicative purposes (one legislative and the other informative): depth of specificity and level of reader accessibility. One communicative purpose will be strictly legislative and governmental, whereas the other communicative purpose will be informative and directed to the public at large.

By 'cognitive structuring', linguists (Bhatia 2014; Langton 2005) mean a practical tool for revealing potential comprehension problems present in the text and the nature of an adequate legal drafting rule. Rather than attempting to isolate syntax from the rest of language in a syntactic component governed by principles and elements specific to that component, the attention is focused on the relation of language structure to extra language items outside language. Cognitive structures, therefore, are the basic mental processes people use to make information meaningful.[17] Other names for cognitive structures include mental structures, mental tools, and patterns of thought (Dewey 1997; Gardner 2004; Goddard 2009). By clarifying cognitive structure, which is one of the most efficient easification strategies, it is possible to:

- recognise the legislative intention,
- reduce information load at specific syntactic points; decrease the occurrence of syntactic discontinuities, and
- choose referential links wherever needed.

The provision will still be equally authoritative, detailed, and adequately specified, serving the same legislative function in the court of law. To say that 'easification measures' are synonymous with 'simplified versions', however, would be a mistake. In fact, a simplified version is meant to be a simple account of an authoritative version to inform citizens about the main legislative intentions and their implications for their personal and public activities (Bhatia 2014, 2021). Although easily accessible to larger non-specialist readers, a simplified version is not necessarily

- all-inclusive,
- informative,
- authoritative,
- authentic, and
- complete in all respects.

As explained elsewhere (Pennisi 2024; Xanthaki and Pennisi 2012), even if the simplified version guarantees that the basic meaning is easily understood by the final addressees (i.e., laypeople), it is highly unlikely it will eventually preserve the imperative nature and the all-inclusiveness of legislative provisions.

The following sections will consider some examples of more recent legislation from the international context and from primary UK legislation, where the latest simplification and easification techniques are tested from the point of view of the theories developed in the field of specialised languages and linguistics.

17.3.1 Simplified Version

A simplified version is not intended to replace the original, and simplification strategies may be successfully applied where an original text needs to be explained to or summarised for non-specialist readers. This is true of the Council of Europe[18] initiative, which felt the need to promote equality in human dignity and human rights education. As the Secretary General of the Council of Europe, Marija Pejčinović Burić, explains in the editorial of the updated version of *Compass. Manual for Human Rights Education with Young People* (hereafter *Compass*),[19]

> It is not enough for children and young people simply to hold human rights. In order to embed a human rights culture and ensure that our young people understand how to access those rights—and to uphold, defend and promote them—they need an education fit for that purpose. Compass was first published in 2002. Since then, it has supported scores of professionals and civil society actors in bringing human rights education into the lives of countless young people in Europe and throughout the world. Translated into 31 languages, it has played an essential role in shaping rights-based approaches to youth policy and youth work.

> This creates a human rights awareness that empowers learners, stays with them through life, and can be passed on to future generations. It is not just about learning, but about enhancing democratic citizenship in the longer-term.[20]

Historically, every society has developed systems to ensure social cohesion by codifying the rights and responsibilities of its citizens. In 1948, the international community agreed on the *Universal Declaration of Human Rights* (hereafter *UDHR*) as a code of rights that would be binding on all States. Since 1948 other human rights documents have been agreed upon, such as *The European Convention on Human Rights in 1950* and *The Convention on the Rights of the Child in 1990.* Human rights are about equality, dignity, respect, freedom, and justice. Among the examples of human rights are the right to life, the right to marriage and family, the right to education, freedom of speech, and freedom from discrimination. Saying that human rights are universal means that they are the same for all human beings in every country. They are inalienable, equally important, and complementary; for instance, the right to participate in free elections depends on freedom of speech.

Since 2002, one of the main purposes of the Secretary General of the Council of Europe has been to create a common democratic and legal area throughout the whole of the European continent, ensuring respect for democracy, the rule of law, and human rights. To achieve this goal, the Council of Europe believes that not only is it important to use words, expressions, and language common to laypeople, but also it is imperative to clarify words and expressions they are unfamiliar with. Therefore, the *Simplified Version of the Universal Declaration of Human Rights* (hereafter the *Simplified UDHR*) in the appendices to the updated version 2023 of *Compass* is a timely and welcome publication. At this point, a lexico-grammatical and textual analysis of both texts, that is, the *UDHR* (i.e., the original document) and the *Simplified UDHR*, reveals interesting insights.

The *UDHR* was adopted in 1948 by the General Assembly of the United Nations (UN) and represents the most important global human rights instrument in the world. In fact, it is so widely accepted that its initial non-binding character has changed, and much of it is nowadays frequently referred to as legally binding on the basis of customary international law.[21] The original text consists of a Preamble and 30 articles setting forth the human rights and fundamental freedoms to which all human beings everywhere in the world are entitled.[22]

The Preamble is rather lengthy and consists of seven clauses starting with the term *whereas* used as the introductory word to a recital in the *UDHR*. These *whereas* clauses not only present the reasons for and the purposes of the *UDHR* but also project the solemnity in this official proclamation.

> *Whereas* recognition of the inherent dignity and of the equal and inalienable rights of all members of the human family is the foundation of freedom, justice and peace in the world,
> *Whereas* disregard and contempt for human rights have resulted in barbarous acts which have outraged the conscience of mankind, and the advent of a world in which human beings shall enjoy freedom of speech and belief [...]
> *Whereas* it is essential, if man [...]
> *Whereas* it is essential to protect [...]
> *Whereas* the peoples of the United Nations [...]
> *Whereas* Member States have pledged themselves to achieve [...]
> *Whereas* a common understanding of these rights and freedoms [...]
> Now, therefore, the General Assembly proclaims this Universal Declaration of Human Rights as a common standard of achievement for all peoples and all nations, to the end that every individual and every organ of society, keeping this Declaration constantly in mind, shall strive by teaching and education to promote respect for these rights and freedoms and by progressive measures, national and international, to secure their universal and effective recognition and observance, both among the peoples of Member States themselves and among the peoples of territories under their jurisdiction.

Remarkably, the Preamble has the case description placed after the main provisory *whereas* clauses, i.e., 'Now, therefore the General Assembly proclaims [...] under their jurisdiction'. Overall, the *UDHR* displays a rather clear structure characterised by a rather excessive use of:

(i) textual-mapping devices breaking down a few articles into different subsections following a numerical order and ranging from two to four subsections.

  Article 23

  (1) Everyone has the right to work, to free choice of employment, to just and favourable conditions of work and to protection against unemployment.
  (2) Everyone, without any discrimination, has the right to equal pay for equal work.
  (3) Everyone who works has the right to just and favourable remuneration ensuring for themselves and their family an existence worthy

of human dignity, and supplemented, if necessary, by other means of social protection.

(4) Everyone has the right to form and to join trade unions for the protection of his interests.

(ii) multiple negative phrasing

Article 11

(1) Everyone charged with a penal offence has the right to be presumed innocent until proved guilty according to law in a public trial at which he has had all the guarantees necessary for his defence.

(2) *No one shall be held guilty of any penal offence on account of any act or omission which did not constitute a penal offence, under national or international law, at the time when it was committed. Nor shall a heavier penalty be imposed than the one that was applicable at the time the penal offence was committed.*

(iii) and the overuse of *shall* that, due to its polysemy, may cause indeterminacy of interpretation[23]

Article 26

(1) Everyone has the right to education. Education shall be free, at least in the elementary and fundamental stages. Elementary education *shall* be compulsory. Technical and professional education *shall* be made generally available and higher education *shall* be equally accessible to all on the basis of merit.

(2) Education *shall* be directed to the full development of the human personality and to the strengthening of respect for human rights and fundamental freedoms. It *shall* promote understanding, tolerance and friendship among all nations, racial or religious groups, and *shall* further the activities of the UN for the maintenance of peace.

The *Simplified UDHR*, on the contrary, renders the original legislative text more accessible and easier to read due to the strategic use of linguistic and textual devices. Such simplified versions should be meant for public awareness, which may include legal intentions, explanations, and typical examples. It is a common practice in sciences, where we have the original reports on experiments and, also, a popular version for non-specialist readers (Bhatia 2014; Langton 2005). The *Simplified UDHR* consists of two parts. In the first part, 'What are human rights?', there is an indication of the main topics regulated by the UDHR and consists of a paragraph (reported below).

> How can people use and defend human rights if they have never learned about them? The Universal Declaration of Human Rights (UDHR) acknowledges this in its preamble, and in Article 26 it gives everyone the right to education that should 'strengthen respect for human rights and fundamental freedoms'. The aim of human rights education is to create a world with a culture of human rights. This is a culture where everyone's rights are respected and rights themselves are respected; a culture where people understand their rights and responsibilities, recognise human rights violations and take action to protect the rights of others. It is a culture where human rights are as much a part of the lives of individuals as language, customs, the arts and ties to place are.
>
> (p. 17)

As the linguistic and textual analysis reveals, there is no loss of intended meaning although the format is quite unusual. This is achieved by using the question 'How can people use and defend human rights if they have never learned about them?' to reveal the legislative intent. Then, the *Simplified UDHR* reports straightforwardly the 30 UDHR articles with the simple naming of the human rights.

The Simplified Version of the Universal Declaration of Human Rights

Article 1
Right to Equality

Article 2
Freedom from Discrimination

Article 3
Right to Life, Liberty, Personal Security

Article 4
Freedom from Slavery

Article 5
Freedom from Torture and Degrading Treatment

Article 6
Right to Recognition as a Person before the Law

Article 7
Right to Equality before the Law

Article 8
Right to Remedy by Competent Tribunal

Article 9
Freedom from Arbitrary Arrest and Exile

Article 10
Right to Fair Public Hearing

Article 11
Right to be Considered Innocent until Proven Guilty

Article 12
Freedom from Interference with Privacy, Family, Home and Correspondence

Article 13
Right to Free Movement in and Out of the Country

Article 14
Right to Asylum in Other Countries from Persecution

Article 15
Right to a Nationality and the Freedom to Change It

Article 16
Right to Marriage and Family

Article 17
Right to Own Property

Article 18
Freedom of Belief and Religion

Article 19
Freedom of Opinion and Information

Article 20
Right of Peaceful Assembly and Association

Article 21
Right to Participate in Government and in Free Elections

Article 22
Right to Social Security

Article 23
Right to Desirable Work and to Join Trade Unions

Article 24
Right to Rest and Leisure

Article 25
Right to Adequate Living Standard

Article 26
Right to Education

Article 27
Right to Participate in the Cultural Life of Community

Article 28
Right to a Social Order That Articulates This Document

Article 29
Community Duties Essential to Free and Full Development

Article 30
Freedom from State or Personal Interference in the above Rights

Here, there is a list of UDHR articles with no Preamble. Clearly, all the unnecessary cross-referencing, overused textual-mapping, and multiple negative phrasing are eventually removed in the *Simplified UDHR*. The overall approach is to simplify the rules in both content and concept to promote transparency and accessibility.

17.3.2 'Easified' Version

According to traditional legal drafting, most legal sentences in common law legislative texts take a direct or indirect form of the legal reasoning formula '*if A* (case) *then B* (legal subject) *shall be / shall do C* (legal action)' (Crystal and Davy 1969; Driedger 1982). Taking this tradition into account, Bhatia (2014, 2021) observes that within common law jurisdictions all necessary information is typically condensed into a single sentence so as not to allow interpretation of the provision out of context. Thus, the construction of a single sentence that carries such an information load has the effect of making it complex in its meaning and less accessible to the intended audience (Fung and Watson-Brown 1994). Such syntactic complexity eventually makes cognitive processing beyond untrained and non-specialist readers.

In this regard, clarifying cognitive structure is one of the most efficient 'easification' strategies. Thanks to the easification strategies, it can be possible to identify the legislative intentions, reduce the information load of each sentence, limit syntactic discontinuities, decrease nominalisations, and use referential links when strictly necessary. At this point, it would be interesting to consider how the 'easification' strategies work and be applied. The extracts reported (Examples 9 and 10) here are some examples of easification.

Example 9

Section 63D material obtained for one purpose and used for another:

(1) Subsection (2) applies if section 63D material which is taken (or, in the case of a DNA profile, derived from a sample taken) from a person in connection with the investigation of an offence leads to the person to whom the material relates being arrested for or charged with, or convicted of, an offence other than the offence under investigation (Protection of Freedoms Act 2012).[24]

It is a relatively simpler provision (Example 9) but serves well as a typical example of a legislative provision bearing a number of difficulties. Thanks to the 'easification' strategies the main provision reported above will be as follows (Example 10).

Example 10

Section 63D material obtained for one purpose and used for another:

(1) Subsection (2) applies (*action rule*) if section 63D material leads to the person being arrested for or charged with, or convicted of, an offence other than the offence under investigation (*stipulation rule + qualification: preparatory*)

and the subsidiary provisions/qualifications will be those following:

to whom the material relates, which is taken (or, in the case of a DNA profile, derived from a sample taken) from a person in connection with the investigation of an offence (*stipulation rule: preparatory + referential*).

To make it easier for the readers to process, some of the difficulties can be removed from this following alternative version by adapting what Bhatia (1993, 2014) calls cognitive structuring.

As a matter of fact, 'easification' strategies do not modify or rewrite content but clarify and make content more accessible. 'Easification' strategies aim to make the text clearer, not simpler, as it is shown in Example 11:

Example 11

Section 63D material obtained for one purpose and used for another:

(1) Subsection (2) applies if section 63D material leads to the person being

- arrested for, or
- charged with, or
- convicted of

an offence other than the offence under investigation to whom the material relates, which is taken

- or derived from a sample taken in the case of a DNA profile,
- from a person in connection with the investigation of an offence.

By regrouping ideas and using bullet points to create one legal subject and one case descriptor, the underlying legal reasoning and the nature of the legal rules are made clearer and easily identifiable.

Indeed, there might be other problems related to the language or textual structure of the legislative text. Let us consider this other example taken from the *Parliamentary Constituencies Act 2020*. In particular, the following extract taken from Section 2(2) is one of the few most complex sections, whereas others are generally easier to process and understand (Example 12).

Example 12

For subsections (1) to (4) (procedure for draft Orders in Council) substitute—

(1) After all four reports under section 3(1) which are required by section 3(2) to be submitted before a particular date have been laid before Parliament under section 3(2ZB), *the Secretary of State or the Minister for the Cabinet Office* must submit to Her Majesty in Council a draft of an Order in Council for giving effect to the recommendations in those of the four reports (if any) which are reports under section 3(1)(a) (report with recommendations). (Parliamentary Constituencies Act 2020)[25]

At first glance, this clause appears to be a classic example of conventional legislative discourse with its quite standard opening case description, which accounts for 72 words of the legislative sentence. More specifically, we have what in legal terminology is known as *legal action* that 'the Secretary of State or the Minister for the Cabinet Office must submit to Her Majesty in Council a draft of an Order in Council'. This sentence has a few linguistic characteristics, one of which is the use of a binomial or multinomial expression, such as 'the Secretary of State or the Minister for the Cabinet Office'. In terms of the cognitive structuring of Section 2(2), another interesting device commonly used in a legislative sentence is what linguists often call 'syntactic discontinuities', of which a good example is the use of 'After all four reports under section 3(1) which are required by section 3(2) to be submitted before a particular date have been laid before Parliament under section 3(2ZB)' and 'for giving effect to the recommendations in those of the four reports (if any) which are reports under section 3(1)(a), that limit 'the performance of any function'. If we remove all the syntactic discontinuity, the 'easified' version of Section 2(2) of the *Parliamentary Constituencies Act 2020* should be the following (Example 13):

Example 13

For subsections (1) to (4) (procedure for draft Orders in Council) substitute—

(1) After all four reports under section 3(1) have been laid before Parliament under section 3(2ZB), *the Secretary of State or the Minister for the Cabinet Office* must submit to Her Majesty in Council a draft of an Order in Council for giving effect to the recommendations in those of the four reports (if any)

- (a) which are reports under section 3(1)(a) (report with recommendations);
- (b) which are [reports] required by section 3(2) to be submitted before a particular date.

Therefore, thanks to the easification strategies, the main provisions in Example 13 will be as follows:

(1) After all four reports under section 3(1) have been laid before Parliament under section 3(2ZB) (*main provision: stipulation rule*), the Secretary of State or the Minister for the Cabinet Office must submit to Her Majesty in Council a draft of an Order in Council for giving effect to the recommendations in those of the four reports (if any) (*main provision: action rule + condition*).

And the subsidiary provision/qualification will be the following:

(a) which are reports under section 3(1)(a) (report with recommendations);
(b) which are [reports] required by section 3(2) to be submitted before a particular date.

As shown above, the legislative provision (i.e., Section 2(2) of the *Parliamentary Constituencies Act 2020*), albeit quite thin in the specification of legal scope, will become even simpler and more accessible.

So far, the analysis of the lexico-grammatical and textual elements that are essential to give an account of how legislative provisions are structured demonstrates that legal texts, and particularly legislative provisions, cannot be considered in isolation from their communicative context(s). By considering legislative provisions from a linguistic point of view, tests of language can surely be conducted in a number of texts and documents belonging to the common law drafting practice to assess the effectiveness of their draft and eventually to ascertain a loss of conceptual focus by legislative drafters.

17.4 Conclusions

Drafting legislative provisions is a very complex and difficult task, which involves both legal knowledge and linguistic awareness. The construction of legal norms is greatly conditioned by specific factors that strictly depend on the context, such as the numerous cultural, linguistic, and legal environments in which it takes place. That poorly drafted provisions constitute a problem for the entire community is quite evident with the increasing number of courts that have been struggling to interpret and apply legislative norms, lawyers finding it difficult to base any advice upon them with any degree of certainty, and citizens being confused about how to conform to them (Galdia 2009). An increasing number of guidelines for better legislative drafting have been provided with the purpose of achieving a greater degree of clarity and consistency, and these have been greatly influential in introducing significant innovations in law-making with a consequent improvement in the quality of legislation.

The need to produce better legislation cannot be met without the contribution of other disciplines such as linguistics, with profitable cooperation between linguists and legislative drafters and the application of linguistic tools when formulating legal provisions that aim to be communicatively effective (Engberg 2013; Williams 2023). The analysis of simplification and 'easification' strategies certainly provides interesting insights into how legislative provisions can be linguistically and textually improved depending on the communicative purposes which have originated them and the context in which they will eventually be applied. Simplification in legislative texts can be achieved by introducing purpose clauses, subheadings, glossaries, etc. However, this added information cannot be placed in all legislative texts. In some cases, their use might oversimplify and distort the content and intended meaning of the original text (Langton 2005). To make the specialist versions easier for processing and interpretation, Bhatia (2014, 2021) suggests the 'easification' of legislative provisions, keeping them clear, precise, unambiguous, all-inclusive, and as transparent as linguistic resources permit.

The present research attempts to demonstrate that, thanks to the linguistic research methodology, it is possible to investigate how meaning and text functions evolve in the process of text production, discover what the functions of the produced legislative texts are, and eventually assess whether the texts' functions match with the original intentions of the drafters.

The final recommendation coming from the results of the analysis conducted here is that there may be additional scope for using innovative drafting techniques that can be applied to match the law's functions with the intention of drafters, thus developing methods that can lead to the desired result.

Notes

1 Childcare Payments Act 2014 (legislation.gov.uk) (accessed 12 October 2024).
2 Ivory Act 2018 (legislation.gov.uk).
3 Increased length often implies more complex relations between a noun and a word, or group of words, that describes a noun phrase or limits its meaning in some way and is placed after it (i.e., postmodifiers).
4 United Kingdom Internal Market Act 2020 (legislation.gov.uk).
5 Fisheries Act 2020 (legislation.gov.uk).
6 Oxford English Dictionary.
7 Childcare Payments Act 2014 (legislation.gov.uk).
8 https://assets.publishing.service.gov.uk/media/66682226bc25f5bc5da6ded0/Land_Registration-Rules-2003_2024-03-07_version.pdf
9 Glossary of Linguistic Terms at https://glossary.sil.org/bibliography/l.
10 glossary.sil.org/term/illocutionary-act.
11 Offensive Weapons Act 2019 (legislation.gov.uk).
12 *Substantial, satisfactory, negligent, unconscionable,* and *reasonable* are examples of indefinite adjectives with borderline indefiniteness (Fjeld 2001).
13 Policing and Crime Act 2009 (legislation.gov.uk).
14 For example, some Offices of Parliamentary Counsel of various English-speaking countries (e.g. Australia, New Zealand, Scotland) specify in their websites that their drafters adopt Plain Language techniques.
15 Langton (2005) distinguishes legal rules in *action rules* (duties, obligations and rights, prohibitions, powers and penalties), *stipulation rules* (how and when they are applied), *definition rules* (applied to the whole or part of the Act), and *qualification rules* (i) preparatory (i.e., when the rule applies); (ii) operational

(i.e., how the rule applies); (iii) referential (i.e., other sections of the same Act or other Acts that are strictly linked thereto).

16 Discourse analysis is a method of analysing the structure of texts or utterances longer than one sentence, taking into account both their linguistic content and their sociolinguistic context; analysis performed using this method (Oxford English Dictionary).

17 It is even more important to recognise the communicative purpose, the intended audience, and the linguistic features of the legislative provisions (Bhatia 1987, 1993; Crystal and Davy 1969; Geeraerts and Cuyckens 2010).

18 https://www.coe.int/en/web/compass/the-universal-declaration-of-human-rights

19 After an introduction to human rights and human rights education (chapter 1), *Compass* consists of other four chapters providing different activities for exploring human rights (chapter 2), ideas and tips to promote human rights in the community and the wider world (chapter 3), background information about human rights and their historical development together with international standards and documents (chapter 4), a summary of the background information to the global Compass themes (chapter 5), plus the simplified versions/summaries of the main declarations (i.e., the *Universal Declaration of Human Rights*), conventions (i.e., *The Convention of the Right of the Child*) and human rights texts (Appendices), and a glossary of frequently used terms (https://www.coe.int/en/web/compass/home).

20 Compass. Manual for Human Rights Education with Young People 2023 (https://rm.coe.int/compass-2023-eng-final-web/1680af992c).

21 Tens of other international and regional instruments, and hundreds of domestic constitutions and other legislation, have drawn inspiration from the *UDHR* (https://www.coe.int/en/web/compass/home).

22 It encompasses both civil and political rights and social, economic, and cultural rights.

23 As has been mentioned previously, the use of *shall* has become extremely rare in legislative provisions.

24 Protection of Freedoms Act 2012 (legislation.gov.uk).

25 Parliamentary Constituencies Act 2020 (legislation.gov.uk).

References

Barnes, Jeffrey. 2006. "The Continuing Debate about 'Plain Language' Legislation: A Law Reform Conundrum." *Statute Law Review* 27(2), 83–132.

Bhatia, Vijay K. 1987. "Textual-mapping in British Legislative Writing." *World Englishes* 1: 1–10. https://doi.org/10.1111/j.1467-971X.1987.tb00172.x

Bhatia, Vijay K. 1993. *Analysing Genre: Language Use in Professional Settings*. London: Longman.

Bhatia, Vijay K. 2004. *Worlds of Written Discourse*. London: Continuum.

Bhatia, Vijay K. 2014. "Linguistic and Socio-pragmatic Considerations in Legislative Drafting." *Legislative Drafting and Linguistics* 2(2): 169–183. https://www.tandfonline.com/doi/abs/10.5235/2050-8840.2.2.169

Bhatia, Vijay K. 2021. "Legal Writing: Specificity." *The Routledge Handbook of Forensic Linguistics*, edited by Malcolm Coulthard, and Alison Johnson, 37–50. London: Routledge.

Bowman, Geoffrey. 2006. "The Art of Legislative Drafting." *Amicus Curiae* 64: 2–9. https://doi.org/10.14296/ac.v2006i64.1117

Campbell, Lisbeth. 1996. "Drafting Styles: Fuzzy or Fussy?". *Murdoch University Electronic Journal of Law* 3(2): 17. https://classic.austlii.edu.au/au/journals/MurdochUeJlLaw/1996/17.html

Crystal, David, and Derek Davy. 1969. *Investigating English Style*. London: Routledge.

Dewey, John. 1997. *How We Think*. New York: Dover Publications Mineola.

Driedger, Elemer A. 1982. *A Manual of Instructions for Legislative and Legal Writing*. Ottawa: Minister of Supply and Services Canada.

Engberg, Jan. 2013. "Legal Linguistics as a Mutual Arena for Cooperation: Recent Developments in the Field of Applied Linguistics and Law." *AILA Review* 26: 24–41. https://doi.org/10.1075/aila.26.03eng

Fairclough, Norman. 1989. *Language and Power*. Harlow: Longman.

Fairclough, Norman. 1995. *The Critical Study of Language*. London: Longman.

Fairclough, Norman. 2003. *Analysing Discourse: Textual Analysis for Social Research*. London: Routledge.

Fjeld, Ruth V. 2001. "Interpretation of Indefinite Adjectives in Legislative Language." *Languages for Special Purposes: Perspectives for the New Millennium*, edited by Felix Mayer, 643–650. Tübingen: Narr.

Fung, Spring Y. C., and Anthony Watson-Brown. 1994. *The Template: A Guide for the Analysis of Complex Legislation*. London: University of London: Institute of Advanced Legal Studies.

Galdia, Marcus. 2009. *Legal Linguistics*. Frankfurt: Peter Lang.

Gardner, Howard. 2004. *Changing Minds: The Art and Science of Changing Our Own and Other People's Minds*. Cambridge, MA: Harvard University Press.

Garzone, Giuliana. 2013. "Variation in the Use of Modality in Legislative Texts: Focus on Shall." *Journal of Pragmatics* 57: 68–81. https://doi.org/10.1016/j.pragma.2013.07.008

Geeraerts, Dirk, and Hubert Cuyckens. 2010. *The Oxford Handbook of Cognitive Linguistics*. Oxford Handbooks Online. https://doi.org/10.1093/oxfordhb/9780199738632.001.0001

Goddard, Murray J. 2009. "The Impact of Human Intuition in Psychology." *Review of General Psychology* 13(2): 167–174. https://journals.sagepub.com/doi/10.1037/a0015104

Gotti, Maurizio. 2011. *Investigating Specialized Discourse*. Bern: Peter Lang.

Gotti, Maurizio, and Marina Dossena. 2001. *Modality in Specialized Texts*. Bern: Peter Lang.

Langacker, Ronald W. 1991. *Foundations of Cognitive Grammar. Vol. 2: Descriptive Application*. Stanford: Stanford University Press.

Langton, Nicola M. 2005. "Cleaning Up the Act: Using Plain English in Legislation." *Clarity* 54: 28–32. https://usercontent.one/wp/www.clarity-international.org/wp-content/uploads/2020/07/Clarity-no-54-bookmarked.pdf?media=1721338114

Mousmouti, Maria. 2019. *Designing Effective Legislation*. Cheltenham and Northampton, MA: Edward Elgar Publishing.

Pennisi, Giulia A. 2024. *A Linguistic Insight into Legislative Drafting: Tradition and Change in the UK Legislation*. Lausanne: Peter Lang.
Scollon, Ron. 2001. "Action and Text: Towards an Integrated Understanding of the Place of Text in Social (Inter)action, Mediated Discourse Analysis and the Problem of Social Action." *Methods of Critical Discourse Analysis*, edited by Ruth Wodak and Michael Meyer, 139–195. London: SAGE Publications.
Solan, Lawrence M. 1993. *The Language of Judges*. Chicago: The University of Chicago Press.
Solan, Lawrence M. 2004. "Private Language, Public Laws: The Central Role of Legislative Intent in Statutory Interpretation." *Social Science Research Network* 93(2): 427–486. https://doi.org/10.2139/ssrn.515022
Stefanou, Constantin. 2011. "Legislative Drafting as a Form of Communication." *Quality of Legislation Principles and Instruments*, edited by Luzius Mader, and Marta Tavares de Almeida, 308–320. Baden-Baden: Nomos.
Tiersma, Peter. 1999. *Legal Language*. Chicago: Chicago University Press.
Tiersma, Peter, and Lawrence M. Solan. 2012. *Oxford Handbook of Language and Law*. Oxford: Oxford University Press.
van Dijk, Teun A. 1985. *Handbook of Discourse Analysis*. London: Academic Press.
van Dijk, Teun A. 1997. *Discourse Studies: A Multidisciplinary Introduction*. London: Sage.
van Dijk, Teun A. 2005. "Contextual Knowledge Management in Discourse Production: A CDA Perspective." *A New Agenda in (Critical) Discourse Analysis*, edited by Ruth Wodak, and Paul Chilton, 71–100. Amsterdam: John Benjamins.
van Dijk, Teun A. 2007. *Discourse Studies*. London: Sage.
Xanthaki, Helen. 2014. *Drafting Legislation: Art and Technology of Rules for Regulation*. Oxford: Hart Publishing.
Xanthaki, Helen. 2022. *Thornton's Legislative Drafting*, 6th edn. London: Bloomsbury Publishing.
Xanthaki, Helen, and Giulia A. Pennisi. 2012. "Crossing the Borders between Legislative Drafting and Linguistics: Linguists to the Aid of Legislative Drafters." *Explorations in Language and Law: Approaches and Perspectives*, edited by Girolamo Tessuto, 83–109. Aprilia: Novalogos.
Williams, Christopher. 2023. *The Impact of Plain Language on Legal English in the United Kingdom*. New York: Routledge.
Williams, Christopher. 2004. "Legal English and Plain Language: An Introduction." *ESP Across Culture*, 111–124. https://edipuglia.it/wp-content/uploads/2015/05/ESP_1_2004.pdf
Wodak, Ruth, and Michael Meyer. 2001. *Methods of Critical Discourse Analysis*. London: Sage.

18 Let Linguists Teach the Drafters

Easification (Layering the Structure) of Regulation (EU) 2023/955 Establishing a Social Climate Fund

Helen Xanthaki

18.1 Effectiveness, Easification, and the Layered Structure

In my recent book on the legislative quality of EU legislation, I proposed a different style for the drafting of EU Acts, both Regulations and Directives,[1] informed by lessons learnt from linguistics. The proposals derive from the pursuit of legislative effectiveness as a means of enhancing regulatory efficacy defined as the achievement of the desired regulatory results.

The prevalent definition of legislative quality for those of us who view legislation as a tool for regulation is legislative effectiveness. Effectiveness requires a departure from formalistic rigidity in the assessment of legislative quality. Of course, clarity, precision, and unambiguity contribute to effectiveness. And clarity is enhanced by easification and gender inclusivity.

Since effectiveness is a contributor to regulatory efficacy, the success of a legislative text is assessed by its contribution to the achievement of the desired regulatory results. To achieve those, the text must speak to the users of the legislation and persuade them to undertake the prescribed action: this is where easification comes in. It is only when users act in the way that the law-makers intended that the law reform is put to effect and the desired (or at least the envisaged) regulatory goals can be reached. But to act in the way requested and required by the regulators, users must be able to receive the regulatory message. Receiving the regulatory message means two things: one, finding it within the text; and, two, understanding it in the way that the legislator meant it.

So easification may be relatively low in the pyramid of legislative values in that it is a tool for clarity, which in turn is a tool for legislative effectiveness, which enhances the much sought-after regulatory efficacy. Yet, despite its academic inferiority, it is all but insignificant in legislative and regulatory practice. Easification can produce critical results in the achievement of accessibility and intelligibility of legislation, which are important parameters for the rule of law.

DOI: 10.4324/9781003430308-22

Yet, as a theory and pursuit? It is virtually unknown in legislative studies and legislative drafting. Most drafters pursue its ancestor, namely plain language. But plain language is flawed when it comes to effectiveness and efficacy. Plain language is bidimensional. A word, a phrase, or a text is either plain or not. Simple or complex. But the addressees of legislation, the legislative audiences, are diverse. The diversity in their understanding of the topic of the law but also the law in and around the legislative text leads to diversity in their topical and legal sophistication. And this leads to diverse needs when it comes to legislative language. What is plain for one may be complex for another. The term 'mens rea' is rather simple for anyone with a legal background, but it is completely lost on those users who have not had the opportunity to study it in law school. Does that make it an inappropriate word for legislation? Easification tells us that the answer cannot be black or white. If the term is used in rules of evidence, then obviously it is plain and appropriate to be used, especially since it conveys a specific meaning awarded to it by case law and legal theory. If the term is used in a criminal provision, then obviously it is complex and the lay users of that text will be unable to identify what it means. As a result, they will be unable to understand what is prohibited as a criminal offence and what is allowed. Borrowing from linguistics and in the application of easification as a tool of communication, drafters may use the term 'archaic' as it admittedly is, provided that the particular audience to whom this specific provision is addressed has the topical and legal sophistication to understand it fully.

But, of course, the choice of the appropriate word for the specific audience over the provision is not the only usage of easification in legislative drafting. A word may be crucial, but it is not at the core of accessibility and intelligibility. Not compared the to the structure of the text. This is where the layered approach to structure comes into play. Since the empirically sound reveal of the three main groups of audiences of legislative texts by the Good Law initiative, easification can be applied to nurture accessibility and intelligibility by using a legislative structure that services each of the three groups of audiences separately, thus contributing to legislative effectiveness in a manner unachievable during the prevalence of plain language.

The layered approach recognises that there are three groups of users. The first group of users are lay users. They lack legal and topical sophistication. They access legislation to learn what rights are awarded to them by the legislation or what obligations are imposed on them. They have little tolerance for long texts. And even a little understanding of complexity and legalese. To facilitate their identification of the main information from the text and to ensure that they manage to read and understand the text, the layered structure places their relevant regulatory messages at the very start of the text, ensuring that they can read the relevant information within the four seconds' to six minutes' attention span recorded by studies of linguistics. The nature of their questions relates to the substantive provisions of the text. In that respect, the layered structure is not different from the traditional structure introduced by Lord Thring, who suggested that substantive provisions should be placed at the beginning of the text.

The second group of users are those who administer the law. They have no or little legal education, but they understand the topic and they are used to applying legislation in the course of their professional duties. These are officials who administer the law, and so they are concerned mostly with procedure. They have a degree of training in reading legislation, and in that respect their attention span is longer than that of lay users. Their messages, administrative in nature, should be placed after the first part of the legislation with substantive provisions. In that respect, the layered approach continues to comply with Lord Thring's structure where matters of procedure follow the substantive provisions. The language used in Part 2 of the legislation is semi-legal.

The third group of users are lawyers and judges, learned audiences, who understand legalese and who can sustain their attention for as long as necessary for the text. Their provisions are technical in nature and can use archaic times, provided that they carry an established meaning understood by all.

The layered approach uses the strengths and weaknesses of each group. And it utilises the now-known information on them to enhance the accessibility of the relevant regulatory messages and intelligibility by offering context to lay users, by offering clear procedural instructions to the group two users, and by ensuring that all technical details are in a form that learned users understand.

When it comes to EU Acts, the layered approach can be quite beneficial for accessibility and legibility. The Act may speak to EU citizens in Part 1. To Member States and their authorities in Part 2. And to EU institutions and learned users in Part 3.

In the application of easification, the following drafting points are put forward for the amelioration of the quality of EU Regulations:

What is proposed is a change of drafting philosophy, where the users lead on drafting dilemmas, rather than tradition or esoteric legalese. This supports the following changes in the drafting style of Regulations:

1 Shorter title pinpointing the topic of the Regulation, leaving the legal requirement for a full name to a citation article at the end of the text
2 Introduction of a table of contents to be used as a roadmap for users
3 Radical culling of recitals by maintaining only those needed for context for EU citizens and transferring the rest to the Notes Annex addressed to learned users
4 Introduction of a new Article 1 on objectives, with clear measurable regulatory goals and evidence-led criteria for effectiveness
5 Culling of definitions and correct use of them solely to extend or delimit the ordinary meaning of the defined term

6 Use of the article on subject matter to list the main points of the Act, thus narrating briefly to the citizen what follows
7 Division of the Regulation into three Parts, addressed to EU citizens, to Member States, and to EU Institutions, respectively, each containing regulatory messages relevant to each group and speaking to them in the appropriate easified language: a layered structure
8 Collection of all authorisation for implementing delegated acts in a list within one Article towards the end of the Regulation
9 Introduction of a citation article as penultimate to the Regulation stating that 'This Regulation is ...' and including the full current title of the Regulation
10 Introduction of review clauses in the article on entry into force
11 Introduction of an Annex on Definitions
12 Introduction of an Annex for Notes and Statement of the Commission, offering space for the political context of the Regulation, for references to relevant EU Acts, and miscellaneous topics

18.2 Layered Structure in Practice: Regulation 2023/955 as a Representative Case Study

This chapter will apply the proposed new easified drafting style for EU Regulations to a recent EU Regulation,[2] which was passed to benefit EU citizens by placing funds at their disposal but does not address them directly or convey that point to them at all. This is an extreme, yet representative of EU legislation, case of complexity, which prevents lay users (the main addressees of the Act) from understanding what are their new benefits and how to make use of them. It also typically invites Member States to plagiarise the benefits to their citizens by attributing the availability of funds and the subsidy to green works to the national funds to which Member States may only contribute 25%. In other words, this is a case where the EU has lost the opportunity to declare that up to 75% of all subsidies to green works undertaken by EU citizens are EU's rather than national. It goes, therefore, beyond easification in the sense of structure and words. And it really impresses upon the point of the current inability of the EU legislator to speak to its citizens and to convey the regulatory messages that affect them in a way that they understand and can act upon. Easification could not have been more absent. Or needed.

Before proceeding with the analysis of the quality of each type of drafting provision within this Act, it is important to note that the scope of this analysis is not to assess whether the current drafting rules for EU Acts have been followed. Instead, the scope of this analysis is to dissect this representative sample of EU Regulations, identify their strengths and weaknesses, and repurpose them as a means of rendering them user-centred and therefore fertile for the easified communication of their regulatory message.

The Regulation	*Comments*
Regulation (EU) 2023/955 of the European Parliament and of the Council of 10 May 2023 establishing a Social Climate Fund and amending Regulation (EU) 2021/1060	The title fails to convey the benefit of the text to EU citizens: this is about the subsidy of green works, which will be administered through the SCF. Easified proposal: **Title: Regulation (EU) 2023/955 on the subsidy to green works for EU citizens via a Social Climate Fund, and amending Regulation (EU) 2021/1060** **Citation Article (at the end of the Regulation): This Act is Regulation (EU) 2023/955 of the European Parliament on the subsidy to green works for EU citizens via a Social Climate Fund, and amending Regulation (EU) 2021/1060**
	The table of contents is published on Eur-Lex but is not in the Act: this deprives the user of a roadmap of provisions.
THE EUROPEAN PARLIAMENT AND THE COUNCIL OF THE EUROPEAN UNION, Having regard to the Treaty on the Functioning of the European Union, and in particular Article 91(1), point (d), Article 192(1) and Article 194(2), and Article 322(1), point (a), thereof, Having regard to the proposal from the European Commission, After transmission of the draft legislative act to the national parliaments, Having regard to the opinion of the European Economic and Social Committee (1), Having regard to the opinion of the Committee of the Regions (2), Acting in accordance with the ordinary legislative procedure (3),	There are 47 recitals that usurp the prime time of users' attention and deprive the text of the opportunity to serve the regulatory message within the attention span of the user. Linguistics set this at anywhere between four seconds and six minutes. Regulators have six minutes within which they have the golden opportunity to be heard by users, especially lay users. It is a real shame that all this valuable time is taken up by recitals. It would be much more sensible to reconsider the scope and utility of recitals and delimit them to what is absolutely necessary in order to offer the user context and to showcase the legitimacy of the EU Act. At the same time as weeding out generic statements of a political character, which have no place in legislation, recitals may be repurposed in an Annex to the EU Act entitled 'Notes' or could be placed within the Statement of the Commission.

The Regulation	*Comments*
Whereas:	
(1) The Paris Agreement([4]), adopted on 12 December 2015 under the United Nations Framework Convention on Climate Change (UNFCCC) (the 'Paris Agreement'), entered into force on 4 November 2016. The Parties to the Paris Agreement have agreed to hold the increase in the global average temperature well below 2°C above pre-industrial levels and to pursue efforts to limit the temperature increase to 1.5°C above pre-industrial levels. That commitment has been reinforced with the adoption under the UNFCCC of the Glasgow Climate Pact on 13 November 2021, in which the Conference of the Parties to the UNFCC, serving as the meeting of the Parties to the Paris Agreement, recognises that the impacts of climate change will be much lower at a temperature increase of 1.5°C, compared with 2°C, and resolves to pursue efforts to limit the temperature increase to 1.5°C.	1 Could be useful for the objectives clause.
(2) The communication of the Commission of 11 December 2019 on 'The European Green Deal' (the 'European Green Deal') sets out a new growth strategy that aims to transform the Union into a sustainable, fair and prosperous society, with a modern, resource-efficient and competitive economy, where there are no net emissions of greenhouse gases at the latest by 2050 and where economic growth is decoupled from resource use. The European Green Deal also aims to restore, protect, conserve and enhance the Union's natural capital, and protect the health and well-being of citizens from environment-related risks and impacts. Finally, it considers that this transition should be just and inclusive, leaving no one behind.	2 Useful in the introductory memorandum or the proposed Notes Annex.
(3) Through the adoption of Regulation (EU) 2021/1119 of the European Parliament and of the Council([5]), the Union has enshrined in legislation the objective of economy-wide climate neutrality by 2050 at the latest, and the aim of achieving negative emissions thereafter. That Regulation also establishes a binding Union domestic reduction target for net greenhouse gas emissions (emissions after deduction of removals) of at least 55% compared to 1990 levels by 2030. All sectors of the economy are expected to contribute to achieving that target.	3 Useful for the objectives clause in detailing the basic success of regulatory efficacy to which the Regulation can contribute.
(4) The conclusions of the European Council of 10–11 December 2020 endorsed the binding Union domestic reduction target for net greenhouse gas emissions, while underlining the importance of considerations of fairness and solidarity and leaving no one behind. Those conclusions were reaffirmed in the conclusions of the European Council of 24–25 May 2021, when the European Council invited the Commission to swiftly put forward its legislative package together with an in-depth examination of the environmental, economic and social impact at Member State level.	4 Useful for an explanatory memorandum or the proposed Notes Annex.
(5) The European Pillar of Social Rights Action Plan, endorsed by the conclusions of the European Council of 24–25 June 2021, highlights the need to strengthen social rights and the European social dimension across all policies of the Union. Principle 20 of the European Pillar of Social Rights states that 'everyone has the right to access essential services of good quality, including water, sanitation, energy, transport, financial services and digital communications. Support for access to such services shall be available for those in need'.	5 Useful for an explanatory memorandum or the proposed Notes Annex.

The Regulation	*Comments*
(6) The Porto Declaration of 8 May 2021 reaffirmed the European Council's pledge to work towards a social Europe strengthening a fair transition and its determination to continue deepening the implementation of the European Pillar of Social Rights at Union and national level, with due regard for respective competences and the principles of subsidiarity and proportionality.	6 Useful for an explanatory memorandum or the proposed Notes Annex.
(7) In order to implement the commitment towards climate neutrality, the Union's climate and energy legislation has been reviewed and amended in order to accelerate greenhouse gas emission reductions.	7 Not necessary.
(8) Those amendments have differing economic and social impacts on the different sectors of the economy, citizens and Member States. In particular, the inclusion of greenhouse gas emissions from buildings, road transport and additional sectors which correspond to industrial activities not covered by Annex I to Directive 2003/87/EC of the European Parliament and of the Council(6) within the scope of that Directive should provide an additional economic incentive to invest in the reduction of fossil fuel consumption and thereby accelerate the reduction of greenhouse gas emissions. Combined with other measures, this should, in the medium to long term, contribute to the reduction of energy poverty and transport poverty, reduce the costs of buildings and road transport, and, where relevant, provide new opportunities for quality job creation and sustainable investments, fully aligned with the goals of the European Green Deal.	8 Useful for an explanatory memorandum or the proposed Notes Annex.
(9) However, resources are needed to finance those investments. In addition, before such investments are made, the cost supported by households and transport users for heating, cooling, cooking, and road transport, is likely to increase as fuel suppliers that are subject to the obligations under the emission trading system for buildings and road transport pass on the costs of carbon to consumers.	9 To be rephrased as justification of the necessity of the Act.
(10) The climate transition will have an economic and social impact that is difficult to asses *sex ante*. Achieving the increased climate ambition will require substantial public and private resources. Investments in energy efficiency measures, as well as renewable energy-based heating systems, such as heating with electric heat pumps, heating and cooling at district level and participation in renewable energy communities, are an effective method of reducing import dependency and emissions while increasing the Union's resilience. Dedicated funding to support vulnerable households, vulnerable micro-enterprises and vulnerable transport users is necessary.	10 General political statement, but it makes an excellent point on the vulnerability of beneficiaries as the target audiences. Could be added to the title as it showcases the social aspect of the regulation. And to the scope. Or deleted.

The Regulation	*Comments*
(11) The increase in the price for fossil fuels can disproportionally affect vulnerable households, vulnerable micro-enterprises and vulnerable transport users who spend a larger part of their income on energy and transport, who, in certain regions, do not have access to alternative, affordable mobility and transport solutions, and who may lack the financial capacity to invest in the reduction of fossil fuel consumption. Geographic specificities, such as islands, outermost regions and territories, rural or remote areas, less accessible peripheries, mountainous areas or areas that are lagging behind, can have specific impacts in the context of transport poverty on the vulnerability of households, micro-enterprises and transport users. Therefore, those geographic specificities should be taken into account when preparing measures and investments in support of vulnerable households, vulnerable micro-enterprises and vulnerable transport users, where applicable and relevant.	11 Useful for an explanatory memorandum or the proposed Notes Annex.
(12) A part of the revenues generated by the inclusion of buildings, road transport and additional sectors within the scope of Directive 2003/87/EC should be used to address the social impacts arising from that inclusion, in order for the transition to be just and inclusive, leaving no one behind. The overall amount of the Social Climate Fund established under this Regulation (the 'Fund') should reflect the level of decarbonisation ambition from the inclusion of greenhouse gas emissions from buildings, road transport and additional sectors within the scope of Directive 2003/87/EC.	12 Relevant only for the provision of funding the fund.
(13) Using part of the revenues to address the social impacts arising from the inclusion of the buildings, road transport and additional sectors within the scope of Directive 2003/87/EC is even more relevant in view of the existing levels of energy poverty. Energy poverty is a situation in which households are unable to access essential energy services that underpin a decent standard of living and health, such as adequate warmth through heating, cooling, as temperatures rise, lighting, and energy to power appliances. In a 2021 Union-wide survey, approximately 34 million Europeans, nearly 6.9% of the population of the Union, said that they could not afford to heat their home sufficiently. Energy poverty is therefore a major challenge for the Union. While social tariffs or temporary direct income support can provide immediate relief to households facing energy poverty in the short term, only targeted structural measures, in particular building renovations, including through access to energy from renewable sources and the active promotion of renewable energy sources through information and awareness-raising measures targeted at households, and building renovations that contribute to the objectives established in Directive 2010/31/EU of the European Parliament and of the Council([7]) can provide lasting solutions and effectively help combat energy poverty. It should be possible for the definition of energy poverty under this Regulation to be updated to reflect the outcome of the negotiations on a Directive of the European Parliament and of the Council on energy efficiency (recast).	13 To be moved to the Notes Annex.

The Regulation	*Comments*
(14) A holistic approach to building renovations that takes into account in a more efficient way people at risk of exclusion, namely those who suffer most from energy poverty in the Union, could lead to less demand for energy. Therefore, the support under the Fund to the buildings sector should aim to improve energy efficiency, leading to a reduction in energy consumption for each household that would be visible in terms of the money saved and, as a result, would provide one means of combating energy poverty. The revision of Directive 2010/31/EU would lay the foundations for those objectives to be achieved and should therefore be taken into account when implementing this Regulation.	14 Lacks legislative content.
(15) Since transport poverty has not yet been defined at Union level, such a definition should be introduced for the purpose of this Regulation. Transport poverty could become an even more pressing issue, as recognised in the Council Recommendation of 16 June 2022 on ensuring a fair transition towards climate neutrality([8]), and result in diminished access to essential socioeconomic activities and services such as employment, education or healthcare, in particular for vulnerable individuals and households. Transport poverty is usually caused by one or a combination of factors such as low income, high fuel expenditures, or a lack of affordable or accessible private or public transport. Transport poverty can particularly affect individuals and households in rural, insular, peripheral, mountainous, remote and less accessible areas or less developed regions or territories, including less developed peri-urban areas and the outermost regions.	15 Lacks legislative content.
(16) The Fund should be established to provide funds to the Member States to support their policies to address the social impacts of the introduction of the emissions trading system for buildings and road transport on vulnerable households, vulnerable micro-enterprises and vulnerable transport users. This should be achieved in particular through temporary direct income support and measures and investments intended to reduce reliance on fossil fuels through increased energy efficiency of buildings, decarbonisation of heating and cooling of buildings, irrespective of who owns those buildings, including the integration of energy from renewable sources, and through granting improved access to zero- and low-emission mobility and transport to the benefit of vulnerable households, vulnerable micro-enterprises and vulnerable transport users. Attention needs to be paid to the different forms of rental housing, including those on the private rental market. Financial support or fiscal incentives, such as deductibility of renovation costs from the rent could be included among the measures in order to take account of tenants and people living in social housing.	16 To be moved to the Notes Annex or even deleted as it is evident.

The Regulation	*Comments*
(17) Each Member State should submit to the Commission a Social Climate Plan (the 'Plan'). The Plans should be submitted by 30 June 2025 so that they can be given careful and timely consideration. The Plans should have an investment component that promotes the long-term solution of reducing fossil fuels reliance and could envisage other measures, including temporary direct income support, to mitigate adverse effects on income in the shorter term. The Plans should pursue two objectives. First, they should provide vulnerable households, vulnerable micro-enterprises and vulnerable transport users with the necessary resources to finance and carry out investments in energy efficiency, decarbonisation of heating and cooling, in zero- and low-emission vehicles and mobility, including through vouchers, subsidies or zero-interest loans. Second, they should mitigate the impact of the increase in the cost of fossil fuels on the most vulnerable and thereby prevent energy poverty and transport poverty during the transitional period until such investments have been carried out. The Plans could support access to affordable energy-efficient housing, including social housing. When implementing measures in support of vulnerable transport users, it should be possible for Member States to prioritise support to zero-emission vehicles in their Plans, provided that it is an affordable and deployable solution.	17 To be moved to the Notes Annex or even deleted as it is evident from the text.
(18) Member States, in consultation with local and regional authorities, economic and social partners and relevant civil society organisations, are best placed to design, implement and, where relevant, amend Plans that are adapted and targeted to their local, regional and national circumstances, their existing policies in the relevant areas and planned use of other relevant Union funds. A public consultation of stakeholders should take place every time the Commission is required to assess a Plan. In that manner, the broad diversity of situations, the specific knowledge of local and regional governments, economic and social partners, relevant civil society organisations, research and innovation institutions, industrial stakeholders and social dialogue representatives, as well as national circumstances can best be reflected and contribute to the effectiveness and efficiency of the overall support to the vulnerable.	18 To be moved to the Notes Annex or even deleted as it is evident.
(19) The Plans should be designed in close cooperation with the Commission and prepared in accordance with the template provided. In order to avoid excessive administrative burdens, it should be possible for Member States to make minor adjustments to or correct clerical errors in the Plans, by a simple notification of those changes to the Commission. Minor adjustments should represent an increase or decrease of less than 5% of a target envisaged in the Plan.	19 To be moved to the Notes Annex or even deleted as it is evident.
(20) Ensuring that the measures and investments are particularly targeted towards households in energy poverty or vulnerable households, vulnerable micro-enterprises and vulnerable transport users is key for a just transition towards climate neutrality. Support measures to promote reductions in greenhouse gas emissions should help Member States to address the social impacts arising from the emissions trading in the buildings and road transport sectors.	20 To be moved to the Notes Annex or even deleted as it is evident.

The Regulation	*Comments*
(21) Pending the impact of those investments on reducing costs and emissions, well targeted direct income support for vulnerable households and vulnerable transport users would contribute to a reduction of energy and mobility costs and would support the just transition. Direct income support should be understood to be a temporary measure accompanying the decarbonisation of the housing and transport sectors. It would not be permanent as it does not address the root causes of energy poverty and transport poverty. Such support should only be used to address direct impacts of the inclusion of greenhouse gas emissions from buildings and road transport within the scope of Directive 2003/87/EC, and should not be used to address electricity or heating costs related to the inclusion of power and heat production in the scope of that Directive. Eligibility for such direct income support should be limited in time. Recipients of direct income support should be targeted, as members of a general group of recipients, by measures and investments aimed at effectively lifting those recipients out of energy poverty and transport poverty. The Plans should therefore include direct income support provided that they also contain measures or investments with lasting impacts targeted at the vulnerable households and vulnerable transport users who receive direct income support.	21 To be moved to the Notes Annex or even deleted as it is evident.
(22) Member States should raise awareness among vulnerable households, vulnerable micro-enterprises and vulnerable transport users by providing targeted, accessible and affordable information, education and advice on cost-effective measures and investments, and available support, including through energy audits of buildings, as well as tailored energy consultations or tailored mobility management services.	22 To be moved to the Notes Annex or even deleted as it is evident from the text.
(23) Taking into account the importance of tackling climate change in accordance with the Paris Agreement commitments, and the commitment to the United Nations Sustainable Development Goals, the measures and investments under this Regulation are intended to be in line with the target that at least 30% of the total amount of the Union budget under the multiannual financial framework for the years 2021 to 2027 laid down in Council Regulation (EU, Euratom) 2020/2093([9]) (the 'MFF 2021–2027') and of the total amount of the European Union Recovery Instrument, established by Council Regulation (EU) 2020/2094([10]), and at least 37% of the total amount of the Recovery and Resilience Facility, established by Regulation (EU) 2021/241 of the European Parliament and of the Council([11]), should be spent on mainstreaming climate objectives. The measures and investments under this Regulation are also intended to be in line with the ambition of providing 7.5% of annual spending under the MFF 2021–2027 to biodiversity objectives in2024 and 10% of annual spending under MFF 2021–2027 to biodiversity objectives in2026 and 2027, while considering the existing overlaps between climate and biodiversity goals.	23 To be used for the objectives clause

The Regulation	*Comments*
For that purpose, the methodology set out in Annex I to Regulation (EU) 2021/1060 of the European Parliament and of the Council(12) should be used to track the expenditures of the Fund. The Fund should support measures and investments that fully respect climate and environmental standards and priorities of the Union and comply with the principle of 'do no significant harm' within the meaning of Article 17 of Regulation (EU) 2020/852 of the European Parliament and of the Council(13). Only such measures and investments should be included in the Plans. Direct income support measures should, as a rule, be considered as having an insignificant foreseeable impact on environmental objectives and, as such, should be considered to be compliant with the principle of 'do no significant harm'. The Commission should issue technical guidance to the Member States well ahead of the preparation of the Plans. The guidance should explain how the measures and investments are to comply with the principle of 'do no significant harm'.	
(24) Women are disproportionately affected by energy poverty and transport poverty, in particular single mothers, who represent 85% of single parent families, as well as single women, women with disabilities, and elderly women living alone. In addition, women have different and more complex mobility patterns. Single parent families with dependent children have a particularly high risk of child poverty. Gender equality and equal opportunities for all, and the mainstreaming of those objectives, as well as accessibility rights of persons with disabilities should be upheld and promoted throughout the preparation and implementation of Plans to ensure that no one is left behind.	24 To be used in the objectives
(25) Active customers, citizen energy communities and peer-to-peer trading of renewable energy can help Member States achieve the objectives of this Regulation through a bottom-up approach initiated by citizens. They empower and engage consumers and enable certain groups of household customers to participate in energy efficiency measures and investments, support the use of renewable energy of households and at the same time contribute to fighting energy poverty. Member States should therefore promote the role of citizen energy communities and renewable energy communities and regard them as eligible beneficiaries of the Fund.	25 To be moved to the Notes Annex or even deleted as it is evident from the text.
(26) Member States should include in the Plans the measures and investments to be financed, the estimated costs of those measures and investments, and the national contribution. When submitting their Plans, Member States should present the estimated total costs excluding the value added tax (VAT) to enable comparability between the Plans. The Plans should also include key milestones and targets so that the effective implementation of the measures and investments can be assessed.	26 To be moved to the Notes Annex or even deleted as it is evident from the text.
(27) The Fund and the Plans should be coherent with and framed by the reforms planned and the commitments made by the Member States under their updated	27 This issubstantive provision for the text

The Regulation	*Comments*
integrated national energy and climate plans in accordance with Regulation (EU) 2018/1999 of the European Parliament and of the Council([14]), under Directive of the European Parliament and the Council on energy efficiency (recast), under the European Pillar of Social Rights Action Plan, under cohesion policy programmes in accordance with Regulation (EU) 2021/1060, under territorial just transition plans in accordance with Regulation (EU) 2021/1056 of the European Parliament and of the Council([15]), under recovery and resilience plans in accordance with Regulation (EU) 2021/241, under the Modernisation Fund, as set out in Article 10d of Directive 2003/87/EC, and under the Member States' long-term building renovation strategies in accordance with Directive 2010/31/EU. To ensure administrative efficiency, where applicable, the information included in the Plans should be consistent with those legislative acts and plans.	
(28) For more efficient planning, Member States should indicate in their Plans the consequences of postponing the emission trading system established in accordance with Chapter IVa of Directive 2003/87/EC, pursuant to Article 30k of that Directive. To that end, all the relevant information to be included in the Plan should be thoroughly distinguished by separating it into two scenarios, namely, by describing and quantifying the necessary adjustments to the measures, investments, milestones, targets, the amount of national contribution and any other relevant element of the Plan.	28 Substantive provision for the text
(29) The Union should support Member States with financial means to implement their Plans through the Fund. Payments from the Fund should be made conditional upon the achievement of the milestones and targets included in the Plans. This would enable national circumstances and priorities to be taken into account, while simplifying financing and facilitating the integration of financing under the Fund with other national spending programmes and while guaranteeing the impact and the integrity of Union spending.	29 To be deleted as superfluous (making a self-evident statement).
(30) The Fund should be exceptionally and temporarily financed by the revenue generated from the auctioning of 50 million allowances pursuant to Article 10a(8b) of Directive 2003/87/EC, 150 million allowances pursuant to Article 30d(3) of that Directive and a volume of additional allowances pursuant to Article 30d(4) of that Directive, which should constitute external assigned revenue. In principle, a maximum amount of EUR 65,000,000,000 should be made available for the implementation of the Fund for the period 2026–2032. The Commission is to ensure the auctioning of allowances covered by Chapter IVa of that Directive. Where the emission trading system established in accordance with that Chapter is postponed until 2028 pursuant to Article 30k of that Directive, the maximum amount available for the implementation of the Fund should be EUR 54,600,000,000. That amount and the annual amounts reflect a greater need of financing at the start of the Fund. The maximum financial allocation should be calculated for each Member State in	30 Substantive provision.

The Regulation	*Comments*
accordance with an allocation methodology providing, in particular, additional support to those Member States that are more impacted by the inclusion of greenhouse gas emissions from buildings and road transport within the scope of Directive 2003/87/EC. Considering that the external assigned revenue is to be made available following the auctioning of allowances pursuant to Articles 10a(8b), 30d(3) and 30d(4) of Directive 2003/87/EC, it is necessary to provide for a derogation from Article 22(2) of Regulation (EU, Euratom) 2018/1046 of the European Parliament and of the Council([16]) to enable the Union to commit each year the amounts necessary for the payments to Member States to be made in accordance with this Regulation for the accommodation of appropriations corresponding to assigned revenue.	
(31) Member States should contribute at least 25% of the estimated total costs of their Plans.	31 To be deleted as it is evident from the text.
(32) The budgetary commitments should be able to be broken down into annual instalments, where appropriate. The agreements with Member States constituting individual legal commitments should take into account, inter alia, the event referred to in Article 30k of Directive 2003/87/EC which could trigger a oneyear delay of the start of emissions trading for buildings, road transport and additional sectors. Those agreements should also take into account any potential financial risks for the Union, which might require an amendment of the individual legal commitments, due to the specificities of the temporary and exceptional financing of the Fund by external assigned revenue generated from allowances of the emission trading system.	32 To be moved to the Notes Annex or even deleted as it is evident from the text.
(33) In order to ensure additional resources for the Fund, the Member States should be able to request a transfer of resources to the Fund from the cohesion policy programmes under shared management, established by Regulation (EU) 2021/1060, subject to the conditions set out in that Regulation. In order to provide Member States with sufficient flexibility in the implementation of their allocations under the Fund, it should be possible to transfer resources from their annual financial allocation to funds under shared management provided for in Regulation (EU) 2021/1060, up to a ceiling of 15%. With a view to alleviating the administrative burden resulting from successive transfers of resources from their annual financial allocation from the Fund to funds under shared management falling within the scope of Regulation (EU) 2021/1060, the corresponding amendment of one or more programmes should, in principle, be required only once, subject to certain conditions to ensure effective financial control. It should be possible to effect further transfers in subsequent years by notifying the financial tables to the Commission, provided that the changes relate exclusively to an increase in the financial resources, without any further changes to the programme concerned.	33 Substantive provision.

The Regulation	*Comments*
(34) The Fund should support measures that respect the principle of additionality of Union funding. The Fund should not be a substitute for recurring national expenditure, except in duly justified cases, including for payments of costs for technical assistance actions indicated in the Plans.	34 Substantive provision.
(35) In order to ensure the efficient, transparent and coherent allocation of funds, and to respect the principle of sound financial management, actions under this Regulation should be consistent with and be complementary to ongoing Union, national and, where appropriate, regional programmes, whilst avoiding double funding from the Fund and other Union programmes for the same expenditure. In particular, the Commission and Member States should ensure effective coordination, at all stages of the process, in order to safeguard the consistency, coherence, complementarity and synergy among sources of funding. To that effect, Member States should be required to present the relevant information on existing or planned Union financing when submitting their Plans to the Commission. Financial support under the Fund should be additional to the support provided under other Union programmes and instruments. Measures and investments financed under the Fund should be able to receive funding from other Union programmes and instruments provided that such support does not cover the same costs.	35 To be moved to the Notes Annex or even deleted as it is evident.
(36) Payments should be made on the basis of a Commission decision authorising the disbursement to the Member State concerned. It is therefore necessary to derogate from Article 116(2) of Regulation (EU, Euratom) 2018/1046, so that the payment deadline can start running from the date of the communication from the Commission to the Member State concerned of that decision and not from the date on which a payment request is received.	36 To be deleted as it is evident from the text.
(37) After the analysis of all the payment requests received in a given round, and if revenues assigned to the Fund in accordance with Article 30d(4) of Directive 2003/87/EC are not sufficient to cover the payment requests submitted by the Member States, the Commission should pay the Member States on a pro-rata basis in order to provide for an equal treatment of Member States. In the following round of payment requests, the Commission should give priority to those Member States with delayed payments from the previous round of payment requests, and only afterwards pay the newly submitted payment requests.	37 To be moved to the Notes Annex or even deleted as it is evident from the text.
(38) In order to facilitate the preparation of the Plans and to ensure transparent rules for monitoring and evaluation, the list of common indicators and the template for the Plans should be included in the Annexes to this Regulation. It should be possible for the Member States to use relevant common indicators to set out the milestones and targets in their Plans. The list of common indicators should contain the common indicators for reporting on the progress and for the purpose of monitoring and evaluation of the implementation of the Plans and of the Fund.	38 To delete as the Commission does the drafting.

The Regulation	*Comments*
(39) The Fund should be implemented in line with the principle of sound financial management, including the effective prevention and prosecution of fraud, tax fraud, tax evasion, corruption and conflicts of interests. The Fund is subject to a general regime of conditionality for the protection of the Union budget in the case of breaches of the principles of the rule of law in the Member States established by Regulation (EU, Euratom) 2020/2092 of the European Parliament and of the Council([17]).	39 To be moved to the Notes Annex.
(40) For the purpose of sound financial management, while respecting the performance-based nature of the Fund, specific rules should be laid down for budget commitments, payments, suspension, and the recovery of funds as well as for the termination of agreements related to financial support. The Member States should take appropriate measures to ensure that the use of funds in relation to measures supported by the Fund complies with applicable Union and national law. Member States should ensure that such support is granted in compliance with the Union State aid rules, where applicable. In particular, they should ensure that fraud, corruption and conflicts of interests are prevented, detected and corrected, and that double funding from the Fund and other Union programmes is avoided. Suspension and the termination of agreements related to financial support, as well as reduction and recovery of the financial allocation, should be possible when the Plan has not been implemented in a satisfactory manner by the Member State concerned or in the case of serious irregularities, namely fraud, corruption and conflicts of interests in relation to the measures supported by the Fund or a serious breach of an obligation under the agreements related to financial support. In the case of the termination of an agreement related to financial support or the reduction and recovery of a financial allocation, those amounts should be allocated to Member States by 31 December 2033 according to the rules for distribution of allowances set out in Article 30d(5) of Directive 2003/87/EC. Appropriate contradictory procedures should be established to ensure that the decisions of the Commission in relation to suspension and recovery of amounts paid or the termination of agreements related to financial support respect the right of Member States to submit observations.	40 To be moved to the Notes Annex, but it is already covered in the new Art. 25.
(41) The Commission should ensure that the financial interests of the Union are protected effectively. While it is primarily the responsibility of the Member State itself to ensure that the Fund is implemented in compliance with relevant Union and national law, the Commission should be able to receive sufficient assurance from Member States in that regard. To that end, in implementing the Fund, Member States should ensure the functioning of an effective and efficient internal control system and should recover amounts unduly paid or misused. In that regard, Member States should be able to rely on their regular national budget management systems. Member States should collect, record and store in an electronic system, standardised categories of data and information allowing the prevention, detection	41 To delete or keep in the Notes Annex or moved to Art. 25.

The Regulation	*Comments*
and correction of serious irregularities in relation to the measures and investments supported by the Fund, namely fraud, corruption and conflicts of interests. The Commission should make available an information and monitoring system, including a single data-mining and risk-scoring tool, to access and analyse that data and information. The Commission should encourage the use of that information and monitoring system with a view to a generalised application by Member States.	
(42) The Commission, the European Anti-Fraud Office (OLAF), the Court of Auditors and, where applicable, the European Public Prosecutor's Office (EPPO) should be able to use the information and monitoring system within their competences and rights.	42 To be moved to the Notes Annex or even deleted as it is evident from the text.
(43) The Member States and the Commission should be allowed to process personal data only where necessary for the purpose of ensuring discharge, audit and control, information, communication and visibility of the use of funds in relation to measures for the implementation under the Fund. Personal data should be processed in accordance with Regulation (EU) 2016/679 of the European Parliament and of the Council([18])or Regulation (EU) 2018/1725 of the European Parliament and of the Council([19]), whichever is applicable.	43 To be moved to the Notes Annex or even deleted as it is evident from the text.
(44) In accordance with Regulation (EU, Euratom) 2018/1046, Regulation (EU, Euratom) No. 883/2013 of the European Parliament and of the Council([20]), and Council Regulations (EC, Euratom) No. 2988/95([21]), (Euratom, EC) No. 2185/96([24]) and (EU) 2017/1939([23]), the financial interests of the Union are to be protected by means of proportionate measures, including measures relating to the prevention, detection, correction and investigation of fraud, corruption and conflicts of interests, and, where appropriate, the imposition of administrative penalties. In particular, in accordance with Regulations (Euratom, EC) No. 2185/96 and (EU, Euratom) No. 883/2013, OLAF has the power to carry out administrative investigations, including on-the-spot checks and inspections, with a view to establishing whether there has been fraud, corruption, conflicts of interests or any other illegal activity affecting the financial interests of the Union. EPPO is empowered, in accordance with Regulation (EU) 2017/1939, to investigate and prosecute fraud, corruption, conflicts of interests and other criminal offences affecting the financial interests of the Union as provided for in Directive (EU) 2017/1371 of the European Parliament and of the Council([24]). In accordance with Regulation (EU, Euratom) 2018/1046, any person or entity receiving Union funds is to fully cooperate in the protection of the financial interests of the Union, grant the necessary rights and access to the Commission, OLAF, the Court of Auditors and, in respect of those Member States participating in enhanced cooperation, EPPO pursuant to Regulation (EU) 2017/1939, and ensure that any third parties involved in the implementation of Union funds grant equivalent rights.	44 To be moved to the Notes Annex or even deleted as it is evident from the text.

The Regulation	*Comments*
(45) Horizontal financial rules adopted by the European Parliament and by the Council pursuant to Article 322 of the Treaty on the Functioning of the European Union (TFEU) apply to this Regulation. Those rules are laid down in Regulation (EU, Euratom) 2018/1046 and determine in particular the procedure for establishing and implementing the Union budget through grants, procurement, prizes and indirect management, and provide for checks on the responsibility of financial actors. Rules adopted pursuant to Article 322 TFEU also include a general regime of conditionality for the protection of the Union budget.	45 To be moved to the Notes Annex or even deleted as it is evident from the text.
(46) Regulation (EU) 2021/1060 should be amended accordingly.	46 To be moved to the Notes Annex or even deleted as it is evident from the text.
(47) Since the objective of this Regulation, namely to contribute to a socially fair transition towards climate neutrality by addressing the social impacts of the inclusion of greenhouse gas emissions from buildings and road transport within the scope of Directive 2003/87/EC, cannot be sufficiently achieved by the Member States but can rather, by reason of its scale and effects, be better achieved at Union level, the Union may adopt measures, in accordance with the principle of subsidiarity as set out in Article 5 of the Treaty on European Union. In accordance with the principle of proportionality as set out in that Article, this Regulation does not go beyond what is necessary in order to achieve that objective,	47 Necessary as evidence of necessity and subsidiarity.
HAVE ADOPTED THIS REGULATION:	Excellent enacting clause, clear, precise, brief.

CHAPTER I *General provisions* *Article 1* **Subject matter and scope** This Regulation establishes the Social Climate Fund (the 'Fund') for the period from 2026 to 2032. The Fund shall provide financial support to Member States for the measures and investments included in their Social Climate Plans (the 'Plans'). The measures and investments supported by the Fund shall benefit households, micro-enterprises and transport users, which are vulnerable and particularly affected by the inclusion of greenhouse gas emissions from buildings and road transport within the scope of Directive 2003/87/EC, in particular households in energy poverty or households in transport poverty.	The first provisions of the text can enhance comprehensibility by offering context: why and what do we legislate? Two provisions are necessary for that: objectives and subject matter. The first conveys why we legislate and what we are aiming to achieve. Subject matter states what tools we use to get to the objectives.

The Regulation	*Comments*
	Subject matter answers the question: which are the main points of the law reform? An easified article on the subject matter should be user-centred, namely speaking the main points of the Regulation from the focal point of the citizen.
Article 2 **Definitions** For the purposes of this Regulation, the following definitions apply: (1) 'energy poverty' means a household's lack of access to essential energy services that underpin a decent standard of living and health, including adequate warmth, cooling, lighting, and energy to power appliances, in the relevant national context, existing social policy and other relevant policies; (2) 'transport poverty' means individuals' and households' inability or difficulty to meet the costs of private or public transport, or their lack of or limited access to transport needed for their access to essential socioeconomic services and activities, taking into account the national and spatial context; (3) 'estimated total costs of the Plan' means the estimated total costs of the measures and investments included in the Plan; (4) 'financial allocation' means non-repayable financial support under the Fund that is available for allocation, or that has been allocated, to a Member State; (5) 'milestone' means a qualitative achievement used to measure progress towards the achievement of a measure or an investment; (6) 'target' means a quantitative achievement used to measure progress towards the achievement of a measure or investment; (7) 'energy from renewable sources' or 'renewable energy' means energy from renewable sources as defined in Article 2, second subparagraph, point (1), of Directive (EU) 2018/2001 of the European Parliament and of the Council[25]; (8) 'household' means a private household as defined in Article 2, point (15), of Regulation (EU) 2019/1700 of the European Parliament and of the Council[26]; (9) 'micro-enterprise' means an enterprise that employs fewer than 10 persons and whose annual turnover or annual balance sheet does not exceed EUR2 million, calculated in accordance with Articles 3 to 6 of Annex I to Commission Regulation (EU) No. 651/2014[27]; (10) 'vulnerable households' means households in energy poverty or households, including low income and lower middle-income ones, that are significantly affected by the price impacts of the inclusion of greenhouse gas emissions from buildings within the scope of Directive 2003/87/EC and lack the means to renovate the building they occupy;	There is no reason to have definitions at the start of the Regulation, taking up more of the limited users' attention span. Those of the lay users who have survived the recitals will now be lost in definitions, thus derailing from the main regulatory message. Those learned users who need definitions are trained and resilient enough to look for them in a Definitions Annex immediately after the body of the text. And so, Article 2 can just be a hanging provision for the definitions annex. Leaving the placement of definitions aside, the drafting of definitions in EU Regulations is flawed. Definitions provide a tool to either extend or delimit the semantic field of the concept that is being defined, such as definition 9. But: a They do not allow for a departure from the common meaning of the concept such as 10. The definition is used erroneously. Instead, the text should have used

The Regulation	*Comments*
(11) 'vulnerable micro-enterprises' means micro-enterprises that are significantly affected by the price impacts of the inclusion of greenhouse gas emissions from buildings or road transport within the scope of Directive 2003/87/EC and that, for the purpose of their activity, lack the means either to renovate the building they occupy, or to purchase zero- and low-emission vehicles or to switch to alternative sustainable modes of transport, including public transport, as relevant; (12) 'vulnerable transport users' means individuals and households in transport poverty, but also individuals and households, including low income and lower middle-income ones, that are significantly affected by the price impacts of the inclusion of greenhouse gas emissions from road transport within the scope of Directive 2003/87/EC and lack the means to purchase zero- and low-emission vehicles or to switch to alternative sustainable modes of transport, including public transport; (13) 'building renovation' means any kind of energy-related building renovation, which has the aim of increasing the energy performance of buildings, such as the insulation of the building envelope, that is to say the walls, roof, floor and the replacement of windows, and the installation of technical building systems, compliant with any relevant national safety standards, including by contributing to the renovation requirements established in the Directive of the European Parliament and of the Council on the energy performance of buildings (recast); (14) 'technical building system' means the technical equipment for space heating, space cooling, ventilation, domestic hot water, building automation and control, on-site renewable energy generation and storage, or a combination of such technical equipment, including those systems using energy from renewable sources, of a building or building unit; (15) 'active customer' means an active customer as defined in Article 2, point (8), of Directive (EU) 2019/944 of the European Parliament and of the Council[28]; (16) 'citizen energy community' means a citizen energy community as defined in Article 2, point (11), of Directive (EU) 2019/944; (17) 'renewable energy community' means a renewable energy community as defined in Article 2, point (16), of Directive (EU) 2018/2001; (18) 'peer-to-peer trading of renewable energy' means peer-to-peer trading of renewable energy as defined in Article 2, point (18), of Directive (EU) 2018/2001; (19) 'zero- and low-emission vehicle' means zero- and low-emission vehicle as defined in Article 3(1), point (m), of Regulation (EU) 2019/631 of the European Parliament and of the Council[29].	the precise term 'energy vulnerable' for which no definition is needed. The result of the use of the same generic term defined differently in EU texts creates ambiguity on the meaning of the term across EU legislation. b Moreover, definitions do not define terms that do not need it, namely terms that carry an ordinary meaning that is neither expended nor delimited, such as 5, 6, and 19. c Finally, definitions cannot introduce a legal provision, such as 10 and 11, which are application provisions. One last drafting point. Definitions should be introduced as follows: '*In this* Regulation the following definition apply' rather than the current '*For the purposes of this Regulation*'. The current expression invites the interpretation of definitions on a teleological basis, which creates ground for individuality and possibly judicial activism. Both of which negate the reason for having definitions anyway.

The Regulation	*Comments*
Article 3 **Objectives** 1 The general objective of the Fund shall be to contribute to a socially fair transition towards climate neutrality by addressing the social impacts of the inclusion of greenhouse gas emissions from buildings and road transport within the scope of Directive 2003/87/EC. 2 The specific objectives of the Fund shall be to support vulnerable households, vulnerable micro-enterprises and vulnerable transport users, through temporary direct income support and through measures and investments intended to increase the energy efficiency of buildings, decarbonisation of heating and cooling of buildings, including through the integration in buildings of renewable energy generation and storage, and to grant improved access to zero- and low-emission mobility and transport.	This provision should have been placed in Art. 1. It should not focus on the Fund but on the subsidy of green works for the energy vulnerable by the EU, thus setting what the EU does for its citizens and its MS, laying out clearly and measurably the regulatory results pursued by the Regulation. An objectives provision, properly drafted, can persuade the user that this is a worthwhile pursuit in which they must participate. It is a crucial tool to ensure participation and therefore legislative effectiveness. But it is also an equally crucial message for the direct communication of the EU with EU citizens to share the policy goals, to instil trust in the objective and the means by which these are to be achieved and to, in the long run, instil loyalty for sustainable integration and longevity. Structure: The main body of the Regulation consists of 3 chapters and 23 Articles. For the analysis of the legislative style of the EU under the focal point of easification, the main comment to be made concerns the structure of the Regulation, namely the sequence of Articles. In the application of the layered structure, the Regulation could be restructured as follows: Art. 1 (now 2 and 1) Objectives and subject matter Art. 2 Definitions with hanging provision and current Art. 2 (culled) to become Annex Part 1 (to the citizens) Art. 3 (new) The right to subsidised green works for the energy vulnerable Art. 4 (now 10 para 1) The fund Art. 5 (now 5) National contribution to the estimated total cost Part 2 (to MS) Chapter 1 The Fund Art. 6 (now 4) Social climate plans Art. 7 (now 7) Principles governing the fund

The Regulation	*Comments*
	Art. 8 (now 8) Eligible measures and Investments to be included in the social climate plans Art. 9 (now 6) Content of social climate plans Art. 10 (now 9) Pass on benefits to households, micro-enterprises, and transport users Chapter 2 The process Art. 11 (now 5) Public consultation Art. 12 (now 16) Commission assessment of the plan Art. 13 (now 17) Commission decision on the plan Art. 14 (now 18) Amendment of social climate plans Art. 15 (now 20) Rules on payment, suspension, and termination of agreements regarding financial allocations Art. 16 (now 25) Transparency Art. 17 (now 22) Coordination and complementarity Art. 18 (now 23) Information, communication, and visibility Art. 19 (now 24) Monitoring of implementation Part 3 (to EU) Art. 20 (now 10) Resources of the Fund (apart from now Art. 1, first paragraph) Art. 21 (now 11) Resources from shared management programs and use of resources Art. 22 (now 12) Implementation Art. 23 (now 13) Additionality and complementary funding Art. 24 (now 14) Maximum financial allocation Art. 25 (now 21) Protection of the financial interests of the Union Art. 26 (now 26) Social climate dialogue Art. 27 (now 27) Evaluation and review of the fund Art. 28 (now 28) Amendment to Regulation EU 2021/1060 Art. 29 (new) Citation Art. 30 (now 29) Entry into force

The Regulation	*Comments*
CHAPTER II *Social Climate Plans* *Article 4* **Social Climate Plans** 1 Each Member State shall submit to the Commission its Plan. The Plan shall contain a coherent set of existing or new national measures and investments to address the impact of carbon pricing on vulnerable households, vulnerable micro-enterprises and vulnerable transport users in order to ensure affordable heating, cooling and mobility, while accompanying and accelerating necessary measures to meet the climate targets of the Union. 2 Each Member State shall ensure consistency between its Plan and its updated integrated national energy and climate plan referred to in Article 14(2) of Regulation (EU) 2018/1999. 3 The Plan may include national measures providing temporary direct income support to vulnerable households and vulnerable transport users to reduce the impact of the increase in the price of fossil fuels resulting from the inclusion of greenhouse gas emissions from buildings and road transport within the scope of Directive 2003/87/EC. 4 The Plan shall include national and, where relevant, local and regional measures and investments, in accordance with Article 8, to: (a) carry out building renovation, and decarbonise heating and cooling of buildings, including the integration of renewable energy generation and storage; (b) increase the uptake of zero- and low-emission mobility and transport. 5 Where a Member State has already in place a national emission trading system for buildings and road transport or carbon tax, the national measures already in place to mitigate social impacts and challenges may be included in the Plan provided that they comply with this Regulation.	This is not a successful way to start the text. The first message should be what is in it for the citizens, be they natural or legal persons. An alternative would be to expressly award access to subsidised green works for those who are energy vulnerable. In other words, instead of introducing this as an obligation of Member States to submit plans to the Commission, they should be an expression of the benevolent provision of the EU to its citizens. And this should be followed by a provision establishing the fund, which will be used for the purposes of materialising this new access to subsidised green works for the energy vulnerable. Thus the current Art. 4 should be transferred to Part 2 of the Act that speaks to Member States and informs them of the details of the plans that they need to submit, the procedure to be followed, and the effect of approved submission (payment, etc.)
Article 5 **Public consultation** 1 Each Member State shall submit a Plan to the Commission following a public consultation with local and regional authorities, representatives of economic and social partners, relevant civil society organisations, youth organisations and other stakeholders. Each Member State shall conduct that consultation in accordance with the requirements of Article 10 of Regulation (EU) 2018/1999 and in compliance with that Member State's national legal framework.	This article details part of the procedure to be followed for the purposes of submitting the plan and should therefore be in Part 2, Chapter 2.

The Regulation	*Comments*
2 Each Member State shall include in its Plan a summary of: (a) the consultation held pursuant to paragraph 1; and (b) how the input of the stakeholders who participated in the consultation is reflected in the Plan. 3 For the purposes of Article 16(3), the Commission shall assess whether the Plan has been developed in consultation with stakeholders in accordance with paragraph 1 of this Article. 4 The Commission shall support Member States by providing examples of good practices of consultations on the Plans in accordance with Article 6(4).	
Article 6 **Content of Social Climate Plans**	
1 The Plan shall set out the following elements: (a) concrete measures and investments in accordance with Articles 4 and8 to reduce the effects referred to in point (d) of this paragraph, together with an explanation of how those measures and investments would contribute effectively to the achievement of the objectives set out in Article 3 within the overall setting of a Member State's relevant policies; (b) where relevant, concrete, mutually coherent and reinforced accompanying measures to accomplish the measures and investments and reduce the effects referred to in point (d); (c) information on existing or planned financing of measures and investments from other Union, international, public or, where relevant, private sources which contribute to the measures and investments set out in the Plan, including information on temporary direct income support; (d) an estimate of the likely effects of the increase in prices resulting from the inclusion of greenhouse gas emissions from buildings and road transport within the scope of Directive 2003/87/EC on households, in particular on incidence of energy poverty and transport poverty, and on micro-enterprises; those effects are to be analysed at the appropriate territorial level as defined by each Member State, taking into account national specificities and elements, such as access to public transport and basic services, and identifying the areas mostly affected; (e) an estimated number of, and the identification of, vulnerable households, vulnerable micro-enterprises and vulnerable transport users; (f) an explanation of how the definitions of energy poverty and transport poverty are to be applied at national level;	The content of social climate plans should be in Part 2, Chapter 1, so that Member States are aware of what they should include in their plans.

The Regulation	*Comments*
(g) where the Plan provides for measures as referred to in Article 4(3), the criteria for the identification of eligible final recipients, the envisaged time limit for the measures in question and their justification on the basis of a quantitative estimate and a qualitative explanation of how those measures are expected to reduce energy poverty, transport poverty and the vulnerability of households to an increase in the price of road transport and heating fuel; (h) envisaged milestones, targets and an indicative comprehensive timetable for the implementation of the measures and investments to be completed by 31 July 2032; (i) where applicable, a timetable for the gradual reduction of support for low-emission vehicles; (j) the estimated total costs of the Plan, accompanied by appropriate justification and explanations of how they are in line with the principle of cost efficiency and commensurate to the expected impact of the Plan; (k) the envisaged national contribution to the estimated total costs of the Plan, calculated in accordance with Article 15; (l) except for the measures referred to in Article 4(3) of this Regulation, an explanation of how the Plan ensures that none of the measures or investments would do significant harm to environmental objectives within the meaning of Article 17 of Regulation (EU) 2020/852; (m) the arrangements for the effective monitoring and implementation of the Plan by the Member State concerned, in particular of the proposed milestones and targets, the relevant common indicators referred to in Annex IV, and if none of those indicators are relevant for a specific measure or investment, additional individual indicators proposed by the Member State concerned; (n) for the preparation and, where available, for the implementation of the Plan, a summary of the public consultation process referred to in Article 5; (o) an explanation of the Member State's system to prevent, detect and correct fraud, corruption and conflicts of interests when using the financial allocation provided under the Fund, and of the arrangements that aim to avoid double funding from the Fund and other Union programmes; (p) where applicable and relevant, an explanation of how geographic specificities, such as islands, outermost regions and territories, rural or remote areas, less accessible peripheries, mountainous areas or areas lagging behind, have been taken into account in the Plan; (q) where relevant, an explanation of how the measures and investments aim to address gender inequality.	

The Regulation	*Comments*
2 The Plan may include technical assistance actions necessary for the effective administration and implementation of the measures and investments. 3 The Plan shall be consistent with the information included in and the commitments made by the Member State under the following: (a) the European Pillar of Social Rights Action Plan; (b) its cohesion policy programmes under Regulation (EU) 2021/1060; (c) its recovery and resilience plan under Regulation (EU) 2021/241; (d) its building renovation plan under the Directive of the European Parliament and of the Council on the energy performance of buildings (recast); (e) its updated integrated national energy and climate plan under Regulation (EU) 2018/1999; and (f) its territorial just transition plans under Regulation (EU) 2021/1056. 4 During the preparation of the Plans, the Commission shall organise an exchange of good practices, including on cost-effective measures and investments to be included in the Plans. Member States may request technical support under the European Local ENergy Assistance (ELENA) facility, established by an Agreement between the Commission and the European Investment Bank in 2009, or under the Technical Support Instrument established by Regulation (EU) 2021/240 of the European Parliament and of the Council([30]). 5 For the purposes of paragraph 1, point (l), of this Article, the Commission shall provide technical guidance to the Member States, tailored to the scope of the Fund, on the compliance of measures and investments with the principle of 'do no significant harm' within the meaning of Article 17 of Regulation (EU) 2020/852. 6 To assist Member States in providing the information referred to in paragraph 1, point (d), of this Article the Commission shall provide a common value to be considered as an estimate for the carbon price resulting from the inclusion of greenhouse gas emissions from buildings, road transport and additional sectors within the scope of Directive 2003/87/EC. 7 Each Member State shall use the template set out in Annex V for the Plan. ***CHAPTER III*** ***Support from the fund for Social Climate Plans*** *Article 7* **Principles governing the Fund** 1 The Fund shall provide financial support to Member States to fund the measures and investments set out in their Plans.	Art. 7 relates to the principles governing the Fund and should be transferred to Part 2 for Member States, Chapter 1, where the details of the plan are provided.

The Regulation	*Comments*
2 Payment of financial support pursuant to paragraph 1 of this Article to each Member State shall be conditional upon that Member State achieving the milestones and targets for the measures and investments in accordance with Article 8 of this Regulation. Those milestones and targets shall be compatible with the Union's climate targets and the objective set out in Regulation (EU) 2021/1119, and shall cover in particular: (a) energy efficiency; (b) building renovation; (c) zero- and low-emission mobility and transport; (d) greenhouse gas emission reductions; (e) reductions in the number of vulnerable households, in particular households in energy poverty, of vulnerable micro-enterprises and of vulnerable transport users. 3 The Fund shall only support measures and investments which comply with the principle of 'do no significant harm' within the meaning of Article 17 of Regulation (EU) 2020/852. 4 The measures and investments supported by the Fund shall reduce fossil fuel dependency and, where relevant, contribute to the implementation of the European Pillar of Social Rights as well as to sustainable and quality jobs in the fields covered by the measures and investments of the Fund.	
Article 8 **Eligible measures and investments to be included in the Social Climate Plans** 1 The Member State may include in the estimated total costs of the Plan the following measures and investments with lasting impacts, provided they principally target vulnerable households, vulnerable micro-enterprises or vulnerable transport users and intend to: (a) support building renovations, in particular for vulnerable households and vulnerable micro-enterprises occupying the worst performing buildings, and including for tenants and people living in social housing; (b) support access to affordable energy-efficient housing, including social housing; (c) contribute to the decarbonisation, such as through electrification, of heating and cooling of, and cooking in, buildings by providing access to affordable and energy-efficient systems, and by integrating renewable energy generation and storage, including through renewable energy communities, citizen energy communities and other active customers to promote the uptake of the self-consumption of renewable energy, such as energy sharing and peer-to-peer trading of renewable energy, connection to smart grids and to district heating networks, that contributes to achieving energy savings or to reducing energy poverty;	Art. 8 includes a dual message, which should be divided into twoparts for an easified layered Regulation. On the one hand, it explains to energy-vulnerable citizens exactly what types of green works can be subsidised and therefore what types of green works they can apply for. On the other hand, it does state what type of investments and measures can Member States include in their Social Climate Plans and therefore needs a more abstract categorisation of such works. It is important that the part of the message addressed to citizens is not lost so far down the text: it should be offered

The Regulation	*Comments*
(d) provide targeted, accessible and affordable information, education, awareness and advice on cost-effective measures and investments, available support for building renovations and energy efficiency, as well as sustainable and affordable mobility and transport alternatives; (e) support public and private entities, including social housing providers, in particular public-private cooperatives, in developing and providing affordable energy efficiency solutions and appropriate funding instruments in line with the social goals of the Fund; (f) provide access to zero- and low-emission vehicles and bicycles, while maintaining technological neutrality, including financial support or fiscal incentives for their purchase as well as for appropriate public and private infrastructure, in particular, where relevant, purchase of zero- and low-emission vehicles, infrastructure for recharging and refuelling and development of a second-hand zero-emission vehicles market; Member States shall aim to ensure that where zero-emission vehicles are an affordable and deployable solution, support to such vehicles is prioritised in their Plans; (g) incentivise the use of affordable and accessible public transport and support private and public entities, including cooperatives, in developing and providing sustainable mobility on demand, shared mobility services and active mobility options. 2 Member States may include in the estimated total costs of the Plans the costs of measures providing direct income support to vulnerable households and vulnerable transport users to reduce the impact of the increase in road transport and heating fuel prices. Such support shall be temporary and decrease over time. Member States may provide temporary direct income support if their Plans contain measures or investments aimed at those vulnerable households and vulnerable transport users in accordance with Article 8(1) of this Regulation. Such support shall be limited to the direct impact of the inclusion of greenhouse gas emissions from buildings and road transport within the scope of Directive 2003/87/EC. The costs of measures providing temporary direct income support shall not represent more than 37.5% of the estimated total costs of the Plan, as referred to in Article 6(1), point (j), of this Regulation. 3 Member States may include in the estimated total costs of the Plans the costs of technical assistance to cover expenses related to training, programming, monitoring, control, audit and evaluation activities which are required for the management of the Fund and the achievement of its objectives, for example studies, information technology (IT) expenses, public consultation of stakeholders, information and communication actions. The costs of such technical assistance shall be up to 2.5% of the estimated total costs of the Plan, as referred to in Article 6(1), point (j).	at the very start of the Regulation so that users can see and understand exactly how this Regulation can impact them and what they can apply for. The suggestion is to include examples of specific green works that are relevant to citizens at the beginning, of the new Art. 3 of Part 1, at the point where citizens are being addressed, and then continue with a more overarching description of those works as stated in this article for the purposes of inciting possible initiatives by Member States to include as many types of works as possible.

The Regulation	*Comments*
Article 9 **Pass-on of benefits to households, micro-enterprises and transport users** 1 Member States may include in the Plans support provided through public or private entities other than vulnerable households, vulnerable micro-enterprises and vulnerable transport users, provided that those entities carry out measures and investments ultimately benefitting vulnerable households, vulnerable micro-enterprises or vulnerable transport users. 2 Member States shall provide for the necessary statutory and contractual safeguards to ensure that the entire benefit is passed on to the vulnerable households, vulnerable micro-enterprises or vulnerable transport users.	Art. 9 carries another dual message on the inclusion in the field of application of nonvulnerable households, micro-enterprises, and transport users. The placement of this provision is very much a regulatory choice. The legislator may decide that this is a technical provision because it doesn't involve a large number of lay users, and therefore the provision of Art. 9 can be transferred to Part 2, Chapter 1, on the Fund and its beneficiaries. Equally, the legislator may decide that this is a message addressed to a number of lay users of such extent that it becomes a very important message, and it should therefore be placed at the very beginning where access to the fund is conveyed to lay users.
Article 10 **Resources of the Fund** 1 A maximum amount of EUR 65,000,000,000 for the period from 1 January 2026 to 31 December 2032 in current prices shall be made available, in accordance with Articles 10a(8b), 30d(3) and 30d(4) of Directive 2003/87/EC, for implementation of the Fund. That amount shall constitute external assigned revenue for the purposes of Article 21(5) of Regulation (EU, Euratom) 2018/1046, without prejudice to Article 30d(4), sixth subparagraph, of Directive 2003/87/EC. The annual amounts allocated to the Fund, within the limit of the maximum amount laid down in the first subparagraph of this paragraph, shall not exceed the amounts referred to in Article 30d(4), fourth subparagraph, of Directive 2003/87/EC. Where the emission trading system established in accordance with Chapter IVa of Directive 2003/87/EC is postponed until 2028 pursuant to Article 30k of that Directive, the maximum amount to be made available to the Fund shall be EUR 54,600,000,000 and the annual amounts allocated to the Fund shall not exceed the respective amounts referred to in the Article 30d(4), fifth subparagraph, of Directive 2003/87/EC.	Art. 10 includes a very important message on the resources for the Fund and is therefore a technical provision addressed to the EU and learned users in Part 3. However, it does convey a very important message for lay users as well in that it expresses the huge amount of funding made available by the EU to vulnerable citizens. The maximum amount of EUR 65,000,000,000 to be made available for the Fund should be included at the very start of the Regulation, where the new Art. 3 would convey the new access to subsidised works.

The Regulation	*Comments*
2 By way of derogation from Article 22(2) of Regulation (EU, Euratom) 2018/1046 and without prejudice to Article 19 of this Regulation, commitment appropriations covering the relevant maximum amount referred to in paragraph 1 of this Article shall be made available automatically at the beginning of each financial year, starting from 1 January 2026, up to the relevant applicable annual amounts referred to in the second and third subparagraphs of paragraph 1. 3 The amounts referred to in paragraph 1 may also cover expenses pertaining to preparatory, monitoring, control, audit and evaluation activities which are required for the management of the Fund and the achievement of its objectives, in particular studies, meetings of experts, consultation of stakeholders, information and communication actions, including inclusive outreach actions, and corporate communication of the political priorities of the Union, insofar as they are related to the objectives of this Regulation, expenses linked to IT networks focusing on information processing and exchange, corporate IT tools, and all other technical and administrative assistance expenses incurred by the Commission for the management of the Fund. Expenses may also cover the costs of other supporting activities such as quality control and monitoring of projects on the ground and the costs of peer counselling and experts for the assessment and implementation of the eligible actions.	On that point, the word 'subsidy' is not used in the Regulation at all. This is not surprising in view of the fact that subsidies have a specific legal meaning in EU law. However, since this is the very core of the regulatory message here and relates to an understanding of the lay users of what exactly is being offered to them, there is a strong argument for extending the meaning of subsidies to include the subsidised works introduced here because the term reflects the ordinary meaning of the word and what specifically is on offer to our citizens by means of this Regulation.
Article 11 **Resources from and to shared management programmes and use of resources** 1 Resources allocated to Member States under shared management may, at their request, be transferred to the Fund subject to the conditions set out in the relevant provisions of Regulation (EU) 2021/1060. The Commission shall implement those resources directly in accordance with Article 62(1), first subparagraph, point (a), of Regulation (EU, Euratom) 2018/1046. Those resources shall be used exclusively for the benefit of the Member State concerned. 2 Member States may request in their Plans submitted in accordance with Article 4(1) of this Regulation for the transfer of up to 15% of their maximum annual financial allocation to the funds under shared management provided for in Regulation (EU) 2021/1060. The transferred resources shall finance measures and investments as referred to in Article 8 of this Regulation and shall be implemented in accordance with the rules of the funds to which the resources are transferred. Resources shall be transferred by Member States through the amendment of one or more programmes, except for programmes under the European territorial cooperation goal (Interreg), in accordance with Article 26a of Regulation (EU) 2021/1060, and shall be implemented in accordance with the rules set out in that Regulation and the rules of the funds to which the resources are transferred.	Art. 11 discusses the resources of the Fund and should follow Art. 10 in Part 3.

The Regulation	*Comments*
3 Member States may entrust the managing authorities of the cohesion policy programmes under Regulation (EU) 2021/1060 with the implementation of measures and investments benefitting from the Fund, where applicable, in view of the synergies with those cohesion policy programmes and in conformity with the objectives of the Fund. Member States shall state their intention to thus entrust those authorities in their Plans. In such cases, the existing management and control systems put in place by Member States, as notified to the Commission, shall be deemed to comply with the requirements of this Regulation. 4 Member States may include in their Plans, as part of the estimated total costs, the payments for additional technical support pursuant to Article 7 of Regulation (EU) 2021/240 and the amount of the cash contribution for the purpose of the Member State compartment pursuant to the relevant provisions of Regulation (EU) 2021/523 of the European Parliament and of the Council(31). Those costs shall not exceed 4% of the maximum financial allocation for the Plan, and the relevant measures, as set out in the Plan, shall comply with this Regulation.	
Article 12 **Implementation** The Fund shall be implemented by the Commission under direct management in accordance with the relevant rules adopted pursuant to Article 322 TFEU, in particular Regulation (EU, Euratom) 2018/1046 and Regulation (EU, Euratom) 2020/2092 on a general regime of conditionality for the protection of the Union budget.	Art. 12 on implementation should be at the very end of Part 3 as it is addressed to the Commission and conveys a message of a technical nature.
Article 13 **Additionality and complementary funding** 1 Support under the Fund shall be additional to the support provided under other Union funds, programmes and instruments. Measures and investments supported under the Fund may receive support from other Union funds, programmes and instruments provided that such support does not cover the same cost. 2 Support from the Fund, including temporary direct income support referred to in Article 4(3), shall be additional and shall not substitute recurring national budgetary expenditure. 3 For technical assistance to Member States, administrative costs directly linked to the implementation of the Plan shall not be considered as recurring national budgetary expenditure.	Art. 13 also conveys a message of a technical nature and should be at the end of Part 3.
Article 14 **Maximum financial allocation** 1 The maximum financial allocation shall be calculated for each Member State in accordance with Article 10 and as specified in Annexes I and II. 2 Each Member State may submit a request up to its maximum financial allocation to implement its Plan.	Art. 4 conveys a message of a technical nature and should be at the end of Part 3.

The Regulation	*Comments*
Article 15 **National contribution to the estimated total costs** Member States shall contribute at least to 25% of the estimated total costs of their Plans.	Art. 15, however, contains a very important message for the citizens' appreciation of what is on offer and who offers the funds. It is important for citizens to know, having identified the huge amount of money put down by the EU, that the national contribution to the Fund is a mere 25% minimum. As a result, this article should be transferred to Part 1 for lay users just after the article on the resources for the Fund.
Article 16 **Commission assessment** 1 The Commission shall assess the Plan and, where applicable, any amendment to that Plan submitted by a Member State in accordance with Article 18, for compliance with this Regulation. When carrying out that assessment, the Commission shall act in close cooperation with the Member State concerned. The Commission may make observations or seek additional information within twomonthsfrom the date of submission of the Plan by the Member State. The Member State shall provide the requested additional information and may revise the Plan if needed, including after the submission of the Plan. The Member State and the Commission may agree to extend the deadline for assessment by a reasonable period if necessary. 2 The Commission shall assess whether transfers requested in accordance with Article 11 meet the objectives of this Regulation. 3 The Commission shall assess the relevance, effectiveness, efficiency and coherence of the Plan, taking into account the specific challenges and the financial allocation of the Member State, as follows: (a) for the purpose of assessing relevance, the Commission shall take into account the following criteria: (i) whether the Plan represents an adequate response to the social impact on and challenges faced by vulnerable households, vulnerable	Art. 16 returns to the topic of the procedure for the compilation of plans by Member States and should therefore be in Part 2, Chapter 2.

The Regulation	*Comments*
micro-enterprises and vulnerable transport users in the Member State concerned from the inclusion of greenhouse gas emissions from buildings and road transport within the scope of Directive 2003/87/EC, in particular households in energy poverty or households in transport poverty, duly taking into account the challenges identified in the assessments of the Commission of the update of the concerned Member State's integrated national energy and climate plan and of its progress pursuant to Article 9(3), and Articles 13 and 29 of Regulation (EU) 2018/1999, as well as in the Commission recommendations to Member States issued pursuant to Article 34 of Regulation (EU) 2018/1999 in view of the Union's 2030 climate and energy targets and long-term objective of climate neutrality in the Union at the latest by 2050; (ii) whether the Plan is expected to ensure that measures and investments included in the Plan do not significantly harm environmental objectives within the meaning of Article 17 of Regulation (EU) 2020/852 and whether the Plan helps reduce fossil fuel dependency; (iii) whether the Plan contains measures and investments that contribute to the green transition, including to addressing the social impacts and challenges resulting therefrom and in particular to the achievement of the Union's 2030 climate and energy targets and long-term objective of climate neutrality in the Union at the latest by 2050 and the 2030 milestones of the Union's Sustainable and Smart Mobility Strategy; (b) for the purpose of assessing effectiveness, the Commission shall take into account the following criteria: (i) whether the Plan is expected to have a lasting impact in the Member State on the challenges addressed by that Plan, in line with the Union's 2030 climate and energy targets and long-term objective of climate neutrality in the Union at the latest by 2050, and in particular on vulnerable households, vulnerable micro-enterprises and vulnerable transport users, in particular households in energy poverty or households in transport poverty;	

The Regulation	*Comments*
(ii) whether the arrangements proposed by the Member State are expected to ensure the effective monitoring and implementation of the Plan, including the envisaged timetable, milestones and targets, and the related indicators; (iii) whether the measures and investments proposed by the Member State are consistent and compliant with the requirements of the Directive of the European Parliament and of the Council on energy efficiency (recast), Directive (EU) 2018/2001, the Regulation of the European Parliament and of the Council on the deployment of alternative fuels infrastructure, and repealing Directive 2014/94/EU of the European Parliament and of the Council, Directive 2009/33/EC of the European Parliament and of the Council([32]) and Directive 2010/31/EU; and (iv) whether the measures and investments proposed by the Member State foster complementarity, synergy, coherence and consistency with the Union instruments referred to in Article 6(3). (c) for the purposes of assessing efficiency, the Commission shall take into account the following criteria: (i) whether the justification provided by the Member State for the amount of the estimated total costs of the Plan is reasonable, plausible, in line with the principle of cost efficiency and commensurate with the expected national environmental and social impact, while also taking into account national specificities that could impact the costs provided in the Plan; (ii) whether the arrangements proposed by the Member State are expected to prevent, detect and correct corruption, fraud and conflicts of interests when using the financial allocation provided under the Fund, including the arrangements that aim to avoid double funding from the Fund and other Union programmes; (iii) whether the milestones and targets proposed by the Member State are efficient, in view of the scope, objectives and eligible actions of the Fund; (d) for the purpose of assessing coherence, the Commission shall take into account whether the Plan contains measures and investments that represent coherent actions.	

The Regulation	*Comments*
Article 17 **Commission decision** 1 On the basis of the assessment carried out in accordance with Article 16, the Commission shall decide on the Plan of a Member State, by means of an implementing act, no later than five months from the date of the submission of that Plan pursuant to Article 4(1). 2 Where the Commission gives a positive assessment of a Plan, the implementing act referred to in paragraph 1 shall set out: (a) the measures and investments to be implemented by the Member State, the amount of the estimated total costs of the Plan, and the milestones and targets; (b) the maximum financial allocation allocated in accordance with Article 14(1) to be paid in instalments, in accordance with Article 20, once the Member State has satisfactorily achieved the relevant milestones and targets identified in relation to the implementation of the Plan; (c) the national contribution; (d) the arrangements and timetable for monitoring and implementation of the Plan, including, where relevant, measures necessary for complying with Article 21; (e) the relevant indicators relating to the achievement of the envisaged milestones and targets; and (f) the arrangements for providing access by the Commission to the underlying relevant data. 3 The maximum financial allocation referred to in paragraph 2, point (b), of this Article shall be determined on the basis of the estimated total costs of the Plan proposed by the Member State, as assessed by reference to the criteria set out in Article 16(3). The amount of the maximum financial allocation referred to in paragraph 2, point (b), of this Article shall be set as follows: (a) where the Plan complies satisfactorily with the criteria set out in Article 16(3), and the amount of the estimated total costs of the Plan minus the national contribution is equal to, or higher than, the maximum financial allocation for that Member State referred to in Article 14(1), the financial allocation allocated to the Member State shall be equal to the total amount of the maximum financial allocation referred to in Article 14(1);	The same applies to Art. 17, which should be transferred to Part 2, Chapter 2, on the procedure for the plans.

The Regulation	*Comments*
(b) where the Plan complies satisfactorily with the criteria set out in Article 16(3), and the amount of the estimated total costs of the Plan minus the national contribution is lower than the maximum financial allocation for that Member State referred to in Article 14(1), the financial allocation allocated to the Member State shall be equal to the amount of the estimated total costs of the Plan minus the national contribution; (c) where the Plan complies satisfactorily with the criteria set out in Article 16(3), but the assessment identifies weaknesses in the internal control systems, the Commission may require that additional measures to address those weaknesses be included in the Plan and be achieved by the Member State before the first payment; (d) where the Plan does not comply satisfactorily with the criteria set out in Article 16(3), no financial allocation shall be allocated to the Member State. 4 Where the Commission gives a negative assessment of a Plan, the decision referred to in paragraph 1 shall include the reasons for that negative assessment. The Member State shall resubmit the Plan, after taking into account the assessment of the Commission. *Article 18* **Amendment of Social Climate Plans**	
1 Where a Plan is no longer achievable, including relevant milestones and targets, or needs to be significantly adjusted, either in whole or in part, by a Member State because of objective circumstances, in particular because of the actual direct effects of the inclusion of greenhouse gas emissions from buildings and road transport within the scope of Directive 2003/87/EC, the Member State concerned shall submit an amended Plan to the Commission in order to include the necessary and duly justified changes. Member States may request technical support, in accordance with Article 11(4), for the preparation of the amended Plan. 2 The Commission shall assess the amended Plan in accordance with Article 16. 3 Where the Commission gives a positive assessment of the amended Plan, it shall in accordance with Article 17(1) adopt a decision setting out the reasons for its positive assessment, by means of an implementing act. By way of derogation from Article 17(1), the Commission shall adopt the decision under this paragraph within three months from the date of the submission of the amended Plan by the Member State concerned. 4 Where the Commission gives a negative assessment of the amended Plan, it shall reject the amended Plan within the period referred to in paragraph 3, after having given the Member State concerned the possibility to present its observations within threemonthsfrom the date of the communication of the Commission's assessment of the amended Plan.	The same applies to Art. 18, which should be transferred to Part 2, Chapter 2, on procedure.

The Regulation	*Comments*
5 By 15 March 2029 each Member State shall assess the appropriateness of its Plan in view of the actual direct effects of the inclusion of greenhouse gas emissions from buildings and road transport within the scope of Directive 2003/87/EC. Those assessments shall be submitted to the Commission together with the integrated national energy and climate progress reports pursuant to Article 17 of Regulation (EU) 2018/1999. 6 In the case of minor adjustments to the Plan, representing an increase or decrease of less than 5% of a target set out in the Plan, such as minor updates in the measures and investments set out in the Plan, or the correction of clerical errors, a Member State shall notify such changes to the Commission.	
Article 19 **Commitment of the financial allocation**	
1 After the Commission has adopted a positive decision as referred to in Article 17 of this Regulation, it shall in due time conclude an agreement with the Member State concerned constituting an individual legal commitment within the meaning of Regulation (EU, Euratom) 2018/1046 for the period 2026–2032, without prejudice to Article 30d(4) and Articles 30i and30k of Directive 2003/87/EC. That agreement shall be concluded at the earliest one year before the year of the start of the auctions under Chapter IVa of Directive 2003/87/EC, or two years before that year, in cases where Article 10(1), third subparagraph, of this Regulation applies. 2 Budgetary commitments may be based on global commitments and, where appropriate, may be broken down into annual instalments spread over several years.	Art. 19 refers to the consequences of a positive decision by the Commission and should be included within the article on the Commission's decision on Plan 9 (current 13 and new 17)
Article 20 **Rules on payments, suspension and termination of agreements regarding financial allocations**	
1 Payments of financial allocations under this Article to the Member State shall be made upon achievement of the relevant agreed milestones and targets indicated in the Plan, as approved in accordance with Article 17, and subject to the availability of funding. Upon such achievement, the Member State shall submit to the Commission a duly reasoned payment request. The Member State shall submit such payment requests to the Commission once or twice a year, by 31 July or by 31 December. 2 Upon receiving a payment request from a Member State, the Commission shall assess whether the relevant milestones and targets set out in the Commission decision referred to in Article 17 have been satisfactorily achieved. The satisfactory achievement of milestones and targets shall presuppose that measures related to previously satisfactorily achieved milestones and targets have not been reversed by the Member State concerned.	Art. 20 should be transferred to Part 2, Chapter 2.

The Regulation	*Comments*
3 Where the Commission makes a positive assessment of an individual payment request, it shall adopt an individual decision authorising the disbursement of the financial allocation in accordance with Regulation (EU, Euratom) 2018/1046, subject to the availability of funding and ensuring the equal treatment of Member States. The Commission shall adopt the individual decision not earlier than two months and not later than three months after the relevant deadline for submission of the payment request in accordance with paragraph 1 of this Article. 4 Where, as a result of the assessment referred to in paragraph 3 of this Article, the Commission establishes that the milestones and targets set out in the Commission decision referred to in Article 17 have not been satisfactorily achieved, the payment of the part of the financial allocation proportional to the unachieved target or milestone shall be suspended. The Member State may present its observations within one month of the communication of the Commission's assessment. The suspension shall only be lifted where the milestones and targets have been satisfactorily achieved as set out in the Commission decision referred to in Article 17. 5 By way of derogation from Article 116(2) of Regulation (EU, Euratom) 2018/1046, the payment deadline shall start running from the date of the communication of the Commission's decision authorising the disbursement of the financial allocation to the Member State concerned pursuant to paragraph 3 of this Article, or from the date of the communication of the lifting of a suspension pursuant to paragraph 4, second subparagraph, of this Article. 6 Where the milestones and targets have not been satisfactorily achieved within a period of nine months from the suspension referred to in paragraph 4, first subparagraph, the Commission shall reduce the amount of the financial allocation proportionately after having given the Member State the possibility to present its observations within two months from the communication of its conclusions as to the achievement of the milestones and targets. 7 Where, within 15 months from the date of the conclusion of relevant agreements referred to in Article 19, no tangible progress has been made in respect of any relevant milestones and targets by the Member State, the Commission shall terminate those agreements and shall decommit the amount of the financial allocation without prejudice to Article 14(3) of Regulation (EU, Euratom) 2018/1046. The Commission shall take a decision on the termination of those agreements after having given the Member State the possibility to present its observations within a period of two months of the communication of the assessment by the Commission that no tangible progress has been made.	

The Regulation	*Comments*
8 All payments shall be made by 31 December 2033.	
9 By way of derogation from Article 116 of Regulation (EU, Euratom) 2018/1046 and paragraph 5 of this Article, if, in a given round of payment requests as referred to in paragraph 1 of this Article, the revenue assigned to the Fund in accordance with Article 30d(4) of Directive 2003/87/EC is not sufficient to cover the submitted payment requests, the Commission shall pay the Member States on a pro-rata basis determined as a share of the payment availabilities to the total approved payments. In the following round of payment requests, the Commission shall give priority to those Member States with delayed payments from the previous round of payment requests, and only later to the newly submitted payment requests.	
10 By way of derogation from Article 12(4), point (c), of Regulation (EU, Euratom) 2018/1046 and without prejudice to Article 30d(4), sixth subparagraph, of Directive 2003/87/EC, the Commission shall allocate to Member States the amounts corresponding to any appropriations that are unused by 31 December 2033 in accordance with the rules for distribution of allowances defined under Article 30d(5) of Directive 2003/87/EC in order to achieve the objectives referred to in Article 3 of this Regulation.	
Article 21 **Protection of the financial interests of the Union**	
1 The Member States, when implementing the Plans, as beneficiaries of funds under the Fund, shall take all the appropriate measures to protect the financial interests of the Union and to ensure that the use of the financial allocations in relation to measures and investments supported by the Fund, including those carried out by public or private entities other than vulnerable households, vulnerable micro-enterprises and vulnerable transport users in accordance with Article 9, complies with applicable Union and national law, in particular regarding the prevention, detection and correction of fraud, corruption and conflicts of interests. To that effect, the Member States shall provide an effective and efficient internal control system as further set out in Annex III and the recovery of amounts wrongly paid or incorrectly used. Member States may rely on their regular national budget management systems.	Art. 21 refers to EU institutions and learner users and should therefore be transferred to Part 3.
2 The agreements referred to in Article 19 shall provide for the following obligations of the Member States: (a) to regularly check that the financing provided has been properly used in accordance with all applicable rules and that any measure or investment under the Plan has been properly implemented in accordance with all applicable rules, in particular regarding the prevention, detection and correction of fraud, corruption and conflicts of interests;	

The Regulation	*Comments*
(b) to take appropriate measures to prevent, detect and correct fraud, corruption, and conflicts of interests as defined in Article 61 of Regulation (EU, Euratom) 2018/1046 affecting the financial interests of the Union and to take legal action to recover funds that have been misappropriated, including in relation to any measure or investment implemented under the Plan; (c) to accompany a payment request by: (i) a management declaration that the financial allocations were used for its intended purpose, that the information submitted with the payment request is complete, accurate and reliable and that the internal control systems put in place give the necessary assurances that the financial allocations were managed in accordance with all applicable rules, in particular rules on avoidance of conflicts of interests, fraud prevention, corruption and double funding from the Fund and other Union programmes in accordance with the principle of sound financial management; and (ii) a summary of the audits carried out in accordance with internationally accepted audit standards, including the scope of those audits in terms of amount of spending covered and period of time covered and an analysis of the weaknesses identified and any corrective action taken; (d) for the purpose of audit and control and to provide for comparable information on the use of financial allocations in relation to measures and investments implemented under the Plan, to collect, record and store in an electronic system and ensure access to the following standardised categories of data: (i) name of the final recipients of the financial allocations, their VAT registration numbers or tax identification numbers and amount of the financial allocations from the Fund; (ii) name of the contractor(s) and sub-contractor(s) and their VAT registration number(s) or tax identification number(s) and value of the contract(s) where the final recipient of the financial allocations is a contracting authority in accordance with Union or national law on public procurement; (iii) first name(s), last name(s), date(s) of birth and VAT registration number(s) or tax identification number(s), of beneficial owner(s) of the recipient of the financial allocations or contractor, as defined in Article 3, point (6), of Directive (EU) 2015/849 of the European Parliament and of the Council([33]); (iv) a list of any measures and investments implemented under the Fund with the total amount of public funding of those measures and investments and indicating the amount of funds paid under other funds financed from the Union budget;	

The Regulation	*Comments*
(e) to expressly authorise the Commission, OLAF, the Court of Auditors and, in respect of those Member States participating in enhanced cooperation pursuant to Regulation (EU) 2017/1939, the EPPO, to exert their rights as provided for in Article 129(1) of Regulation (EU, Euratom) 2018/1046 and to impose obligations on all final recipients of the financial allocations paid for implementing the measures and investments included in the Plan, or to all other persons or entities involved in their implementation to expressly authorise the Commission, OLAF, the Court of Auditors and, where applicable, EPPO to exert their rights as provided for in Article 129(1) of Regulation (EU, Euratom) 2018/1046 and to impose similar obligations on all final recipients of funds disbursed; (f) to keep records in accordance with Article 132 of Regulation (EU, Euratom) 2018/1046, the point of reference being the payment transaction relevant to the respective measure or investment. The information referred to in point (d)(ii) of the first subparagraph of this Article shall be required only where the value of public procurement is greater than the Union thresholds set out in Article 4 of Directive 2014/24/EU of the European Parliament and of the Council([34]). Regarding subcontractors, that information shall be required only: (a) for the first level of sub-contracting; (b) where that information is recorded regarding the respective contractor; and (c) for sub-contracts with a total value greater than EUR50,000. 3 Personal data as referred to in paragraph 2, point (d), of this Article shall be processed by Member States and by the Commission for the purpose, and corresponding duration, of discharge, audit and control proceedings, and information, communication and visibility activities, related to the use of financial allocations related to the implementation of the agreements referred to in Article 19. The personal data shall be processed in accordance with Regulation (EU) 2016/679 or Regulation (EU) 2018/1725, whichever is applicable. Within the framework of the discharge procedure to the Commission, in accordance with Article 319 TFEU, the Fund shall be subject to reporting under the integrated financial and accountability reporting referred to in Article 247 of Regulation (EU, Euratom) 2018/1046, and, in particular, separately in the annual management and performance report. 4 The agreements referred to in Article 19 shall also provide for the right of the Commission to reduce proportionately the support under the Fund and recover any amount due to the Union budget, in cases of fraud, corruption, and conflict of interests affecting the financial interests of the Union that have not been corrected by the Member State, or a serious breach of an obligation resulting from such agreements.	

The Regulation	*Comments*
When deciding on the amount of the recovery and reduction the Commission shall respect the principle of proportionality and shall take into account the seriousness of the fraud, corruption and conflict of interests affecting the financial interests of the Union, or of a breach of an obligation. The Commission shall give the Member State the opportunity to present its observations before the reduction is made.	
CHAPTER IV ***Complementarity, monitoring and evaluation***	
Article 22 **Coordination and complementarity**	
The Commission and the Member States concerned shall, in a manner commensurate to their respective responsibilities, foster synergies and ensure effective coordination between the Fund and the Union programmes and instruments referred to in Article 6(3) of this Regulation, and the Modernisation Fund under Article 10d of Directive 2003/87/EC. For that purpose, they shall: (a) ensure complementarity, synergy, coherence and consistency among different instruments at Union, national and, where appropriate, local or regional levels, both in the planning phase and during implementation; (b) optimise mechanisms for coordination to avoid duplication of effort; and (c) ensure close cooperation between those responsible for implementation and control at Union, national and, where appropriate, local or regional levels to achieve the objectives of the Fund.	Art. 22 refers to the procedure related to the fund and should therefore be in Part 2, Chapter 2.
Article 23 **Information, communication and visibility**	
1 Member States shall make the data referred to in Article 21(2), point (d)(i), (ii) and (iv), of this Regulation publicly available and keep them up to date on a single website in open, machine-readable formats, as set out in Article 5(1) of Directive (EU) 2019/1024 of the European Parliament and of the Council[35], which shall allow data to be sorted, searched, extracted, compared and reused. The information referred to in Article 21(2), points (d)(i) and (ii), of this Regulation shall not be published in the cases referred to in Article 38(3) of Regulation (EU, Euratom) 2018/1046 or in the case of temporary direct income support to vulnerable households.	Art. 23 is addressed to Member States and should therefore be in Part 2, Chapter 2, as this is a matter of procedure.

The Regulation	*Comments*
2 The recipients of support from the Fund shall be informed of the origin of those funds, including where they benefit from those funds through intermediaries. That information shall include the emblem of the Union and an appropriate funding statement that reads 'funded by the European Union – Social Climate Fund' on documents and communication material relating to the implementation of the measure intended for the recipients. The recipients of support from the Fund, except the support for natural persons or where there is risk of commercially sensitive information being made public, shall ensure the visibility of the Union funding, in particular when promoting the actions and their results, by providing coherent, effective and proportionate targeted information to multiple audiences, including the media and the public. 3 The Commission shall implement information and communication actions relating to the Fund, to actions taken pursuant to this Regulation and to the results obtained, including, where appropriate and with the agreement of the national authorities, through joint communication activities with the national authorities and the representation offices of the European Parliament and of the Commission in the Member State concerned.	
Article 24 **Monitoring of implementation**	
1 Each Member State shall, on a biennial basis, report to the Commission on the implementation of its Plan together with its integrated national energy and climate progress report pursuant to Article 17 of Regulation (EU) 2018/1999 and in accordance with Article 28 thereof. The monitoring of implementation shall be targeted and proportionate to the activities carried out in the Plan. The Member States shall include the indicators set out in Annex IV to this Regulation in their progress report. 2 The Commission shall monitor the implementation of the Fund and measure the achievement of its objectives. The monitoring of implementation shall be targeted and proportionate to the activities carried out under the Fund. 3 The performance reporting system of the Commission shall ensure that data for monitoring the implementation of the activities and results are collected efficiently, effectively and in a timely manner. To that end, proportionate reporting requirements shall be imposed on recipients of support from the Fund. 4 The Commission shall use the common indicators set out in Annex IV for reporting on the progress and for the purpose of monitoring and evaluation of the Fund towards the achievement of the objectives set out in Article 3.	Art. 24 is addressed to Member States, is a matter of procedure, and should therefore be transferred to Part 2, Chapter 2.

The Regulation	*Comments*
Article 25 **Transparency**	
1 The Commission shall transmit the Plans submitted by Member States and the decisions, as made public by the Commission, simultaneously and on equal terms to the European Parliament and the Council without undue delay. 2 Information transmitted by the Commission to the Council in the context of this Regulation or its implementation shall simultaneously be made available to the European Parliament, subject to confidentiality arrangements if necessary. 3 The competent committees of the European Parliament may invite the Commission to provide information on the state of play of the assessment by the Commission of the Plans.	Art. 25 reverts to the procedure related to the plan and should therefore be transferred to Part 2, Chapter 2. However, it is tempting to place it in Part 3 as it is addressed to the EU. Nonetheless, it complements the tail end of the procedure related to the plan and the funding, and it is therefore best suited for a procedural provision at the end of Part 2.
Article 26 **Social climate dialogue**	
1 In order to enhance the dialogue between the Union institutions, in particular the European Parliament and the Commission, and to ensure greater transparency and accountability, the competent committees of the European Parliament may invite the Commission twice a year to discuss the following matters: (a) the Plans submitted by Member States; (b) the assessment by the Commission of the Plans submitted by Member States; (c) the status of achievement of the milestones and targets set out in the Plans submitted by Member States; (d) payment, suspension and termination procedures, including any observation presented and remedial measures taken by Member States to ensure the satisfactory achievement of the milestones and targets set out in the Plans submitted by them. 2 The Commission shall take account of any elements arising from the views expressed through the social climate dialogue, including the resolutions of the European Parliament if provided.	Art. 26 is addressed to the Parliament and the Commission and should therefore be in Part 3.
CHAPTER V ***Final provisions***	
Article 27 **Evaluation and review of the Fund**	
1 Two years after the start of the implementation of the Plans, the Commission shall provide the European Parliament, the Council, the European Economic and Social Committee and the Committee of the Regions with an evaluation report on the implementation and functioning of the Fund, taking into account the results of the first reports submitted by Member States in accordance with Article 24, and shall submit, where appropriate, any proposals for amendments to this Regulation.	Art. 27 is a provision of a technical nature that is addressed to the EU institutions, and it should therefore be in Part 3.

The Regulation	*Comments*
2 The evaluation report referred to in paragraph 1 shall, in particular, assess: (a) the extent to which the objectives of the Fund set out in Article 3 have been achieved, the efficiency of the use of the resources and the Union added value; (b) on a country-by-country basis, the efficiency of measures and investments and the use of the direct income support in light of the achievement of the milestones and targets set out in the Plans; (c) how the definitions of energy poverty and transport poverty are applied in Member States, based on the information referred to in Article 6(1), point (f), as well as whether amendments to such definitions are necessary; (d) the continued relevance of all objectives, and measures and investments set out in Article 8 of this Regulation in light of the impact on greenhouse gas emissions of the inclusion of greenhouse gas emissions from buildings and road transport within the scope of Directive 2003/87/EC and of the national measures taken to meet the binding annual greenhouse gas emission reductions by Member States pursuant to Regulation (EU) 2018/842 of the European Parliament and of the Council([36]), as well as the continued relevance of the assigned revenues in relation to possible developments concerning the auctioning of allowances under the emission trading system for buildings, road transport and additional sectors pursuant to Chapter IVa of Directive 2003/87/EC and other relevant considerations. 3 By 31December 2033, the Commission shall provide the European Parliament, the Council, the European Economic and Social Committee and the Committee of the Regions with an independentex postevaluation report. Theex postevaluation report shall consist of a global assessment of the Fund and shall include information on its impact. 4 Without prejudging the multiannual financial framework post 2027, in the event revenue generated from the auctioning of allowances referred to in Article 30d(5) of Directive 2003/87/EC is established as an own resource in accordance with Article 311(3) TFEU, the Commission shall, as appropriate, present the necessary proposals in order to ensure, within the framework of the multiannual financial framework post 2027, the effectiveness and continuity of the implementation of the Fund, which is temporarily and exceptionally financed by external assigned revenue generated from allowances of the emission trading system.	

The Regulation	*Comments*
Article 28 **Amendment to Regulation (EU) 2021/1060** The following Article is inserted in Regulation (EU) 2021/1060:	Art. 28 is a technical provision, and it is wisely at the end of the Regulation. It is definitely a Part 3 provision.
'Article 26a **Resources transferred from the Social Climate Fund** 1 Resources transferred from the Social Climate Fund, established by Regulation (EU) 2023/955 of the European Parliament and of the Council(*1)shall be implemented in accordance with this Regulation and the provisions governing the Fund to which the resources are transferred and shall be definitive. Such resources shall constitute external assigned revenue for the purpose of Article 21(5) of Regulation (EU, Euratom) 2018/1046 and shall be additional to the resources referred to in Article 110 of this Regulation. 2 Where Member States implement the resources referred to in paragraph 1 of this Article under shared management, they shall submit programme amendments in accordance with Article 24 of this Regulation concerning one or more programmes. Member States shall plan the use of such resources for achieving the climate objectives set out for the Union budget in accordance with Article 6(1) of this Regulation. Those resources shall contribute to achieving relevant objectives of the Social Climate Fund as set out in Article 3 of Regulation (EU) 2023/955 and shall be used to support measures and investments set out in Article 8 of that Regulation. They shall be programmed under one or more dedicated priorities corresponding to one or more specific objectives of the Fund to which the resources are transferred and for one or more categories of regions, where applicable, with an indication of the yearly breakdown of resources. They shall not be taken into account for the calculation of compliance with thematic concentration requirements as set out in Fund-specific rules. 3 Where the Commission has already approved a Member State's request for an amendment of a programme relating to a transfer of resources from the Social Climate Fund, for any further transfer of resources in subsequent years, the Member State may submit a notification of financial tables instead of an amendment of a programme, provided that the proposed changes relate exclusively to an increase of the financial resources, without any further changes to the programme.	It is at this point that the new article on citation, including the whole text of the title of the Regulation, could be introduced. This would alleviate the obligation to place it at the very beginning of the title, thus burdening the user with technical information that complicates and elongates the title without any benefit to lay users.

The Regulation	*Comments*
4 By way of derogation from Article 18 and Article 86(1), second subparagraph, of this Regulation, the resources transferred in accordance with this Article and Article 11(2) of Regulation (EU) 2023/955 shall not be taken into account for the mid-term review and the flexibility amount. 5 By way of derogation from Article 14(3) of Regulation (EU, Euratom) 2018/1046, the time limit after which the Commission shall decommit the amounts in accordance with Article 105(1) of this Regulation shall start from the year in which the corresponding budgetary commitments are made. Resources shall not be transferred to programmes under the European territorial cooperation goal (Interreg). *Article 29* **Entry into force**	
This Regulation shall enter into force on the twentieth day following that of its publication in theOfficial Journal of the European Union. It shall apply from 30 June 2024, the date by which the Member States are to bring into force the laws, regulations and administrative provisions necessary to comply with Directive (EU) 2023/959 of the European Parliament and of the Council[37] amending Directive 2003/87/EC as regards Chapter IVa of Directive 2003/87/EC. This Regulation shall be binding in its entirety and directly applicable in all Member States. Done at Strasbourg, 10May 2023. For the European Parliament The President R. METSOLA For the Council The President J. ROSWALL	Art. 29 on entry into force should be expressed in the most clear and concrete of terms. Although this is not particularly relevant to this specific Regulation, as it refers to access to subsidised works that can be used only when the Funds are complete, it would make enormous sense for the EU to try and even postdate EU Acts as a means of stating a specific date for a start point for EU Regulations, especially those that award specific rights/ benefits to lay users.

Having commented on the text of the Regulation, let's see it clean with all the changes to an easified layered structure:

REGULATION (EU) 2023/955 Establishing a Social Climate Fund and amending Regulation (EU) 2021/1060 Table of Contents

Article 1(a) and (b) (original 3 and 1) (original 2 and 23)	Objectives and subject matter
Article 2 (d) (original 2)	Definitions in Annex
Part 1: To EU citizens	
Article 3 (new) (original 30)	The right to subsidised green works for the energy vulnerable
Article 4 (new and original 10 first para)	Establishment of the Social Climate Fund
Article 5 (original 15)	National contributions to the Social Climate Fund
Part 2: To Member States	
Chapter I	*The Social Climate Fund*
Art. 6 (original 4)	Social climate plans
Article 7 (original 7)	Principles governing the fund
Article 8 (original 8)	Eligible measures and Investments to be included in the Social Climate Plans
Article 9 (original 6) (original 28)	Content of Social Climate Plans
Article 10 (original 9)	Pass on benefits to households, micro-enterprises and transport users
Chapter II	*Procedure and administration of the Social Climate Fund*
Article 11 (original 5)	Public consultation
Article 12 (original 16)	Commission assessment of the plan
Article 13 (original 17)	Commission decision on the plan
Article 14 (original 18)	Amendment of social climate plans
Article 15 (original 20) (original 33(11))	Rules on payment, suspension and termination of agreements regarding financial allocations
Article 16 (original 25)	Transparency
Article 17 (original 22)	Coordination and complementarity
Article 18 (original 23)	Information, communication and visibility
Article 19 (original 24)	Monitoring of implementation
Part 3 (to EU)	
Article 20 (original 10, 28)	Resources of the Fund (apart from now Art. 1, first paragraph)

Article 21 (original 11)	Art. 21 (now 11) Resources from shared management programs and use of resources
Article 22 (original 12)	Art. 22 (now 12) Implementation
Article 23 (original 13)	Art. 23 (now 13) Additionality and complementary funding
Article 24 (original 14)	Art. 24 (now 14) Maximum financial allocation
Article 25 (original 21)	Art. 25 (now 21) Protection of the financial interests of the Union
Article 26 (original 26)	Art. 26 (now 26) Social climate dialogue
Article 27 (original 27)	Art. 27 (now 27) Evaluation and review of the fund
Article 28 (original 28)	Art. 28 (now 28) Amendment to Regulation EU 2021/1060
Article 29 (new)	Citation
Article 30 (original 29)	Entry into force
Annex 1	DEFINITIONS
Annex 2	NOTES AND COMMISSION STATEMENT

In the annex to this chapter, this easified layered structure is put to effect by a group of professional drafters, as an aid to the appreciation of the difference that it can really make to accessibility and effectiveness. This is an exercise on structure so minimal words have been amended.

18.3 Conclusions

The quest for better legislation cannot be more vibrant than it is today. Legislative studies have made leaps of advances in the past 20 years. Legislative effectiveness as a synonym to legislative quality is now widely accepted, as is the use of legislation as a tool for regulation, namely for the achievement of the desired regulatory results. The focus on words as the main topic for legislative drafting and legislative studies has given way to more academic overarching debates. It is understood that the wrong choice of a word may still allow the text to be effective and contribute to the desired regulatory results. However, the design of the legislative solution and its translation to structure is directly linked to effectiveness. This is the main mischief in legislation today. Structure is at the forefront of legislative innovation potential.

It is unfortunate that legislative studies remain oblivious to the methodologies and lessons that can be borrowed and applied by disciplines that have been studying similar topics for a much longer period of time. The inspiration and lessons learnt by the study of language are certainly one of the main examples of the loss of the opportunity to gain from other disciplines.

The structure of legislation remains a text-centred technique that suffers from its erroneous perception as a purely technical matter. But structure is not just a technical matter. It is a reflection of legislative design, which can only be achieved successfully, if the groups of legislative audiences and their characteristics are taken into account.

Easification as a concept identified and developed in the study of language can come to the rescue of legislative drafters. The acceptance that there are three distinct audiences in legislation with diverse characteristics and diverse needs for information can change the way in which legislation is structured. And this can in turn enhance the accessibility and legibility of legislation. If the language of provisions takes into account the level of topical and legal sophistication of the users to whom the specific provision is addressed, comprehensibility is greatly enhanced. The message is communicated in an optimal way, ensuring that it is received as it was transmitted.

But also the use of easification for the purposes of prioritising legislative messages can enhance approachability and accessibility too. To identify the regulatory messages legislative audiences have different requirements. Lay users require immediate, quick information on the rights and obligations imposed on them, namely the substantive provisions, at the very start of a legislative text, and in a way that can be understood by unsophisticated users. Matters of procedure belong to Part 2 where their users strive to administer the law as expected, may understand semi-legal messages, and follow matters of administration. Finally, issues of a technical nature, namely legal and interpretation, belong to the end of the text, where learned users can read and understand a language that expresses complex legal concepts in complex legal language.

This chapter used the layered approach to an EU Regulation. This representative case study demonstrated the crucial effect that a layered structure can have for the purposes of accessibility and legibility of EU Regulations. The lessons learnt are detailed and technical. But perhaps the most important conclusion of this chapter is that the requirement for effective legislation can be met only with a change of legislative mentality. In other words, legislators, including the EU, must change the way in which they express legislation. Depart from the formalities of the past. And put them aside for the purposes of communicating to each group of users, EU citizens,

Member States, EU institutions, and learned users in a language that they understand.

But why change? Because better communication means better implementation. Better implementation means a better possibility of reaching regulatory efficacy. And regulatory efficacy means that the legislation actually contributed to the achievement of the desired regulatory results, i.e. the success of the regulatory effort.

Moreover, and perhaps most importantly, better communication via the layered approach facilitates the exchange of messages between the legislators, including the EU, and the legislative audiences. This creates a new channel of direct communication between the legislator and the citizen. This offers a unique opportunity for the legislator to explain why legislation is necessary, what is the benefit of legislation for the citizen (short or long term), and how the legislation will be monitored to ensure the production of the desired regulatory results. This approach renders the citizen participatory in the regulatory effort. The sense of ownership re-establishes a benevolent relationship of loyalty to the legislator. And, the longer term creates a sentiment of trust, which in turn enhances implementation and regulatory success.

This chapter showcases the direct relationship between the studies of language and legislation as one of concentric circles. Topics are shared. Solutions are transferable. Cross fertilisation is highly beneficial. And the hope is for even further points of contact.

Annex

By Nicole Sardiello-Zamboni, Aarohi Vikas Pillai, Denise Yasmine H. Eixas and Kimberley Shepherd[3]

Regulation (EU) 2023/955 on the subsidy of green works for the energy vulnerable via a Social Climate Fund, and amending Regulation (EU) 2021/1060

Preamble	
Article 1 (original Art. 3 and Art. 1) and (recitals (1), (3), (8), (23), (24), (31))	Objectives and subject matter
Article 2 (original Art. 2)	Definitions in Annex
Part 1: To EU citizens	
Article 3 (original Art. 8 para 1)	The right of access to funding for green works for the energy vulnerable

Article 4 (original Art. 1) and (original Art. 10 para 1)	Establishment of the social climate fund
Article 5 (original 15)	National contributions to the social climate plans
Part 2: To Member States	
Chapter I	*The Social Climate Fund and Plans*
Article 6 (original Art. 4)	Social Climate Plans
Article 7 (original Art. 7) and (recital (34) and (27))	Principles governing the Fund and Plans
Article 8 (original Art. 8)	Eligible measures and investments to be included in the Social Climate Plans
Article 9 (original Art. 6) (recital (28))	Content of Social Climate Plans
Article 10 (original Art. 9)	Pass on benefits to households, micro-enterprises and transport users
Chapter II	*Procedure and administration of the Social Climate Fund*
Article 11 (original Art. 5)	Public consultation
Article 12 (original Art. 16)	Commission assessment of the Plan
Article 13 (original Art. 17) and (original Art. 19)	Commission decision on the Plan
Article 14 (original Art. 18)	Amendment of Social Climate Plans
Article 15 (original Art. 20) and (recital (33))	Rules on payment, suspension and termination of agreements regarding financial allocations
Article 16 (original Art. 25)	Transparency
Article 17 (original Art. 22)	Coordination and complementarity
Article 18 (original Art. 23)	Information, communication and visibility
Article 19 (original Art. 4)	Monitoring of implementation
Part 3 (to EU)	
Article 20 (original Art. 10 para 2 and 3)	Resources of the Fund
Article 21 (original Art. 11)	Resources from shared management programs and use of resources
Article 22 (original Art. 12)	Implementation
Article 23 (original Art. 13)	Additionality and complementary funding

Article 24 (original Art. 14)	Maximum financial allocation
Article 25 (original Art. 21)	Protection of the financial interests of the Union
Article 26 (original Art. 26)	Social climate dialogue
Article 27 (original Art. 27)	Evaluation and review of the fund
Article 28 (original Art. 28)	Amendment to Regulation EU 2021/1060
Article 29 (new)	Citation
Article 30 (original Art. 29)	Entry into force
Annex 1	DEFINITIONS
Annex 2	NOTES AND COMMISSION STATEMENT

Preamble

THE EUROPEAN PARLIAMENT AND THE COUNCIL OF THE EUROPEAN UNION,

Having regard to the Treaty on the Functioning of the European Union, and in particular Article 91(1), point (d), Article 192(1) and Article 194(2), and Article 322(1), point (a), thereof,

Having regard to the proposal from the European Commission,

After transmission of the draft legislative act to the national parliaments,

Having regard to the opinion of the European Economic and Social Committee ([1]),

Having regard to the opinion of the Committee of the Regions ([2]),

Acting in accordance with the ordinary legislative procedure ([3]),

Whereas:

A part of the revenues generated by the inclusion of buildings, road transport and additional sectors within the scope of Directive 2003/87/EC should be used to address the social impacts arising from that inclusion, in order for the transition to be just and inclusive, leaving no one behind. The overall amount of the Social Climate Fund established under this Regulation (the 'Fund') should reflect the level of decarbonisation ambition from the inclusion of greenhouse gas emissions from buildings, road transport and additional sectors within the scope of Directive 2003/87/EC.

Resources are needed to finance those investments. In addition, before such investments are made, the cost supported by households and transport users for heating, cooling, cooking, and road transport, is likely to increase as fuel suppliers that are subject to the obligations under the emission trading system for buildings and road transport pass on the costs of carbon to consumers.

Since the objective of this Regulation, namely to contribute to a socially fair transition towards climate neutrality by addressing the social impacts of the inclusion of greenhouse gas emissions from buildings and road transport within the scope of Directive 2003/87/EC, cannot be sufficiently achieved by the Member States but can rather, by reason of its scale and effects, be better achieved at Union level, the Union may adopt measures, in accordance with the principle of subsidiarity as set out in Article 5 of the Treaty on European Union. In accordance with the principle of proportionality as set out in that Article, this Regulation does not go beyond what is necessary in order to achieve that objective,

HAVE ADOPTED THIS REGULATION:
Article 1
Objectives and subject matter

1 The objectives of this Regulation are:

(a) To contribute to the Paris Agreement target to hold the increase in the global average temperature well below 2°C above pre-industrial levels and to pursue efforts to limit the temperature increase to 1.5°C above pre-industrial levels.
(b) To contribute to the Paris Agreement and the commitment to the United Nations Sustainable Development Goals target that at least 30% of the total amount of the Union budget under the multiannual financial framework for the years 2021 to 2027 laid down in Council Regulation (EU, Euratom) 2020/2093 ([9]) (the 'MFF 2021–2027') and of the total amount of the European Union Recovery Instrument, established by Council Regulation (EU) 2020/2094 ([10]), and at least 37% of the total amount of the Recovery and Resilience Facility, established by Regulation (EU) 2021/241 of the European Parliament and of the Council ([11]), should be spent on mainstreaming climate objectives.
(c) To contribute to the provision of 7.5% of annual spending under the MFF 2021–2027 to biodiversity objectives in 2024 and 10% of annual spending under MFF 2021–2027 to biodiversity objectives in 2026 and 2027, while considering the existing overlaps between climate and biodiversity goals.
(d) To contribute to the objective of Regulation (EU) 2021/1119 of the European Parliament and of the Council that establishes a binding

Union domestic reduction target for net greenhouse gas emissions (emissions after deduction of removals) of at least 55% compared to 1990 levels by 2030.

(e) To enable the subsidisation of green works that directly reduce energy poverty and support energy-vulnerable households, micro-enterprises, and transport users across Member States.
(f) To mitigate the economic and social impacts of the transition to climate neutrality, particularly in light of the extension of carbon pricing to buildings and road transport, by supporting Member States in implementing structural investments that increase energy efficiency, reduce fossil fuel dependence, and lower household energy costs.
(g) To reduce the number of energy and transport vulnerable by 15% and increase the funds allocated for this purpose by the Member States by at least 25%.
(h) To support women who are disproportionately affected by energy poverty and transport poverty, in particular single mothers, who represent 85% of single parent families, as well as single women, women with disabilities, and elderly women living alone.
(i) To support single parent families with dependent children who have a particularly high risk of child poverty.

2 This Regulation:

(a) Establishes an EU fund for EUR 65,000,000,000 to financially support up to 75% of green works undertaken by energy-vulnerable households, micro-enterprises, and transport users who suffer from climate change.
(b) Introduces the procedure for the planning and funding of a minimum of 25% of green works by the national funds of the Member States.
(c) Provides safety processes for the protection of the financial interests of the EU through standardized procedures in application of EU financial rules.
(d) Uses the methodology set out in Annex I to Regulation (EU) 2021/1060 of the European Parliament and of the Council ([12]) to track the expenditures of the Fund for measures and investments that fully respect climate and environmental standards and priorities of the Union and comply with the principle of 'do no significant harm' within the meaning of Article 17 of Regulation (EU) 2020/852 of the European Parliament and of the Council ([13]).

Part 1: To EU Citizens

Article 3

The Right of Access to Funding for Green Works for the Energy Vulnerable

Vulnerable households, vulnerable micro-enterprises, and vulnerable transport users have the right to access funding for the following green works to:

(a) support building renovations, in particular for vulnerable households and vulnerable micro-enterprises occupying the worst performing buildings, and including for tenants and people living in social housing;
(b) support access to affordable energy-efficient housing, including social housing;
(c) contribute to the decarbonisation, such as through electrification, of heating and cooling of, and cooking in, buildings by providing access to affordable and energy-efficient systems, and by integrating renewable energy generation and storage, including through renewable energy communities, citizen energy communities and other active customers to promote the uptake of the self-consumption of renewable energy, such as energy sharing and peer-to-peer trading of renewable energy, connection to smart grids and to district heating networks, that contributes to achieving energy savings or to reducing energy poverty;
(d) provide targeted, accessible and affordable information, education, awareness and advice on cost-effective measures and investments, available support for building renovations and energy efficiency, as well as sustainable and affordable mobility and transport alternatives;
(e) support public and private entities, including social housing providers, in particular public-private cooperatives, in developing and providing affordable energy efficiency solutions and appropriate funding instruments in line with the social goals of the Fund;
(f) provide access to zero- and low-emission vehicles and bicycles, while maintaining technological neutrality, including financial support or fiscal incentives for their purchase as well as for appropriate public and private infrastructure, in particular, where relevant, purchase of zero- and low-emission vehicles, infrastructure for recharging and refuelling and development of a second-hand zero-emission vehicles market; Member States shall aim to ensure that where zero-emission vehicles are an affordable and deployable solution, support to such vehicles is prioritised in their Plans;
(g) incentivise the use of affordable and accessible public transport and support private and public entities, including cooperatives, in developing

and providing sustainable mobility on demand, shared mobility services and active mobility options.

Article 4

Establishment of the Social Climate Fund

1 The EU establishes the Social Climate Fund (the 'Fund') for the period from 2026 to 2032.
2 The Fund shall provide financial support to Member States for the measures and investments included in their Social Climate Plans (the 'Plans').
3 The measures and investments supported by the Fund shall benefit households, micro-enterprises and transport users, which are vulnerable and particularly affected by the inclusion of greenhouse gas emissions from buildings and road transport within the scope of Directive 2003/87/EC, in particular households in energy poverty or households in transport poverty.
4 A maximum amount of EUR 65,000,000,000 for the period from 1 January 2026 to 31 December 2032 in current prices shall be made available, in accordance with Articles 10a(8b), 30d(3) and 30d(4) of Directive 2003/87/EC, for implementation of the Fund. That amount shall constitute external assigned revenue for the purposes of Article 21(5) of Regulation (EU, Euratom) 2018/1046, without prejudice to Article 30d(4), sixth subparagraph, of Directive 2003/87/EC.
5 The annual amounts allocated to the Fund, within the limit of the maximum amount laid down in paragraph 4, shall not exceed the amounts referred to in Article 30d(4), fourth subparagraph, of Directive 2003/87/EC.
6 Where the emission trading system established in accordance with Chapter IVa of Directive 2003/87/EC is postponed until 2028 pursuant to Article 30k of that Directive, the maximum amount to be made available to the Fund shall be EUR 54,600,000,000 and the annual amounts allocated to the Fund shall not exceed the respective amounts referred to in the Article 30d(4), fifth subparagraph, of Directive 2003/87/EC.

Article 5

National contribution to the Social Climate Plans

Member States shall contribute at least to 25% of the estimated total costs of their Plans.

Part II: To the Members States

Chapter 1: The Fund and Plans

Article 6

Social Climate Plans

1 Each Member State shall submit to the Commission its Plan.
2 Each Member State shall ensure consistency between its Plan and its updated integrated national energy and climate plan referred to in Article 14(2) of Regulation (EU) 2018/1999.
3 The Plan shall contain a coherent set of existing or new national measures and investments to address the impact of carbon pricing on vulnerable households, vulnerable micro-enterprises and vulnerable transport users in order to ensure affordable heating, cooling and mobility, while accompanying and accelerating necessary measures to meet the climate targets of the Union.
4 The Plan may include national measures providing temporary direct income support to vulnerable households and vulnerable transport users to reduce the impact of the increase in the price of fossil fuels resulting from the inclusion of greenhouse gas emissions from buildings and road transport within the scope of Directive 2003/87/EC.
5 The Plan shall include national and, where relevant, local and regional measures and investments, in accordance with Article 3 and Article 8 of this Regulation, to:

   (a) carry out building renovation, and decarbonise heating and cooling of buildings, including the integration of renewable energy generation and storage;
   (b) increase the uptake of zero- and low-emission mobility and transport.

6 Where a Member State has already in place a national emission trading system for buildings and road transport or carbon tax, the national measures already in place to mitigate social impacts and challenges may be included in the Plan provided that they comply with this Regulation.

Article 7

Principles Governing the Fund and Plans

1 The Fund shall provide financial support to Member States to fund the measures and investments set out in their Plans.
2 Payment of financial support pursuant to paragraph 1 of this Article to each Member State shall be conditional upon that Member State

achieving the milestones and targets for the measures and investments in accordance with Article 8 of this Regulation.

3 The milestones and targets referred to in paragraph 2 of this Article shall be compatible with the Union's climate targets and the objective set out in Regulation (EU) 2021/1119, and shall cover in particular:

(a) energy efficiency;
(b) building renovation;
(c) zero- and low-emission mobility and transport;
(d) greenhouse gas emission reductions; and
(e) reductions in the number of vulnerable households, in particular households in energy poverty, of vulnerable micro-enterprises and of vulnerable transport users.

4 The Fund should support measures that respect the principle of additionality of Union funding. The Fund should not be a substitute for recurring national expenditure, except in duly justified cases, including for payments of costs for technical assistance actions indicated in the Plans.

5 The Fund shall only support measures and investments which comply with the principle of 'do no significant harm' within the meaning of Article 17 of Regulation (EU) 2020/852.

6 The measures and investments supported by the Fund shall reduce fossil fuel dependency and, where relevant, contribute to the implementation of the European Pillar of Social Rights as well as to sustainable and quality jobs in the fields covered by the measures and investments of the Fund.

7 The Fund and the Plans should be coherent with and framed by the reforms planned and the commitments made by the Member States under their updated integrated national energy and climate plans in accordance with Regulation (EU) 2018/1999 of the European Parliament and of the Council ([14]), under Directive of the European Parliament and the Council on energy efficiency (recast), under the European Pillar of Social Rights Action Plan, under cohesion policy programmes in accordance with Regulation (EU) 2021/1060, under territorial just transition plans in accordance with Regulation (EU) 2021/1056 of the European Parliament and of the Council ([15]), under recovery and resilience plans in accordance with Regulation (EU) 2021/241, under the Modernisation Fund, as set out in Article 10d of Directive 2003/87/EC, and under the Member States' long-term building renovation strategies in accordance with Directive 2010/31/EU. To ensure administrative efficiency, where applicable, the information included in the Plans should be consistent with those legislative acts and plans.

Article 8

Eligible Measures and Investments to Be Included in the Social Climate Plans

1 Member States may include in the estimated total costs of the Plans the costs of measures providing direct income support to vulnerable households and vulnerable transport users to reduce the impact of the increase in road transport and heating fuel prices. Such support shall be temporary and decrease over time.
2 Member States may provide temporary direct income support if their Plans contain measures or investments aimed at those vulnerable households and vulnerable transport users in accordance with Article 3 of this Regulation. Such support shall be limited to the direct impact of the inclusion of greenhouse gas emissions from buildings and road transport within the scope of Directive 2003/87/EC. The costs of measures providing temporary direct income support shall not represent more than 37.5% of the estimated total costs of the Plan, as referred to in Article 9(1), point (j), of this Regulation.
3 Member States may include in the estimated total costs of the Plans the costs of technical assistance to cover expenses related to training, programming, monitoring, control, audit and evaluation activities which are required for the management of the Fund and the achievement of its objectives, for example studies, information technology (IT) expenses, public consultation of stakeholders, information and communication actions. The costs of such technical assistance shall be up to 2.5% of the estimated total costs of the Plan, as referred to in Article 9(1), point (j) of this Regulation.

Article 9

Content of Social Climate Plans

1 The Plan shall set out the following elements:

(a) concrete measures and investments in accordance with Articles 6 and 8 of this Regulation to reduce the effects referred to in point (d) of this paragraph, together with an explanation of how those measures and investments would contribute effectively to the achievement of the objectives set out in Article 1 of this Regulation within the overall setting of a Member State's relevant policies;
(b) where relevant, concrete, mutually coherent and reinforced accompanying measures to accomplish the measures and investments and reduce the effects referred to in point (d);
(c) information on existing or planned financing of measures and investments from other Union, international, public or, where

relevant, private sources which contribute to the measures and investments set out in the Plan, including information on temporary direct income support;

(d) an estimate of the likely effects of the increase in prices resulting from the inclusion of greenhouse gas emissions from buildings and road transport within the scope of Directive 2003/87/EC on households, in particular on incidence of energy poverty and transport poverty, and on micro-enterprises; those effects are to be analysed at the appropriate territorial level as defined by each Member State, taking into account national specificities and elements, such as access to public transport and basic services, and identifying the areas mostly affected;

(e) an estimated number of, and the identification of, vulnerable households, vulnerable micro-enterprises and vulnerable transport users;

(f) an explanation of how the definitions of energy poverty and transport poverty are to be applied at national level;

(g) where the Plan provides for measures as referred to in Article 6(3) of this Regulation, the criteria for the identification of eligible final recipients, the envisaged time limit for the measures in question and their justification on the basis of a quantitative estimate and a qualitative explanation of how those measures are expected to reduce energy poverty, transport poverty and the vulnerability of households to an increase in the price of road transport and heating fuel;

(h) envisaged milestones, targets and an indicative comprehensive timetable for the implementation of the measures and investments to be completed by 31 July 2032;

(i) where applicable, a timetable for the gradual reduction of support for low-emission vehicles;

(j) the estimated total costs of the Plan, accompanied by appropriate justification and explanations of how they are in line with the principle of cost efficiency and commensurate to the expected impact of the Plan;

(k) the envisaged national contribution to the estimated total costs of the Plan, calculated in accordance with Article 5 of this Regulation;

(l) except for the measures referred to in Article 6(3) of this Regulation, an explanation of how the Plan ensures that none of the measures or investments would do significant harm to environmental objectives within the meaning of Article 17 of Regulation (EU) 2020/852;

(m) the arrangements for the effective monitoring and implementation of the Plan by the Member State concerned, in particular of the proposed milestones and targets, the relevant common indicators referred to in Annex IV, and if none of those indicators are relevant for a specific measure or investment, additional individual indicators proposed by the Member State concerned;

(n) for the preparation and, where available, for the implementation of the Plan, a summary of the public consultation process referred to in Article 11 of this Regulation;

(o) an explanation of the Member State's system to prevent, detect and correct fraud, corruption and conflicts of interests when using the financial allocation provided under the Fund, and of the arrangements that aim to avoid double funding from the Fund and other Union programmes;

(p) where applicable and relevant, an explanation of how geographic specificities, such as islands, outermost regions and territories, rural or remote areas, less accessible peripheries, mountainous areas or areas lagging behind, have been taken into account in the Plan;

(q) where relevant, an explanation of how the measures and investments aim to address gender inequality.

2 The Plan may include technical assistance actions necessary for the effective administration and implementation of the measures and investments.

3 The Plan shall be consistent with the information included in and the commitments made by the Member State under the following:

(a) the European Pillar of Social Rights Action Plan;

(b) its cohesion policy programmes under Regulation (EU) 2021/1060;

(c) its recovery and resilience plan under Regulation (EU) 2021/241;

(d) its building renovation plan under the Directive of the European Parliament and of the Council on the energy performance of buildings (recast);

(e) its updated integrated national energy and climate plan under Regulation (EU) 2018/1999; and

(f) its territorial just transition plans under Regulation (EU) 2021/1056.

4 For more efficient planning, Member States should indicate in their Plans the consequences of postponing the emission trading system established in accordance with Chapter IVa of Directive 2003/87/EC, pursuant to Article 30k of that Directive. To that end, all the relevant information to be included in the Plan should be thoroughly distinguished by separating it into two scenarios, namely, by describing and quantifying the necessary adjustments to the measures, investments, milestones, targets, the amount of national contribution and any other relevant element of the Plan.

5 During the preparation of the Plans, the Commission shall organise an exchange of good practices, including on cost-effective measures and investments to be included in the Plans. Member States may

request technical support under the European Local ENergy Assistance (ELENA) facility, established by an Agreement between the Commission and the European Investment Bank in 2009, or under the Technical Support Instrument established by Regulation (EU) 2021/240 of the European Parliament and of the Council (30).

6 For the purposes of paragraph 1, point (l), of this Article, the Commission shall provide technical guidance to the Member States, tailored to the scope of the Fund, on the compliance of measures and investments with the principle of 'do no significant harm' within the meaning of Article 17 of Regulation (EU) 2020/852.

7 To assist Member States in providing the information referred to in paragraph 1, point (d), of this Article the Commission shall provide a common value to be considered as an estimate for the carbon price resulting from the inclusion of greenhouse gas emissions from buildings, road transport and additional sectors within the scope of Directive 2003/87/EC.

8 Each Member State shall use the template set out in Annex V for the Plan.

Article 10

Pass on Benefits to Households, Micro-Enterprises and Transport Users

1 Member States may include in the Plans support provided through public or private entities other than vulnerable households, vulnerable micro-enterprises and vulnerable transport users, provided that those entities carry out measures and investments ultimately benefitting vulnerable households, vulnerable micro-enterprises or vulnerable transport users.

2 Member States shall provide for the necessary statutory and contractual safeguards to ensure that the entire benefit is passed on to the vulnerable households, vulnerable micro-enterprises or vulnerable transport users.

Chapter 2: The Process

Article 11

Public Consultation

1 Each Member State shall submit a Plan to the Commission following a public consultation with local and regional authorities, representatives of economic and social partners, relevant civil society organisations, youth organisations and other stakeholders. Each Member State shall conduct that consultation in accordance with the requirements of Article 10 of Regulation (EU) 2018/1999 and in compliance with that Member State's national legal framework.

2 Each Member State shall include in its Plan a summary of:

(a) the consultation held pursuant to paragraph 1; and
(b) how the input of the stakeholders who participated in the consultation is reflected in the Plan.

3 For the purposes of Article 12(3) of this regulation, the Commission shall assess whether the Plan has been developed in consultation with stakeholders in accordance with paragraph 1 of this Article.
4 The Commission shall support Member States by providing examples of good practices of consultations on the Plans in accordance with Article 9(5) of this Regulation.

Article 12

Commission Assessment of the Plan

1 The Commission shall assess the Plan and, where applicable, any amendment to that Plan submitted by a Member State in accordance with Article 14, for compliance with this Regulation.
2 When carrying out the assessment pursuant to paragraph 1 of this Article, the Commission:

(a) shall act in close cooperation with the Member State concerned; and
(b) may make observations or seek additional information within two months from the date of submission of the Plan by the Member State.

3 The Member State shall provide the requested additional information referred to in paragraph 2 of this Article and may revise the Plan if needed, including after the submission of the Plan. The Member State and the Commission may agree to extend the deadline for assessment by a reasonable period if necessary.
4 The Commission shall assess whether transfers requested in accordance with Article 21 meet the objectives of this Regulation.
5 The Commission shall assess the relevance, effectiveness, efficiency and coherence of the Plan, taking into account the specific challenges and the financial allocation of the Member State, as follows:

(a) for the purpose of assessing relevance, the Commission shall take into account the following criteria:

(i) whether the Plan represents an adequate response to the social impact on and challenges faced by vulnerable households, vulnerable micro-enterprises and vulnerable transport users in the Member State concerned from the inclusion of greenhouse gas emissions from buildings and road transport within the scope of Directive 2003/87/EC, in particular households in energy poverty or households in transport poverty, duly taking into account the challenges identified in the assessments of the Commission of the update of the concerned Member State's integrated national energy and climate plan and of its progress pursuant to Article 9(3), and Articles 13 and 29 of Regulation (EU) 2018/1999, as well as in the Commission recommendations to Member States issued pursuant to Article 34 of Regulation (EU) 2018/1999 in view of the Union's 2030 climate and energy targets and long-term objective of climate neutrality in the Union at the latest by 2050;

(ii) whether the Plan is expected to ensure that measures and investments included in the Plan do not significantly harm environmental objectives within the meaning of Article 17 of Regulation (EU) 2020/852 and whether the Plan helps reduce fossil fuel dependency;

(iii) whether the Plan contains measures and investments that contribute to the green transition, including to addressing the social impacts and challenges resulting therefrom and in particular to the achievement of the Union's 2030 climate and energy targets and long-term objective of climate neutrality in the Union at the latest by 2050 and the 2030 milestones of the Union's Sustainable and Smart Mobility Strategy;

(b) for the purpose of assessing effectiveness, the Commission shall take into account the following criteria:

(i) whether the Plan is expected to have a lasting impact in the Member State on the challenges addressed by that Plan, in line with the Union's 2030 climate and energy targets and long-term objective of climate neutrality in the Union at the latest by 2050, and in particular on vulnerable households, vulnerable micro-enterprises and vulnerable transport users, in particular households in energy poverty or households in transport poverty;

(ii) whether the arrangements proposed by the Member State are expected to ensure the effective monitoring and implementation of the Plan, including the envisaged timetable, milestones and targets, and the related indicators;

(iii) whether the measures and investments proposed by the Member State are consistent and compliant with the requirements of the Directive of the European Parliament and of the Council on energy efficiency (recast), Directive (EU) 2018/2001, the Regulation of the European Parliament and of the Council on the deployment of alternative fuels infrastructure, and repealing Directive 2014/94/EU of the European Parliament and of the Council, Directive 2009/33/EC of the European Parliament and of the Council (32) and Directive 2010/31/EU; and

(iv) whether the measures and investments proposed by the Member State foster complementarity, synergy, coherence and consistency with the Union instruments referred to in Article 9(3).

(c) for the purposes of assessing efficiency, the Commission shall take into account the following criteria:

(i) whether the justification provided by the Member State for the amount of the estimated total costs of the Plan is reasonable, plausible, in line with the principle of cost efficiency and commensurate with the expected national environmental and social impact, while also taking into account national specificities that could impact the costs provided in the Plan;

(ii) whether the arrangements proposed by the Member State are expected to prevent, detect and correct corruption, fraud and conflicts of interests when using the financial allocation provided under the Fund, including the arrangements that aim to avoid double funding from the Fund and other Union programmes;

(iii) whether the milestones and targets proposed by the Member State are efficient, in view of the scope, objectives and eligible actions of the Fund;

(d) for the purpose of assessing coherence, the Commission shall take into account whether the Plan contains measures and investments that represent coherent actions.

Article 13

Commission Decision on the Plan

1 On the basis of the assessment carried out in accordance with Article 12 of this Regulation, the Commission shall decide on the Plan of a Member State, by means of an implementing act, no later than five months from the date of the submission of that Plan pursuant to Article 6(1) of this Regulation.

2 Where the Commission gives a positive assessment of a Plan, the implementing act referred to in paragraph 1 shall set out:

(a) the measures and investments to be implemented by the Member State, the amount of the estimated total costs of the Plan, and the milestones and targets;

(b) the maximum financial allocation allocated in accordance with Article 24(1) of this Regulation to be paid in instalments, in accordance with Article 15 of this Regulation, once the Member State has satisfactorily achieved the relevant milestones and targets identified in relation to the implementation of the Plan;
(c) the national contribution;
(d) the arrangements and timetable for monitoring and implementation of the Plan, including, where relevant, measures necessary for complying with Article 25 of this Regulation;
(e) the relevant indicators relating to the achievement of the envisaged milestones and targets; and
(f) the arrangements for providing access by the Commission to the underlying relevant data.

3 The maximum financial allocation referred to in paragraph 2, point (b), of this Article shall be determined on the basis of the estimated total costs of the Plan proposed by the Member State, as assessed by reference to the criteria set out in Article 12(5) of this Regulation.
4 The amount of the maximum financial allocation referred to in paragraph 2, point (b), of this Article shall be set as follows:

(a) where the Plan complies satisfactorily with the criteria set out in Article 12(5) of this Regulation, and the amount of the estimated total costs of the Plan minus the national contribution is equal to, or higher than, the maximum financial allocation for that Member State referred to in Article 24(1) of this Regulation, the financial allocation allocated to the Member State shall be equal to the total amount of the maximum financial allocation referred to in Article 14(1);
(b) where the Plan complies satisfactorily with the criteria set out in Article 12(5) of this Regulation, and the amount of the estimated total costs of the Plan minus the national contribution is lower than the maximum financial allocation for that Member State referred to in Article 24(1), the financial allocation allocated to the Member State shall be equal to the amount of the estimated total costs of the Plan minus the national contribution;
(c) where the Plan complies satisfactorily with the criteria set out in Article 12(5) of this Regulation, but the assessment identifies weaknesses in the internal control systems, the Commission may require that additional measures to address those weaknesses be included in the Plan and be achieved by the Member State before the first payment;
(d) where the Plan does not comply satisfactorily with the criteria set out in Article 12(5) of this Regulation, no financial allocation shall be allocated to the Member State.

5 If the Commission has adopted a positive decision in accordance with this Article, it shall in due time conclude an agreement with the Member State concerned constituting an individual legal commitment within the meaning of Regulation (EU, Euratom) 2018/1046 for the period 2026–2032, without prejudice to Article 30d(4) and Articles 30i and 30k of Directive 2003/87/EC. That agreement shall be concluded at the earliest one year before the year of the start of the auctions under Chapter IVa of Directive 2003/87/EC, or two years before that year, in cases where Article 4(6) of this Regulation applies.

6 Budgetary commitments may be based on global commitments and, where appropriate, may be broken down into annual instalments spread over several years.

7 Where the Commission gives a negative assessment of a Plan, the decision referred to in paragraph 1 shall include the reasons for that negative assessment and the Member State shall resubmit the Plan, after taking into account the assessment of the Commission.

Article 14

Amendment of Social Climate Plans

1 Where a Plan is no longer achievable, including relevant milestones and targets, or needs to be significantly adjusted, either in whole or in part, by a Member State because of objective circumstances, in particular because of the actual direct effects of the inclusion of greenhouse gas emissions from buildings and road transport within the scope of Directive 2003/87/EC, the Member State concerned shall submit an amended Plan to the Commission in order to include the necessary and duly justified changes. Member States may request technical support, in accordance with Article 21(4) of this Regulation, for the preparation of the amended Plan.

2 The Commission shall assess the amended Plan in accordance with Article 12 of this Regulation.

3 Where the Commission gives a positive assessment of the amended Plan, it shall in accordance with Article 13(1) of this Regulation adopt a decision setting out the reasons for its positive assessment, by means of an implementing act. By way of derogation from Article 13(1) of this Regulation, the Commission shall adopt the decision under this paragraph within three months from the date of the submission of the amended Plan by the Member State concerned.

4 Where the Commission gives a negative assessment of the amended Plan, it shall reject the amended Plan within the period referred to in paragraph 3, after having given the Member State concerned the possibility to present its observations within three months from the

date of the communication of the Commission's assessment of the amended Plan.

5 By 15 March 2029 each Member State shall assess the appropriateness of its Plan in view of the actual direct effects of the inclusion of greenhouse gas emissions from buildings and road transport within the scope of Directive 2003/87/EC. Those assessments shall be submitted to the Commission together with the integrated national energy and climate progress reports pursuant to Article 17 of Regulation (EU) 2018/1999.

6 In the case of minor adjustments to the Plan, representing an increase or decrease of less than 5% of a target set out in the Plan, such as minor updates in the measures and investments set out in the Plan, or the correction of clerical errors, a Member State shall notify such changes to the Commission.

Article 15

Rules on Payment, Suspension and Termination of Agreements Regarding Financial Allocations

1 Payments of financial allocations under this Article to the Member State shall be made upon achievement of the relevant agreed milestones and targets indicated in the Plan, as approved in accordance with Article 13 of this Regulation, and subject to the availability of funding. Upon such achievement, the Member State shall submit to the Commission a duly reasoned payment request and the Member State shall submit such payment requests to the Commission once or twice a year, by 31 July or by 31 December.

2 Upon receiving a payment request from a Member State, the Commission shall assess whether the relevant milestones and targets set out in the Commission decision referred to in Article 13 of this Regulation have been satisfactorily achieved. The satisfactory achievement of milestones and targets shall presuppose that measures related to previously satisfactorily achieved milestones and targets have not been reversed by the Member State concerned.

3 Where the Commission makes a positive assessment of an individual payment request, it shall adopt an individual decision authorising the disbursement of the financial allocation in accordance with Regulation (EU, Euratom) 2018/1046, subject to the availability of funding and ensuring the equal treatment of Member States. The Commission shall adopt the individual decision not earlier than two months and not later than three months after the relevant deadline for submission of the payment request in accordance with paragraph 1 of this Article.

4 Where, as a result of the assessment referred to in paragraph 3 of this Article, the Commission establishes that the milestones and targets set

out in the Commission decision referred to in Article 13 of this Regulation have not been satisfactorily achieved, the payment of the part of the financial allocation proportional to the unachieved target or milestone shall be suspended. The Member State may present its observations within one month of the communication of the Commission's assessment. The suspension shall only be lifted where the milestones and targets have been satisfactorily achieved as set out in the Commission decision referred to in Article 13.

5 By way of derogation from Article 116(2) of Regulation (EU, Euratom) 2018/1046, the payment deadline shall start running from the date of the communication of the Commission's decision authorising the disbursement of the financial allocation to the Member State concerned pursuant to paragraph 3 of this Article, or from the date of the communication of the lifting of a suspension pursuant to paragraph 4, second subparagraph, of this Article.

6 Where the milestones and targets have not been satisfactorily achieved within a period of nine months from the suspension referred to in paragraph 4, first subparagraph, the Commission shall reduce the amount of the financial allocation proportionately after having given the Member State the possibility to present its observations within two months from the communication of its conclusions as to the achievement of the milestones and targets.

7 Where, within 15 months from the date of the conclusion of relevant agreements referred to in Article 13(5) and (6) of this Regulation, no tangible progress has been made in respect of any relevant milestones and targets by the Member State, the Commission shall terminate those agreements and shall decommit the amount of the financial allocation without prejudice to Article 14(3) of Regulation (EU, Euratom) 2018/1046. The Commission shall take a decision on the termination of those agreements after having given the Member State the possibility to present its observations within a period of two months of the communication of the assessment by the Commission that no tangible progress has been made.

8 All payments shall be made by 31 December 2033.

9 By way of derogation from Article 116 of Regulation (EU, Euratom) 2018/1046 and paragraph 5 of this Article, if, in a given round of payment requests as referred to in paragraph 1 of this Article, the revenue assigned to the Fund in accordance with Article 30d(4) of Directive 2003/87/EC is not sufficient to cover the submitted payment requests, the Commission shall pay the Member States on a pro-rata basis determined as a share of the payment availabilities to the total approved payments. In the following round of payment requests, the Commission shall give priority to those Member States with delayed payments

from the previous round of payment requests, and only later to the newly submitted payment requests.

10 By way of derogation from Article 12(4), point (c), of Regulation (EU, Euratom) 2018/1046 and without prejudice to Article 30d(4), sixth subparagraph, of Directive 2003/87/EC, the Commission shall allocate to Member States the amounts corresponding to any appropriations that are unused by 31 December 2033 in accordance with the rules for distribution of allowances defined under Article 30d(5) of Directive 2003/87/EC in order to achieve the objectives referred to in Article 3 of this Regulation.

11 In order to ensure additional resources for the Fund, the Member States should be able to request a transfer of resources to the Fund from the cohesion policy programmes under shared management, established by Regulation (EU) 2021/1060, subject to the conditions set out in that Regulation. In order to provide Member States with sufficient flexibility in the implementation of their allocations under the Fund, it should be possible to transfer resources from their annual financial allocation to funds under shared management provided for in Regulation (EU) 2021/1060, up to a ceiling of 15%. With a view to alleviating the administrative burden resulting from successive transfers of resources from their annual financial allocation from the Fund to funds under shared management falling within the scope of Regulation (EU) 2021/1060, the corresponding amendment of one or more programmes should, in principle, be required only once, subject to certain conditions to ensure effective financial control. It should be possible to effect further transfers in subsequent years by notifying the financial tables to the Commission, provided that the changes relate exclusively to an increase in the financial resources, without any further changes to the programme concerned.

Article 16

Transparency

1 The Commission shall transmit the Plans submitted by Member States and the decisions, as made public by the Commission, simultaneously and on equal terms to the European Parliament and the Council without undue delay.

2 Information transmitted by the Commission to the Council in the context of this Regulation or its implementation shall simultaneously be made available to the European Parliament, subject to confidentiality arrangements if necessary.

3 The competent committees of the European Parliament may invite the Commission to provide information on the state of play of the assessment by the Commission of the Plans.

Article 17

Coordination and Complementarity

1 The Commission and the Member States concerned shall, in a manner commensurate to their respective responsibilities, foster synergies and ensure effective coordination between the Fund and the Union programmes and instruments referred to in Article 9(3) of this Regulation, and the Modernisation Fund under Article 10d of Directive 2003/87/EC. For that purpose, they shall:

(a) ensure complementarity, synergy, coherence and consistency among different instruments at Union, national and, where appropriate, local or regional levels, both in the planning phase and during implementation;
(b) optimise mechanisms for coordination to avoid duplication of effort; and
(c) ensure close cooperation between those responsible for implementation and control at Union, national and, where appropriate, local or regional levels to achieve the objectives of the Fund.

Article 18

Information, Communication and Visibility

1 Member States shall make the data referred to in Article 25(2), point (d)(i), (ii) and (iv), of this Regulation publicly available and keep them up to date on a single website in open, machine-readable formats, as set out in Article 5(1) of Directive (EU) 2019/1024 of the European Parliament and of the Council (35), which shall allow data to be sorted, searched, extracted, compared and reused. The information referred to in Article 25(2), points (d)(i) and (ii), of this Regulation shall not be published in the cases referred to in Article 38(3) of Regulation (EU, Euratom) 2018/1046 or in the case of temporary direct income support to vulnerable households.
2 The recipients of support from the Fund shall be informed of the origin of those funds, including where they benefit from those funds through intermediaries. That information shall include the emblem of the Union and an appropriate funding statement that reads 'funded by the European Union – Social Climate Fund' on documents and communication material relating to the implementation of the measure intended for the recipients. The recipients of support from the Fund, except the support for natural persons or where there is risk of commercially sensitive information being made public, shall ensure the visibility of the Union funding, in particular when promoting the actions and their results, by

providing coherent, effective and proportionate targeted information to multiple audiences, including the media and the public.

3 The Commission shall implement information and communication actions relating to the Fund, to actions taken pursuant to this Regulation and to the results obtained, including, where appropriate and with the agreement of the national authorities, through joint communication activities with the national authorities and the representation offices of the European Parliament and of the Commission in the Member State concerned.

Article 19

Monitoring of Implementation

1 Each Member State shall, on a biennial basis, report to the Commission on the implementation of its Plan together with its integrated national energy and climate progress report pursuant to Article 17 of Regulation (EU) 2018/1999 and in accordance with Article 28 thereof. The monitoring of implementation shall be targeted and proportionate to the activities carried out in the Plan. The Member States shall include the indicators set out in Annex IV to this Regulation in their progress report.

2 The Commission shall monitor the implementation of the Fund and measure the achievement of its objectives. The monitoring of implementation shall be targeted and proportionate to the activities carried out under the Fund.

3 The performance reporting system of the Commission shall ensure that data for monitoring the implementation of the activities and results are collected efficiently, effectively and in a timely manner. To that end, proportionate reporting requirements shall be imposed on recipients of support from the Fund.

4 The Commission shall use the common indicators set out in Annex IV for reporting on the progress and for the purpose of monitoring and evaluation of the Fund towards the achievement of the objectives set out in Article 1 of this Regulation.

Part 3: To EU

Article 20

Resources of the Fund

1 By way of derogation from Article 22(2) of Regulation (EU, Euratom) 2018/1046 and without prejudice to Article 13(5) and (6) of

this Regulation, commitment appropriations covering the relevant maximum amount referred to in Article 4(4) of this Regulation shall be made available automatically at the beginning of each financial year, starting from 1 January 2026, up to the relevant applicable annual amounts referred to in Article 4(5) and (6) of this Regulation.

2 The amounts referred to in paragraph 1 may also cover expenses pertaining to preparatory, monitoring, control, audit and evaluation activities which are required for the management of the Fund and the achievement of its objectives, in particular studies, meetings of experts, consultation of stakeholders, information and communication actions, including inclusive outreach actions, and corporate communication of the political priorities of the Union, insofar as they are related to the objectives of this Regulation, expenses linked to IT networks focusing on information processing and exchange, corporate IT tools, and all other technical and administrative assistance expenses incurred by the Commission for the management of the Fund. Expenses may also cover the costs of other supporting activities such as quality control and monitoring of projects on the ground and the costs of peer counselling and experts for the assessment and implementation of the eligible actions.

Article 21

Resources from and to Shared Management Programmes and Use of Resources

1 Resources allocated to Member States under shared management may, at their request, be transferred to the Fund subject to the conditions set out in the relevant provisions of Regulation (EU) 2021/1060. The Commission shall implement those resources directly in accordance with Article 62(1), first subparagraph, point (a), of Regulation (EU, Euratom) 2018/1046. Those resources shall be used exclusively for the benefit of the Member State concerned.

2 Member States may request in their Plans submitted in accordance with Article 6(1) and (3) of this Regulation for the transfer of up to 15% of their maximum annual financial allocation to the funds under shared management provided for in Regulation (EU) 2021/1060. The transferred resources shall finance measures and investments as referred to in Article 3 and Article 8 of this Regulation and shall be implemented in accordance with the rules of the funds to which the resources are transferred. Resources shall be transferred by Member States through the amendment of one or more programmes, except for programmes under the European territorial cooperation goal (Interreg), in accordance with Article 26a of Regulation (EU) 2021/1060, and shall be implemented in

accordance with the rules set out in that Regulation and the rules of the funds to which the resources are transferred.

3 Member States may entrust the managing authorities of the cohesion policy programmes under Regulation (EU) 2021/1060 with the implementation of measures and investments benefitting from the Fund, where applicable, in view of the synergies with those cohesion policy programmes and in conformity with the objectives of the Fund. Member States shall state their intention to thus entrust those authorities in their Plans. In such cases, the existing management and control systems put in place by Member States, as notified to the Commission, shall be deemed to comply with the requirements of this Regulation.

4 Member States may include in their Plans, as part of the estimated total costs, the payments for additional technical support pursuant to Article 7 of Regulation (EU) 2021/240 and the amount of the cash contribution for the purpose of the Member State compartment pursuant to the relevant provisions of Regulation (EU) 2021/523 of the European Parliament and of the Council ([31]). Those costs shall not exceed 4% of the maximum financial allocation for the Plan, and the relevant measures, as set out in the Plan, shall comply with this Regulation.

Article 22

Implementation

The Fund shall be implemented by the Commission under direct management in accordance with the relevant rules adopted pursuant to Article 322 TFEU, in particular Regulation (EU, Euratom) 2018/1046 and Regulation (EU, Euratom) 2020/2092 on a general regime of conditionality for the protection of the Union budget.

Article 23

Additionality and Complementary Funding

1 Support under the Fund shall be additional to the support provided under other Union funds, programmes and instruments. Measures and investments supported under the Fund may receive support from other Union funds, programmes and instruments provided that such support does not cover the same cost.

2 Support from the Fund, including temporary direct income support referred to in Article 6(4), shall be additional and shall not substitute recurring national budgetary expenditure.

3 For technical assistance to Member States, administrative costs directly linked to the implementation of the Plan shall not be considered as recurring national budgetary expenditure.

Article 24

Maximum Financial Allocation

1 The maximum financial allocation shall be calculated for each Member State in accordance with Article 4(4), (5) and (6) of this Regulation and as specified in Annexes I and II.
2 Each Member State may submit a request up to its maximum financial allocation to implement its Plan.

Article 25

Protection of the Financial Interests of the Union

1 The Member States, when implementing the Plans, as beneficiaries of funds under the Fund, shall take all the appropriate measures to protect the financial interests of the Union and to ensure that the use of the financial allocations in relation to measures and investments supported by the Fund, including those carried out by public or private entities other than vulnerable households, vulnerable micro-enterprises and vulnerable transport users in accordance with Article 10, complies with applicable Union and national law, in particular regarding the prevention, detection and correction of fraud, corruption and conflicts of interests. To that effect, the Member States shall provide an effective and efficient internal control system as further set out in Annex III and the recovery of amounts wrongly paid or incorrectly used. Member States may rely on their regular national budget management systems.
2 The agreements referred to in Article 13(5) shall provide for the following obligations of the Member States:

(a) to regularly check that the financing provided has been properly used in accordance with all applicable rules and that any measure or investment under the Plan has been properly implemented in accordance with all applicable rules, in particular regarding the prevention, detection and correction of fraud, corruption and conflicts of interests;
(b) to take appropriate measures to prevent, detect and correct fraud, corruption, and conflicts of interests as defined in Article 61 of Regulation (EU, Euratom) 2018/1046 affecting the financial interests of the Union and to take legal action to recover funds that have been misappropriated, including in relation to any measure or investment implemented under the Plan;
(c) to accompany a payment request by:

(i) a management declaration that the financial allocations were used for its intended purpose, that the information submitted with the payment request is complete, accurate and reliable and that the internal control systems put in place give the necessary assurances that the financial allocations were managed in accordance with all applicable rules, in particular rules on avoidance of conflicts of interests, fraud prevention, corruption and double funding from the Fund and other Union programmes in accordance with the principle of sound financial management; and

(ii) a summary of the audits carried out in accordance with internationally accepted audit standards, including the scope of those audits in terms of amount of spending covered and period of time covered and an analysis of the weaknesses identified and any corrective action taken;

(d) for the purpose of audit and control and to provide for comparable information on the use of financial allocations in relation to measures and investments implemented under the Plan, to collect, record and store in an electronic system and ensure access to the following standardised categories of data:

(i) name of the final recipients of the financial allocations, their VAT registration numbers or tax identification numbers and amount of the financial allocations from the Fund;
(ii) name of the contractor(s) and sub-contractor(s) and their VAT registration number(s) or tax identification number(s) and value of the contract(s) where the final recipient of the financial allocations is a contracting authority in accordance with Union or national law on public procurement;
(iii) first name(s), last name(s), date(s) of birth and VAT registration number(s) or tax identification number(s), of beneficial owner(s) of the recipient of the financial allocations or contractor, as defined in Article 3, point (6), of Directive (EU) 2015/849 of the European Parliament and of the Council ([33]);
(iv) a list of any measures and investments implemented under the Fund with the total amount of public funding of those measures and investments and indicating the amount of funds paid under other funds financed from the Union budget;

(e) to expressly authorise the Commission, OLAF, the Court of Auditors and, in respect of those Member States participating in enhanced cooperation pursuant to Regulation (EU) 2017/1939, the EPPO, to exert their rights as provided for in Article 129(1) of Regulation (EU, Euratom) 2018/1046 and to impose obligations on all final recipients of the financial allocations paid for implementing the measures and investments included in the Plan, or to all other persons or entities involved in their implementation to expressly authorise the Commission, OLAF, the Court of Auditors and, where applicable, EPPO to exert their rights as provided for in Article 129(1) of Regulation (EU, Euratom) 2018/1046 and to impose similar obligations on all final recipients of funds disbursed;

(f) to keep records in accordance with Article 132 of Regulation (EU, Euratom) 2018/1046, the point of reference being the payment transaction relevant to the respective measure or investment.

The information referred to in point (d)(ii) of the first subparagraph of this Article shall be required only where the value of public procurement is greater than the Union thresholds set out in Article 4 of Directive 2014/24/EU of the European Parliament and of the Council (34). Regarding subcontractors, that information shall be required only:

(a) for the first level of sub-contracting;
(b) where that information is recorded regarding the respective contractor; and
(c) for sub-contracts with a total value greater than EUR 50,000.

3 Personal data as referred to in paragraph 2, point (d), of this Article shall be processed by Member States and by the Commission for the purpose, and corresponding duration, of discharge, audit and control proceedings, and information, communication and visibility activities, related to the use of financial allocations related to the implementation of the agreements referred to in Article 13(5) of this Regulation. The personal data shall be processed in accordance with Regulation (EU) 2016/679 or Regulation (EU) 2018/1725, whichever is applicable. Within the framework of the discharge procedure to the Commission, in accordance with Article 319 TFEU, the Fund shall be subject to reporting under the integrated financial and accountability reporting referred to in Article 247 of Regulation (EU, Euratom) 2018/1046, and, in particular, separately in the annual management and performance report.

4 The agreements referred to in Article 13(5) of this Regulation shall also provide for the right of the Commission to reduce proportionately the support under the Fund and recover any amount due to the Union budget, in cases of fraud, corruption, and conflict of interests affecting the financial interests of the Union that have not been corrected by the Member State, or a serious breach of an obligation resulting from such agreements. When deciding on the amount of the recovery and reduction the Commission shall respect the principle of proportionality and shall take into account the seriousness of the fraud, corruption and conflict of interests affecting the financial interests of the Union, or of a breach of an obligation. The Commission shall give the Member State the opportunity to present its observations before the reduction is made.

Article 26

Social Climate Dialogue

1 In order to enhance the dialogue between the Union institutions, in particular the European Parliament and the Commission, and to ensure greater transparency and accountability, the competent committees of the European Parliament may invite the Commission twice a year to discuss the following matters:

(a) the Plans submitted by Member States;
(b) the assessment by the Commission of the Plans submitted by Member States;
(c) the status of achievement of the milestones and targets set out in the Plans submitted by Member States;
(d) payment, suspension and termination procedures, including any observation presented and remedial measures taken by Member States to ensure the satisfactory achievement of the milestones and targets set out in the Plans submitted by them.

2 The Commission shall take account of any elements arising from the views expressed through the social climate dialogue, including the resolutions of the European Parliament if provided.

Article 27

Evaluation and Review of the Fund

1 Two years after the start of the implementation of the Plans, the Commission shall provide the European Parliament, the Council, the European Economic and Social Committee and the Committee of the Regions with an evaluation report on the implementation and functioning of the Fund, taking into account the results of the first reports submitted by Member States in accordance with Article 19, and shall submit, where appropriate, any proposals for amendments to this Regulation.

2 The evaluation report referred to in paragraph 1 shall, in particular, assess:

(a) the extent to which the objectives of the Fund set out in Article 3 have been achieved, the efficiency of the use of the resources and the Union added value;
(b) on a country-by-country basis, the efficiency of measures and investments and the use of the direct income support in light of the achievement of the milestones and targets set out in the Plans;
(c) how the definitions of energy poverty and transport poverty are applied in Member States, based on the information referred to in Article 9(1), point (f), as well as whether amendments to such definitions are necessary;

(d) the continued relevance of all objectives, and measures and investments set out in Article 8 of this Regulation in light of the impact on greenhouse gas emissions of the inclusion of greenhouse gas emissions from buildings and road transport within the scope of Directive 2003/87/EC and of the national measures taken to meet the binding annual greenhouse gas emission reductions by Member States pursuant to Regulation (EU) 2018/842 of the European Parliament and of the Council ([36]), as well as the continued relevance of the assigned revenues in relation to possible developments concerning the auctioning of allowances under the emission trading system for buildings, road transport and additional sectors pursuant to Chapter IVa of Directive 2003/87/EC and other relevant considerations.

3 By 31 December 2033, the Commission shall provide the European Parliament, the Council, the European Economic and Social Committee and the Committee of the Regions with an independent *ex post* evaluation report. The *ex post* evaluation report shall consist of a global assessment of the Fund and shall include information on its impact.
4 Without prejudging the multiannual financial framework post 2027, in the event revenue generated from the auctioning of allowances referred to in Article 30d(5) of Directive 2003/87/EC is established as an own resource in accordance with Article 311(3) TFEU, the Commission shall, as appropriate, present the necessary proposals in order to ensure, within the framework of the multiannual financial framework post 2027, the effectiveness and continuity of the implementation of the Fund, which is temporarily and exceptionally financed by external assigned revenue generated from allowances of the emission trading system

Article 28

Amendment to Regulation (EU) 2021/1060

The following Article is inserted in Regulation (EU) 2021/1060:

'Article 26a

Resources transferred from the Social Climate Fund

1 Resources transferred from the Social Climate Fund, established by Regulation (EU) 2023/955 of the European Parliament and of the Council ([*1]) shall be implemented in accordance with this Regulation and the provisions governing the Fund to which the resources are transferred and shall be definitive. Such resources shall constitute external assigned

revenue for the purpose of Article 21(5) of Regulation (EU, Euratom) 2018/1046 and shall be additional to the resources referred to in Article 110 of this Regulation.

2 Where Member States implement the resources referred to in paragraph 1 of this Article under shared management, they shall submit programme amendments in accordance with Article 24 of this Regulation concerning one or more programmes. Member States shall plan the use of such resources for achieving the climate objectives set out for the Union budget in accordance with Article 6(1) of this Regulation. Those resources shall contribute to achieving relevant objectives of the Social Climate Fund as set out in Article 3 of Regulation (EU) 2023/955 and shall be used to support measures and investments set out in Article 8 of that Regulation. They shall be programmed under one or more dedicated priorities corresponding to one or more specific objectives of the Fund to which the resources are transferred and for one or more categories of regions, where applicable, with an indication of the yearly breakdown of resources. They shall not be taken into account for the calculation of compliance with thematic concentration requirements as set out in Fund-specific rules.

3 Where the Commission has already approved a Member State's request for an amendment of a programme relating to a transfer of resources from the Social Climate Fund, for any further transfer of resources in subsequent years, the Member State may submit a notification of financial tables instead of an amendment of a programme, provided that the proposed changes relate exclusively to an increase of the financial resources, without any further changes to the programme.

4 By way of derogation from Article 18 and Article 86(1), second subparagraph, of this Regulation, the resources transferred in accordance with this Article and Article 11(2) of Regulation (EU) 2023/955 shall not be taken into account for the mid-term review and the flexibility amount.

5 By way of derogation from Article 14(3) of Regulation (EU, Euratom) 2018/1046, the time limit after which the Commission shall decommit the amounts in accordance with Article 105(1) of this Regulation shall start from the year in which the corresponding budgetary commitments are made. Resources shall not be transferred to programmes under the European territorial cooperation goal (Interreg).

Article 29

Citation

This Regulation is Regulation (EU) 2023/955 of the European Parliament and of the Council of 10 May 2023 establishing a Social Climate Fund and amending Regulation (EU) 2021/1060.

Article 30

Entry into Force

This Regulation shall enter into force on the twentieth day following that of its publication in the *Official Journal of the European Union.*

It shall apply from 30 June 2024, the date by which the Member States are to bring into force the laws, regulations and administrative provisions necessary to comply with Directive (EU) 2023/959 of the European Parliament and of the Council ([37]) amending Directive 2003/87/EC as regards Chapter IVa of Directive 2003/87/EC.

This Regulation shall be binding in its entirety and directly applicable in all Member States.

Done at Strasbourg, 10 May 2023.
For the European Parliament
The President
R. METSOLA
For the Council
The President
J. ROSWALL

Annex 1

Definitions

In this Regulation the following definitions apply:

1 'energy poverty' means a household's lack of access to essential energy services that underpin a decent standard of living and health, including adequate warmth, cooling, lighting, and energy to power appliances, in the relevant national context, existing social policy and other relevant policies;
2 'transport poverty' means individuals' and households' inability or difficulty to meet the costs of private or public transport, or their lack of or limited access to transport needed for their access to essential socio-economic services and activities, taking into account the national and spatial context;
3 'estimated total costs of the Plan' means the estimated total costs of the measures and investments included in the Plan;
4 'financial allocation' means non-repayable financial support under the Fund that is available for allocation, or that has been allocated, to a Member State;
5 'milestone' means a qualitative achievement used to measure progress towards the achievement of a measure or an investment;

6 'target' means a quantitative achievement used to measure progress towards the achievement of a measure or investment;
7 'energy from renewable sources' or 'renewable energy' means energy from renewable sources as defined in Article 2, second subparagraph, point (1), of Directive (EU) 2018/2001 of the European Parliament and of the Council (25);
8 'household' means a private household as defined in Article 2, point (15), of Regulation (EU) 2019/1700 of the European Parliament and of the Council (26);
9 'micro-enterprise' means an enterprise that employs fewer than ten persons and whose annual turnover or annual balance sheet does not exceed EUR 2 million, calculated in accordance with Articles 3 to 6 of Annex I to Commission Regulation (EU) No. 651/2014 (27);
10 'vulnerable households' means households in energy poverty or households, including low income and lower middle-income ones, that are significantly affected by the price impacts of the inclusion of greenhouse gas emissions from buildings within the scope of Directive 2003/87/EC and lack the means to renovate the building they occupy;
11 'vulnerable micro-enterprises' means micro-enterprises that are significantly affected by the price impacts of the inclusion of greenhouse gas emissions from buildings or road transport within the scope of Directive 2003/87/EC and that, for the purpose of their activity, lack the means either to renovate the building they occupy, or to purchase zero- and low-emission vehicles or to switch to alternative sustainable modes of transport, including public transport, as relevant;
12 'vulnerable transport users' means individuals and households in transport poverty, but also individuals and households, including low income and lower middle-income ones, that are significantly affected by the price impacts of the inclusion of greenhouse gas emissions from road transport within the scope of Directive 2003/87/EC and lack the means to purchase zero- and low-emission vehicles or to switch to alternative sustainable modes of transport, including public transport;
13 'building renovation' means any kind of energy-related building renovation, which has the aim of increasing the energy performance of buildings, such as the insulation of the building envelope, that is to say the walls, roof, floor and the replacement of windows, and the installation of technical building systems, compliant with any relevant national safety standards, including by contributing to the renovation requirements established in the Directive of the European Parliament and of the Council on the energy performance of buildings (recast);
14 'technical building system' means the technical equipment for space heating, space cooling, ventilation, domestic hot water, building

automation and control, on-site renewable energy generation and storage, or a combination of such technical equipment, including those systems using energy from renewable sources, of a building or building unit;

15 'active customer' means an active customer as defined in Article 2, point (8), of Directive (EU) 2019/944 of the European Parliament and of the Council ([28]);

16 'citizen energy community' means a citizen energy community as defined in Article 2, point (11), of Directive (EU) 2019/944;

17 'renewable energy community' means a renewable energy community as defined in Article 2, point (16), of Directive (EU) 2018/2001;

18 'peer-to-peer trading of renewable energy' means peer-to-peer trading of renewable energy as defined in Article 2, point (18), of Directive (EU) 2018/2001;

19 'zero- and low-emission vehicle' means zero- and low- emission vehicle as defined in Article 3(1), point (m), of Regulation (EU) 2019/631 of the European Parliament and of the Council.

Annex 2

Notes and Commission Statements

(1) The communication of the Commission of 11 December 2019 on 'The European Green Deal' (the 'European Green Deal') sets out a new growth strategy that aims to transform the Union into a sustainable, fair and prosperous society, with a modern, resource-efficient and competitive economy, where there are no net emissions of greenhouse gases at the latest by 2050 and where economic growth is decoupled from resource use. The European Green Deal also aims to restore, protect, conserve and enhance the Union's natural capital, and protect the health and well-being of citizens from environment-related risks and impacts. Finally, it considers that this transition should be just and inclusive, leaving no one behind.

(2) The conclusions of the European Council of 10–11 December 2020 endorsed the binding Union domestic reduction target for net greenhouse gas emissions, while underlining the importance of considerations of fairness and solidarity and leaving no one behind. Those conclusions were reaffirmed in the conclusions of the European Council of 24–25 May 2021, when the European Council invited the Commission to swiftly put forward its legislative package together with an in-depth examination of the environmental, economic and social impact at Member State level

(3) The European Pillar of Social Rights Action Plan, endorsed by the conclusions of the European Council of 24–25 June 2021, highlights the need to strengthen social rights and the European social dimension across all policies of the Union. Principle 20 of the European Pillar of Social Rights states that 'everyone has the right to access essential services of good quality, including water, sanitation, energy, transport, financial services and digital communications. Support for access to such services shall be available for those in need.'

(4) The increase in the price for fossil fuels can disproportionally affect vulnerable households, vulnerable micro-enterprises and vulnerable transport users who spend a larger part of their income on energy and transport, who, in certain regions, do not have access to alternative, affordable mobility and transport solutions, and who may lack the financial capacity to invest in the reduction of fossil fuel consumption. Geographic specificities, such as islands, outermost regions and territories, rural or remote areas, less accessible peripheries, mountainous areas or areas that are lagging behind, can have specific impacts in the context of transport poverty on the vulnerability of households, micro-enterprises and transport users. Therefore, those geographic specificities should be taken into account when preparing measures and investments in support of vulnerable households, vulnerable micro-enterprises and vulnerable transport users, where applicable and relevant.

(5) Using part of the revenues to address the social impacts arising from the inclusion of the buildings, road transport and additional sectors within the scope of Directive 2003/87/EC is even more relevant in view of the existing levels of energy poverty. Energy poverty is a situation in which households are unable to access essential energy services that underpin a decent standard of living and health, such as adequate warmth through heating, cooling, as temperatures rise, lighting, and energy to power appliances. In a 2021 Union-wide survey, approximately 34 million Europeans, nearly 6.9% of the population of the Union, said that they could not afford to heat their home sufficiently. Energy poverty is therefore a major challenge for the Union. While social tariffs or temporary direct income support can provide immediate relief to households facing energy poverty in the short term, only targeted structural measures, in particular building renovations, including through access to energy from renewable sources and the active promotion of renewable energy sources through information and awareness-raising measures targeted at households, and building renovations that contribute to the objectives established in Directive 2010/31/EU of the European Parliament

and of the Council [7] can provide lasting solutions and effectively help combat energy poverty. It should be possible for the definition of energy poverty under this Regulation to be updated to reflect the outcome of the negotiations on a Directive of the European Parliament and of the Council on energy efficiency (recast).

(6) Pending the impact of those investments on reducing costs and emissions, well targeted direct income support for vulnerable households and vulnerable transport users would contribute to a reduction of energy and mobility costs and would support the just transition. Direct income support should be understood to be a temporary measure accompanying the decarbonisation of the housing and transport sectors. It would not be permanent as it does not address the root causes of energy poverty and transport poverty. Such support should only be used to address direct impacts of the inclusion of greenhouse gas emissions from buildings and road transport within the scope of Directive 2003/87/EC, and should not be used to address electricity or heating costs related to the inclusion of power and heat production in the scope of that Directive. Eligibility for such direct income support should be limited in time. Recipients of direct income support should be targeted, as members of a general group of recipients, by measures and investments aimed at effectively lifting those recipients out of energy poverty and transport poverty. The Plans should therefore include direct income support provided that they also contain measures or investments with lasting impacts targeted at the vulnerable households and vulnerable transport users who receive direct income support.

(7) In order to ensure the efficient, transparent and coherent allocation of funds, and to respect the principle of sound financial management, actions under this Regulation should be consistent with and be complementary to ongoing Union, national and, where appropriate, regional programmes, whilst avoiding double funding from the Fund and other Union programmes for the same expenditure. In particular, the Commission and Member States should ensure effective coordination, at all stages of the process, in order to safeguard the consistency, coherence, complementarity and synergy among sources of funding. To that effect, Member States should be required to present the relevant information on existing or planned Union financing when submitting their Plans to the Commission. Financial support under the Fund should be additional to the support provided under other Union programmes and instruments. Measures and investments financed under the Fund should be able to receive funding from other Union programmes and instruments provided that such support does not cover the same costs.

(8) After the analysis of all the payment requests received in a given round, and if revenues assigned to the Fund in accordance with Article 30d(4) of Directive 2003/87/EC are not sufficient to cover the payment requests submitted by the Member States, the Commission should pay the Member States on a pro-rata basis in order to provide for an equal treatment of Member States. In the following round of payment requests, the Commission should give priority to those Member States with delayed payments from the previous round of payment requests, and only afterwards pay the newly submitted payment requests.

(9) In order to facilitate the preparation of the Plans and to ensure transparent rules for monitoring and evaluation, the list of common indicators and the template for the Plans should be included in the Annexes to this Regulation. It should be possible for the Member States to use relevant common indicators to set out the milestones and targets in their Plans. The list of common indicators should contain the common indicators for reporting on the progress and for the purpose of monitoring and evaluation of the implementation of the Plans and of the Fund.

(10) The Fund should be implemented in line with the principle of sound financial management, including the effective prevention and prosecution of fraud, tax fraud, tax evasion, corruption and conflicts of interests. The Fund is subject to a general regime of conditionality for the protection of the Union budget in the case of breaches of the principles of the rule of law in the Member States established by Regulation (EU, Euratom) 2020/2092 of the European Parliament and of the Council ([17]).

(11) For the purpose of sound financial management, while respecting the performance-based nature of the Fund, specific rules should be laid down for budget commitments, payments, suspension, and the recovery of funds as well as for the termination of agreements related to financial support. The Member States should take appropriate measures to ensure that the use of funds in relation to measures supported by the Fund complies with applicable Union and national law. Member States should ensure that such support is granted in compliance with the Union State aid rules, where applicable. In particular, they should ensure that fraud, corruption and conflicts of interests are prevented, detected and corrected, and that double funding from the Fund and other Union programmes is avoided. Suspension and the termination of agreements related to financial support, as well as reduction and recovery of the financial allocation, should be possible when the Plan has not been implemented in a satisfactory manner by the Member State concerned or in the case of serious irregularities,

namely fraud, corruption and conflicts of interests in relation to the measures supported by the Fund or a serious breach of an obligation under the agreements related to financial support. In the case of the termination of an agreement related to financial support or the reduction and recovery of a financial allocation, those amounts should be allocated to Member States by 31 December 2033 according to the rules for distribution of allowances set out in Article 30d(5) of Directive 2003/87/EC. Appropriate contradictory procedures should be established to ensure that the decisions of the Commission in relation to suspension and recovery of amounts paid or the termination of agreements related to financial support respect the right of Member States to submit observations.

(12) The Member States and the Commission should be allowed to process personal data only where necessary for the purpose of ensuring discharge, audit and control, information, communication and visibility of the use of funds in relation to measures for the implementation under the Fund. Personal data should be processed in accordance with Regulation (EU) 2016/679 of the European Parliament and of the Council ([18]) or Regulation (EU) 2018/1725 of the European Parliament and of the Council ([19]), whichever is applicable.

Notes

1 Helen Xanthaki, *Legislative Drafting for the EU: Transposition Techniques as a Roadmap for Better Legislation and a Sustainable EU* (2024, Elgar Publishers, Cheltenham).

2 https://eur-lex.europa.eu/legal-content/EN/TXT/?uri=CELEX%3A32023R0955&qid=1739004216469#cpt_V.

3 Lawyers and drafters.

Index

Note: **Bold** page numbers refer to tables; *italic* page numbers refer to figures and page numbers followed by "n" denote endnotes.

Kolibri 360 GmbH
Ferdinand-Jühlke-Straße 7
99095 Erfurt, Deutschland
produktsicherheit@kolibri360.de